Earth Science

interactive SCIENCE

Go to MyScienceOnline.com to experience science in a whole new way.

Interactive tools such as My Planet Diary connect you to the latest science happenings.

MY PLANET DIARY

- **Search Earth's Journal** for important science news from around the world.

- **Use Earth's Calendar** to find out when cool scientific events occur.

- **Explore science Links** to find even more exciting information about our planet.

- **Visit Jack's Blog** to be the first to know about what is going on in science!

PEARSON

Glenview, Illinois • Boston, Massachusetts • Chandler, Arizona • Upper Saddle River, New Jersey

Program Authors

You're an author!

As you write in this science book, your answers and personal discoveries will be recorded for you to keep, making this book unique to you. That is why you are one of the primary authors of this book.

✏ **In the space below, print your name, school, town, and state. Then write a short autobiography that includes your interests and accomplishments.**

YOUR NAME _____

SCHOOL _____

TOWN, STATE _____

AUTOBIOGRAPHY _____

_____

_____

_____

_____

_____

Your Photo

Acknowledgments appear on pages 730–733, which constitute an extension of this copyright page.

ISBN-13: 978-0-13-320921-1
ISBN-10: 0-13-320921-0
12 17

Earth Science
interactive
SCIENCE

ON THE COVER
Garnet
In general, a mineral has a well-defined chemical composition. Different circumstances and impurities during the mineral's formation can produce a certain amount of variability. In the case of garnets this variability is considerable, because the word *garnet* encompasses several distinct mineral species. While garnets share some chemical characteristics and crystal structure, samples from different sites may differ in color, shape, and other properties.

Program Authors

KATHRYN THORNTON, Ph.D.
Professor and Associate Dean, School of Engineering and Applied Science, University of Virginia, Charlottesville, Virginia
Selected by NASA in May 1984, Dr. Kathryn Thornton is a veteran of four space flights. She has logged more than 975 hours in space, including more than 21 hours of extravehicular activity. As an author on the *Scott Foresman Science* series, Dr. Thornton's enthusiasm for science has inspired teachers around the globe.

DON BUCKLEY, M.Sc.
Information and Communications Technology Director, The School at Columbia University, New York, New York
A founder of New York City Independent School Technologists (NYCIST) and long-time chair of New York Association of Independent Schools' annual IT conference, Mr. Buckley has taught students on two continents and created multimedia and Internet-based instructional systems for schools worldwide.

ZIPPORAH MILLER, M.A.Ed.
Associate Executive Director for Professional Programs and Conferences, National Science Teachers Association, Arlington, Virginia
Ms. Zipporah Miller is a former K–12 science supervisor and STEM coordinator for the Prince George's County Public School District in Maryland. She is a science education consultant who has overseen curriculum development and staff training for more than 150 district science coordinators.

MICHAEL J. PADILLA, Ph.D.
Associate Dean and Director, Eugene P. Moore School of Education, Clemson University, Clemson, South Carolina
A former middle school teacher and a leader in middle school science education, Dr. Michael Padilla has served as president of the National Science Teachers Association and as a writer of the National Science Education Standards. He is professor of science education at Clemson University.

MICHAEL E. WYSESSION, Ph.D.
Associate Professor of Earth and Planetary Science, Washington University, St. Louis, Missouri
An author on more than 50 scientific publications, Dr. Wysession was awarded the prestigious Packard Foundation Fellowship and Presidential Faculty Fellowship for his research in geophysics. Dr. Wysession is an expert on Earth's inner structure and has mapped various regions of Earth using seismic tomography. He is known internationally for his work in geoscience education and outreach.

Instructional Design Author

GRANT WIGGINS, Ed.D.
President, Authentic Education, Hopewell, New Jersey
Dr. Wiggins is a co-author with Jay McTighe of *Understanding by Design, 2nd Edition* (ASCD 2005). His approach to instructional design provides teachers with a disciplined way of thinking about curriculum design, assessment, and instruction that moves teaching from covering content to ensuring understanding.

UNDERSTANDING BY DESIGN® and UbD® are trademarks of ASCD, and are used under license.

Planet Diary Author

JACK HANKIN
Science/Mathematics Teacher, The Hilldale School, Daly City, California, Founder, Planet Diary Web site
Mr. Hankin is the creator and writer of Planet Diary, a science current events Web site. He is passionate about bringing science news and environmental awareness into classrooms and offers numerous Planet Diary workshops at NSTA and other events to train middle and high school teachers.

ELL Consultant

JIM CUMMINS, Ph.D.
Professor and Canada Research Chair, Curriculum, Teaching and Learning department at the University of Toronto
Dr. Cummins focuses on literacy development in multilingual schools and the role of technology in promoting student learning across the curriculum. *Interactive Science* incorporates essential research-based principles for integrating language with the teaching of academic content based on his instructional framework.

Reading Consultant

HARVEY DANIELS, Ph.D.
Professor of Secondary Education, University of New Mexico, Albuquerque, New Mexico
Dr. Daniels is an international consultant to schools, districts, and educational agencies. He has authored or coauthored 13 books on language, literacy, and education. His most recent works are *Comprehension and Collaboration: Inquiry Circles in Action* and *Subjects Matter: Every Teacher's Guide to Content-Area Reading*.

Reviewers

Contributing Writers

Edward Aguado, Ph.D.
Professor, Department of
 Geography
San Diego State University
San Diego, California

Elizabeth Coolidge-Stolz, M.D.
Medical Writer
North Reading, Massachusetts

Donald L. Cronkite, Ph.D.
Professor of Biology
Hope College
Holland, Michigan

Jan Jenner, Ph.D.
Science Writer
Talladega, Alabama

Linda Cronin Jones, Ph.D.
Associate Professor of Science and
 Environmental Education
University of Florida
Gainesville, Florida

T. Griffith Jones, Ph.D.
Clinical Associate Professor
 of Science Education
College of Education
University of Florida
Gainesville, Florida

Andrew C. Kemp, Ph.D.
Teacher
Jefferson County Public Schools
Louisville, Kentucky

Matthew Stoneking, Ph.D.
Associate Professor of Physics
Lawrence University
Appleton, Wisconsin

R. Bruce Ward, Ed.D.
Senior Research Associate
Science Education Department
Harvard-Smithsonian Center for
 Astrophysics
Cambridge, Massachusetts

Content Reviewers

Paul D. Beale, Ph.D.
Department of Physics
University of Colorado at Boulder
Boulder, Colorado

Jeff R. Bodart, Ph.D.
Professor of Physical Sciences
Chipola College
Marianna, Florida

Joy Branlund, Ph.D.
Department of Earth Science
Southwestern Illinois College
Granite City, Illinois

Marguerite Brickman, Ph.D.
Division of Biological Sciences
University of Georgia
Athens, Georgia

Bonnie J. Brunkhorst, Ph.D.
Science Education and Geological
 Sciences
California State University
San Bernardino, California

Michael Castellani, Ph.D.
Department of Chemistry
Marshall University
Huntington, West Virginia

Charles C. Curtis, Ph.D.
Research Associate Professor
 of Physics
University of Arizona
Tucson, Arizona

Diane I. Doser, Ph.D.
Department of Geological
 Sciences
University of Texas
El Paso, Texas

Rick Duhrkopf, Ph.D.
Department of Biology
Baylor University
Waco, Texas

Alice K. Hankla, Ph.D.
The Galloway School
Atlanta, Georgia

Mark Henriksen, Ph.D.
Physics Department
University of Maryland
Baltimore, Maryland

Chad Hershock, Ph.D.
Center for Research on Learning
 and Teaching
University of Michigan
Ann Arbor, Michigan

Jeremiah N. Jarrett, Ph.D.
Department of Biology
Central Connecticut State
 University
New Britain, Connecticut

Scott L. Kight, Ph.D.
Department of Biology
Montclair State University
Montclair, New Jersey

Jennifer O. Liang, Ph.D.
Department of Biology
University of Minnesota–Duluth
Duluth, Minnesota

Candace Lutzow-Felling, Ph.D.
State Arboretum of Virginia &
 Blanding Experimental Farm
Boyce, Virginia

Joseph F. McCullough, Ph.D.
Physics Program Chair
Cabrillo College
Aptos, California

Heather Mernitz, Ph.D.
Department of Physical Science
Alverno College
Milwaukee, Wisconsin

Sadredin C. Moosavi, Ph.D.
Department of Earth and
 Environmental Sciences
Tulane University
New Orleans, Louisiana

David L. Reid, Ph.D.
Department of Biology
Blackburn College
Carlinville, Illinois

Scott M. Rochette, Ph.D.
Department of the Earth Sciences
SUNY College at Brockport
Brockport, New York

Karyn L. Rogers, Ph.D.
Department of Geological
 Sciences
University of Missouri
Columbia, Missouri

Laurence Rosenhein, Ph.D.
Department of Chemistry
Indiana State University
Terre Haute, Indiana

Sara Seager, Ph.D.
Department of Planetary Sciences
 and Physics
Massachusetts Institute of
 Technology
Cambridge, Massachusetts

Tom Shoberg, Ph.D.
Missouri University of Science
 and Technology
Rolla, Missouri

Patricia Simmons, Ph.D.
North Carolina State University
Raleigh, North Carolina

William H. Steinecker, Ph.D.
Research Scholar
Miami University
Oxford, Ohio

Paul R. Stoddard, Ph.D.
Department of Geology and
 Environmental Geosciences
Northern Illinois University
DeKalb, Illinois

John R. Villarreal, Ph.D.
Department of Chemistry
The University of Texas–Pan
 American
Edinburg, Texas

John R. Wagner, Ph.D.
Department of Geology
Clemson University
Clemson, South Carolina

Jerry Waldvogel, Ph.D.
Department of Biological Sciences
Clemson University
Clemson, South Carolina

Donna L. Witter, Ph.D.
Department of Geology
Kent State University
Kent, Ohio

Edward J. Zalisko, Ph.D.
Department of Biology
Blackburn College
Carlinville, Illinois

Special thanks to the Museum of
Science, Boston, Massachusetts,
and Ioannis Miaoulis, the
Museum's president and director,
for serving as content advisors for
the technology and design strand
in this program.

Teacher Reviewers

Herb Bergamini
The Northwest School
Seattle, Washington

David R. Blakely
Arlington High School
Arlington, Massachusetts

Jane E. Callery
Capital Region Education Council
Hartford, Connecticut

Jeffrey C. Callister
Former Earth Science Instructor
Newburgh Free Academy
Newburgh, New York

Colleen Campos
Cherry Creek Schools
Aurora, Colorado

Scott Cordell
Amarillo Independent School
District
Amarillo, Texas

Dan Gabel
Consulting Teacher, Science
Montgomery County Public
Schools
Montgomery County, Maryland

Wayne Goates
Kansas Polymer Ambassador
Intersociety Polymer Education
Council (IPEC)
Wichita, Kansas

Katherine Bobay Graser
Mint Hill Middle School
Charlotte, North Carolina

Darcy Hampton
Science Department Chair
Deal Middle School
Washington, D.C.

Sean S. Houseknecht
Elizabethtown Area Middle School
Elizabethtown, Pennsylvania

Tanisha L. Johnson
Prince George's County Public
Schools
Lanham, Maryland

Karen E. Kelly
Pierce Middle School
Waterford, Michigan

Dave J. Kelso
Manchester Central High School
Manchester, New Hampshire

Beverly Crouch Lyons
Career Center High School
Winston-Salem, North Carolina

Angie L. Matamoros, Ed.D.
ALM Consulting
Weston, Florida

Corey Mayle
Durham Public Schools
Durham, North Carolina

Keith W. McCarthy
George Washington Middle
School
Wayne, New Jersey

Timothy McCollum
Charleston Middle School
Charleston, Illinois

Bruce A. Mellin
Cambridge College
Cambridge, Massachusetts

John Thomas Miller
Thornapple Kellogg High School
Middleville, Michigan

Randy Mousley
Dean Ray Stucky Middle School
Wichita, Kansas

Yolanda O. Peña
John F. Kennedy Junior High
School
West Valley, Utah

Kathleen M. Poe
Fletcher Middle School
Jacksonville Beach, Florida

Judy Pouncey
Thomasville Middle School
Thomasville, North Carolina

Vickki Lynne Reese
Mad River Middle School
Dayton, Ohio

Bronwyn W. Robinson
Director of Curriculum
Algiers Charter Schools
Association
New Orleans, Louisiana

Shirley Rose
Lewis and Clark Middle School
Tulsa, Oklahoma

Linda Sandersen
Sally Ride Academy
Whitefish Bay, Wisconsin

Roxanne Scala
Schuyler-Colfax Middle School
Wayne, New Jersey

Patricia M. Shane, Ph.D.
Associate Director
Center for Mathematics & Science
Education
University of North Carolina
at Chapel Hill
Chapel Hill, North Carolina

Bradd A. Smithson
Science Curriculum Coordinator
John Glenn Middle School
Bedford, Massachusetts

Sharon Stroud
Consultant
Colorado Springs, Colorado

Master Teacher Board

Emily Compton
Park Forest Middle School
Baton Rouge, Louisiana

Georgi Delgadillo
East Valley School District
Spokane Valley, Washington

Treva Jeffries
Toledo Public Schools
Toledo, Ohio

James W. Kuhl
Central Square Middle School
Central Square, New York

Bonnie Mizell
Howard Middle School
Orlando, Florida

Joel Palmer, Ed.D.
Mesquite Independent School
District
Mesquite, Texas

Leslie Pohley
Largo Middle School
Largo, Florida

Susan M. Pritchard, Ph.D.
Washington Middle School
La Habra, California

Anne Rice
Woodland Middle School
Gurnee, Illinois

Richard Towle
Noblesville Middle School
Noblesville, Indiana

Table of Contents

Lab zone® Enter the Lab zone for hands-on inquiry.

Chapter Lab Investigation:
• Directed Inquiry: Modeling Mantle Convection Currents • Open Inquiry: Modeling Mantle Convection Currents

Inquiry Warm-Ups: • What Is a System? • Earth's Interior • Tracing Heat Flow • What Is the Land Like Around Your School? • How Can You Flatten the Curved Earth? • Can a Map Show Relief?

Quick Labs: • Parts of Earth's System • What Forces Shape Earth? • How Do Scientists Find Out What's Inside Earth? • Build a Model of Earth • How Can Heat Cause Motion in a Liquid? • Surface Features • Modeling Landforms • 2-D and 3-D Maps • Measuring in Degrees • Where in the World? • A Map in a Pan

my science online.com

Go to MyScienceOnline.com to interact with this chapter's content. Keyword: Introducing Earth

> **UNTAMED SCIENCE**
• Beyond the Dirt

> **PLANET DIARY**
• Introducing Earth

> **INTERACTIVE ART**
• The Earth System • Heat Transfer • Topographic Maps

> **ART IN MOTION**
• Convection in Earth's Mantle

> **REAL-WORLD INQUIRY**
• Exploring Earth's Layers

Lab zone® Enter the Lab zone for hands-on inquiry.

Chapter Lab Investigation:
• Directed Inquiry: Testing Rock Flooring
• Open Inquiry: Testing Rock Flooring

Inquiry Warm-Ups: • How Does the Rate of Cooling Affect Crystals? • How Do Rocks Compare? • Liquid to Solid • Acid Test for Rocks • A Sequined Rock • Recycling Rocks

Quick Labs: • Classifying Objects as Minerals • Identifying Minerals • Crystal Hands • Classify These Rocks • How Do Igneous Rocks Form? • The Rocks Around Us • How Does Pressure Affect Particles of Rock? • What Causes Layers? • How Do Grain Patterns Compare? • Which Rock Came First?

my science online.com

Go to MyScienceOnline.com to interact with this chapter's content.
Keyword: Minerals and Rocks

> **UNTAMED SCIENCE**
• Climbing Through the Rock Cycle

> **PLANET DIARY**
• Minerals and Rocks

> **INTERACTIVE ART**
• Crystal Systems • Rock Cycle

> **ART IN MOTION**
• Formation of Igneous Rock

> **REAL-WORLD INQUIRY**
• What Would You Build With?

Enter the Lab zone
for hands-on inquiry.

Chapter Lab Investigation:
• Directed Inquiry: Modeling Sea-Floor Spreading
• Open Inquiry: Modeling Sea-Floor Spreading

Inquiry Warm-Ups: • How Are Earth's Continents Linked Together? • What Is the Effect of a Change in Density? • Plate Interactions

Quick Labs: • Moving the Continents • Mid-Ocean Ridges • Reversing Poles • Mantle Convection Currents

my science online

Go to MyScienceOnline.com to interact with this chapter's content.
Keyword: Plate Tectonics

> **UNTAMED SCIENCE**
• Diving Toward Divergence

> **PLANET DIARY**
• Plate Tectonics

> **INTERACTIVE ART**
• Continental Drift • Sea-Floor Spreading

> **ART IN MOTION**
• Changing Earth's Crust

> **REAL-WORLD INQUIRY**
• Predicting Plate Motions

 Enter the Lab zone for hands-on inquiry.

Chapter Lab Investigation:
• Directed Inquiry: Finding the Epicenter
• Open Inquiry: Finding the Epicenter

Inquiry Warm-Ups: • How Does Stress Affect Earth's Crust? • How Do Seismic Waves Travel Through Earth? • How Can Seismic Waves Be Detected?

Quick Labs: • Effects of Stress • Modeling Faults • Modeling Stress • Properties of Seismic Waves • Measuring Earthquakes • Design a Seismograph • Earthquake Patterns

MY SCIENCE online.com

Go to MyScienceOnline.com to interact with this chapter's content. Keyword: Earthquakes

> UNTAMED SCIENCE
• Why Quakes Shake

> PLANET DIARY
• Earthquakes

> INTERACTIVE ART
• Seismic Waves • Earthquake Engineering

> ART IN MOTION
• Stresses and Faults

> REAL-WORLD INQUIRY
• Placing a Bay Area Stadium

CHAPTER 5

Volcanoes

Enter the Lab zone for hands-on inquiry.

△ **Chapter Lab Investigation:**
 • Directed Inquiry: Gelatin Volcanoes
 • Open Inquiry: Gelatin Volcanoes

△ **Inquiry Warm-Ups:** • Moving Volcanoes
 • How Fast Do Liquids Flow? • How Do
 Volcanoes Change Land?

△ **Quick Labs:** • Where Are Volcanoes
 Found on Earth's Surface? • Volcanic Stages
 • Identifying Volcanic Landforms • How Can
 Volcanic Activity Change Earth's Surface?

my science online.com

**Go to MyScienceOnline.com to
interact with this chapter's content.
Keyword: Volcanoes**

▷ **UNTAMED SCIENCE**
• Why Some Volcanoes Explode

▷ **PLANET DIARY**
• Volcanoes

▷ **INTERACTIVE ART**
• Composite Volcano • Volcanoes and
Volcanic Landforms

▷ **ART IN MOTION**
• Volcanic Boundaries and Hot Spots

▷ **REAL-WORLD INQUIRY**
• Monitoring a Volcano

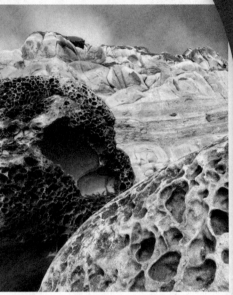

Lab zone® Enter the Lab zone for hands-on inquiry.

Chapter Lab Investigation:
• Directed Inquiry: Investigating Soils and Drainage
• Open Inquiry: Investigating Soils and Drainage

Inquiry Warm-Ups: How Fast Can It Fizz?
• What Is Soil? • How Can You Keep Soil From Washing Away?

Quick Labs: Freezing and Thawing
• Rusting Away • It's All on the Surface
• The Contents of Soil • Using It Up • Soil Conservation

MY SCIENCE ONLINE.com

Go to MyScienceOnline.com to interact with this chapter's content.
Keyword: **Weathering and Soil**

> **UNTAMED SCIENCE**
• Tafoni, No Bologna

> **PLANET DIARY**
• Weathering and Soil

> **INTERACTIVE ART**
• The Forces of Weathering • Soil Layers

> **ART IN MOTION**
• Mechanical and Chemical Weathering

> **REAL-WORLD INQUIRY**
• Being Smart About Soil

Lab zone® Enter the Lab zone for hands-on inquiry.

Chapter Lab Investigation:
• Directed Inquiry: Sand Hills
• Open Inquiry: Sand Hills

Inquiry Warm-Ups: • How Does Gravity Affect Materials on a Slope? • How Does Moving Water Wear Away Rocks? • How Do Glaciers Change the Land? • What Is Sand Made Of? • How Does Moving Air Affect Sediment?

Quick Labs: • Weathering and Erosion • Raindrops Falling • Erosion Cube • Surging Glaciers • Modeling Valleys • Shaping a Coastline • Desert Pavement

my science online .com

Go to MyScienceOnline.com to interact with this chapter's content. **Keyword: Erosion and Deposition**

> **UNTAMED SCIENCE**
• Carving a Canyon

> **PLANET DIARY**
• Erosion and Deposition

> **ART IN MOTION**
• Effects of Glaciers

> **INTERACTIVE ART**
• Mass Movement • Effects of Waves

> **REAL-WORLD INQUIRY**
• Why Live Where It Floods?

 Enter the Lab zone for hands-on inquiry.

△ **Chapter Lab Investigation:**
• Directed Inquiry: Exploring Geologic Time Through Core Samples
• Open Inquiry: Exploring Geologic Time Through Core Samples

△ **Inquiry Warm-Ups:** • What's In a Rock? • Which Layer Is the Oldest? • How Long Till It's Gone? • This Is Your Life! • How Could Planet Earth Form in Space? • Dividing History

△ **Quick Labs:** • Sweet Fossils • Modeling Trace Fossils • Modeling the Fossil Record • How Did It Form? • The Dating Game • How Old Is It? • Going Back in Time • Learning From Fossils • Graphing the Fossil Record • Modeling an Asteroid Impact • Cenozoic Timeline

my science online.com

Go to MyScienceOnline.com to interact with this chapter's content. Keyword: A Trip Through Geologic Time

▷ **UNTAMED SCIENCE**
• Riding the Geo-vator

▷ **ART IN MOTION**
• Change Over Geologic Time

▷ **INTERACTIVE ART**
• Fossil Formation • Piecing Together the Past • Index Fossils

▷ **REAL-WORLD INQUIRY**
• How Do You Find the Age of a Rock?

 Enter the Lab zone for hands-on inquiry.

Chapter Lab Investigation:
• Directed Inquiry: Design and Build a Solar Cooker
• Open Inquiry: Design and Build a Solar Cooker

Inquiry Warm-Ups: • What's in a Piece of Coal? • Can You Capture Solar Energy? • Which Bulb Is More Efficient?

Quick Labs: • Observing Oil's Consistency • Fossil Fuels • Producing Electricity • Human Energy Use • Future Energy Use

MY SCIENCE ONLINE.com

Go to MyScienceOnline.com to interact with this chapter's content.
Keyword: Energy Resources

> **UNTAMED SCIENCE**
• Farming the Wind

> **PLANET DIARY**
• Energy Resources

> **INTERACTIVE ART**
• Hydroelectric Power Plant • Nuclear Power Plant

> **ART IN MOTION**
• Oil: Long to Form, Quick to Use

> **REAL-WORLD INQUIRY**
• Energy Conservation

 Lab zone®   **Enter the Lab zone for hands-on inquiry.**

Chapter Lab Investigation:
• Directed Inquiry: Water From Trees
• Modeling Ocean Currents
• Open Inquiry: Water From Trees
• Modeling Ocean Currents

Inquiry Warm-Ups: • Where Does the Water Come From? • Mapping Surface Waters • Where Does the Water Go? • What Can You Learn Without Seeing? • How Do Waves Change a Beach? • Bottom to Top

Quick Labs: • Water, Water Everywhere • Water on Earth • What Is a Watershed? • Modeling How a Lake Forms • How Can Algal Growth Affect Pond Life? • Soil Percolation • An Artesian Well • Ocean Conditions • The Shape of the Ocean Floor • Making Waves • Modeling Current • Deep Currents

my science online.com

Go to MyScienceOnline.com to interact with this chapter's content. Keyword: Water

▷ **UNTAMED SCIENCE**
• Water Cyclists

▷ **PLANET DIARY**
• Water

▷ **INTERACTIVE ART**
• Water Cycle • Water Motion

▷ **ART IN MOTION**
• How Does Groundwater Collect?

▷ **REAL-WORLD INQUIRY**
• Water Cycle, Interrupted

▷ **VIRTUAL LAB**
• How Does the Density of Sea Water Change?

Lab zone® Enter the Lab zone for hands-on inquiry.

Chapter Lab Investigation:
• Directed Inquiry: Heating Earth's Surface
• Open Inquiry: Heating Earth's Surface

Inquiry Warm-Ups: • How Long Will the Candle Burn? • Does Air Have Mass? • Is Air There? • Does a Plastic Bag Trap Heat? • What Happens When Air Is Heated? • Does the Wind Turn?

Quick Labs: • Breathe In, Breathe Out
• What Is the Source of Earth's Energy?
• Properties of Air • Soda Bottle Barometer
• Effects of Altitude on the Atmosphere
• Layers of the Atmosphere • Calculating Temperature Changes • How Does the Sun's Energy Reach Earth? • Measuring Temperature • Temperature and Height • Build a Wind Vane • Modeling Global Wind Belts

my science ONLINE.com

Go to MyScienceOnline.com to interact with this chapter's content.
Keyword: The Atmosphere

> **UNTAMED SCIENCE**
• Gliding Through the Atmosphere

> **INTERACTIVE ART**
• Measuring Air Pressure • Global Winds

> **ART IN MOTION**
• Greenhouse Effect

> **VIRTUAL LAB**
• What Do Temperature and Volume Have to Do With Air Pressure?

 Enter the Lab zone for hands-on inquiry.

Chapter Lab Investigation:
• Directed Inquiry: Reading a Weather Map
• Open Inquiry: Reading a Weather Map

Inquiry Warm-Ups: • Where Did the Water Go? • How Does Fog Form? • How Can You Make Hail? • How Do Fluids of Different Densities Move? • Can You Make a Tornado? • Predicting Weather

Quick Labs: • Water in the Air • Measuring to Find the Dew Point • How Clouds Form • Identifying Clouds • Types of Precipitation • Floods and Droughts • Tracking Air Masses • Weather Fronts • Cyclones and Anticyclones • Where Do Hurricanes Come From? • Storm Safety • Modeling Weather Satellites

my science online.com

Go to MyScienceOnline.com to interact with this chapter's content.
Keyword: **Weather**

> **UNTAMED SCIENCE**
• Twisted Adventures

> **PLANET DIARY**
• Weather

> **INTERACTIVE ART**
• Water Cycle • Weather Fronts • Different Conditions, Different Storms

> **ART IN MOTION**
• How Does Precipitation Form?

> **REAL-WORLD INQUIRY**
• Predicting the Weather

Lab **Enter the Lab zone**
zone **for hands-on inquiry.**

△ **Chapter Lab Investigation:**
  • Directed Inquiry: Sunny Rays and Angles
  • Open Inquiry: Sunny Rays and Angles

△ **Inquiry Warm-Ups:** • How Does Latitude
Affect Climate? • How Do Climates Differ?
• What Story Can Tree Rings Tell? • What Is
the Greenhouse Effect?

△ **Quick Labs:** • Inferring United States
Precipitation Patterns • Classifying Climates
• Making and Interpreting a Climograph
• Climate Clues • Earth's Movement and
Climate • Greenhouse Gases and Global
Warming

my science
online.com

Go to MyScienceOnline.com to
interact with this chapter's content.
Keyword: Climate and Climate Change

▷ **UNTAMED SCIENCE**
• Searching for the Perfect Climate

▷ **PLANET DIARY**
• Climate and Climate Change

▷ **INTERACTIVE ART**
• Continental Drift • Climate Change:
Causes, Effects, Solutions

▷ **ART IN MOTION**
• Greenhouse Effect

▷ **VIRTUAL LAB**
• Climate Connections

 Lab zone ® **Enter the Lab zone for hands-on inquiry.**

Chapter Lab Investigation:
• Directed Inquiry: Reasons for the Seasons
• Open Inquiry: Reasons for the Seasons

Inquiry Warm-Ups: • Earth's Sky • What Causes Day and Night? • What Factors Affect Gravity? • How Does the Moon Move? • When Is High Tide? • Why Do Craters Look Different From Each Other?

Quick Labs: • Observing the Night Sky • Watching the Sky • Sun Shadows • What's Doing the Pulling? • Around and Around We Go • Moon Phases • Eclipses • Modeling the Moon's Pull of Gravity • Moonwatching

my science online.com

Go to MyScienceOnline.com to interact with this chapter's content. **Keyword:** Earth, Moon, and Sun

UNTAMED SCIENCE
• Phased by the Moon!

PLANET DIARY
• Earth, Moon, and Sun

INTERACTIVE ART
•Constellations •Seasons and Earth's Revolution •Solar and Lunar Eclipses

ART IN MOTION
• Cause of Tides

VIRTUAL LAB
• What Affects Gravity?

 Enter the Lab zone for hands-on inquiry.

Chapter Lab Investigation:
• Directed Inquiry: Speeding Around the Sun
• Open Inquiry: Speeding Around the Sun

Inquiry Warm-Ups: • What Is at the Center? • How Big Is Earth? • How Can You Safely Observe the Sun? • Ring Around the Sun • How Big Are the Planets? • Collecting Micrometeorites

Quick Labs: • Going Around in Circles • A Loopy Ellipse • Clumping Planets • Layers of the Sun • Viewing Sunspots • Characteristics of the Inner Planets • Greenhouse Effect • Under Pressure • Make a Model of Saturn • Changing Orbits

my science online

Go to MyScienceOnline.com to interact with this chapter's content.
Keyword: The Solar System

> UNTAMED SCIENCE
• 100 Meters to Neptune

> PLANET DIARY
• The Solar System

> INTERACTIVE ART
• Objects of the Solar System • Anatomy of the Sun

> ART IN MOTION
• Formation of the Solar System

> VIRTUAL LAB
• Why Isn't Pluto a Planet?

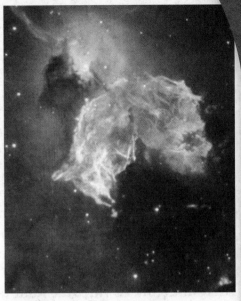

 Lab zone® Enter the Lab zone for hands-on inquiry.

Chapter Lab Investigation:
• Directed Inquiry: Design and Build a Telescope
• Open Inquiry: Design and Build a Telescope

Inquiry Warm-Ups: • How Does Distance Affect an Image? • Stringing Along • How Stars Differ • What Determines How Long Stars Live? • Why Does the Milky Way Look Hazy? • How Does the Universe Expand?

Quick Labs: • Observing a Continuous Spectrum • How Far Is That Star? • Measuring the Universe • Star Bright • Interpreting the H-R Diagram • Life Cycle of Stars • Death of a Star

my science online.com

Go to MyScienceOnline.com to interact with this chapter's content. Keyword: Stars, Galaxies, and the Universe

> UNTAMED SCIENCE
• Reaching Into Deep Space

> PLANET DIARY
• Stars, Galaxies, and the Universe

> INTERACTIVE ART
• Refracting and Reflecting Telescopes
• Universe at Different Scales • Lives of Stars

> ART IN MOTION
• Expanding Universe

> REAL-WORLD INQUIRY
• How Can Light Help You Find Life?

Enter the Lab zone for hands-on inquiry.

Chapter Lab Investigation:
• Directed Inquiry: Recycling Paper
• Waste, Away!
• Open Inquiry: Recycling Paper
• Waste, Away!

Inquiry Warm-Ups: • How Do You Decide?
• Using Resources • How Does Mining Affect
the Land? • What's in the Trash? • How Does
the Scent Spread? • How Does the Water
Change?

Quick Labs: • Environmental Issues
• Comparing Costs and Benefits • Natural
Resources • Land Use • Modeling Soil
Conservation • It's in the Numbers • Half-
Life • How Acid is Your Rain? • Analyzing
Ozone • It's in the Air • Where's the Water?
• Cleaning Up Oil Spills • Getting Clean

my science online.com

Go to MyScienceOnline.com to
interact with this chapter's content.
Keyword: Land, Air, and Water
Resources

> UNTAMED SCIENCE
• Manatee Survival

> PLANET DIARY
• Land, Air, and Water Resources

> INTERACTIVE ART
• Exploring Environmental Impact • Recycled
Materials • Air Pollution

> REAL-WORLD INQUIRY
• Mutation Mystery

Untamed Science™

Video Series: Chapter Adventures

Untamed Science created this captivating video series for **interactive** SCIENCE featuring a unique segment for every chapter of the program.

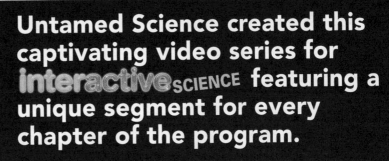

Featuring videos such as

Interactive Science

Interactive Science is a program that features 3 pathways to match the way you learn.

• The write-in student edition enables you to become an active participant as you read about science.

• A variety of hands-on activities will not only engage you but also provide you with a deep understanding of science concepts.

• Go to MyScienceOnline.com to access a wide array of digital resources built especially for students like you!

 Interact with your textbook.

 Interact with inquiry.

 Interact online.

interactive SCIENCE

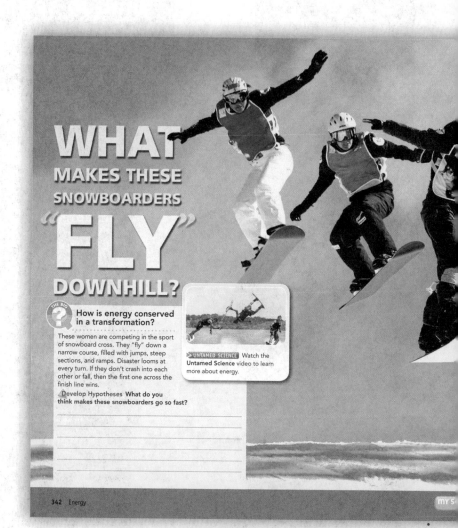

WHAT MAKES THESE SNOWBOARDERS "FLY" DOWNHILL?

THE BIG ? How is energy conserved in a transformation?

These women are competing in the sport of snowboard cross. They "fly" down a narrow course, filled with jumps, steep sections, and ramps. Disaster looms at every turn. If they don't crash into each other or fall, then the first one across the finish line wins.

Develop Hypotheses What do you think makes these snowboarders go so fast?

_____

_____

_____

_____

> UNTAMED SCIENCE Watch the **Untamed Science** video to learn more about energy.

342 Energy

my s

 Get Engaged!

At the start of each chapter, you will see two questions: an Engaging Question and the Big Question. Each chapter's Big Question will help you start thinking about the Big Ideas of Science. Look for the Big Q symbol throughout the chapter! . . . .

Start with the Big Question

CHAPTER 10

Energy

Energy ▷ UNTAMED SCIENCE ▷ THE BIG QUESTION 343

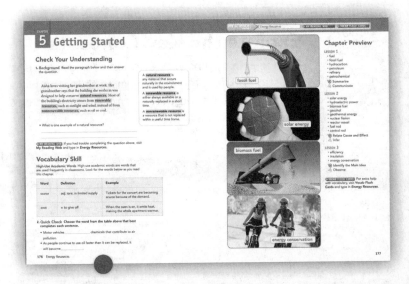

Build Reading, Inquiry, and Vocabulary Skills

- In every lesson you will learn new Reading 🔄 and Inquiry skills △ to help you read and think like a scientist.

- Go online to MyScienceOnline.com and click on My Reading Web to get additional reading at your level.

my science online.com

Go Online!

At MyScienceOnline.com, you will find a variety of engaging digital resources such as the Untamed Science videos. Follow the Untamed Science video crew as they travel the globe exploring the Big Ideas of Science.

Unlock the Big Question

MY SCIENCE ONLINE.com

Go to MyScienceOnline.com to access a wide array of digital resources such as Virtual Labs, additional My Planet Diary activities, and Got It? assessments with instant feedback.

Explore the Key Concepts

Each lesson begins with a series of Key Concept questions. The interactivities in each lesson will help you understand these concepts and Unlock the Big Question.

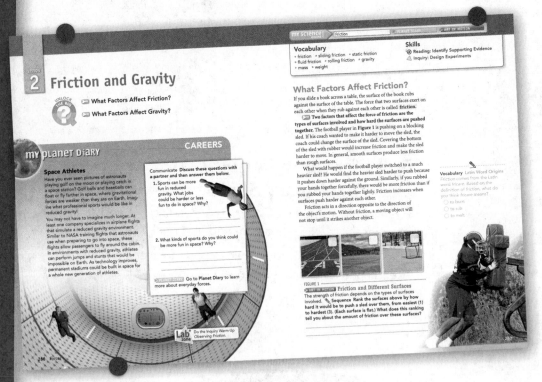

MY PLANET DIARY

At the start of each lesson, My Planet Diary will introduce you to amazing events, significant people, and important discoveries in science or help you to overcome common misconceptions about science concepts.

apply it!

Elaborate further with the Apply It activities. This is your opportunity to take what you've learned and apply those skills to new situations.

Lab zone

Look for the Lab zone triangle. This means that it's time to do a hands-on inquiry lab. In every lesson, you'll have the opportunity to do a hands-on inquiry activity that will help reinforce your understanding of the lesson topic. • • • • • • • • • • • • • • • • • •

Land Reclamation Fortunately, it is possible to replace land damaged by erosion or mining. The process of restoring an area of land to a more productive state is called **land reclamation**. In addition to restoring land for agriculture, land reclamation can restore habitats for wildlife. Many different types of land reclamation projects are currently underway all over the world. But it is generally more difficult and expensive to restore damaged land and soil than it is to protect those resources in the first place. In some cases, the land may not return to its original state.

FIGURE 4 • • • • • • • • • • • • • • • • • •
Land Reclamation
These pictures show land before and after it was mined.

✎ **Communicate** Below the pictures, write a story about what happened to the land.

🔑 **Assess Your Understanding**

1a. Review Subsoil has (less/more) plant and animal matter than topsoil.

b. Explain What can happen to soil if plants are removed?

c. Apply Concepts Wha___
that could prevent ___
land reclamation?___

got it? • • • • • • • • • • • • • • • • • •

○ I get it! Now I know that soil management is important because ___

○ I need extra help with ___

Go to **MY SCIENCE** S **COACH** online for help with this subject.

Do the Quick Lab
Modeling Soil Conservation.

[partial text at left edge]
tile area becomes depleted
ecome a desert. The
as that previously were
___uh fih KAY shun).
___. For example, a **drought**
___lls in an area. During
___ the exposed soil easily
___ cattle and sheep and
___e desertification, too.
___eople cannot grow crops
___has occurred. As a result,
___Desertification is severe in
___ere are moving to the
___ themselves on the land.

Key
■ Existing desert
■ High-risk area
■ Moderate-risk area

___n areas where there
___ on the map to support

___fication, what are some
___s effects?

got it?

Evaluate Your Progress

After answering the Got It question, think about how you're doing. Did you get it or do you need a little help? Remember, **MY SCIENCE** S **COACH** is there for you if you need extra help.

Assess the Big Question

Explore the Big Question

At one point in the chapter, you'll have the opportunity to take all that you've learned to further explore the Big Question.

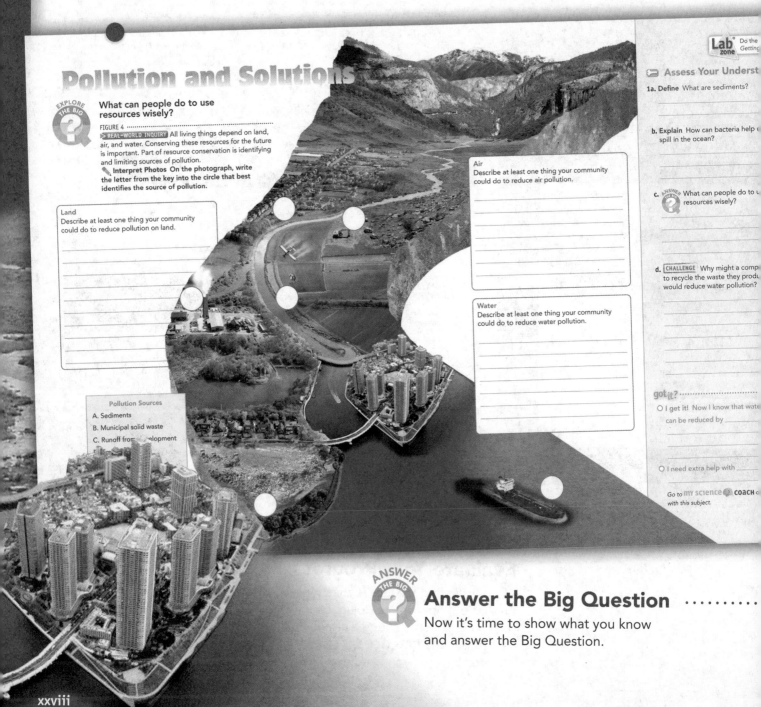

Pollution and Solutions

What can people do to use resources wisely?

FIGURE 4 ....
REAL-WORLD INQUIRY All living things depend on land, air, and water. Conserving these resources for the future is important. Part of resource conservation is identifying and limiting sources of pollution.

✎ **Interpret Photos** On the photograph, write the letter from the key into the circle that best identifies the source of pollution.

Land
Describe at least one thing your community could do to reduce pollution on land.

Air
Describe at least one thing your community could do to reduce air pollution.

Water
Describe at least one thing your community could do to reduce water pollution.

Pollution Sources
A. Sediments
B. Municipal solid waste
C. Runoff from development

Lab Do the
zone Getting

☞ Assess Your Underst

1a. Define What are sediments?

b. Explain How can bacteria help spill in the ocean?

c. What can people do to u
resources wisely?

d. CHALLENGE Why might a comp
to recycle the waste they prod
would reduce water pollution?

got it? ....

○ I get it! Now I know that wate
can be reduced by

○ I need extra help with

Go to MY SCIENCE COACH c
with this subject.

Answer the Big Question ....

Now it's time to show what you know and answer the Big Question.

Review What You've Learned

Use the Chapter Study Guide to review the
Big Question and prepare for the test.

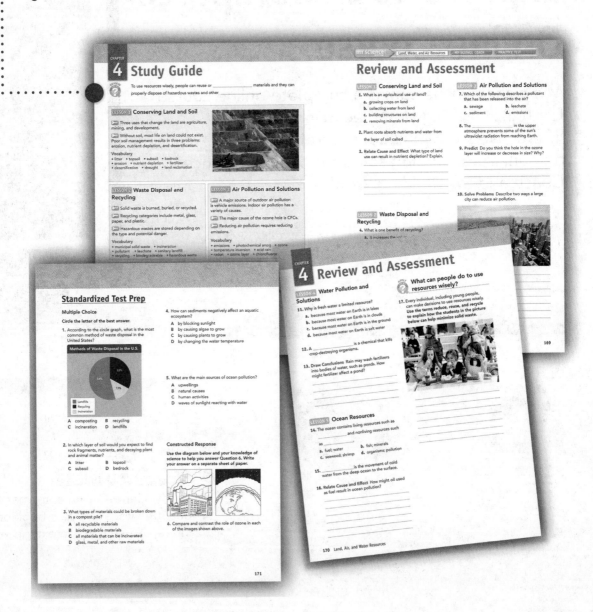

Practice Taking Tests

Apply the Big Question and take a practice test in
standardized test format.

Explore Your Complete Online Course

MyScienceOnline.com is a complete online course featuring exciting Untamed Science Videos, Interactive Art Simulations, and innovative personalized learning solutions like My Science Coach and My Reading Web.

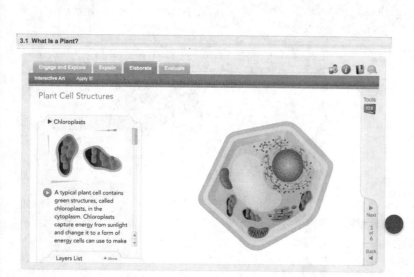

> INTERACTIVE ART

At MyScienceOnline.com, many of the beautiful visuals in your book become interactive so you can extend your learning.

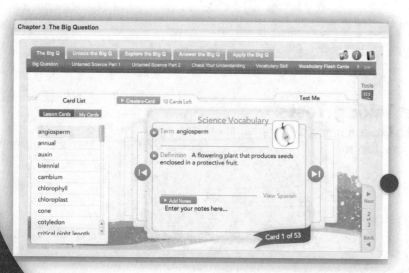

> VOCAB FLASH CARDS

Practice chapter vocabulary with interactive flash cards. Each card has an image, definitions in English and Spanish, and space for your own notes.

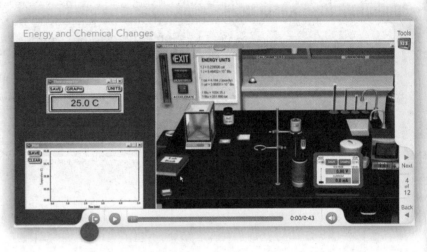

▷ VIRTUAL LAB

Get more practice with realistic virtual labs. Interact with on-line labs without costly equipment or clean-up.

Your Online Student Edition

Create an online notebook! Highlight important information and create sticky notes. Notes and highlights are saved in your own personal Online Student Edition.

? BIG IDEAS OF SCIENCE

Have you ever worked on a jigsaw puzzle? Usually a puzzle has a theme that leads you to group the pieces by what they have in common. But until you put all the pieces together you can't solve the puzzle. Studying science is similar to solving a puzzle. The big ideas of science are like puzzle themes. To understand big ideas, scientists ask questions. The answers to those questions are like pieces of a puzzle. Each chapter in this book asks a big question to help you think about a big idea of science. By answering the big questions, you will get closer to understanding the big idea.

✎ **Before you read each chapter, write about what you know and what more you'd like to know.**

BIGIDEA

Scientists use scientific inquiry to explain the natural world.

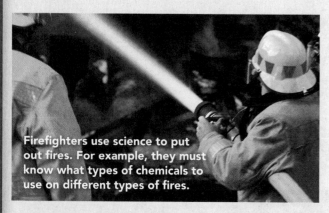

Firefighters use science to put out fires. For example, they must know what types of chemicals to use on different types of fires.

What do you already know about how science affects your everyday life? ✎ **What more would you like to know?**

_____
_____
_____
_____
_____
_____
_____
_____

BIGIDEA

Scientists use mathematics in many ways.

The spring scale measures the weight of the oranges, which is a measure of the force of gravity on the oranges.

Which measurement tools have you used in everyday life? ✎ **Which math skills do you need to practice?**

_____
_____
_____
_____
_____
_____
_____
_____

BIGIDEA
Earth is a continually changing planet.

Over millions of years, the Colorado River cut through layers of solid rock to form the Grand Canyon in Arizona.

What do you already know about changes on Earth? **What more would you like to know?**

_____

_____

_____

Big Questions:

🔹 What is the structure of Earth? Chapter 1

🔹 How do rocks form? Chapter 2

🔹 How do moving plates change Earth's crust? Chapter 3

🔹 Why do earthquakes occur more often in some places than in others? Chapter 4

🔹 How does a volcano erupt? Chapter 5

🔹 What processes break down rock? Chapter 6

🔹 What processes shape the surface of the land? Chapter 7

After reading the chapters, write what you have learned about the Big Idea.

_____

_____

_____

BIGIDEA
Earth is 4.6 billion years old and the rock record contains its history.

This fossil of a turtle is millions of years old.

What do you already know about Earth's history? **What more would you like to know?**

_____

_____

_____

Big Question:

🔹 How do scientists study Earth's past? Chapter 8

After reading the chapter, write what you have learned about the Big Idea.

_____

_____

_____

_____

_____

_____

_____

BIGIDEA
Living things interact with their environment.

People depend on the ocean's living resources, such as codfish, for food.

What do you already know about how you get food, water, and shelter from your surroundings?

✎ **What more would you like to know?**

_____

_____

_____

_____

Big Questions:

❓ What are some of Earth's energy sources?
Chapter 9

❓ How do people use Earth's resources?
Chapter 17

✎ **After reading the chapters, write what you have learned about the Big Idea.**

_____

_____

_____

BIGIDEA
Earth's land, water, air, and life form a system.

A severe storm, drought, or wildfire could cause changes in Yellowstone National Park that would affect these bison.

What do you already know about how changes in one part of Earth can affect another part?

✎ **What would you like to know?**

_____

_____

_____

Big Questions:

❓ How does fresh water cycle on Earth?
Chapter 10

❓ How does the sun's energy affect Earth's atmosphere? Chapter 11

❓ How do meteorologists predict the weather? Chapter 12

❓ What factors affect Earth's climate?
Chapter 13

✎ **After reading the chapters, write what you have learned about the Big Idea.**

_____

_____

_____

_____

BIG IDEA

Earth is part of a system of objects that orbit the sun.

Jupiter, its moons, and Earth are all parts of the solar system. Each of them is held in its orbit by gravity.

What do you already know about Earth and the other objects in the solar system? ✎ **What more would you like to know?**

_____

_____

Big Questions:

❓ How do Earth, the moon, and the sun interact? Chapter 14

❓ Why are objects in the solar system different from each other? Chapter 15

✎ **After reading the chapters, write what you have learned about the Big Idea.**

_____

_____

_____

BIG IDEA

The universe is very old, very large, and constantly changing.

This galaxy, visible near the Big Dipper, is so far away that light from it takes 12 million years to reach Earth!

What do you already know about the universe? ✎ **What more would you like to know?**

_____

_____

_____

Big Question:

❓ How do astronomers learn about distant objects in the universe? Chapter 16

✎ **After reading the chapter, write what you have learned about the Big Idea.**

_____

_____

_____

_____

HOW DEEP INTO EARTH CAN THIS CLIMBER GO?

What is the structure of Earth?

Descending into a canyon, this climber will get nearer to the center of Earth. But how close will he get? As climbers move down through narrow, dark passages of rock and dirt, they sometimes have to dig their way through. Some spelunkers, or cave explorers, have even descended into caves over 2,000 meters deep—the length of nearly 22 football fields!

Predict If this climber could go all the way down to Earth's center, what materials other than dirt and solid rock might he find along the way? Explain your answer.

_____

_____

_____

_____

> **UNTAMED SCIENCE** Watch the **Untamed Science** video to learn more about Earth's structure.

Introducing Earth

1 Getting Started

Check Your Understanding

1. **Background** Read the paragraph below and then answer the question.

On a field trip, Paula sees that beach cliffs near the sea have worn away. "Where do the cliffs go?" she asks. Her teacher says, "The cliffs are exposed to natural **forces** all year. The harsh weather breaks the cliffs into pieces. **Gravity** causes the pieces to fall to the sea. Waves then shape the pieces into small **particles**, which wash away."

> A **force** is a natural power that acts on an object.
>
> **Gravity** is the force that makes objects fall toward Earth's center.
>
> A **particle** is a very small fragment of a much larger object.

• What forces change the beach cliffs each year?

_____

_____

> **MY READING WEB** If you had trouble answering the question above, visit **My Reading Web** and type in *Introducing Earth.*

Vocabulary Skill

Identify Related Word Forms You can increase your vocabulary by learning related word forms. If you know that the noun *energy* means "the ability to do work," you can figure out the meaning of the adjective *energetic.*

Verb	Noun	Adjective
destroy to reduce to pieces	destruction the process of reducing to pieces	destructive tending to cause damage or to reduce to pieces
radiate to release energy	radiation energy released in the form of rays or waves	radiant released as waves or rays

2. **Quick Check** Review the words related to *destroy.* Then circle the correct form of the word *destroy* in the following sentence.

• The (destruction/destructive) winds of a hurricane can be very dangerous.

system

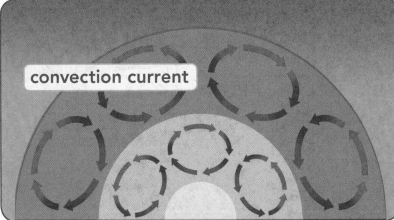

convection current

mountain

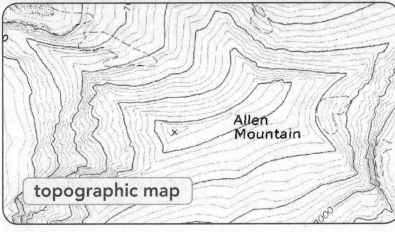

topographic map

Allen Mountain

Chapter Preview

LESSON 1
- system • energy • atmosphere
- geosphere • hydrosphere
- biosphere • constructive force
- destructive force

🔁 Ask Questions
△ Draw Conclusions

LESSON 2
- seismic wave • pressure • crust
- basalt • granite • mantle
- lithosphere • asthenosphere
- outer core • inner core

🔁 Identify Supporting Evidence
△ Interpret Data

LESSON 3
- radiation • convection
- conduction • density
- convection current

🔁 Relate Cause and Effect
△ Communicate

LESSON 4
- topography • elevation
- relief • landform • plain
- mountain • mountain range
- plateau • landform region

🔁 Sequence
△ Classify

LESSON 5
- globe • map
- map projection • symbol
- key • scale • degree
- equator • hemisphere
- prime meridian • latitude
- longitude

🔁 Identify the Main Idea
△ Measure

LESSON 6
- topographic map • contour line
- contour interval • index contour

🔁 Compare and Contrast
△ Make Models

> VOCAB FLASH CARDS For extra help with vocabulary, visit **Vocab Flash Cards** and type in *Introducing Earth*.

3

The Earth System

🔑 **What Are the Main Parts of the Earth System?**

🔑 **How Do Constructive and Destructive Forces Change Earth?**

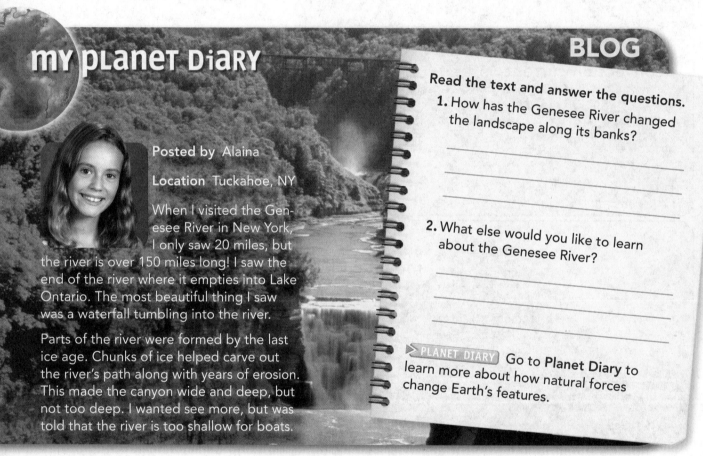

my planet Diary

BLOG

Posted by Alaina

Location Tuckahoe, NY

When I visited the Genesee River in New York, I only saw 20 miles, but the river is over 150 miles long! I saw the end of the river where it empties into Lake Ontario. The most beautiful thing I saw was a waterfall tumbling into the river.

Parts of the river were formed by the last ice age. Chunks of ice helped carve out the river's path along with years of erosion. This made the canyon wide and deep, but not too deep. I wanted see more, but was told that the river is too shallow for boats.

Read the text and answer the questions.

1. How has the Genesee River changed the landscape along its banks?

_____

_____

_____

2. What else would you like to learn about the Genesee River?

_____

_____

_____

▷ **PLANET DIARY** Go to **Planet Diary** to learn more about how natural forces change Earth's features.

What Are the Main Parts of the Earth System?

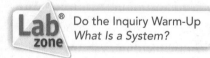
Do the Inquiry Warm-Up
What Is a System?

The Grand Canyon is made up of different parts. Rock forms the canyon walls. Water flows through the canyon in the form of a river, which carves away the rock. Animals such as deer drink the river's water. And air fills the canyon, allowing the animals to breathe. All these parts work together. So the environment of the Grand Canyon can be thought of as a system. A **system** is a group of parts that work together as a whole. **Figure 1** shows how air, water, rock, and life work together in another part of Earth.

Vocabulary

- system • energy • atmosphere • geosphere
- hydrosphere • biosphere • constructive force
- destructive force

Skills

↻ Reading: Ask Questions

△ Inquiry: Draw Conclusions

Earth as a System The Earth system involves a constant flow of matter through different parts. For example, you may know that in the *water cycle,* water evaporates from the ocean, rises into the atmosphere, and then falls from the sky as rain. The rainwater then flows into and over Earth, and then back into the ocean.

You might be surprised to learn that rock, too, cycles through the Earth system. For example, new rock can form from molten material inside Earth called *magma.* This material can rise to the surface and harden on land to form new rock. The new rock can then erode into small pieces. The pieces can be washed into the ocean, where they may sink to the bottom as small particles, or *sediment.* If enough of the small particles collect, the weight of the sediment can crush all the particles together. The particles can then be cemented together to form new rock. The flow of rock through the Earth system is called the *rock cycle.*

The constant flow, or cycling, of matter through the Earth system is driven by energy. **Energy** is the ability to do work. The energy that drives the Earth system has two main sources: heat from the sun and heat flowing out of Earth as it cools.

FIGURE 1 ························

All Systems Go!

The many parts of the Earth system all work together.

✎ **Develop Hypotheses Look at the photograph. Choose one part of the Earth system—rock, water, air, or life—and describe how the other parts might be affected if the first part were removed.**

_____
_____
_____
_____
_____
_____
_____
_____
_____
_____
_____
_____
_____
_____
_____

FIGURE 2 ··························

▷ INTERACTIVE ART The Earth System

Earth's four spheres can affect one another.

✏️ **Interpret Photos** Read the descriptions of Earth's four spheres. On the lines in each box, write the spheres that are interacting with each other in the small photograph next to the box.

Parts of the Earth System

Earth contains air, water, land, and life. Each of these parts forms its own part, or "sphere." 🔑 **The Earth system has four main spheres: the atmosphere, the hydrosphere, the geosphere, and the biosphere. As a major source of energy for Earth processes, the sun can be considered part of the Earth system as well.** Each part of the Earth system can be studied separately. But the four parts are interconnected, as shown in **Figure 2**.

One of the most important parts of the Earth system is—you! Humans greatly affect the air, water, land, and life of Earth. For instance, the amount of paved land, including roads and parking lots, in the United States is now larger than the state of Georgia.

Atmosphere

Earth's outermost layer is a mixture of gases—mostly nitrogen and oxygen. It also contains dust particles, cloud droplets, and the rain and snow that form from water vapor. It contains Earth's weather, and is the foundation for the different climates around the world. Earth's **atmosphere** (AT muh sfeer) is the relatively thin envelope of gases that forms Earth's outermost layer.

_____

_____

Geosphere

Nearly all of Earth's mass is found in Earth's solid rocks and metals, in addition to other materials. Earth's **geosphere** (GEE uh sfeer) has three main parts: a metal core, a solid middle layer, and a rocky outer layer.

_____

_____

Hydrosphere

About three quarters of Earth is covered by a relatively thin layer of water. Earth's water can take the form of oceans, glaciers, rivers, lakes, groundwater, and water vapor. Of the surface water, most is the salt water of the ocean. Only a tiny part of the hydrosphere is fresh water that is drinkable by humans. The **hydrosphere** (HY druh sfeer) contains all of Earth's water.

_____

_____

Feedback Within a System For years, the ice in glaciers at Glacier National Park in Montana has been melting. The melting is caused by rising temperatures. As the volume of ice in the glaciers has decreased, the land around the glaciers has become warmer. The warmer land melts the glaciers even faster.

Melting of the glaciers in Glacier National Park is an example of a process called *feedback*. When feedback occurs, a system returns—or feeds back—to itself data about a change in the system. In Glacier National Park, the ground around the melting glaciers feeds back warmer temperatures to the glaciers. Feedback can increase the effects of a change, as in the case of warming glaciers, or slow the effects down. Feedback demonstrates how changes in one part of the Earth system might affect the other parts. For example, the feedback of melting glaciers affects the geosphere (the ground), hydrosphere (glaciers), and atmosphere (climate).

🔄 **Ask Questions** Write a question about feedback. Then read the text and answer your question.

_____
_____
_____
_____
_____
_____
_____

 Lab zone® Do the Quick Lab *Parts of Earth's System.*

🔑 **Assess Your Understanding**

1a. Review The Earth system consists of the sun and four main _____

b. Classify The sphere that contains humans is the _____

c. Evaluate the Impact on Society Give one example of how humans affect the hydrosphere. Then explain how this change impacts society.

_____
_____
_____

got it? ....

O **I get it!** Now I know that the main parts of the Earth system are _____

_____
_____

O **I need extra help with** _____

Go to MY SCIENCE COACH *online for help with this subject.*

Biosphere
Life exists at the tops of mountains, deep underground, at the bottom of the ocean, and high up in the atmosphere. In fact, life exists in all kinds of conditions. But life as we know it cannot exist without water. The parts of Earth that contain living organisms make up the **biosphere** (BI uh sfeer).

_____
_____
_____

How Do Constructive and Destructive Forces Change Earth?

Suppose you left a movie camera running in one spot for the next 100 million years and then you watched the movie in fast motion. You would see lands forming and mountains rising up—but you would also see them eroding back down again. 🔑 **Lands are constantly being created and destroyed by competing forces.**

Constructive Forces The Himalayas are Earth's highest mountains. But rock in the Himalayas contains *fossils,* or remains, of ocean animals such as ammonites. How could creatures that once lived at the bottom of the sea be found at the top of the world?

The Himalayas are the result of the collision of two sections of Earth's *lithosphere,* or Earth's top layer of stiff, solid rock. This layer is broken into huge pieces, or *plates,* that move slowly over Earth. The slow movement of Earth's plates is called *plate tectonics.*

The Himalayas are the result of the collision of the plate that carries India with the plate that carries China. Over millions of years, as these plates collided, their edges were squeezed slowly upward. This process lifted up the ocean floor and formed the Himalayas, shown in **Figure 3.**

Forces that construct, or build up, mountains are called **constructive forces.** 🔑 **Constructive forces shape the land's surface by building up mountains and other landmasses.** Volcanoes build up Earth's surface by spewing lava that hardens into rock. Earthquakes build landmasses by lifting up mountains and rock.

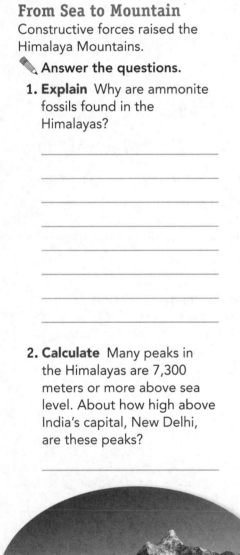

FIGURE 3 ·············

From Sea to Mountain
Constructive forces raised the Himalaya Mountains.

✎ **Answer the questions.**

1. **Explain** Why are ammonite fossils found in the Himalayas?

_____

_____

_____

_____

_____

_____

_____

2. **Calculate** Many peaks in the Himalayas are 7,300 meters or more above sea level. About how high above India's capital, New Delhi, are these peaks?

_____

Ammonite

AFGHANISTAN
CHINA
Eurasian Plate
PAKISTAN
New Delhi ✪
NEPAL
HIMALAYAS
BHUTAN
Indo-Australian Plate
BANGLADESH
INDIA
INDIAN OCEAN

Key
⌒ Plate boundary
Elevation
Meters
4,500
3,000
1,800
900
300
150
0

Destructive Forces While the Himalayas are being built up, they are also being torn down. Ice, rain, wind, and changing temperatures tear the rock apart. This process is called *weathering*. After the rock is torn apart, gravity pulls it downward. Eventually, rivers and streams carry away most of the eroded material.

Because forces such as ice, rain, wind, and changing temperatures wear down, or destroy, landmasses, they are called **destructive forces.** 🔑 **Destructive forces destroy and wear away landmasses through processes like erosion and weathering.** *Erosion* is the wearing down and carrying away of land by natural forces such as water, ice, or wind.

Vocabulary Identify Related Word Forms Use the text and your knowledge of the word *weather* to write a definition of *weathering*.

_____

_____

_____

_____

Since 1983, lava from Kilauea has covered more than 100 square kilometers of land in Hawaii. Here, lava flows into the Pacific Ocean. When it reaches the water, it cools quickly. The cooled lava hardens to form new rock.

❶ Draw Conclusions The forces that cause lava to erupt are (constructive/destructive) forces.

❷ CHALLENGE Other than the weather, what force wears down the new rock formed by the magma from Kilauea?

_____

_____

Lab zone Do the Quick Lab *What Forces Shape Earth?*

🔑 **Assess Your Understanding**

2a. Review Forces that erode mountains are called (constructive/destructive) forces.

b. List List the destructive forces that act on mountains to erode them.

_____

_____

c. Relate Cause and Effect How do destructive forces change Earth?

_____

_____

_____

_____

got it? ....

○ **I get it!** Now I know that constructive and destructive forces change Earth by _____

○ **I need extra help with** _____

Go to my science 💬 COACH online for help with this subject.

9

LESSON

2 Earth's Interior

UNLOCK THE BIG

🔑 How Do Geologists Learn About Earth's Interior?

🔑 What Are the Features of Earth's Crust, Mantle, and Core?

my planet Diary

Inside Earth

Deep inside Earth, our planet is constantly changing. Dr. Samuel B. Mukasa, a geochemist at the University of Michigan, studies some of these changes. He examines rocks in Antarctica that have been brought up to Earth's surface by magma. When he examines these rocks, he looks for elements that occur only in very small amounts. These elements can offer telltale signs of processes occurring near the boundary between Earth's crust and its mantle—or even at deeper levels. By studying rocks at Earth's surface, Dr. Mukasa is helping us understand Earth's interior.

CAREERS

Read the text and then answer the question.

How is Dr. Mukasa able to study Earth's interior without actually seeing it?

_____
_____
_____
_____
_____

▷ PLANET DIARY Go to **Planet Diary** to learn more about Earth's interior.

Lab® Do the Inquiry Warm-Up **zone** *Earth's Interior.*

How Do Geologists Learn About Earth's Interior?

Processes that affect Earth's surface are often a result of what's going on inside Earth. But what's inside Earth? This question is very difficult to answer, because geologists are unable to see deep inside Earth. But geologists have found other methods to study the interior of Earth. 🔑 **Geologists have used two main types of evidence to learn about Earth's interior: direct evidence from rock samples and indirect evidence from seismic waves.**

Vocabulary
- seismic wave • pressure • crust • basalt
- granite • mantle • lithosphere • asthenosphere
- outer core • inner core

Skills
↻ Reading: Identify Supporting Evidence
△ Inquiry: Interpret Data

Evidence From Rock Samples Geologists have drilled holes as deep as 12.3 kilometers into Earth. The drills bring up samples of rock. These rocks give geologists clues about Earth's structure and conditions deep inside Earth, where the rocks formed. In addition, volcanoes sometimes blast rock to the surface from depths of more than 100 kilometers. These rocks provide more information about Earth's interior. Also, in laboratories, geologists have re-created conditions inside Earth to see how rock behaves. For instance, they focus laser beams on pieces of rock while squeezing the rock with great force.

Evidence From Seismic Waves To study Earth's interior, geologists use an indirect method. When earthquakes occur, they produce **seismic waves** (SYZ mik). Geologists record the seismic waves and study how they travel through Earth. The speed of seismic waves and the paths they take give geologists clues about the structure of the planet. That is, the paths of seismic waves reveal areas inside Earth where the makeup or form of material changes. To better understand how seismic waves can reveal Earth's interior, look at how the paths of ocean waves "reveal" the island shown in **Figure 1.**

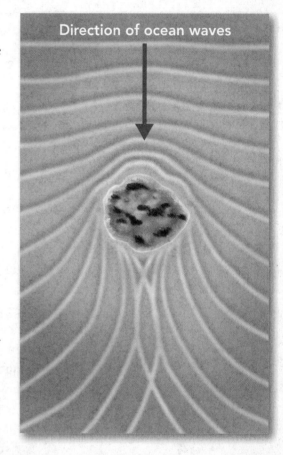

Direction of ocean waves

FIGURE 1 ···
Waves
Paths of ocean waves change when the waves reach an island.

✎ **Infer** Geologists have found that the paths of seismic waves change when the waves reach specific depths inside Earth. What can you infer about Earth's structure from this observation?

_____
_____
_____
_____

Lab zone ® Do the Quick Lab *How Do Scientists Find Out What's Inside Earth?*

🔑 Assess Your Understanding

got it? ··

O **I get it!** Now I know that to learn about Earth's interior, geologists use two main types of evidence: _____

_____

O **I need extra help with** _____

Go to MY SCIENCE ⓢ COACH online for help with this subject.

11

What Are the Features of Earth's Crust, Mantle, and Core?

Today, scientists know that Earth's interior is made up of three main layers. Each of Earth's layers covers the layers beneath it, much like the layers of an onion. 🔑 **The three main layers of Earth are the crust, the mantle, and the core. These layers vary greatly in size, composition, temperature, and pressure.**

Although each layer of Earth has its own characteristics, some properties apply throughout all of Earth. For example, the deeper inside Earth, the greater the mass of the rock that is pressing down from above. **Pressure** results from a force pressing on an area. Because of the weight of the rock above, pressure inside Earth increases with depth. 🔑 **The deeper down inside Earth, the greater the pressure.** Look at **Figure 2.** Pressure inside Earth increases much like pressure in the swimming pool increases.

The mass of rock that presses down from above affects the temperature inside Earth. 🔑 **The temperature inside Earth increases as depth increases.** Just beneath Earth's surface, the surrounding rock is cool. But at about 20 meters down, the rock starts to get warmer. For every 40 meters of depth from that point, the temperature typically rises 1 Celsius degree. The rapid rise in temperature continues for several tens of kilometers. Eventually, the temperature increases more slowly, but steadily. The high temperatures inside Earth are the result of the great pressures squeezing rock and the release of energy from radioactive substances. Some heat is also left over from the formation of Earth 4.6 billion years ago.

FIGURE 2 ·······························

Pressure and Depth

The deeper that this swimmer goes, the greater the pressure from the surrounding water.

✏️ **Compare and Contrast** How is the water in the swimming pool similar to Earth's interior? How is it different? (*Hint:* Consider both temperature and pressure in your answer.)

_____

_____

_____

_____

_____

_____

_____

_____

_____

Depth
0

0.5 m

1 m

Pressure increases

1.5 m

2 m

The Crust In the summer, you might climb a mountain or hike down into a shaded valley. During each of these activities, you are interacting with Earth's **crust,** the layer of rock that forms Earth's outer skin. 🔑 **The crust is a layer of solid rock that includes both dry land and the ocean floor.** The main elements in the crust are oxygen and silicon, as shown in **Figure 3.**

The crust is much thinner than the layer that lies beneath it. In most places, the crust is between 5 and 40 kilometers thick. It is thickest under high mountains—where it can be as thick as 80 kilometers—and thinnest beneath the ocean.

The crust that lies beneath the ocean is called oceanic crust. The composition of oceanic crust is nearly constant. Its overall composition is much like basalt, with small amounts of ocean sediment on top. **Basalt** (buh SAWLT) is a dark, fine-grained rock.

Continental crust, the crust that forms the continents, contains many types of rocks. So, unlike oceanic crust, its composition varies greatly. But overall the composition of continental crust is much like granite. **Granite** is a rock that usually is a light color and has coarse grains. Both granite and basalt have more oxygen and silicon than they have any other element.

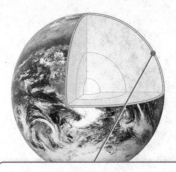

> Read the text on this page and then fill in the missing information below.
>
> Layer: _____
>
> Thickness: _____

FIGURE 3 ························
Earth's Crust
The crust is Earth's outer layer of solid rock.

The Earth's Crust

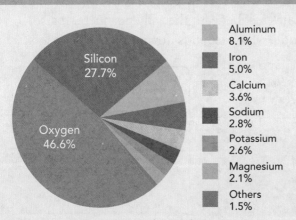

Silicon 27.7%	Aluminum 8.1%
Oxygen 46.6%	Iron 5.0%
	Calcium 3.6%
	Sodium 2.8%
	Potassium 2.6%
	Magnesium 2.1%
	Others 1.5%

Note: Percentages given are by weight.

The circle graph above shows the composition of Earth's crust.

✏️ **Use the graph and the text on this page to complete the activities below.**

1. **Read Graphs** In total, how much of Earth's crust is made up of oxygen and silicon?

   _____

2. **Summarize** Fill in the missing information in the two charts at the right.

Oceanic crust

Oceanic crust

Typical rock: _____

Relative grain size: _____

Color: _____

Continental crust

Typical rock: _____

Relative grain size: _____

Color: _____

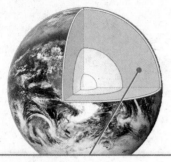

Read the text on this page and then fill in the missing information below.

Layer: _____

Thickness: _____

_____

The Mantle

About 40 kilometers beneath dry land, the rock in Earth's interior changes. Rock here contains more magnesium and iron than rock above it. The rock below the boundary is the solid material of the **mantle**, a layer of hot rock. 🔑 **The mantle is made of rock that is very hot, but solid.** Scientists divide the mantle into layers based on the physical characteristics of those layers. Overall, the mantle is nearly 3,000 kilometers thick.

The Lithosphere

The uppermost part of the mantle is brittle rock, like the rock of the crust. Both the crust and the uppermost part of the mantle are strong, hard, and rigid. So geologists often group the crust and uppermost mantle into a single layer called the **lithosphere** (LITH uh sfeer). As shown in **Figure 4,** Earth's lithosphere averages about 100 kilometers thick.

The Asthenosphere

Below the lithosphere, the material is hotter and under increasing pressure. As a result, the part of the mantle just beneath the lithosphere is less rigid than the rock above. Over thousands of years this part of the mantle can bend like a metal spoon. But it's still solid. If you kicked it, you would stub your toe. This soft layer is called the **asthenosphere** (as THEN uh sfeer).

The Mesosphere

Beneath the asthenosphere, the mantle is hot but more rigid. The stiffness of the *mesosphere* is the result of increasingly high pressure. This layer includes a region called the transition zone, which lies just beneath the asthenosphere. It also includes the lower mantle, which extends down to Earth's core.

FIGURE 4 ·······························

Mantle Piece

Earth's mantle is nearly 3,000 kilometers thick. The rigid lithosphere rests on the softer material of the asthenosphere.

✏️ **Describe** Fill in the information in the boxes next to the diagram of the upper mantle.

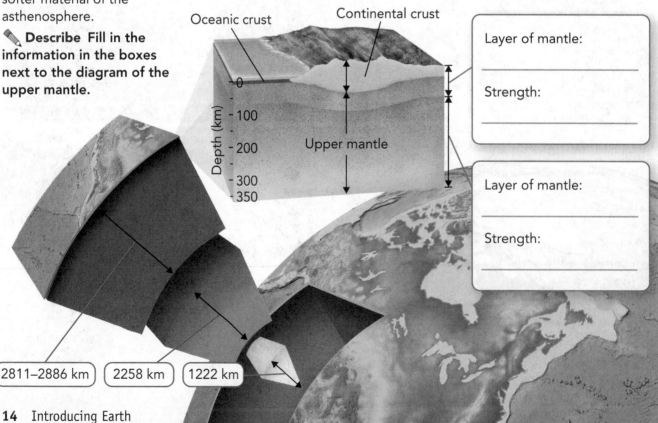

Oceanic crust

Continental crust

Depth (km)

0
-100
-200
-300
-350

Upper mantle

Layer of mantle:
_____
Strength:
_____

Layer of mantle:
_____
Strength:
_____

2811–2886 km   2258 km   1222 km

The Core Below the mantle lies Earth's core.  **The core is made mostly of the metals iron and nickel. It consists of two parts—a liquid outer core and a solid inner core.** The outer core is 2,258 kilometers thick. The inner core is a solid ball. Its radius is 1,222 kilometers. The total radius of the core is 3,480 kilometers. Earth's core occupies the center of the planet.

Outer Core and Inner Core The **outer core** is a layer of molten metal surrounding the inner core. Despite enormous pressure, the outer core is liquid. The **inner core** is a dense ball of solid metal. In the inner core, extreme pressure squeezes the atoms of iron and nickel so much that they cannot spread out to become liquid.

Currently, most evidence suggests that both parts of the core are made of iron and nickel. But scientists have found data suggesting that the core also contains oxygen, sulfur, and silicon.

Read the text on this page and then fill in the missing information below.

Layer: _____

Radius: _____

FIGURE 5 ....

The Core of It
Earth's core consists of two separate layers.

✎ **Review** Put each term below in its proper place in the Venn diagram.

solid metal	molten metal
iron	nickel
dense ball	liquid layer

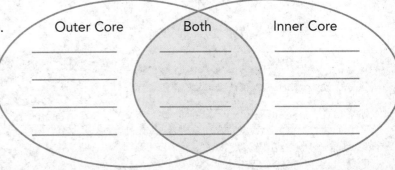

Outer Core Both Inner Core

do the
math! Analyzing Data

Temperature Inside Earth
The graph shows how temperatures change between Earth's surface and the core.

① **Read Graphs** Between what depths does Earth's temperature increase the slowest?

_____

② [CHALLENGE] Why does the graph show a temperature of 16°C at 0 meters of depth?

_____

_____

③ ⬠ **Interpret Data** How does temperature change with depth in Earth's interior?

_____

_____

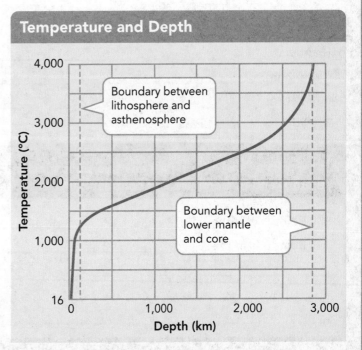

Temperature and Depth

Boundary between lithosphere and asthenosphere

Boundary between lower mantle and core

Temperature (°C)

Depth (km)

······ Identify Supporting
Evidence How can iron filings
provide evidence that a bar
magnet has a magnetic field?

_____

_____

_____

_____

_____

The Core and Earth's Magnetic Field Scientists think that movements in the liquid outer core create Earth's magnetic field. Because Earth has a magnetic field, the planet acts like a giant bar magnet. Earth's magnetic field affects the whole planet.

To understand how a magnetic field affects an object, look at the bar magnet shown in **Figure 6.** If you place the magnet on a piece of paper and sprinkle iron filings on the paper, the iron filings line up with the bar's magnetic field. If you could surround Earth with iron filings, they would form a similar pattern.

When you use a compass, the compass needle aligns with the lines of force in Earth's magnetic field. These lines meet at Earth's magnetic poles. So the needle points to Earth's *magnetic* north pole, which is not the same location as Earth's *geographic* North Pole.

EXPLORE THE BIG ? Earth's Interior

What is the structure of Earth?

FIGURE 7 ··

▶ REAL-WORLD INQUIRY Earth is divided into distinct layers. Each layer has its own characteristics.

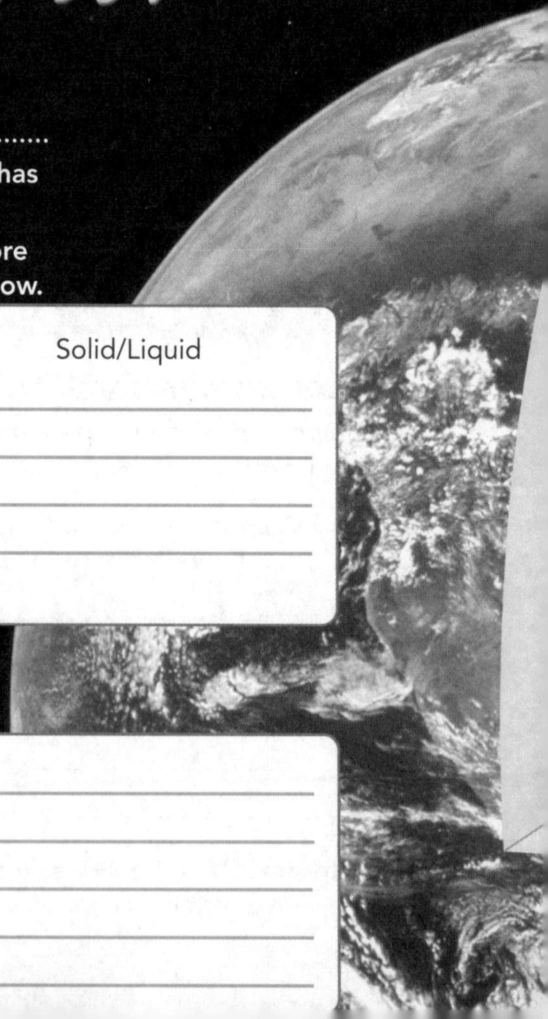

1. Summarize Draw each of Earth's layers. Include both the outer core and the inner core. Label each layer. Then, complete the chart below.

	Thickness/Radius	Composition	Solid/Liquid
Crust:			
Mantle:			
Outer core:			
Inner core:			
TOTAL:	6,371 km		

2. Compare and Contrast Pick any two points inside Earth and label them A and B. Compare and contrast Earth at those two points.

My Point A is in the _____

My Point B is in the _____

_____

_____

_____

FIGURE 6 ···

Earth's Magnetic Field

Earth's magnetic field has a north and south pole, like the magnetic field at each end of a magnet.

✏️ **Name** Which pole will a compass needle in North America point to? (Underline the correct label for the pole on the globe.)

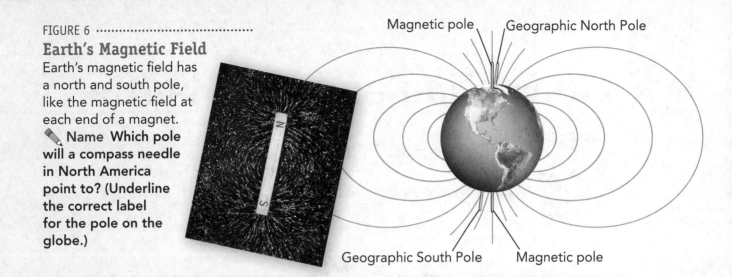

Magnetic pole   Geographic North Pole

Geographic South Pole   Magnetic pole

Lab zone® Do the Quick Lab *Build a Model of Earth.*

🔑 Assess Your Understanding

1a. Identify Earth's thin outer layer of solid rock is called (the crust/the mantle/ the core).

b. ANSWER THE BIG ❓ **Summarize** What is the structure of Earth?

_____

_____

_____

got it? ···

○ **I get it!** Now I know that each of the three main layers of Earth has its own features, as follows: _____

_____

_____

_____

_____

○ I need extra help with _____

Go to MY SCIENCE COACH *online for help with this subject.*

17

Convection and the Mantle

🔑 **How Is Heat Transferred?**

🔑 **How Does Convection Occur in Earth's Mantle?**

my planeT DiaRY

Lighting Up the Subject

Misconception: Rock cannot flow.

Did you know that the solid rock in Earth's mantle can flow like a fluid? To learn how, look at this image of a lava lamp. Heat from a bulb causes solid globs of wax at the bottom of the lamp to expand. As they expand, the globs become less dense. The globs then rise through the more dense fluid that surrounds them.

In Earth's mantle, great heat and pressure create regions of rock that are less dense than the rock around them. Over millions of years, the less dense rock slowly rises—like the solid globs in the lava lamp!

MISCONCEPTION

✎ **Compare and Contrast** Think about your own observations of liquids that flow. Then answer the question below.

How is flowing rock different from flowing water?

_____

_____

_____

_____

▷ **PLANET DIARY** Go to **Planet Diary** to learn more about Earth's mantle.

 Lab zone® Do the Inquiry Warm-Up *Tracing Heat Flow.*

How Is Heat Transferred?

Heat is constantly being transferred inside Earth and all around Earth's surface. For example, the warm sun heats the cooler ground. In fact, heat always moves from a warmer object to a cooler object. When an object is heated, the particles that make up the object move faster. The faster-moving particles have more energy.

The movement of energy from a warmer object to a cooler object is called heat transfer. 🔑 **There are three types of heat transfer: radiation, convection, and conduction.** Look at **Figure 1** to see examples of heat transfer.

Vocabulary

- radiation • convection
- conduction • density
- convection current

Skills

↻ Reading: Relate Cause and Effect

△ Inquiry: Communicate

Radiation

The sun constantly transfers light and heat through the air, warming your skin. The transfer of energy that is carried in rays like light is called **radiation**.

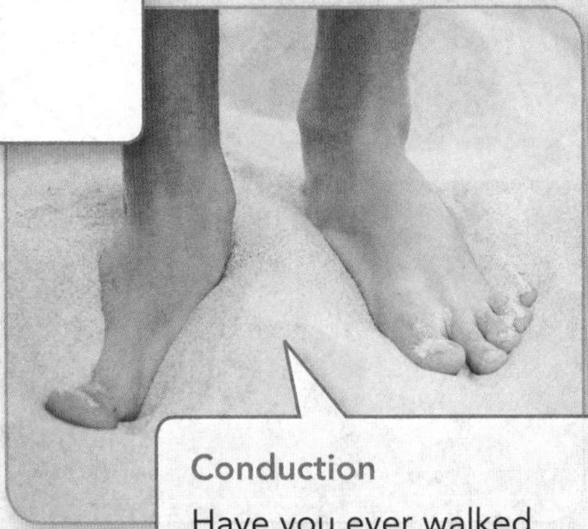

Conduction

Have you ever walked barefoot over hot sand? Your feet can feel as if they are burning! That is because the sand transfers its heat to your skin. Heat transfer between materials that are touching is called **conduction**.

Convection

Seagulls often soar on warm air currents. The currents are created as warm air rises from the ground. The warm air heats cooler air above it. Heat transfer by the movement of a fluid is called **convection**.

FIGURE 1 ....

▷ INTERACTIVE ART **Heat Transfer**

In each type of heat transfer, heat moves from a warmer object to a colder object.

△ **Communicate** Work with a classmate to think of other examples of conduction, convection, and radiation. (*Hint:* Think of different ways to cook food.) Write your answers in the spaces provided.

Radiation

_____

_____

Conduction

_____

_____

Convection

_____

_____

 Lab zone ® Do the Quick Lab *How Can Heat Cause Motion in a Liquid?*

🔑 Assess Your Understanding

got it? ....

○ **I get it!** Now I know that the three types of heat transfer are _____

_____

○ **I need extra help with** _____

Go to MY SCIENCE ⓢ COACH *online for help with this subject.*

19

How Does Convection Occur in Earth's Mantle?

Recall that Earth's mantle and core are extremely hot. How is heat transferred within Earth?

Convection Currents When you heat soup on a stove, convection occurs in the soup. That is, the soup at the bottom of the pot gets hot and expands. As the soup expands, its density decreases. **Density** is a measure of how much mass there is in a given volume of a substance. For example, most rock is more dense than water because a given volume of rock has more mass than the same volume of water.

The warm, less dense soup above the heat source moves upward and floats over the cooler, denser soup, as shown in **Figure 2.** Near the surface, the warm soup cools, becoming denser. Gravity then pulls the colder soup back down to the bottom of the pot. Here, it is reheated and rises again.

A constant flow begins. Cooler, denser soup sinks to the bottom of the pot. At the same time, warmer, less dense soup rises. The flow that transfers heat within a fluid is called a **convection current.** **Heating and cooling of a fluid, changes in the fluid's density, and the force of gravity combine to set convection currents in motion.** Without heat, convection currents eventually stop.

✏️

Relate Cause and Effect
What three processes or forces combine to set convection currents in motion?

_____

_____

_____

_____

_____

FIGURE 2 ·······························
Convection Currents
In a pot of soup, convection currents flow as the hotter, less dense soup rises and the cooler, more dense soup sinks.

apply it!

Hot springs are common in Yellowstone National Park. Here, melted snow and rainwater seep to a depth of 3,000 meters, where a shallow magma chamber heats the rock of Earth's crust. The rock heats the water to over 200°C and keeps it under very high pressure.

❶ **Compare and Contrast** The heated water is (more/less) dense than the melted snow and rainwater.

❷ [CHALLENGE] What might cause convection currents in a hot spring?

_____

_____

Convection Currents in Earth

Inside Earth, heat from the core and the mantle act like the stove that heats the pot of soup. That is, large amounts of heat are transferred by convection currents within the core and mantle. 🔑 **Heat from the core and the mantle itself causes convection currents in the mantle.** To see how these currents work in the core and mantle, look at **Figure 3.**

How is it possible for mantle rock to flow? Over millions of years, the great heat and pressure in the mantle have caused solid mantle rock to warm and flow very slowly. Many geologists think plumes of mantle rock rise slowly from the bottom of the mantle toward the top. The hot rock eventually cools and sinks back through the mantle. Over and over, the cycle of rising and sinking takes place. Convection currents like these have been moving inside Earth for more than four billion years!

There are also convection currents in the outer core. These convection currents cause Earth's magnetic field.

FIGURE 3 ·······························

> **ART IN MOTION** **Mantle Convection**

✏ **Interpret Diagrams** Place the following labels in the boxes for Points A and B:

hotter	less dense	sinks
colder	more dense	rises

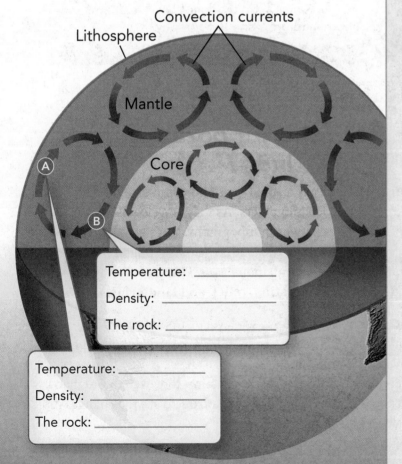

Convection currents

Lithosphere

Mantle

Core

A

B

Temperature: _____
Density: _____
The rock: _____

Temperature: _____
Density: _____
The rock: _____

did you know?

Convection currents may form on planets other than Earth. For example, scientists believe that the Great Red Spot on Jupiter may be the result of storms that have convection currents.

Lab zone ® Do the Lab Investigation *Modeling Mantle Convection Currents.*

🔑 Assess Your Understanding

1a. Explain A convection current transfers (heat /air) within a fluid.

b. Infer In which part of Earth's core do convection currents occur? _____

c. Predict What would happen to the convection currents in the mantle if Earth's interior eventually cooled down? Why?

_____
_____
_____
_____
_____

got it? ······································

O **I get it!** Now I know that convection currents in the mantle are caused by_____

_____
_____

O **I need extra help with** _____

Go to **my science** COACH *online for help with this subject.*

Exploring Earth's Surface

🔑 What Does the Topography of an Area Include?

🔑 What Are the Main Types of Landforms?

my planeT DiaRY

DISCOVERY

Lewis and Clark

In 1804, an expedition set out from near St. Louis to explore the land between the Mississippi River and the Pacific Ocean. The United States had just purchased a part of this vast territory from France. Few had traveled far to the west.

Led by Meriwether Lewis and William Clark, the expedition first traveled up the Missouri River. Then the group crossed the Rocky Mountains and followed the Columbia River to the Pacific Ocean.

If you were going on an expedition to explore unknown territory, what supplies would you bring with you?

_____

_____

_____

▶ PLANET DIARY Go to **Planet Diary** to learn more about landforms and topography.

Lab zone® Do the Inquiry Warm-Up
*What Is the Land Like
Around Your School?*

What Does the Topography of an Area Include?

On the journey to the Pacific, the Lewis and Clark expedition traveled more than 5,000 kilometers. As they traveled, Lewis and Clark observed many changes in topography. **Topography** (tuh PAWG ruh fee) is the shape of the land. An area's topography may be flat, sloping, hilly, or mountainous. 🔑 **The topography of an area includes the area's elevation, relief, and landforms.**

Elevation The height above sea level of a point on Earth's surface is its **elevation.** When Lewis and Clark started their expedition, they were about 140 meters above sea level. By the time they reached Lemhi Pass in the Rocky Mountains, they were more than 2,200 meters above sea level. Look at **Figure 1** to see the changes in elevation along Lewis and Clark's route.

Vocabulary

- topography • elevation • relief • landform
- plain • mountain • mountain range • plateau
- landform region

Skills

↻ Reading: Sequence

△ Inquiry: Classify

Relief The difference in elevation between the highest and lowest parts of an area is its **relief.** Early in their journey, Lewis and Clark encountered flat or rolling land that had low relief, or small differences in elevation. In the Rocky Mountains, they crossed huge mountains separated by deep valleys. These areas had high relief, or great differences in elevation.

Landforms If you followed the route of the Lewis and Clark expedition, you would see many different landforms. A **landform** is a feature of topography, such as a hill or valley, formed by the processes that shape Earth's surface. Different landforms have different combinations of elevation and relief.

FIGURE 1 ·····················

Lewis & Clark's Journey

The route of the Lewis and Clark expedition crossed regions that differed greatly in elevation and relief. ✎ **Calculate** Circle the highest and lowest points on their route. What is the relief between these two points?

_____

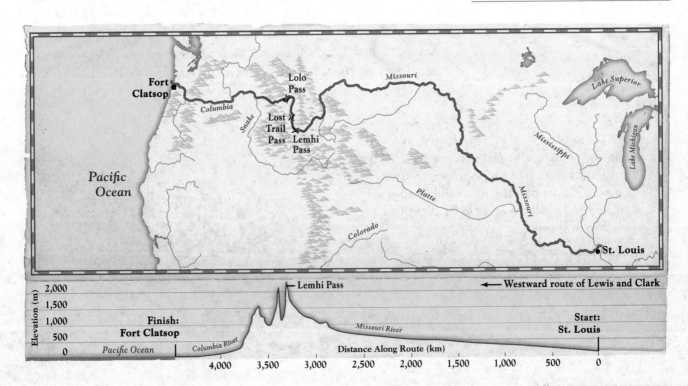

Assess Your Understanding

got it? ·····································

○ I get it! Now I know topography of an area includes _____

○ I need extra help with _____

Go to my science ⓢ COACH online for help with this subject.

Lab zone ® Do the Quick Lab
Surface Features.

What Are the Main Types of Landforms?

Landforms vary greatly in size and shape. They include level plains extending as far as the eye can see, rounded hills that you could climb on foot, and jagged mountains difficult to hike through. 🔑 **Three major types of landforms are plains, mountains, and plateaus.**

Plains A **plain** is a landform made up of nearly flat or gently rolling land with low relief. A plain that lies along a seacoast is called a coastal plain. In North America, a coastal plain extends around the continent's eastern and southeastern shores. Coastal plains have both low elevation and low relief.

A plain that lies away from the coast is called an interior plain. Interior plains are often low and have low relief, but their elevations can vary. The broad interior plains of North America are called the Great Plains.

The Great Plains extend north from Texas into Canada. The Great Plains also extend west to the Rocky Mountains from the states of North and South Dakota, Nebraska, Kansas, Oklahoma, and Texas. At the time of the Lewis and Clark expedition, the Great Plains were a vast grassland.

FIGURE 2 ···

Landforms

Plains, mountains, and plateaus are three of the many land-forms that make up the topography of Earth's surface.

✏️ **Apply Concepts** Below each photograph, identify the landform and circle its typical elevation and relief.

Landform: _____

Elevation: High / Low

Relief: High / Low

Mountains

A **mountain** is a landform with high elevation and high relief. A mountain's base can cover an area of several square kilometers or more. Mountains usually exist as part of a mountain range. A **mountain range** is a group of mountains that are closely related in shape, structure, area, and age. After crossing the Great Plains, the Lewis and Clark expedition crossed a rugged mountain range in Idaho called the Bitterroot Mountains.

The different mountain ranges in a region make up a mountain system. The Bitterroot Mountains are one mountain range in the mountain system known as the Rocky Mountains.

Mountain ranges and mountain systems in a long, connected chain form a larger unit called a mountain belt. The Rocky Mountains are part of a great mountain belt that stretches down the western sides of North America and South America.

Plateaus

A landform that has high elevation and a more or less level surface is called a **plateau.** A plateau is rarely perfectly smooth on top. Streams and rivers may cut into the plateau's surface. The Columbia Plateau in Washington State is an example. The Columbia River, which the Lewis and Clark expedition followed, slices through this plateau. The many layers of rock that make up the Columbia Plateau rise as high as 1,500 meters.

Sequence Place these features in order from smallest to largest: mountain system, mountain range, mountain belt, mountain.

_____

_____

_____

_____

Landform: _____
Elevation: High / Low
Relief: High / Low

Landform: _____
Elevation: High / Low
Relief: High / Low

25

Landform Regions

A large area of land where the topography is made up mainly of one type of landform is called a **landform region.** The Great Plains and the Rocky Mountains are examples of major landform regions, as are the Great Basin, the Colorado Plateau, the Sierra Nevada Coastal Range, and the Atlantic Coastal Plain. All of the land in one major landform region tends to have much in common. For example, the land of the Atlantic Coastal Plain is generally of low elevation and relief. The plain forms an apron of rocky material that slopes gently down from the Appalachian Mountains to the ocean. The Great Basin is mostly desert land at high elevation. Much of the Great Basin is made up of broad valleys separated by mountain ranges.

Other terms can be used to describe landform regions. For example, an upland is a region of hilly topography. The Superior Uplands, located near Lake Superior, include hilly terrain. A lowland is a region of plains with low elevation. The Central Lowlands are an area of plains bordered by areas of higher elevation.

did you know?

The highest elevation in the United States is Mt. McKinley, Alaska, at 6,194 meters. The lowest is Death Valley, California, at 86 meters below sea level.

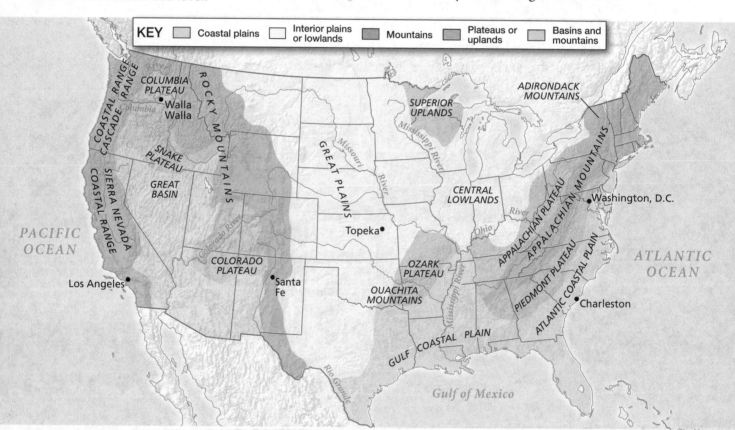

KEY   Coastal plains   Interior plains or lowlands   Mountains   Plateaus or uplands   Basins and mountains

FIGURE 3

Landform Regions of the United States

The United States has many different landform regions.

✏️ **Classify** Circle your home state (or another state) on the map and classify it by landform region(s).

apply it!

Use the picture to answer the questions.

1 Use words to describe the topography shown in the picture.

_____

_____

2 **Classify** Classify the picture by the type of landform region.

_____

Rocky Mountains

Colorado Plateau

Great Plains

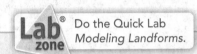

Lab zone Do the Quick Lab
Modeling Landforms.

Assess Your Understanding

1a. List What are the three main types of landforms?

_____

_____

b. Compare and Contrast How are plateaus and mountains alike? How are they different?

_____

_____

_____

c. Apply Concepts Which landform would be hardest to hike through? Why?

_____

_____

_____

got it? ....

O **I get it!** Now I know that the main types

of landforms are _____

_____

O **I need extra help with** _____

Go to **MY SCIENCE** Ⓢ **COACH** *online for help with this subject.*

UNLOCK THE BIG ?

🔑 **How Do Maps and Globes Represent Earth?**

🔑 **How Is Distance Measured in Degrees?**

🔑 **What Are Latitude and Longitude?**

my planet diary

DISCOVERY

Measuring Earth

Around 240 B.C., near the day of the summer solstice, the Greek scientist Eratosthenes (276–194 B.C.) calculated Earth's size. On that day, the sun was directly overhead at noon when viewed from the city of Syene, and its image was reflected in a well. At the same moment in Alexandria, to the north, the sun was not directly overhead. Instead, it appeared about $\frac{1}{50}$ of a circle south of the point directly overhead. Eratosthenes reasoned that the distance between the cities would be about $\frac{1}{50}$ of the distance around Earth. He multiplied the distance between the cities by 50 and found that Earth's circumference was 39,400 kilometers. This figure is very close to the modern measurement of 40,075 kilometers.

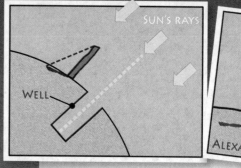

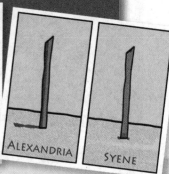

SUN'S RAYS

WELL

ALEXANDRIA   SYENE

✏️ **Communicate** Write your answer to each question below. Then discuss your answers with a partner.

1. What science skills did Eratosthenes use when he estimated Earth's circumference?

_____

_____

2. On the summer solstice, would a stick cast a shadow where you live? Why or why not?

_____

_____

_____

▶ PLANET DIARY   Go to **Planet Diary** to learn more about reading maps.

Lab zone ®   Do the Inquiry Warm-Up *How Can You Flatten the Curved Earth?*

Vocabulary
- globe • map • map projection • symbol
- key • scale • degree • equator • hemisphere
- prime meridian • latitude • longitude

Skills
⟳ Reading: Identify the Main Idea
△ Inquiry: Measure

How Do Maps and Globes Represent Earth?

Maps and globes show the shape, size, and position of features on Earth's surface. A **globe** is a sphere that represents Earth's entire surface. A **map** is a flat model of all or part of Earth's surface as seen from above. **Maps and globes are drawn to scale and use symbols to represent features on Earth's surface. To show Earth's curved surface on a flat map, mapmakers use map projections.**

Map Projection
A **map projection** is a framework of lines that helps to transfer points on Earth's three-dimensional surface onto a flat map. Continents, oceans, islands, rivers, and lakes might appear to have somewhat different sizes and shapes due to the map projection used. A Mercator projection is just one of many projections that allow mapmakers to show a curved Earth on a flat surface. On a Mercator projection, the size and shape of landmasses become more and more distorted toward the north and south poles.

Vocabulary Use Context to Determine Meaning Show you understand the word *model* by explaining how a globe is a model of Earth.

_____

_____

_____

_____

_____

_____

_____

FIGURE 1 ················
Mercator Projection
A Mercator projection is based on a cylinder with grid lines that has been flattened.

✏ **Interpret Maps Look at the landmasses on both the globe and the map. How are the images alike and how are they different on the two maps?**

_____

_____

_____

_____

_____

_____

_____

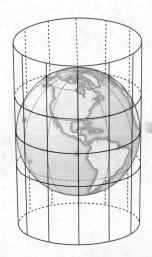

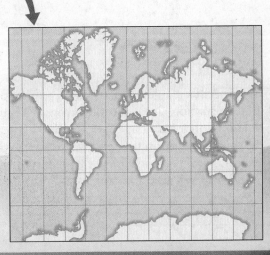

FIGURE 2 ············

▷INTERACTIVE ART What's in a Map?

A map is drawn to scale, uses symbols explained in a key, and usually has a compass rose to show direction.

WELCOME TO Central City

Key

- 🏫 School
- ❓ Tourist information
- Ⓗ Hospital
- 🍴 Restaurant
- 🛍 Shopping center
- - - Cycle route

Symbols and Key

Mapmakers use shapes and pictures called **symbols** to stand for features on Earth's surface. A symbol can represent a physical feature, such as a river, lake, mountain, or plain. A symbol can also stand for a human-made feature, such as a highway, city, or airport. A map's **key,** or legend, is a list of all the symbols used on the map, with an explanation of their meanings. Maps also include a compass rose or north arrow. The compass rose helps relate directions on the map to directions on Earth's surface. North usually is located at the top of the map.

Elm Park

Market Plaza

First Street · Second Street · Third Street · Fourth Street · Fifth Street

Main Street

Map Scale

Ratio scale 1 : 2,500

Bar scale

| 0 | 100 | 200 | 300 ft |

| 0 | 25 | 50 | 75 | 100 m |

Equivalent units scale
1 cm = 25 m

Scale

A map's **scale** relates distance on a map to distance on Earth's surface. Scale is often given as a ratio. For example, one unit on a map could equal 2,500 units on the ground. So 1 centimeter on the map would represent 2,500 centimeters, or 25 meters. This scale, "one to two thousand five hundred," would be written as the ratio "1 : 2,500." **Figure 2** shows three ways of giving a map's scale.

✏️ **Identify the Main Idea** How do mapmakers relate distance on a map to distances on Earth's surface?

_____

_____

do the math! Sample Problem

Scale and Ratios

A ratio compares two numbers by division. For example, the scale of a particular map is given as a ratio of 1 : 250,000. At this scale, the distance between two points on the map measures 23.5 cm. How would you find the actual distance?

STEP 1 **Write the scale as a fraction.**

$$\frac{1}{250,000}$$

STEP 2 Write a proportion. Let d represent the distance between the two points.

$$\frac{1}{250,000} = \frac{23.5 \text{ cm}}{d}$$

STEP 3 Write the cross products. (*Hint:* To convert cm to km, divide d by 100,000.)

$$1 \times d = 250,000 \times 23.5 \text{ cm}$$

$$d = 5,875,000 \text{ cm, or } 58.75 \text{ km}$$

·· Practice! ··

Use the formula in the sample problem to solve the problem below.

Calculate A map's scale is 1 : 25,000. If two points are 4.7 cm apart on the map, how far apart are they on the ground?

✏️ **Answer the following questions.**

1. What is the scale of this map in equivalent units?

   _____

2. Circle all the locations on the map where you can buy food.

3. Create a symbol for a gas station and draw it at the southwest corner of Fourth St. and Main St. The distance on the map between the school and the gas station is about 6 cm. According to the scale, how far is that distance on Earth's surface?

   _____

Lab zone® Do the Quick Lab 2-D and 3-D Maps.

🔑 Assess Your Understanding

1a. Describe A (symbol/key) is a picture that stands for a feature on Earth's surface.

b. Summarize What are some physical features that can be shown on a map?

_____

_____

_____

got it? ······································

○ I get it! Now I know that maps and globes are _____

_____

○ I need extra help with _____

   Go to **MY SCIENCE** ⓢ **COACH** *online for help with this subject.*

How Is Distance Measured in Degrees?

When you play checkers, the grid of squares helps you to keep track of where each piece should be. To find a point on Earth's surface, you need a reference system like the grid of squares on a checkerboard. Of course, Earth itself does not have grid lines, but most maps and globes show a grid. Because Earth is a sphere, the grid curves to cover the entire planet. Two of the lines that make up the grid, the equator and prime meridian, are the base lines for measuring distances on Earth's surface. 🔑 **Distances on Earth are measured in degrees from the equator and the prime meridian.**

Measuring in Degrees
You probably know that degrees are used to measure the distance around a circle. As you can see in **Figure 3,** a **degree** (°) is $\frac{1}{360}$ of the distance around a circle. Degrees can also be used to measure distances on the surface of a sphere. On Earth's surface, degrees are a measure of an angle formed by lines drawn from the center of Earth to points on the surface. To locate points precisely, degrees are further divided into smaller units called minutes and seconds. There are 60 minutes in a degree and 60 seconds in a minute.

FIGURE 3 ·······························

Degrees Around
Distances around a circle are measured in degrees.

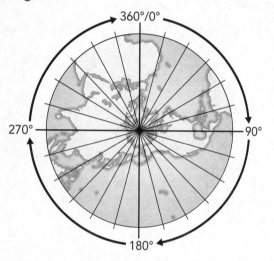

✎ **How many degrees are there in one quarter of the distance around the circle?** _____

apply it!

This tangerine is made up of ten equal wedges. The circle shows how the wedges have been grouped into four pieces for serving. Using a protractor, measure the number of degrees in the pieces of the tangerine.

❶ △**Measure** One single wedge has a measure of _____

_____

❷ Two of the pieces are equal in measure. How many degrees does each one measure? _____

❸ The tangerine's biggest piece has a measure of

_____

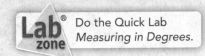

Lab zone ® Do the Quick Lab
Measuring in Degrees.

FIGURE 4

Equator and Prime Meridian

The equator and prime meridian divide Earth's surface into hemispheres.

✎ **Measure** What is the angle between the equator and prime meridian?

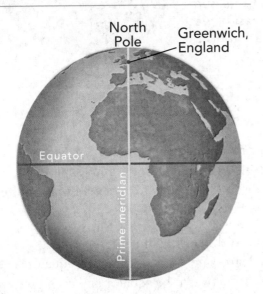

North Pole

Greenwich, England

Equator

Prime meridian

The Equator
Halfway between the North and South poles, the **equator** forms an imaginary line that circles Earth. The equator divides Earth into the Northern and Southern hemispheres. A **hemisphere** (HEM ih sfeer) is one half of the sphere that makes up Earth's surface. If you started at the equator and traveled to one of the poles, you would travel 90°, one quarter of the distance in a full circle.

The Prime Meridian
Another imaginary line, called the **prime meridian,** makes a half circle from the North Pole to the South Pole. The prime meridian passes through Greenwich, England. Places east of the prime meridian are in the Eastern Hemisphere. Places west of the prime meridian are in the Western Hemisphere.

If you started at the prime meridian and traveled west along the equator, you would travel 360° before returning to your starting point. At 180° east or west of the prime meridian, another imaginary half circle lies directly opposite the prime meridian.

🔑 Assess Your Understanding

2a. Identify The _____ and the _____ are two base lines used to locate points on Earth's surface.

b. Explain How are these base lines used?

_____
_____
_____

c. Compare and Contrast How are these base lines similar? How are these base lines different?

_____
_____
_____
_____
_____
_____
_____
_____

got it? ....

○ **I get it!** Now I know that distances on Earth are measured_____

_____
_____

○ **I need extra help with** _____

_____

Go to **my science ⑤ coach** *online for help with this subject.*

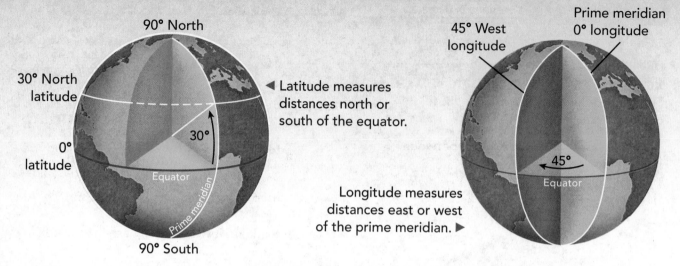

90° North

30° North
latitude

0°
latitude

90° South

30°

Equator

Prime meridian

◄ Latitude measures
distances north or
south of the equator.

45° West
longitude

Prime meridian
0° longitude

45°

Equator

Longitude measures
distances east or west
of the prime meridian. ▶

What Are Latitude and Longitude?

Using the equator and prime meridian, mapmakers have constructed a grid made up of lines of latitude and longitude. 🔑 **The lines of latitude and longitude form a grid that can be used to find locations anywhere on Earth.**

Latitude The equator is the starting line for measuring **latitude,** or distance in degrees north or south of the equator. The latitude at the equator is 0°. Between the equator and each pole are 90 evenly spaced, parallel lines called lines of latitude. Each degree of latitude is equal to about 111 kilometers. In navigation, latitude can be determined by observing the position of the sun and measuring the angle it forms with the horizon.

apply it!

Every point on Earth's surface has a particular latitude and longitude.

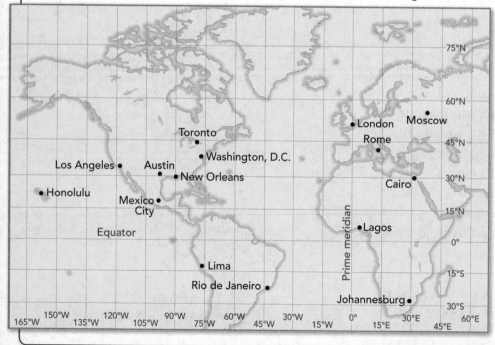

Interpret Maps Use the map to answer the following questions.

1. What is Mexico City's latitude?

_____

2. What city is located near latitude 30° S and longitude 30° E?

_____

3. Which three cities are all located at or near 30° N latitude?

_____

_____

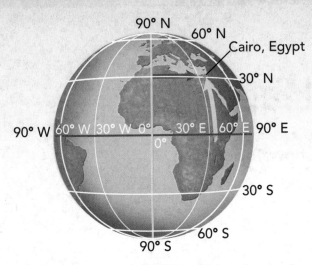

A line of latitude is defined by the angle it makes with the equator and the center of Earth. **Figure 5** shows how lines drawn from the center of Earth to the equator and from the center of Earth to 30° North form an angle of 30°.

Longitude
The distance in degrees east or west of the prime meridian is called **longitude.** There are 360 lines of longitude that run from north to south, meeting at the poles. Each line represents one degree of longitude. A degree of longitude equals about 111 kilometers at the equator. But at the poles, where the lines of longitude come together, the distance decreases to zero.

The prime meridian, which is the starting line for measuring longitude, is at 0°. The longitude lines in each hemisphere are numbered from 0° to 180°. Half of the lines of longitude are in the Eastern Hemisphere and half are in the Western Hemisphere.

Each line of longitude is defined by the angle it makes with the prime meridian and Earth's center. As shown in **Figure 5**, lines from the center of Earth to the prime meridian and from the center of Earth to 45° West form an angle of 45° at the equator. A compass, which always points north, indicates that west is to the left of a starting point and east is to the right.

Using Latitude and Longitude
The location of any point on Earth's surface can be expressed in terms of the latitude and longitude lines that cross at that point. For example, you can see on the map that New Orleans is located where the line for 30° North latitude crosses the line for 90° West longitude. Notice that each longitude line crosses the latitude lines, including the equator, at a right angle.

FIGURE 5 ···

Latitude and Longitude
Points on Earth's surface can be located using the grid of latitude and longitude lines.

✎ **Interpret Maps** What are the latitude and longitude of Cairo, Egypt?

_____

Lab zone®   Do the Quick Lab
                Where in the World?

🗝 Assess Your Understanding

3a. Identify You can express the location of any point on Earth by using

_____ and _____.

b. Explain How are these lines used to locate a point on Earth's surface?

_____

_____

_____

c. Make Judgments Would it be a good idea if every country measured longitude from its own prime meridian? Why or why not?

_____

_____

_____

_____

_____

got it? ···

○ **I get it!** Now I know that to find a location

anywhere on Earth _____

_____

○ **I need extra help with** _____

_____

Go to my science ⓢ coach *online for help with this subject.*

35

Topographic Maps

🔑 **How Do Maps Show Topography?**

my planet Diary

Geocaching

In May of 2000, people began to play a new version of the game hide-and-seek. Improvements to satellites meant that people could use a GPS (Global Positioning System) device to precisely locate any place—or thing. People started hiding objects in the woods or on mountains, and then used GPS data to post these locations on the Internet. They challenged other people to find the objects, and the sport of geocaching (*geo* means "earth"; *cache* means "storage place") was born! With GPS technology, nothing is hidden long, but searchers still might need to use maps in their quest. A cache can be found anywhere, so people searching for the cache need to rely on topographic maps.

FUN FACTS

✎ **Communicate** Write your answer to each question below. Then discuss your answers with a partner.

1. What technological advance made the sport of geocaching possible?

_____

_____

_____

2. If you were a geocacher, where would you hide a cache? Why?

_____

_____

_____

_____

_____

_____

▶ PLANET DIARY   Go to **Planet Diary** to learn more about topographic maps.

Lab zone® Do the Inquiry Warm-Up *Can a Map Show Relief?*

Vocabulary
- topographic map
- contour interval
- contour line
- index contour

Skills
- Reading: Compare and Contrast
- Inquiry: Make Models

How Do Maps Show Topography?

A **topographic map** (tahp uh GRAF ik) is a map showing the surface features of an area. Topographic maps portray the land as if you were looking down on it from above. They provide accurate information on the elevation, relief, and slope of the ground.

Reading Contour Lines 🔑 **Mapmakers use contour lines to show elevation, relief, and slope on topographic maps.** On a topographic map, a **contour line** connects points of equal elevation. In the United States, most topographic maps give contour intervals in feet rather than meters.

The change in elevation from one contour line to the next is called the **contour interval.** The contour interval for a given map is always the same. For example, the map in **Figure 1** has a contour interval of 160 feet. If you start at one contour line and count up 10 contour lines, you have reached an elevation 1,600 feet higher. Every fifth contour line is known as an **index contour.** These lines are darker and heavier than the others.

🖉

↩ **Compare and Contrast**
Explain the difference between an index contour and a regular contour line.

_____

_____

_____

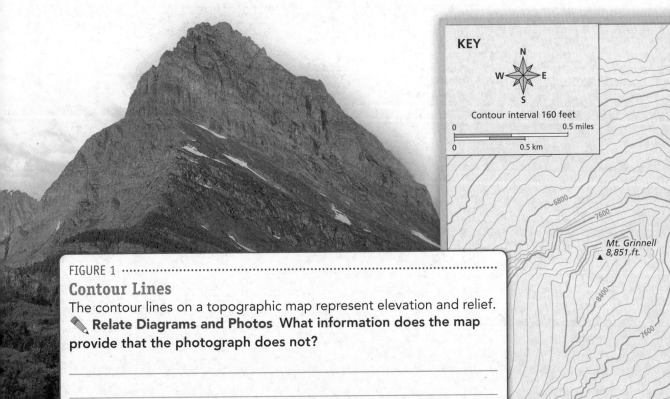

KEY

Contour interval 160 feet

0 — 0.5 miles

0 — 0.5 km

Mt. Grinnell
8,851 ft.

6800
7600
8400
7600
6800
6000

FIGURE 1 ·····················
Contour Lines
The contour lines on a topographic map represent elevation and relief.
🖉 **Relate Diagrams and Photos** What information does the map provide that the photograph does not?

_____

_____

Mapping a Mountain

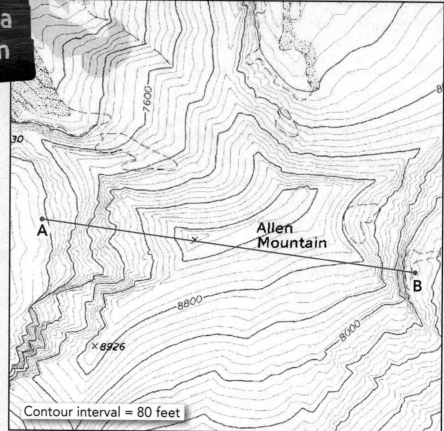

Contour interval = 80 feet

FIGURE 2 ....

> INTERACTIVE ART

✎ **Interpreting Maps** Study the topographic map and then answer the questions.

1. What is the highest elevation on the map?_____

   _____

2. Draw a topographic profile, or side view, of the elevations between Points A and B. Use the index contour lines on the map to plot the points on the graph below, and create your own profile of the mountain.

3. Why would you want to use a topographic map when climbing a mountain?

   _____

   _____

   _____

   _____

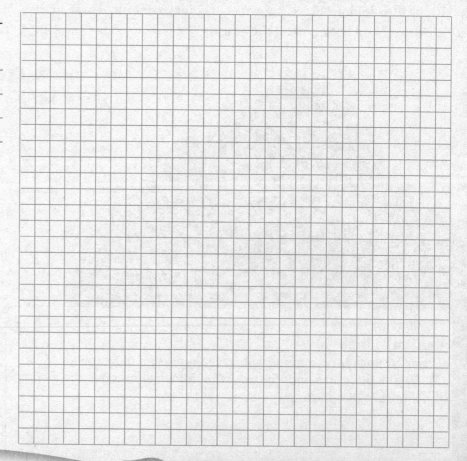

Reading a Topographic Map
Looking at a topographic map with so many squiggles, you may feel as if you are gazing into a bowl of spaghetti. But with practice, you can learn to read a topographic map. First, you must become familiar with the map's scale and interpret the map's contour lines.

In the United States, many topographic maps are drawn at a scale of 1 : 24,000, or 1 centimeter equals 0.24 kilometers. At this scale, maps can show features such as rivers and coastlines. Large buildings, airports, and major highways appear as outlines. Symbols are used to show houses and other small features.

To find the elevation of a feature, begin at the labeled index contour, which is a heavier line than regular contour lines. Then, count the number of contour lines up or down to the feature.

Reading contour lines is the first step toward "seeing" an area's topography. Look at the topographic map on the previous page. The closely spaced contour lines indicate steep slopes. The widely spaced contour lines indicate gentle slopes or relatively flat areas. A contour line that forms a closed loop with no other contour lines inside it indicates a hilltop. A closed loop with dashes inside indicates a depression, or hollow in the ground.

The shape of contour lines also helps to show ridges and valleys. V-shaped contour lines pointing downhill indicate a ridge line. V-shaped contour lines pointing uphill indicate a valley. A stream in the valley flows toward the open end of the V.

apply it!

Look at the topographic map below, and answer the following questions.

❶ What sort of feature is shown by the map? How do you know?

_____

_____

_____

❷ **CHALLENGE** How deep is the depression?

_____

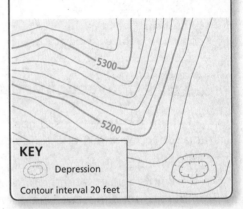

KEY

⬭ Depression

Contour interval 20 feet

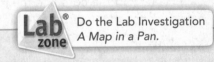

Do the Lab Investigation
A Map in a Pan.

🔑 Assess Your Understanding

1a. ⛰ Make Models How does a topographic map serve as a good model of a mountain? What is it missing?

_____

_____

_____

_____

b. How is a map a model of Earth?

_____

_____

_____

_____

_____

got it? . . . .

○ I get it! Now I know that a topographic map shows _____

○ I need extra help with _____

Go to **MY SCIENCE COACH** *online for help with this subject.*

Study Guide

Earth consists of three main layers. The _____ is the outermost layer. The _____ is made up of rock that is hot but solid. The _____ occupies Earth's center.

LESSON 1 The Earth System

🔑 The Earth system has four main spheres: the atmosphere, the hydrosphere, the geosphere, and the biosphere. The sun can be considered part of the Earth system.

🔑 Lands are constantly being created and destroyed by constructive forces and destructive forces.

Vocabulary
• system • energy • atmosphere
• geosphere • hydrosphere • biosphere
• constructive force • destructive force

LESSON 2 Earth's Interior

🔑 Geologists have used direct evidence from rock samples and indirect evidence from seismic waves to learn about Earth's interior.

🔑 The temperature and pressure inside Earth increase as depth increases.

🔑 The three main layers of Earth are the crust, the mantle, and the core.

Vocabulary
• seismic wave • pressure • crust • basalt
• granite • mantle • lithosphere
• asthenosphere • outer core • inner core

LESSON 3 Convection and the Mantle

🔑 There are three types of heat transfer: radiation, convection, and conduction.

🔑 Heating and cooling of a fluid, changes in the fluid's density, and the force of gravity combine to set convection currents in motion.

🔑 Heat from the core and the mantle itself causes convection currents in the mantle.

Vocabulary
• radiation • convection • conduction
• density • convection current

LESSON 4 Exploring Earth's Surface

🔑 The topography of an area includes the area's elevation, relief, and landforms.

🔑 Three major types of landforms are plains, mountains, and plateaus.

Vocabulary
• topography • elevation • relief • landform
• plain • mountain • mountain range • plateau
• landform region

LESSON 5 Models of Earth

🔑 Maps and globes are drawn to scale and use symbols to represent features on Earth's surface.

🔑 Distances on Earth are measured in degrees from the equator and the prime meridian.

🔑 The lines of latitude and longitude form a grid that can be used to find locations anywhere on Earth.

Vocabulary
• globe • map • map projection • symbol • key
• scale • degree • equator • hemisphere
• prime meridian • latitude • longitude

LESSON 6 Topographic Maps

🔑 Mapmakers use contour lines to show elevation, relief, and slope on topographic maps.

Vocabulary
• topographic map
• contour line
• contour interval
• index contour

Review and Assessment

LESSON 1 The Earth System

1. Which is part of Earth's hydrosphere?

    a. liquid outer core   **b.** solid inner core

    c. granite   **d.** ocean water

2. Earth's system has two sources of energy, which are _____

_____

_____

3. Classify Are the forces that cause lava to erupt from a volcano and flow over Earth's surface constructive or destructive forces? Explain.

_____

_____

_____

_____

LESSON 2 Earth's Interior

4. To learn about Earth's structure, geologists use seismic waves, which are _____

_____

_____

5. Sequence Name each layer of Earth, starting from Earth's center. Include both layers of the core and all layers of the mantle.

_____

_____

_____

_____

6. **Write About It** Compare and contrast oceanic crust with continental crust. In your answer, be sure to consider the composition and thickness of both types of crust.

LESSON 3 Convection and the Mantle

7. What is the transfer of heat by direct contact of particles of matter called?

    a. conduction   **b.** radiation

    c. convection   **d.** pressure

8. Compared to air and water, most rock has a high density, which means it has _____

_____

_____

9. Explain What conditions allow rock in the mantle to flow?

_____

_____

_____

LESSON 4 Exploring Earth's Surface

10. Which is a landform that has a low elevation and a mostly flat surface?

    a. valley   **b.** coastal plain

    c. mountain   **d.** plateau

11. A landform's height above sea level is its elevation, while its relief is the _____

_____

_____

12. Predict Landform regions feature mainly one type of landform. How would you expect humans to use land in a region of plains?

_____

_____

_____

_____

_____

LESSON 5 Models of Earth

13. The equator divides Earth into two equal halves. What are these halves called?

a. projections   b. degrees

c. hemispheres   d. pixels

14. Interpret Maps What are the latitude and longitude of point A?

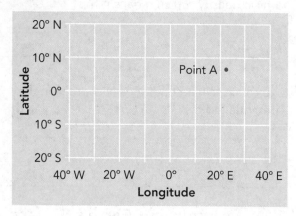

_____

_____

LESSON 6 Topographic Maps

15. On a topographic map, how is relief shown?

a. contour lines   b. projections

c. pixels   d. lines of latitude

16. Applying Concepts To show a shallow, 1.5-meter-deep depression in the ground, would you use a 1-meter contour interval or a 5-meter contour interval?

_____

_____

_____

17. Write About It Charlene is planning a 5K run to benefit local recycling efforts. She wants the run to be open to all ages and fitness levels. How can she use a topographic map to plan a good route for different groups such as families with children or regular runners?

What is the structure of Earth?

18. Suppose you could travel to the center of Earth. You must design a special vehicle for your journey. What equipment should your vehicle include so that it could travel through each layer of Earth shown below? Also, what conditions should your vehicle be able to withstand? Consider temperature, pressure, and the hardness of each layer of Earth.

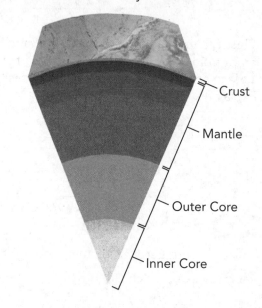

Crust

Mantle

Outer Core

Inner Core

_____

_____

_____

_____

_____

_____

_____

_____

_____

_____

_____

Standardized Test Prep

Multiple Choice

Circle the letter of the best answer.

1. This contour map shows land topography.

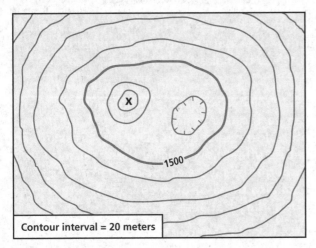

What is the elevation of the point marked X, the top of the mountain, on the map?

A 1,400 meters   **B** 1,485 meters
C 1,500 meters   **D** 1,540 meters

2. Which part of Earth's system forms a nearly continuous shell around Earth?

A lithosphere   **B** hydrosphere
C atmosphere   **D** geosphere

3. Which part of Earth's interior is made mostly of nickel and iron and has liquid and solid parts?

A lithosphere   **B** crust
C asthenosphere **D** core

4. What is one result of convection currents in Earth's outer core?

A erosion
B Earth's magnetic field
C melted glaciers
D Earth's force of gravity

5. How is longitude measured?

A in degrees north or south of the equator
B in degrees north or south of the prime meridian
C in degrees east or west of the prime meridian
D in degrees east or west of the equator

Constructed Response

Use the illustration below and your knowledge of science to help you answer Question 6. Write your answer on a separate piece of paper.

6. Describe how Earth's spheres are interacting in the scene pictured below. Also describe any notable constructive and destructive forces.

A Slice of Earth

If you could dig a hole that went straight through to the other side of the world, on your way down you'd see all of the layers underneath Earth's surface.

Of course, digging that kind of hole would be impossible. But if we want to see a slice of Earth, and all its layers, we have another tool. Seismic tomography lets us see Earth's layers as 3-D images. A computer uses data on the size and speed of seismic waves to make these images.

The sudden release of stored energy under Earth's crust sends seismic waves in all directions and causes an earthquake. The waves travel out from the center of the earthquake. Density, pressure, and temperature affect how quickly these seismic waves move through the layers of rock underground. Waves can also bend or bounce back where they meet a boundary between layers.

Scientists are able to record the speed and size of the seismic waves from thousands of earthquakes. Combining data recorded at different places allows scientists to use computers to create models of Earth's interior.

Knowing exactly what is lying beneath our feet is helping scientists learn more about tectonic processes, such as mountain building, as well as helping us find important mineral resources.

Research It Seismic tomography has been compared to CAT (computerized axial tomography) scans. How are they similar? How are they different? Research them both and create a graphic organizer outlining the similarities and differences.

This seismic tomography image shows a cross-section of Earth's crust and mantle. The colors show materials of different densities that are rising or sinking as part of convection currents in the mantle. The blue line on the map shows that this "slice" of Earth extends from the Pacific Ocean eastward to western Africa. ▶

Save the Seeds, Save the World

Bananas may be in trouble. So may some species of wheat. In fact a number of species of plants face threats to their survival. Scientists think that Earth's climate is changing. And as it changes, so does the biosphere. Some plants are becoming more vulnerable to disease or to insect pests. Human development also threatens some plants' habitats. With all these changes to the biosphere, plant species are becoming extinct at an increasing rate.

The Svalbard Global Seed Vault may be helping to preserve samples of important resources. Tucked into the permafrost in Svalbard—an island north of Norway that is farther north than almost any other landmass on Earth—the Seed Vault protects seeds that come from almost every important food crop in the world. The seeds of bananas, strawberries, rice, and beans are all preserved (along with many other species) in case they go extinct. Many seeds come from developing countries, which have a lot of biodiversity. Because the Seed Vault is in the cryosphere—the frozen portion of the hydrosphere—scientists think that Svalbard will remain frozen even if climate change continues to cause the glaciers farther south to melt.

The Seed Vault can store up to 4.5 million seeds at –18°C. Even if the power goes out, the seeds will stay frozen because the permafrost will keep the temperature of the vaults below –3.5°C.

Inside the Svalbard Global Seed Vault ▲

Write About It Scientists have observed signs of global climate change. Changes to Earth's climate are affecting many other Earth systems. For example, sea levels are rising, and sea ice is melting. Write an essay explaining how these changes might lead to the extinction of a specific plant species.

HOW DID THIS ROCK GET HERE?

How do rocks form?

The famous naturalist John Muir first climbed to the summit of Cathedral Peak in 1869. Located in the Sierra Nevada Range in California, it is 3,308 meters in elevation. Cathedral Peak is mostly composed of granite, a mixture of quartz, feldspar, and other minerals such as hornblende and mica. Looking down from this tall, narrow peak, you would probably feel like you were on top of the world!

△ Develop Hypotheses **How might this towering piece of rock have gotten here?**

_____

_____

_____

_____

_____

▷ UNTAMED SCIENCE Watch the **Untamed Science** video to learn more about minerals and rocks.

Minerals and Rocks

2 Getting Started

Check Your Understanding

1. Background Read the paragraph below and then answer the question.

Judy filled a glass jar with water. She put a lid on the jar and put the jar in the freezer. Overnight, the water, which was a **liquid,** froze into ice, which is a **solid.** But Judy had forgotten that ice occupies a larger **volume** than the same mass of water. So when the water froze, it expanded and cracked the jar.

> A **liquid** is a substance that flows and whose shape, but not volume, can be changed.
>
> A **solid** is a substance that resists changing shape.
>
> **Volume** is the amount of space that matter occupies.

• What variable changed to turn the liquid water into solid ice?

_____

_____

> **MY READING WEB** If you had trouble completing the question above, visit **My Reading Web** and type in **Minerals and Rocks.**

Vocabulary Skill

Latin Word Origins Many science words in English come from Latin. For example, *granite* comes from the Latin *granum*, meaning "grain." Granite is a rock that has large, visible grains.

Latin Word	Meaning of Latin Word	Example
erosus	eaten away	erosion, *n.* a process by which a mountain is broken into pieces
folium	leaf	foliated, *adj.* with thin, flat layers
caementum	stones and chips from a quarry	cementation, *n.* process in which bits of rock are glued together

2. Quick Check Choose the word from the table that best completes the sentence.

• Rocks that have their grains arranged in flat layers are said to be

_____

crystal

texture

clastic rock

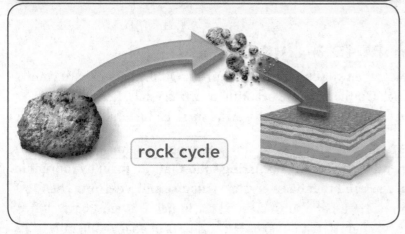

rock cycle

Chapter Preview

LESSON 1

- mineral • inorganic • crystal
- streak • luster
- Mohs hardness scale • cleavage
- fracture • geode • crystallization
- solution • vein

🔁 **Relate Text and Visuals**
△ **Form Operational Definitions**

LESSON 2

- rock-forming mineral • granite
- basalt • grain • texture
- igneous rock • sedimentary rock
- metamorphic rock

🔁 **Identify the Main Idea**
△ **Observe**

LESSON 3

- extrusive rock
- intrusive rock

🔁 **Relate Cause and Effect**
△ **Interpret Data**

LESSON 4

- sediment • weathering • erosion
- deposition • compaction
- cementation • clastic rock
- organic rock • chemical rock

🔁 **Identify the Main Idea**
△ **Infer**

LESSON 5

- foliated

🔁 **Relate Cause and Effect**
△ **Observe**

LESSON 6

- rock cycle

🔁 **Sequence**
△ **Classify**

> **VOCAB FLASH CARDS** For extra help with vocabulary, visit **Vocab Flash Cards** and type in *Minerals and Rocks.*

Properties of Minerals

UNLOCK THE BIG

🔑 **What Is a Mineral?**

🔑 **How Are Minerals Identified?**

🔑 **How Do Minerals Form?**

my pLaneT DiaRY

BLOG

Posted by: MacKenzie

Location: Brewerton, New York

I used to go to summer camp. We went on a good field trip to an underground cavern. When we got inside, I thought I was in a dragon's mouth. Later, I found out that those teeth were stalactites and stalagmites. Stalactites hang from the ceiling and stalagmites grow from the ground.

Communicate Discuss the question with a partner. Write your answer below.

Stalactites and stalagmites are usually made up of the mineral calcite. This mineral dissolves easily in acidic water. How do you think calcite hardened to form the features in the cave?

_____

_____

_____

_____

▶ PLANET DIARY Go to **Planet Diary** to learn more about minerals.

Lab zone Do the Inquiry Warm-Up *How Does the Rate of Cooling Affect Crystals?*

What Is a Mineral?

Look at the two substances in **Figure 1**. On the left is a hard chunk of coal. On the right are beautiful quartz crystals. Both are solid materials that form beneath Earth's surface. But which is a mineral?

Defining Minerals How are minerals defined? 🔑 **A mineral is a naturally occurring solid that can form by inorganic processes and that has a crystal structure and a definite chemical composition.** For a substance to be a **mineral**, it must have all five of these characteristics. So, is either quartz or coal a mineral?

Vocabulary

- mineral • inorganic • crystal • streak • luster
- Mohs hardness scale • cleavage • fracture
- geode • crystallization • solution • vein

Skills

↪ **Reading:** Relate Text and Visuals
△ **Inquiry:** Form Operational Definitions

Naturally Occurring

All minerals are substances that are formed by natural processes. Quartz forms naturally as molten material called magma cools and hardens beneath Earth's surface. Coal forms naturally from the remains of plants that are squeezed tightly together.

Solid

A mineral is always a solid, with a definite volume and shape. The particles that make up a solid are packed together very tightly, so they cannot move like the particles that make up a liquid. Coal and quartz are solids.

Crystal Structure

The particles of a mineral line up in a pattern that repeats over and over again. The repeating pattern of a mineral's particles forms a solid called a **crystal.** A crystal has flat sides, called faces, that meet at sharp edges and corners. The quartz in **Figure 1** has a crystal structure. In contrast, most coal lacks a crystal structure.

Forms by Inorganic Processes

All minerals must be able to form by **inorganic** processes. That is, every mineral must be able to form from materials that were not a part of living things. Quartz can form naturally as magma cools. Coal comes only from living things—the remains of plants that lived millions of years ago. But some minerals that can form from inorganic processes may also be produced by living things.

Definite Chemical Composition

A mineral has a definite chemical composition. This means that a mineral always contains certain elements in definite proportions. An element is a substance composed of a single kind of atom.

Quartz always contains one atom of silicon for every two atoms of oxygen. The elements in coal can vary over a wide range.

Quartz

Coal

FIGURE 1 ·····················

Are They or Aren't They?

To be classified as a mineral, a substance must satisfy five requirements.

✎ **Classify** Complete the checklist. Are quartz and coal minerals or only naturally occurring substances?

_____

_____

_____

Mineral Characteristics	Quartz	Coal
Naturally occurring	✔	✔
Can form by inorganic processes		
Solid		
Crystal structure		
Definite chemical composition		

Minerals, Compounds, and Elements

Almost all minerals are compounds. In a compound, two or more elements are combined so that the elements no longer have distinct properties. For example, the mineral cinnabar is composed of the elements sulfur and mercury. Sulfur is bright yellow. Mercury is a silvery liquid at room temperature. But cinnabar has solid, shiny, red crystals.

Different minerals have a different combination of elements. For example, a crystal of quartz has one atom of silicon for every two atoms of oxygen. This ratio is constant for all varieties of quartz. Each mineral in the garnet group of minerals has three atoms of silicon for every twelve atoms of oxygen. But garnets also contain other elements, in set ratios. **Figure 2** shows one variety of garnet.

Some elements occur in nature in a pure form, and not as part of a compound. Elements such as copper, silver, and gold are also minerals. Almost all pure, solid elements are metals.

FIGURE 2 ·······························

Elements and Compounds in Minerals

Quartz and the garnet minerals contain the elements silicon and oxygen. At room temperature, pure silicon is a hard, dark gray solid. Oxygen is a colorless gas.

✎ **Describe** Choose either quartz or garnet. Then, choose silicon or oxygen. When your element is part of a mineral, how is it different from its pure form?

_____
_____
_____
_____
_____
_____
_____

Rose quartz

Almandine garnet

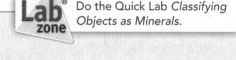
Do the Quick Lab *Classifying Objects as Minerals.*

🗝 Assess Your Understanding

1a. Summarize All minerals must be able to form from (organic/inorganic) processes.

b. Explain What, specifically, makes a process inorganic?

_____
_____

c. Classify Amber is a material used in jewelry. It forms only by the process of pine tree resin hardening into stone. Is amber a mineral? Explain.

_____
_____
_____

got it? ··

○ **I get it!** Now I know that to be classified as a mineral, a substance must be _____

_____
_____

○ **I need extra help with** _____

Go to MY SCIENCE ⬤ COACH *online for help with this subject.*

How Are Minerals Identified?

Geologists have identified more than 4,000 minerals. But telling these minerals apart can often be a challenge. 🗝 **Each mineral has characteristic properties that can be used to identify it.**

Color

Both minerals shown here are the color gold. But only one is the mineral gold. In fact, only a few minerals have their own characteristic color.

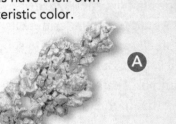

B

A

FIGURE 3 ······························
Is All That Glitters Really Gold?
Both minerals shown here are gold in color.

✏️ **Identify** Circle the mineral that you think is gold. (Answer at bottom of page.)

Streak

The **streak** of a mineral is the color of its powder. Although the color of a mineral can vary, its streak does not. However, the streak color and the mineral color are often different. For example, pyrite has a gold color but its streak is greenish black.

FIGURE 4 ······························
Scratching the Surface
The color of any particular mineral's streak does not vary.

✏️ **Infer** Which is more useful when identifying a mineral: the mineral's color or the mineral's streak?

_____

_____

Galena   Hematite   Malachite

Luster

Luster is the term used to describe how light is reflected from a mineral's surface. For example, minerals such as galena that contain metals often have a metallic luster. Quartz has a glassy luster. Other terms used to describe luster include earthy, silky, waxy, and pearly.

Metallic   Silky   Waxy, greasy, or pearly

Galena   Malachite   Talc

FIGURE 5 ······························
Upon Reflection
Geologists use many terms to describe the luster of minerals.

✏️ **Describe** Choose any item in your classroom that reflects light. In one word, describe its luster.

Item: _____

Luster: _____

A. Gold B. Pyrite

53

did you

know?

Apatite is a mineral included in the Mohs hardness scale. Enamel on mature teeth consists mainly of apatite crystals.

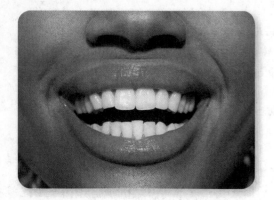

Hardness

When you want to identify a mineral, one of the most useful clues to use is the mineral's hardness. In 1812, Austrian Friedrich Mohs, a mineral expert, invented a scale to help identify minerals by how hard they are. The **Mohs hardness scale** is used to rank the hardness of minerals. The scale assigns a mineral's hardness a ranking from 1 to 10, as shown in **Figure 6.**

Hardness can be determined by a scratch test. A mineral can scratch any mineral softer than itself, but can be scratched by any mineral that is harder. For example, suppose you found a deposit of azurite. Azurite is not on the Mohs scale, but you would like to determine its hardness. So you take a small sample and try to scratch it with talc, gypsum, and calcite. But none of these minerals scratch your sample. Apatite, rated 5 on the scale, does scratch it. Therefore, the hardness of azurite is probably about 4.

FIGURE 6

Mohs Hardness Scale

Geologists determine a mineral's hardness by comparing it to the hardness of the minerals on the Mohs scale.

✎ **Explain** Read the description of each mineral at the right. Place each mineral's name in its proper location in the scale.

Topaz It can scratch quartz but not corundum.

Gypsum A fingernail can easily scratch it.

Apatite A steel knife can scratch it.

Diamond Extremely hard, it can scratch all known common minerals.

Quartz It can scratch feldspar but not topaz.

1 Talc
The softest mineral, talc flakes when scratched by a fingernail.

2 _____

3 Calcite
A fingernail cannot scratch it, but a copper penny can.

4 Fluorite
A steel knife can easily scratch it.

5 _____

Increasing hardness

do the math!

Calculating Density

For many minerals, different samples of a mineral all have the same density. So geologists can use density to help identify mineral samples. To do so, they use the following formula.

$$\text{Density} = \frac{\text{Mass}}{\text{Volume}}$$

You find a sample of the mineral magnetite. The sample has a mass of 151.0 g and a volume of 29.0 cm³. What is the density of magnetite?

_____

_____

_____

Density Each mineral has a characteristic density. Recall that density is the mass in a given space, or mass per unit volume. No matter how large or small the mineral sample is, the density of that mineral always remains the same. For example, the density of quartz is 2.6 g/cm³. The density of diamond is 3.5 g/cm³.

To measure density, geologists use a balance to first determine the precise mass of a mineral sample. Then they place the mineral in water to determine how much water the sample displaces. The volume of the displaced water equals the volume of the sample. The mineral's density can then be calculated using the formula below.

$$\text{Density} = \frac{\text{Mass}}{\text{Volume}}$$

You can compare the density of two mineral samples of about the same size. Just pick them up and heft them, or feel their weight, in your hands. The sample that feels heavier is probably also denser.

6 Feldspar
It can't be scratched by a steel knife but can scratch window glass.

7 _____

8 _____

9 Corundum
It can scratch topaz.

10 _____

55

Halite

Quartz

FIGURE 7 ....
> INTERACTIVE ART Crystal Structure

Each mineral has its own crystal structure.

🖊 **Answer the questions.**

1. **List** What two features do geologists use to classify crystals?

_____

_____

_____

_____

2. CHALLENGE Does a quartz crystal have more or fewer faces than a halite crystal?

_____

Crystal Structure

The atoms that make up a mineral line up in a regular pattern. This pattern repeats over and over. The repeating pattern of a mineral's atoms forms a mineral's crystal structure. All the crystals of a mineral have the same crystal structure. Scientists can use crystal structure to identify very small mineral samples. For example, scientists can bounce a powerful beam of particles off very small crystals. Because the atoms that make up minerals line up in regular patterns, these beams produce distinct patterns of light.

As shown in **Figure 7,** different minerals have crystals that are shaped differently. Halite crystals are cubic. That is, they are shaped like a cube. You can break a large piece of halite into smaller pieces. But the smaller pieces still contain crystals that are perfect cubes.

Geologists classify crystals by the number of faces, or sides, on the crystal. They also measure the angles at which the faces meet.

What Do You Know?

🖊 **Interpret Photographs** The photograph shows crystals of the mineral stibnite. Read the text about how minerals are identified. Then identify which of stibnite's characteristic properties you can infer from the photograph. Which properties would you need to test before being able to identify the mineral?

_____

_____

_____

_____

_____

_____

_____

_____

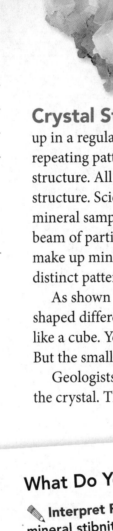

Cleavage and Fracture

You may be familiar with how the mineral mica can split apart to form flat sheets. A mineral that splits easily along flat surfaces has the property called **cleavage.**

Whether a mineral has cleavage depends on how the atoms in its crystals are arranged. The way atoms are arranged in mica allows it to split easily in one direction. **Figure 8** shows cleavage in mica.

Most minerals do not split apart evenly. Instead, they have a characteristic type of fracture. **Fracture** describes how a mineral looks when it breaks apart in an irregular way. For example, when quartz breaks, it produces curved, shell-like surfaces.

Special Properties

Some minerals can be identified by special physical properties. Calcite bends light to produce double images, as shown in **Figure 9.** Other minerals conduct electricity, glow when placed under ultraviolet light, or are magnetic.

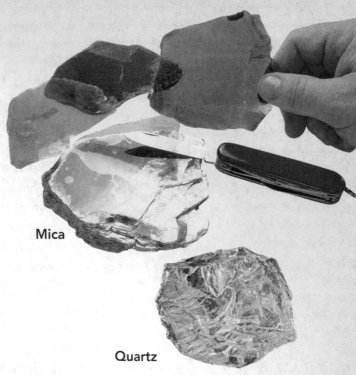

Mica

Quartz

FIGURE 8 ....
Fracture and Cleavage
How a mineral breaks apart can help to identify it.

⚠ **Form Operational Definitions** Observe the examples of cleavage and fracture above. Based on your observations, write a definition of cleavage in your own words.

_____

_____

FIGURE 9 ....
Special Properties
Calcite bends light to produce a double image.

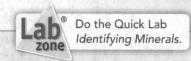

Lab zone® Do the Quick Lab *Identifying Minerals.*

🔑 Assess Your Understanding

2a. Summarize Geologists identify minerals by examining their _____

_____

_____

_____

b. Design Experiments Lodestone is magnetic. How might you identify whether a mineral sample might be lodestone?

_____

_____

_____

got it? ....

○ **I get it!** Now I know that the characteristic properties used to identify minerals are _____

_____

○ **I need extra help with** _____

Go to **MY SCIENCE** ⑤ **COACH** online for help with this subject.

How Do Minerals Form?

On a rock-collecting field trip, you find an egg-shaped rock about the size of a football. Later, at a geologic laboratory, you split the rock open. The rock is hollow! Its inside surface sparkles with large amethyst crystals. Amethyst is a type of quartz.

You have found a geode, as shown in **Figure 10**. A **geode** (JEE ohd) is a rounded, hollow rock that is often lined with mineral crystals. Geologists believe that crystals probably form inside a geode when water containing dissolved minerals seeps into a crack or hollow in a rock. Slowly, crystallization occurs, lining the inside with large crystals that are often perfectly formed. **Crystallization** is the process by which atoms are arranged to form a material that has a crystal structure. 🗝 **In general, minerals can form in three ways. Some minerals form from organic processes. Other minerals can crystallize from materials dissolved in solutions. Finally, many minerals crystallize as magma and lava cool.**

Organic Minerals All minerals can form by inorganic processes. 🗝 **However, some minerals can also form by organic processes.** For instance, ocean animals such as clams and corals produce shells and skeletons made out of the mineral calcite.

FIGURE 10 ·······························

Geodes
Water seeping into a crack in a rock can result in the formation of a geode.

✎ **Sequence** Complete the graphic organizer to show how a geode forms in four steps.

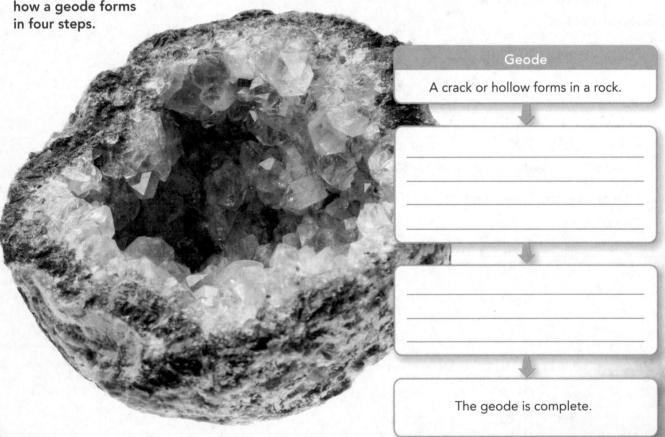

Geode
A crack or hollow forms in a rock.

↓

_____
_____
_____
_____

↓

_____
_____
_____

↓

The geode is complete.

Minerals From Solutions Sometimes the elements and compounds that form minerals can be dissolved in water to form solutions. A **solution** is a mixture in which one substance is dissolved in another. 🗝 **When elements and compounds that are dissolved in water leave a solution, crystallization occurs.** Minerals can form in this way in bodies of water on Earth's surface. But the huge selenite crystals shown in **Figure 11** formed from a solution of hot water that cooled underground.

Minerals Formed by Evaporation

Some minerals form when solutions evaporate. For example, when the water in salt water evaporates, it leaves behind salt crystals.

In a similar way, deposits of the mineral halite formed over millions of years when ancient seas slowly evaporated. Such halite deposits are found in the American Southwest and along the Gulf Coast. Gypsum and calcite can also form by evaporation. Sometimes, gypsum forms in the shape of a rose.

A gypsum "rose"

Minerals From Hot Water Solutions

Deep underground, magma can heat water to a high temperature. The hot water can dissolve the elements and compounds that form minerals. When the hot water solution begins to cool, the elements and compounds leave the solution and crystallize as minerals. For example, quartz can crystallize from out of a hot water solution. Pure silver is also often deposited from a hot water solution. Gold, too, can be deposited in this way.

Pure metals that crystallize from hot water solutions underground often form veins. A **vein** is a narrow channel or slab of a mineral that is different from the surrounding rock.

Silver

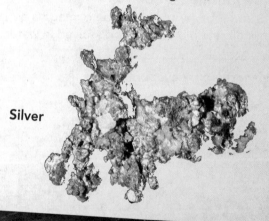

FIGURE 11 ·······················
Selenite
These huge selenite crystals in a cave in Mexico formed from the crystallization of minerals in a solution.

·············· ✎ ··············

⟳ Relate Text and Visuals
Review the text on this page and on the previous page. Underline the name of each mineral the first time it is mentioned. Then place each mineral in its correct place in **Figure 12**.

Minerals From Magma and Lava

Many minerals form from magma and lava. ⟬⟭ **Minerals form as hot magma cools inside the crust, or as lava hardens on the surface. When these liquids cool to a solid state, they form crystals.** The size of the crystals depends on several factors. The rate at which the magma cools, the amount of gas the magma contains, and the chemical composition of the magma all affect crystal size.

Magma and lava are often rich in oxygen and silicon. Minerals that contain these elements are called *silicates*. Together, silicates make up a majority of Earth's crust.

Minerals From Magma

Magma that remains deep below the surface cools slowly over thousands of years. Slow cooling leads to the formation of large crystals. Quartz, feldspar, tourmaline, and mica are common silicate minerals that form from magma.

Tourmaline

Minerals From Lava

If magma erupts to the surface and becomes lava, the lava will cool quickly. There will be no time for large crystals to form. Instead, small crystals form. Leucite and olivine are silicate minerals that can form in lava.

Olivine

FIGURE 12 ···

Where Minerals Form

Minerals can form by crystallization of magma and lava or by crystallization of materials dissolved in water.

Minerals formed by evaporation
_____
_____

Minerals formed as lava cools
_____

Minerals formed in hot water solutions
_____
_____

Veins

Minerals formed as magma cools
_____
_____

Water containing dissolved minerals

Cooling magma

Where Mineral Resources Are Found

Earth's crust is made up mostly of the common rock-forming minerals combined in various types of rock. Less common minerals are not found evenly throughout the crust. Instead, several processes can concentrate these minerals, or bring them together, in deposits. An *ore* is a deposit of valuable minerals contained in rocks. Iron ores may contain the iron-bearing minerals pyrite, magnetite, and hematite. Lead ores may contain galena. These ores are mined and the iron or lead is separated from the rock. Graphite and sulfur are sometimes also mined. **Figure 13** shows some major mining areas.

FIGURE 13 ·····························

Ores

✎ **Interpret Maps** Copper, aluminum, zinc, iron, and nickel can be used in making refrigerators. Which of these metals might the United States need to import for its refrigerators?

_____

_____

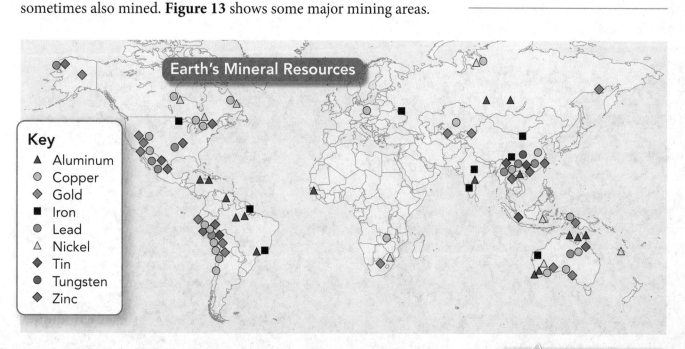

Earth's Mineral Resources

Key
- ▲ Aluminum
- ◯ Copper
- ◆ Gold
- ■ Iron
- ● Lead
- △ Nickel
- ◆ Tin
- ● Tungsten
- ◆ Zinc

Lab zone® Do the Quick Lab *Crystal Hands.*

🔑 Assess Your Understanding

3a. Review Magma below Earth's surface cools (slowly/quickly).

b. Predict Slow cooling of magma leads to what size mineral crystals?

_____

_____

c. Develop Hypotheses A certain rock has large crystals of feldspar, mica, and quartz. Explain how and where the rock might have formed.

_____

_____

_____

_____

got it? ··

◯ **I get it!** Now I know that the three general ways minerals form are when _____

_____

_____

◯ **I need extra help with** _____

Go to MY SCIENCE Ⓢ COACH online for help with this subject.

61

Classifying Rocks

UNLOCK THE BIG ?

🔑 How Do Geologists Classify Rocks?

my planeT DiaRY

FIELD TRIP

The Lonely Giant

In the midst of Wyoming stands a lonely giant: Mount Moran. Its peak stands more than 3,800 meters above sea level. If you climb Mount Moran, you'll crawl across slabs of rock. These slabs formed deep beneath Earth's surface. Here, great temperatures and pressures changed one type of rock into the rock of the slabs. As you continue to climb, a thick, vertical strip of darker stone suddenly appears. This rock is volcanic rock. Finally, when you reach the top, you find a 15-meter cap of sandstone. This rock formed when many tiny particles were squeezed tightly together over millions of years. So Mount Moran contains rocks that formed in three different ways.

Read the text and then answer the questions.

1. In your own words, describe one way in which rocks formed on Mount Moran.

_____

_____

2. If you were climbing Mount Moran, how might you be able to tell one rock from another?

_____

_____

▷ PLANET DIARY Go to **Planet Diary** to learn more about the three main groups of rocks.

Lab zone® Do the Inquiry Warm-Up *How Do Rocks Compare?*

Vocabulary
- rock-forming mineral • granite • basalt • grain
- texture • igneous rock • sedimentary rock
- metamorphic rock

Skills
- Reading: Identify the Main Idea
- Inquiry: Observe

How Do Geologists Classify Rocks?

If you were a geologist, how would you examine a rock for the first time? You might look at the outside surfaces. But you would also probably use a hammer to break open a small sample of the rock and look at the inside. **To study a rock sample, geologists observe the rock's mineral composition, color, and texture.**

Mineral Composition and Color Rocks are made of mixtures of minerals and other materials. Some rocks contain only a single mineral. Other rocks contain several minerals. The granite in **Figure 1,** for example, is made up of quartz, feldspar, mica, and hornblende. About 20 minerals make up most of the rocks of Earth's crust. These minerals are known as **rock-forming minerals.** The minerals that make up granite are rock-forming minerals.

A rock's color provides clues to the rock's mineral composition. For example, **granite** is generally a light-colored rock that has high silica content. That is, it is rich in the elements silicon and oxygen. **Basalt** is a dark-colored rock that has a lower silica content than granite has. But unlike granite, basalt has mineral crystals that are too small to be seen with the naked eye. As with minerals, color alone does not provide enough information to identify a rock.

FIGURE 1 ·····························

Granite
Granite is generally made up of only a few common minerals.

Observe How would you describe the overall color of this rock? What minerals cause the color (or colors) you chose?

_____

_____

_____

_____

_____

_____

Feldspar

Hornblende

Quartz

Mica

Granite

Texture Most rocks are made up of particles of minerals or other rocks, which geologists call **grains.** Grains give the rock its texture. **Texture** is the look and feel of a rock's surface. To describe the texture of a rock, geologists use terms that are based on the size, shape, and pattern of the grains.

Grain Size

Rocks with grains that are large and easy to see are said to be coarse grained. Fine-grained rocks have grains that are so small they can be seen only with a microscope.

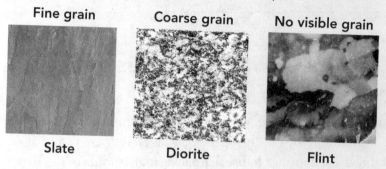

Fine grain
Slate

Coarse grain
Diorite

No visible grain
Flint

Grain Shape

In some rocks, grain shape results from the shape of the mineral crystals that form the rock. Other rocks have a grain shape that results from rounded or jagged bits of several rocks.

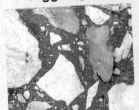

Rounded grain
Conglomerate

Jagged grain
Breccia

Grain Pattern

In banded rocks, grains can lie in a pattern of flat layers or can form swirls or colored bands. Nonbanded rocks have grains that do not lie in any visible pattern.

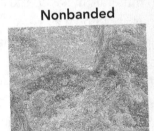

Nonbanded
Quartzite

Banded
Gneiss

apply it!

This photograph shows part of a coarse-grained rock. Read the text on this page and then answer the questions.

1 Observe Is this rock banded or nonbanded? _____

2 Infer Based on this rock's appearance, what type of rock might it be? _____

3 CHALLENGE Gneiss forms when very high pressure and temperature are applied to existing rock. How might these conditions explain the wavy pattern in this rock?

_____
_____
_____
_____

Origin Using the characteristics of color, texture, and mineral composition, geologists can classify a rock according to its origin. A rock's origin is the way that the rock formed. 🔑 **Geologists have classified rocks into three major groups: igneous rock, sedimentary rock, and metamorphic rock.**

Each of these groups of rocks forms in a different way, as shown in **Figure 2. Igneous rock** (IG nee us) forms from the cooling of magma or lava. The magma hardens underground to form rock. The lava erupts, cools, and hardens to form rock on Earth's surface.

Most **sedimentary rock** (sed uh MEN tur ee) forms when small particles of rocks or the remains of plants and animals are pressed and cemented together. Sedimentary rock forms in layers that are buried below the surface. **Metamorphic rock** (met uh MAWR fik) forms when a rock is changed by heat or pressure, or by chemical reactions. Most metamorphic rock forms deep underground.

🔁 **Identify the Main Idea**
Read the text on this page. Underline how each of the three major groups of rocks forms.

FIGURE 2 ·······················
Rock Origins
Rocks are classified by the way they formed.

✎ **Interpret Diagrams** Using the sentences you underlined, label each diagram with the rock origin it represents.

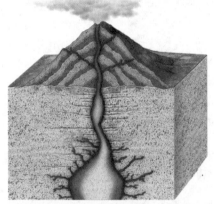

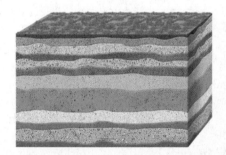

_____   _____   _____

Lab zone® Do the Quick Lab *Classify These Rocks.*

🔑 **Assess Your Understanding**

1a. Review Geologists classify rocks according to their _____

b. Explain How do igneous rocks form?

_____

_____

c. Classify Pumice is a type of rock that forms from molten material that erupts violently from a volcano. To what group of rock does pumice belong?

_____

_____

got it? ·····························

○ I get it! Now I know that geologists classify rocks into three major groups called _____

_____

○ I need extra help with _____

Go to MY SCIENCE ⬤ⁱ COACH online for help with this subject.

Igneous Rocks

UNLOCK THE BIG ?

🔑 How Do Geologists Classify Igneous Rocks?

🔑 How Are Igneous Rocks Used?

my planeT DiaRY

Arctic Diamonds

If you were looking for diamonds, where would you start? Maybe in a helicopter flying over the Arctic Circle?

In the 1980s, a pair of geologists used a helicopter to search for diamonds in Canada. The pair knew that diamonds form more than 100 kilometers under Earth's surface. They also knew that after diamonds form, powerful eruptions of magma can thrust the diamonds to the surface through volcanic pipes. As the magma cools and hardens, the diamonds are trapped inside volcanic rock.

The geologists found a source for diamonds after searching for several years. Now, diamond mines in Canada produce one of the world's most valuable crops of diamonds!

Discuss this question with a group of classmates. Write your answer below.

If you wanted to try to find diamonds, what type of rock might you look for? Why?

_____

_____

_____

▷ PLANET DIARY Go to **Planet Diary** to learn more about volcanic rocks.

Lab zone® Do the Inquiry Warm-Up *Liquid to Solid.*

How Do Geologists Classify Igneous Rocks?

Look at **Figure 1.** All the rocks shown in the figure are igneous rocks. But do all these rocks look the same? No, because even though all igneous rocks form from magma or lava, igneous rocks can look vastly different from each other. 🔑 **Igneous rocks are classified by their origin, texture, and mineral composition.**

Vocabulary
- extrusive rock
- intrusive rock

Skills
- Reading: Relate Cause and Effect
- Inquiry: Interpret Data

Origin Igneous rock may form on or beneath Earth's surface. **Extrusive rock** is igneous rock formed from lava that erupted onto Earth's surface. Basalt is the most common extrusive rock.

Igneous rock that formed when magma hardened beneath the surface of Earth is called **intrusive rock.** The most abundant type of intrusive rock in continental crust is granite. Granite forms tens of kilometers below Earth's surface and over hundreds of thousands of years or longer.

Texture Different igneous rocks may have similar mineral compositions and yet have very different textures. The texture of an igneous rock depends on the size and shape of its mineral crystals. The only exceptions to this rule are the different types of volcanic glass—igneous rock that lacks a crystal structure.

Rapidly cooling lava forms fine-grained igneous rocks with small crystals or no crystals at all. Slowly cooling magma forms coarse-grained rocks, such as granite, with large crystals. So, intrusive and extrusive rocks usually have different textures. For example, intrusive rocks have larger grains than extrusive rocks. Extrusive rocks have a fine-grained or glassy texture. **Figure 1** shows the textures of different igneous rocks.

Vocabulary Latin Word Origins *Ignis* means "fire" in Latin. What is "fiery" about igneous rocks?

_____

_____

_____

_____

FIGURE 1 ·······

> ART IN MOTION **Igneous Rock Origins and Textures** The texture of igneous rock varies according to its origin.

Interpret Diagrams Did the rocks in the photographs form at A or B? Write your answers in the spaces provided.

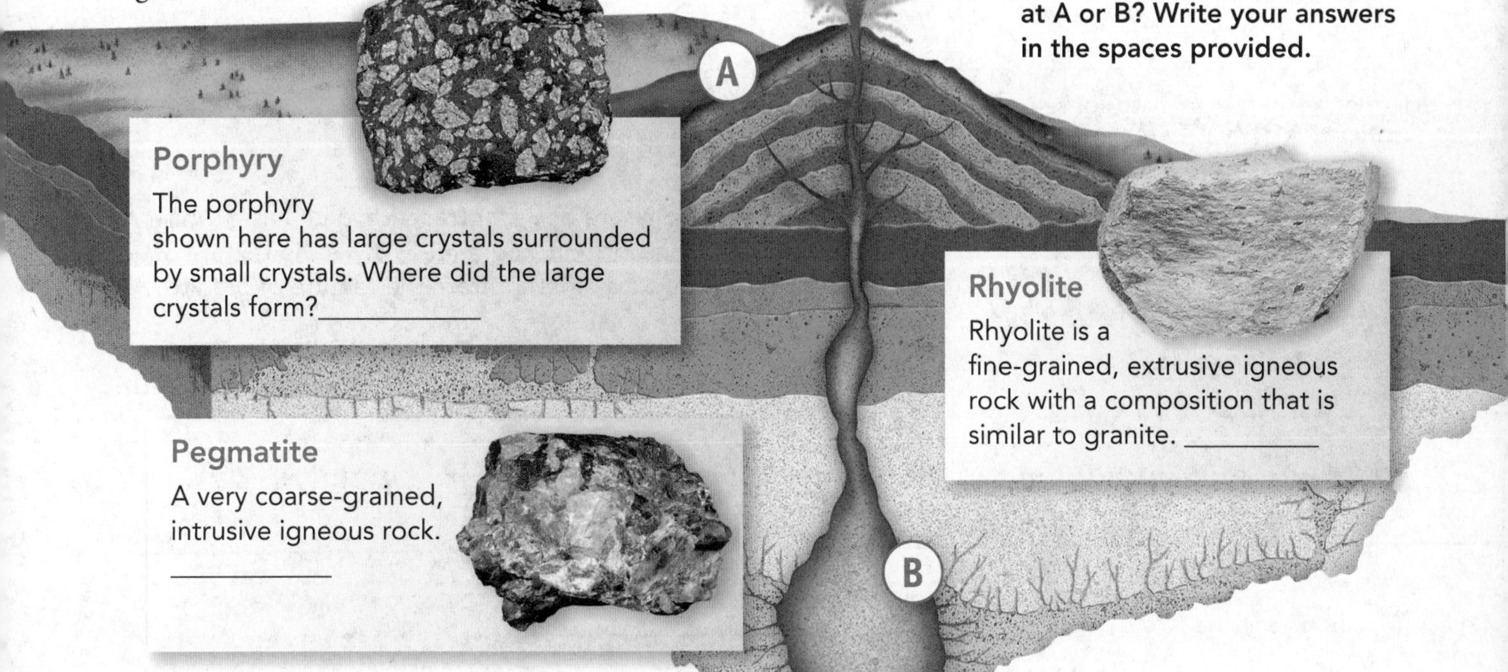

Porphyry
The porphyry shown here has large crystals surrounded by small crystals. Where did the large crystals form?_____

Rhyolite
Rhyolite is a fine-grained, extrusive igneous rock with a composition that is similar to granite. _____

Pegmatite
A very coarse-grained, intrusive igneous rock.

_____

Diorite is a coarse-grained intrusive igneous rock. It is a mixture of feldspar and dark-colored minerals such as hornblende and mica. The proportion of feldspar and dark minerals in diorite can vary.

1 ⚠ **Interpret Data** What mineral is most abundant in the sample of diorite illustrated by the graph?

_____

2 CHALLENGE How would the color of the diorite change if it contained less hornblende and more feldspar? Explain.

_____

_____

_____

_____

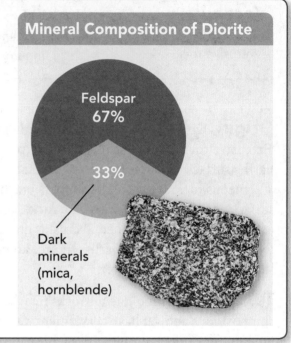

Mineral Composition of Diorite

Feldspar
67%

33%

Dark minerals (mica, hornblende)

⟳ **Relate Cause and Effect**

What determines the color of granite?

○ Its mineral composition

○ Its density

Mineral Composition Recall that the silica content of magma and lava can vary. Lava that is low in silica usually forms dark-colored rocks such as basalt. Basalt contains feldspar as well as certain dark-colored minerals, but does not contain quartz.

Magma that is high in silica usually forms light-colored rocks, such as granite. Granite's mineral composition determines its color, which can be light gray, red, or pink. Granite that is rich in reddish feldspar is a speckled pink. But granite rich in hornblende and dark mica is light gray with dark specks. Quartz crystals in granite add light gray or smoky specks.

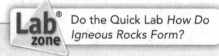

Lab zone Do the Quick Lab *How Do Igneous Rocks Form?*

🗝 **Assess Your Understanding**

1a. Identify Rhyolite is an (intrusive/extrusive) igneous rock.

b. Summarize How does rhyolite form?

_____

_____

c. Compare and Contrast Rhyolite has a similar composition to granite. Why is the texture of rhyolite different from the texture of granite?

_____

_____

_____

got it? ·

○ **I get it!** Now I know that igneous rocks are classified according to their _____

_____

○ I need extra help with _____

Go to **MY SCIENCE ⑤ COACH** online for help with this subject.

How Are Igneous Rocks Used?

Many igneous rocks are hard, dense, and durable. ⟶ **People throughout history have used igneous rock for tools and building materials.**

Granite has a long history of use as a building material. More than 3,500 years ago, the ancient Egyptians used granite to build statues. About 600 years ago, the Incas of Peru built fortresses out of great blocks of granite and other igneous rock. You can see part of one of their fortresses in **Figure 2.** In the United States during the 1800s and early 1900s, granite was widely used to build bridges and public buildings. Today, thin, polished sheets of granite are used in curbstones and floors. Another igneous rock, basalt, can be used for cobblestones. It can also be crushed and used as a material in landscaping and in roads.

Igneous rocks such as pumice and obsidian also have important uses. The rough surface of pumice forms when gas bubbles are trapped in fast-cooling lava, leaving spaces in the rock. The rough surface makes pumice a good abrasive for cleaning and polishing. Ancient Native Americans used obsidian to make sharp tools for cutting and scraping. Obsidian cools very quickly, without forming crystals. So it has a smooth, shiny texture like glass. Perlite, formed by the rapid cooling of magma or lava, is often mixed with soil and used for starting vegetable seeds.

FIGURE 2 ·······················
Building Blocks
Igneous rock has long been used as a building material, such as for this Incan fortress in Peru.

✎ **Work With Design Constraints** A fortress must be strong enough to withstand violent attacks. Why might the Incas have chosen igneous rock to build their fortress near Ollantaytambo in Peru?

_____
_____
_____
_____

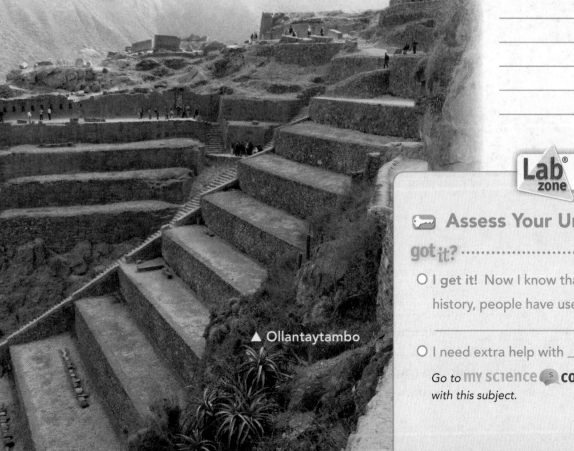

▲ Ollantaytambo

Lab ® Do the Quick Lab
zone *The Rocks Around Us.*

⟶ Assess Your Understanding

got it? ·······························

○ **I get it!** Now I know that throughout history, people have used igneous rocks for _____

_____

○ **I need extra help with** _____

Go to my science ⑤ coach *online for help with this subject.*

Sedimentary Rocks

🔑 How Do Sedimentary Rocks Form?

🔑 What Are the Three Major Types of Sedimentary Rocks?

🔑 How Are Sedimentary Rocks Used?

my planet Diary

The Cutting Edge

If you had to carve tools out of stone, would you know which rocks to use? Dr. Beverly Chiarulli, an archaeologist at Indiana University of Pennsylvania, studies stone tools that were used by people in Pennsylvania 10,000 years ago. Dr. Chiarulli has found that these people crafted spearheads out of the sedimentary rocks called chert and jasper. Chert is hard and has a very fine texture. It is brittle, but does not fracture along thin, even planes. So, chert can be shaped somewhat easily by flaking off chips, producing the sharp edges needed for spearheads.

CAREERS

Read the text and then answer the question.

What properties of chert allow it to be carved into sharp spearheads?

_____

_____

_____

_____

▶ PLANET DIARY Go to **Planet Diary** to learn more about sedimentary rocks.

Lab ® Do the Inquiry Warm-Up
zone *Acid Test for Rocks.*

How Do Sedimentary Rocks Form?

The banks of a cool stream may be made up of tiny sand grains, mud, and pebbles. Shells, leaves, and even bones may also be mixed in. All of these particles are examples of sediment. **Sediment** is small, solid pieces of material that come from rocks or living things.

Sedimentary rocks form when sediment is deposited by water and wind, as shown in **Figure 1.** 🔑 **Most sedimentary rocks are formed through a sequence of processes: weathering, erosion, deposition, compaction, and cementation.**

Vocabulary
- sediment • weathering • erosion • deposition
- compaction • cementation • clastic rock
- organic rock • chemical rock

Skills
- ☉ Reading: Identify the Main Idea
- △ Inquiry: Infer

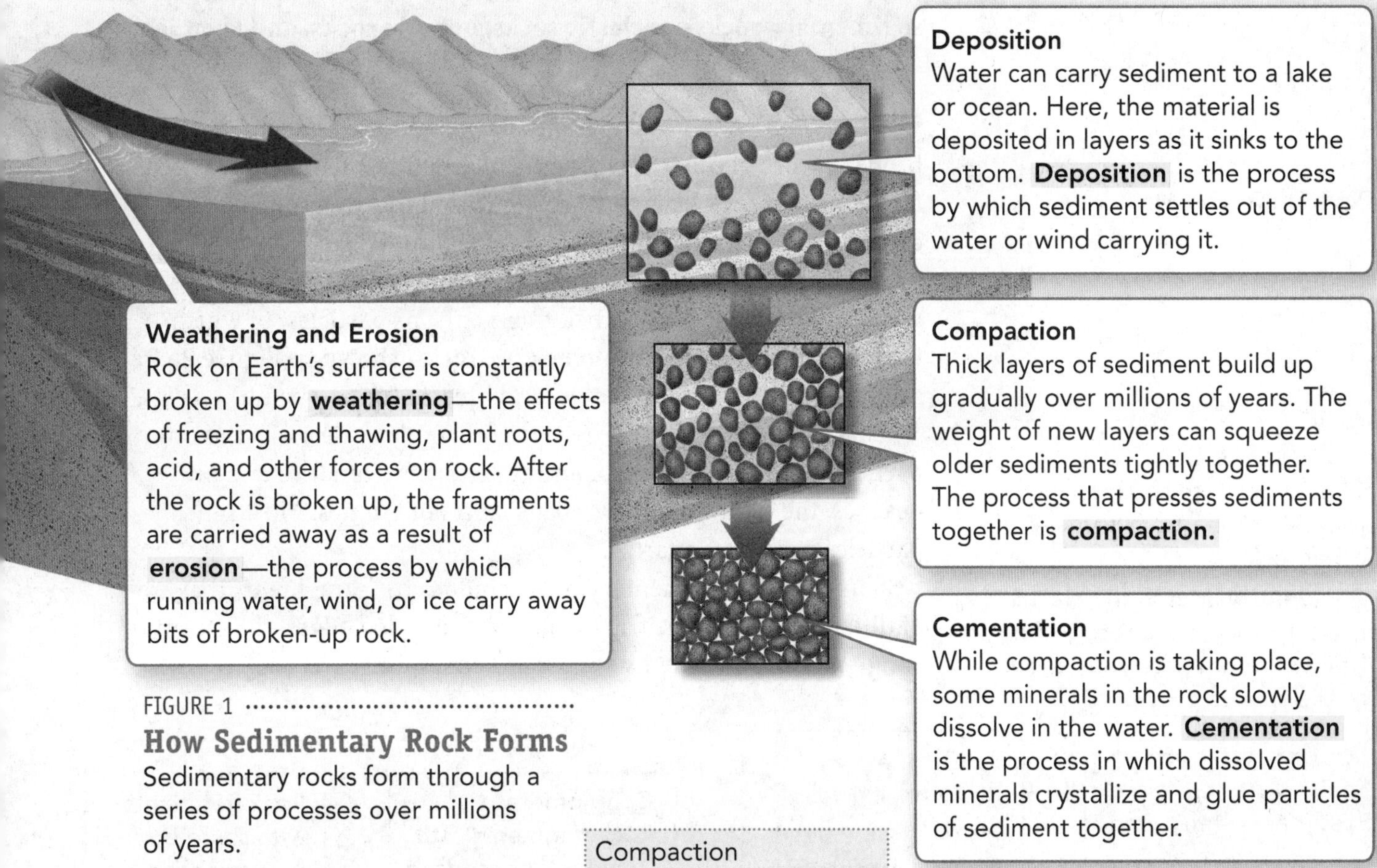

Deposition
Water can carry sediment to a lake or ocean. Here, the material is deposited in layers as it sinks to the bottom. **Deposition** is the process by which sediment settles out of the water or wind carrying it.

Weathering and Erosion
Rock on Earth's surface is constantly broken up by **weathering**—the effects of freezing and thawing, plant roots, acid, and other forces on rock. After the rock is broken up, the fragments are carried away as a result of **erosion**—the process by which running water, wind, or ice carry away bits of broken-up rock.

Compaction
Thick layers of sediment build up gradually over millions of years. The weight of new layers can squeeze older sediments tightly together. The process that presses sediments together is **compaction.**

Cementation
While compaction is taking place, some minerals in the rock slowly dissolve in the water. **Cementation** is the process in which dissolved minerals crystallize and glue particles of sediment together.

FIGURE 1 ·······················

How Sedimentary Rock Forms
Sedimentary rocks form through a series of processes over millions of years.

✎ **Sequence** Put the terms listed in the word bank in the proper sequence to show how mountains can change into sedimentary rock.

Compaction
Cementation
Weathering and erosion
Deposition

Lab zone Do the Quick Lab *How Does Pressure Affect Particles of Rock?*

🔑 Assess Your Understanding

got it? ···

○ **I get it!** Now I know that most sedimentary rocks are formed through the processes of _____

_____

○ **I need extra help with** _____

Go to MY SCIENCE ⑤ COACH online for help with this subject.

71

What Are the Three Major Types of Sedimentary Rocks?

Geologists classify sedimentary rocks according to the type of sediments that make up the rock. 🔑 **The three major groups of sedimentary rocks are clastic rocks, organic rocks, and chemical rocks.** Different processes form each of these types of rocks.

Clastic Rocks Most sedimentary rocks are made up of broken pieces of other rocks. A **clastic rock** is a sedimentary rock formed when rock fragments are squeezed together. The fragments can range in size from clay particles that are too small to be seen without a microscope to large, heavy boulders. Clastic rocks are grouped by the size of the rock fragments, or particles, of which they are made. Some common clastic rocks, shown in **Figure 2,** are shale, sandstone, conglomerate, and breccia (BRECH ee uh).

Shale forms from tiny particles of clay. Water deposits the clay particles in thin, flat layers. Sandstone forms from the sand on beaches, the ocean floor, riverbeds, and sand dunes. Most sand particles consist of quartz.

Some clastic sedimentary rocks contain rock fragments that are of different sizes. If the fragments have rounded edges, they form conglomerate. Fragments with sharp edges form breccia.

⟳ Identify the Main Idea

Clastic rocks are grouped by the size of the _____ _____ they contain.

FIGURE 2 ·····················

Clastic Rocks
Clastic rocks are sedimentary rocks that form from particles of other rocks.

✎ **Identify** Match the clastic rocks to the four photographs below them. Write your answer in the spaces provided.

Shale
Fossils are often found in shale, which tends to split into flat pieces.

Sandstone
Many small holes between sand grains allow sandstone to absorb water.

Conglomerate
Rock fragments with rounded edges make up conglomerate.

Breccia
Rock fragments with sharp edges form breccia.

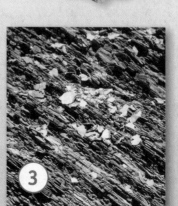

Organic Rocks

Organic Rocks You may be familiar with the rocks called coal and limestone, shown in **Figure 3.** Both are sedimentary rocks. But instead of forming from particles of other rocks, they form from the remains of material that was once living. **Organic rock** forms where the remains of plants and animals are deposited in layers. The term "organic" refers to substances that once were part of living things or were made by living things.

Coal forms from the remains of swamp plants buried in water. As layer upon layer of plant remains build up, the weight of the layers squeezes the decaying plants together. Over millions of years, they slowly change into coal.

Limestone forms in the ocean, where many living things, such as coral, clams, and oysters, have hard shells or skeletons made of calcite. When these ocean animals die, their shells pile up on the ocean floor. Over millions of years, compaction and cementation can change the thick sediment into limestone.

FIGURE 3 ....

Organic Rocks
Organic rocks such as limestone and coal are sedimentary rocks that form from the remains of living things.

✎ **Sequence** Complete the graphic organizers to show how coal and limestone form.

Coal

Remains of swamp plants are buried in water.

↓

_____

_____

↓

_____

_____

Over millions of years, coal forms.

Limestone

Ocean animals with hard shells or skeletons die.

↓

_____

_____

↓

_____

_____

↓

Sediment is slowly changed to limestone.

These rock "towers" in Mono Lake, California, are made of tufa, a form of limestone. Tufa forms from water solutions that contain dissolved materials. The towers formed under water. They became exposed when the water level in the lake dropped as a result of water needs for the city of Los Angeles. Read the text about the major types of sedimentary rocks. Then answer the questions.

1 Classify Tufa is a (clastic/organic/chemical) sedimentary rock.

2 Infer What mineral was dissolved in the waters of Mono Lake and later crystallized to form the rock towers?

_____

3 CHALLENGE When acid comes into contact with calcite, the acid bubbles. How can geologists use acid to confirm that the rock towers are made of limestone?

_____

_____

_____

_____

Chemical Rocks Limestone can also form when calcite that is dissolved in lakes, seas, or underground water comes out of a solution and forms crystals. This kind of limestone is considered a chemical rock. **Chemical rock** forms when minerals dissolved in a water solution crystallize. Chemical rocks can also form from mineral deposits that are left when seas or lakes evaporate. For example, rock salt is made of the mineral halite, which forms by evaporation.

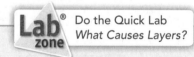
Do the Quick Lab
What Causes Layers?

Assess Your Understanding

1a. Review Shale forms from tiny particles of (clay/sand/mica).

b. Describe How is clay deposited to form shale?

_____

_____

_____

c. Infer You come across a thick deposit of shale that forms a layer in the ground. What can you infer about the area's past environment?

_____

_____

_____

_____

got it? ....

○ **I get it!** Now I know that the three major types of sedimentary rocks are _____

○ **I need extra help with** _____

Go to **MY SCIENCE** ⬤ᔆ **COACH** online for help with this subject.

How Are Sedimentary Rocks Used?

People have used sedimentary rocks throughout history for many different purposes, including for tools and building materials. Chert was used to make spearheads by people who lived in Pennsylvania more than 10,000 years ago. Other people also made arrowheads out of flint for thousands of years. Flint is a hard rock, yet it can be shaped to a point. It forms when small particles of silica settle out of water.

Sedimentary rocks such as sandstone and limestone have been used as building materials for thousands of years. Both types of stone are soft enough to be cut easily into blocks or slabs. The White House in Washington, D.C., is built of sandstone. Today, builders use sandstone and limestone on the outside walls of buildings, such as the building shown in **Figure 4.** Limestone also has industrial uses. For example, it is used in making cement and steel.

FIGURE 4 ·······················
> REAL-WORLD INQUIRY
Building With Limestone
Limestone is a popular building material. However, acid rain reacts with the calcite in limestone, damaging buildings made from it.

✏ **Evaluate the Design** Do the benefits of constructing limestone buildings outweigh the damage acid rain causes to these buildings? Explain.

_____

_____

Carnegie Library (Jeffersonville, Indiana) ▼

Lab zone® Do the Lab Investigation *Testing Rock Flooring.*

Assess Your Understanding

got it? ··

O **I get it!** Now I know that throughout history, people have used sedimentary rocks for _____

O **I need extra help with** _____

Go to **my science** ⓢ **coach** *online for help with this subject.*

Metamorphic Rocks

🔑 **What Are Metamorphic Rocks?**

my planet Diary

Rock Dough

Misconception:
Rocks do not change form.

Did you know that heat can change a rock's form without melting it? To understand how, think of what happens when you bake cookies. You might mix flour, eggs, sugar, and baking powder in a bowl. When you bake the raw dough in a hot oven, the dough changes into cookies.

Heat can change rock, too. If hot magma or lava come near rock, the heat can "bake" the rock. The ingredients in the rock—the minerals—might not melt. But the heat can still change the rock into a new form!

MISCONCEPTION

Read the text and then answer the question below.
Does rock have to melt in order to change form? Explain.

_____

_____

_____

_____

_____

_____

▷ PLANET DIARY Go to Planet Diary to learn more about how rocks can change form.

Lab ® Do the Inquiry Warm-Up
zone A Sequined Rock.

What Are Metamorphic Rocks?

You may be surprised to learn that heat can change rock like a hot oven changes raw cookie dough. But deep inside Earth, both heat and pressure are much greater than at Earth's surface. When great heat and pressure are applied to rock, the rock can change both its shape and its composition. 🔑 **Any rock that forms from another rock as a result of changes in heat or pressure (or both heat and pressure) is a metamorphic rock.**

Vocabulary
• foliated

Skills
↻ Reading: Relate Cause and Effect
△ Inquiry: Observe

How Metamorphic Rocks Form
Metamorphic rock can form out of igneous, sedimentary, or other metamorphic rock. Many metamorphic rocks are found in mountains or near large masses of igneous rock. Why are metamorphic rocks commonly found in these locations? The answer lies inside Earth.

The heat that can change a rock into metamorphic rock can come from pockets of magma. For instance, pockets of magma can rise through the crust. The high temperatures of these pockets can change rock into metamorphic rock. Collisions between Earth's plates can also push rock down toward the heat of the mantle.

Very high pressure can also change rock into metamorphic rock. For instance, plate collisions cause great pressure to be applied to rocks while mountains are being formed. The pressure can deform, or change the physical shape of, the rock, as shown in **Figure 1**. Also, the deeper that a rock is buried in the crust, the greater the pressure on that rock. Under very high temperature or pressure (or both), the minerals in a rock can be changed into other minerals. At the same time, the appearance, texture, and crystal structure of the minerals in the rock change. The rock eventually becomes a metamorphic rock.

FIGURE 1 ·····················
Metamorphic Rock
The rock in the photograph was once sedimentary rock. Now, it is metamorphic rock.

✎ **Develop Hypotheses** What changed the rock? Make sure your answer explains the rock's current appearance.

_____
_____
_____
_____
_____

Deformed metamorphic rock in eastern Connecticut ▲

77

How Metamorphic Rocks Are Classified

While metamorphic rocks are forming, intense heat changes the size and shape of the grains, or mineral crystals, in the rock. Extreme pressure squeezes rock so that the mineral grains may line up in flat, parallel layers. **Geologists classify metamorphic rocks according to the arrangement of the grains making up the rocks.**

Foliated Rocks Metamorphic rocks that have their grains arranged in either parallel layers or bands are said to be foliated. **Foliated** describes the thin, flat layering found in most metamorphic rocks. For instance, the crystals in granite can be flattened to create the foliated texture of gneiss. Slate is also a common foliated rock. Heat and pressure change the sedimentary rock shale into slate. Slate is basically a denser, more compact version of shale. But as shale changes into slate, the mineral composition of the shale can change.

Nonfoliated Rocks Some metamorphic rocks are nonfoliated. The mineral grains in these rocks are arranged randomly. Marble and quartzite are metamorphic rocks that have a nonfoliated texture. Quartzite forms out of quartz sandstone. The weakly cemented quartz particles in the sandstone recrystallize to form quartzite, which is extremely hard. Quartzite looks smoother than sandstone, as shown in **Figure 2**. Finally, marble usually forms when limestone is subjected to heat and pressure deep beneath the surface.

FIGURE 2 ·························
Presto!
Great heat and pressure can change one type of rock into another.

Classify Label each rock *sedimentary*, *igneous*, or *metamorphic*. Indicate whether the metamorphic rocks are foliated. Then shade the correct arrowhead to show which rock can form from the other rock.

How Metamorphic Rocks Are Used

Marble and slate are two of the most useful metamorphic rocks. Marble has an even grain, so it can be cut into thin slabs or carved into many shapes. And marble is easy to polish. So architects and sculptors use marble for many statues and buildings, such as the Tower of Pisa. Like marble, slate comes in many colors, including gray, red, and purple. Because it is foliated, slate splits easily into flat pieces. These pieces can be used for roofing, outdoor walkways, and as trim for stone buildings. **The metamorphic rocks marble and slate are important materials for building and sculpture.**

Tower of Pisa ▶

apply it!

Although marble, quartzite, and slate are all metamorphic rocks, they are used in different ways.

1 Observe Look around your school or neighborhood. What examples of metamorphic rock can you find? How is each metamorphic rock used? Write your answers in the notebook at the right.

2 CHALLENGE Why are chess pieces sometimes made of marble?

_____

_____

_____

Lab zone
Do the Quick Lab *How Do Grain Patterns Compare?*

Assess Your Understanding

1a. Define What is a metamorphic rock?

_____

_____

_____

_____

b. Identify Faulty Reasoning Suppose great heat completely melts a certain deposit of rock, which then hardens into new rock. You might think that the new rock is metamorphic. But it isn't. Why not?

_____

_____

_____

_____

got it? ....

○ **I get it!** Now I know that certain metamorphic rocks are used for _____

○ **I need extra help with** _____

Go to MY SCIENCE COACH *online for help with this subject.*

79

6 The Rock Cycle

🔑 **What Is the Rock Cycle?**

my pLaneT DiaRY

Rolling Along

The Himalaya Mountains are eroding at a rate of about 2.5 millimeters per year. That's about one tenth as fast as your fingernails grow! But the Himalayas were formed millions of years ago. So imagine the total mass of rock that has fallen down the mountain and that has then been swept out to sea. Over millions of years, the piled weight of eroded particles will squeeze the bits together on the sea floor. New rock will form. Then, ancient bits of the Himalayas will be recycled inside new rock.

FUN FACT

Read the text and then answer the question.

How could small pieces of the Himalayas form new rock?

_____

_____

▷ PLANET DIARY Go to **Planet Diary** to learn more about the rock cycle.

Lab® Do the Inquiry Warm-Up
zone *Recycling Rocks.*

What Is the Rock Cycle?

Natural forces act on the Himalayas. In fact, rock in Earth's crust is always changing. 🔑 **Forces deep inside Earth and at the surface produce a slow cycle that builds, destroys, and changes the rocks in the crust.** The **rock cycle** is a series of processes that occur on Earth's surface and in the crust and mantle that slowly change rocks from one kind to another. For example, weathering can break down granite into sediment that later forms sandstone.

Vocabulary
• rock cycle

Skills
↻ Reading: Sequence
△ Inquiry: Classify

One Pathway Through the Rock Cycle

One Pathway Through the Rock Cycle There are many pathways by which rocks move through the rock cycle. For example, Stone Mountain, near Atlanta, Georgia, is made of granite. The granite in Stone Mountain, shown in **Figure 1,** formed millions of years ago below Earth's surface as magma cooled.

After the granite had formed, the forces of mountain building slowly pushed the granite upward. Then, over millions of years, weathering and erosion began to wear away the granite. Today, particles of granite constantly break off the mountain and become sand. Streams carry the sand to the ocean. What might happen next?

Over millions of years, layers of sand might pile up on the ocean floor. Slowly, the sand would be compacted by its own weight. Or perhaps calcite that is dissolved in the ocean water would cement the particles together. Over time, the quartz that once formed the granite of Stone Mountain could become sandstone, which is a sedimentary rock.

Sediment could keep piling up on the sandstone. Eventually, pressure would compact the rock's particles until no spaces were left between them. Silica, the main ingredient in quartz, would replace the calcite cement. The rock's texture would change from gritty to smooth. After millions of years, the standstone would have changed into the metamorphic rock quartzite.

↻ **Sequence** Number the materials that move through the rock cycle at Stone Mountain in the sequence given in the text:

_____ Sand

_____ Granite

_____ Quartzite

FIGURE 1 ·····················
Stone Mountain
The granite in Stone Mountain is moving through the rock cycle.

✎ **Answer the questions.**

1. △ **Classify** As shown in the photograph, trees can grow on the mountain. Their roots might break up the granite. What step of the rock cycle do the trees play a role in?

_____

2. [CHALLENGE] Does the rock cycle stop after the quartzite has formed? Explain.

_____

_____

_____

_____

_____

_____

81

EXPLORE
THE BIG
?

The Rock Cycle

How do rocks form?

FIGURE 2 •••••••••••••••••••••••••••••••••••••

✏️ ▶ INTERACTIVE ART **Be a Rock Star!**
Through melting, weathering and erosion, and heat and pressure, the rock cycle constantly changes rocks from one type into another type.

Interpret Diagrams Study the diagram. Then fill in each blank arrow with the correct term: *melting, weathering and erosion,* or *heat and pressure.* (*Hint:* To fit your answers, abbreviate "weathering and erosion" as "w & e.")

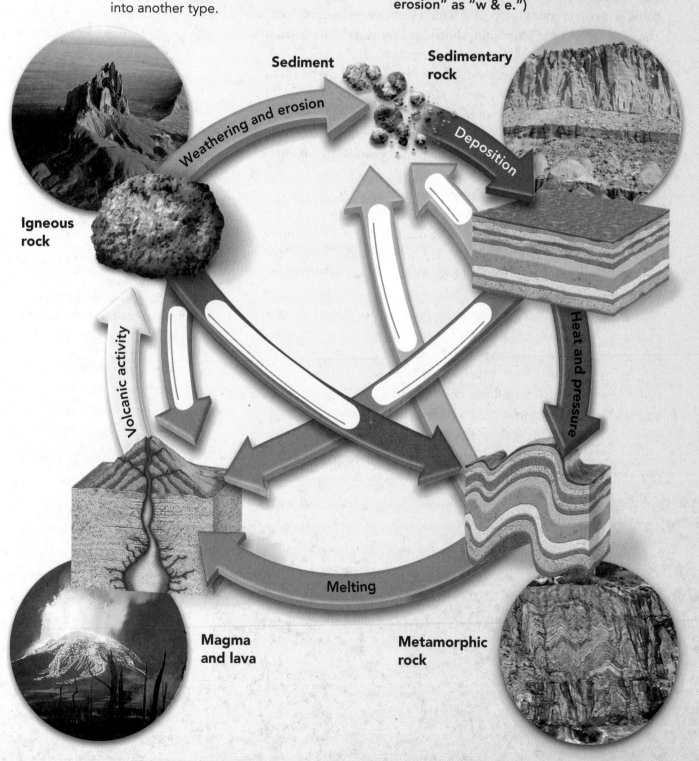

Sediment

Sedimentary rock

Weathering and erosion

Deposition

Igneous rock

Volcanic activity

Heat and pressure

Melting

Magma and lava

Metamorphic rock

The Rock Cycle and Plate Tectonics

The changes of the rock cycle are closely related to plate tectonics. Recall that Earth's lithosphere is made up of huge plates. These plates move slowly over Earth's surface as the result of convection currents in Earth's mantle. As the plates move, they carry the continents and ocean floors with them. Plate movements help drive the rock cycle by helping to form magma, the source of igneous rocks.

Where oceanic plates move apart, magma formed from melted mantle rock moves upward and fills the gap with new igneous rock. Where an oceanic plate is subducted beneath a continental plate, magma forms and rises. The result is a volcano made of igneous rock. A collision of continental plates may push rocks so deep that they melt to form magma, leading to the formation of igneous rock.

Sedimentary rock can also result from plate movement. For example, the collision of continental plates can be strong enough to push up a mountain range. Then, weathering and erosion begin. The mountains are worn away. This process leads to the formation of sedimentary rock.

Finally, a collision between continental plates can push rocks down deep beneath the surface. Here, heat and pressure could change the rocks to metamorphic rock.

Conservation of Material in the Rock Cycle

Constructive and destructive forces build up and destroy Earth's landmasses. But as the rock in Earth's crust moves through the rock cycle, material is not lost or gained. For example, a mountain can erode to form sediment, all of which can eventually form new rock.

Lab zone ® Do the Quick Lab *Which Rock Came First?*

apply it!

New rock forms on the ocean floor at the mid-Atlantic ridge. Here, two plates move apart.

❶ (Igneous/Sedimentary) rock forms at point A.

❷ How can rock that is formed at the mid-Atlantic ridge be changed into sedimentary rock?

_____

_____

_____

_____

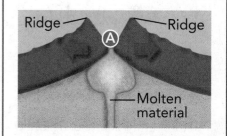

Ridge — Ⓐ — Ridge

— Molten material

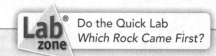

🗝 Assess Your Understanding

1a. Name The rock cycle builds, destroys, and changes the rock in Earth's (crust/core).

b. ANSWER THE BIG ❓ **Describe** How do rocks form?

_____

_____

got it? ....

O **I get it!** Now I know that the rock cycle is _____

_____

_____

O **I need extra help with** _____

Go to MY SCIENCE Ⓢ **COACH** *online for help with this subject.*

Study Guide

REVIEW THE BIG ?

In the rock cycle, rocks form through three main processes: _____,
_____, and _____.

LESSON 1 Properties of Minerals

🔑 A mineral is a natural solid that can form by inorganic processes and that has a crystal structure and a definite chemical composition.

🔑 Each mineral has characteristic properties.

🔑 Minerals form from cooling of magma and lava, from solutions, or from organic processes.

Vocabulary
• mineral • inorganic • crystal • streak • luster
• Mohs hardness scale • cleavage • fracture
• geode • crystallization • solution • vein

LESSON 2 Classifying Rocks

🔑 To study a rock sample, geologists observe the rock's mineral composition, color, and texture.

🔑 Geologists have classified rocks into three major groups: igneous rock, sedimentary rock, and metamorphic rock.

Vocabulary
• rock-forming mineral • granite • basalt
• grain • texture • igneous rock
• sedimentary rock • metamorphic rock

LESSON 3 Igneous Rocks

🔑 Igneous rocks are classified by their origin, texture, and mineral composition.

🔑 People throughout history have used igneous rock for tools and building materials.

Vocabulary
• extrusive rock
• intrusive rock

LESSON 4 Sedimentary Rocks

🔑 Most sedimentary rocks form by weathering, erosion, deposition, compaction, cementation.

🔑 Three major types of sedimentary rocks are clastic rocks, organic rocks, and chemical rocks.

🔑 People use sedimentary rocks for tools and building materials.

Vocabulary
• sediment • weathering • erosion
• deposition • compaction • cementation
• clastic rock • organic rock • chemical rock

LESSON 5 Metamorphic Rocks

🔑 Any rock that forms from another rock as a result of changes in heat or pressure (or both) is a metamorphic rock.

🔑 Geologists classify metamorphic rocks according to the arrangement of the grains making up the rocks.

🔑 The metamorphic rocks marble and slate are important materials for building and sculpture.

Vocabulary
• foliated

LESSON 6 The Rock Cycle

🔑 Forces deep inside Earth and at the surface produce a slow cycle that builds, destroys, and changes the rocks in the crust.

Vocabulary
• rock cycle

Review and Assessment

LESSON 1 Properties of Minerals

1. Streak is the color of a mineral's

   a. luster.   **b.** cleavage.

   c. powder.   **d.** fracture.

2. During crystallization, _____ are arranged to form a material with a crystal structure.

3. Compare and Contrast Fill in the table to compare the characteristics of a mineral and a material that is not a mineral.

	Hematite	Brick
Natural	✔	✘
Can form by inorganic processes		
Solid		
Crystal structure		
Definite chemical composition		

LESSON 2 Classifying Rocks

4. A rock that forms from many small fragments of other rocks is a(n)

   a. igneous rock.   **b.** sedimentary rock.

   c. metamorphic rock.   **d.** extrusive rock.

5. The 20 or so minerals that make up most of the rocks of Earth's crust are known as

_____

Use the photograph to answer Question 6.

6. Interpret Photographs Describe the texture of this rock.

_____

_____

LESSON 3 Igneous Rocks

7. What kind of igneous rock usually contains large crystals?

   a. organic   **b.** clastic

   c. intrusive   **d.** extrusive

8. An igneous rock's color is primarily determined by its _____

9. Relate Cause and Effect What conditions lead to the formation of large crystals in an igneous rock?

_____

_____

10. **Write About It** Describe the texture of granite. Also describe granite's mineral composition and explain granite's origin.

LESSON 4 Sedimentary Rocks

11. You find a deposit of organic limestone. In what type of setting did it probably form?

   a. the ocean   **b.** a volcano

   c. a swamp   **d.** sand dunes

12. Shale is a clastic rock, meaning that it forms when _____ are squeezed or cemented together (or both).

13. Name A certain rock contains large, jagged pieces of other rocks, cemented by fine particles. What type of rock is this? Explain.

_____

_____

_____

14. **Write About It** You find a rock with fossils in it. Is this rock more likely to be a sedimentary rock than an igneous rock? Explain.

LESSON 5 **Metamorphic Rocks**

15. A metamorphic rock in which the grains line up in layers is called a

  a. chemical rock.   **b.** clastic rock.

  c. nonorganic rock. **d.** foliated rock.

16. Two types of foliated rock are

_____

17. Infer Why do you think slate might be denser than shale?

_____

_____

18. Develop Hypotheses Why do the crystals in gneiss line up in bands?

_____

_____

_____

LESSON 6 **The Rock Cycle**

19. The process by which metamorphic rock changes to igneous rock begins with

  a. melting.   **b.** erosion.

  c. deposition. **d.** crystallization.

20. _____ can turn igneous rock into sediment.

21. [Write About It] Use the diagram to describe two ways metamorphic rock can change into sedimentary rock.

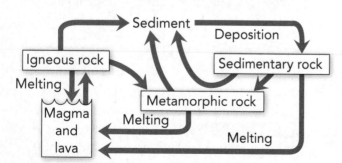

22. While hiking through a mountain range, you use a chisel and hammer to remove the three rock samples shown below. Classify the rocks you found as either igneous, sedimentary, or metamorphic. Then, describe the textures of each rock. Also describe the processes that formed each rock.

_____

_____

_____

_____

_____

_____

_____

_____

_____

_____

_____

_____

_____

_____

Standardized Test Prep

Multiple Choice

Circle the letter of the best answer.

1. The diagrams below show four different mineral samples.

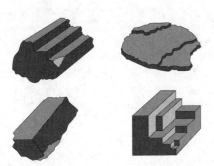

   Which mineral property is best shown by the samples?

   A crystal structure

   B cleavage

   C hardness

   D color

2. You find a rock in which the grains are arranged in wavy, parallel bands of white and black crystals. What kind of rock have you probably found?

   A igneous   B sedimentary

   C metamorphic D extrusive

3. Which statement best describes how an extrusive igneous rock forms?

   A Magma cools quickly on Earth's surface.

   B Magma cools slowly to form granite.

   C Magma cools quickly below Earth's surface.

   D Magma cools slowly beneath Earth's surface.

4. Which rock cycle process causes many sedimentary rocks to have visible layers?

   A eruption   B intrusion

   C crystallization D deposition

5. If heat and pressure inside Earth cause the texture and crystal structure of a rock to change, what new material is formed?

   A metamorphic rock

   B sedimentary rock

   C igneous rock

   D chemical rock

Constructed Response

Use the diagram below and your knowledge of science to help you answer Question 6. Write your answer on a separate piece of paper.

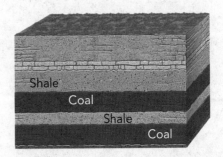

6. Describe the environment that probably existed millions of years ago where these rocks formed. Explain your reasoning.

STRUGGLING TO SURVIVE

An old problem has resurfaced in Arizona and New Mexico. The Navajo homeland in this region rests on one of the richest uranium reserves in the United States. Uranium mining in this area first began in the 1950s and stopped in the 1970s. When the mining companies left, many of them did not remove radioactive waste or seal the mine tunnels. This has greatly affected the health of the Navajo people who live and work near the old mines.

Years later, mining companies have come back to the Navajo homeland and the area around it. This time, they want to use solution mining, which uses water to flush out the uranium ore. This method is less dangerous than underground mining, but it can still contaminate the groundwater. And because the area is mostly desert, mining could use up scarce water.

Uranium is used for fuel in nuclear reactors that generate electricity. These reactors do not add carbon to the atmosphere, so some people think we should use them, instead of coal-fired power plants, to meet our electricity needs. The Navajo who live in an area with both coal and uranium must try to make decisions that will be good for their community both in the present and in the future.

Research It Working in a group, research (a) the uses of uranium, (b) the environmental impact of uranium mining, (c) the effect mining has had on the Navajo people's health, and (d) the effect mining has had on Navajo communities, environment, and people. As a group, write a paper weighing the costs and benefits of using solution mining to extract uranium ore.

Abandoned Uranium Mines (AUM) on the Navajo Nation

Waiter there's a MINERAL in my soup!

While minerals form part of Earth's crust, they do not simply stay there until somebody picks them up. The minerals that make up Earth's crust are made up of elements that living things need, such as calcium. Over time, the minerals containing elements dissolve in water. Elements become part of our food because vegetables absorb them from the soil. When we eat the vegetables, we also take in the elements.

Calcium is one of the most important elements for your body because it helps build strong bones and teeth. It can be found in dairy products like milk, yogurt, and cheese, as well as broccoli and canned salmon.

Iron helps transport oxygen from your lungs to the rest of your body, and helps form red blood cells. Beef, tuna, eggs, and whole wheat bread are great sources of iron.

Potassium helps your muscles and nervous system work properly. Bananas, tomatoes, oranges, potatoes with skins, and peanuts are rich in potassium.

Zinc helps your immune system stay strong. A healthy immune system helps you fight off illnesses and infections. Zinc can be found in pork, lamb, beans, and lentils.

Design It Plan one day's worth of meals (breakfast, lunch, dinner). Include as many foods rich in essential elements as possible in your plan.

IS THIS CRACK IN EARTH GROWING?

How do moving plates change Earth's crust?

You may think that Earth's crust is one huge, solid piece. In fact, Earth's surface is broken into several pieces—like a cracked eggshell. One of the cracks runs through the middle of this lake in Iceland.

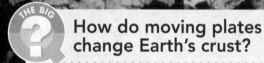 **Infer** Why do you think this crack in Earth's crust might get wider?

_____

_____

_____

_____

_____

_____

_____

▶ UNTAMED SCIENCE Watch the **Untamed Science** video to learn more about Earth's crust.

Plate Tectonics

3 Getting Started

Check Your Understanding

1. Background Read the paragraph below and then answer the question.

Maria took a train from Oregon to Georgia. The train rode across the entire **continent** of North America. It rode up and down the Rocky Mountains, which form a **boundary** between America's east and west. The conductor said, "These mountains are part of Earth's **crust**."

> A **continent** is a large landmass.
>
> A **boundary** is the point or line where one region ends and another begins.
>
> The **crust** is the outer layer of Earth.

- What is the crust?

_____

_____

▶ MY READING WEB If you had trouble answering the question above, visit **My Reading Web** and type in *Plate Tectonics.*

Vocabulary Skill

Use Prefixes A prefix is a word part that is added at the beginning of a root or base word to change its meaning. Knowing the meaning of prefixes will help you figure out new words.

Prefix	Meaning	Example
mid-	at or near the middle	mid-ocean ridge, *n.* a chain of mountains that runs along the middle of the ocean floor
sub-	below, beneath, under	subduction, *n.* a process by which part of Earth's crust sinks downward

2. Quick Check Choose the word from the table that best completes the sentence below.

- Oceanic crust is pushed beneath continental crust during

_____ .

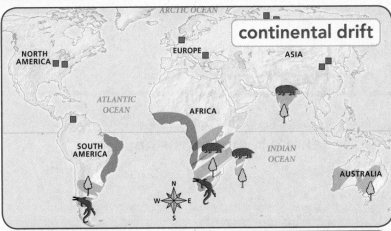

continental drift

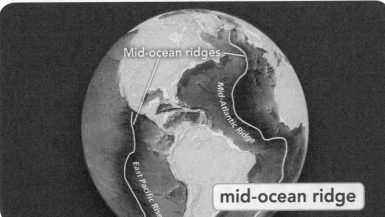

mid-ocean ridge

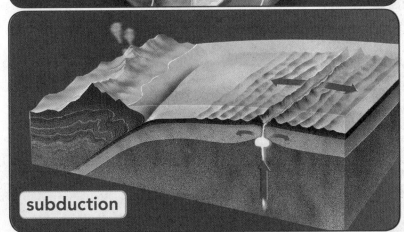

subduction

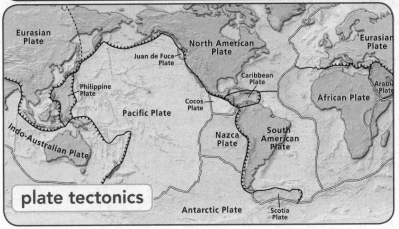

plate tectonics

Chapter Preview

LESSON 1
- continental drift
- Pangaea
- fossil

↻ **Ask Questions**
△ **Infer**

LESSON 2
- mid-ocean ridge
- sea-floor spreading
- deep-ocean trench
- subduction

↻ **Relate Text and Visuals**
△ **Develop Hypotheses**

LESSON 3
- plate
- divergent boundary
- convergent boundary
- transform boundary
- plate tectonics
- fault
- rift valley

↻ **Relate Cause and Effect**
△ **Calculate**

> VOCAB FLASH CARDS For extra help
with vocabulary, visit **Vocab Flash
Cards** and type in *Plate Tectonics.*

Drifting Continents

UNLOCK THE BIG ?

🔑 **What Was Wegener's Hypothesis About the Continents?**

my planet DiaRY

A Puzzled Look

Scientists have long noticed that Earth's continents look as though they could fit together like pieces of a jigsaw puzzle. This was an idea that Alfred Wegener suggested in 1910. "Doesn't the east coast of South America fit exactly against the west coast of Africa, as if they had once been joined?" he asked. "This is an idea I'll have to pursue."

VOICES FROM HISTORY

Communicate Discuss Wegener's idea with a partner. Then answer the questions.

1. Why did Wegener think that the continents might once have been joined?

_____

_____

_____

2. If you were Wegener, what other evidence would you look for to show that the continents had once been joined?

_____

_____

▷ PLANET DIARY Go to **Planet Diary** to learn more about the continents.

Lab zone® Do the Inquiry Warm-Up *How Are Earth's Continents Linked Together?*

What Was Wegener's Hypothesis About the Continents?

Have you ever looked at a world map and noticed how the coastlines of Africa and South America seem to match up? For many years, scientists made this same observation! In 1910, a German scientist named Alfred Wegener (VAY guh nur) became curious about why some continents look as though they could fit together.

Vocabulary

- continental drift
- Pangaea
- fossil

Skills

- Reading: Ask Questions
- Inquiry: Infer

According to Wegener, the continents of Earth had moved. **Wegener's hypothesis was that all the continents were once joined together in a single landmass and have since drifted apart.** Wegener's idea that the continents slowly moved over Earth's surface became known as **continental drift.**

According to Wegener, the continents were joined together in a supercontinent, or single landmass, about 300 million years ago. Wegener called the supercontinent **Pangaea** (pan JEE uh).

Over tens of millions of years, Pangaea began to break apart. The pieces of Pangaea slowly moved to their present locations, shown in **Figure 1.** These pieces became the continents as formed today. In 1915, Wegener published his evidence for continental drift in a book called *The Origin of Continents and Oceans*.

Evidence From Land Features
Land features on the continents provided Wegener with evidence for his hypothesis. On the next page, **Figure 2** shows some of this evidence. For example, Wegener pieced together maps of Africa and South America. He noticed that mountain ranges on the continents line up. He noticed that coal fields in Europe and North America also match up.

Pangaea means "all lands" in Greek. Why is this a suitable name for a supercontinent?

_____

_____

_____

_____

_____

FIGURE 1 ....

Piecing It All Together

The coastlines of some continents seem to fit together like a jigsaw puzzle.

✎ **Use the map to answer the questions.**

1. **Interpret Maps** Draw an arrow to match the numbered coast with the lettered coast that seems to fit with it.

   ❶   ⓐ
   ❷   ⓑ
   ❸   ⓒ
   ❹   ⓓ

2. △ **Infer** How would a continent's climate change if it drifted closer to the equator?

_____

_____

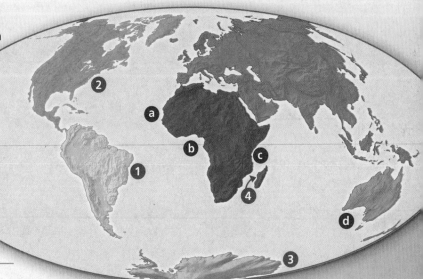

FIGURE 2 ·····························

▶ INTERACTIVE ART **Pangaea and Continental Drift**

Many types of evidence suggest that Earth's landmasses were once joined together.

⚠ **Infer** On the top map of Pangaea, draw where each piece of evidence on the bottom map would have been found. Use a different symbol or color for each piece of evidence, and provide a key. Then label the continents.

Evidence From Fossils

Wegener also used fossils to support his hypothesis for continental drift. A **fossil** is any trace of an ancient organism that has been preserved in rock. For example, *Glossopteris* (glaw SAHP tuh ris) was a fernlike plant that lived 250 million years ago. *Glossopteris* fossils have been found in Africa, South America, Australia, India, and Antarctica, as shown in **Figure 2**. The occurrence of *Glossopteris* on landmasses that are now separated by oceans indicates that Pangaea once existed.

Other examples include fossils of the freshwater reptiles *Mesosaurus* and *Lystrosaurus*. These fossils have also been found in places now separated by oceans. Neither reptile could have swum great distances across salt water. Wegener inferred that these reptiles lived on a single landmass that had since split apart.

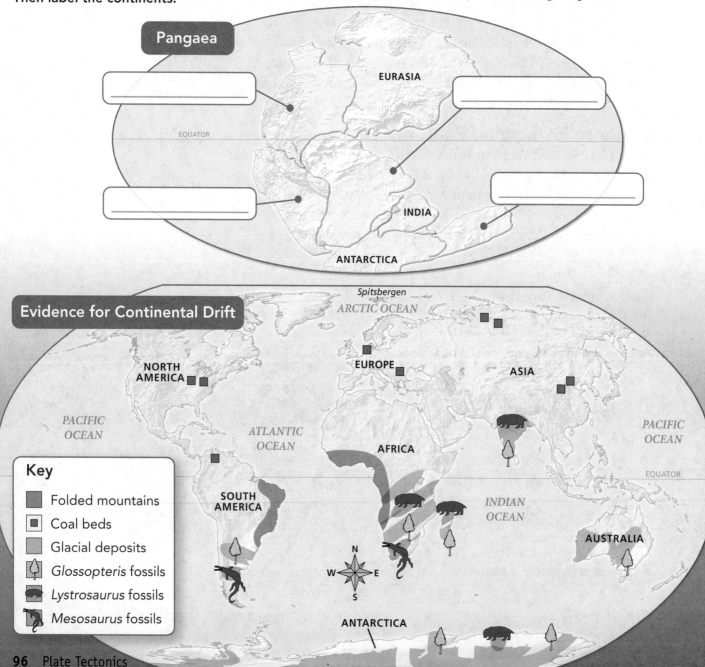

Pangaea

EURASIA

EQUATOR

INDIA

ANTARCTICA

Evidence for Continental Drift

Spitsbergen
ARCTIC OCEAN

NORTH AMERICA

EUROPE

ASIA

PACIFIC OCEAN

ATLANTIC OCEAN

AFRICA

PACIFIC OCEAN

EQUATOR

Key

- Folded mountains
- Coal beds
- Glacial deposits
- *Glossopteris* fossils
- *Lystrosaurus* fossils
- *Mesosaurus* fossils

SOUTH AMERICA

INDIAN OCEAN

AUSTRALIA

N W E S

ANTARCTICA

Evidence From Climate

Wegener used evidence of climate change to support his hypothesis. As a continent moves toward the equator, its climate gets warmer. As a continent moves toward the poles, its climate gets colder. In either case, the continent carries along with it the fossils and rocks that formed at all of its previous locations.

For example, fossils of tropical plants are found on Spitsbergen, an island in the Arctic Ocean. When these plants lived about 300 million years ago, the island must have had a warm, mild climate. Wegener said the climate changed because the island moved.

Wegener's Hypothesis Rejected

Wegener attempted to explain how continental drift took place. He suggested that the continents plowed across the ocean floors. But Wegener could not provide a satisfactory explanation for the force that pushes or pulls the continents. Because Wegener could not identify the cause of continental drift, most geologists of his time rejected his idea.

✎ **Ask Questions** Write a question relating to climate and Wegener's hypothesis. Read the text and answer your question.

_____

_____

_____

_____

_____

_____

_____

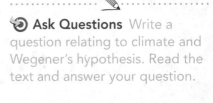

apply it!

Deep scratches have been found in rocks in South Africa. Such scratches are caused only by glaciers that move across continents. But the climate of South Africa is too mild today for glaciers to form.

1 **Infer** South Africa was once (colder/warmer) than it is today.

2 **CHALLENGE** What can you infer about South Africa's former location?

_____

_____

Lab zone ® Do the Quick Lab *Moving the Continents.*

🗝 Assess Your Understanding

1a. Review Based on evidence from land features, fossils, and climate, Wegener concluded that continents (sink/rise/move).

b. Predict Wegener said that because continents move, they can collide with each other. How could colliding continents explain the formation of mountains?

_____

_____

_____

_____

got it?

○ **I get it!** Now I know Wegener's hypothesis about the continents stated that _____

_____

_____

_____

○ **I need extra help with** _____

Go to **MY SCIENCE** Ⓢ **COACH** online for help with this subject.

Sea-Floor Spreading

What Are Mid-Ocean Ridges?

What Is Sea-Floor Spreading?

What Happens at Deep-Ocean Trenches?

MY PLANET DIARY

DISCOVERY

Marie Tharp

Have you ever tried to draw something you can't see? By 1952, geologists Marie Tharp and Bruce Heezen had set to work mapping the ocean floor. Tharp drew details of the ocean floor based on data taken from ships. The data showed how the height of the ocean floor varied. Tharp's maps, which were first published in 1957, helped to confirm the hypothesis of continental drift.

Think about what structures might lie beneath Earth's oceans. Then answer the question.

Do you think the ocean has valleys and mountains? Explain.

_____

_____

_____

_____

> PLANET DIARY Go to Planet Diary to learn more about the ocean floor.

Lab zone® Do the Inquiry Warm-Up What Is the Effect of a Change in Density?

What Are Mid-Ocean Ridges?

When scientists such as Marie Tharp drew maps showing features of the ocean floor, they made a surprising discovery. In certain places, the floor of the ocean appeared to be stitched together like the seams of a baseball! The seams curved along the ocean floors for great distances, as shown in **Figure 1.**

Scientists found that the seams formed mountain ranges that ran along the middle of some ocean floors. Scientists called these mountain ranges **mid-ocean ridges.** **Mid-ocean ridges form long chains of mountains that rise up from the ocean floor.**

Vocabulary

- mid-ocean ridge
- deep-ocean trench
- sea-floor spreading
- subduction

Skills

- Reading: Relate Text and Visuals
- Inquiry: Develop Hypotheses

In the mid-1900s, scientists mapped mid-ocean ridges using *sonar*. Sonar is a device that uses sound waves to measure the distance to an object. Scientists found that mid-ocean ridges extend into all of Earth's oceans. Most mid-ocean ridges lie under thousands of meters of water. Scientists also discovered that a steep-sided valley splits the tops of some mid-ocean ridges. The ridges form the longest mountain ranges on Earth. They are longer than the Rockies in North America and longer than the Andes in South America.

FIGURE 1 ·

Ocean Floors

Mid-ocean ridges rise from the sea floor like stitches on the seams of a baseball.

✏ **Interpret Diagrams** Look at the diagram below. Then use the scale to answer each question. Be sure to measure from the *front* of the diagram.

1. How far below sea level is the peak of the ridge?

_____

2. How high does the ridge rise from the sea floor?

_____

3. CHALLENGE How deep below the peak is the valley marking the center of the ridge?

_____

Mid-ocean ridges

Mid-Atlantic Ridge

East Pacific Rise

Vertical scale exaggerated

Depth (km)

0
1
2
3
4

Lab zone® Do the Quick Lab *Mid-Ocean Ridges*.

🔑 Assess Your Understanding

got it? ·

○ I get it! Now I know that mid-ocean ridges form _____

_____

○ I need extra help with _____

Go to MY SCIENCE ⓢ COACH online for help with this subject.

What Is Sea-Floor Spreading?

By the 1960s, geologists had learned more about mid-ocean ridges. They found that mid-ocean ridges continually add new material to the ocean floor. They called this process **sea-floor spreading.**

Sea-floor spreading begins at a mid-ocean ridge, which forms along a crack in the oceanic crust. Along the ridge, new molten material from inside Earth rises, erupts, cools, and hardens to form a solid strip of rock. **Sea-floor spreading adds more crust to the ocean floor. At the same time, older strips of rock move outward from either side of the ridge.**

Figure 2 shows evidence that geologists have found for sea-floor spreading.

Pillow lava on the ocean floor

Evidence From Ocean-Floor Material

In the central valley of mid-ocean ridges, scientists have found rocks shaped like pillows. Such rocks form only when molten material hardens quickly after erupting under water.

Evidence From Magnetic Stripes

Rock on the ocean floor forms from molten material. As the material erupts, cools, and hardens, magnetic minerals inside the rock line up in the direction of Earth's magnetic poles. These minerals form unseen magnetic "stripes" on the ocean floor. But the magnetic poles occasionally reverse themselves. So each stripe defines a period when molten material erupted and hardened while Earth's magnetic poles did not change.

Scientists found that the pattern of magnetic stripes on one side of a mid-ocean ridge is usually a mirror image of the pattern on the other side of the ridge. The matching patterns show that the crust on the two sides of the ridge spread from the ridge at the same time and at the same rate.

Ridge

Magnetic striping on both sides of the Juan de Fuca ridge

Evidence From Drilling Samples

Scientists drilled into the ocean floor to obtain rock samples. They found that the farther away from a ridge a rock sample was taken, the older the rock was. The youngest rocks were always found at the center of the ridges. Recall that at the ridge center, molten material erupts and cools to form new crust. The rocks' age showed that sea-floor spreading had taken place.

Ocean floor samples taken in 2006

FIGURE 2

> INTERACTIVE ART Sea-Floor Spreading

Some mid-ocean ridges have a valley that runs along their center. Evidence shows that molten material erupts through this valley. The material then hardens to form the rock of the ocean floor.

✎ **Color the right half of the diagram to show magnetic striping. How does your drawing show evidence of sea-floor spreading?**

_____

_____

_____

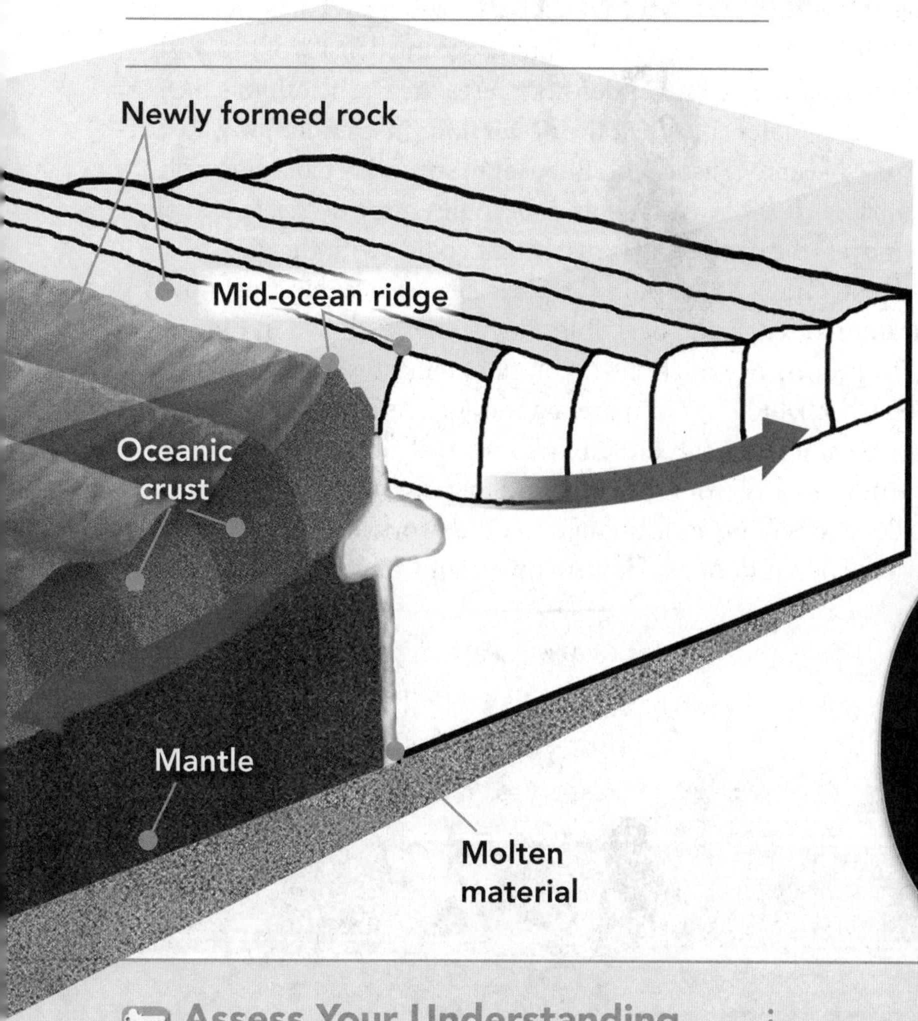

⊙ Relate Text and Visuals

How does the diagram show that new crust forms from molten material?

_____

_____

_____

_____

_____

_____

_____

Newly formed rock

Mid-ocean ridge

Oceanic crust

Mantle

Molten material

did you know?

Scientists used the small submarine *Alvin* to explore the ocean floor. Did you know that *Alvin* was built to withstand the great pressure 4 kilometers down in the ocean?

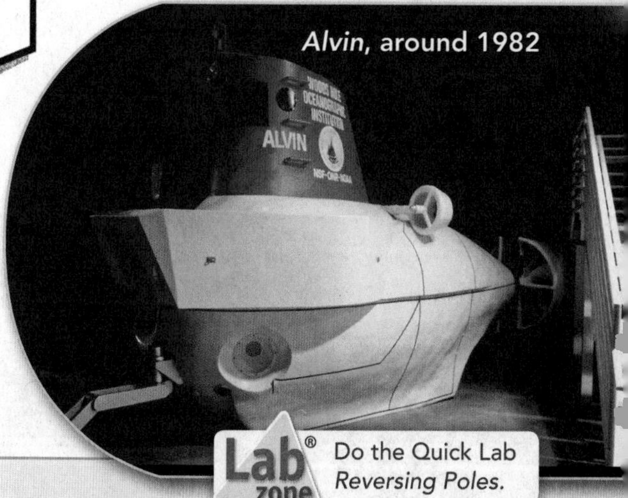

Alvin, around 1982

ALVIN

Lab zone® Do the Quick Lab *Reversing Poles.*

🔑 Assess Your Understanding

1a. Review In sea-floor spreading, new crust is added at a (mid-ocean ridge/magnetic stripe).

b. Apply Concepts Suppose Earth's magnetic polarity changed many times over a short period. What pattern of striping at a mid-ocean ridge would you expect to find?

_____

_____

got it?

○ **I get it!** Now I know that sea-floor spreading is the process in which _____

_____

○ **I need extra help with** _____

Go to MY SCIENCE ⓢ COACH *online for help with this subject.*

What Happens at Deep-Ocean Trenches?

Does the ocean floor keep getting wider without stopping? No, eventually the ocean floor plunges into deep underwater canyons. These canyons are called **deep-ocean trenches.** At a deep-ocean trench, the oceanic crust bends downward. 🔑 **In a process taking tens of millions of years, part of the ocean floor sinks back into the mantle at deep-ocean trenches.**

The Process of Subduction When a washcloth is placed in water, the water soaks into it. So, the density of the washcloth increases. The higher density causes the washcloth to sink.

Changes in density affect the ocean floor in a similar way. Recall that new oceanic crust is hot. But as it moves away from the mid-ocean ridge, it cools. As it cools, it becomes more dense. Eventually, as it moves, the cool, dense crust might collide with the edge of a continent. Gravity then pulls the older, denser oceanic crust down beneath the trench and back into the mantle, as shown in **Figure 3.**

The process by which the ocean floor sinks beneath a deep-ocean trench and back into the mantle again is called **subduction** (sub DUC shun). As subduction occurs, crust closer to a mid-ocean ridge moves away from the ridge and toward a deep-ocean trench. Sea-floor spreading and subduction often work together. They move the ocean floor as if it were on a giant conveyor belt.

FIGURE 3 ·······························

Subduction

Oceanic crust created along a mid-ocean ridge is destroyed at a deep-ocean trench. During the process of subduction, oceanic crust sinks down beneath the trench into the mantle.

✎ **Summarize** Label the mantle, the mid-ocean ridge, and the deep-ocean trench. For locations A and B, circle the correct choice for each statement.

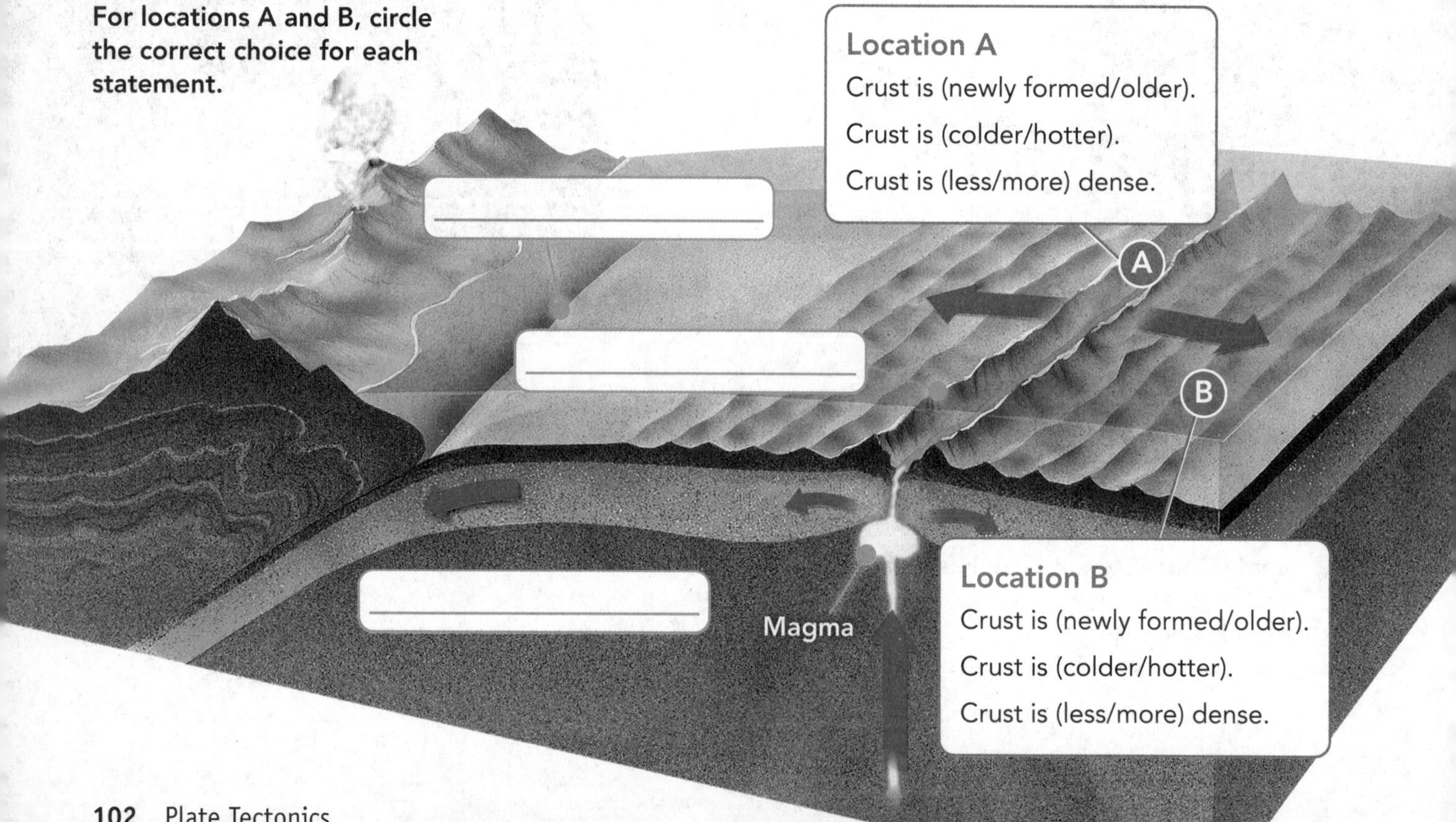

Location A
Crust is (newly formed/older).
Crust is (colder/hotter).
Crust is (less/more) dense.

Location B
Crust is (newly formed/older).
Crust is (colder/hotter).
Crust is (less/more) dense.

Magma

apply it!

The deepest part of the ocean is along the Mariana Trench. This trench is one of several trenches (shown in yellow) in the Pacific Ocean. After reading the main text in this lesson, answer the questions below.

❶ **Infer** At the Pacific Ocean's deep-ocean trenches, oceanic crust is (spread/subducted).

❷ **Develop Hypotheses** The Pacific Ocean is shrinking. Explain this fact in terms of subduction at deep-ocean trenches and spreading at mid-ocean ridges.

_____
_____
_____
_____
_____
_____
_____

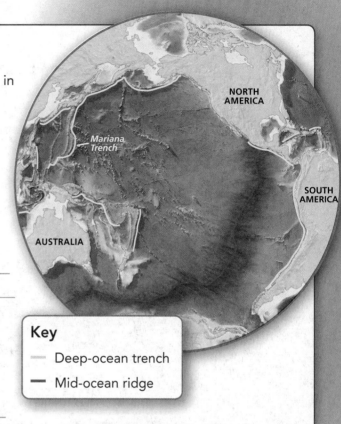

NORTH AMERICA

Mariana Trench

SOUTH AMERICA

AUSTRALIA

Key

— Deep-ocean trench

— Mid-ocean ridge

Subduction and Earth's Oceans

The processes of subduction and sea-floor spreading can change the size and shape of the oceans. Because of these processes, the ocean floor is renewed about every 200 million years. That is the time it takes for new rock to form at the mid-ocean ridge, move across the ocean, and sink into a trench.

The sizes of Earth's oceans are determined by how fast new crust is being created at mid-ocean ridges and how fast old crust is being swallowed up at deep-ocean trenches. An ocean surrounded by many trenches may shrink. An ocean with few trenches will probably grow larger.

For example, the Atlantic Ocean is expanding. This ocean has only a few short trenches. As a result, the spreading ocean floor has almost nowhere to go. Along the continental margins, the oceanic crust of the Atlantic Ocean floor is attached to the continental crust of the continents around the ocean. So as the Atlantic's ocean floor spreads, the continents along its edges also move. Over time, the whole ocean gets wider.

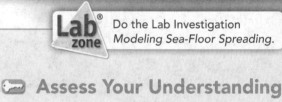

Lab zone ® Do the Lab Investigation *Modeling Sea-Floor Spreading.*

🔑 Assess Your Understanding

2a. Review Subduction takes place at (mid-ocean ridges/deep-ocean trenches).

b. Relate Cause and Effect Why does subduction occur?

_____
_____
_____
_____

got it? •••••••••••••••••••••••••••••••

○ **I get it!** Now I know that at deep-ocean

trenches _____

_____

○ **I need extra help with** _____

Go to my science ⑤ coach *online for help with this subject.*

LESSON
3 The Theory of Plate Tectonics

🔑 What Is the Theory of Plate Tectonics?

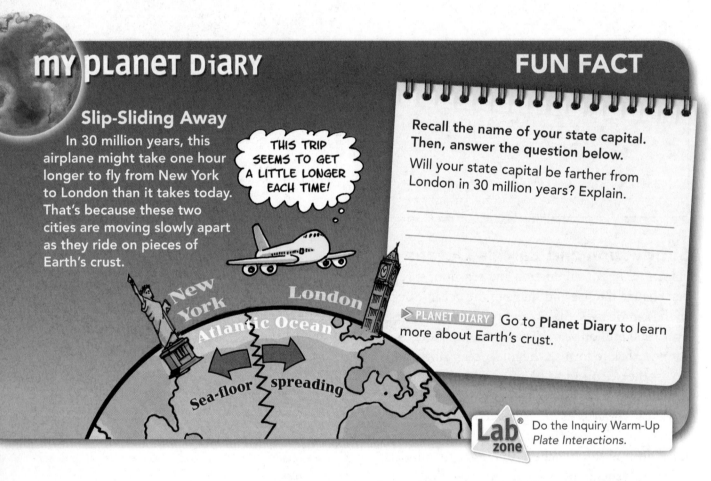

my planet Diary

Slip-Sliding Away

In 30 million years, this airplane might take one hour longer to fly from New York to London than it takes today. That's because these two cities are moving slowly apart as they ride on pieces of Earth's crust.

THIS TRIP SEEMS TO GET A LITTLE LONGER EACH TIME!

New York · London · Atlantic Ocean · Sea-floor spreading

FUN FACT

Recall the name of your state capital. Then, answer the question below.

Will your state capital be farther from London in 30 million years? Explain.

_____

_____

_____

_____

> **PLANET DIARY** Go to **Planet Diary** to learn more about Earth's crust.

Lab zone Do the Inquiry Warm-Up *Plate Interactions.*

What Is the Theory of Plate Tectonics?

Have you ever dropped a hard-boiled egg? The eggshell cracks into uneven pieces. Earth's lithosphere, its solid outer shell, is like that eggshell. It is broken into pieces separated by cracks. These pieces are called **plates.** Earth's major tectonic plates are shown in **Figure 1.**

104 Plate Tectonics

Vocabulary

- plate • divergent boundary • convergent boundary
- transform boundary • plate tectonics • fault
- rift valley

Skills

↻ Reading: Relate Cause and Effect
△ Inquiry: Calculate

Earth's plates meet at boundaries. Along each boundary, plates move in one of three ways. Plates move apart, or diverge, from each other at a **divergent boundary** (dy VUR junt). Plates come together, or converge, at a **convergent boundary** (kun VUR junt). Plates slip past each other along a **transform boundary.**

In the mid-1960s, geologists combined what they knew about sea-floor spreading, Earth's plates, and plate motions into a single theory called **plate tectonics.** 🔑 **The theory of plate tectonics states that Earth's plates are in slow, constant motion, driven by convection currents in the mantle.** Plate tectonics explains the formation, movement, and subduction of Earth's plates.

Mantle Convection and Plate Motions What

force is great enough to move the continents? Earth's plates move because they are the top part of the large convection currents in Earth's mantle. During subduction, gravity pulls denser plate edges downward, into the mantle. The rest of the plate also moves. The motion of the plates is like the motion of liquid in a pot of soup heating on a stove.

FIGURE 1 ·······················

▷ REAL-WORLD INQUIRY

Earth's Plates

Plate boundaries divide the lithosphere into large plates.

✏ **Interpret Maps** Draw arrows at all the boundaries of the Pacific plate, showing the directions in which plates move. (*Hint:* First, study the map key.)

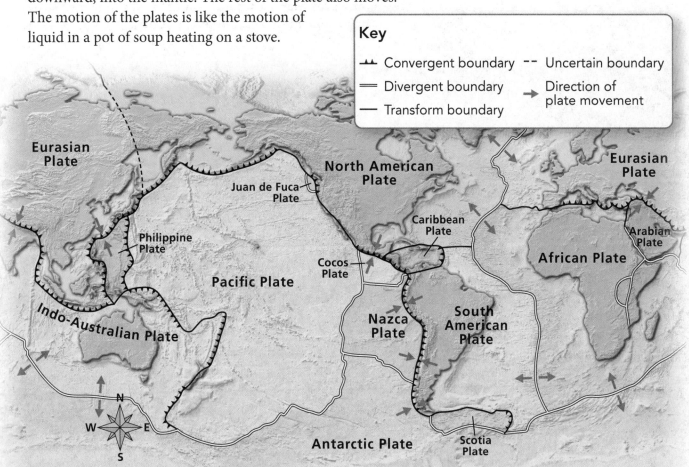

Key

- ⊥⊥ Convergent boundary
- ═ Divergent boundary
- — Transform boundary
- -- Uncertain boundary
- → Direction of plate movement

Eurasian Plate

North American Plate

Juan de Fuca Plate

Eurasian Plate

Caribbean Plate

Arabian Plate

Philippine Plate

African Plate

Cocos Plate

Pacific Plate

Indo-Australian Plate

Nazca Plate

South American Plate

N W E S

Antarctic Plate

Scotia Plate

Relate Cause and Effect

What has caused the location of Earth's continents to change over time?

Plate Motions Over Time Scientists use satellites to measure plate motion precisely. The plates move very slowly—from about 1 to 12 centimeters per year. The North American and Eurasian plates move apart at a rate of 2.5 centimeters per year. That's about as fast as your fingernails grow. Because the plates have been moving for tens to hundreds of millions of years, they have moved great distances.

Over time, the movement of Earth's plates has greatly changed the location of the continents and the size and shape of the oceans. As plates move, they change Earth's surface, producing earthquakes, volcanoes, mountain ranges, and deep-ocean trenches. Geologists have evidence that, before Pangaea existed, other supercontinents formed and split apart over the last billion years. Pangaea itself formed when Earth's landmasses moved together about 350 to 250 million years ago. Then, about 200 million years ago, Pangaea began to break apart, as shown in **Figure 2**.

FIGURE 2 ···

> INTERACTIVE ART **Plate Motion**

Since the breakup of Pangaea, the continents have taken about 200 million years to move to their present location.

Use the maps to answer the questions.

1. **Interpret Maps** List three examples of continents that have drifted apart from each other.

_____

_____

_____

_____

2. **CHALLENGE** Which two landmasses that were not connected to each other in Pangaea have collided on Earth today?

_____

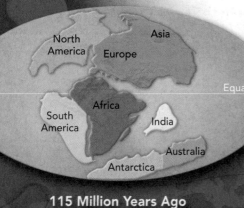

200 Million Years Ago

115 Million Years Ago

Earth Today

Plate Boundaries

Plate Boundaries Recall that the edges of Earth's plates meet at plate boundaries. **Faults**—breaks in Earth's crust where rocks have slipped past each other—form along these boundaries. Convection currents in Earth's mantle cause the plates to move. As the plates move, they collide, pull apart, or grind past each other. These movements produce great changes in Earth's surface and on the ocean floor. These changes include the formation of volcanoes, mountain ranges, and deep-ocean trenches.

Divergent Boundaries Can a crack in Earth's crust be so wide that people can walk through it? In Iceland it can! There, two plates move slowly away from each other. **Figure 3** shows part of the crack that has formed as these two plates have moved apart over time.

Recall that plates move away from each other at a divergent boundary. Most divergent boundaries occur along the mid-ocean ridges, where new crust is added during sea-floor spreading. But in a few places, the mid-ocean ridge rises above sea level. Volcanic activity of the mid-Atlantic ridge is also seen in Iceland.

Where pieces of Earth's crust diverge on land, a deep valley called a **rift valley** forms. Several rift valleys make up the East African rift system. There, the crust is slowly pulling apart over a wide area.

FIGURE 3 ·······················

Breaking Up Is Hard to Do

Two plates separate to form a great crack in Iceland, marking a divergent boundary.

✎ **Interpret Diagrams** Draw arrows on the diagram to show how plates move at a divergent boundary. Then describe how the plates move.

_____

_____

_____

Vocabulary Prefixes Read the text about the three types of plate boundaries. Circle the correct meaning of each prefix given here.

Di- = (away/together/along)

Con- = (away/together/along)

Trans- = (away/together/along)

do the math!

Plates move at very slow rates. These rates are from about 1 to 12 cm per year. To calculate rates of motion, geologists use the following formula.

$$\text{Rate} = \frac{\text{Distance}}{\text{Time}}$$

✎ **Calculate** The Pacific plate is sliding past the North American plate. In 10 million years, the plate will move 500 km. What is the Pacific plate's rate of motion? Express your answer in centimeters per year.

107

FIGURE 4

The Andes

The Andes Mountains formed at a convergent boundary.

✎ **Interpret Diagrams** Draw arrows on the diagram to show how plates move when they converge. Then describe how the plates move.

_____

_____

_____

Convergent Boundaries The Andes Mountains run for 8,900 kilometers along the west coast of South America. Here, two plates collide. Recall that a boundary where two plates come together, or collide, is called a convergent boundary.

What happens when two plates collide? The density of the plates determines which one comes out on top. Oceanic crust becomes cooler and denser as it spreads away from the mid-ocean ridge. Where two plates carrying oceanic crust meet at a trench, the plate that is more dense sinks under the less dense plate.

A plate carrying oceanic crust can also collide with a plate carrying continental crust. Oceanic crust is more dense than continental crust. The more dense oceanic crust can push up the less dense continental crust. This process has formed the Andes, as shown in **Figure 4.** Meanwhile, the more dense oceanic crust also sinks as subduction occurs. Water eventually leaves the sinking crust and rises into the wedge of the mantle above it. This water lowers the melting point of the mantle in the wedge. As a result, the mantle partially melts and rises up as magma to form volcanoes.

Two plates carrying continental crust can also collide. Then, neither piece of crust is dense enough to sink far into the mantle. Instead, the collision squeezes the crust into high mountain ranges.

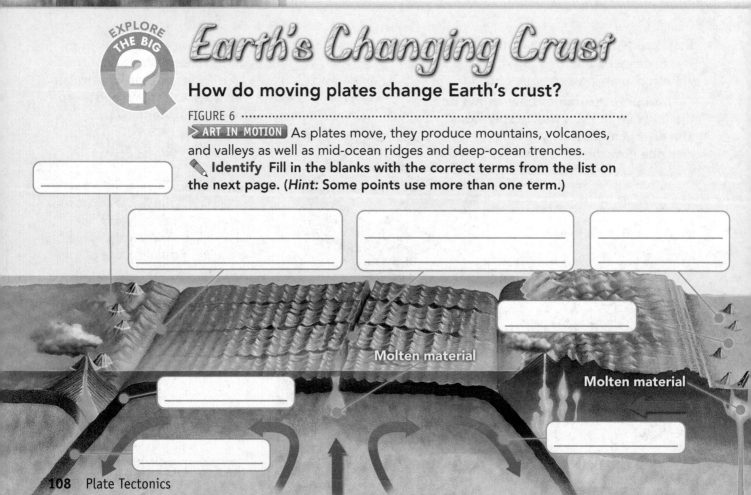

EXPLORE THE BIG ?

Earth's Changing Crust

How do moving plates change Earth's crust?

FIGURE 6

▶ **ART IN MOTION** As plates move, they produce mountains, volcanoes, and valleys as well as mid-ocean ridges and deep-ocean trenches.

✎ **Identify** Fill in the blanks with the correct terms from the list on the next page. (*Hint:* Some points use more than one term.)

Molten material

Molten material

108 Plate Tectonics

Transform Boundaries Recall that a transform boundary is a place where two plates slip past each other, moving in opposite directions. Beneath the surface of a transform boundary, the sides of the plates are rocky and jagged. So, the two plates can grab hold of each other and "lock" in place. Forces inside the crust can later cause the two plates to unlock. Earthquakes often occur when the plates suddenly slip along the boundary that they form. However, crust is neither created nor destroyed at transform boundaries. The San Andreas fault, shown in **Figure 5,** is one example of a transform boundary.

FIGURE 5 ·····················
Fault Line
The San Andreas fault in California marks a transform boundary.

✏ **Interpret Diagrams** Draw arrows on the diagram to show how plates move at a transform boundary. Then describe how the plates move.

_____

_____

_____

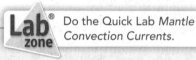

Do the Quick Lab *Mantle Convection Currents.*

🔑 Assess Your Understanding

1a. Review Moving plates form convergent, divergent, or _____ boundaries.

b. ANSWER THE BIG **Summarize** How do moving plates change Earth's crust?

_____

_____

_____

_____

_____

_____

_____

_____

got **it?** ·····························

○ **I get it!** Now I know that the three types of plate boundaries are _____

_____

○ I need extra help with _____

Go to MY SCIENCE ⓢ COACH *online for help with this subject.*

Rift valley	Mountains	Convection
Volcanoes	Subduction	Oceanic crust
Sea-floor spreading	Mid-ocean ridge	Convergent boundary
Transform boundary	Continental crust	Deep-ocean trench
Divergent boundary		

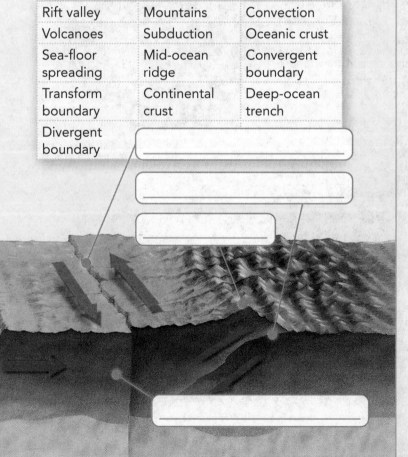

Study Guide

New crust forms at _____. Crust is subducted and destroyed at _____. Mountains form where plates _____.

LESSON 1 Drifting Continents

🔑 Wegener's hypothesis was that all the continents were once joined together in a single landmass and have since drifted apart.

Vocabulary
- continental drift
- Pangaea
- fossil

LESSON 2 Sea-Floor Spreading

🔑 Mid-ocean ridges form long chains of mountains that rise up from the ocean floor.

🔑 Sea-floor spreading adds more crust to the ocean floor. At the same time, older strips of rock move outward from either side of the ridge.

🔑 In a process taking tens of millions of years, part of the ocean floor sinks back into the mantle at deep-ocean trenches.

Vocabulary
- mid-ocean ridge
- sea-floor spreading
- deep-ocean trench
- subduction

LESSON 3 The Theory of Plate Tectonics

🔑 The theory of plate tectonics states that Earth's plates are in slow, constant motion, driven by convection currents in the mantle.

Vocabulary
- plate • divergent boundary
- convergent boundary
- transform boundary
- plate tectonics • fault
- rift valley

Review and Assessment

LESSON 1 Drifting Continents

1. What did Wegener think happens during continental drift?

  a. Continents move. **b.** Continents freeze.

  c. The mantle warms. **d.** Convection stops.

2. Wegener thought that all the continents were once joined together in a supercontinent that he called _____.

3. Draw The drawing shows North America and Africa. Circle the parts of the coastlines of the two continents that were joined in Pangaea.

North America

Africa

4. Make Judgments Wegener proposed that mountains form when continents collide, crumpling up their edges. Was Wegener's idea about how mountains form consistent with his hypothesis of continental drift? Explain.

_____

_____

_____

5. **Write About It** Michelle is a scientist working in Antarctica. She learns that fossils of *Glossopteris* have been found on Antarctica. Her colleague Joe, working in India, has also found *Glossopteris* fossils. Write a letter from Michelle to her colleague explaining how these fossils could be found in both places. Define *continental drift* in your answer and discuss how it explains the fossil findings.

LESSON 2 Sea-Floor Spreading

6. In which areas does subduction of the ocean floor take place?

  a. rift valleys **b.** the lower mantle

  c. mid-ocean ridges **d.** deep-ocean trenches

7. A mid-ocean ridge is a _____ _____ that rises up from the ocean floor.

8. Compare and Contrast Look at the diagram. Label the area where new crust forms.

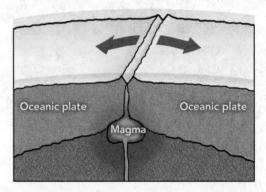

Oceanic plate   Oceanic plate

Magma

9. Apply Concepts Why are the oldest parts of the ocean floor no older than about 200 million years?

_____

_____

_____

10. Sequence Place the following steps of sea-floor spreading in their correct sequence.

  A. The molten material cools and hardens, forming a strip of rock along the ocean floor.

  B. The strip of rock moves away from the ridge.

  C. Molten material from inside Earth rises to the ocean floor at a mid-ocean ridge.

_____

11. **Write About It** How is pillow lava evidence of sea-floor spreading?

3 Review and Assessment

The Theory of Plate Tectonics

12. At which boundary do two plates pull apart?

    a. convergent   **b.** transform

    c. divergent   **d.** mantle-crust

13. When a divergent boundary occurs on land, it forms a _____.

Use the diagram to answer Questions 14–15.

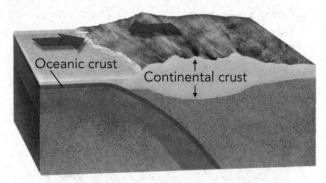

14. Classify What type of plate boundary is shown in the diagram?

_____

15. Predict What type of landforms will result from the plate movement shown in the diagram?

_____

16. Compare and Contrast How does the density of oceanic crust differ from that of continental crust? Why is this difference important?

_____

_____

_____

_____

17. math! It takes 100,000 years for a plate to move about 2 kilometers. What is the rate of motion in centimeters per year?

_____

How do moving plates change Earth's crust?

18. Summarize Suppose Earth's landmasses someday all move together again. Describe the changes that would occur in Earth's oceans and Earth's landmasses. Use the map and the theory of plate tectonics to explain your ideas.

_____

_____

_____

_____

_____

_____

_____

_____

_____

_____

_____

_____

_____

_____

_____

_____

_____

Standardized Test Prep

Multiple Choice

Circle the letter of the best answer.

1. The diagram shows a process in Earth's crust.

Which statement best describes the process in the diagram?

A Converging plates form mountains.

B Converging plates form volcanoes.

C Diverging plates form mountains.

D Diverging plates form a rift valley.

2. What is one piece of evidence that caused Wegener to think that continents moved?

A He found an old map of the world that showed movement.

B He found similar fossils on different continents that are separated by oceans.

C He proved his hypothesis with an experiment that measured movement.

D He observed the continents moving with his own eyes.

3. Which of the following is evidence for sea-floor spreading?

A matching patterns of magnetic stripes found in the crust of the ocean floor

B new rock found farther from mid-ocean ridges than older rock

C pieces of different crust found on different continents

D changes in climate on the continent of Africa

4. What happens to new oceanic crust at a mid-ocean ridge?

A It forms new mountains under the water.

B It climbs up the mantle to form a trench.

C It gets hotter and sinks into a trench.

D It is so dense that gravity pulls it into a deep-ocean trench.

5. What force causes the movement of Earth's plates?

A convection currents

B pressure

C sound waves

D cooling

Constructed Response

Use the map below and your knowledge of science to help you answer Question 6. Write your answer on a separate piece of paper.

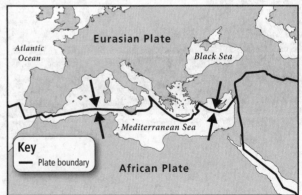

6. The African plate is moving toward the Eurasian plate at a rate of a few centimeters per year. How will this area change in 100 million years? In your answer, consider how the continents will change and how the Mediterranean Sea will change.

ALVIN:2.0

AN EXTREME MAKEOVER

For years, *Alvin*, the world's oldest research submarine, has worked hard. *Alvin* carries scientists deep into the ocean. The research submarine has made over 4,400 dives—some as deep as 4,500 meters beneath the water's surface. With the help of *Alvin*, scientists have discovered everything from tube worms to the wreck of the *Titanic*. But *Alvin* allows scientists to see only the top 63 percent of the ocean. The rest of the ocean lies even deeper than 4,500 meters, where *Alvin* can't go.

Enter *Alvin 2.0*—*Alvin's* replacement. It is bigger and faster, with more windows and improved sensors. It can go down to 6,500 meters and carry heavier samples. Even better, *Alvin 2.0* allows scientists to see most of the ocean—only 1 percent of the ocean lies deeper than 6,500 meters!

With better and deeper access to the ocean, scientists are excited about all of the new and weird discoveries they'll make with *Alvin 2.0*.

▼ Presenting . . . the new *Alvin!*

Design It Research more about *Alvin 2.0's* features. Think about a new feature that you would like to add to *Alvin 2.0*. What needs would your feature meet? Draw or describe a design for the part, and explain how it will work on the new model.

Museum of Science

An Ocean Is Born

In one of the hottest, driest places in the world, Earth's crust is cracking.

In the Afar region of Ethiopia, Earth's tectonic plates are moving apart. Here, Earth's crust is so thin that magma has been able to break through the surface. As the plates drifted farther apart, the crust sank to form a valley that is 59 kilometers long!

Today volcanoes, earthquakes, and hydrothermal fields tell us how thin the crust is, and how the plates are pulling apart. Eventually, this valley could sink deep enough to allow salt water from the nearby Red Sea to move in and form an ocean. This ocean could split Africa apart. Although it could take millions of years for an actual ocean to form, scientists are excited to witness the steps that will lead to its birth.

Research It Research a major change in Earth's surface caused by plate movement. Try to find at least two different accounts of the event. Create a timeline or a storyboard showing when and how the change occurred.

▲ Tectonic plates are pulling apart in this dry, hot area in the Afar region of Ethiopia.

▲ Lava seeps out of a crack in the lava lake on top of Erfa Ale, the highest mountain in the Afar region. Scientists must wear protective clothing in this extremely hot, dangerous environment.

115

WHAT COULD CAUSE THIS BUILDING TO TOPPLE?

Why do earthquakes occur more often in some places than in others?

Earthquakes can strike without a moment's notice. The ground can buckle and buildings can topple, as happened to this building in Taiwan in 1999. These disasters may seem like random events. But the structure of Earth suggests a different conclusion. **Predict** Do you think geologists can predict where and when an earthquake will occur? Explain.

> UNTAMED SCIENCE Watch the **Untamed Science** video to learn more about earthquakes.

Earthquakes

皇峰電腦資訊公司

TEL

4 Getting Started

Check Your Understanding

1. **Background** Read the paragraph below and then answer the question.

Ann's parents couldn't move the huge boulder from their yard. The **force** of their pushing didn't budge the rock. "Let's crush it," said Ann's mom. She went on, "Smaller pieces will each have smaller **mass** and **volume**. Then we can move the rock one piece at a time."

> A **force** is a push or pull exerted on an object.
>
> **Mass** is a measure of the amount of matter an object contains and its resistance to movement.
>
> **Volume** is the amount of space that matter occupies.

- What features of the boulder make it hard to move?

> **MY READING WEB** If you had trouble completing the question above, visit **My Reading Web** and type in *Earthquakes.*

Vocabulary Skill

Identify Multiple Meanings Some familiar words have more than one meaning. Words you use every day may have different meanings in science. Look at the different meanings of the words below.

Word	Everyday Meaning	Scientific Meaning
fault	*n.* blame or responsibility Example: The team's loss was not the fault of any one person.	*n.* a crack or break in rock along which rock surfaces can slip Example: A fault ran through the cliff.
focus	*v.* to concentrate Example: Focus your attention on reading, writing, and arithmetic.	*n.* the area where rock that is under stress begins to break, causing an earthquake Example: The focus of the earthquake was 70 kilometers below Earth's surface.

2. **Quick Check** Circle the sentence below that uses the scientific meaning of the word *fault.*

- Errors in the test were the test writer's **fault.**
- The San Andreas **fault** runs along the coast of California.

plateau

strike-slip fault

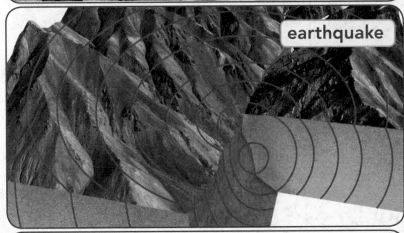

earthquake

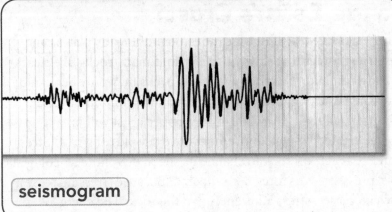

seismogram

Chapter Preview

LESSON 1

- stress
- tension
- compression
- shearing
- normal fault
- reverse fault
- strike-slip fault
- plateau

⤾ **Relate Cause and Effect**
△ **Make Models**

LESSON 2

- earthquake
- focus
- epicenter
- P wave
- S wave
- surface wave
- seismograph
- Modified Mercalli scale
- magnitude
- Richter scale
- moment magnitude scale

⤾ **Sequence**
△ **Infer**

LESSON 3

- seismogram

⤾ **Identify the Main Idea**
△ **Predict**

> **VOCAB FLASH CARDS** For extra help with vocabulary, visit **Vocab Flash Cards** and type in *Earthquakes.*

Forces in Earth's Crust

🔑 How Does Stress Change Earth's Crust?

🔑 How Do Faults Form?

🔑 How Does Plate Movement Create New Landforms?

my planet Diary

Still Growing!

Mount Everest in the Himalayas is the highest mountain on Earth. Climbers who reach the peak stand 8,850 meters above sea level. You might think that mountains never change. But forces inside Earth push Mount Everest at least several millimeters higher each year. Over time, Earth's forces slowly but constantly lift, stretch, bend, and break Earth's crust in dramatic ways!

MISCONCEPTION

✏️ **Communicate** Discuss the following question with a classmate. Write your answer below.

How long do you think it took Mount Everest to form? Hundreds of years? Thousands? Millions? Explain.

_____

_____

_____

_____

▶ PLANET DIARY Go to **Planet Diary** to learn more about forces in Earth's crust.

Lab® zone Do the Inquiry Warm-Up *How Does Stress Affect Earth's Crust?*

How Does Stress Change Earth's Crust?

Rocks are hard and stiff. But the movement of Earth's plates can create strong forces that slowly bend or fold many rocks like a caramel candy bar. Like the candy bar, some rocks may only bend and stretch when a strong force is first applied to them. But beyond a certain limit, all rocks in Earth's brittle upper crust will break.

Forces created by plate movement are examples of stress. **Stress** is a force that acts on rock to change its shape or volume. Geologists often express stress as force per unit area. Because stress increases as force increases, stress adds energy to the rock. The energy is stored in the rock until the rock changes shape or breaks.

Vocabulary

- stress • tension • compression • shearing
- normal fault • reverse fault • strike-slip fault • plateau

Skills

⊙ Reading: Relate Cause and Effect
△ Inquiry: Make Models

Three kinds of stress can occur in the crust—tension, compression, and shearing. 🗝 **Tension, compression, and shearing work over millions of years to change the shape and volume of rock.** Most changes in the crust occur only very slowly, so that you cannot directly observe the crust bending, stretching, or breaking. **Figure 1** shows the three types of stress.

Tension Rock in the crust can be stretched so that it becomes thinner in the middle. This process can make rock seem to act like a piece of warm bubble gum. The stress force that pulls on the crust and thins rock in the middle is called **tension**. Tension occurs where two plates pull apart.

Compression One plate pushing against another plate can squeeze rock like a giant trash compactor. The stress force that squeezes rock until it folds or breaks is called **compression**. Compression occurs where two plates come together.

Shearing Stress that pushes a mass of rock in two opposite directions is called **shearing**. Shearing can cause rock to break and slip apart or to change its shape. Shearing occurs where two plates slip past each other.

Before stress

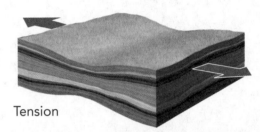
Tension

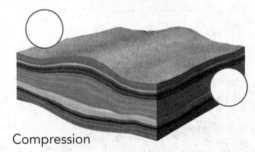
Compression

Shearing

FIGURE 1 ···

▷**ART IN MOTION** **Stress in Earth's Crust**
Stress can push, pull, or squeeze rock in Earth's crust.
✎ **Apply Concepts** Look at the pair of arrows in the second diagram. These arrows show how tension affects rock. Draw a pair of arrows on the third diagram to show how compression affects rock. Then, draw a pair of arrows on the bottom diagram to show how shearing acts on rock.

Lab zone® Do the Quick Lab
Effects of Stress.

🗝 Assess Your Understanding

got it? ··

○ **I get it!** Now I know that stress changes Earth's crust by changing the _____

_____

○ I need extra help with _____

Go to **my science COACH** *online for help with this subject.*

How Do Faults Form?

Recall that a fault is a break in the rock of the crust where rock surfaces slip past each other. Most faults occur along plate boundaries, where the forces of plate motion push or pull the crust so much that the crust breaks. 🔑 **When enough stress builds up in rock, the rock breaks, creating a fault.** There are three main types of faults: normal faults, reverse faults, and strike-slip faults.

Normal Faults The Rio Grande River flows through a wide valley in New Mexico. Here, tension has pulled apart two pieces of Earth's crust, forming the valley. Where rock is pulled apart by tension in Earth's crust, normal faults form. In a **normal fault,** the fault cuts through rock at an angle, so one block of rock sits over the fault, while the other block lies under the fault. The block of rock that sits over the fault is called the *hanging wall.* The rock that lies under the fault is called the *footwall.* The diagram of the normal fault in **Figure 2** shows how the hanging wall sits over the footwall. When movement occurs along a normal fault, the hanging wall slips downward. Normal faults occur where two plates diverge, or pull apart.

FIGURE 2 ···

▷ ART IN MOTION   Faults

The three main types of faults are defined by the direction in which rock moves along the fault. ✎ **Observe** In the descriptions below the first two diagrams, fill in the blanks to indicate how rock moves. In both of these diagrams, label the hanging wall and footwall.

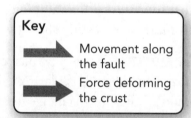

Key

➡ Movement along the fault

➡ Force deforming the crust

Normal fault

In a normal fault, the hanging wall _____

_____ relative to the footwall.

Reverse fault

In a reverse fault, the hanging wall moves

_____ relative to the footwall.

Reverse Faults
The northern Rocky Mountains rise high above the western United States and Canada. These mountains were gradually lifted up over time by movement along reverse faults. A **reverse fault** has the same structure as a normal fault, but the blocks move in the reverse direction. That is, the hanging wall moves up and the footwall moves down. **Figure 2** shows a reverse fault. Reverse faults form where compression pushes the rock of the crust together.

Strike-Slip Faults
The hilly plains in southern California are split by the San Andreas fault, shown in **Figure 2.** Here, shearing has produced a strike-slip fault. In a **strike-slip fault,** the rocks on either side of the fault slip past each other sideways, with little up or down motion. A strike-slip fault that forms the boundary between two plates is called a transform boundary. The San Andreas fault is an example of a transform boundary.

Lab zone Do the Quick Lab *Modeling Faults.*

Strike-slip fault

Rocks on either side of a strike-slip fault move past each other.

apply it!

The low angle of a thrust fault allows rock in the hanging wall to be pushed great distances. For example, over millions of years, rock along the Lewis thrust fault in Glacier National Park has moved 80 kilometers.

1 Identify Based on the arrows showing fault movements in the diagram, a thrust fault is a type of (normal fault/reverse fault).

2 CHALLENGE Why might the type of rock in the hanging wall of the Lewis thrust fault be different from the type of rock in the footwall?

_____
_____
_____
_____

Assess Your Understanding

1a. Review When enough stress builds up in brittle rock, the rock breaks, causing a _____ to form.

b. Infer A geologist sees a fault along which blocks of rock in the footwall have moved higher relative to blocks of rock in the hanging wall. What type of fault is this?

_____

got it?

○ **I get it!** Now I know that faults form when _____

○ **I need extra help with** _____

Go to my science **COACH** *online for help with this subject.*

123

How Does Plate Movement Create New Landforms?

Most changes in the crust occur so slowly that they cannot be observed directly. But what if you could speed up time so that a billion years passed by in minutes? Then, you could watch the movement of Earth's plates fold, stretch, and uplift the crust over wide areas. **Over millions of years, the forces of plate movement can change a flat plain into features such as anticlines and synclines, folded mountains, fault-block mountains, and plateaus.**

Folding Earth's Crust Have you ever skidded on a rug that wrinkled up as your feet pushed it across the floor? Sometimes plate movements can cause Earth's crust to fold much like the rug. Then, rocks stressed by compression may bend without breaking.

How Folds Form Folds are bends in rock that form when compression shortens and thickens Earth's crust. A fold can be a few centimeters across or hundreds of kilometers wide. **Figure 3** shows folds in rock that were exposed when a road was cut through a hillside in California.

Vocabulary Identify Multiple Meanings Underline the sentence that uses the scientific meaning of *fold*.

- The rock looked as crushed as my shirts if I don't fold them.
- Rock that bends without breaking may form a fold.

FIGURE 3 ·····
Folded Rock
Folds in rock shorten and thicken the Earth's crust. Over time, this process can form mountains.
Make Models Hold down the right edge of this page. Then, push the left edge toward the center of the book. Is this activity a good model for showing how folded rock forms? Explain.

_____
_____
_____
_____
_____
_____
_____

Place your fingers here and push the left edge of the page.

How Anticlines and Synclines Form Geologists use the terms *anticline* and *syncline* to describe upward and downward folds in rock. A fold in rock that bends upward into an arch is an anticline (AN tih klyn), as shown in **Figure 4**. A fold in rock that bends downward to form a V shape is a syncline (SIN klyn). Anticlines and synclines are found in many places where compression forces have folded the crust. The central Appalachian Mountains in Pennsylvania are folded mountains made up of anticlines and synclines.

How Folded Mountains Form The collision of two plates can cause compression and folding of the crust over a wide area. Folding produced some of the world's largest mountain ranges. The Himalayas in Asia and the Alps in Europe formed when pieces of the crust folded during the collision of two plates. These mountains formed over millions of years.

FIGURE 4 ....

Anticlines and Synclines
Compression can cause folds in the crust. Two types of folding are anticlines, which arch up, and synclines, which dip down.
Relate Cause and Effect Draw arrows to show the direction in which forces act to compress the crust. (*Hint*: Review the information on compression in this lesson.) Then label the anticline and the syncline.

Stretching Earth's Crust

If you traveled by car from Salt Lake City to Los Angeles, you would cross the Great Basin. This region contains many mountains separated by broad valleys, or basins. The mountains form from tension in Earth's crust that causes faulting. Such mountains are called fault-block mountains.

How do fault-block mountains form? Where two plates move away from each other, tension forces create many normal faults. Suppose two normal faults cause valleys to drop down on either side of a block of rock. This process is shown in the diagram that accompanies the photograph in **Figure 5**. As the hanging wall of each normal fault slips downward, the block in between now stands above the surrounding valleys, forming a fault-block mountain.

✎ **Relate Cause and Effect**
When two normal faults cause valleys to drop down on either side of a block of rock, what type of landform results?

_____

_____

FIGURE 5 ....

Tension and Normal Faults

As tension forces pull the crust apart, two normal faults can form a fault-block mountain range, as you can see in the diagram below. The mountain range in the photograph is in the Great Basin. Valleys can also form as a result of two normal faults.

✎ **Predict** Label the hanging wall and the two footwalls in diagram A. In diagram B, draw the new position of the hanging wall after movement occurs. Describe what happens.

_____

_____

_____

_____

A Before movement occurs along the faults.

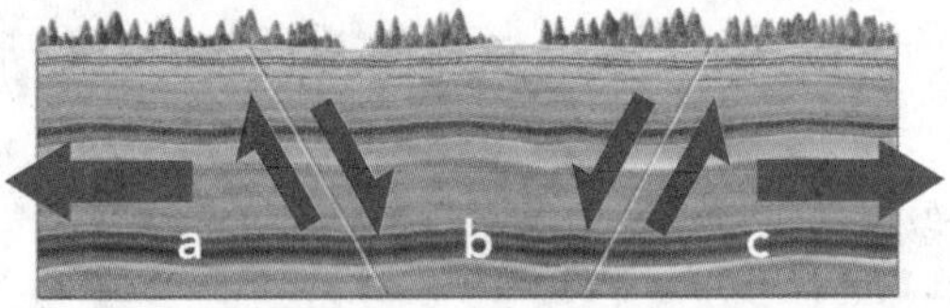

a. _____

b. _____

c. _____

B Draw the outcome after movement occurs along the faults.

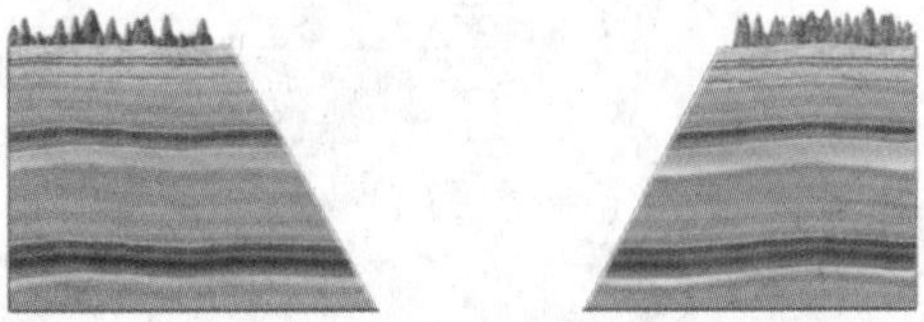

Fault-block mountains

Key

Movement along the fault

Force deforming the crust

Uplifting Earth's Crust The forces that raise mountains can also uplift, or raise, plateaus. A **plateau** is a large area of flat land elevated high above sea level. Some plateaus form when forces in Earth's crust push up a large, flat block of rock. Like a fancy sandwich, a plateau consists of many different flat layers, and is wider than it is tall. Forces deforming the crust uplifted the Colorado Plateau in the "Four Corners" region of Arizona, Utah, Colorado, and New Mexico. **Figure 6** shows one part of that plateau in northern Arizona.

FIGURE 6
The Kaibab Plateau
The Kaibab Plateau forms the North Rim of the Grand Canyon. The plateau is the flat-topped landform in the right half of the photograph.

Look at the sequence of drawings below. In your own words, describe what happens in the last two diagrams.

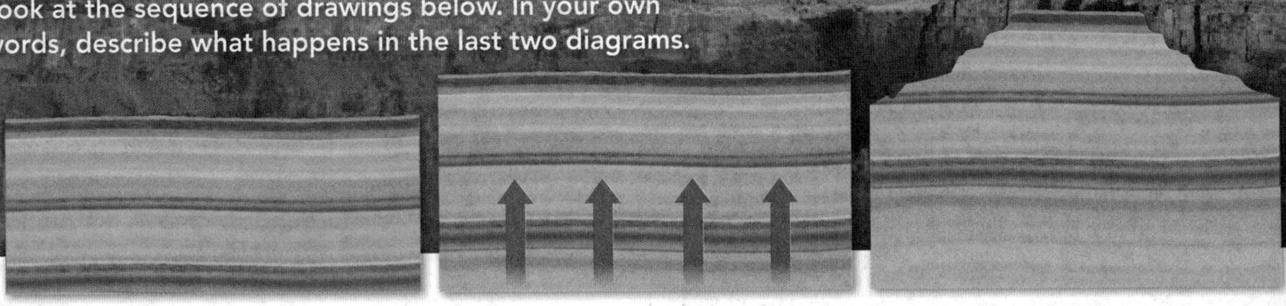

A flat, layered block of rock lies somewhere in Earth's crust.

Lab zone® Do the Quick Lab *Modeling Stress.*

Assess Your Understanding

2a. Review Normal faults often occur when two plates (come together/pull apart).

b. Interpret Diagrams Look at the diagram that accompanies the photograph in **Figure 5**. Does the block of rock in the middle move up as a result of movement along the normal faults? Explain.

got it?

○ **I get it!** Now I know that plate movements create new features by _____

○ **I need extra help with** _____

Go to MY SCIENCE COACH *online for help with this subject.*

Earthquakes and Seismic Waves

UNLOCK
THE BIG
?

🔑 **What Are Seismic Waves?**

🔑 **How Are Earthquakes Measured?**

🔑 **How Is an Epicenter Located?**

my planet diary

Witness to Disaster

On May 12, 2008, a major earthquake struck China. American reporter Melissa Block was conducting a live radio interview in that country at the moment the earthquake struck.

"What's going on?" Block asked. She remained on the air and continued: "The whole building is shaking. The whole building is SHAKING."

Block watched as the ground moved like waves beneath her feet. The top of the church across the street started to fall down. For minutes, the ground continued to vibrate under Block's feet. The earthquake that day killed about 87,000 people.

—NPR.com

DISASTER

✏ **Communicate** Discuss these questions with a group of classmates. Write your answers below.

1. What does Melissa Block's experience tell you about the way the ground can move during an earthquake?

_____

_____

2. How do you think you would react during an earthquake or other disaster?

_____

_____

_____

> PLANET DIARY Go to **Planet Diary** to learn more about earthquakes.

Lab ® Do the Inquiry Warm-Up
zone *How Do Seismic Waves Travel Through Earth?*

Vocabulary

- earthquake • focus • epicenter • P wave
- S wave • surface wave • seismograph
- Modified Mercalli scale • magnitude • Richter scale
- moment magnitude scale

Skills

⊙ Reading: Sequence

△ Inquiry: Infer

What Are Seismic Waves?

Earth is never still. Every day, worldwide, several thousand earthquakes are detected. An **earthquake** is the shaking and trembling that results from movement of rock beneath Earth's surface. Most earthquakes are too small to notice. But a large earthquake can crack open the ground, shift mountains, and cause great damage.

Cause of Earthquakes The forces of plate movement cause earthquakes. Plate movements produce stress in Earth's crust, adding energy to rock and forming faults. Stress increases along a fault until the rock slips or breaks, causing an earthquake. In seconds, the earthquake releases an enormous amount of stored energy. Some of the energy released during an earthquake travels in the form of seismic waves. ▬ **Seismic waves are vibrations that are similar to sound waves. They travel through Earth carrying energy released by an earthquake.** The speed and path of the waves in part depend on the material through which the waves travel.

Earthquake

Path of seismic waves

• A

• B

C

apply it!

Earthquakes start below the surface of Earth. But an earthquake's seismic waves do not carry energy only upward, toward Earth's surface. They also carry energy downward, through Earth's interior.

❶ Look at the drawing showing Earth's interior. At which point(s) can seismic waves be detected?

○ A only
○ A and B
○ A, B, and C

❷ △**Infer** At which point do you think the seismic waves will have the most energy? Why?

_____

_____

_____

_____

○ **Sequence** Number the
following in the order in which
seismic waves would be felt:

__ At an earthquake's epicenter

__ At a distance of 500 km from
the earthquake's focus

__ At the earthquake's focus

FIGURE 1 ································

▶ **INTERACTIVE ART** **Seismic Waves**
The diagram shows how seismic
waves traveled during an earthquake
along the Denali fault.

✎ Explain **Match the two points
in the diagram to the two terms
below them. Then, write a short,
science-based news article that
describes how, why, and where
the earthquake took place.
Include a headline.**

Types of Seismic Waves

Types of Seismic Waves Like a pebble thrown
into a pond, the seismic waves of an earthquake race out in
every direction from the earthquake's focus. The **focus**
(FOH kus) is the area beneath Earth's surface where rock that
was under stress begins to break or move. This action triggers the earthquake. The point on the surface directly above
the focus is called the **epicenter** (EP uh sen tur).

Most earthquakes start in the lithosphere, within about
100 kilometers beneath Earth's surface. Seismic waves carry
energy from the earthquake's focus. This energy travels
through Earth's interior and across Earth's surface. That happened in 2002, when a powerful earthquake ruptured the
Denali fault in Alaska, shown in **Figure 1.**

There are three main categories of seismic waves. These
waves are P waves, S waves, and surface waves. But an earthquake sends out only P and S waves from its focus. Surface
waves can develop wherever P and S waves reach the surface.

earthBL🌎G

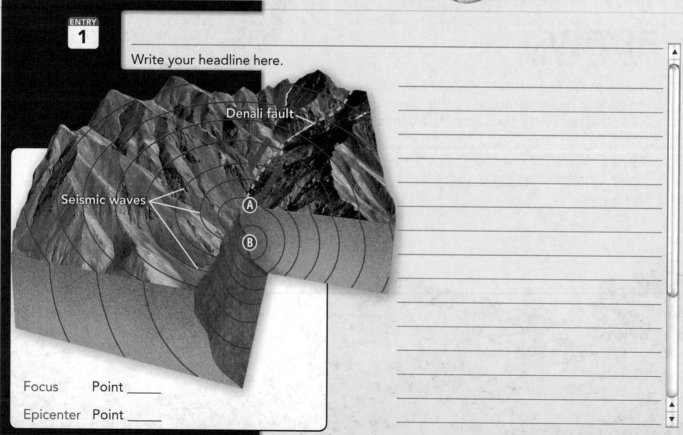

ENTRY 1

Write your headline here.

Denali fault

Seismic waves

Ⓐ

Ⓑ

Focus   Point _____

Epicenter Point _____

P Waves The first waves to arrive are primary waves, or P waves. **P waves** are seismic waves that compress and expand the ground like an accordion. Like the other types of seismic waves, P waves can damage buildings. Look at **Figure 2A** to see how P waves move.

S Waves After P waves come secondary waves, or S waves. **S waves** are seismic waves that can vibrate from side to side (as shown in **Figure 2B**) or up and down. Their vibrations are at an angle of 90° to the direction that they travel. When S waves reach the surface, they shake structures violently. While P waves travel through both solids and liquids, S waves cannot move through liquids.

Surface Waves When P waves and S waves reach the surface, some of them become surface waves. **Surface waves** move more slowly than P and S waves, but they can produce severe ground movements. These waves produce movement that is similar to waves in water, where the water's particles move in a pattern that is almost circular. Surface waves can make the ground roll like ocean waves (**Figure 2C**) or shake buildings from side to side.

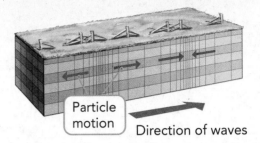
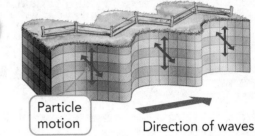
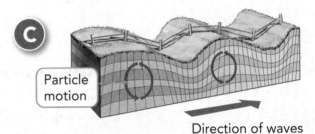

FIGURE 2 ·····························

P, S, and Surface Waves
Earthquakes release stored energy as seismic waves.
✎ **Describe** Draw a line from each type of seismic wave to the movement it causes.

P waves	can vibrate the ground from side to side
S waves	can make the ground roll like ocean waves
Surface waves	compress and expand the ground

 Lab zone® Do the Quick Lab
Properties of Seismic Waves.

🔑 **Assess Your Understanding**

1a. Review The energy released by an earthquake moves out from the earthquake's

_____ in the form of seismic waves.

b. Predict Small earthquakes occur along a certain fault several times a year. Why might geologists worry if no earthquakes occur for 25 years?

_____

_____

_____

got it? ··

○ **I get it!** Now I know that seismic waves are_____

_____

○ **I need extra help with** _____

Go to **my science** ⬡ᔆ **COACH** *online for help with this subject.*

131

How Are Earthquakes Measured?

Geologists monitor earthquakes by measuring the seismic waves they produce. This is done in two ways. ⟶ **The amount of earthquake damage or shaking that is felt is rated using the Modified Mercalli scale. The magnitude, or size, of an earthquake is measured on a seismograph using the Richter scale or moment magnitude scale.** A **seismograph** is an instrument that records and measures an earthquake's seismic waves.

The Modified Mercalli Scale

The **Modified Mercalli scale** rates the amount of shaking from an earthquake. The shaking is rated by people's observations, without the use of any instruments. This scale is useful in regions where there aren't many instruments to measure an earthquake's strength. The table in **Figure 3** describes the 12 steps of the Mercalli scale. To rank examples of damage, look at the photographs in **Figure 3.**

The Richter Scale
An earthquake's **magnitude** is a single number that geologists assign to an earthquake based on the earthquake's size. There are many magnitude scales. These scales are based on the earliest magnitude scale, called the **Richter scale.** Magnitude scales like the Richter scale rate the magnitude of small earthquakes based on the size of the earthquake's waves as recorded by seismographs. The magnitudes take into account that seismic waves get smaller the farther a seismograph is from an earthquake.

Rank	Description
I–III	People notice vibrations like those from a passing truck. Unstable objects disturbed.
IV–VI	Some windows break. Plaster may fall.
VII–IX	Moderate to heavy damage. Buildings jolted off foundations.
X–XII	Great destruction. Cracks appear in ground. Waves seen on surface.

FIGURE 3 ································

> **INTERACTIVE ART** Modified Mercalli Scale
The Modified Mercalli scale uses Roman numerals to rate the damage and shaking at any given location, usually close to the earthquake. ✎ **Classify Assign a Modified Mercalli rating to each photograph.**

The Moment Magnitude Scale

Geologists use the **moment magnitude scale** to rate the total energy an earthquake releases. News reports may mention the Richter scale, but the number quoted is almost always an earthquake's moment magnitude. To assign a magnitude to an earthquake, geologists use data from seismographs and other sources. The data allow geologists to estimate how much energy the earthquake releases. **Figure 4** gives the magnitudes of some recent, strong earthquakes.

Comparing Magnitudes

An earthquake's moment magnitude tells geologists how much energy was released by an earthquake. Each one-point increase in magnitude represents the release of roughly 32 times more energy. For example, a magnitude 6 earthquake releases 32 times as much energy as a magnitude 5 earthquake.

An earthquake's effects increase with magnitude. Earthquakes with a magnitude below 5 are small and cause little damage. Those with a magnitude above 6 can cause great damage. The most powerful earthquakes, with a magnitude of 8 or above, are rare. In the 1900's, only three earthquakes had a magnitude of 9 or above. More recently, the 2004 Sumatra earthquake had a magnitude of 9.2.

FIGURE 4 ···

Earthquake Magnitude

The table gives the moment magnitudes of some recent earthquakes.

Magnitude	Location	Date
9.2	Sumatra (Indian Ocean)	December 2004
7.9	China	May 2008
7.6	Turkey	August 1999
6.6	Japan	October 2004
5.4	California	July 2008

CHALLENGE Approximately how many times stronger was the earthquake in Turkey than the earthquake in Japan?

did you know?

About 98 percent of Antarctica is covered by ice. Large shifts in the ice here can cause "ice quakes." Did you know that these "ice quakes" can be the equivalent of magnitude 7 earthquakes?

Lab zone® | Do the Quick Lab *Measuring Earthquakes.*

Assess Your Understanding

2a. Identify The _____ scale rates earthquakes based on the amount of energy that is released.

b. Infer Suppose the moment magnitude of an earthquake is first thought to be 6, but is later found to be 8. Would you expect the earthquake damage to be more or less serious? Why?

_____

_____

_____

got it? ···

○ **I get it!** Now I know that to measure earthquakes, geologists use seismic waves to determine _____

_____

○ I need extra help with _____

_____

Go to my science ⓢ coach *online for help with this subject.*

How Is an Epicenter Located?

When an earthquake occurs, geologists try to pinpoint the earthquake's epicenter. Why? Locating the epicenter helps geologists identify areas where earthquakes may occur in the future. **Geologists use seismic waves to locate an earthquake's epicenter.** To do this, they use data from thousands of seismograph stations set up all over the world. However, you can use a simpler method to find an earthquake's epicenter.

Recall that seismic waves travel at different speeds. P waves arrive at a seismograph first. Then S waves follow close behind. Look at the graph, P and S Waves, below. Suppose you know when P waves arrived at a seismograph after an earthquake, and when S waves arrived. You can read the graph to find the distance from the seismograph to the epicenter. Notice that the farther away an earthquake is from a given point, the greater the time between the arrival of the P waves and the S waves.

Suppose you know the distance of three seismograph stations from an epicenter. You can then draw three circles to locate the epicenter. Look at **Figure 5.** The center of each circle is a particular seismograph's location. The radius of each circle is the distance from that seismograph to the epicenter. The point where the three circles intersect is the location of the epicenter.

do the math!

Seismic Wave Speeds

Seismographs at five observation stations recorded the arrival times of the P and S waves produced by an earthquake. These data were used to draw the graph.

① **Read Graphs** What variable is shown on the x-axis of the graph? What variable is shown on the y-axis?

_____

② **Estimate** How long did it take the S waves to travel 2,000 km?

_____

③ **Estimate** How long did it take the P waves to travel 2,000 km?

_____

④ **Calculate** What is the difference in the arrival times of the P waves and the S waves at 2,000 km? At 4,000 km?

_____

_____

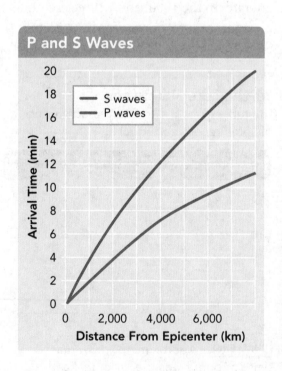

P and S Waves

- S waves
- P waves

Arrival Time (min) — y-axis: 0, 2, 4, 6, 8, 10, 12, 14, 16, 18, 20

Distance From Epicenter (km) — x-axis: 0, 2,000, 4,000, 6,000

FIGURE 5 ·······························

Determining an Earthquake's Epicenter

The map shows how to find the epicenter of an earthquake using data from three seismographic stations. ✎ **Interpret Maps** Suppose a fourth seismographic station is located in San Diego. What was the approximate difference in arrival times of P and S waves here?

_____

Hint: Use the map scale to determine how far San Diego is from the epicenter. Then, use the graph on the previous page to find your answer.

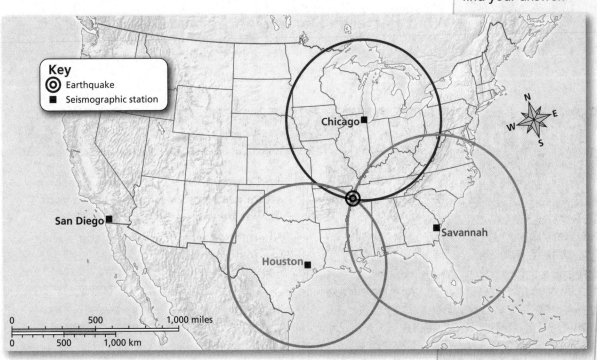

Key
◎ Earthquake
■ Seismographic station

Chicago ■

San Diego ■

Houston ■

Savannah ■

0   500   1,000 miles

0   500   1,000 km

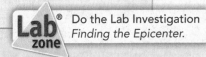
Do the Lab Investigation
Finding the Epicenter.

🔑 Assess Your Understanding

3a. Review Geologists use _____ to locate an earthquake's epicenter.

b. Identify What can geologists measure to tell how far an earthquake's epicenter is from a particular seismograph?

_____

_____

c. Apply Concepts Suppose an earthquake occurs somewhere in California. Could a seismograph on Hawaii be used to help locate the epicenter of the earthquake? Why or why not?

_____

_____

_____

_____

got it? ·······························

○ **I get it!** Now I know that geologists can locate an earthquake's epicenter by using_____

_____

○ **I need extra help with** _____

Go to my SCIENCE ⓢ **COACH** *online for help with this subject.*

Monitoring Earthquakes

 UNLOCK THE BIG **?**

🔑 **How Do Seismographs Work?**

🔑 **What Patterns Do Seismographic Data Reveal?**

MY PLANET DIARY

Whole Lot of Shaking Going On

Is the ground moving under your school? A project that will monitor shaking underneath the entire nation might help you find out!

In 2004, scientists in the USArray project placed 400 seismographs across the western United States. Every month, 18 seismographs are picked up and moved east, "leapfrogging" the other seismographs. The map below shows one arrangement of the array. The seismic data that are obtained will help scientists learn more about our active Earth!

FUN FACT

✏️ **Communicate** Discuss this question with a group of classmates. Write your answer below.

When the array arrives in your state, what information might it provide?

_____

_____

_____

_____

▶ PLANET DIARY Go to **Planet Diary** to learn more about monitoring earthquakes.

Key
▲ Seismograph

Lab zone Do the Inquiry Warm-Up *How Can Seismic Waves Be Detected?*

Vocabulary
• seismogram

Skills
⊙ Reading: Identify the Main Idea
△ Inquiry: Predict

How Do Seismographs Work?

Today, seismographs are complex electronic devices. Some laptop computers and car air bags contain similar devices that detect shaking. But a simple seismograph, like the one in **Figure 1,** can consist of a heavy weight attached to a frame by a spring or wire. A pen connected to the weight rests its point on a drum that can rotate. As the drum rotates, the pen in effect draws a straight line on paper wrapped tightly around the drum. 🔑 **Seismic waves cause a simple seismograph's drum to vibrate, which in turn causes the pen to record the drum's vibrations.** The suspended weight with the pen attached moves very little. This allows the pen to stay in place and record the drum's vibrations.

Measuring Seismic Waves When you write a sentence, the paper stays in one place while your hand moves the pen. But in a seismograph, it's the pen that remains stationary while the paper moves. Why is this? All seismographs make use of a basic principle of physics: Whether it is moving or at rest, every object resists any change to its motion. A seismograph's heavy weight resists motion during an earthquake. But the rest of the seismograph is anchored to the ground and vibrates when seismic waves arrive.

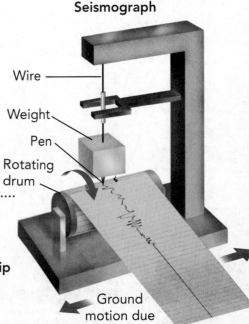

Seismograph

Wire

Weight

Pen

Rotating drum

Ground motion due to seismic waves

FIGURE 1 ···

Recording Seismic Waves
In a simple seismograph, a pen attached to a suspended weight records an earthquake's seismic waves.

✏ **Make Models** To mimic the action of a seismograph, hold the tip of a pencil on the right edge of the seismograph paper below. Have a classmate pull the right edge of the book away from your pencil while the classmate also "vibrates" the book side to side.

FIGURE 2

Seismograms

When an earthquake's seismic waves reach a simple seismograph, the seismograph's drum vibrates. The vibrations are recorded by the seismograph's pen, producing a seismogram, as shown on the top diagram.

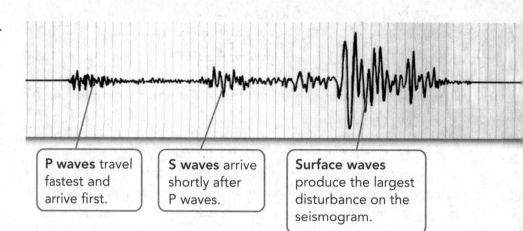

P waves travel fastest and arrive first.

S waves arrive shortly after P waves.

Surface waves produce the largest disturbance on the seismogram.

[CHALLENGE] An aftershock is a smaller earthquake that occurs after a larger earthquake. Draw the seismogram that might be produced by a seismograph during an earthquake and its aftershock. Label the earthquake and the aftershock.

Reading a Seismogram You have probably seen the zig-zagging lines used to represent an earthquake. The pattern of lines, called a **seismogram,** is the record of an earthquake's seismic waves produced by a seismograph. Study the seismogram in **Figure 2.** Notice when the P waves, S waves, and surface waves arrive. The height of the lines drawn by the seismograph is greater for a more severe earthquake or an earthquake closer to the seismograph.

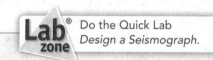
Do the Quick Lab
Design a Seismograph.

🔖 Assess Your Understanding

1a. Review The height of the lines on a seismogram is (greater/less) for a stronger earthquake.

b. Interpret Diagrams What do the relatively straight, flat portions of the seismogram at the top of **Figure 2** represent?

_____

_____

_____

_____

got it?

○ **I get it!** Now I know that a simple seismograph works when _____

_____

_____

_____

○ **I need extra help with** _____

Go to MY SCIENCE COACH online for help with this subject.

Earthquakes

What Patterns Do Seismographic Data Reveal?

Geologists use seismographs to monitor earthquakes. Other devices that geologists use detect slight motions along faults. Yet even with data from many different devices, geologists cannot yet predict when and where an earthquake might strike. **But from past seismographic data, geologists have created maps of where earthquakes occur around the world. The maps show that earthquakes often occur along plate boundaries.** Recall that where plates meet, plate movement stores energy in rock that makes up the crust. This energy is eventually released in an earthquake.

Earthquake Risk in North America Earthquake risk largely depends on how close a given location is to a plate boundary. In the United States, two plates meet along the Pacific coast in California, Washington state, and Alaska, causing many faults. Frequent earthquakes occur in California, where the Pacific plate and the North American plate meet along the San Andreas fault. In Washington, earthquakes result from the subduction of the Juan de Fuca plate beneath the North American plate. Recall that during subduction, one plate is forced down under another plate.

⤺ **Identify the Main Idea**
Underline the sentence in the second paragraph that describes the main factor in determining earthquake risk for a given location.

The map shows areas where serious earthquakes are likely to occur, based on the location of past earthquakes across the United States.

❶ **Interpret Maps** The map indicates that serious earthquakes are most likely to occur (on the east coast/in the midsection/on the west coast) of the United States.

❷ **Predict** Based on the evidence shown in the map, predict where you think plate boundaries lie. Explain your reasoning.

_____
_____
_____
_____
_____
_____
_____
_____
_____
_____
_____

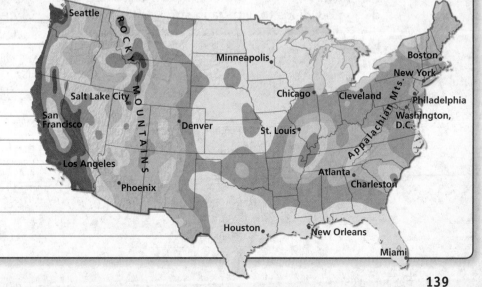

Key

Lowest risk — Highest risk

Earthquake Risk Around the World

Earthquake Risk Around the World Many of the world's earthquakes occur in a vast area of geologic activity called the Ring of Fire. In this area, plate boundaries form a ring around the Pacific Ocean. Volcanoes as well as earthquakes are common along these boundaries. The Ring of Fire includes the west coast of Central America and the west coast of South America. Strong earthquakes have occurred in countries along these coasts, where plates converge. Across the Pacific Ocean, the Pacific Plate collides with several other plates. Here, Japan, Indonesia, New Zealand, and New Guinea are seismically very active. One of the most powerful earthquakes ever recorded occurred off the coast of Japan on March 11, 2011.

India, China, and Pakistan also have been struck by large earthquakes. In this area of the world, the Indo-Australian Plate collides with the Eurasian Plate. Earthquakes are also common where the Eurasian Plate meets the Arabian and African plates.

 EXPLORE THE BIG ?

Earthquakes and Plate Tectonics

Why do earthquakes occur more often in some places than in others?

FIGURE 3 ....

> **REAL-WORLD INQUIRY** Earthquakes Around the World

Earthquakes are closely linked to plate tectonics. The map shows where past earthquakes have occurred in relation to plate boundaries.

✏ **Make Judgments** Draw an outline tracing the plate boundaries that make up the Ring of Fire. Then, look at North America. Draw a star where buildings should be built to withstand earthquakes. Put an X where there is less need to design buildings to withstand strong shaking. Do the same for another continent (not Antarctica). Explain your answers.

_____

_____

_____

_____

_____

_____

_____

_____

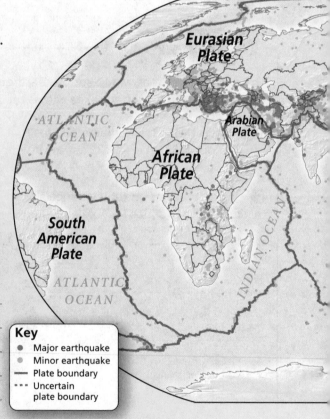

Key
- ● Major earthquake
- ● Minor earthquake
- — Plate boundary
- --- Uncertain plate boundary

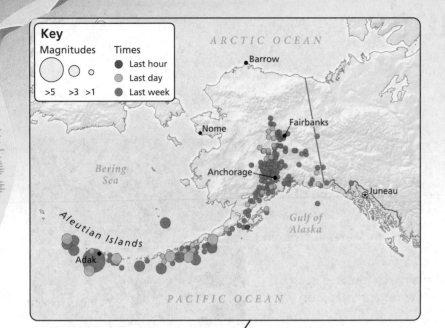

Key

Magnitudes

○ ○ ○
>5 >3 >1

Times

● Last hour
● Last day
● Last week

Earthquakes in Alaska

Look at the map of Alaska. Earthquakes here are the result of subduction. ✎ **Infer** Draw the plate boundary. Then draw arrows on either side of the boundary to show the direction in which the plates move relative to each other.

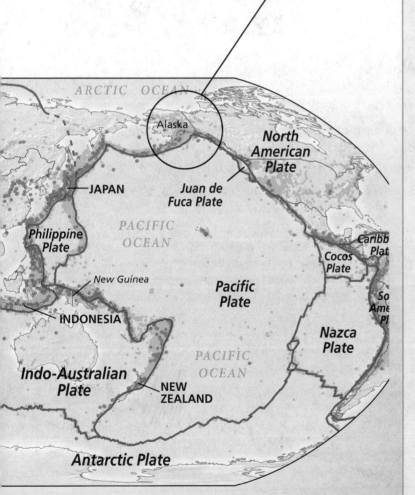

Lab® Do the Quick Lab
zone *Earthquake Patterns.*

🔑 Assess Your Understanding

2a. Review The _____ stored in rocks as a result of plate movement can be released in an earthquake.

b. **ANSWER THE BIG ❓** Why do earthquakes occur more often in some places than in others?

_____
_____
_____
_____
_____
_____

got **it?** ....

○ **I get it!** Now I know that seismographic data reveal that _____
_____
_____

○ **I need extra help with** _____
_____

Go to **MY SCIENCE ⑤ COACH** *online for help with this subject.*

CHAPTER

4 Study Guide

REVIEW THE BIG Q

Earthquakes often occur along _____ , where _____
_____ stores energy in rock that makes up the crust.

LESSON 1 Forces in Earth's Crust

🔑 Tension, compression, and shearing work over millions of years to change the shape and volume of rock.

🔑 When enough stress builds up in rock, the rock breaks, creating a fault.

🔑 Plate movement can change a flat plain into features such as folds, folded mountains, fault-block mountains, and plateaus.

Vocabulary
- stress • tension • compression • shearing
- normal fault • reverse fault • strike-slip fault • plateau

LESSON 2 Earthquakes and Seismic Waves

🔑 Seismic waves carry energy produced by an earthquake.

🔑 The amount of earthquake damage or shaking that is felt is rated using the Modified Mercalli scale. An earthquake's magnitude, or size, is measured using the Richter scale or moment magnitude scale.

🔑 Geologists use seismic waves to locate an earthquake's epicenter.

Vocabulary
- earthquake • focus • epicenter • P wave • S wave
- surface wave • seismograph • Modified Mercalli scale
- magnitude • Richter scale • moment magnitude scale

LESSON 3 Monitoring Earthquakes

🔑 Seismic waves cause a simple seismograph's drum to vibrate, which in turn causes the pen to record the drum's vibrations.

🔑 From past seismographic data, geologists have created maps of where earthquakes occur around the world. The maps show that earthquakes often occur along plate boundaries.

Vocabulary
- seismogram

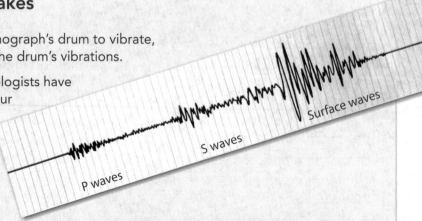

P waves

S waves

Surface waves

Review and Assessment

LESSON 1 Forces in Earth's Crust

1. Which force squeezes Earth's crust to make the crust shorter and thicker?

  a. tension   **b.** normal

  c. shearing   **d.** compression

2. Rocks on either side of a _____ fault slip past each other with little up and down motion.

3. List Give two examples of mountain ranges in the world that have been caused by folding.

_____

_____

_____

4. Interpret Diagrams What type of stress is shown in the diagram below?

_____

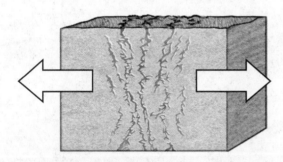

5. Relate Cause and Effect Plateaus are large, flat, elevated areas of land. What is one way plateaus can form?

_____

_____

_____

6. **Write About It** Compression causes folds called anticlines and synclines. How do these features resemble each other? How do they differ from one another?

LESSON 2 Earthquakes and Seismic Waves

7. Which of these scales rates earthquake damage at a particular location?

  a. focus   **b.** Modified Mercalli

  c. Richter   **d.** moment magnitude

8. The point on Earth's surface directly above an earthquake's focus is called _____

_____

9. Interpret Diagrams Label the diagram to show the directions an S wave travels and vibrates.

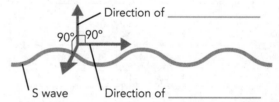

10. Explain How is the energy released by an earthquake related to its moment magnitude?

_____

_____

11. Interpret Data Can geologists use data from only two seismographic stations to locate an earthquake's epicenter? Explain.

_____

_____

_____

12. math! Seismograph A records P waves at 6:05 P.M. and S waves at 6:10 P.M. Seismograph B records P waves at 6:10 P.M. and S waves at 6:25 P.M. What is the difference in the arrival times at each device? Which device is closer to the earthquake's epicenter?

_____

_____

143

LESSON 3 Monitoring Earthquakes

13. In which type of location is earthquake risk the greatest?

    a. at plate centers   **b.** on big plates

    c. at plate boundaries   **d.** on small plates

14. Very high, jagged lines on a seismogram indicate that an earthquake is either _____

_____

Use the graph to answer questions 15–16.

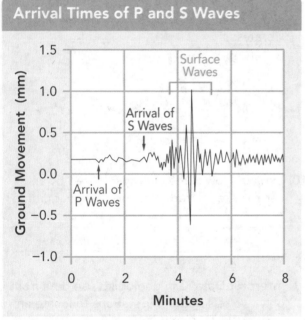

Arrival Times of P and S Waves

15. Read Graphs Which type of seismic waves produced the largest ground movement?

_____

16. Interpret Data What was the difference in arrival times for the P waves and the S waves?

_____

17. [Write About It] There is a high risk of earthquakes along the San Andreas fault in California. What is happening in Earth's crust along the fault to cause this high earthquake risk? Use the theory of plate tectonics in your answer.

APPLY THE BIG Q Why do earthquakes occur more often in some places than in others?

18. An architect is hired to design a skyscraper in the Indonesian city of Jakarta, which is near the Ring of Fire. The architect must follow special building codes that the city has written. What might those codes be for and why are they important in Jakarta?

_____

_____

_____

_____

_____

_____

_____

_____

Standardized Test Prep

Multiple Choice

Circle the letter of the best answer.

1. The diagram below shows a mass of rock affected by stress.

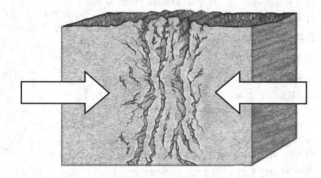

   What type of stress process is shown in this diagram?

   A pulling apart   B tension
   C compression   D shearing

2. An earthquake occurs along a fault when

   A energy in the rock along the fault does not change for a long period of time.
   B stress in the rock along the fault causes the rock to melt.
   C enough energy builds up in the rock along the fault to cause the rock to break or slip.
   D energy in the rock along the fault is changed to heat.

3. Which scale would a geologist use to estimate the total energy released by an earthquake?

   A Modified Mercalli scale
   B Richter scale
   C epicenter scale
   D moment magnitude scale

4. When an earthquake occurs, seismic waves travel

   A only through the hanging wall.
   B only through the footwall.
   C outward from the focus.
   D inward to the epicenter.

5. Where are the areas that are at greatest risk from earthquakes?

   A in the center of plates
   B where plates meet
   C in the middle of the ocean
   D where land meets water

Constructed Response

Use the diagram below and your knowledge of science to help you answer Question 6. Write your answer on a separate piece of paper.

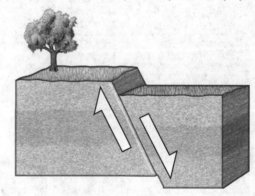

6. Explain the process that forms a normal fault and leads to an earthquake along the fault. Describe the fault, the type of stress that produces it, and events that occur before and during the earthquake.

Seismic-SAFE BUILDINGS

Suppose you are on the highest floor of a tall building in your town. An earthquake strikes. What features might help the building withstand the powerful effects of an earthquake?

Tension ties firmly "tie" the floors and ceilings of the building to the walls, and work to absorb and scatter earthquake energy.

Base isolators are pads under the first floor that separate, or isolate, the building from its foundation. The pads stop some of an earthquake's energy from entering the building.

Cross braces form a network of steel on the outside of the building to stiffen its frame.

Dampers work like shock absorbers in a car, absorbing some of the energy of seismic waves.

Design It Use cardboard, craft sticks, and modeling clay to build a model of a seismic-safe building. Place your model on a table, and drop a heavy book next to it. Then try bumping the table to shake the model sideways. How well does your building stand up? What changes could you make to improve your structure's stability?

▲ Cross braces on the outside of the building help to support the frame.

What Do the Toads Know?

On May 12, 2008, a strong earthquake struck China. Within days, bloggers claimed that many signs had predicted the earthquake. One blogger wrote that thousands of toads moved through the area just before the earthquake. Another claimed to have seen ponds that emptied and dried up.

Write About It Write an entry that you might post in a blog. Do you believe the bloggers' claims about signs that might predict an earthquake? What evidence would you look for to determine whether the bloggers' claims were scientifically accurate?

FORENSIC SEISMOLOGY

In May 2008, India tested two nuclear devices by exploding them underground. Days later, Pakistan conducted similar tests. The world learned of these tests because these explosions caused seismic waves.

How did geologists know the seismic waves were produced by nuclear explosions and not by earthquakes? Seismic waves from underground nuclear explosions produce a different seismogram pattern than earthquakes do.

Research It Research how the seismograms produced by nuclear explosions differ from those produced by earthquakes, and make a poster illustrating the differences.

▲ An underground nuclear test destroyed these test buildings at Pokaran, India, in 1998.

147

WHAT
CAUSED
THIS
EXPLOSION?

How does a volcano erupt?

Vivid orange and red sparks shower the night sky. A small crowd stands by and watches this beautiful scene light up the night. Could this be a fireworks display gone crazy? You've probably guessed that it is a volcano erupting. This volcano is actually exploding, sending hot gases, ash, and lava into the air. **Infer** **What could cause a volcano to blow up?**

_____

_____

_____

_____

_____

_____

> UNTAMED SCIENCE   Watch the **Untamed Science** video to learn more about volcanoes.

Volcanoes

5 Getting Started

Check Your Understanding

1. **Background** Read the paragraph below and then answer the question.

Mr. Carenni said, "For today's activity, let's make a model of Earth's crust. We can think of the **crust** as a thin film of ice resting on top of a much thicker layer of hard, packed snow. Now let's suppose that the ice breaks into pieces. On Earth, these pieces are called **plates.** The edges of the plates are called **boundaries.** "

> The **crust** is Earth's rocky, outer layer.
>
> A **plate** is one of the large pieces that Earth's crust is broken into.
>
> **Boundaries** are lines along which something ends.

• Suppose two pieces of ice are pushed slowly together. What might happen to the edges of the pieces?

_____

_____

> **MY READING WEB** If you had trouble answering the question above, visit **My Reading Web** and type in *Volcanoes.*

Vocabulary Skill

High-Use Academic Words High-use words are words that are used frequently in academic reading, writing, and discussions. These words are different from key terms because they appear in many subject areas.

Word	Definition	Example
surface	*n.* the exterior or outermost layer of an object	The *surface* of Earth is very rocky.
stage	*n.* a point in a process	Middle age is one *stage* of life.
hazard	*n.* a possible danger	Forest fires can be a *hazard* for people living near the woods.

2. **Quick Check** Choose the word from the table that best completes the sentence.

• When a volcano erupts, the lava can be a _____

for cities and towns nearby.

hot spot

crater

volcanic neck

caldera

Chapter Preview

LESSON 1

- volcano
- magma
- lava
- Ring of Fire
- island arc
- hot spot

⊙ Relate Text and Visuals
△ Develop Hypotheses

LESSON 2

- magma chamber
- pipe
- vent
- lava flow
- crater
- silica
- pyroclastic flow
- dormant
- extinct

⊙ Outline
△ Communicate

LESSON 3

- caldera
- cinder cone
- composite volcano
- shield volcano
- volcanic neck
- dike
- sill
- batholith

⊙ Relate Cause and Effect
△ Predict

> VOCAB FLASH CARDS For extra help with vocabulary, visit **Vocab Flash Cards** and type in *Volcanoes.*

Volcanoes and Plate Tectonics

🔑 **Where Are Volcanoes Found on Earth's Surface?**

my planet diary

FIELD TRIP

Mountain of Fire, Mountain of Ice

Climbers who struggle up the snow-packed slopes of Mount Erebus on Antarctica may be in for an unpleasant surprise. Balls of scorching molten rock three meters across might come hurtling out of the air and land just steps from climbers' feet! Why? Because Mount Erebus is one of Earth's southernmost volcanoes.

Scientists believe that Mount Erebus lies over an area where material from Earth's mantle rises and then melts. The melted material reaches the surface at Mount Erebus.

Read the text and then answer the question.

How did Mount Erebus form?

_____

_____

_____

_____

_____

_____

▷ PLANET DIARY   Go to **Planet Diary** to learn more about volcanoes.

Lab zone Do the Inquiry Warm-Up *Moving Volcanoes.*

Where Are Volcanoes Found on Earth's Surface?

The eruption of a volcano can be awe-inspiring. Molten material can be spewed high into the atmosphere. Villages can be buried in volcanic ash. A **volcano** is a mountain that forms in Earth's crust when molten material, or magma, reaches the surface. **Magma** is a molten mixture of rock-forming substances, gases, and water from the mantle. When magma reaches the surface, it is called **lava.** After magma and lava cool, they form solid rock.

Vocabulary
- volcano
- magma
- lava
- Ring of Fire
- island arc
- hot spot

Skills
↻ Reading: Relate Text and Visuals
△ Inquiry: Develop Hypotheses

Volcanoes and Plate Boundaries

Are volcanoes found randomly across Earth? No, in general, volcanoes form a regular pattern on Earth. To understand why, look at the map in **Figure 1.** Notice how volcanoes occur in many great, long belts. 🗝 **Volcanic belts form along the boundaries of Earth's plates.**

Volcanoes can occur where two plates pull apart, or diverge. Here, plate movements cause the crust to fracture. The fractures in the crust allow magma to reach the surface. Volcanoes can also occur where two plates push together, or converge. As the plates push together, one plate can sink beneath the other plate. Water that is brought down with the sinking plate eventually helps to form magma, which rises to the surface.

The **Ring of Fire,** shown in **Figure 1,** is one major belt of volcanoes. It includes the many volcanoes that rim the Pacific Ocean. The Ring of Fire includes the volcanoes along the coasts of North and South America and those in Japan and the Philippines.

↻ **Relate Text and Visuals**
Volcanoes often form belts along plate boundaries. How does **Figure 1** illustrate that this statement holds true for North America?

_____
_____
_____
_____
_____
_____

FIGURE 1 ·······················
The Ring of Fire
The Ring of Fire is a belt of volcanoes that circles the Pacific Ocean. As with most of Earth's volcanoes, these volcanoes form along boundaries of tectonic plates.

△ **Develop Hypotheses** Circle a volcano on the map that does not fall along a plate boundary. Why did this volcano form here? Write your answer below. Revise your answer after finishing the lesson.

Original Hypothesis: _____
_____
_____
_____
_____

Revised Hypothesis: _____
_____
_____
_____

Key
▦ Plate boundary
△ Volcano

153

FIGURE 2 ·······························
▷ ART IN MOTION

Volcanoes and Converging Boundaries

Volcanoes often form where two plates collide.

✎ **Compare and Contrast** Shade the arrows to show the direction of plate movement. Then compare and contrast the ways volcanoes form at A and B.

_____

_____

_____

_____

_____

_____

_____

_____

_____

Diverging Boundaries Volcanoes form along the mid-ocean ridges, where two plates move apart. Mid-ocean ridges form long, underwater mountain ranges that sometimes have a rift valley down their center. Along the rift valley, lava pours out of cracks in the ocean floor. This process gradually builds new mountains. Volcanoes also form along diverging plate boundaries on land. For example, large volcanoes are found along the Great Rift Valley in East Africa.

Converging Boundaries Many volcanoes form near converging plate boundaries, where two oceanic plates collide. Through subduction, the older, denser plate sinks into the mantle and creates a deep-ocean trench. Water in the sinking plate eventually leaves the crust and rises into the wedge of the mantle above it. As a result, the melting point of the mantle in the wedge is lowered. So, the mantle partially melts. The magma that forms as a result rises up. This magma can break through the ocean floor, creating volcanoes.

The resulting volcanoes sometime create a string of islands called an **island arc.** Look at **Figure 2.** The curve of an island arc echoes the curve of its deep-ocean trench. Major island arcs include Japan, New Zealand, the Aleutians, and the Caribbean islands.

Volcanoes also occur where an oceanic plate is subducted beneath a continental plate. Collisions of this type produced the volcanoes of the Andes Mountains in South America. In the United States, plate collisions also produced the volcanoes of the Pacific Northwest, including Mount St. Helens and Mount Rainier.

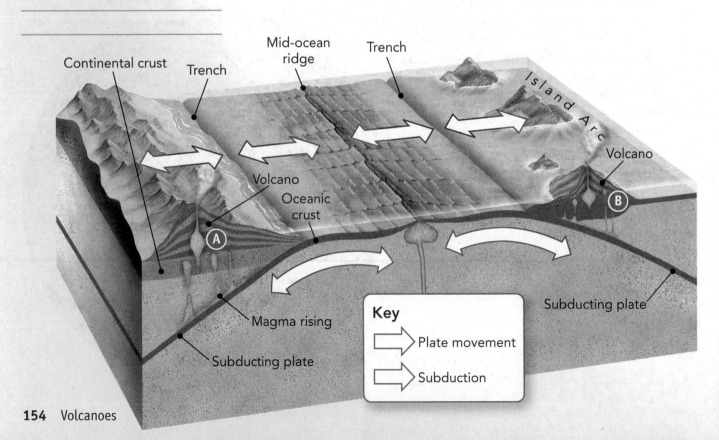

Key
⇨ Plate movement
⇨ Subduction

Hot Spots Not all volcanoes form along plate boundaries. Some volcanoes are the result of "hot spots" in Earth's mantle. A **hot spot** is an area where material from deep within Earth's mantle rises through the crust and melts to form magma. 🔑 **A volcano forms above a hot spot when magma erupts through the crust and reaches the surface.** Hot spots stay in one place for many millions of years while the plate moves over them. Some hot spot volcanoes lie close to plate boundaries. Others lie in the middle of plates. Yellowstone National Park in Wyoming marks a huge hot spot under the North American plate.

apply it!

The Hawaiian Islands have formed one by one as the Pacific plate drifts slowly over a hot spot. This process has taken millions of years.

1 The hot spot is currently forming volcanic mountains on the island of (Oahu/Maui/Hawaii).

2 Do you think Maui will erupt again? Why or why not?

_____

_____

3 [CHALLENGE] Which island is older—Kauai or Maui? Why?

_____

_____

_____

Pacific Ocean

Kauai   Oahu   Maui

Hawaiian Islands

Hawaii

Motion of Pacific plate

Hot spot

🔑 **Assess Your Understanding**

1a. Define A volcano is a mountain that forms in Earth's crust when _____ reaches the surface.

b. Explain Can volcanoes form under water? Why or why not?

_____

_____

_____

Lab ® zone Do the Quick Lab *Where Are Volcanoes Found on Earth's Surface?*

got it?

○ **I get it!** Now I know that volcanoes are found in the following two general locations: _____

_____

_____

○ **I need extra help with** _____

Go to MY SCIENCE 🅢 COACH *online for help with this subject.*

Volcanic Eruptions

UNLOCK THE BIG

🔑 **What Happens When a Volcano Erupts?**

🔑 **What Are the Stages of Volcanic Activity?**

my planet diary

Hotheaded!

Can lava look like hair from the top of your head? It often does in Hawaii! Here, hikers may come across thin strands of hardened material that shimmer like gold in the sunlight. These thin strands are Pele's hair (PAY layz). Pele is the Hawaiian goddess of volcanoes and fire. Her "hair" is actually volcanic glass! It forms when tiny drops of molten lava fly into the air. The wind stretches these drops into threads that are as thin as hair. The glass strands then settle in crevices in the ground, forming clumps.

Read the text. Then answer the question.

How does Pele's hair form?

_____

_____

_____

_____

_____

▶ PLANET DIARY Go to **Planet Diary** to learn more about lava.

Lab zone® Do the Inquiry Warm-Up *How Fast Do Liquids Flow?*

What Happens When a Volcano Erupts?

Lava begins as magma. Magma usually forms in the somewhat soft layer of hot, solid rock that lies in the upper mantle, just below a layer of harder rock. The magma is less dense than the material that is around it. So it rises into any cracks in the rock above. If this magma reaches the surface, a volcano can form.

Vocabulary

- magma chamber • pipe • vent • lava flow • crater
- silica • pyroclastic flow • dormant • extinct

Skills

- ⟳ Reading: Outline
- △ Inquiry: Communicate

Inside a Volcano A volcano is more than a large, cone-shaped mountain. Inside a volcano is a system of passageways through which magma moves, as shown in **Figure 1.**

- **Magma chamber** All volcanoes have a pocket of magma beneath the surface. Beneath a volcano, magma collects in a **magma chamber.** During an eruption, the magma forces its way through one or more cracks in Earth's crust.
- **Pipe** Magma moves upward through a **pipe,** a long tube that extends from Earth's crust up through the top of the volcano, connecting the magma chamber to Earth's surface.
- **Vent** Molten rock and gas leave the volcano through an opening called a **vent.** Some volcanoes have a single central vent at the top. But volcanoes often have vents on the sides also.
- **Lava flow** A **lava flow** is the spread of lava as it pours out of a vent.
- **Crater** A **crater** is a bowl-shaped area that may form at the top of a volcano around the central vent.

Vocabulary High-Use Academic Words A system is a group of parts that function as a whole. Describe why a volcano might be considered a system.

_____
_____
_____
_____
_____

FIGURE 1 ··
> INTERACTIVE ART **Inside a Volcano**
A volcano is made up of many different parts.
✎ **Identify** Place each word in its proper place in the diagram.

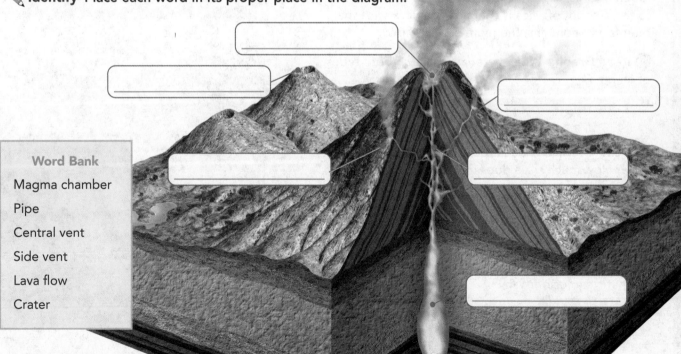

Word Bank

Magma chamber

Pipe

Central vent

Side vent

Lava flow

Crater

A Volcanic Eruption

Perhaps you know that dissolved carbon dioxide gas is trapped in every can of soda. But did you know that dissolved gases are trapped in magma? These dissolved gases are under great pressure. During an eruption, as magma rises toward the surface, the pressure of the surrounding rock on the magma decreases. The dissolved gases begin to expand, forming bubbles. These bubbles are much like the bubbles in the soda can. As pressure falls within the magma, the size of the gas bubbles increases greatly. These expanding gases exert great force. **When a volcano erupts, the force of the expanding gases pushes magma from the magma chamber through the pipe until it flows or explodes out of the vent.** Once magma escapes from the volcano and becomes lava, the remaining gases bubble out.

Two Types of Volcanic Eruptions

Some volcanic eruptions occur gradually, over days, months, or even years. Others are great explosions. **Geologists classify volcanic eruptions as quiet or explosive.** Whether an eruption is quiet or explosive depends in part on the magma's silica content and whether the magma is thin and runny or thick and sticky. **Silica** is a material found in magma that forms from the elements oxygen and silicon. Temperature also helps determine how fluid, or runny, magma is.

do the math!

Magma Composition

Magma varies in composition. It is classified according to the amount of silica it contains. The less silica that the magma contains, the more easily it flows.

1 Read Graphs What materials make up both types of magma?

_____

2 Read Graphs Which type of magma has more silica? How much silica does this magma contain?

_____

_____

3 CHALLENGE Which of these magmas do you think might erupt in a dramatic explosion? Why?

_____

_____

_____

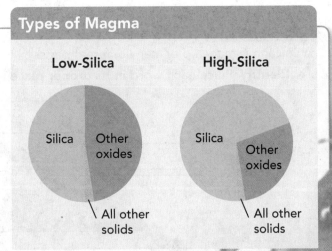

Types of Magma

Low-Silica / High-Silica

Silica — Other oxides — All other solids

Quiet Eruptions A volcano erupts quietly if its magma is hot or low in silica. Hot, low-silica magma is thin and runny and flows easily. The gases in the magma bubble out gently. Low-silica lava oozes quietly from the vent and can flow for many kilometers.

Quiet eruptions can produce different types of lava, as shown in **Figure 2.** The different types of lava harden into different types of rock. Pahoehoe (pah HOH ee hoh ee) forms from fast-moving, hot lava that is thin and runny. The surface of pahoehoe looks like a solid mass of ropelike coils. Aa (AH ah) forms from lava that is cooler and thicker. The lava that aa forms from is also slower-moving. Aa has a rough surface consisting of jagged lava chunks.

Mostly quiet eruptions formed the Hawaiian Islands. On the island of Hawaii, lava pours from the crater near the top of Kilauea. Lava also flows out of long cracks on the volcano's sides. In general, the temperature of magma and lava can range from about 750°C to 1175°C—hot enough to melt copper! Quiet eruptions have built up the island of Hawaii over hundreds of thousands of years.

FIGURE 2 ···
Lava From Quiet Eruptions
Quiet eruptions can produce two different types of lava.

✎ **Interpret Photographs** Which lava is hardening to form aa? Which is hardening to form pahoehoe? Write your answers in the spaces provided. Then, in your own words, describe the texture of each type of rock.

_____

_____

_____

_____

_____

_____

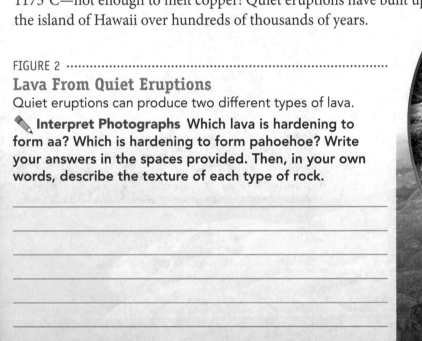

Types of Volcanic Eruptions
1. Quiet eruption
   a. Kilauea
   b. _____
2. Explosive eruption
   a. _____
   b. High-silica magma

Explosive Eruptions A volcano erupts explosively if its magma is high in silica. High-silica magma is thick and sticky. This type of magma can build up in the volcano's pipe, plugging it like a cork in a bottle. Dissolved gases, including water vapor, cannot escape from the thick magma. The trapped gases build up pressure until they explode. The erupting gases and steam push the magma out of the volcano with incredible force. That's what happened during the eruption of Mount St. Helens in Washington State. This eruption is shown in **Figure 3.**

An explosive eruption throws lava powerfully into the air where it breaks into fragments that quickly cool and harden into pieces of different sizes. The smallest pieces are volcanic ash. Volcanic ash is made up of fine, rocky particles as small as a speck of dust. Pebble-sized particles are called cinders. Larger pieces, called bombs, may range from the size of a golf ball to the size of a car.

FIGURE 3 ···

What a Blast!
The explosive eruption of Mount St. Helens in 1980 blew off the top of the mountain.
✏️ **Explain** Read the text in this section. In your own words, explain how dissolved gases caused Mount St. Helens to erupt explosively.

_____
_____
_____
_____
_____
_____

Before 1980 eruption

During 1980 eruption

After 1980 eruption

Volcano Hazards Both quiet eruptions and explosive eruptions can cause damage far from a crater's rim. For example, during a quiet eruption, lava flows from vents, setting fire to, and often burying, everything in its path. A quiet eruption can cover large areas with a thick layer of lava.

During an explosive eruption, a volcano can belch out a mixture of dangerous materials such as hot rock and ash. This mixture of materials can form a fast-moving cloud that rushes down the sides of the volcano. A **pyroclastic flow** (py roh KLAS tik) is the mixture of hot gases, ash, cinders, and bombs that flow down the sides of a volcano when it erupts explosively. Landslides of mud, melted snow, and rock can also form from an explosive eruption. **Figure 4** shows one result of an explosive eruption.

FIGURE 4 ....
Volcano Hazards
In 1991, Mount Pinatubo in the Philippines erupted explosively.

⬚ Communicate What hazards did Mount Pinatubo present to towns near the volcano? Consider the effects of lava, ash, and gases. Work in a small group. List your answers here.

_____

_____

_____

_____

_____

_____

_____

Lab® Do the Lab
zone Investigation
Gelatin Volcanoes.

🔑 **Assess Your Understanding**

1a. Review Two types of volcanic eruptions are

_____

b. Infer Some volcanoes have great glaciers on their slopes. Why might these glaciers be a hazard if a volcano erupts?

_____

_____

_____

_____

got it?

⚪ **I get it!** Now I know that when a volcano erupts, the force of the expanding gases

_____

_____

_____

⚪ I need extra help with _____

Go to MY SCIENCE ⓢ COACH *online for help with this subject.*

161

What Are the Stages of Volcanic Activity?

The activity of a volcano may last from less than a decade to more than 10 million years. But most long-lived volcanoes do not erupt continuously. You can see the pattern of activity by looking at the eruptions of volcanoes in the Cascade Range, shown in **Figure 5**. Mount Jefferson has not erupted in at least 15,000 years. Will it ever erupt again? 🔑 **Geologists often use the terms active, dormant, or extinct to describe a volcano's stage of activity.**

An active, or live, volcano is one that is erupting or has shown signs that it may erupt in the near future. A **dormant,** or sleeping, volcano is a volcano that scientists expect to awaken in the future and become active. An **extinct,** or dead, volcano is a volcano that is unlikely to ever erupt again. For example, hot-spot volcanoes may become extinct after they drift away from the hot spot.

Changes in activity in and around a volcano may give warning shortly before a volcano erupts. Geologists use special instruments to detect these changes. For example, tiltmeters can detect slight surface changes in elevation and tilt caused by magma moving underground. Geologists can also monitor gases escaping from the volcano. They monitor the many small earthquakes that occur around a volcano before an eruption. The upward movement of magma triggers these earthquakes. Also, rising temperatures in underground water may signal that magma is nearing the surface.

Key

→ Direction of plate movement

— Plate boundary

FIGURE 5 ··

Cascade Volcanoes

The Cascade volcanoes have formed as the Juan de Fuca plate sinks beneath the North American plate.

✎ **Develop Hypotheses** Answer the questions.

1. Circle the three volcanoes that appear to be the most active.
2. Why might geologists still consider Mount Jefferson to be an active volcano?

_____

_____

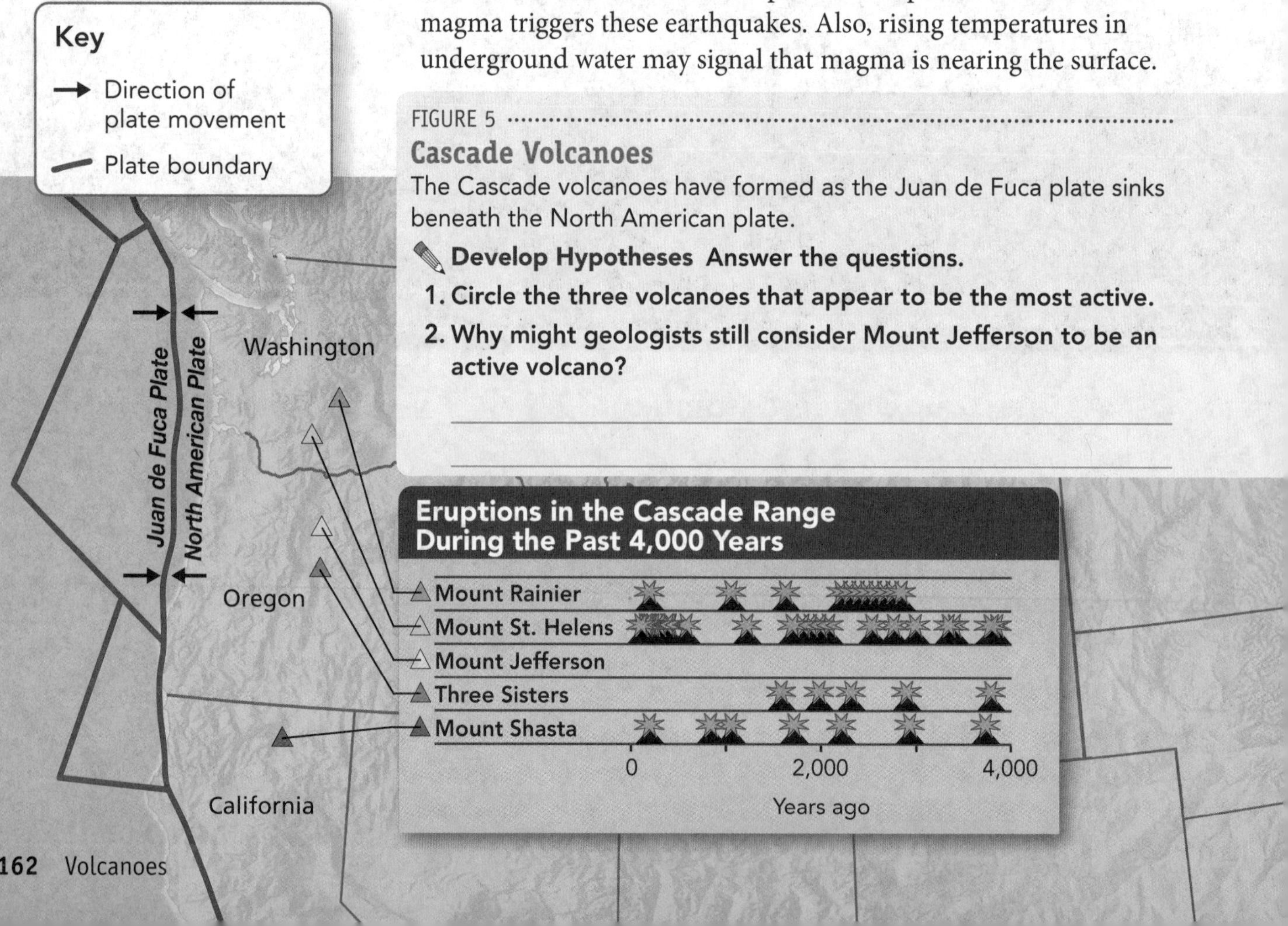

Juan de Fuca Plate

North American Plate

Washington

Oregon

California

Eruptions in the Cascade Range During the Past 4,000 Years

	0	2,000	4,000
Mount Rainier			
Mount St. Helens			
Mount Jefferson			
Three Sisters			
Mount Shasta			

Years ago

EXPLORE THE BIG ?

MT. RAINIER

How does a volcano erupt?

FIGURE 6 ··
> REAL-WORLD INQUIRY Mount Rainier is part of the Cascade volcanoes. All past eruptions of Mount Rainier have included ash and lava.

Magma at Mount Rainier

60% Silica **40%** Other material

North American plate

Seattle

Mount Rainier

Juan de Fuca plate

✎ **Predict** How might Mount Rainier erupt in the future? Use the information given here. Include the role of plate tectonics in your answer. Also discuss Mount Rainier's history and its current stage of activity. (*Hint:* Look at Figure 5.)

_____

_____

_____

_____

_____

_____

_____

_____

_____

_____

_____

_____

Lab zone® Do the Quick Lab *Volcanic Stages.*

🔑 Assess Your Understanding

2a. Identify A volcano that is currently erupting is called an (active/dormant/extinct) volcano.

b. ANSWER THE BIG ? How does a volcano erupt?

_____

_____

_____

_____

_____

got it?

○ I get it! Now I know that the three stages in the life cycle of a volcano are _____

_____

_____

○ I need extra help with _____

_____

Go to MY SCIENCE ⓢ COACH online for help with this subject.

Volcanic Landforms

🔑 **What Landforms Do Lava and Ash Create?**

🔑 **What Landforms Does Magma Create?**

MY PLANET DIARY

BLOG

Posted by: Jackson

Location: West Hills, California

I was subjected to the sight of an active, dangerous volcano. We were on Hawaii, in a small aircraft over the Big Island.

The volcano was quite large—maybe a few miles in diameter. Out of the top of this volcano, there was an immense pillar of smoke, being blown out to sea by the Hawaiian winds. Judging by the patterns of the hardened lava on the slopes of the volcano, it was a shield volcano. The whole area was literally oozing with volcanic activity. Quite a few large depressions had formed where presumably there had been a magma pocket that collapsed in on itself.

Answer the questions below.

1. What landforms were created by the volcano that Jackson saw?

   _____
   _____
   _____

2. If you had a chance to visit Hawaii, would you prefer to see a volcano from an airplane or from the ground? Explain.

   _____
   _____
   _____
   _____

▶ PLANET DIARY Go to **Planet Diary** to learn more about volcanic landforms.

Lab zone ® Do the Inquiry Warm-Up *How Do Volcanoes Change Land?*

Vocabulary

- caldera • cinder cone • composite volcano
- shield volcano • volcanic neck • dike • sill
- batholith

Skills

- Reading: Relate Cause and Effect
- Inquiry: Predict

What Landforms Do Lava and Ash Create?

Lava has built up much of the islands of Hawaii. In fact, for much of Earth's history, volcanic activity on and beneath Earth's surface has built up Earth's land areas and formed much of the ocean crust. **Volcanic eruptions create landforms made of lava, ash, and other materials. These landforms include shield volcanoes, cinder cone volcanoes, composite volcanoes, and lava plateaus. Other landforms include calderas, which are the huge holes left by the collapse of volcanoes.** A caldera is shown in **Figure 1**.

FIGURE 1 ·······························

How a Caldera Forms

Crater Lake in Oregon fills an almost circular caldera.

✎ **Interpret Diagrams In your own words, describe what is happening in the sequence of diagrams below.**

Calderas

Large eruptions can empty the main vent and magma chamber beneath a volcano. With nothing to support it, the mountain top may collapse inward. A **caldera** (kal DAIR uh) is the hole left when a volcano collapses. A lake can form, filling the hole. If the volcano erupts again, a steep-walled cone may form in the middle.

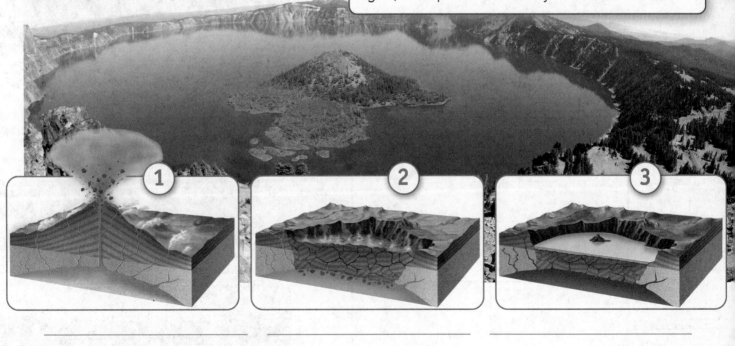

1   2   3

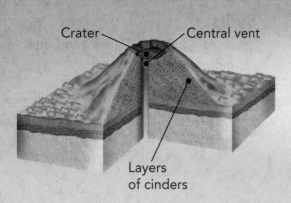

Crater   Central vent

Layers
of cinders

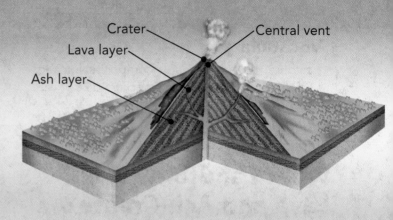

Crater   Central vent
Lava layer
Ash layer

Cinder Cone Volcanoes

If a volcano's magma has high silica content, it will be thick and sticky. So the volcano can erupt explosively, producing ash, cinders, and bombs. These materials can build up around the vent in a steep, cone-shaped hill or small mountain that is called a **cinder cone.** For example, Paricutín in Mexico erupted in 1943 in a farmer's cornfield. The volcano built up a cinder cone that was about 400 meters high.

Composite Volcanoes

Sometimes, the silica content of magma can vary. So eruptions of lava flows alternate with explosive eruptions of ash, cinder, and bombs. The result is a composite volcano. **Composite volcanoes** are tall, cone-shaped mountains in which layers of lava alternate with layers of ash. Mount Fuji in Japan and Mount St. Helens in Washington State are composite volcanoes. Composite volcanoes can be more than 4,800 meters tall.

FIGURE 2 ....

Volcanic Mountains

Lava from volcanoes cools and hardens to form lava plateaus and three types of mountains.

✎ **Read the text at the top of these two pages. Then answer the questions.**

1. **Classify** Identify the type of volcanic landform shown in each of the two photographs at the right.
2. [CHALLENGE] Use the graphic organizer to compare and contrast two types of volcanoes.

	Volcano Type: _____	Volcano Type: _____
Typical size		
Shape		
How the volcano forms		

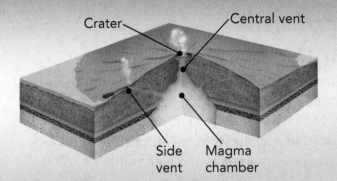

Crater   Central vent

Side vent   Magma chamber

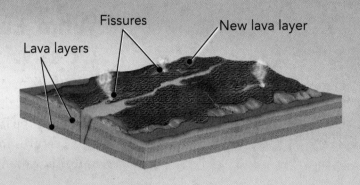

Fissures   New lava layer

Lava layers

Shield Volcanoes

At some spots on Earth's surface, thin layers of lava pour out of a vent and harden on top of previous layers. Such lava flows slowly build a wide, gently sloping mountain called a **shield volcano.** Hot spot volcanoes that form on the ocean floor are usually shield volcanoes. For example, in Hawaii, Mauna Loa rises 9,000 meters from the ocean floor!

Lava Plateaus

Lava can flow out of several long cracks in an area. The thin, runny lava floods the area and travels far before cooling and solidifying. After millions of years, repeated floods of lava can form high, level plateaus. These plateaus are called lava plateaus. The Columbia Plateau is a lava plateau that covers parts of Washington State, Oregon, and Idaho.

apply it!

The Hawaiian Islands are very fertile, or able to support plant growth. In fact, many areas near volcanoes have rich, fertile soil. The rich soil forms after hard lava and ash break down. The ash releases substances that plants need to grow.

1 **Predict** What type of industry might you expect to find on land near volcanoes?

_____

2 **Analyze Costs and Benefits** Lava flows could force people to flee their homes on the island of Hawaii. But in 2006, sales from crops on the island totaled over $153 million. Are the risks worth the rewards? Explain.

_____

_____

_____

> **Lab zone** Do the Quick Lab *Identifying Volcanic Landforms.*

🔑 Assess Your Understanding

1a. Review Volcanic landforms can be built up by (lava only/ash only/both lava and ash).

b. Explain Suppose lava from a certain volcano has built up a steep, cone-shaped hill around a central vent. What can you conclude about the kind of lava that formed the volcano?

_____

_____

_____

got it?

○ **I get it!** Now I know that lava and ash can create the following landforms: _____

_____

_____

○ **I need extra help with** _____

Go to **my science coach** *online for help with this subject.*

What Landforms Does Magma Create?

Sometimes magma cools and hardens into rock before reaching the surface. Over time, forces such as flowing water, ice, or wind may strip away the layers above the hardened magma and expose it. 🔑 **Features formed by magma include volcanic necks, dikes, and sills, as well as dome mountains and batholiths.**

Volcanic Necks
Look at **Figure 3.** The landform that looks like a giant tooth stuck in the ground is Shiprock in New Mexico. Shiprock formed when magma hardened in an ancient volcano's pipe. Later, the softer rock around the pipe wore away, exposing the harder rock inside. A **volcanic neck** forms when magma hardens in a volcano's pipe and the surrounding rock later wears away.

Dikes and Sills
Magma that forces itself across rock layers hardens into a **dike.** Magma that squeezes between horizontal rock layers hardens to form a **sill.**

🔄 **Relate Cause and Effect**
What type of landform can be created when magma hardens in a volcano's pipe?

○ Sill
○ Dike
○ Volcanic neck

FIGURE 3 ·····························

▶ INTERACTIVE ART **Volcanic Necks, Dikes, and Sills**
A dike extends outward from Shiprock, a volcanic neck in New Mexico.

✏️ **Identify** Label the formations. How can you tell which is which?

_____
_____
_____

Volcanic neck

Dike

Sill

CANADA
British Columbia batholith
Idaho batholith
PACIFIC OCEAN
UNITED STATES
Sierra Nevada batholith
Baja batholith

Key
■ Batholith
0   200 mi
0   200 km

Dome Mountains Bodies of hardened magma can create dome mountains. A dome mountain forms when uplift pushes a large body of hardened magma toward the surface. The hardened magma forces the layers of rock to bend upward into a dome shape. Eventually, the rock above the dome mountain wears away, leaving it exposed. This process formed the Black Hills in South Dakota.

Batholiths How large can landforms created by magma be? Look at the map in **Figure 4.** A **batholith** (BATH uh lith) is a mass of rock formed when a large body of magma cools inside the crust. Batholiths form the core of many mountain ranges. Over millions of years, the overlying rock wears away, allowing the batholith to move upward. Flowing water and grinding ice slowly carve the batholith into mountains.

FIGURE 4 ·······························
Batholiths
Batholiths are common in the western United States. The mountains shown here are part of the Sierra Nevada batholith.

✎ **Measure** About how long is the Sierra Nevada batholith? (*Hint:* Use the map and map key.)

_____

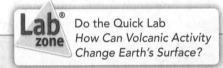

Do the Quick Lab
How Can Volcanic Activity Change Earth's Surface?

⚷ Assess Your Understanding

2a. Review Dikes and sills are two examples of landforms created when (magma/lava) forces its way through cracks in the upper crust.

b. Identify What feature forms when magma cuts across rock layers?

_____

c. Infer Which is older—a dike or the rock layers the dike cuts across? Explain.

_____
_____
_____

got it? ·······························

○ I get it! Now I know that magma creates landforms such as _____
_____

○ I need extra help with _____

Go to MY SCIENCE ⑤ COACH online for help with this subject.

A volcano erupts when the force of expanding gases pushes _____ from the magma chamber through the _____ until it flows or explodes out of the _____.

LESSON 1 Volcanoes and Plate Tectonics

🔑 Volcanic belts form along the boundaries of Earth's plates.

🔑 A volcano forms above a hot spot when magma erupts through the crust and reaches the surface.

Vocabulary
- volcano • magma • lava
- Ring of Fire • island arc
- hot spot

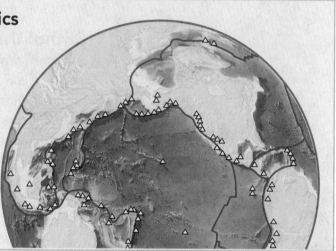

LESSON 2 Volcanic Eruptions

🔑 When a volcano erupts, the force of the expanding gases pushes magma from the magma chamber through the pipe until it flows or explodes out of the vent.

🔑 Geologists classify volcanic eruptions as quiet or explosive.

🔑 Geologists often use the terms active, dormant, or extinct to describe a volcano's stage of activity.

Vocabulary
- magma chamber • pipe • vent • lava flow
- crater • silica • pyroclastic flow • dormant • extinct

LESSON 3 Volcanic Landforms

🔑 Volcanic eruptions create landforms made of lava, ash, and other materials. These landforms include shield volcanoes, cinder cone volcanoes, composite volcanoes, and lava plateaus. Other landforms include calderas, or the huge holes left by the collapse of volcanoes.

🔑 Features formed by magma include volcanic necks, dikes, and sills, as well as dome mountains and batholiths.

Vocabulary
- caldera • cinder cone • composite volcano
- shield volcano • volcanic neck • dike • sill
- batholith

Review and Assessment

LESSON 1 Volcanoes and Plate Tectonics

1. At what point does magma become lava?

   a. below a vent   **b.** inside a pipe

   c. at Earth's surface   **d.** in Earth's mantle

2. Magma reaches the surface by erupting through a volcano, which is a _____

_____

3. Explain Does magma consist only of rock-forming materials? Explain.

_____

_____

_____

4. Relate Cause and Effect What causes volcanoes to form along a mid-ocean ridge?

_____

_____

_____

_____

5. Interpret Diagrams Look at the diagram below. Draw an arrow to indicate the direction of plate movement.

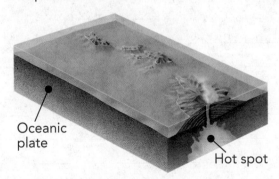

Oceanic plate

Hot spot

6. 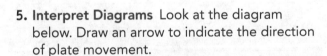 **Write About It** What role do converging plates play in the formation of volcanoes?

LESSON 2 Volcanic Eruptions

7. What type of rock forms from thin and runny, fast-moving lava?

   a. pyroclastic   **b.** silica

   c. aa   **d.** pahoehoe

8. As magma rises to the surface during an eruption, pressure on the magma decreases, allowing gas bubbles to _____

9. Define What is an extinct volcano?

_____

_____

10. Predict How might a volcano be hazardous for plants and animals that live nearby?

_____

_____

_____

_____

11. A certain volcano has erupted only explosively in the past. Another volcano has erupted only quietly. The magma composition for both volcanoes is shown below. Circle the chart showing the magma composition for the volcano that erupted quietly. Explain.

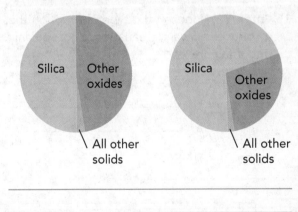

_____

_____

_____

_____

LESSON 3 Volcanic Landforms

12. What type of volcanic mountain is composed of layers of lava that alternate with layers of ash?

    a. cinder cone   **b.** composite volcano

    c. shield volcano   **d.** caldera

13. Sometimes magma creates batholiths, which are _____

_____

_____

14. Name What type of volcano forms when thin layers of lava pour out of a vent and harden on top of previous layers?

_____

Use the illustration to answer the question below.

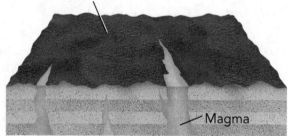

Lava plateau

Magma

15. Infer Why doesn't the type of eruption that produces a lava plateau produce a volcanic mountain instead?

_____

_____

_____

_____

_____

16. Write About It Compare and contrast dikes and sills.

How does a volcano erupt?

17. You are a blogger who interviews geologists. A certain geologist has just returned from studying a nearby volcano. The geologist tells you that the volcano may soon erupt. Write three questions you would ask the geologist about her evidence, her prediction about the type of eruption that will occur, and about the role of plate tectonics in the eruption. Write an answer for each of your questions.

_____

_____

_____

_____

_____

_____

_____

_____

_____

_____

_____

_____

_____

_____

_____

_____

_____

Standardized Test Prep

Multiple Choice

Circle the letter of the best answer.

1. What volcanic feature is forming in the diagram below?

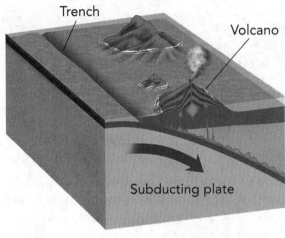

Trench

Volcano

Subducting plate

   A   island arc
   B   mid-ocean ridge
   C   caldera
   D   diverging boundary

2. Which of the following landforms is formed by magma?

   A   caldera
   B   dome mountain
   C   cinder cone volcano
   D   composite volcano

3. What type of feature can form when magma hardens between horizontal layers of rock?

   A   volcanic neck   B   dike
   C   cinder cone   D   sill

4. Which is the first step in the formation of a hot-spot volcano?

   A   Material in the mantle rises and melts.
   B   Lava erupts and forms an island.
   C   Two plates move apart.
   D   Magma flows through a pipe.

5. Which is potentially the most far-reaching hazard of a volcanic eruption?

   A   ash, dust, and gases
   B   landslide
   C   pyroclastic flow
   D   explosion and fire

Constructed Response

Use the diagram below and your knowledge of science to help you answer Question 6. Write your answer on a separate piece of paper.

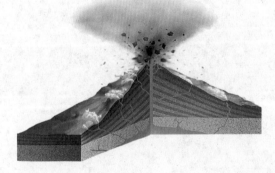

6. A geologist observes the area around a large volcano. She decides that this volcano must once have had an explosive eruption. What evidence might have led her to this conclusion? Discuss the type of magma that produces an explosive eruption and the rocks that would result from an explosive eruption.

Congratulations,
It's an Island!

Island of Surtsey today. People are not allowed to live on the island, but scientists who have permission to research there have built a research station.

On November 15, 1963, a fiery eruption shot out from the icy sea, off the south coast of Iceland, spewing gigantic clouds of ash.

A new island, Surtsey, formed. A volcanic eruption began 130 meters under the sea and forced volcanic ash to the surface. Eventually, the layers of lava and ash formed a volcanic cone that rose above sea level—the birth of Surtsey.

Eruptions continued for nearly four years as steady flows of lava moved outward and cooled in the sea. By the end, Surtsey had an area of 2.7 square kilometers.

It takes a long time for a new island to cool down! At the very base of the island, water flows through layers of loose rocks. When it makes contact with the extremely hot magma chamber deep under the sea, the water evaporates. Steam travels through the layers of porous rock at the base of the island, heating the island up.

To protect Surtsey's environment, the government of Iceland allows only a handful of scientists to visit the delicate new environment. Surtsey is a natural laboratory that gives scientists valuable information on how plant and animal populations begin on a volcanic island.

Research It The arrival of living things on Surtsey is an example of primary succession. Research the organisms that live on Surtsey, or in another area of newly formed lava rock. Make a storyboard showing primary succession on Surtsey or on the area you have researched.

Volcanologists have a seriously hot job. They investigate how, where, and when volcanoes all over the world erupt. You might find a volcanologist studying on the slopes of Mount St. Helens in Washington State, or investigating the crater of Krakatoa in Indonesia. They also try to predict eruptions.

Volcanologists have to take safety very seriously—after all, they work around actively erupting volcanoes! They have to watch out for volcanic gases and landslides. Volcanology is not all about adventures in the field, though. Volcanologists study Earth sciences, math, and physics in order to understand what they observe in the field. They also spend time writing about what they learn, so that other people can learn from their research.

Research It Research the history of a volcano that has been studied by volcanologists. Based on your research, describe how the volcano has erupted and try to predict if and when it might erupt again.

A Dangerous Job

AN EXPLOSIVE SECRET

Scientists once believed that explosive volcanic eruptions could not happen deep under water. Instead, they thought, lava seeped slowly from undersea volcanoes.

But in 2008, scientists found jagged pieces of glassy volcanic rock around undersea volcanoes in the Arctic Ocean. Seeping lava does not cause jagged glassy rocks. Explosive eruptions do.

The Gakkel Ridge is a long crack in the floor of the Arctic Ocean. The two sides of the crack are spreading apart slowly. As a result, gas builds up in pockets of magma beneath the ridge. Eventually the pressure of this gas causes explosive volcanic eruptions. The eruptions release lava, heat, gases, and trace metals into the ocean water. The jagged rocks that scientists found came from these explosions.

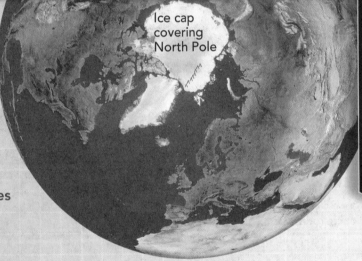

Ice cap covering North Pole

▲ The Gakkel Ridge (in red) is located under the Arctic Ocean.

Research It Research volcanic activity along another mid-ocean ridge, such as the Juan de Fuca Ridge. Prepare a graphic organizer comparing the timing, intensity, and volcanic activities along the two mid-ocean ridges.

WHY DOES THIS ROCK LOOK LIKE A SPONGE?

What processes break down rock?

What could make a rock so full of holes? These rock formations, called *tafoni*, are found along the coast of California at Salt Point State Park. **Develop Hypotheses** Explain what you think caused the holes in these rock formations.

_____

_____

_____

_____

_____

_____

_____

> UNTAMED SCIENCE Watch the **Untamed Science** video to learn more about the forces that break down rock.

Weathering and Soil

6 Getting Started

Check Your Understanding

1. Background Read the paragraph below and then answer the question.

The **minerals** that make up a rock determine some of the rock's properties. The properties of a rock can change in two ways: **physical changes** and **chemical changes.** Physical changes change the shape or size of a rock, but not its composition. Chemical changes can change minerals into other substances, changing the composition of the rock.

> **Minerals** are naturally occurring, inorganic solids that have specific crystal structures and specific chemical compositions.
>
> A **physical change** is any change that does not alter the chemical composition of a substance.
>
> A **chemical change** produces one or more new substances.

- How can you tell if a physical change has occurred in a rock?

_____

_____

▶ **MY READING WEB** If you had trouble answering the question above, visit **My Reading Web** and type in *Weathering and Soil.*

Vocabulary Skill

Suffixes A suffix is a letter or group of letters added to the end of a word to change its meaning and often its part of speech. The suffix *-ation* added to a verb can form a noun that means "process of" or "action of." For example, the suffix *-ation* added to *observe* forms the noun *observation.*

Suffix	Meaning	Part of Speech	Examples
-ation, -sion	Process of, action of	Noun	Abrasion, oxidation, conservation
-ing	Showing continuous action	Noun or adjective	Weathering, plowing

2. Quick Check Circle the correct words to complete the sentence.

- People who (conserve/conservation) energy are contributing to energy (conserve/conservation).

mechanical weathering

soil

decomposer

contour plowing

Chapter Preview

LESSON 1
- uniformitarianism
- erosion
- weathering
- mechanical weathering
- chemical weathering
- abrasion
- frost wedging
- oxidation
- permeable

⟳ **Relate Cause and Effect**
△ **Control Variables**

LESSON 2
- soil
- bedrock
- humus
- fertility
- loam
- pH scale
- soil horizon
- topsoil
- subsoil
- decomposer

⟳ **Ask Questions**
△ **Form Operational Definitions**

LESSON 3
- natural resource
- soil conservation
- crop rotation
- contour plowing
- conservation plowing

⟳ **Summarize**
△ **Observe**

> **VOCAB FLASH CARDS** For extra help with vocabulary, visit **Vocab Flash Cards** and type in *Weathering and Soil.*

179

Rocks and Weathering

UNLOCK THE BIG
?

🔑 **What Breaks Down Rocks?**

🔑 **What Causes Weathering?**

🔑 **How Fast Does Weathering Occur?**

my planet Diary   DISCOVERY

Wearing Away Mars

Does this scene look like a desert? It is—but not on Earth! These rocks are found on Mars. Blowing sand wears away some rocks on the surface. Fog containing acid dissolves and breaks down other rocks. Over time, the rocks break down into small particles, covering the planet with reddish sand.

Lab zone® Do the Inquiry Warm-Up *How Fast Can It Fizz?*

✏️ **Communicate** After you read about the rocks on Mars, answer these questions with a partner.

1. What are two processes that break down rocks on Mars?

   _____

   _____

2. Give an example of rocks you have seen that were changed by natural processes.

   _____

   _____

   _____

▶ **PLANET DIARY** Go to **Planet Diary** to learn more about rocks and weathering.

What Breaks Down Rocks?

Even the hardest rocks wear down over time—on Earth or on Mars. Natural processes break down rocks and carry the pieces away.

How do scientists know what processes shaped Earth in the past? Geologists make inferences based on the principle of **uniformitarianism** (yoon uh fawrm uh TAYR ee un iz um). This principle states that the geologic processes that operate today also operated in the past. Scientists can infer that ancient landforms and features formed through the same processes they observe today.

Vocabulary
- uniformitarianism • erosion • weathering
- mechanical weathering • chemical weathering
- abrasion • frost wedging • oxidation • permeable

Skills
↻ Reading: Relate Cause and Effect
△ Inquiry: Control Variables

Erosion Erosion (ee ROH zhun) is the process of wearing down and carrying away rocks. Erosion includes the breaking of rocks into smaller pieces. It also involves the removal of rock particles by wind, water, ice, or gravity.

Weathering Weathering is the process that breaks down rock and other substances. Heat, cold, water, ice, and gases all contribute to weathering. The forces that wear down mountains like those in **Figure 1** also cause bicycles to rust, paint to peel, and sidewalks to crack. **Erosion works continuously to weather and carry away rocks at Earth's surface.**

FIGURE 1 ·······························

Effects of Weathering
The Sierra Nevada (below) are much younger than the Appalachians (right). ✎ Predict **How might the Sierras change in the future? Explain your answer.**

_____

_____

_____

Lab zone® Do the Quick Lab
Freezing and Thawing.

Assess Your Understanding

got it? ·······························

○ I get it! Now I know that erosion and weathering _____

_____

○ I need extra help with _____

   Go to my science ⟨s⟩ coach *online for help with this subject.*

What Causes Weathering?

If you hit a rock with a hammer, the rock may break into pieces. Some forces of weathering break rock into pieces, as a hammer does. The type of weathering in which rock is physically broken into smaller pieces is called **mechanical weathering**. A second type of weathering, called chemical weathering, also breaks down rock. **Chemical weathering** is the process that breaks down rock through chemical changes.

Mechanical Weathering If you have seen rocks that are cracked or split in layers, then you have seen rocks that have undergone mechanical weathering. Mechanical weathering usually works slowly. But over very long periods of time, it does more than wear down rocks. Mechanical weathering, as part of erosion, eventually wears away whole mountains.

FIGURE 2 ·····························
> INTERACTIVE ART Forces of
Mechanical Weathering
✎ **Classify** Match each description to an example shown in the photos on the next page.

[CHALLENGE] How might more than one agent of mechanical weathering operate in the same place?

_____
_____
_____
_____
_____

1 Animal Actions

Animals that burrow in the ground—including moles, gophers, prairie dogs, and some insects—loosen and break apart rocks in the soil.

2 Freezing and Thawing

When water freezes in a crack in a rock, it expands and makes the crack bigger. The process of frost wedging also widens cracks in sidewalks and causes potholes in streets.

3 Plant Growth

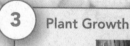

Plant roots enter cracks in rocks. As roots grow, they force the cracks apart. Over time, the roots of even small plants can pry apart cracked rocks.

4 Release of Pressure

As erosion removes material from the surface of a mass of rock, pressure on the rock is reduced. This release of pressure causes the outside of the rock to crack and flake off like the layers of an onion.

5 Abrasion

Sand and other rock particles that are carried by wind, water, or ice can wear away exposed rock surfaces like sandpaper on wood.

Agents of Mechanical Weathering 🔑 The
natural agents of mechanical weathering include freezing and
thawing, release of pressure, plant growth, actions of animals, and
abrasion. **Abrasion** (uh BRAY zhun) refers to the wearing away of
rock by rock particles carried by water, ice, wind, or gravity. Human
activities, such as mining and farming, can also cause weathering.

In cool climates, the most important agent of mechanical
weathering is the freezing and thawing of water. Water seeps into
cracks in rocks and freezes there, expanding as it freezes. The ice
then forces the rock apart. Wedges of ice in rocks widen and deepen
cracks. This process is called **frost wedging.** When the ice melts,
water seeps deeper into the cracks. With repeated freezing and
thawing, the cracks slowly expand until pieces of rock break off.

Chemical Weathering

Chemical weathering can produce new minerals as it breaks down rock. For example, granite is made up of several minerals, including feldspars. As a result of chemical weathering, the feldspar minerals eventually change to clay.

Chemical and mechanical weathering often work together. Chemical weathering creates holes or soft spots in rock, so the rock breaks apart more easily. As rocks break into pieces, more surface area is exposed to chemical weathering, as shown in **Figure 3**.

Agents of Chemical Weathering

The agents of chemical weathering include water, oxygen, carbon dioxide, living organisms, and acid rain.

Water Water weathers some rock by dissolving it. Water also carries other substances that dissolve or break down rock, including oxygen, carbon dioxide, and other chemicals.

FIGURE 3

Weathering and Surface Area

Weathering breaks rock into smaller pieces. While the pieces are usually irregularly shaped, you can model the process with cubes. The diagram shows what would happen if a rock cube broke into smaller cubes.

✎ **Calculate** By how much does the surface area increase? How would the rate of weathering change?

_____

_____

_____

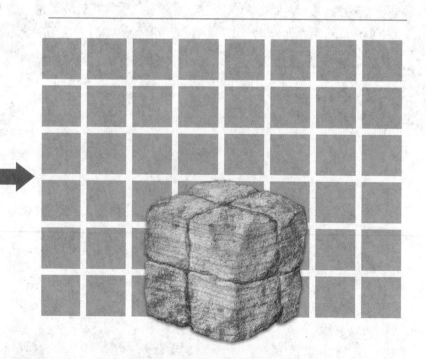

FIGURE 4 ··································

> ART IN MOTION **Chemical Weathering**
Acid rain chemically weathered the statue of the lion.
✎ **Infer** Which agent of chemical weathering most likely formed this limestone cavern?

_____

_____

_____

Oxygen The oxygen gas in air is an important cause of chemical weathering. Iron combines with oxygen in the presence of water in a process called **oxidation.** The product of iron oxidation is rust. Rust makes rock soft and crumbly and gives it a red or brown color.

Carbon Dioxide Another gas found in air, carbon dioxide, also causes chemical weathering when it dissolves in water. The result is a weak acid called carbonic acid. Carbonic acid easily weathers some kinds of rocks, such as marble and limestone.

Living Organisms As a plant's roots grow, they produce weak acids that slowly dissolve rock around the roots. Lichens—plantlike organisms that grow on rocks—also produce weak acids.

Acid Rain Rainwater is naturally slightly acidic. Burning coal, oil, and gas for energy can pollute the air with sulfur, carbon, and nitrogen compounds. These compounds react with water vapor in clouds, making acids that are stronger than normal rainwater. These acids mix with raindrops and fall as acid rain. Acid rain causes very rapid chemical weathering of rock.

Lab zone ® Do the Quick Lab *Rusting Away.*

🔑 **Assess Your Understanding**

1a. Define (Mechanical/chemical) weathering physically breaks rock into smaller pieces.

b. Classify Circle the examples of chemical weathering. Underline the examples of mechanical weathering. Freezing and thawing, oxidation, water dissolving chemicals, abrasion, acid rain

c. Predict Many ancient monuments are made of marble. Some are located in highly polluted cities. How might the pollution affect the monuments?

_____

_____

_____

got it? ·····································

○ **I get it!** Now I know that weathering is

caused by_____

_____

○ **I need extra help with** _____

Go to **MY SCIENCE COACH** *online for help with this subject.*

How Fast Does Weathering Occur?

Visitors to New England's historic cemeteries may notice a surprising fact. Slate tombstones carved in the 1700s are less weathered and easier to read than marble gravestones from the 1800s. Why is this so? Some kinds of rocks weather more rapidly than others. **The most important factors that determine the rate at which weathering occurs are the type of rock and the climate.**

Type of Rock The minerals that make up the rock determine how fast it weathers. Rocks that are made of minerals that do not dissolve easily will weather slowly. Rocks weather faster if they are made of minerals that do dissolve easily.

Some rocks weather more easily because they are permeable. **Permeable** (PUR mee uh bul) means that a material is full of tiny, connected air spaces that allow water to seep through it. The spaces increase the surface area of the rock. As water seeps through the spaces in the rock, it carries chemicals that dissolve the rock. The water also removes material broken down by weathering.

do the math!

Which Weathered Faster?

The data table shows how much stone was lost due to weathering for two identical pieces of limestone from different locations.

1 Graph Use the data to make a double-line graph. Be sure to label the axes and provide a key and a title.

2 Draw Conclusions (Stone A/Stone B) weathered at a faster rate.

Weathering Rates of Limestone		
Time (years)	Thickness of Stone Lost (mm)	
	Stone A	Stone B
200	1.75	0.80
400	3.50	1.60
600	5.25	2.40
800	7.00	3.20
1,000	8.75	4.00

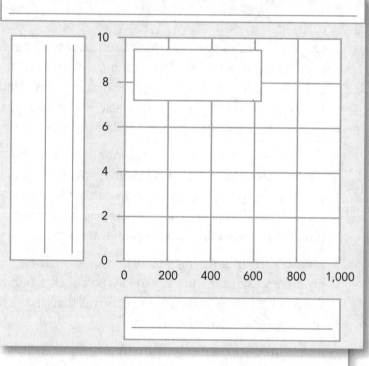

3 Infer What can you infer caused the difference in the rates of weathering?

_____

_____

_____

Climate
Climate refers to the average weather conditions in an area. Both chemical and mechanical weathering occur faster in wet climates. Rainfall provides the water needed for chemical changes as well as for freezing and thawing.

Chemical reactions occur faster at higher temperatures. That is why chemical weathering occurs more quickly where the climate is both hot and wet. Human activities, such as those that produce acid rain, also increase the rate of weathering.

 Relate Cause and Effect
Underline the reason that chemical weathering occurs faster in hot climates.

Tombstones 1 and 2 are both around 200 years old and are in the same cemetery.

1 (Stone 1/Stone 2) has weathered more.

2 What might explain the difference?

_____
_____
_____

3 **Control Variables** How do you know that the type of rock is the only difference between the tombstones?

_____
_____

Stone 1

Stone 2

Lab zone Do the Quick Lab
It's All on the Surface.

🔑 Assess Your Understanding

2a. **Relate Cause and Effect** Why does permeable rock weather more quickly than less permeable rock?

_____
_____
_____

b. Infer Why are tombstones in a cemetery useful for comparing rates of weathering?

_____
_____
_____

got it?

○ **I get it!** Now I know that the rate of weathering depends on_____

○ **I need extra help with** _____

Go to MY SCIENCE **COACH** *online for help with this subject.*

187

How Soil Forms

UNLOCK THE BIG

🔑 **What Is Soil?**

🔑 **How Do Living Things Affect Soil?**

my planet Diary

Life Beneath Your Feet

The soil beneath your feet may not look very interesting, but it's packed with life! Many microscopic organisms live in soil and affect the lives of other organisms. Some bacteria, like the *Pseudomonas* shown above, can protect plants from disease. Hundreds of thousands of soil mites can live in a single square meter of soil. And tiny worms called nematodes eat plants, bacteria, fungi, and even other nematodes!

Bacterium

FUN FACT

Use what you have read and your experiences to answer the questions below.

1. What are some examples of organisms that live in soil?

_____

_____

_____

2. Describe soil you have seen or touched. What did it feel like? How did it smell? What creatures did you see in it?

_____

_____

_____

_____

_____

▶ PLANET DIARY Go to **Planet Diary** to learn more about soil.

Nematode

Mite

Lab zone® Do the Inquiry Warm-Up *What Is Soil?*

Vocabulary
- soil • bedrock • humus • fertility • loam
- pH scale • soil horizon • topsoil • subsoil
- decomposer

Skills
🔁 Reading: Ask Questions
△ Inquiry: Form Operational Definitions

What Is Soil?

Have you ever seen a plant growing in a crack in a rock? It may look like the plant is growing on solid rock, but it isn't. Plants can only grow when soil begins to form in the cracks. **Soil** is the loose, weathered material on Earth's surface in which plants can grow.

Soil Composition 🔑 **Soil is a mixture of rock particles, minerals, decayed organic material, water, and air.** One of the main ingredients of soil comes from bedrock. **Bedrock** is the solid layer of rock beneath the soil. Once bedrock is exposed to air, water, and living things, it gradually weathers into smaller and smaller particles that are the most common components of soil.

The particles of rock in soil are classified by size as gravel, sand, silt, and clay. **Figure 1** shows the relative sizes of these particles. Together, gravel, sand, silt, and clay make up the portion of soil that comes from weathered rock.

The decayed organic material in soil is called humus. **Humus** (HYOO mus) is a dark-colored substance that forms as plant and animal remains decay. Humus helps create spaces in soil for air and water. Humus also contains nutrients that plants need.

FIGURE 1 ··

Soil Particle Size
The particles shown here have been enlarged.

✏️ **Graph** Mark where a 1.5-mm particle would fall on the graph. What type of particle is it? _____

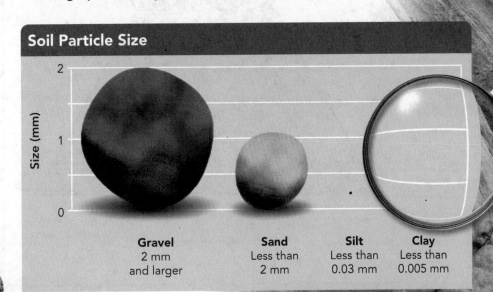

Soil Particle Size

Size (mm)

Gravel	Sand	Silt	Clay
2 mm and larger	Less than 2 mm	Less than 0.03 mm	Less than 0.005 mm

189

Vocabulary **Suffixes** How does adding the suffix *-ity* change the form of the word *fertile*?

_____

_____

_____

🔄 **Ask Questions** Before you read the section Soil pH, write a question that you would like answered. Then write the answer.

_____

_____

_____

_____

Soil Fertility Fertile soil is rich in the nutrients that plants need to grow. The **fertility** of soil is a measure of how well the soil supports plant growth. Soil that is rich in humus generally has high fertility. Sandy soil containing little humus has low fertility.

Soil Texture Sandy soil feels coarse and grainy, but soil with lots of clay feels smooth and silky. These differences are differences in texture. Soil texture depends on the size of the soil particles.

Soil texture is important for plant growth. Soil that is mostly clay may hold too much water and not enough air. In contrast, sandy soil loses water quickly. Plants may die for lack of air or water. Soil that is made up of about equal parts of clay, sand, and silt is called **loam.** Loam is the best soil for growing most plants.

Soil pH Soil can be acidic or basic. Acidic substances react with some metals and turn blue litmus paper red. Basic substances feel slippery and turn red litmus paper blue. The **pH scale** measures acidity. A substance with a pH less than 4 is strongly acidic. A substance with a pH of 7 is neither acidic nor basic. (Pure water has a pH of 7.) A substance with a pH greater than 10 is strongly basic. Most garden plants grow best in soil with a pH between 6 and 7.5. Some soils can have a pH as low as 4, which is quite acidic.

apply it!

This diagram is called the soil texture triangle. To use the triangle, first find the percentages of silt, sand, and clay in a soil sample. Then locate each percentage on its side of the triangle. The point where the lines meet tells you the type of soil. (This example shows clay loam soil that is 40% silt, 30% clay, and 30% sand.)

❶ **Interpret Diagrams** What percentage of silty clay loam is silt? (*Hint:* Look at the corners of the silty clay loam area.)

_____

_____

❷ **Interpret Diagrams** A soil sample has 20% silt, 10% clay, and 70% sand. What kind of soil is it? (*Hint:* Draw lines to find out.)

_____

❸ **Form Operational Definitions** How would you define silty clay soil?

_____

_____

The Process of Soil Formation 🔑 **Soil forms as rock is broken down by weathering and mixes with other materials on the surface.** Soil forms constantly wherever bedrock weathers. Soil formation continues over a long period of time.

Gradually, soil develops layers called horizons. A **soil horizon** is a layer of soil that differs in color, texture, and composition from the layers above or below it. **Figure 2** shows how scientists classify soil into three horizons.

C Horizon The C horizon forms as bedrock begins to weather. The rock breaks up into small particles.

A Horizon The A horizon is made up of **topsoil,** a crumbly, dark brown soil that is a mixture of humus, clay, and other minerals. Topsoil forms as plants add organic material to the soil, and plant roots weather pieces of rock.

B Horizon The B horizon, often called **subsoil,** usually consists of clay and other particles of rock, but little humus. It forms as rainwater washes these materials down from the A horizon.

FIGURE 2 ······························
Soil Layers
✏️ **Use the diagram to answer the questions.**

1. **Compare and Contrast** Which layer contains the most organic material?

_____

2. **CHALLENGE** In what climates would you expect soil to form fastest? Why?

_____

_____

_____

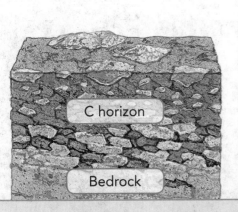

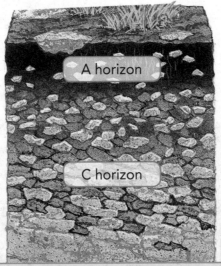

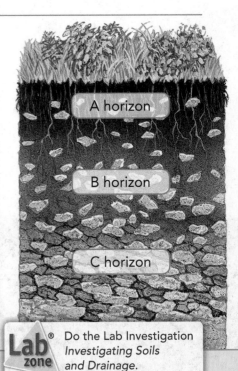

C horizon

Bedrock

A horizon

C horizon

A horizon

B horizon

C horizon

Lab zone ® Do the Lab Investigation *Investigating Soils and Drainage.*

🔑 Assess Your Understanding

1a. List What are three characteristics used to describe soil?

_____

b. Compare and Contrast How are the A, B, and C horizons different?

_____

_____

_____

_____

got it? ································

○ **I get it!** Now I know that soil forms from _____

_____

_____

_____

○ **I need extra help with** _____

Go to **MY SCIENCE** 🅢 **COACH** *online for help with this subject.*

How Do Living Things Affect Soil?

Many organisms live in soil. 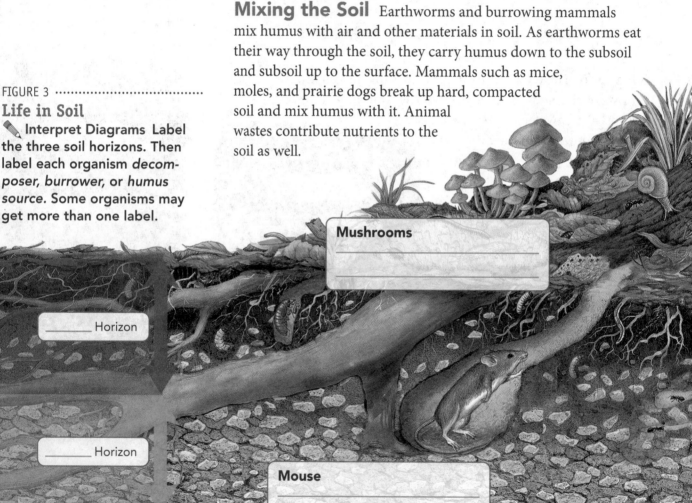 Some soil organisms make humus, the material that makes soil fertile. Other soil organisms mix the soil and make spaces in it for air and water.

Forming Humus Dead leaves, roots, and other plant materials contribute most of the organic remains that form humus. Humus forms in a process called decomposition. **Decomposers** are the organisms that break the remains of dead organisms into smaller pieces and digest them with chemicals. This material then mixes with the soil as humus. Soil decomposers include fungi (such as mushrooms), bacteria, worms, and other organisms.

Mixing the Soil Earthworms and burrowing mammals mix humus with air and other materials in soil. As earthworms eat their way through the soil, they carry humus down to the subsoil and subsoil up to the surface. Mammals such as mice, moles, and prairie dogs break up hard, compacted soil and mix humus with it. Animal wastes contribute nutrients to the soil as well.

FIGURE 3 ··························

Life in Soil

Interpret Diagrams Label the three soil horizons. Then label each organism *decomposer*, *burrower*, or *humus source*. Some organisms may get more than one label.

Mushrooms
_____
_____

_____ Horizon

_____ Horizon

_____ Horizon

Mouse
_____
_____

Bedrock

EXPLORE THE BIG Q ?

From Rock to Soil

What processes break down rock?

FIGURE 4 ···

> INTERACTIVE ART   The illustrations show a rock and rich, fertile soil. In the remaining boxes, draw the steps that could change the rock into the soil. Label the processes in each drawing. Include at least two types of weathering.

_____   _____   _____   _____   _____
_____   _____   _____   _____   _____

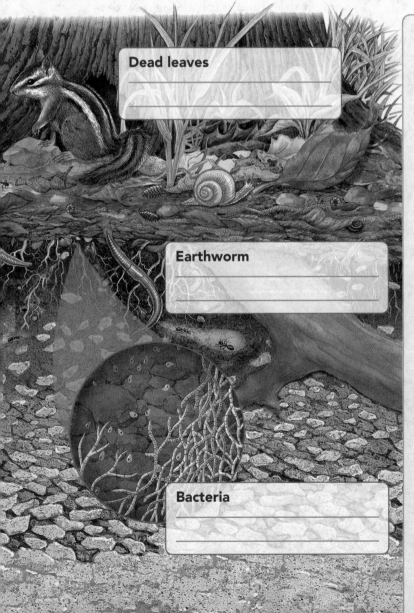

Dead leaves
_____
_____

Earthworm
_____
_____

Bacteria
_____
_____

Lab® zone   Do the Quick Lab
The Contents of Soil.

🗝 Assess Your Understanding

2a. Identify Organisms contribute to soil
formation by _____
and _____

b. Describe List two types of decomposers.
_____

c. ANSWER THE BIG Q ? What processes break down
rock? Include the processes of soil
formation in your answer.
_____
_____
_____
_____

got it? ···

○ **I get it!** Now I know that living things affect
soil by _____
_____

○ **I need extra help with** _____

Go to MY SCIENCE ⓢ COACH *online for help
with this subject.*

193

Soil Conservation

🔑 **How Can Soil Lose Its Value?**

🔑 **How Can Soil Be Conserved?**

MY PLANET DIARY

DISASTER

The Dust Bowl

In the 1800s, farmers began to settle the Great Plains of the central United States. Some were used to thin, rocky soil. They were excited to find prairies full of thick, rich soil covered with grasses. Farmers quickly plowed up most of the available land. By 1930, almost all of the Great Plains had been turned into farms or ranches.

But as they plowed, farmers dug up plants that held the soil together. Then a long drought in the 1930s caused the soil to dry out. The soil in parts of the Great Plains, including Texas, Oklahoma, Kansas, and Colorado, turned to dust. Without plants to hold the soil in place, it blew away. Wind caused huge dust storms and clouds of black dirt. Farms throughout the central United States were destroyed. The area most affected by this became known as the Dust Bowl.

Look at the photograph and review the information about the Dust Bowl. Then answer the questions below.

1. What happened during the Dust Bowl?

_____

_____

_____

2. Why do you think the Dust Bowl is considered a disaster?

_____

_____

_____

_____

▶ PLANET DIARY Go to **Planet Diary** to learn more about how soil can be damaged.

Lab zone® Do the Inquiry Warm-Up *How Can You Keep Soil From Washing Away?*

Vocabulary
- natural resource
- crop rotation
- conservation plowing
- soil conservation
- contour plowing

Skills
- Reading: Summarize
- Inquiry: Observe

How Can Soil Lose Its Value?

Today, much of the area affected by the Dust Bowl is once again covered with farms. But the Dust Bowl was a reminder of how important soil is for humans.

The Value of Soil A **natural resource** is anything in the environment that humans use. Soil is one of Earth's most valuable natural resources because everything that lives on land, including humans, depends directly or indirectly on soil. Plants depend directly on the soil to live and grow. Humans and animals depend on plants—or on other animals that depend on plants—for food.

Fertile soil is valuable because there is a limited supply of it. Less than one eighth of the land on Earth has soils that are well suited for farming. Soil is also in limited supply because it takes a long time to form. It can take hundreds of years for just a few centimeters of soil to form.

FIGURE 1 ··
Prairie Grasses
Prairie soils like those found on the Great Plains are still among the most fertile in the world.

✏ **Make Generalizations** Based on the illustration below, how do you think prairie grasses protect soil?

_____

_____

✏ **Summarize** Write two sentences to summarize the value of soil.

_____

_____

_____

_____

_____

_____

apply it!

The two photos show samples of different soils.

1 ◭ **Observe** List two visible differences between the two soil samples.

_____

_____

_____

_____

_____

2 [CHALLENGE] Which sample would you predict is more fertile? (Sample A/Sample B)

Soil Damage and Loss Human actions and changes in the environment can affect soil. ☞ **The value of soil is reduced when soil loses its fertility or when topsoil is lost due to erosion.**

Loss of Fertility Soil can be damaged when it loses its fertility. This can happen through loss of moisture and nutrients. This type of soil damage occurred in large parts of the southern United States in the late 1800s, where cotton was the only crop. Cotton used up many nutrients in the soil, and those nutrients were not replaced.

Loss of Topsoil Whenever soil is exposed, water and wind can quickly erode it. Plant cover can protect soil from erosion in several ways. Plants break the force of falling rain, and plant roots hold the soil together.

Wind erosion is most likely to occur in areas where farming methods are not suited to dry conditions. For example, wind erosion contributed to the Dust Bowl on the Great Plains. Farmers plowed up the prairie grasses that held the soil together. Without roots to hold it, the soil blew away more easily.

Lab® zone Do the Quick Lab
Using It Up.

☞ Assess Your Understanding

1a. Explain Why is soil valuable?

_____

_____

_____

b. Relate Cause and Effect How does wind erosion affect the value of soil?

_____

_____

_____

got it? ....

○ **I get it!** Now I know that soil can lose value when _____

_____

○ **I need extra help with** _____

Go to MY SCIENCE ⬤ COACH *online for help with this subject.*

How Can Soil Be Conserved?

Today, many farmers use methods of soil conservation. **Soil conservation** is the management of soil to limit its destruction. 🔑 **Soil can be conserved through practices such as contour plowing, conservation plowing, and crop rotation.**

Changes in Crops Some crops, such as corn and cotton, take up large amounts of nutrients from the soil. Others, such as peanuts, alfalfa, and beans, help restore soil fertility. These plants, called legumes, have small lumps on their roots that contain nitrogen-fixing bacteria. These bacteria make the important nutrient nitrogen available in a form that plants can use.

In **crop rotation,** a farmer plants different crops in a field each year. One year, the farmer plants a crop such as corn or cotton. The next year, the farmer plants crops that use fewer soil nutrients, such as oats, barley, or rye. The year after that the farmer sows legumes to restore the nutrient supply.

Changes in Plowing In **contour plowing,** farmers plow their fields along the curves of a slope instead of in straight rows. This method helps slow the runoff of excess rainfall and prevents it from washing the soil away. In **conservation plowing,** dead weeds and stalks of the previous year's crop are plowed into the ground to help return soil nutrients, retain moisture, and hold soil in place.

Nodules containing bacteria

FIGURE 2 ·······················

> REAL-WORLD INQUIRY

Farming Methods
Peanuts (above) are useful for crop rotation. The bacteria on their roots make nitrogen available. Contour plowing (left) is one way to conserve soil.

✎ **Make Judgments** Which method would you recommend to a farmer who wanted to maintain soil fertility?

_____

_____

_____

_____

Lab zone Do the Quick Lab *Soil Conservation.*

🔑 Assess Your Understanding

got it? ··

○ I get it! Now I know that soil can be conserved by_____

_____

○ I need extra help with _____

Go to **my science COACH** online for help with this subject.

6 Study Guide

Processes of _____ and _____ break down rocks and carry them away. The broken rocks combine with _____ to make soil.

LESSON 1 Rocks and Weathering

🔑 Erosion works continuously to weather and carry away rocks at Earth's surface.

🔑 The natural agents of mechanical weathering include freezing and thawing, release of pressure, plant growth, actions of animals, and abrasion. The agents of chemical weathering include water, oxygen, carbon dioxide, living organisms, and acid rain.

🔑 The most important factors that determine the rate at which weathering occurs are the type of rock and the climate.

Vocabulary
• uniformitarianism • erosion • weathering • mechanical weathering
• chemical weathering • abrasion • frost wedging • oxidation • permeable

---

LESSON 2 How Soil Forms

🔑 Soil is a mixture of rock particles, minerals, decayed organic material, water, and air. Soil forms as rock is broken down by weathering and mixes with other materials on the surface.

🔑 Some soil organisms make humus, the material that makes soil fertile. Other soil organisms mix the soil and make spaces in it for air and water.

Vocabulary
• soil • bedrock • humus • fertility • loam • pH scale
• soil horizon • topsoil • subsoil • decomposer

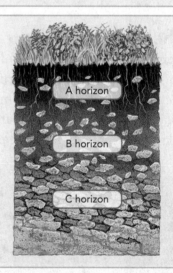

LESSON 3 Soil Conservation

🔑 The value of soil is reduced when soil loses its fertility and when topsoil is lost due to erosion.

🔑 Soil can be conserved through practices such as contour plowing, conservation plowing, and crop rotation.

Vocabulary
• natural resource • soil conservation • crop rotation
• contour plowing • conservation plowing

Review and Assessment

LESSON 1 Rocks and Weathering

1. The process that splits rock through freezing and thawing is called

   a. abrasion.

   b. dissolving.

   c. erosion.

   d. frost wedging.

2. Which of the following is caused by acid rain?

   a. abrasion

   b. dissolving of rock

   c. release of pressure

   d. oxidation

3. **Classify** Classify each of the following as mechanical or chemical weathering.

   Cracks in a sidewalk next to a tree

   _____

   Limestone with holes like Swiss cheese

   _____

   A rock that slowly turns reddish brown

   _____

4. **Predict** If mechanical weathering breaks a rock into pieces, how would this affect the rate at which the rock weathers chemically?

   _____

   _____

5. **Write About It** A community group wants to build a monument in a city park. They want the monument to last for a long time. They ask you for advice on choosing long-lasting stone for the monument. Write a proposal explaining what factors would affect how long the monument would last.

LESSON 2 How Soil Forms

6. Soil that is made up of roughly equal parts of clay, sand, and silt is called

   a. loam.

   b. sod.

   c. subsoil.

   d. topsoil.

7. The decayed organic material in soil is called

   a. bedrock.

   b. humus.

   c. silt.

   d. subsoil.

8. **Identify** What are two roles living things play in soil formation?

   _____

   _____

Use the graph to answer Question 9.

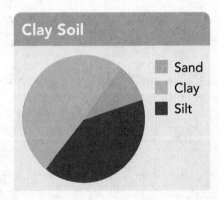

Clay Soil

- Sand
- Clay
- Silt

9. **Pose Questions** The graph shows a farmer's soil sample. What questions would the farmer need to answer before choosing whether to plant soybeans in this soil?

   _____

   _____

   _____

   _____

LESSON 3 **Soil Conservation**

10. Which technique returns nutrients to soil?

    a. chemical weathering

    b. contour plowing

    c. crop rotation

    d. wind erosion

11. What role do grasses play in conserving the soil of the prairies?

    a. holding the soil in place

    b. increasing wind erosion

    c. decreasing the amount of fertile soil

    d. making nitrogen available to plants

12. Draw Conclusions Why is soil important to people and to other living things?

_____

_____

_____

_____

_____

_____

13. Relate Cause and Effect How did human activities contribute to the Dust Bowl?

_____

_____

_____

_____

_____

14. 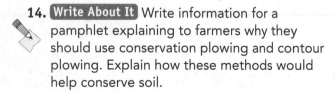 **Write About It** Write information for a pamphlet explaining to farmers why they should use conservation plowing and contour plowing. Explain how these methods would help conserve soil.

 What processes break down rock?

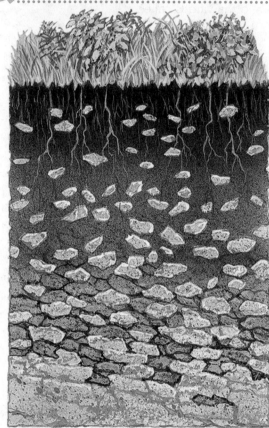

15. Examine the soil sample shown above. Find the A, B, and C horizons. Describe the processes that formed each layer of the soil. Remember to include examples of weathering in your description.

_____

_____

_____

_____

_____

_____

_____

_____

_____

_____

Standardized Test Prep

Multiple Choice

Circle the letter of the correct answer.

1. Use the picture to answer the question.

   What **most likely** caused the weathering shown in the picture?

   A abrasion   B ice wedging
   C plant growth   D animal actions

2. What is the **most** important role that burrowing animals play in the formation of soil?

   A breaking down organic materials
   B decomposing dead animals
   C holding soil in place
   D mixing air and water into the soil

3. Fertile soil is an important natural resource because

   A no new soil can be produced.
   B everything that lives on land depends on soil.
   C there is an unlimited supply of fertile soil.
   D plants cannot grow in fertile soil.

4. In which type of climate would a limestone monument weather **most** quickly?

   A a cold, dry climate
   B a hot, dry climate
   C a cold, wet climate
   D a hot, wet climate

5. A farmer wants to reduce the amount of runoff in his fields. Which of the following is he **most likely** trying to avoid?

   A topsoil erosion
   B conservation plowing
   C crop rotation
   D chemical weathering

Constructed Response

Use the diagram and your knowledge of science to answer the question. Write your answer on another piece of paper.

30% sand
30% silt
40% clay

70% sand
10% silt
20% clay

6. Examine the soil samples above. Describe the soil in each pot. Predict whether each soil would be good for growing most kinds of plants and explain your reasoning.

HASTA LA VISTA, REGULAR CONCRETE

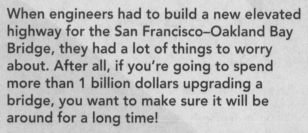

▲ The new fly-ash concrete bridge, beside the old metal bridge.

Museum of Science

When engineers had to build a new elevated highway for the San Francisco–Oakland Bay Bridge, they had a lot of things to worry about. After all, if you're going to spend more than 1 billion dollars upgrading a bridge, you want to make sure it will be around for a long time!

The supports of the bridge needed to stand in salt water and mud. Chemicals called sulfates in salt water and soil can weather the concrete and weaken the structure. Sulfates also cause weathering by allowing salt crystals to form on the bridge. But when fly ash is mixed into concrete, it protects the concrete against the weathering effects of the sulfates. Fly ash is powder left behind after coal has been burned. This waste product is usually dumped in landfills.

The engineers of the huge concrete elevated highway used a mixture of concrete and fly ash to build the bridge supports. This improved concrete is helping the bridge to stand up to everything nature throws its way.

Analyze It Identify how weathering has affected a local site, such as a bridge or a monument. Find out what materials were used to build the site, and research what other materials might better withstand weathering. Write a paragraph making the case for using these different materials in future building projects.

THE Plant Doctor

Even as a young boy, George Washington Carver understood plants. Born into slavery in the 1860s, Carver spent his days studying plants. He observed that some plants needed a lot of sunlight and some needed very little. He experimented with mixtures of sand, soil, and clay to find out the kind of soil each plant needed. He knew so much about plants, neighbors called him the "plant doctor."

Carver received a master of science degree from Iowa State Agricultural College and began to teach and do research at Tuskegee Institute. Because Southern farmers grew only cotton, their soil was in poor condition and had started to erode. Carver taught farmers that crop rotation would enrich the soil. Many farmers found that the crops Carver suggested grew better in their soil, and that his methods made the soil healthier. Crop rotation is now a common farming technique.

Research It Dr. Carver taught farmers in the South to plant peanuts, sweet potatoes, and soybeans. The success of these crops often left farmers with more than they could use or sell. Research the many uses discovered by Dr. Carver for one of these crops and present them in a poster.

Dr. Carver inspecting plants in a research greenhouse ▶

WHAT RESHAPED THESE ROCKS?

What processes shape the surface of the land?

Smooth and colorful, the sandstone walls of Antelope Canyon look more like a sculpture than like natural rock. Located in Arizona, this slot canyon was carved by nature. From above, the opening of the canyon is so narrow that you can jump across. But be careful, some areas of the canyon are more than 30 meters deep!

Infer How could nature have carved these rocks?

_____

_____

_____

_____

_____

▶ **UNTAMED SCIENCE** Watch the **Untamed Science** video to learn more about erosion and deposition.

Erosion and Deposition

7 Getting Started

Check Your Understanding

1. Background Read the paragraph below and then answer the question.

A giant **mass** of mud blocked the road after a storm. "How did it get there?" asked Gail. "During the storm, the nearby river rose really fast, so the **force** of the water pushed it there," said her dad. "Spring flooding is part of the natural **cycle** of the seasons."

> **Mass** is an amount of matter that has an indefinite size and shape.
>
> **Force** is the push or pull exerted on an object.
>
> A **cycle** is a sequence of events that repeats over and over.

- Why does it take the force of fast-moving water to move a large mass of mud?

_____

_____

> **MY READING WEB** If you had trouble completing the question above, visit **My Reading Web** and type in *Erosion and Deposition*.

Vocabulary Skill

Word Origins Many science words come to English from other languages. By learning the meaning of a few common Latin roots, you can determine the meaning of new science words.

Latin Word	Meaning of Latin Word	Example
sedere	sit, settle	sediment, *n.* pieces of rock or soil moved by the process of erosion
flare	blow	deflation, *n.* the process by which wind removes surface materials

2. Quick Check Use the chart to answer the question.

- How does the Latin word *sedere* relate to the word *sediment*?

_____

_____

mass movement

flood plain

glacier

sand dune

Chapter Preview

LESSON 1
- erosion • sediment • deposition
- gravity • mass movement
- ↻ Relate Text and Visuals
- △ Infer

LESSON 2
- runoff • rill • gully • stream
- tributary • flood plain • meander
- oxbow lake • delta • alluvial fan
- groundwater • stalactite
- stalagmite • karst topography
- ↻ Identify Supporting Evidence
- △ Develop Hypotheses

LESSON 3
- glacier • continental glacier
- ice age • valley glacier
- plucking • till • moraine • kettle
- ↻ Relate Cause and Effect
- △ Draw Conclusions

LESSON 4
- headland • beach
- longshore drift • spit
- ↻ Summarize
- △ Communicate

LESSON 5
- deflation • sand dune • loess
- ↻ Ask Questions
- △ Predict

▸ VOCAB FLASH CARDS For extra help with vocabulary, visit **Vocab Flash Cards** and type in *Erosion and Deposition.*

Mass Movement

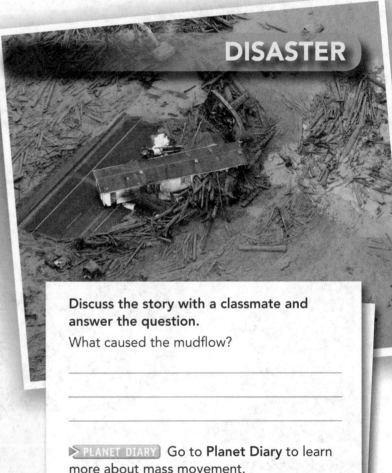

🔑 **What Processes Wear Down and Build Up Earth's Surface?**

🔑 **What Are the Different Types of Mass Movement?**

my planet Diary

Mudflow Hits Town

In December 2007, severe storms hit the northwestern United States. These storms started landslides in the hills above Woodson, Oregon. When landslide debris dammed a creek in the hills, a deep lake formed. If the debris gave way, a mudflow could run downhill and damage the town.

Fortunately, a landowner called the Oregon Department of Forestry (ODF). People were quickly evacuated and a nearby highway was closed. It wasn't long before the pile of debris collapsed, allowing the water to escape. A large mudflow swept away homes, cars, and trees! But thanks to the ODF, no one was harmed.

Lab zone Do the Inquiry Warm-Up *How Does Gravity Affect Materials on a Slope?*

DISASTER

Discuss the story with a classmate and answer the question.

What caused the mudflow?

_____

_____

_____

▶ **PLANET DIARY** Go to **Planet Diary** to learn more about mass movement.

What Processes Wear Down and Build Up Earth's Surface?

On a rainy day, you may have seen water carrying soil and gravel down a driveway. That's an example of **erosion**—the process by which natural forces move weathered rock and soil from one place to another. Gravity, moving water, glaciers, waves, and wind are all agents, or causes, of erosion.

Vocabulary
- erosion • sediment • deposition
- gravity • mass movement

Skills
- Reading: Relate Text and Visuals
- Inquiry: Infer

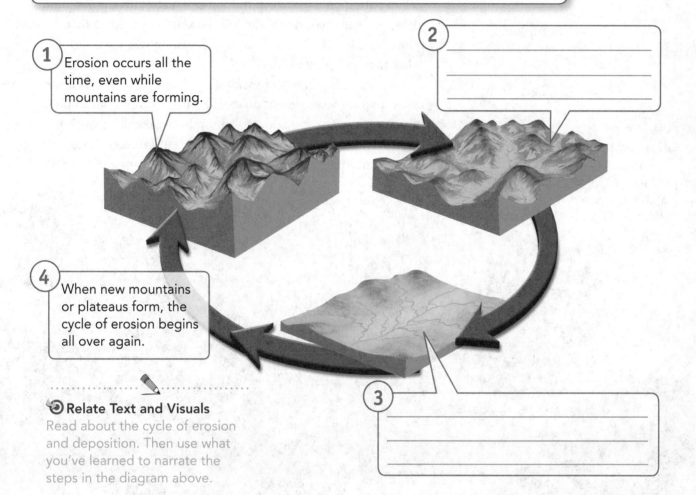

1 Erosion occurs all the time, even while mountains are forming.

2

4 When new mountains or plateaus form, the cycle of erosion begins all over again.

3

Relate Text and Visuals
Read about the cycle of erosion and deposition. Then use what you've learned to narrate the steps in the diagram above.

The process of erosion moves material called **sediment.** Sediment may consist of pieces of rock or soil, or the remains of plants and animals. **Deposition** occurs where the agents of erosion deposit, or lay down, sediment. Deposition changes the shape of the land. You may have watched a playing child who picked up several toys, carried them across a room, and then put them down. This child was acting something like an agent of erosion and deposition.

 Weathering, erosion, and deposition act together in a cycle that wears down and builds up Earth's surface. Erosion and deposition are at work everywhere on Earth. As a mountain wears down in one place, new landforms build up in other places. The cycle of erosion and deposition is never-ending.

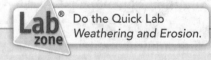
Lab zone — Do the Quick Lab *Weathering and Erosion.*

🔑 Assess Your Understanding
got it? ....

○ **I get it!** Now I know the three major processes that shape Earth's surface are
_____
_____
_____

○ **I need extra help with** _____
Go to MY SCIENCE ⓢ COACH *online for help with this subject.*

What Are the Different Types of Mass Movement?

You're sitting on a bicycle at the top of a hill. With a slight push, you can coast down the hill. **Gravity** is the force that pulls you and your bike downward. It also moves rock and other materials downhill.

Gravity causes **mass movement,** any one of several processes that move sediment downhill. Mass movement can be rapid or slow. Erosion and deposition both take place during a mass movement event. 🔑 **The different types of mass movement include landslides, mudflows, slumps, and creep.**

FIGURE 1 ·····································

▶ **INTERACTIVE ART** **Mass Movement**
✎ **Interpret Diagrams** Read about the types of mass movement. Then match each description with its corresponding diagram.

A

B

C

D

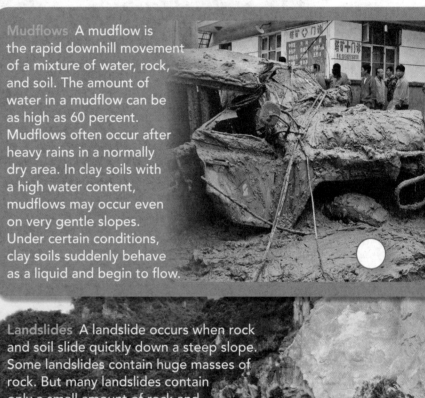

Mudflows A mudflow is the rapid downhill movement of a mixture of water, rock, and soil. The amount of water in a mudflow can be as high as 60 percent. Mudflows often occur after heavy rains in a normally dry area. In clay soils with a high water content, mudflows may occur even on very gentle slopes. Under certain conditions, clay soils suddenly behave as a liquid and begin to flow.

Landslides A landslide occurs when rock and soil slide quickly down a steep slope. Some landslides contain huge masses of rock. But many landslides contain only a small amount of rock and soil. Some landslides occur where road builders have cut highways through hills or mountains, leaving behind unstable slopes.

apply it!

Infer A fence runs across a steep hillside. The fence is tilted downhill and forms a curve rather than a straight line. What do you think happened?

_____

_____

_____

_____

Slumps If you slump your shoulders, the entire upper part of your body drops down. In the type of mass movement known as slumps, a mass of rock and soil suddenly slips down a slope. Unlike a landslide, the material in a slump moves down in one large mass. It looks as if someone pulled the bottom out from under part of the slope. A slump often occurs when water soaks the bottom of soil that is rich in clay.

Creep Creep is the very slow downhill movement of rock and soil. It can even occur on gentle slopes. Creep often results from the freezing and thawing of water in cracked layers of rock beneath the soil. Like the movement of an hour hand on a clock, creep is so slow you can barely notice it. But you can see the effects of creep in vertical objects such as telephone poles and tree trunks. Creep may tilt these objects at unusual angles.

Lab zone Do the Lab Investigation _Sand Hills._

Assess Your Understanding

1a. Review What is mass movement?

_____

_____

_____

b. Relate Cause and Effect What force causes all types of mass movement? Explain.

_____

_____

_____

got it? ....

○ **I get it!** Now I know that mass movement is the _____

_____

○ **I need extra help with** _____

Go to **my science** **coach** online for help with this subject.

Water Erosion

UNLOCK THE BIG ?

🔑 How Does Moving Water Cause Erosion?

🔑 What Land Features Are Formed by Water Erosion and Deposition?

The Great Blue Hole

The boat leaves at 5:30 A.M. But you don't mind the early hour because it's the trip of a lifetime: a visit to the Great Blue Hole of Belize.

The Great Blue Hole is actually the remains of a cave formed by erosion. Several factors, including rising sea levels, caused the roof of the cave to collapse. This resulted in a natural depression called a sinkhole.

The Great Blue Hole is more than 300 meters wide and 125 meters deep. It's possibly the deepest and most massive sinkhole in the world. If you want to explore it, you have to scuba dive through the roof. It's an impressive example of what nature can accomplish over time!

Read the story. Then answer the question.
How was the Great Blue Hole formed?

_____

_____

_____

> PLANET DIARY Go to **Planet Diary** to learn more about water erosion.

Do the Inquiry Warm-Up *How Does Moving Water Wear Away Rocks?*

How Does Moving Water Cause Erosion?

Erosion by water begins with a splash of rain. Some rainfall sinks into the ground. Some evaporates or is taken up by plants. The rest of the water runs off over the land surface. 🔑 **Moving water is the major agent of the erosion that has shaped Earth's land surface.**

Vocabulary
- runoff • rill • gully • stream • tributary
- flood plain • meander • oxbow lake • delta
- alluvial fan • groundwater • stalactite
- stalagmite • karst topography

Skills
↻ **Reading:** Identify Supporting Evidence
△ **Inquiry:** Develop Hypotheses

Runoff As water moves over the land, it carries particles with it. This moving water is called **runoff.** When runoff flows in a thin layer over the land, it may cause a type of erosion called sheet erosion. The amount of runoff in an area depends on five main factors. The first factor is the amount of rain an area gets. A second factor is vegetation. Grasses, shrubs, and trees reduce runoff by absorbing water and holding soil in place. A third factor is the type of soil. Some types of soils absorb more water than others. A fourth factor is the shape of the land. Steeply sloped land has more runoff than flatter land. Finally, a fifth factor is how people use land. For example, a paved parking lot absorbs no water. All the rain that falls on it becomes runoff. Runoff also increases when farmers cut down crops, since this removes vegetation from the land.

Generally, more runoff means more erosion. In contrast, factors that reduce runoff will reduce erosion. Even though deserts have little rainfall they often have high runoff and erosion because they have few plants and thin soil. In wet areas, runoff and erosion may be low because there are more plants to help protect the soil.

↻ **Identify Supporting Evidence** As you read the paragraph on the left, number each of the factors that affect runoff.

Factor	Example

FIGURE 1 ·············
Factors Affecting Runoff
✎ **Complete the task below.**

1. **List** Record the five main factors affecting runoff.

2. **Identify** Using a specific location, such as a park, identify an example for each factor.

3. **Communicate** Explain to a partner what the runoff would be like at your location.

Stream Formation

Stream Formation Because of gravity, runoff and the material it contains flow downhill. As this water moves across the land, it runs together to form rills, gullies, and streams.

Rills and Gullies As runoff travels, it forms tiny grooves in the soil called **rills.** When many rills flow into one another, they grow larger, forming a gully. A **gully** is a large groove, or channel, in the soil that carries runoff after a rainstorm. As water flows through gullies, it moves soil and rocks with it, thus enlarging the gullies through erosion. Gullies only contain water during a rainstorm and for a short time after it rains.

Streams and Rivers Gullies join together to form a larger channel called a stream. A **stream** is a channel along which water is continually flowing down a slope. Unlike gullies, streams rarely dry up. Small streams are also called creeks or brooks. As streams flow together, they form larger and larger bodies of flowing water. A large stream is often called a river.

Tributaries A stream grows into a larger stream or river by receiving water from tributaries. A **tributary** is a stream or river that flows into a larger river. For example, the Missouri and Ohio rivers are tributaries of the Mississippi River. A drainage basin, or watershed, is the area from which a river and its tributaries collect their water.

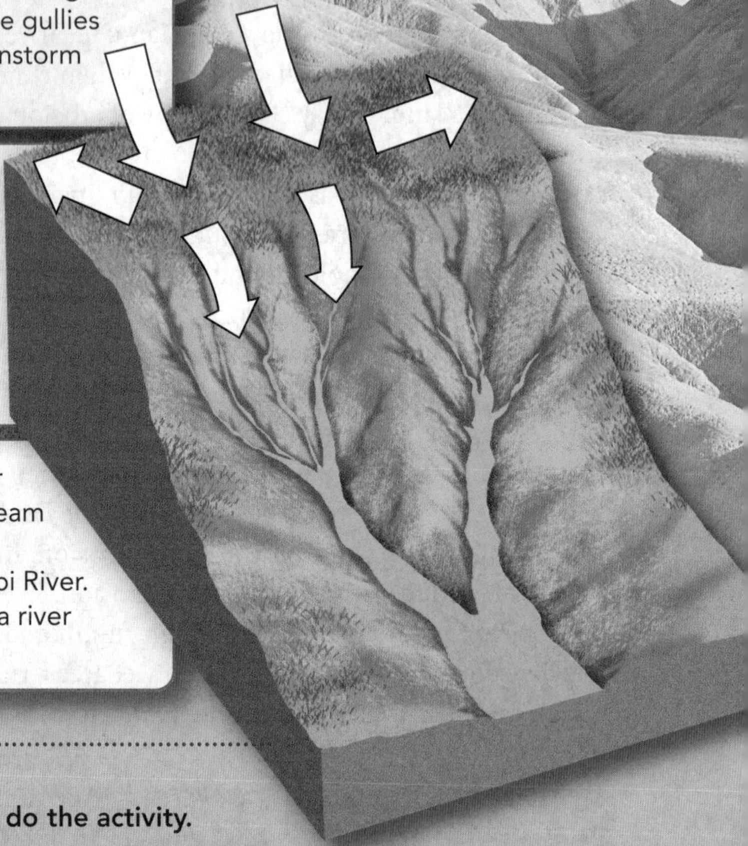

FIGURE 2 ....
Stream Formation

✎ **Relate Text and Visuals After you read, do the activity.**

1. Shade in the arrows that indicate the direction of sheet erosion.
2. Circle the terms *rills, gully,* and *stream* in the text. Then draw a line from the word to examples of them in the picture.

Lab ® Do the Quick Lab
zone *Raindrops Falling.*

🔑 Assess Your Understanding

1a. Review How does runoff affect the rate of erosion?

_____

_____

b. Sequence Put these in order of size from smallest to biggest: creek, rill, gully, river.

_____

_____

got it? ....

○ **I get it!** Now I know what runoff does: _____

_____

○ **I need extra help with** _____

Go to MY SCIENCE ⬤ⁱ COACH *online for help with this subject.*

What Land Features Are Formed by Water Erosion and Deposition?

Walking in the woods in summer, you can hear the racing water of a river before you see the river itself. When you reach the river's banks, you see water rushing by. Sand and pebbles tumble along the river bottom. As it swirls downstream, the water also carries twigs, leaves, and bits of soil. In sheltered pools, insects skim the water's calm surface. Beneath the surface, a rainbow trout swims in the clear water. As the seasons change, so does the river. In winter, the surface of the river may freeze. But during spring, it may flood. Throughout the year, the river continues to erode Earth's surface.

FIGURE 3 ···

River Erosion

✏ **Interpret Photos** How does a river's ability to erode change with the seasons? (*Hint:* Look at how the amount of water changes during each season.)

Spring

Summer

Fall

Winter

_____

_____

_____

_____

_____

Water Erosion Many rivers begin on steep mountain slopes. Near their source, these rivers can be fast-flowing and generally follow a straight, narrow course. The steep slopes along the river erode rapidly, resulting in a deep, V-shaped valley. As a river flows from the mountains to the sea, it forms many features. 🔑 **Through erosion, a river creates valleys, waterfalls, flood plains, meanders, and oxbow lakes.**

Waterfalls Waterfalls may occur where a river meets an area of rock that is very hard and erodes slowly. The river flows over this rock and then flows over softer rock downstream. Softer rock wears away faster than harder rock. Eventually a waterfall develops where the softer rock was removed. Areas of rough water called rapids also occur where a river tumbles over hard rock.

FIGURE 4 ·····················
Waterfalls
✏️ **Apply Concepts**
Where do you think the layers of hard and soft rock are located? Label the areas on the diagram to show your answer.

Flood Plain Lower down on its course, a river usually flows over more gently sloping land. The river spreads out and erodes the land, forming a wide river valley. The flat, wide area of land along a river is a flood plain. On a wide flood plain, the valley walls may be kilometers away from the river itself. A river often covers its flood plain when it overflows its banks during a flood. When the flood water finally retreats, it deposits sediment as new soil. This makes a river valley fertile.

Meanders A river often develops meanders where it flows through easily eroded rock or sediment. A **meander** is a looplike bend in the course of a river. As the river winds from side to side, it tends to erode the outer bank and deposit sediment on the inner bank of a bend. Over time, a meander becomes more curved.

Because of the sediment a river carries, it can erode a very wide flood plain. Along this part of a river's course, its channel may be deep and wide. The southern stretch of the Mississippi River meanders on a wide, gently sloping flood plain.

Oxbow Lakes Sometimes a meandering river forms a feature called an oxbow lake. As the photo below shows, an **oxbow lake** is a meander that has been cut off from the river. An oxbow lake may form when a river floods. During the flood, high water finds a straighter route downstream. As the flood waters fall, sediments dam up the ends of a meander, forming an oxbow lake.

FIGURE 5 ·····································

Oxbow Lakes

A meander may gradually form an oxbow lake.

✎ **Make Models** Draw steps 2 and 4 to show how an oxbow lake forms and describe the last step.

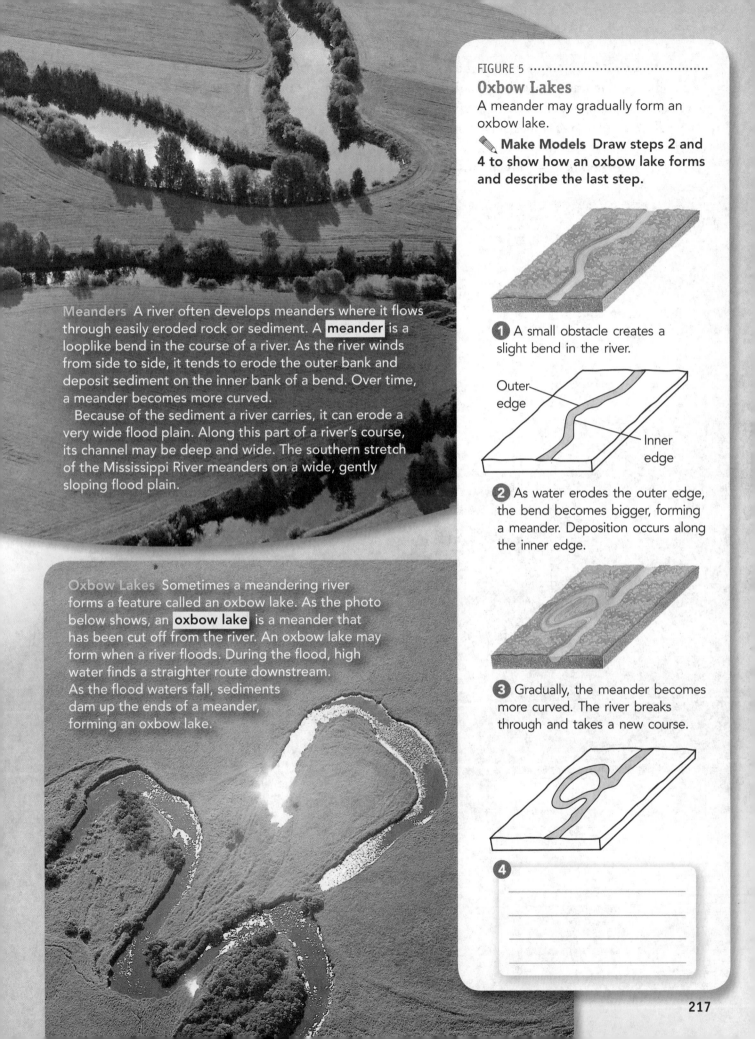

1 A small obstacle creates a slight bend in the river.

Outer edge

Inner edge

2 As water erodes the outer edge, the bend becomes bigger, forming a meander. Deposition occurs along the inner edge.

3 Gradually, the meander becomes more curved. The river breaks through and takes a new course.

4 _____
_____
_____
_____

Water Deposition

As water moves, it carries sediment with it. Any time moving water slows down, it drops, or deposits, some of the sediment. In this way, soil can be added to a river's flood plain. As the water slows down, large stones quit rolling and sliding. Fine particles fall to the river's bed as the river flows even more slowly. 🔑 **Deposition creates landforms such as alluvial fans and deltas.**

Deltas A river ends its journey when it flows into a still body of water, such as an ocean or a lake. Because the river water is no longer flowing downhill, the water slows down. At this point, the sediment in the water drops to the bottom. Sediment deposited where a river flows into an ocean or lake builds up a landform called a **delta.** Deltas can be a variety of shapes. Some are arc-shaped, others are triangle-shaped. The delta of the Mississippi River, shown here, is an example of a type of delta called a "bird's foot" delta.

Alluvial Fans Where a stream flows out of a steep, narrow mountain valley, the stream suddenly becomes wider and shallower. The water slows down. Here sediments are deposited in an alluvial fan. An **alluvial fan** is a wide, sloping deposit of sediment formed where a stream leaves a mountain range. As its name suggests, this deposit is shaped like a fan.

Key

▨ Mississippi delta

LOUISIANA

MISSISSIPPI

TEXAS

Mississippi River

New Orleans

0   50   100 mi
0   50   100 km

Gulf of Mexico

FIGURE 6 ·······················
Deposits by Rivers
✎ **Interpret Photos** Use the pictures above to describe the difference between an alluvial fan and a delta.

_____

_____

_____

_____

_____

_____

EXPLORE THE BIG **?**

Rolling Through the Hills

What processes shape the surface of the land?

FIGURE 7 ··

▷ **REAL-WORLD INQUIRY** You're a tour guide in the area pictured below, and your tour group wants to learn more about some of the features they are seeing.

✎ **Relate Evidence and Explanation** Identify the two missing features on the image below. Then summarize what you would say about them to your tour group.

Waterfalls and Rapids Waterfalls and rapids are common where the river passes over harder rock.

V-Shaped Valley Near its source, the river flows through a deep, V-shaped valley. As the river flows, it cuts the valley deeper.

Tributary The river receives water and sediment from a tributary—a smaller river or stream that flows into it.

Oxbow Lake An oxbow lake is a meander cut off from the river by deposition of sediment.

Flood Plain A flood plain forms where the river's power of erosion widens its valley rather than deepening it.

Valley Widening As the river approaches sea level, it meanders more and develops a wider valley and broader flood plain.

219

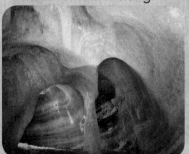

Groundwater Erosion

When rain falls and snow melts, not all of the water evaporates or becomes runoff. Some water soaks into the ground. There it fills the openings in the soil and trickles into cracks and spaces in layers of rock. **Groundwater** is the term geologists use for this underground water. Like running water on the surface, groundwater affects the shape of the land.

Groundwater can cause erosion through a process of chemical weathering. Rainwater is naturally acidic. In the atmosphere, water combines with carbon dioxide to form a weak acid called carbonic acid. Carbonic acid can break down limestone. Groundwater containing carbonic acid flows into any cracks in the limestone. Then some of the limestone dissolves and is carried away in a solution of water. This process gradually hollows out pockets in the rock. Over time, these pockets develop into large holes underground, called caves or caverns.

Cave Formations

The action of carbonic acid on limestone can also result in deposition. Inside limestone caves, deposits called stalactites and stalagmites often form. Water containing carbonic acid and calcium from limestone drips from a cave's roof. Carbon dioxide escapes from the solution, leaving behind a deposit of calcite. A deposit that hangs like an icicle from the roof of a cave is known as a **stalactite** (stuh LAK tyt). Slow dripping builds up a cone-shaped **stalagmite** (stuh LAG myt) from the cave floor.

FIGURE 8

Groundwater Erosion and Deposition

✎ **Explain** How do erosion and deposition shape caves? Take notes as you read. Then discuss with a classmate.

Process of Erosion	Process of Deposition

Karst Topography In rainy regions where there is a layer of limestone near the surface, groundwater erosion can significantly change the shape of the land. Streams are rare, because water easily sinks down into the weathered limestone. Deep valleys and caverns are common. If the roof of a cave collapses because of the erosion of the underlying limestone, the result is a depression called a sinkhole. This type of landscape is called **karst topography** after a region in Eastern Europe.

This sinkhole is in Russia's Perm region.

apply it!

Study the map and answer the questions below.

1 Name three states in which you can find karst topography.

_____

2 **Develop Hypotheses** Why do you think karst topography occurs in these areas?

_____
_____
_____

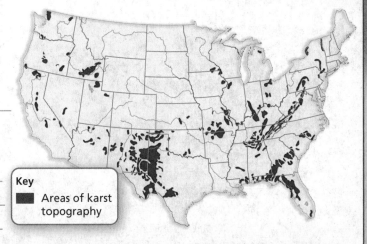

Key

■ Areas of karst topography

Do the Quick Lab *Erosion Cube.*

🗝 Assess Your Understanding

2a. List Name two features of water erosion.

_____

b. CHALLENGE What is carbonic acid and how does it affect rock?

_____
_____
_____

c. ANSWER THE BIG ? What processes shape the surface of the land?

_____
_____
_____
_____
_____

got it? ....

○ **I get it!** Now I know that features of erosion and deposition include _____

_____

○ I need extra help with _____

Go to MY SCIENCE ⬤ COACH online for help with this subject.

Glacial Erosion

UNLOCK
THE BIG
?

🔑 **How Do Glaciers Form and Move?**

🔑 **How Do Glaciers Cause Erosion and Deposition?**

my planet diary

Why Are Glaciers Blue?

If snow is white, why do glaciers look blue? When sunlight hits snow, it bounces right back. Snow is made up of microscopic crystals. It is light and not very dense. As more snow falls, its weight turns some of the crystals underneath into water and vapor. The water and vapor refreeze. This process creates larger, denser ice crystals. Over time, the weight of the snow and the ice on the surface makes these crystals even denser. These are the kind of ice crystals that make up glaciers. When sunlight hits glaciers, these dense ice crystals absorb the red and yellow light. Only the blue light escapes!

FUN FACTS

After you read, answer the questions below with a classmate.

1. What makes glaciers look blue?

_____

_____

_____

2. In addition to color, what might be some other differences between snow and glacial ice?

_____

_____

_____

_____

▶ PLANET DIARY Go to **Planet Diary** to learn more about glacial erosion and deposition.

 Lab zone Do the Inquiry Warm-Up *How Do Glaciers Change the Land?*

Vocabulary
- glacier • continental glacier
- ice age • valley glacier • plucking
- till • moraine • kettle

Skills
↻ Reading: Relate Cause and Effect
△ Inquiry: Draw Conclusions

How Do Glaciers Form and Move?

On a boat trip off the coast of Alaska you sail by evergreen forests and snowcapped mountains. As you round a point of land, you see an amazing sight. A great mass of ice winds like a river between rows of mountains. This river of ice is a glacier. Geologists define a **glacier** as any large mass of ice that moves slowly over land. 🗝 **Glaciers can form only in an area where more snow falls than melts.** There are two kinds of glaciers—continental glaciers and valley glaciers.

Continental Glaciers A **continental glacier** is a glacier that covers much of a continent or large island. It can spread out over millions of square kilometers. Today, continental glaciers cover about 10 percent of Earth's land. They cover Antarctica and most of Greenland. 🗝 **Continental glaciers can flow in all directions as they move.** They spread out much as pancake batter spreads out in a frying pan. Many times in the past, continental glaciers have covered larger parts of Earth's surface. These times are known as **ice ages.** About 1 million years ago, continental glaciers covered nearly one third of Earth's land. The glaciers advanced and retreated, or melted back, several times. They most recently retreated about 10,000 years ago.

FIGURE 1 ·
Continental Glaciers
You're traveling across Antarctica from Point A to Point H on the route below. The cross section shows changes in the ice sheet along your journey.

✎ **Interpret Diagrams** What changes in elevation and ice depth will you encounter?

_____
_____
_____
_____
_____
_____
_____
_____
_____
_____
_____

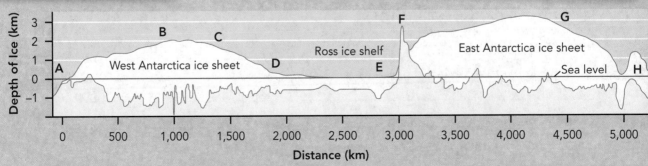

Valley Glaciers

A **valley glacier** is a long, narrow glacier that forms when snow and ice build up high in a mountain valley. The sides of mountains keep these glaciers from spreading out in all directions. Instead, they usually move down valleys that have already been cut by rivers. Valley glaciers are found on many high mountains. Although they are much smaller than continental glaciers, valley glaciers can be tens of kilometers long.

High in mountain valleys, temperatures rarely rise above freezing. Snow builds up year after year. The weight of more and more snow compacts the snow at the bottom into ice. 🔑 **Gravity constantly pulls a glacier downhill.** Once the layer of snow and ice is more than about 30 to 40 meters deep, the glacier begins to move.

Valley glaciers flow at a rate of a few centimeters to a few meters per day. But a valley glacier that surges, or slides quickly, can move as much as 6 kilometers in a year.

apply it!

When glaciers recede, they leave behind evidence of their existence.

❶ Observe What was the landscape like before glaciers formed?

_____

_____

❷ Draw Conclusions What did the glaciers do to the area?

_____

_____

_____

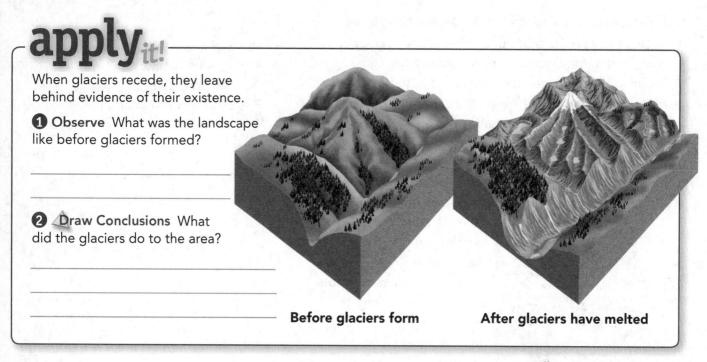

Before glaciers form   **After glaciers have melted**

Lab zone® Do the Quick Lab *Surging Glaciers*.

🔑 Assess Your Understanding

got it?

○ **I get it!** Now I know that glaciers differ in how they move: _____

_____

○ **I need extra help with** _____

Go to **MY SCIENCE** ⓢ **COACH** online for help with this subject.

How Do Glaciers Cause Erosion and Deposition?

The movement of a glacier changes the land beneath it. Although glaciers work slowly, they are a major force of erosion. 🔑 **The two processes by which glaciers erode the land are plucking and abrasion.**

Glacial Erosion As a glacier flows over the land, it picks up rocks in a process called **plucking.** Beneath a glacier, the weight of the ice can break rocks apart. These rock fragments freeze to the bottom of the glacier. When the glacier moves, it carries the rocks with it, as shown in **Figure 2.** Plucking can move huge boulders.

Many rocks remain on the bottom of the glacier, and the glacier drags them across the land. This process, called abrasion, gouges and scratches the bedrock.

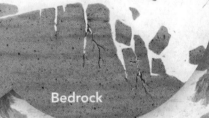

Bedrock

FIGURE 2 ·······················

Glacial Erosion

🖊 **After you read about glaciers, do the activity.**

1. **Identify** Draw an arrow in the diagram above to show the direction the ice is moving.

2. **Explain** In your own words, describe the glacial erosion taking place in the diagram.

_____

_____

_____

_____

_____

_____

225

Relate Cause and Effect As you read, underline the cause of glacial deposition and circle the effects.

Glacial Deposition

A glacier gathers a huge amount of rock and soil as it erodes the land in its path. **When a glacier melts, it deposits the sediment it eroded from the land, creating various landforms.** These landforms remain for thousands of years after the glacier has melted. The mixture of sediments that a glacier deposits directly on the surface is called **till.** Till is made up of particles of many different sizes. Clay, silt, sand, gravel, and boulders can all be found in till.

The till deposited at the edges of a glacier forms a ridge called a **moraine.** A terminal moraine is the ridge of till at the farthest point reached by a glacier. Part of Long Island in New York is a terminal moraine from the continental glaciers of the last ice age.

Retreating glaciers also create features called kettles. A **kettle** is a small depression that forms when a chunk of ice is left in glacial till. When the ice melts, the kettle remains. The continental glacier of the last ice age left behind many kettles. Kettles often fill with water, forming small ponds or lakes called kettle lakes. Such lakes are common in areas such as Wisconsin, that were once covered with ice.

FIGURE 3 ·······

> ART IN MOTION **Glacial Landforms**

 After you read, complete this activity.

1. **Classify** Identify the features of erosion and deposition in the scene below. Record your answers in the boxes provided on the next page.

2. CHALLENGE Identify the feature in the photo on the next page. Describe how it formed.

Cirque A cirque is a bowl-shaped hollow eroded by a glacier.

Horn When glaciers carve away the sides of a mountain, the result is a horn, a sharpened peak.

Fiord A fiord forms when the level of the sea rises, filling a valley once cut by a glacier.

Arête An arête is a sharp ridge separating two cirques.

Glaciers have shaped the land in Denali National Park, Alaska.

Features of Erosion	Features of Deposition	Photo Feature

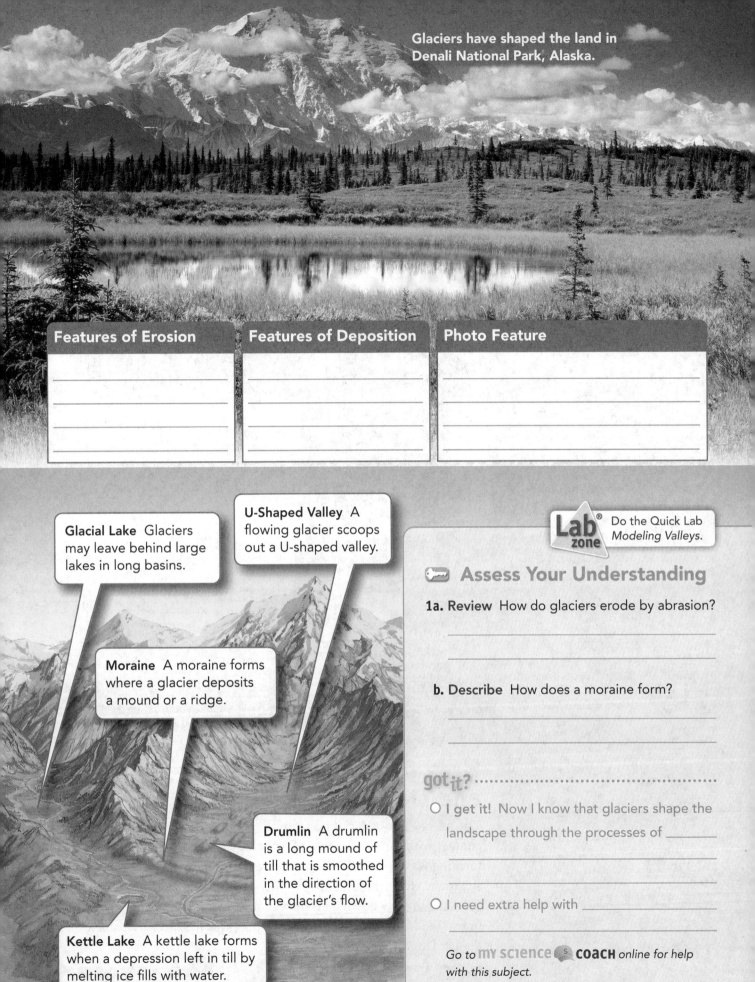

Glacial Lake Glaciers may leave behind large lakes in long basins.

U-Shaped Valley A flowing glacier scoops out a U-shaped valley.

Moraine A moraine forms where a glacier deposits a mound or a ridge.

Drumlin A drumlin is a long mound of till that is smoothed in the direction of the glacier's flow.

Kettle Lake A kettle lake forms when a depression left in till by melting ice fills with water.

Lab zone® Do the Quick Lab *Modeling Valleys.*

🔑 Assess Your Understanding

1a. Review How do glaciers erode by abrasion?

_____

_____

b. Describe How does a moraine form?

_____

_____

got**it?** ....

○ **I get it!** Now I know that glaciers shape the landscape through the processes of _____

_____

_____

○ **I need extra help with** _____

_____

Go to MY SCIENCE ⬤ⁿ COACH *online for help with this subject.*

227

Wave Erosion

 **How Do Waves Cause Erosion and Deposition?**

MY PLANET DIARY

BLOG

Posted by: Lila

Location: Camden, Maine

I was returning home from an island picnic on our 24-foot motor boat, when the wind whipped up. The water in the bay became rough. The waves were splashing up the sides of the boat. Even though my dad slowed down, our boat slammed into wave after wave. My head hit the ceiling of the cabin, as I got bounced each time the boat hit a wave. Anything not strapped down slipped toward the back of the boat. It was scary!

After you read about Lila's trip, answer the question.

How did the waves affect Lila's boat ride?

_____

_____

_____

> PLANET DIARY   Go to **Planet Diary** to learn more about wave erosion and deposition.

 Lab zone   Do the Inquiry Warm-Up *What Is Sand Made Of?*

How Do Waves Cause Erosion and Deposition?

The energy in waves comes from the wind. When the wind makes contact with the water some of its energy transfers to the water, forming waves. As a wave approaches land the water becomes shallower. The friction between the wave and the bottom causes the wave to slow down, and the water moves forward as the wave breaks. This forward-moving water provides the force that shapes the land along the shoreline.

Vocabulary
- headland
- beach
- longshore drift
- spit

Skills
- Reading: Summarize
- Inquiry: Communicate

Erosion by Waves

Waves shape the coast through erosion by breaking down rock and moving sand and other sediment. One way waves erode the land is by impact. Large waves can hit rocks along the shore with great force. This energy in waves can break apart rocks. Over time, waves can make small cracks larger. Eventually, the waves cause pieces of rock to break off. Waves also erode by abrasion. As a wave approaches shallow water, it picks up sediment, including sand and gravel. This sediment is carried forward by the wave. When the wave hits land, the sediment wears away rock like sandpaper wearing away wood.

Waves coming to shore gradually change direction. The change in direction occurs as different parts of a wave begin to drag on the bottom. The waves in **Figure 1** change direction as they approach the shore. The energy of these waves is concentrated on headlands. A **headland** is a part of the shore that sticks out into the ocean. It is made of harder rock that resists erosion by the waves. But, over time, waves erode the headlands and even out the shoreline.

Summarize Read the text about wave erosion and explain how a wave erodes by abrasion.

_____

_____

_____

_____

_____

FIGURE 1 ·····················

Wave Erosion

Identify Shade in the arrows that indicate where the greatest energy of the waves is concentrated.

Headland

Deposition

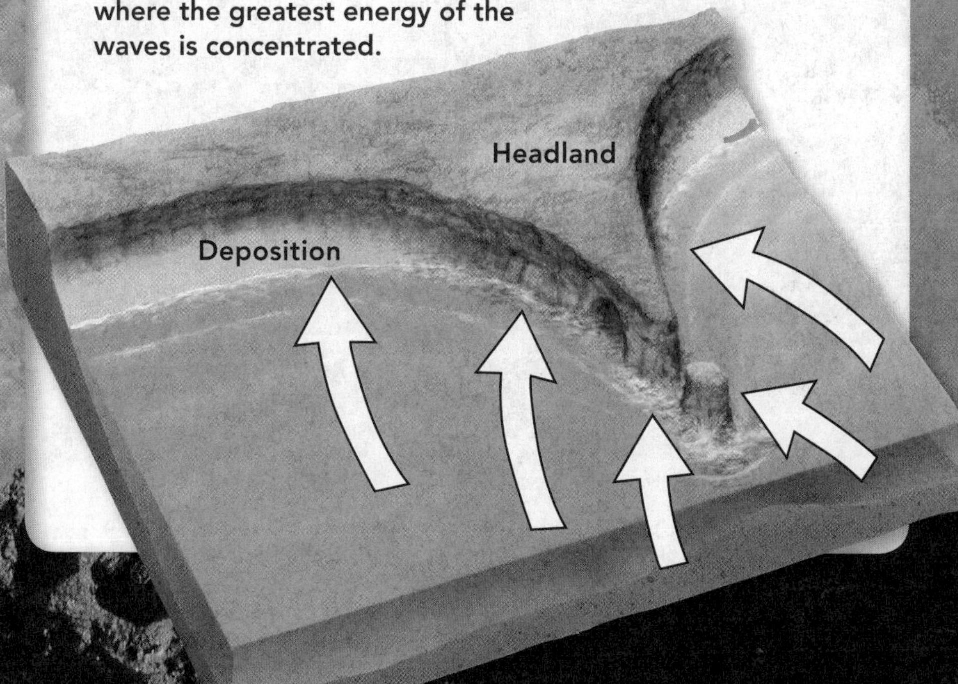

Landforms Created by Wave Erosion Think of an ax striking the trunk of a tree. The cut gets bigger and deeper with each strike of the blade. Finally the tree falls. In a similar way, ocean waves that hit a steep, rocky coast erode the base of the land there. Where the rock is softer, the waves erode the land faster. Over time the waves may erode a hollow area in the rock called a sea cave. Eventually, waves may erode the base of a cliff so much that the rock above collapses. The result is a wave-cut cliff. A sea arch is another feature of wave erosion that forms when waves erode a layer of softer rock that underlies a layer of harder rock. If an arch collapses, a pillar of rock called a sea stack may result.

Deposits by Waves Deposition occurs when waves slow down, causing the water to drop its sediment. 🔑 **Waves shape a coast when they deposit sediment, forming coastal features such as beaches, sandbars, barrier beaches, and spits.**

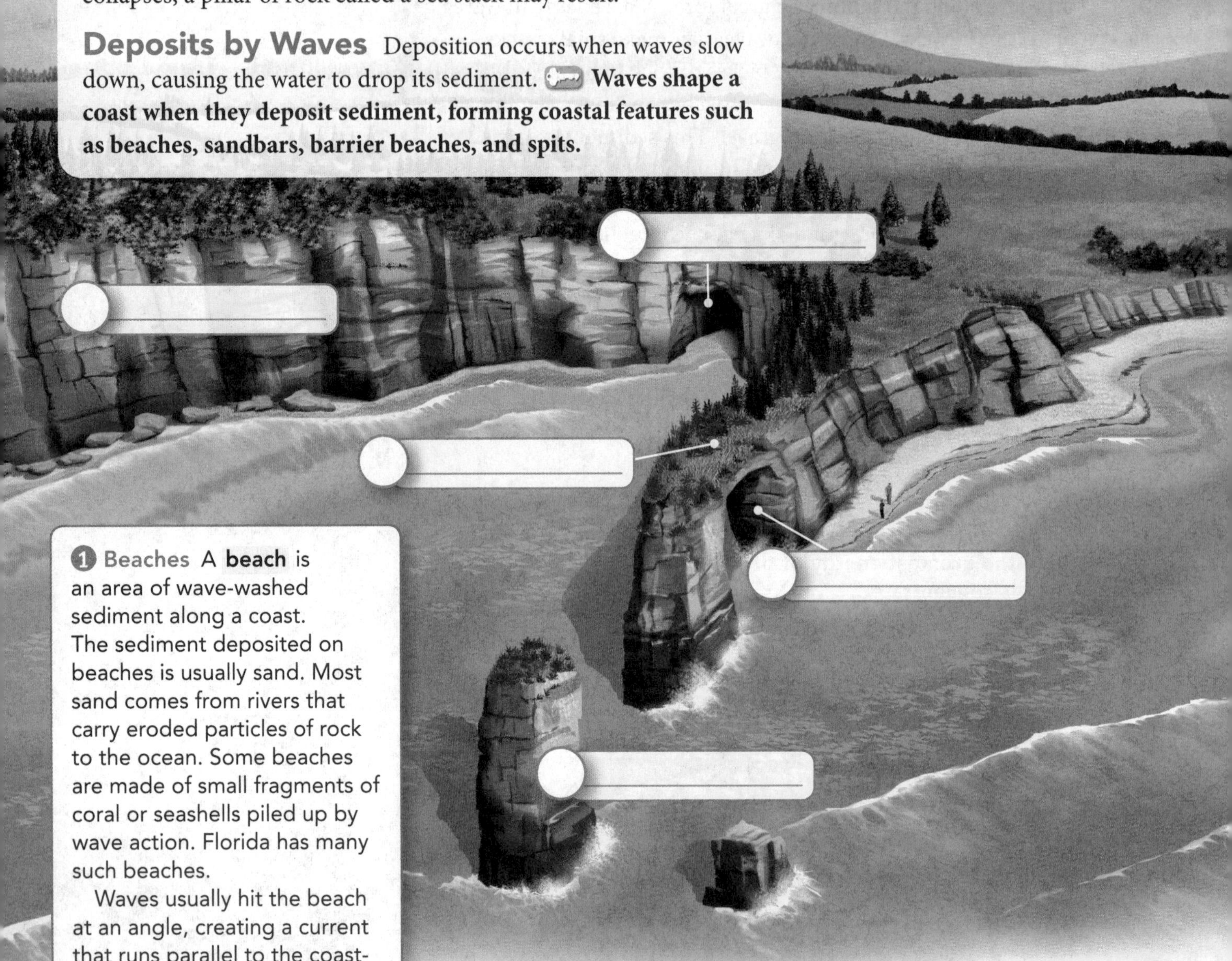

❶ Beaches A **beach** is an area of wave-washed sediment along a coast. The sediment deposited on beaches is usually sand. Most sand comes from rivers that carry eroded particles of rock to the ocean. Some beaches are made of small fragments of coral or seashells piled up by wave action. Florida has many such beaches.

Waves usually hit the beach at an angle, creating a current that runs parallel to the coastline. As waves repeatedly hit the beach, some of the beach sediment moves down the beach with the current, in a process called **longshore drift**.

FIGURE 2 ∙∙
> INTERACTIVE ART **The Changing Coast**

✏ **Apply Concepts** Use what you've learned about features of wave erosion and deposition to complete the activity.

1. Identify the landforms above. Label them in the spaces on the art.

2. Write an *E* or a *D* in each circle to indicate whether the landform was shaped by erosion or deposition.

2 Sandbars and Barrier Beaches Incoming waves carrying sand may build up sandbars, long ridges of sand parallel to the shore. A barrier beach is similar to a sandbar. A barrier beach forms when storm waves pile up large amounts of sand above sea level, forming a long, narrow island parallel to the coast. Barrier beaches are found in many places along the Atlantic coast of the United States, such as the Outer Banks of North Carolina. People have built homes on many of these barrier beaches. But the storm waves that build up the beaches can also wash them away. Barrier beach communities must be prepared for the damage that hurricanes and other storms can bring.

apply it!

Communicate How could a sea cave become a sea arch? Discuss with a classmate and write your conclusions below.

_____

_____

_____

_____

_____

Sediment

Longshore drift

3 Spits One result of longshore drift is the formation of a **spit.** A spit is a beach that projects like a finger out into the water. Spits form as a result of deposition by longshore drift. Spits occur where a headland or other obstacle interrupts longshore drift, or where the coast turns abruptly.

Lab zone® Do the Quick Lab *Shaping a Coastline.*

🔑 Assess Your Understanding

1a. Identify List two ways waves erode rock.

_____

b. List What are two features formed by wave depostion?

_____

_____

got it? ....

○ **I get it!** Now I know that waves shape the

coast by _____

_____

○ **I need extra help with** _____

Go to MY SCIENCE 🅢 COACH *online for help with this subject.*

Wind Erosion

🔑 **How Does Wind Cause Erosion and Deposition?**

my planeT DiaRY

Saving the Navajo Rangelands

How does wind erosion affect humans? You don't have to go far to find out. In the Southwest, sand dunes cover one third of Navajo Nation lands where sheep and cattle graze. Increasing drought is harming the plants that hold the dunes in place. As a result, the wind is moving the dunes on the Navajo rangelands. This makes it harder for living things to survive. Geologist Margaret Hiza Redsteer studies wind erosion. She left the Navajo Nation land to attend college, but she's come back to help. Recently, Dr. Redsteer met with Chinese scientists to learn how they stabilize dunes. Now, she'll use these methods to help slow erosion on the Navajo rangelands.

Lab zone Do the Inquiry Warm-Up *How Does Moving Air Affect Sediment?*

CAREERS

Read about Dr. Margaret Hiza Redsteer and answer the questions with a classmate.

1. Why are the dunes eroding on the Navajo land?

_____

_____

_____

2. Do you think it's important for scientists to problem solve together? Explain.

_____

_____

_____

_____

▶ **PLANET DIARY** Go to **Planet Diary** to learn more about wind erosion.

How Does Wind Cause Erosion and Deposition?

Wind can be a powerful force in shaping the land in areas where there are few plants to hold the soil in place. In the east African nation of Eritrea, sandstorms like the one in the photo are common. Strong winds blowing over loose soil can reduce visibility.

Vocabulary
- deflation
- loess
- sand dune

Skills
- Reading: Ask Questions
- Inquiry: Predict

Deflation Wind causes erosion mainly by deflation. Geologists define **deflation** as the process by which wind removes surface materials. You can see the process of deflation in **Figure 1**. When wind blows over the land, it picks up the smallest particles of sediment, such as clay and silt. The stronger the wind, the larger the particles it can pick up. Slightly heavier particles, such as sand, might skip or bounce for a short distance. But sand soon falls back to the ground. Strong winds can roll heavier sediment particles over the ground. In deserts, deflation can sometimes create an area of rock fragments called *desert pavement.* There, wind has blown away the smaller sediment, leaving behind rocky materials.

Abrasion Abrasion by wind-carried sand can polish rock, but it causes relatively little erosion. Geologists think that most desert landforms are the result of weathering and water erosion.

Vocabulary Word Origins
The Latin word *flare* means "to blow." How does *flare* relate to the word *deflation*?

_____

_____

_____

FIGURE 1 ....

Wind Erosion
The image shows three ways that wind moves particles.

✎ **Apply Concepts** After you read, complete the activity.

1. In each circle, draw the particles that would be moved by the wind. (*Hint:* Use the key.)

2. Complete each sentence with one of the following words: fine, medium, large.

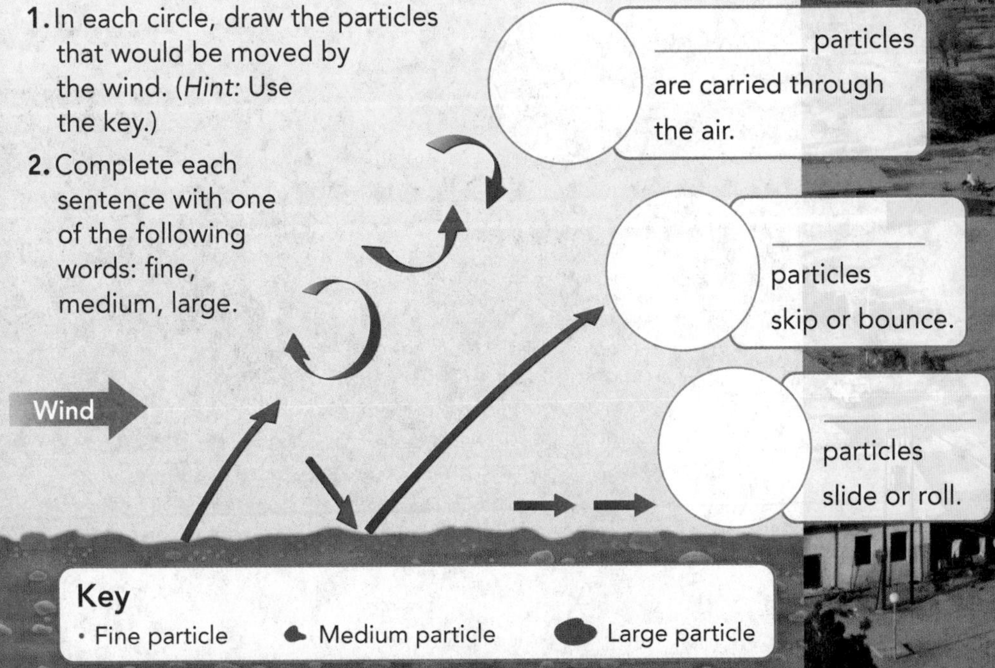

Wind →

_____ particles are carried through the air.

_____ particles skip or bounce.

_____ particles slide or roll.

Key
- Fine particle
- Medium particle
- Large particle

Ask Questions Read the headings on this page, then write down one question you have. After you read, try to answer your question.

_____

_____

_____

_____

Deposits by Wind All the sediment picked up by wind eventually falls to the ground. This happens when the wind slows down or an obstacle, such as a boulder or a clump of grass, traps the windblown sand sediment. 🔑 **Wind erosion and deposition may form sand dunes and loess deposits.** When the wind meets an obstacle, the result is usually a deposit of windblown sand called a sand dune. The shape of sand dunes is determined by the direction of the wind, the amount of sand, and the presence of plants.

Sand Dunes You can see sand dunes on beaches and in deserts where wind-blown sediment has built up. Sand dunes come in many shapes and sizes. Some are long, with parallel ridges, while others are U-shaped. They can also be very small or very large. Some sand dunes in China are 500 meters high. Sand dunes move over time. Little by little, the sand shifts with the wind from one side of the dune to the other. Sometimes plants begin growing on a dune. Plant roots can help to anchor the dune in one place.

Loess Deposits Sediment that is smaller than sand, such as particles of clay and silt, is dropped far from its source in large deposits. This fine, wind-deposited sediment is loess (LOH es). There are large loess deposits in central China and in states such as Nebraska, South Dakota, Iowa, Missouri, and Illinois. Loess helps to form fertile soil. Many areas with thick loess deposits are valuable farmlands.

FIGURE 2 ·······················
Dune Formation
✎ **Draw Conclusions** Why do these dunes have different shapes?

_____

_____

_____

_____

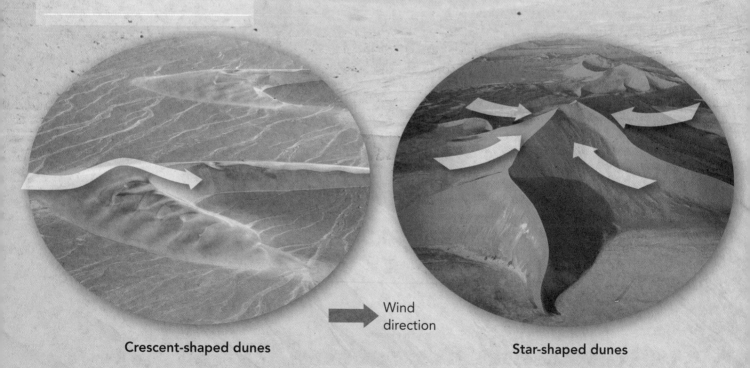

Crescent-shaped dunes

Wind direction

Star-shaped dunes

apply it!

Look at the photos and answer the questions with a classmate.

1 ⚠️ **Predict** Which dune do you think is likely to erode faster? Why?

_____

_____

_____

_____

2 Why do you think plants grew on Dune B?

_____

_____

3 How could sand dunes be held in place to prevent them from drifting onto a parking lot?

_____

_____

_____

Dune A

Dune B

Lab zone ® Do the Quick Lab
Desert Pavement.

🔑 Assess Your Understanding

1a. Review What is deflation?

_____

_____

b. Relate Cause and Effect What causes wind to deposit sand or other sediment?

_____

_____

c. [CHALLENGE] In a desert, a soil mixture of sand and small rocks is exposed to wind erosion. How would the land surface change over time?

_____

_____

_____

_____

got it? ....

○ **I get it!** Now I know that wind causes erosion through _____

○ I need extra help with _____

Go to MY SCIENCE Ⓢ COACH *online for help with this subject.*

7 Study Guide

The surface of the land is shaped by the processes of erosion and deposition caused by gravity, _____, _____, glaciers, and _____.

LESSON 1 Mass Movement

🔑 Weathering, erosion, and deposition act together in a cycle that wears down and builds up Earth's surface.

🔑 The different types of mass movement include landslides, mudflows, slumps, and creep.

Vocabulary
• erosion • sediment • deposition
• gravity • mass movement

LESSON 2 Water Erosion

🔑 Moving water is the major agent of erosion that has shaped Earth's land surface. Groundwater erodes through chemical weathering.

🔑 Through erosion, a river forms valleys, waterfalls, flood plains, meanders, and oxbow lakes. Deposition forms alluvial fans and deltas.

Vocabulary
• runoff • rill • gully • stream • tributary
• flood plain • meander • oxbow lake
• delta • alluvial fan • groundwater
• stalactite • stalagmite • karst topography

LESSON 3 Glacial Erosion

🔑 Glaciers can form only in an area where more snow falls than melts.

🔑 Continental glaciers can flow in all directions as they move.

🔑 Gravity constantly pulls a glacier downhill.

🔑 Glaciers erode the land through plucking and abrasion. When a glacier melts, it deposits the sediment it eroded from the land.

Vocabulary
• glacier • continental glacier • ice age
• valley glacier • plucking • till • moraine • kettle

LESSON 4 Wave Erosion

🔑 Waves shape the coast through erosion by breaking down rock and moving sand and other sediment.

🔑 Waves shape a coast when they deposit sediment, forming coastal features such as beaches, sandbars, barrier beaches, and spits.

Vocabulary
• headland • beach
• longshore drift • spit

LESSON 5 Wind Erosion

🔑 Wind erosion and deposition may form sand dunes and loess deposits.

Vocabulary
• deflation
• sand dune
• loess

Review and Assessment

LESSON 1 Mass Movement

1. What is the process by which weathered rock, sediment, and soil are moved from place to place?

    a. runoff   **b.** delta formation

    c. erosion   **d.** longshore drift

2. Freezing and thawing of water can cause creep, which is _____

_____

3. Compare and Contrast How are landslides and mudflows similar? How are they different?

_____

_____

_____

_____

4. Sequence Identify the steps in the erosion cycle. Explain why it has no beginning or end.

_____

_____

_____

_____

_____

_____

5. Relate Cause and Effect What type of mass movement is shown below? Explain.

_____

_____

LESSON 2 Water Erosion

6. Which feature typically contains water only during a rainstorm and right after it rains?

    a. a river   **b.** a rill

    c. a gully   **d.** a stream

7. Sediments are deposited in an alluvial fan because _____

_____

8. Sequence Complete the flowchart about stream formation.

Stream Formation

Raindrops strike ground.

↓

Runoff forms.

↓

a. _____

↓

b. _____

↓

c. _____

↓

d. _____

9. Make Judgments Your family looks at a new house right on a riverbank. Why might they hesitate to buy this house?

_____

_____

_____

_____

10. **Write About It** Explain to visitors to your valley how the lake called *Oxbow Lake* formed. Use words and a drawing.

237

CHAPTER 7 Review and Assessment

LESSON 3 Glacial Erosion

11. What do you call a mass of rock and soil deposited directly by a glacier?

    a. kettle   **b.** till

    c. slump   **d.** loess

12. When glaciers drag attached rocks across the land, they _____

_____

13. Solve Problems You're in the mountains studying a valley glacier. What methods would you use to tell if it is advancing or retreating?

_____

_____

_____

_____

_____

LESSON 4 Wave Erosion

14. What is a rocky part of the shore that sticks out in the ocean?

    a. spit   **b.** barrier beach

    c. rill   **d.** headland

15. Waves change direction as they near shore

    because _____

_____

16. Apply Concepts Under what conditions would you expect abrasion to cause the most erosion on a beach?

_____

_____

_____

17. [Write About It] You're walking on a beach and see a spit. Explain how a spit could have formed from a rocky headland.

LESSON 5 Wind Erosion

18. What do you call the erosion of sediment by wind?

    a. drifting   **b.** deposition

    c. plucking   **d.** deflation

19. Compare and Contrast How is wind deflation different from wind abrasion?

_____

_____

_____

_____

_____

20. Relate Cause and Effect How does a loess deposit form?

_____

_____

_____

APPLY THE BIG ? What processes shape the surface of the land?

21. Suppose you are a geologist traveling in a region that has limestone bedrock and plenty of rainfall. What features would you expect to find in this landscape? How do they form?

_____

_____

_____

_____

_____

_____

_____

_____

_____

Standardized Test Prep

Multiple Choice

Circle the letter of the best answer.

1. The diagram shows a meander. Where would sediment likely be eroded to help form an oxbow?

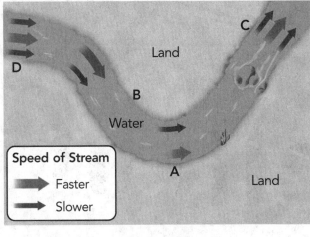

A at A   B at B
C at C   D at D

2. What is the slow, downhill mass movement of rock and soil caused by gravity?

A creep   B a glacier
C a landslide   D runoff

3. What is an alluvial fan?

A a landform created by wind deposition
B a landform created by water erosion
C a landform created by glacial erosion
D a landform created by water deposition

4. What is the name for a small depression created by the melting of a chunk of ice in glacial sediment?

A till   B kettle
C moraine   D spit

5. What "drifts" in longshore drift?

A a chunk of glacier   B a river's course
C beach sediment   D groundwater

Constructed Response

Use the diagram below and your knowledge of science to help you answer Question 6. Write your answer on a separate piece of paper.

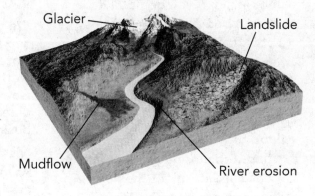

6. Describe how gravity affects the erosion of Earth's surface in mass movement, running water, and glaciers.

239

Floodwater Fallout

In June 2008, large portions of Illinois, Indiana, Iowa, Michigan, Minnesota, Missouri, and Wisconsin were under water. Weeks of rain and spring melting caused rivers in these states to overflow their banks and flood the surrounding flood plains. Where water broke through levees, families were evacuated, roads closed, and several counties were declared disaster zones. Farmland, homes, and businesses located on flood plains suffered billions of dollars' worth of damage.

We can't control the weather. When melting snow and heavy rains cause rivers to flood, some of the water may overflow onto undeveloped riverbanks and wetlands. In these places, the soil absorbs some of the water, and trees and other plants often survive the damage. But when rivers flood houses, streets, and businesses, the water can't drain. It destroys homes and businesses, causing huge amounts of damage.

At least ten million households in the United States are located on flood plains. Levees and dams protect some communities. In others, public officials make laws to prevent building on flood plains. To encourage communities to take action, the government offers flood insurance for cities and towns that take steps to reduce flood damage. We cannot stop the rain from falling or the rivers from flooding, but we can take new approaches to reduce the damage.

Communicate It Find out if your community is located on a flood plain. If you do not live near a flood plain, learn about a community that is on one. Research what plans exist for helping people during and after a flood. Suppose developers want to build homes on the flood plains in your community. What problems might this cause? What benefits might the new development bring? Write a letter to a public official giving your opinion. Support your opinion with facts from your research.

Any Way the Wind Blows

Mars is a pretty cool place. Gusts of wind blow frosty sand dunes around and cause strange streaks of sand and frost. When the Mars Rovers arrived on Mars in 2004, scientists at the National Aeronautics and Space Administration got their first chance to learn about wind and erosion on another planet. The rovers captured pictures of grains of Martian sand (called "blueberries" by the scientists) and of the patterns of dust and rock on the surface of Mars. From these pictures, scientists learned a lot about wind erosion.

By measuring these Martian blueberries and recording where they landed on the surface, scientists could estimate how strong Martian winds must be. Looking at the patterns of sand and bare rock, they could tell which directions the winds on Mars blow. Data showed that they blow from either the northwest or the southeast.

Scientists used all their measuring, counting, and other observations to design a computer model. The model can describe what happens to a planet's sandy surface when the wind starts blowing. By counting millions of blueberries on Mars, scientists are learning how to track wind erosion anywhere in the solar system!

Research It Dr. Douglas Jerolmack is a geophysicist who helped prove there is wind on Mars. Research Dr. Jerolmack's observations. Write a paragraph giving reasons why Dr. Jerolmack's scientific claims are considered to be valid (true).

▲ Scientists measured "blueberries"—grains of Martian sand and dust.

WHAT CAN YOU LEARN FROM A BUG?

How do scientists study Earth's past?

Long ago, a fly got stuck in resin from a tree. Today, that fly is a fossil that scientists can study. It's a clue to what Earth was like on the day the fly got stuck. △ Develop Hypotheses **What do you think scientists can learn from fossils like this?**

▶ UNTAMED SCIENCE Watch the **Untamed Science** video to learn more about fossils.

_____

_____

_____

_____

_____

_____

_____

A Trip Through Geologic Time

8 Getting Started

Check Your Understanding

1. Background Read the paragraph below and then answer the question.

Forces inside Earth move large pieces, or plates, of Earth's crust very slowly over long periods of time. These forces are explained by **plate tectonics.** Where these plates meet, volcanic eruptions can produce **igneous rocks.** Over time, rivers, wind, and ice can break down the rocks and carry **sediment** to new places.

The theory of **plate tectonics** states that pieces of Earth's upper layers move slowly, carried by convection currents inside Earth.

An **igneous rock** forms when melted material hardens inside Earth or on the surface.

Sediment is made up of small pieces of rock and other material.

• How do volcanic eruptions produce rocks?

_____

_____

> **MY READING WEB** If you had trouble answering the question above, visit **My Reading Web** and type in *A Trip Through Geologic Time.*

Vocabulary Skill

Prefixes The root of a word is the part of the word that carries the basic meaning. A prefix is a word part placed in front of the root to change the meaning of the root or to form a new word. Look at the examples in the table below.

Prefix	Meaning	Example
in-	inside, inward	intrusion, *n.*
ex-	outside, outward	extrusion, *n.*
super-	over, above	superposition, *n.*

2. Quick Check The root *–trusion* means "pushing." What might *extrusion* mean?_____

fossil

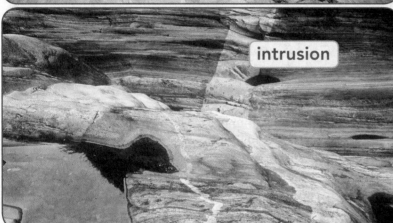

intrusion

law of superposition

vertebrate

Chapter Preview

LESSON 1
- fossil • mold • cast
- petrified fossil • carbon film
- trace fossil • paleontologist
- evolution • extinct

⟳ **Compare and Contrast**
△ **Pose Questions**

LESSON 2
- relative age • absolute age
- law of superposition • extrusion
- intrusion • fault • index fossil
- unconformity

⟳ **Relate Text and Visuals**
△ **Infer**

LESSON 3
- radioactive decay • half-life

⟳ **Identify the Main Idea**
△ **Calculate**

LESSON 4
- geologic time scale • era
- period

⟳ **Summarize**
△ **Make Models**

LESSON 5
- comet

⟳ **Sequence**
△ **Communicate**

LESSON 6
- invertebrate • vertebrate
- amphibian • reptile
- mass extinction • mammal

⟳ **Identify Supporting Evidence**
△ **Classify**

> VOCAB FLASH CARDS For extra help with vocabulary, visit **Vocab Flash Cards** and type in *A Trip Through Geologic Time.*

UNLOCK THE BIG ?

🔑 **What Are Fossils?**

🔑 **What Are the Kinds of Fossils?**

🔑 **What Do Fossils Show?**

my planet diary

DISCOVERY

A Dinosaur Named Sue

On a hot day in August 1990, Sue Hendrickson was hunting for fossils near the town of Faith, South Dakota. She found some little pieces of bone below a cliff. When she looked up at the cliff, she saw more bones. These bones weren't little. They were enormous! She and other scientists determined that they were the bones of a *Tyrannosaurus rex*. In fact, she'd found the largest and most complete skeleton of a *Tyrannosaurus* ever discovered. Today, the skeleton, nicknamed "Sue," is on display at the Field Museum in Chicago.

✏️ **Communicate** Write your answer to each question below. Then discuss your answers with a partner.

1. What science skills did Sue Hendrickson use when she discovered Sue?

_____

_____

2. What do you think scientists can learn by studying dinosaur skeletons?

_____

_____

_____

> PLANET DIARY Go to **Planet Diary** to learn more about fossils.

Lab zone Do the Inquiry Warm-Up *What's in a Rock?*

What Are Fossils?

Sue is one of the most nearly complete dinosaur fossils ever found. **Fossils** are the preserved remains or traces of living things. **Most fossils form when living things die and are buried by sediment. The sediment slowly hardens into rock and preserves the shapes of the organisms.** Sediment is made up of rock particles or the remains of living things. Most fossils form from animals or plants that once lived in or near quiet water such as swamps, lakes, or shallow seas where sediment builds up. In **Figure 1,** you can see how a fossil might form.

When an organism dies, its soft parts often decay quickly or are eaten by animals. That is why only hard parts of an organism generally leave fossils. These hard parts include bones, shells, teeth, seeds, and woody stems. It is rare for the soft parts of an organism to become a fossil.

FIGURE 1 ·····························

> INTERACTIVE ART **How a Fossil Forms**
A fossil may form when sediment quickly covers an organism's body.

An organism dies and sinks to the bottom of a lake.

The organism is covered by sediment.

✎ **Sequence** What happens next?

_____

_____

Do the Quick Lab
Sweet Fossils.

Assess Your Understanding
got it? ···

○ I get it! Now I know that fossils are_____

○ I need extra help with _____

Go to MY SCIENCE COACH online for help with this subject.

247

What Are the Kinds of Fossils?

🔖 **Fossils found in rock include molds and casts, petrified fossils, carbon films, and trace fossils. Other fossils form when the remains of organisms are preserved in substances such as tar, amber, or ice.** Look at examples of the kinds of fossils in **Figure 2.**

Molds and Casts The most common fossils are molds and casts. A **mold** is a hollow area in sediment in the shape of an organism or part of an organism. A mold forms when the organism is buried in sediment. Later, water may deposit minerals and sediment into a mold, forming a cast. A **cast** is a solid copy of the shape of an organism. Molds and casts can preserve fine details.

Petrified Fossils A fossil may form when the remains of an organism become petrified. The term *petrified* means "turned into stone." **Petrified fossils** are fossils in which minerals replace all of an organism, or a part, such as a dinosaur bone. This can also happen to wood, such as tree trunks. Water carrying minerals seeps into spaces in the plant's cells. Over time, the water evaporates, leaving the minerals behind.

Carbon Films Another type of fossil is a **carbon film,** an extremely thin coating of carbon on rock. When sediment buries an organism, some gases escape from the sediment, leaving carbon behind. Eventually, only a thin film of carbon remains. This process can preserve the delicate parts of plant leaves and insects.

🌀 **Compare and Contrast** How are carbon films and preserved remains different?

_____

_____

_____

_____

_____

_____

FIGURE 2 ·······························
Types of Fossils
In addition to petrified fossils, fossils may be molds and casts, carbon films, trace fossils, or preserved remains.

✎ **Classify** Identify each fossil shown here by its type.

Where They Walked
This footprint shows how a dinosaur walked. Fossil type:

_____

Raised Fern
This fossil shows the texture of a leaf. Fossil type:

_____

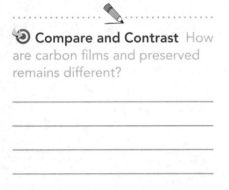

Hollow Fern
Can you see the veins in this plant leaf? Fossil type:

_____

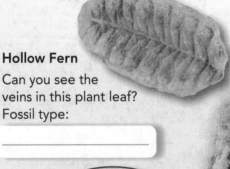

Fine Details
This fossil preserves a thin layer that shows the details of an ancient insect. Fossil type:

_____

apply it!

This fossil is of an ancient organism called *Archaeopteryx*. Study the photograph and then answer the questions.

1 What type of fossil is this?

_____

2 **Pose Questions** List two questions about the organism that studying this fossil could help you answer.

_____

_____

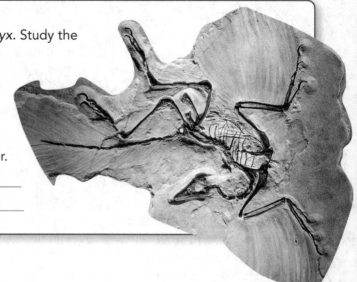

Trace Fossils

Trace fossils provide evidence of the activities of ancient organisms. A fossilized footprint is one example. In such a fossil, a print is buried by sediment, which slowly becomes solid rock. Trails and burrows can also become trace fossils.

Preserved Remains

Some processes can preserve entire organisms. For example, some organisms become trapped in sticky tar or tree resin. When the resin hardens, it becomes a substance called amber. Freezing can also preserve remains.

Frozen in Time
Ice preserved even the fur and skin of this woolly mammoth for thousands of years. Fossil type:

_____

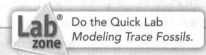

From Wood to Stone
Minerals replaced other materials inside this tree, producing the colors shown here. Fossil type:

_____

Lab zone Do the Quick Lab *Modeling Trace Fossils.*

Assess Your Understanding

1a. Identify A (mold/trace fossil) can form when sediment buries the hard part of an organism.

b. Explain A petrified fossil forms when

_____ replace parts of

a(n) _____ .

c. Make Generalizations What might you learn from a carbon film that you could not learn from a cast?

_____

_____

got it?

O **I get it!** Now I know that the kinds of fossils are _____

_____

_____

O **I need extra help with** _____

Go to **MY SCIENCE COACH** online for help with this subject.

What Do Fossils Show?

Would you like to hunt for fossils all over the world? And what could you learn from them? Scientists who study fossils are called **paleontologists** (pay lee un TAHL uh jists). Together, all the information that paleontologists have gathered about past life is called the fossil record. 🦴 **The fossil record provides evidence about the history of life and past environments on Earth. The fossil record also shows how different groups of organisms have changed over time.**

Fossils and Past Environments Paleontologists use fossils to build up a picture of Earth's past environments. The fossils found in an area tell whether the area was a shallow bay, an ocean bottom, or a freshwater swamp.

Fossils also provide evidence about the past climate of a region. For example, coal has been found in Antarctica. But coal forms only from the remains of plants that grow in warm, swampy regions. The presence of coal shows that the climate of Antarctica was once much warmer than it is today. **Figure 3** shows another example of how fossils show change in an environment.

FIGURE 3 ·······························

▶ **INTERACTIVE ART** **Wyoming, 50 Million Years Ago**
Today, as you can see in the postcard, Wyoming has areas of dry plateaus. But 50 million years ago, the area was very different. ✎ **Infer** Identify the organism or kind of organism shown by fossils a, b, and c.

Palms

a

b

c

Crocodilian

Bat

CHALLENGE What features of *Hyracotherium* show that it is related to horses?

_____

_____

_____

_____

Gar

Change and the Fossil Record

Change and the Fossil Record The fossil record also reveals changes in organisms. Older rocks contain fossils of simpler organisms. Younger rocks contain fossils of both simple and more complex organisms. In other words, the fossil record shows that life on Earth has evolved, or changed over time. **Evolution** is the change in living things over time.

The fossil record shows that millions of types of organisms have evolved as climate and other factors changed over time. Some, such as the dinosaurs, have become extinct. A type of organism is **extinct** if it no longer exists and will never again live on Earth.

Scientists use fossils to reconstruct extinct organisms and determine how they may be related to living organisms. For example, the animals called *Hyracotherium* in **Figure 3** are related to modern horses.

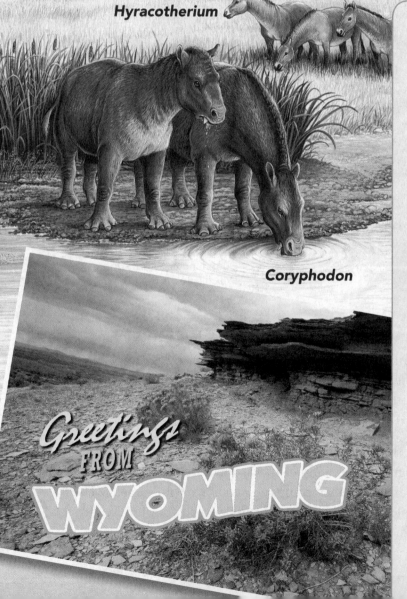

Sequoia

Uintatherium

Hyracotherium

Coryphodon

Greetings FROM WYOMING

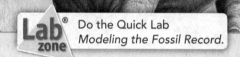

Lab zone Do the Quick Lab *Modeling the Fossil Record.*

🔑 Assess Your Understanding

2a. Explain What does the fossil record show about how life has changed over time?

_____

_____

_____

b. Apply Concepts Give an example of a question you could ask about a fossil of an extinct organism.

_____

_____

_____

got it? ···

○ **I get it!** Now I know that the fossil record shows _____

_____

_____

○ **I need extra help with** _____

Go to my science 🔎 **COACH** *online for help with this subject.*

The Relative Age of Rocks

- How Old Are Rock Layers?

- How Can Rock Layers Change?

my planet Diary

Posted by Owen

Location Tacoma, WA

A couple of summers ago, my dad took me rock climbing for the first time. I went to a place called Frenchman Coulee in central Washington. It was really cool because the rock was basalt, which forms in giant pillars. It starts as lava, and then cools and you can see the different lava flows in the rock. Another cool thing is that Frenchman Coulee, which is a canyon, was gouged out by huge Ice Age floods.

✎ **Communicate** Discuss the question below with a partner. Then answer it on your own.

How do you think scientists figure out the age of the basalt layers at Frenchman Coulee?

_____

_____

_____

_____

▷ PLANET DIARY Go to **Planet Diary** to learn more about the age of rock layers.

 Do the Inquiry Warm-Up
Which Layer Is the Oldest?

How Old Are Rock Layers?

If you found a fossil in a rock, you might start by asking, "What is it?" Your next question would probably be, "How old is it?" The first step is to find the age of the rock.

Relative and Absolute Age Geologists have two ways to express the age of a rock. The **relative age** of a rock is its age compared to the ages of other rocks. You have probably used the idea of relative age when comparing your age with someone else's. For example, if you say that you are older than your brother but younger than your sister, you are describing your relative age.

Vocabulary
- relative age • absolute age • law of superposition
- extrusion • intrusion • fault • index fossil
- unconformity

Skills
⟳ Reading: Relate Text and Visuals
△ Inquiry: Infer

The relative age of a rock does not provide its absolute age. The **absolute age** of a rock is the number of years that have passed since the rock formed. It may be impossible to know a rock's absolute age exactly, so geologists often use both absolute and relative ages.

Rock Layers Fossils are most often found in layers of sedimentary rock. Geologists use the **law of superposition** to determine the relative ages of sedimentary rock layers. 🔑 **According to the law of superposition, in undisturbed horizontal sedimentary rock layers the oldest layer is at the bottom. Each higher layer is younger than the layers below it.** The deeper you go, the older the rocks are.

Figure 1 shows rock layers in the Grand Canyon. Rock layers like these form a record of Earth's history. Scientists can study this record to understand how Earth and life on Earth have changed.

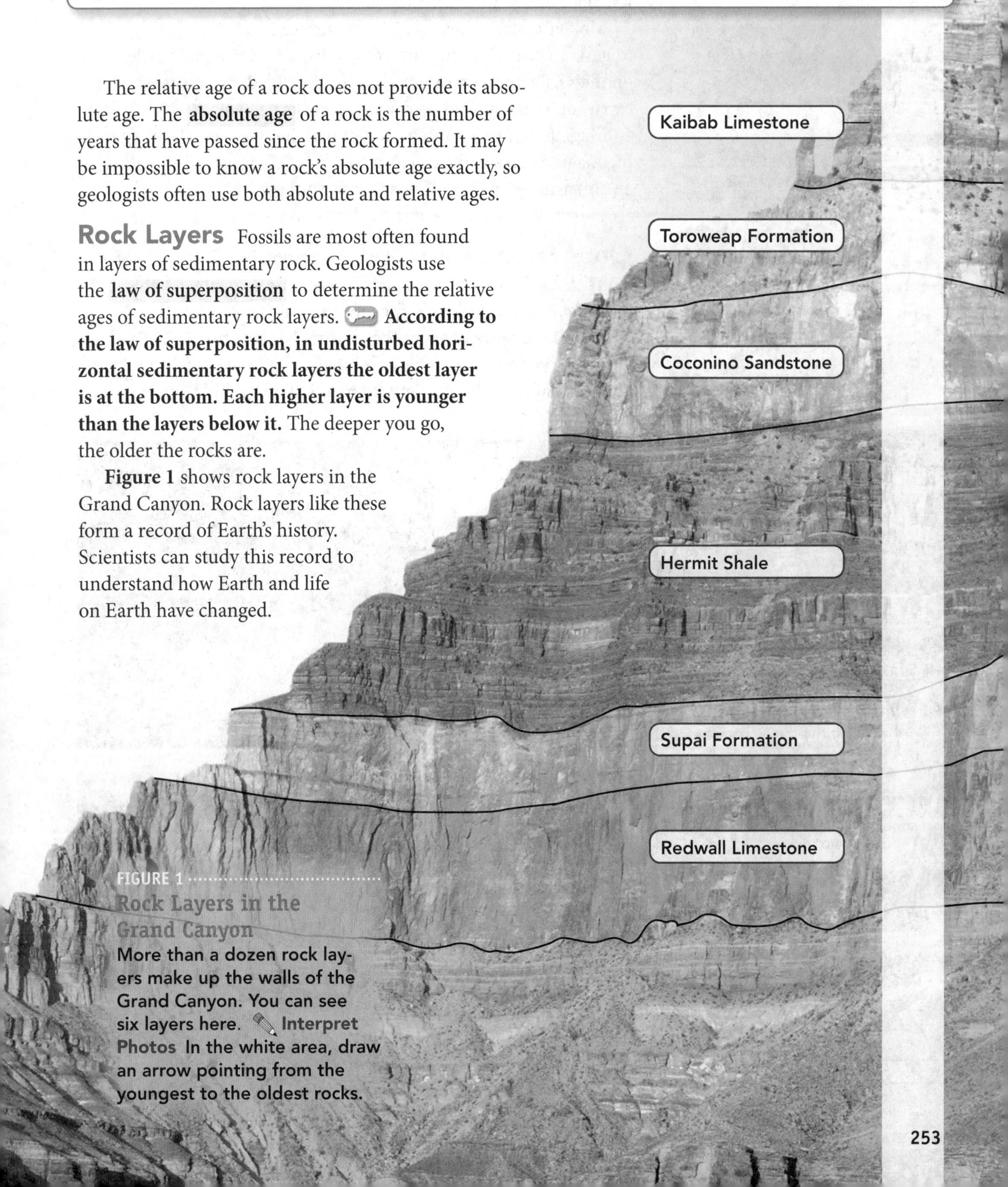

Kaibab Limestone

Toroweap Formation

Coconino Sandstone

Hermit Shale

Supai Formation

Redwall Limestone

FIGURE 1 ·········
Rock Layers in the Grand Canyon
More than a dozen rock layers make up the walls of the Grand Canyon. You can see six layers here. ✎ Interpret Photos In the white area, draw an arrow pointing from the youngest to the oldest rocks.

253

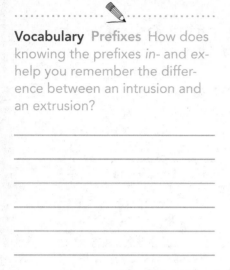

Vocabulary Prefixes How does knowing the prefixes *in-* and *ex-* help you remember the difference between an intrusion and an extrusion?

_____

_____

_____

_____

_____

_____

apply it!

The diagram below shows rock layers found at a site.

❶ Circle the area on the diagram that shows an intrusion.

❷ Shade the oldest layer on the diagram.

❸ **Infer** What can you infer about the relative ages of areas B and E?

_____

_____

_____

_____

_____

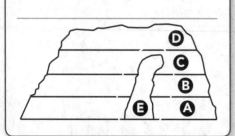

Clues From Igneous Rock There are other clues to the relative ages of rocks besides the position of rock layers. To determine relative age, geologists also study extrusions and intrusions of igneous rock, faults, and index fossils.

Molten material beneath Earth's surface is called magma. Magma that reaches the surface is called lava. Lava that hardens on the surface and forms igneous rock is called an **extrusion.** An extrusion is always younger than the rocks below it.

Magma may push into bodies of rock below the surface. There, the magma cools and hardens into a mass of igneous rock called an **intrusion.** An intrusion is always younger than the rock layers around and beneath it. **Figure 2** shows an intrusion.

Clues From Faults More clues come from the study of faults. A **fault** is a break in Earth's crust. Forces inside Earth cause movement of the rock on opposite sides of a fault.

A fault is always younger than the rock it cuts through. To determine the relative age of a fault, geologists find the relative age of the youngest layer cut by the fault. **Figure 3** shows a fault.

FIGURE 2 ················
Intrusion
An intrusion cuts through rock layers.

Intrusion

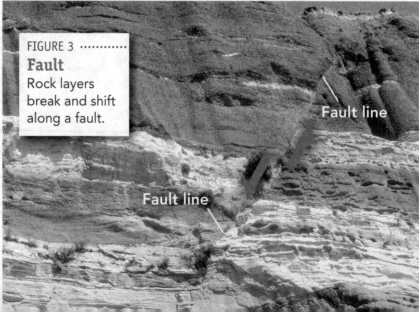

FIGURE 3 ············
Fault
Rock layers break and shift along a fault.

Fault line

Fault line

How Do Fossils Show Age?

To date rock layers, geologists first find the relative age of a layer of rock at one location. Then they can match layers in other locations to that layer.

Certain fossils, called index fossils, help geologists match rock layers. To be useful as an **index fossil,** a fossil must be widely distributed and represent an organism that existed for a geologically short period of time. **Index fossils are useful because they tell the relative ages of the rock layers in which they occur.** Scientists infer that layers with matching index fossils are the same age.

You can use index fossils to match rock layers. Look at **Figure 4,** which shows rock layers from four different locations. Notice that two of the fossils are found in only one of these rock layers. These are the index fossils.

FIGURE 4 ·······················
> **INTERACTIVE ART** Index Fossils

Scientists use index fossils to match rock layers.

✎ **Interpret Diagrams** Label the layers to match the first area shown. Circle the fossil or fossils that you can use as index fossils. What can you infer about the history of Location 4?

_____

_____

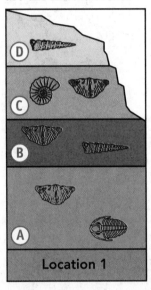

Location 1

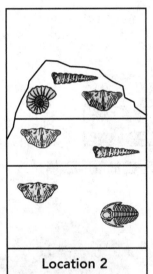

Location 2

Location 3

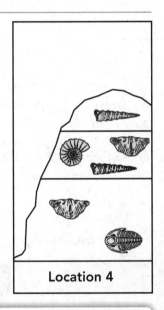

Location 4

Lab zone® Do the Lab Investigation *Exploring Geologic Time Through Core Samples.*

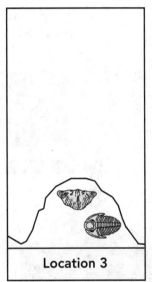 Assess Your Understanding

1a. Explain In an area with several different rock layers, which is oldest? Explain.

_____

_____

_____

b. Infer How could a geologist match the rock layers in one area to rock layers found in another area?

_____

_____

_____

_____

got it? ···

○ **I get it!** Now I know that you can find the relative age of rocks by_____

_____

○ I need extra help with_____

Go to MY SCIENCE ⓢ COACH *online for help with this subject.*

How Can Rock Layers Change?

The geologic record of sedimentary rock layers is not complete. In fact, most of Earth's geologic record has been lost to erosion. 🗝 **Gaps in the geologic record and folding can change the position in which rock layers appear.** Motion along faults can also change how rock layers line up. These changes make it harder for scientists to reconstruct Earth's history. **Figure 5** shows how the order of rock layers may change.

Gaps in the Geologic Record
When rock layers erode away, an older rock surface may be exposed. Then deposition begins again, building new rock layers. The surface where new rock layers meet a much older rock surface beneath them is called an unconformity. An **unconformity** is a gap in the geologic record. It shows where rock layers have been lost due to erosion.

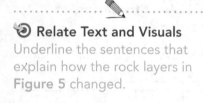

Relate Text and Visuals
Underline the sentences that explain how the rock layers in Figure 5 changed.

FIGURE 5 ·······················

Unconformities and Folding
✎ **Draw Conclusions** Shade the oldest and youngest layers in the last two diagrams. Label the unconformity. Circle the part of the fold that is overturned.

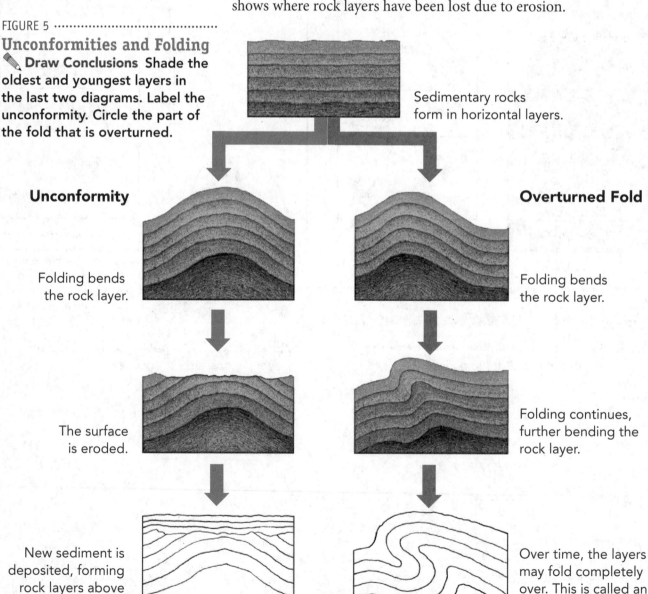

Sedimentary rocks form in horizontal layers.

Unconformity

Folding bends the rock layer.

The surface is eroded.

New sediment is deposited, forming rock layers above the unconformity.

Overturned Fold

Folding bends the rock layer.

Folding continues, further bending the rock layer.

Over time, the layers may fold completely over. This is called an overturned fold.

Folding Sometimes, forces inside Earth fold rock layers so much that the layers are turned over completely. In this case, the youngest rock layers may be on the bottom!

No one place holds a complete geologic record. Geologists compare rock layers in many places to piece together as complete a sequence as possible.

apply it!

Study the photo. Then answer the questions.

❶ What does the photo show? (an unconformity/folding)

❷ What evidence do you see for your answer to Question 1?

_____

❸ CHALLENGE What can you infer about the history of this area?

_____
_____
_____

Lab zone Do the Quick Lab *How Did It Form?*

🔑 Assess Your Understanding

2a. List Name two ways rock layers can change.

_____

b. Explain How does folding change rock layers?

_____
_____
_____

c. Draw Conclusions Two locations include a layer of rock with a particular index fossil. In one location, the layer occurs in a higher position than in the other. What can you conclude about the history of the two areas?

_____
_____
_____

got it? .....

○ **I get it!** Now I know that rock layers can change due to _____
_____

○ **I need extra help with** _____

Go to **my science COACH** *online for help with this subject.*

Radioactive Dating

UNLOCK THE BIG Q

🔑 What Is Radioactive Decay?

🔑 What Is Radioactive Dating?

my planet Diary

VOICES FROM HISTORY

Marie Curie

In 1896, French scientists named Marie and Pierre Curie heard about experiments that had been done by another scientist, Henri Becquerel (bek uh REL). Marie Curie later described what happened:

> Becquerel had shown that by placing some uranium salt on a photographic plate, covered with black paper, the plate would be affected as if light had fallen on it. The effect is produced by special rays which are emitted by the uranium salt.... My determinations showed that the emission of the rays is an atomic property of the uranium.

The property that Becquerel and the Curies discovered was called radioactivity. Today, radioactivity is used for many purposes—including finding the age of rocks!

After you read Marie Curie's description, answer the following questions.

1. What did Marie and Pierre Curie discover about radioactivity?

_____

_____

_____

2. What does the discovery of radioactivity tell you about how scientists work together?

_____

_____

_____

▶ PLANET DIARY   Go to **Planet Diary** to learn more about the uses of radioactivity.

Lab zone®   Do the Inquiry Warm-Up *How Long Till It's Gone?*

Vocabulary
- radioactive decay
- half-life

Skills
- Reading: Identify the Main Idea
- Inquiry: Calculate

What Is Radioactive Decay?

Most elements usually do not change. But some elements can break down, or decay, over time. These elements release particles and energy in a process called **radioactive decay.** These elements are said to be radioactive. **During radioactive decay, the atoms of one element break down to form atoms of another element.**

Half-Life The rate of decay of each radioactive element never changes. The **half-life** of a radioactive element is the time it takes for half of the radioactive atoms to decay. You can see in **Figure 1** how a radioactive element decays over time.

FIGURE 1 ·································

Half-Life
The half-life of a radioactive element is the amount of time it takes for half of the radioactive atoms to decay.

✎ **Graph** What pattern do you see in the graph? Use the pattern to complete the last bar.

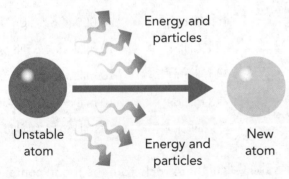

Energy and particles

Unstable atom → New atom

Energy and particles

Decay of Radioactive Element

100% | 50% | 75% | 87.5% |

50% | 25% | 12.5% |

Start | 1 | 2 | 3 | 4
Number of Half-Lives

■ Amount of radioactive element remaining
■ Amount of new element formed

Lab zone® Do the Quick Lab
The Dating Game.

Assess Your Understanding

got it? ··

○ I get it! Now I know that radioactive decay occurs when _____

_____

○ I need extra help with _____

Go to MY SCIENCE ⑤ COACH online for help with this subject.

What Is Radioactive Dating?

Radioactive elements occur naturally in igneous rocks. Scientists use the rate at which these elements decay to calculate the rock's age. As a radioactive element within the igneous rock decays, it changes into another element. So the composition of the rock changes slowly over time. The amount of the radioactive element decreases. But the amount of the new element increases.

Determining Absolute Ages

Geologists use radioactive dating to determine the absolute ages of rocks. 🔑 **In radioactive dating, scientists first determine the amount of a radioactive element in a rock. Then they compare that amount with the amount of the stable element into which the radioactive element decays.** They use this information and the half-life of the element to calculate the age of the rock.

Potassium-Argon Dating

Scientists often date rocks using potassium-40. This form of potassium decays to stable argon-40 and has a half-life of 1.3 billion years. Potassium-40 is useful in dating the most ancient rocks because of its long half-life.

Elements Used in Radioactive Dating

Radioactive Element	Half-life (years)	Dating Range (years)
Carbon-14	5,730	500–50,000
Potassium-40	1.3 billion	50,000–4.6 billion
Rubidium-87	48.8 billion	10 million–4.6 billion
Thorium-232	14 billion	10 million–4.6 billion
Uranium-235	713 million	10 million–4.6 billion
Uranium-238	4.5 billion	10 million–4.6 billion

do the math!

Radioactive Dating

A rock contains 25% of the potassium-40 it started with. How old is the rock?

STEP 1 Determine how many half-lives have passed.
After one half-life, 50% of the potassium would remain. After two half-lives, 25% of the potassium would remain. So two half-lives have passed.

STEP 2 Find the half-life of potassium-40.
The half-life of potassium-40 is 1.3 billion years.

STEP 3 Multiply the half-life by the number of half-lives that have passed.
1.3 billion years/half-life × 2 half-lives = 2.6 billion years, so the rock is about 2.6 billion years old.

1 Calculate A rock from the moon contains 12.5% of the potassium-40 it began with. How old is the rock? (*Hint:* 12.5% = $\frac{1}{8}$)

_____

_____

2 Calculate A fossil contains $\frac{1}{16}$ of the carbon-14 it began with. How old is the fossil?

_____

_____

Carbon-14 Dating

Carbon-14 is a radioactive form of carbon. All plants and animals contain carbon, including some carbon-14. After an organism dies, the carbon-14 in the organism's body decays. It changes to stable nitrogen-14. To determine the age of a sample, scientists measure the amount of carbon-14 that is left in the organism's remains. Carbon-14 has been used to date fossils such as frozen mammoths and the skeletons of prehistoric humans.

Carbon-14 has a half-life of only 5,730 years. For this reason, it generally can't be used to date fossils or rocks older than about 50,000 years. The amount of carbon-14 left would be too small to measure accurately. Also, most rocks do not contain much carbon.

Identify the Main Idea
Underline the main idea in the first paragraph to the left.

FIGURE 2 ....

> **REAL-WORLD INQUIRY** **Using Carbon-14 Dating**
Scientists have dated these skeletons to 5,000–6,000 years ago. But they do not use radioactive dating to find the age of stone artifacts made by people.
Make Generalizations Why not?

_____

_____

_____

_____

_____

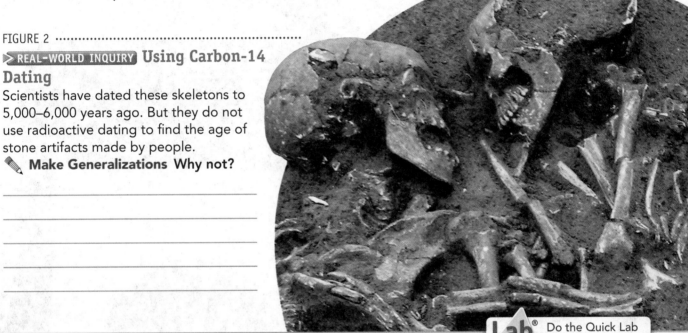

Lab zone® Do the Quick Lab *How Old Is It?*

Assess Your Understanding

1a. Identify Scientists use the method of (radioactive dating/relative dating) to find the absolute age of a rock.

b. Apply Concepts The half-life of thorium-232 is 14 billion years. A rock with 25% of its thorium-232 remaining is _____ years old.

c. CHALLENGE A scientist finds stone tools in the ruins of an ancient house. The house also has ashes in a fireplace. How could the scientist estimate the age of the stone tools?

_____

_____

_____

_____

got it? ....

O **I get it!** Now I know that radioactive dating is done by _____

_____

O **I need extra help with** _____

Go to my science s COACH *online for help with this subject.*

The Geologic Time Scale

🔑 **What Is the Geologic Time Scale?**

my planet Diary

SCIENCE STATS

Earth's History in a Day

Suppose you could squeeze all of Earth's 4.6-billion-year history into one 24-hour day. The table shows the times at which some major events would take place.

	Time	First Appearance
A	Midnight	Earth
B	3:00 A.M.	Rocks
C	4:00 A.M.	Bacteria
D	2:00 P.M.	Algae
E	8:30–9:00 P.M.	Seaweeds and jellyfish
F	10:00 P.M.	Land plants
G	10:50 P.M.	Dinosaurs
H	11:39 P.M.	Mammals
I	11:58:43 P.M.	Humans

Use the data in the table to answer these questions.

1. ✏️ **Sequence** Write the letter for each event on the clock diagram.

2. Did anything surprise you about the data? If so, what?

_____

_____

▶ PLANET DIARY Go to **Planet Diary** to learn more about Earth's history.

Lab zone® Do the Inquiry Warm-Up *This Is Your Life!*

Vocabulary
- geologic time scale
- era • period

Skills
- Reading: Summarize
- Inquiry: Make Models

What Is the Geologic Time Scale?

When you speak of the past, what names do you use for different spans of time? You probably use names such as century, decade, year, month, week, and day. But these units aren't very helpful for thinking about much longer periods of time. Scientists needed to develop a way to talk about Earth's history.

Because the time span of Earth's past is so great, geologists use the geologic time scale to show Earth's history. The **geologic time scale** is a record of the geologic events and the evolution of life forms as shown in the fossil record.

Scientists first developed the geologic time scale by studying rock layers and index fossils worldwide. With this information, scientists placed Earth's rocks in order by relative age. Later, radioactive dating helped determine the absolute age of the divisions in the geologic time scale. **Figure 1** shows some of the earliest known rocks.

Summarize Write two or three sentences to summarize the information on this page.

_____

_____

_____

_____

_____

_____

FIGURE 1 ·····················
Ancient Rocks
The Isua rocks in Greenland are among the oldest rocks on Earth. They formed after heat and pressure changed sedimentary rocks that formed under early oceans.

263

FIGURE 2 ························

The Geologic Time Scale

The divisions of the geologic time scale are used to date events in Earth's history.

✎ **Calculate** After you read the next page, calculate and fill in the duration of each period. Then use the time scale to identify the period in which each organism below lived.

Organism: *Wiwaxia*
Age: about 500 million years
Period: _____

Organism: *Velociraptor*
Age: about 80 million years
Period: _____

Organism: *Smilodon*
Age: about 12,000 years
Period: _____

	PERIOD	MILLIONS OF YEARS AGO	DURATION (MILLIONS OF YEARS)
Cenozoic Era	QUATERNARY		
		1.8	
	NEOGENE		
		23	
	PALEOGENE		
		66	
Mesozoic Era	CRETACEOUS		
		146	
	JURASSIC		
		200	
	TRIASSIC		
		251	
Paleozoic Era	PERMIAN		
		299	
	CARBONIFEROUS		
		359	
	DEVONIAN		
		416	
	SILURIAN		
		444	
	ORDOVICIAN		
		488	
	CAMBRIAN		
		542	
Precambrian Time			
		4,600	

Dividing Geologic Time As geologists studied the fossil record, they found major changes in life forms at certain times. They used these changes to mark where one unit of geologic time ends and the next begins. Therefore, the divisions of the geologic time scale depend on events in the history of life on Earth. **Figure 2** shows the major divisions of the geologic time scale.

Precambrian Time Geologic time begins with a long span of time called Precambrian Time (pree KAM bree un). Precambrian Time, which covers about 88 percent of Earth's history, ended 542 million years ago. Few fossils survive from this time period.

Eras Geologists divide the time between Precambrian Time and the present into three long units of time called **eras.** They are the Paleozoic Era, the Mesozoic Era, and the Cenozoic Era.

Periods Eras are subdivided into units of geologic time called **periods.** You can see in **Figure 2** that the Mesozoic Era includes three periods: the Triassic Period, the Jurassic Period, and the Cretaceous Period.

The names of many of the geologic periods come from places around the world where geologists first described the rocks and fossils of that period. For example, the name *Cambrian* refers to Cambria, a Latin name for Wales. The rocks shown below are in Wales. The dark bottom layer dates from the Cambrian period.

apply it!

Refer to the geologic time scale shown in **Figure 2** to answer the questions below.

Suppose you want to make a model of the geologic time scale. You decide to use a scale of 1 cm = 1 million years.

1 Not counting Precambrian time, which era would take up the most space? _____

2 Make Models How long would the Mesozoic Era be in your model? _____

3 CHALLENGE Suppose you used a different scale: 1 m = 1 million years. What would be one advantage and one disadvantage of this scale?

_____
_____
_____
_____
_____

Lab zone® Do the Quick Lab *Going Back in Time.*

🔑 Assess Your Understanding

1a. Define The geologic time scale is a record of _____ and _____ .

b. Sequence Number the following periods in order from earliest to latest.

Neogene _____   Jurassic _____

Quaternary _____   Triassic _____

Cretaceous _____

c. Draw Conclusions Refer to My Planet Diary and **Figure 2**. During which period did modern humans arise?

_____

got it? ....

○ I get it! Now I know that geologic time _____

○ I need extra help with _____

Go to my science ⑤ coach *online for help with this subject.*

Early Earth

UNLOCK THE BIG ?

🔑 **How Did Earth Form?**

my planet Diary

CAREERS

Exploring Life Under Water

Dr. Anna-Louise Reysenbach always loved water sports. She was also interested in organisms that live in strange, extreme environments. Now, as a biology professor at Portland State University in Oregon, she gets to combine her two loves—and learn about early life on Earth!

Dr. Reysenbach uses submersibles, or submarines, to study bacteria that live deep under the ocean. No sunlight reaches these depths. There, hot water carrying dissolved minerals from inside Earth flows out through vents. Some kinds of bacteria use chemical energy from this material to make food, much as plants use the energy from sunlight. Scientists think that these bacteria are very similar to some of the earliest forms of life on Earth.

✏️ **Communicate** Discuss the work of Dr. Reysenbach with a partner. Then answer these questions on your own.

1. How are the bacteria near ocean vents different from many other organisms on Earth?

_____

_____

_____

2. Would you like to work under water in a submersible? Why, or why not?

_____

_____

_____

_____

▷ **PLANET DIARY** Go to **Planet Diary** to learn more about deep ocean vents.

Lab zone® Do the Inquiry Warm-Up *How Could Planet Earth Form in Space?*

Vocabulary
• comet

Skills
↻ Reading: Sequence
△ Inquiry: Communicate

How Did Earth Form?

Using radioactive dating, scientists have determined that the oldest rocks ever found on Earth are about 4 billion years old. But scientists think Earth formed even earlier than that.

The Age of Earth According to these scientists' hypothesis, the moon formed from material knocked loose when a very young Earth collided with another object. This means Earth and the moon are about the same age. Scientists have used radioactive dating to find the age of moon rocks that astronauts brought back to Earth. The oldest moon rocks are about 4.6 billion years old. Scientists infer that Earth is also roughly 4.6 billion years old—only a little older than those moon rocks.

Earth Takes Shape 🔑 **Scientists think that Earth began as a ball of dust, rock, and ice in space. Gravity pulled this mass together.** As Earth grew larger, its gravity increased, pulling in more dust, rock, and ice nearby.

The energy from collisions with these materials raised Earth's temperature until the planet was very hot. Scientists think that Earth may have become so hot that it melted. Denser materials sank toward the center, forming Earth's dense, iron core. Less dense, molten material hardened over time to form Earth's outer layers—the solid crust and mantle.

FIGURE 1 ··
Early Earth
This artist's illustration shows Earth shortly after the moon formed. Earth was hot and volcanic, and contained no liquid water. The moon was much closer to Earth than it is today. Over time, Earth's surface began to cool, forming solid land.

✎ **Make Generalizations**
Could life have existed on Earth at the time shown in the illustration? Why, or why not?

_____

_____

_____

_____

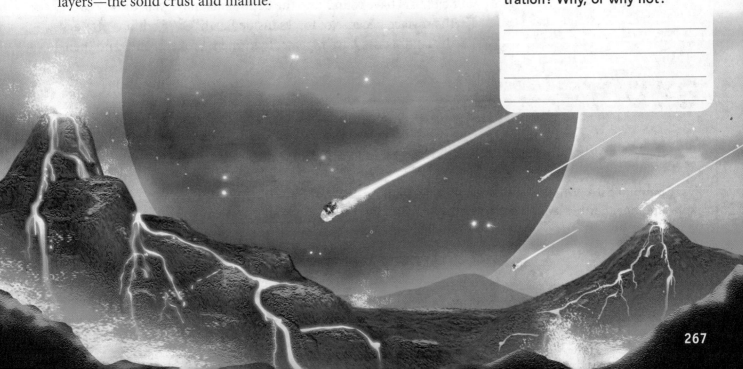

FIGURE 2 ·······························

Development of the Atmosphere
The illustration shows the difference between Earth's first and second atmospheres.

✎ **Relate Text and Visuals**
Fill in the missing information for each atmosphere.

First atmosphere
Gases included:

_____

Blown away by:

_____

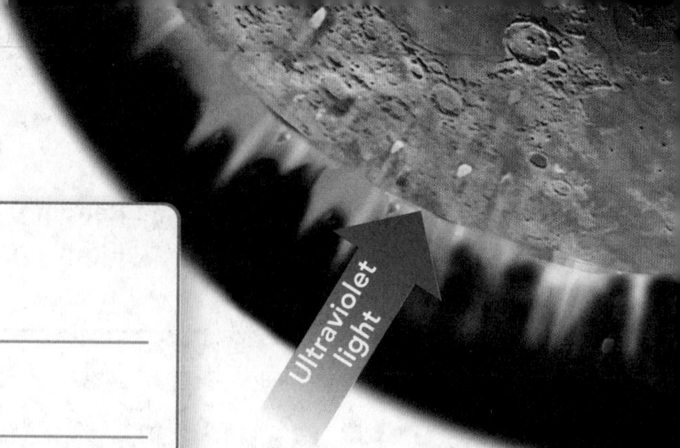

Ultraviolet light

⟳ **Sequence** How did Earth's oceans develop over time?

1. _____
   _____
   _____

2. _____
   _____
   _____

3. _____
   _____
   _____

The Atmosphere Early Earth may have included light gases such as hydrogen and helium. Then the sun released strong bursts of particles called the solar wind. Earth's gravity could not hold the light gases, and the solar wind blew away Earth's first atmosphere.

After Earth lost its first atmosphere, a second atmosphere formed. Volcanic eruptions and collisions with comets added carbon dioxide, water vapor, nitrogen, and other gases to the atmosphere. A **comet** is a ball of dust, gas, and ice that orbits the sun. **Figure 2** shows the first and second atmospheres.

The Oceans At first, Earth's surface was too hot for water to remain a liquid. All water remained as water vapor. As Earth's surface cooled, the water vapor began to condense to form rain. The rainwater gradually accumulated and formed oceans. The oceans absorbed much of the carbon dioxide from the atmosphere.

The Continents During early Precambrian Time, much of Earth's rock cooled and hardened. Less than 500 million years after Earth formed, the rock at the surface formed continents.

Scientists have found that the continents move very slowly over Earth's surface because of forces inside Earth. Over billions of years, Earth's landmasses have repeatedly formed, broken apart, and then crashed together again.

apply it!

❶ Draw a diagram showing Earth's structure after oceans began to form.

❷ ✎ **Communicate** Write a caption for your diagram explaining how Earth changed over time.

_____

_____

_____

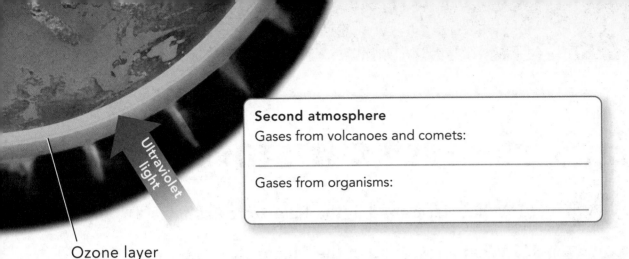

Ultraviolet light

Ozone layer

Early Organisms Scientists cannot pinpoint when or where life began on Earth. But scientists have found fossils of single-celled organisms in rocks that formed about 3.5 billion years ago. Scientists think that all other forms of life on Earth arose from these simple organisms. **Figure 3** shows remains of organisms similar to these early life forms. The bacteria Dr. Reysenbach studies are probably similar to these early organisms.

About 2.5 billion years ago, many organisms began using energy from the sun to make food. This process is called photosynthesis. One waste product of photosynthesis is oxygen. As organisms released oxygen, the amount of oxygen in the atmosphere slowly grew. Some oxygen changed into a form called ozone. The atmosphere developed an ozone layer that blocked the ultraviolet rays of the sun. Shielded from these rays, organisms could live on land.

FIGURE 3 ·····················
Stromatolites
These stromatolite fossils
(stroh MAT uh lyt) from Australia
are the remains of reefs built
by early organisms. Some
similar fossils are more
than three billion
years old.

 Do the Quick Lab
Learning From Fossils.

🔑 **Assess Your Understanding**

1a. Identify Earth formed _____ years ago.

b. 🔄 **Sequence** Write the numbers 1, 2, and 3 to show the correct order of the events below.

_____ Ozone layer forms.

_____ Earth loses its first atmosphere.

_____ Volcanoes and collisions with comets add water vapor to the atmosphere.

c. **CHALLENGE** How would Earth's atmosphere be different if organisms capable of photosynthesis had not evolved?

_____

_____

got it? ·····································

○ **I get it!** Now I know that key features of early Earth were _____

_____

_____

_____

○ **I need extra help with** _____

Go to MY SCIENCE ⒮ COACH *online for help with this subject.*

Eras of Earth's History

🔑 What Happened in the Paleozoic Era?

🔑 What Happened in the Mesozoic Era?

🔑 What Happened in the Cenozoic Era?

my planet diary

FUN FACT

Mystery Metal

The rock layers in the photo hold evidence in one of the great mysteries of science: What killed the dinosaurs?

Find the thin, pale layer of rock marked by the ruler. This layer formed at the end of the Cretaceous period. It contains unusually high amounts of the metal iridium. At first, scientists could not explain the amount of iridium in this layer.

Iridium is more common in asteroids than on Earth. Many scientists now infer that an asteroid struck Earth. The impact threw dust into the air, blocking sunlight for years. About half the plant and animal species on Earth—including the dinosaurs—died out.

Think about what you know about fossils and Earth's history as you answer these questions.

1. What have many scientists inferred from the iridium found at the Cretaceous boundary?

_____

_____

_____

2. What are some questions you have about the history of life on Earth?

_____

_____

_____

▶ PLANET DIARY Go to **Planet Diary** to learn more about mass extinctions.

Lab zone®

Do the Inquiry Warm-Up *Dividing History.*

Vocabulary
- invertebrate
- vertebrate
- amphibian
- reptile
- mass extinction
- mammal

Skills
- Reading: Identify Supporting Evidence
- Inquiry: Classify

What Happened in the Paleozoic Era?

The extinction of the dinosaurs is one of the most famous events in Earth's history, but it is just one example of the changes that have taken place. Through most of Earth's history, the only living things were single-celled organisms.

Near the end of Precambrian time, more complex living things evolved. Feathery, plantlike organisms anchored themselves to the seafloor. Jellyfish-like organisms floated in the oceans. Scientists have found fossils of such organisms in Australia, Russia, China, and southern Africa. But a much greater variety of living things evolved during the next phase of geologic time—the Paleozoic Era.

The Cambrian Explosion During the Cambrian Period, life took a big leap forward. **At the beginning of the Paleozoic Era, a great number of different kinds of organisms evolved. For the first time, many organisms had hard parts, including shells and outer skeletons.** Paleontologists call this event the Cambrian Explosion because so many new life forms appeared within a relatively short time.

FIGURE 1 ·····················

Cambrian Life

The photo below shows a fossil of a Cambrian organism called *Anomalocaris*. The illustration shows one artist's idea of what *Anomalocaris* (the large organism) and other organisms looked like.

✏️ **Interpret Photos** What does the fossil tell you about what *Anomalocaris* looked like?

_____

_____

271

did you

know?

In 1938, a fisherman in South Africa caught a fish he'd never seen before: a coelacanth (SEE luh kanth). Coelacanths evolved during the Devonian Period, but scientists thought they had been extinct for at least 65 million years. Since 1938, more of these "living fossils" have been found living deep in the Indian Ocean.

FIGURE 2 ·······················

Changing Landscapes

✎ **Summarize** Based on the text and illustrations, describe the organisms in each period and how they differed from those in the previous period.

Silurian _____

_____

_____

_____

_____

Invertebrates Develop At this time, all animals lived in the sea. Many were animals without backbones, or **invertebrates.** Invertebrates such as jellyfish, worms, and sponges made their home in the Cambrian ocean.

Brachiopods and trilobites were also common in the Cambrian seas. Brachiopods resembled modern clams, but are only distantly related to them. Trilobites were a huge and varied group of arthropods (AR thru pahds), animals with jointed legs and many body segments.

New Organisms Arise Invertebrates soon shared the seas with a new type of organism. During the Ordovician (awr duh VISH ee un) Period, the first vertebrates evolved. A **vertebrate** is an animal with a backbone. Jawless fishes with suckerlike mouths were the first vertebrates.

The First Land Plants Until the Silurian (sih LOOR ee un) Period, only one-celled organisms lived on the land. But during the Silurian Period, plants became abundant. These first, simple plants grew low to the ground in damp areas. By the Devonian Period (dih VOH nee un), plants that could grow in drier areas had evolved. Among these plants were the earliest ferns.

Early Fishes Both invertebrates and vertebrates lived in the Devonian seas. Even though the invertebrates were more numerous, the Devonian Period is often called the Age of Fishes. Every main group of fishes was present in the oceans at this time. Most fishes now had jaws, bony skeletons, and scales on their bodies. Sharks appeared in the late Devonian Period.

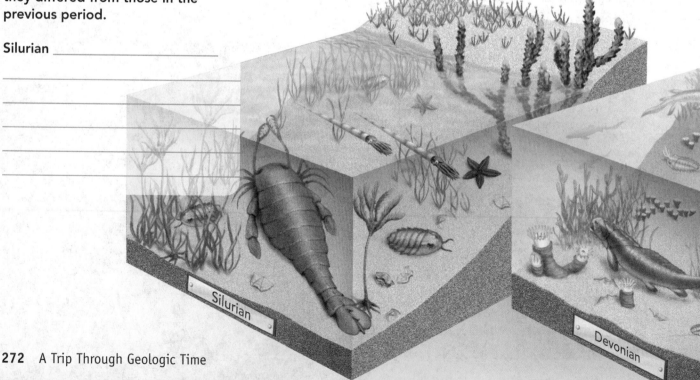

Silurian

Devonian

Animals Reach Land

🔑 **The Devonian Period was also when animals began to spread widely on land.** The first insects evolved during the Silurian Period, but vertebrates reached land during the Devonian. The first land vertebrates were lungfish with strong, muscular fins. The first amphibians evolved from these lungfish. An **amphibian** (am FIB ee un) is an animal that lives part of its life on land and part of its life in water.

The Carboniferous Period

Throughout the rest of the Paleozoic, other vertebrates evolved from amphibians. For example, small reptiles developed during the Carboniferous Period. **Reptiles** have scaly skin and lay eggs that have tough, leathery shells.

During the Carboniferous Period, winged insects evolved into many forms, including huge dragonflies and cockroaches. Giant ferns and cone-bearing plants formed vast swampy forests called coal forests. The remains of the coal-forest plants formed thick deposits of sediment that changed into coal over hundreds of millions of years.

✏️

🔄 **Identify Supporting Evidence** Underline the evidence that supports the statement, "The Devonian Period was also when animals began to spread widely on land."

Devonian _____

Carboniferous _____

Carboniferous

273

What two effects did the formation of Pangaea have?

_____

_____

_____

_____

Pangaea During the Permian Period, between 299 and 250 million years ago, Earth's continents moved together to form a great landmass, or supercontinent, called Pangaea (pan JEE uh). The formation of Pangaea caused deserts to expand in the tropics. At the same time, sheets of ice covered land closer to the South Pole.

Mass Extinction 🔑 **At the end of the Permian Period, most species of life on Earth died out.** This was a **mass extinction,** in which many types of living things became extinct at the same time. Scientists estimate that about 90 percent of all ocean species died out. So did about 70 percent of species on land. Even widespread organisms like trilobites became extinct.

Scientists aren't sure what caused this extinction. Some think an asteroid struck Earth, creating huge dust clouds. Massive volcanic eruptions spewed carbon dioxide and sulfur dioxide into the atmosphere. Temperatures all over Earth rose during this time, too. The amount of carbon dioxide in the oceans increased and the amount of oxygen declined, though scientists aren't sure why. All these factors may have contributed to the mass extinction.

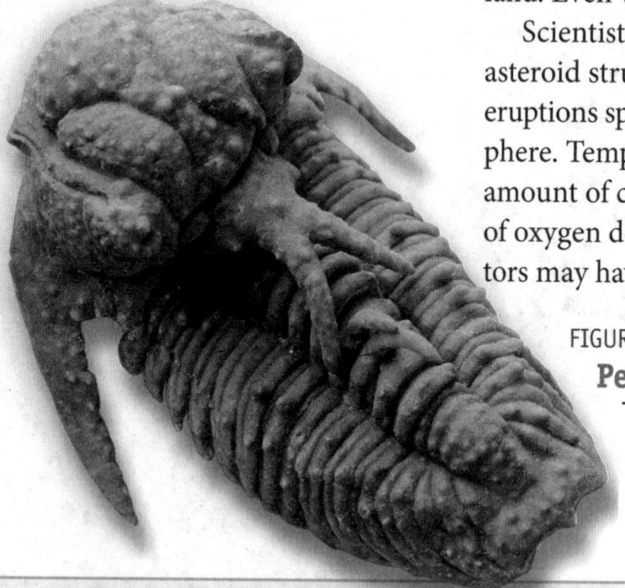

FIGURE 3 ·······························

Permian Trilobite

Throughout the Paleozoic, trilobites such as this Permian example were one of the most successful groups of organisms. But no species of trilobites survived the Permian mass extinction.

Lab ® Do the Quick Lab
zone *Graphing the Fossil Record.*

🔑 Assess Your Understanding

1a. List What are the periods of the Paleozoic Era?

_____

_____

_____

b. Sequence Number the following organisms in order from earliest to latest appearance.

amphibians _____   jawless fishes _____

trilobites _____   bony fishes _____

c. Relate Cause and Effect Name two possible causes of the mass extinction at the end of the Paleozoic.

_____

_____

_____

_____

_____

_____

got**it?** ·······························

○ **I get it!** Now I know that the main events in the Paleozoic Era were _____

_____

○ **I need extra help with** _____

Go to **MY SCIENCE** 🔘 **COACH** online for help with this subject.

What Happened in the Mesozoic Era?

When you think of prehistoric life, do you think of dinosaurs? If so, you're thinking of the Mesozoic Era.

The Triassic Period Some living things managed to survive the Permian mass extinction. Plants and animals that survived included fish, insects, reptiles, and cone-bearing plants called conifers. **Reptiles were so successful during the Mesozoic Era that this time is often called the Age of Reptiles.** The first dinosaurs appeared about 225 million years ago, during the Triassic (tri AS ik) Period.

Mammals also first appeared during the Triassic Period. A **mammal** is a vertebrate that can control its body temperature and feeds milk to its young. Mammals in the Triassic Period were very small, about the size of a mouse.

The Jurassic Period During the Jurassic Period (joo RAS ik), dinosaurs became common on land. Other kinds of reptiles evolved to live in the ocean and in the air. Scientists have identified several hundred different kinds of dinosaurs.

One of the first birds, called *Archaeopteryx,* appeared during the Jurassic Period. The name *Archaeopteryx* means "ancient winged one." Many paleontologists now think that birds evolved from dinosaurs.

apply it!

The illustrations show a flying reptile called *Dimorphodon* and one of the earliest birds, *Archaeopteryx.*

❶ Identify two features the two animals have in common.

_____

_____

❷ Identify one major difference between the two animals.

_____

_____

❸ Classify Which animal is *Archaeopteryx?* How do you know it is related to birds?

_____

_____

FIGURE 4

The End of the Dinosaurs

Many scientists hypothesize that an asteroid hit Earth near the present-day Yucatán Peninsula, in southeastern Mexico.

✏️ CHALLENGE Write a short story summarizing the events shown in the illustration.

_____

_____

_____

_____

_____

_____

_____

_____

_____

_____

The Cretaceous Period

Reptiles, including dinosaurs, were still widespread throughout the Cretaceous Period (krih TAY shus). Birds began to replace flying reptiles during this period. Their hollow bones made them better adapted to their environment than the flying reptiles, which became extinct.

Flowering plants first evolved during the Cretaceous. Unlike conifers, flowering plants produce seeds that are inside a fruit. The fruit helps the seeds spread.

Another Mass Extinction 🔑

At the close of the Cretaceous Period, about 65 million years ago, another mass extinction occurred. Scientists hypothesize that this mass extinction occurred when an asteroid from space struck Earth. This mass extinction wiped out more than half of all plant and animal groups, including the dinosaurs.

When the asteroid hit Earth, the impact threw huge amounts of dust and water vapor into the atmosphere. Dust and heavy clouds blocked sunlight around the world for years. Without sunlight, plants died, and plant-eating animals starved. The dust later formed the iridium-rich rock layer you read about at the beginning of the lesson. Some scientists think that climate changes caused by increased volcanic activity also helped cause the mass extinction.

THE DEATH OF THE DINOSAURS

BY TERRY DACTYL

Lab zone ® Do the Quick Lab Modeling an Asteroid Impact.

🔑 **Assess Your Understanding**

got it? ....

○ I get it! Now I know that the main developments in the Mesozoic Era were _____

_____

○ I need extra help with _____

Go to MY SCIENCE ⓢ COACH online for help with this subject.

What Happened in the Cenozoic Era?

During the Mesozoic Era, mammals had to compete with dinosaurs for food and places to live. ⟳ **The extinction of dinosaurs created an opportunity for mammals. During the Cenozoic Era, mammals evolved to live in many different environments—on land, in water, and even in the air.**

The Paleogene and Neogene Periods During the Paleogene and Neogene periods, Earth's climates were generally warm and mild, though they generally cooled over time. In the oceans, mammals such as whales and dolphins evolved. On land, flowering plants, insects, and mammals flourished. Grasses first began to spread widely. Some mammals became very large, as did some birds.

The Quaternary Period Earth's climate cooled and warmed in cycles during the Quaternary Period, causing a series of ice ages. Thick glaciers covered parts of Europe and North America. The latest warm period began between 10,000 and 20,000 years ago. Over thousands of years, most of the glaciers melted.

In the oceans, algae, coral, mollusks, fish, and mammals thrived. Insects and birds shared the skies. Flowering plants and mammals such as bats, cats, dogs, cattle, and humans became common. The fossil record suggests that modern humans may have evolved as early as 190,000 years ago. By about 12,000 to 15,000 years ago, humans had migrated to every continent except Antarctica.

FIGURE 5 ·····································

Giant Mammals

Many giant mammals evolved in the Cenozoic Era. This *Megatherium* is related to the modern sloth shown to the right, but was up to six meters tall.

✎ **Measure About how many times taller was *Megatherium* than a modern sloth?** _____

Geologic History

How do scientists study Earth's past?

FIGURE 6 ··
This timeline shows key events in Earth's history. Use what you have learned to fill in the missing information.

	Precambrian Time	Paleozoic		
ERA				
MILLIONS OF YEARS AGO	**4,600**	**542**	**488**	**444**
PERIOD				

Geologic Events

Precambrian Time
- Earth forms about 4.6 billion years ago.
- Oceans form and cover Earth about 4 billion years ago.
- First sedimentary rocks form more than 3.8 billion years ago.

▶ **CAMBRIAN**

- Shallow seas cover much of the land.
- Ancient continents lie near or south of the equator.

▶ **ORDOVICIAN**
- Warm, shallow seas cover much of Earth.
- Ice cap covers what is now North Africa.

▶ **SILURIAN**

- Coral reefs develop.
- Early continents collide with what is now North America, forming mountains.

Development of Life
_____
_____
_____
_____
_____

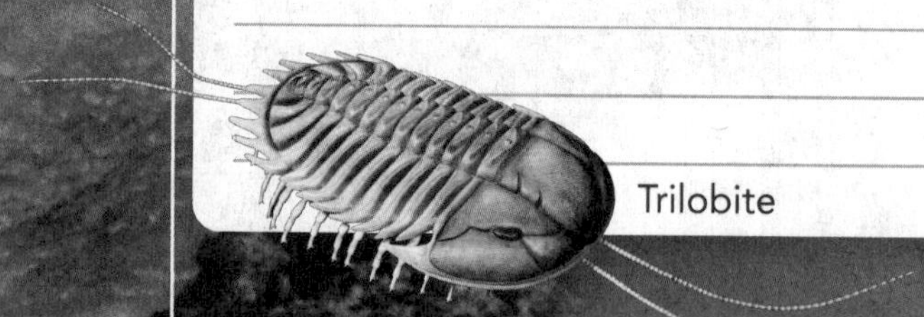

Trilobite

Development of Life
_____
_____
_____
_____
_____

Sea scorpion

Early plant

Development of Life
_____
_____
_____
_____

Sea pen

Development of Life

Ammonite

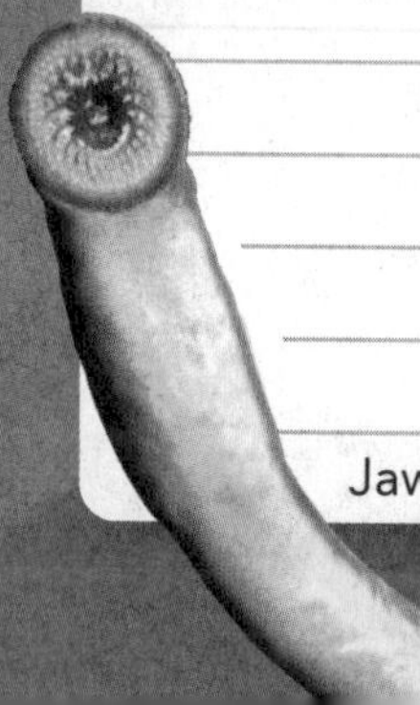

_____
_____
_____
_____

Jawless fish

Note: To make the timeline easier to read, periods are shown at about the same size, though some were longer than others. They are not drawn to scale.

Giant dragonfly (Carboniferous)

359

416

299

▶ **DEVONIAN**

- Seas rise and fall over what is now North America.

▶ **CARBONIFEROUS**

- Early Appalachian Mountains form.
- North America and northern Europe lie in warm, tropical region.

▶ **PERMIAN**

- Deserts become larger in tropical regions.
- The supercontinent Pangaea forms as all continents join together.

Development of Life

_____
_____
_____
_____
_____
_____

Club moss

Development of Life

_____
_____
_____
_____
_____

Bony fish

Early amphibian

Development of Life

_____
_____
_____
_____
_____

Dimetrodon

279

Geologic History

ERA	Mesozoic		
			146
MILLIONS OF YEARS AGO	251	200	
PERIOD	▶ TRIASSIC	▶ JURASSIC	▶ CRETACEOUS

Geologic Events

▶ **TRIASSIC**
- Pangaea holds together for much of the Triassic.
- Hot, dry conditions dominate the center of Pangaea.

▶ **JURASSIC**
- Pangaea breaks apart as North America separates from Africa and South America.

▶ **CRETACEOUS**
- Continents move toward their present-day positions as South America splits from Africa.

Development of Life

Coelophysis

Plateosaurus

Development of Life

Early mammal

Development of Life

Gigantosaurus

Barosaurus

Cenozoic

66

▶ **PALEOGENE**

- Australia becomes a separate continent.
- Heavy volcanic activity occurs in the Pacific and Atlantic Oceans.

23

▶ **NEOGENE**

- Climates change frequently, generally becoming drier.
- Grasslands spread.
- The Andes and Himalayas form.
- North and South America are connected.

1.8

▶ **QUATERNARY**

- Thick glaciers advance and retreat over much of North America and Europe, parts of South America and Asia, and all of Antarctica.

Development of Life

Bat

Hyracotherium

Development of Life

Titanis (giant bird)

Development of Life

Woolly mammoth

Lab zone Do the Quick Lab _Cenozoic Timeline._

🔑 Assess Your Understanding

2a. Identify (Grasses/Flowering plants) first spread widely in the Cenozoic Era.

b. Explain What factors allowed new organisms to spread during the Cenozoic Era?

c. ANSWER THE BIG ❓ How do scientists study Earth's past? Use an example from this chapter in your answer.

got it? ....

○ **I get it!** Now I know that important events in the Cenozoic Era included _____

○ **I need extra help with** _____

  Go to MY SCIENCE COACH online for help with this subject.

8 Study Guide

Scientists study _____ in order to draw inferences about how _____ have changed over time.

LESSON 1 Fossils

🔑 Most fossils form when sediment hardens into rock, preserving the shapes of organisms.

🔑 Fossils include molds, casts, petrified fossils, carbon films, trace fossils, and preserved remains.

🔑 Fossils provide evidence about Earth's history.

Vocabulary
- fossil • mold • cast • petrified fossil
- carbon film • trace fossil • paleontologist
- evolution • extinct

LESSON 2 The Relative Age of Rocks

🔑 In horizontal sedimentary rock layers, the oldest layer is generally at the bottom. Each layer is younger than the layers below it.

🔑 Gaps in the geologic record and folding can change the position in which rock layers appear.

Vocabulary
- relative age • absolute age
- law of superposition • extrusion • intrusion
- fault • index fossil • unconformity

LESSON 3 Radioactive Dating

🔑 During radioactive decay, the atoms of one element break down to form atoms of another element.

🔑 In radioactive dating, scientists compare the amount of a radioactive element in a rock with the amount of the stable element into which the radioactive element decays.

Vocabulary
- radioactive decay
- half-life

LESSON 4 The Geologic Time Scale

🔑 Because the time span of Earth's past is so great, geologists use the geologic time scale to show Earth's history.

Vocabulary
- geologic time scale
- era
- period

LESSON 5 Early Earth

🔑 Scientists think that Earth began as a ball of dust, rock, and ice in space. Gravity pulled this mass together.

Vocabulary
- comet

LESSON 6 Eras of Earth's History

🔑 During the Paleozoic Era, a great number of different organisms evolved.

🔑 Reptiles spread widely during the Mesozoic Era.

🔑 During the Cenozoic Era, mammals evolved to live in many different environments.

Vocabulary
- invertebrate • vertebrate • amphibian • reptile
- mass extinction • mammal

Review and Assessment

LESSON 1 Fossils

1. A hollow area in sediment in the shape of all or part of an organism is called a

   a. mold.   **b.** cast.

   c. trace fossil.   **d.** carbon film.

2. A series of dinosaur footprints in rock are an example of a(n) _____ fossil.

3. Develop Hypotheses Which organism has a better chance of leaving a fossil: a jellyfish or a bony fish? Explain.

_____

_____

_____

Use the picture below to answer Questions 4–5.

4. Classify What type of fossil is shown?

_____

5. Infer This fossil was found in a dry, mountainous area. What can you infer about how the area has changed over time?

_____

_____

_____

6. 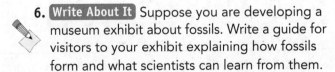 **Write About It** Suppose you are developing a museum exhibit about fossils. Write a guide for visitors to your exhibit explaining how fossils form and what scientists can learn from them.

LESSON 2 The Relative Age of Rocks

7. A gap in the geologic record that occurs when sedimentary rocks cover an eroded surface is called a(n)

   a. intrusion.   **b.** unconformity.

   c. fault.   **d.** extrusion.

8. A geologist finds an area of undisturbed sedimentary rock. The _____ layer is most likely the oldest.

9. Apply Concepts A geologist finds identical index fossils in a rock layer in the Grand Canyon in Arizona and in a rock layer in northern Utah, more than 675 kilometers away. What can she infer about the ages of the two rock layers?

_____

_____

LESSON 3 Radioactive Dating

10. The time it takes for half of a radioactive element's atoms to decay is its

   a. era.   **b.** half-life.

   c. relative age.   **d.** absolute age.

11. Calculate The half-life of carbon-14 is 5,730 years. A basket has 25% of its carbon-14 remaining. About how old is the basket?

_____

12. Solve Problems Uranium-235 has a half-life of 713 million years. Would uranium-235 or carbon-14 be more useful for dating a fossil from Precambrian time? Explain.

_____

_____

_____

_____

8 Review and Assessment

LESSON 4 The Geologic Time Scale

13. The geologic time scale is subdivided into

    a. relative ages.   **b.** absolute ages.

    c. unconformities.   **d.** eras and periods.

14. Scientists developed the geologic time scale by studying _____

_____

15. Sequence Which major division of geologic time came first?

_____

Which period of geologic time occurred most recently?

_____

LESSON 5 Early Earth

16. Which of the following was found in Earth's first atmosphere?

    a. carbon dioxide   **b.** hydrogen

    c. oxygen   **d.** ozone

17. Over time, Earth's rock hardened and formed land called _____

18. Explain How do scientists think that Earth's oceans formed?

_____

_____

_____

19. **Write About It** Do you agree or disagree with the following statement? "Without photosynthesis, land animals and plants could not have evolved." Use evidence to justify your answer.

LESSON 6 Eras of Earth's History

20. The earliest multicelled organisms were

    a. invertebrates.   **b.** land plants.

    c. vertebrates.   **d.** bacteria.

21. Explain How did Earth's environments change from the Neogene to the Quaternary Period?

_____

_____

22. Evaluate Science in the Media If you see a movie in which early humans fight dinosaurs, how would you judge the scientific accuracy of that movie? Give reasons for your judgment.

_____

_____

_____

_____

_____

APPLY THE BIG ? How do scientists study Earth's past?

23. Look at the fossil below. What can you infer about the organism and its environment? Be sure to give evidence for your inferences.

_____

_____

_____

_____

_____

Standardized Test Prep

Multiple Choice

Circle the letter of the correct answer.

1. Use the table to answer the question.

Geologic Time Scale	
Time Period	**Duration (Millions of Years)**
Cenozoic Era	66
Mesozoic Era	185
Paleozoic Era	291
Precambrian Time	about 4,058

A class is designing an outdoor model to show the geologic time scale from Precambrian Time through the present. If they use a scale of 1 m = 100 million years, how long will their model be?

A 46,000 m   **B** 460 m
C 46 m   **D** 4.6 m

2. A leaf falls into a shallow lake and is rapidly buried in the sediment. The sediment changes to rock over millions of years. Which type of fossil would *most likely* be formed?

A carbon film

B cast

C preserved remains

D trace fossil

3. What change in Earth's atmosphere allowed organisms to live on land?

A a collision with a comet

B the development of the ozone layer

C a strong burst of particles from the sun

D the absorption of carbon dioxide by oceans

4. Which of the following organisms lived during the Paleozoic Era?

A dinosaurs

B flowering plants

C grasses

D trilobites

5. Scientists can determine the absolute age of rocks using

A fault lines.

B index fossils.

C radioactive dating.

D the law of superposition.

Constructed Response

Use the diagram below and your knowledge of science to answer Question 6. Write your answer on a separate sheet of paper.

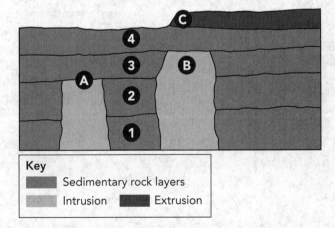

6. Write the order in which the rock areas shown formed. Justify your answer using evidence from the diagram.

PUTTING THE PUZZLE TOGETHER

Imagine you are putting together a puzzle, but you don't have all the pieces. That's the problem for scientists trying to determine exactly what an animal looked like. Paleontologists may find only some of the bones of a prehistoric animal. They may find bones from more than one of the same kind of animal.

Scientists build reconstructions of the animals based on the fossils they have and observations of living relatives of the animal. Computed tomography (CT) scans help scientists make virtual fossils. They start with the pieces they have and then fill in the rest of the puzzle virtually. For example, if the scientists have found a fossil of the right jaw bone, the computers are able to help them model the left jaw bone, and build virtual models of the entire head.

Bones tell a story that scientists can understand. It's much harder to figure out the size and shape of the muscles or the color of the animal. Different scientists will build slightly different reconstructions of the same kind of animal. Because so many pieces of the puzzle are missing, it may be impossible to have a perfectly accurate reconstruction. Because the organisms are extinct, scientists may never know for sure.

Write About It Research the different ways in which paleontologists have reconstructed *Tyrannosaurus rex*. Choose one change and explain how it differed from a previous reconstruction. Why did paleontologists think this was a good change?

Paleontologist Jack Horner can use CT scans to create a 3-D model of this Lambeosaur skull. ▶

Teen Finds Fossils

In early 2007, sixteen-year-old Sierra Sarti-Sweeney went for a walk at Boca Ciega Millennium Park in Seminole, Florida. She wanted to take some nature pictures. She did not expect to stumble on a mammoth!

During her walk, Sierra noticed bones in a stream bed. With her older brother, Sean, she brought the bones to local scientists. The bone Sierra found was the tooth of a prehistoric Columbian mammoth. Archaeologists say that the tooth and other fossils Sierra found could be as much as 100,000 years old!

Since Sierra's find, digging at the site has uncovered even more bones, including those from prehistoric camels, 2-meter turtles, and saber-toothed cats. According to scientists, the findings suggest that this part of Florida was once like the African savanna region.

For Sierra, the experience was exciting. She even had a call from a late-night television host. Finding the tooth confirmed Sierra's desire to be a zoologist and to keep looking at the world around her.

Design It Plan an exhibit of Sierra's findings. What would people want to know and see? Make a brochure advertising your exhibit and develop a presentation of the fossils found at Boca Ciega Millennium Park.

FROZEN EVIDENCE

In the giant ice cap at the South Pole, a continuous record of snow exists reaching back more than 800,000 years. Scientists have drilled 3.2 kilometers down into the ice. From the cores they pull up, scientists learn about the temperature and the different gases in the air when each layer was formed.

These cores show that temperatures go up and down in cycles. Long ice ages (about 90,000 years) follow short warm periods (about 10,000 years). The climate record also shows that temperatures and amounts of carbon dioxide change together. If carbon dioxide levels rise, temperatures also rise.

Research It Find at least three sources that explain the ice cores project. Write an essay critiquing the explanations provided. Note any bias, misinformation, or missing information.

Researchers extract samples from the ice at the South Pole. ▲

HOW CAN WIND KEEP YOUR LIGHTS ON?

What are some of Earth's energy sources?

This man is repairing a wind turbine at a wind farm in Texas. Most wind turbines are at least 30 meters off the ground where the winds are fast. Wind speed and blade length help determine the best way to capture the wind and turn it into power. **Develop Hypotheses** **Why do you think people are working to increase the amount of power we get from wind?**

_____

_____

_____

_____

_____

▶ UNTAMED SCIENCE Watch the **Untamed Science** video to learn more about energy resources.

Energy Resources

CHAPTER

9

Getting Started

Check Your Understanding

1. Background Read the paragraph below and then answer the question.

Aisha loves visiting her grandmother at work. Her grandmother says that the building she works in was designed to help conserve **natural resources.** Most of the building's electricity comes from **renewable resources,** such as sunlight and wind, instead of from **nonrenewable resources,** such as oil or coal.

> A **natural resource** is any material that occurs naturally in the environment and is used by people.
>
> A **renewable resource** is either always available or is naturally replaced in a short time.
>
> A **nonrenewable resource** is a resource that is not replaced within a useful time frame.

• What is one example of a natural resource?

_____

_____

▶ MY READING WEB If you had trouble completing the question above, visit **My Reading Web** and type in *Energy Resources.*

Vocabulary Skill

High-Use Academic Words High-use academic words are words that are used frequently in classrooms. Look for the words below as you read this chapter.

Word	Definition	Example
scarce	*adj.* rare; in limited supply	Tickets for the concert are becoming *scarce* because of the demand.
emit	*v.* to give off	When the oven is on, it *emits* heat, making the whole apartment warmer.

2. Quick Check Choose the word from the table above that best completes each sentence.

• Motor vehicles _____ chemicals that contribute to air pollution.

• As people continue to use oil faster than it can be replaced, it will become _____.

fossil fuel

solar energy

biomass fuel

energy conservation

Chapter Preview

LESSON 1
- fuel
- fossil fuel
- hydrocarbon
- petroleum
- refinery
- petrochemical

↻ **Summarize**
△ **Communicate**

LESSON 2
- solar energy
- hydroelectric power
- biomass fuel
- gasohol
- geothermal energy
- nuclear fission
- reactor vessel
- fuel rod
- control rod

↻ **Relate Cause and Effect**
△ **Infer**

LESSON 3
- efficiency
- insulation
- energy conservation

↻ **Identify the Main Idea**
△ **Observe**

> **VOCAB FLASH CARDS** For extra help with vocabulary, visit **Vocab Flash Cards** and type in *Energy Resources.*

Fossil Fuels

UNLOCK THE BIG ?

🔑 What Are the Three Major Fossil Fuels?

🔑 Why Are Fossil Fuels Nonrenewable Resources?

my planet diary

DISASTERS

Hurricane Energy Crisis

On August 29, 2005, Hurricane Katrina struck the Gulf Coast. The storm flooded cities and towns. In New Orleans, tens of thousands of people were stranded on rooftops. Hundreds of thousands of evacuees fled to other parts of the country. Katrina also created another kind of crisis. The Gulf Coast has many factories that produce oil and gas for the entire country. These factories were shut down because of winds, power outages, and flooding. Gas stations ran out of gas. Prices soared. Many people couldn't afford to heat their homes. Some people burned wood instead. Others just got cold. The hurricane had created an energy crisis.

 Lab zone® Do the Inquiry Warm-Up *What's in a Piece of Coal?*

Communicate Discuss the questions with a group of classmates. Then write your answers below.

1. Due to global climate changes, more hurricanes are expected to hit the Gulf Coast. What might happen to gas and oil production?

_____

_____

2. How might alternative fuels provide a solution?

_____

_____

_____

_____

> PLANET DIARY Go to **Planet Diary** to learn more about fossil fuels.

Vocabulary

- fuel • fossil fuel • hydrocarbon
- petroleum • refinery
- petrochemical

Skills

↩ Reading: Summarize

△ Inquiry: Communicate

What Are the Three Major Fossil Fuels?

Whether you travel in a car or a bus, walk, or ride your bike, you use some form of energy. The source of that energy is fuel. A **fuel** is a substance that provides energy, such as heat, light, motion, or electricity. This energy is the result of a chemical change.

Most of the energy used today comes from organisms that lived hundreds of millions of years ago. As these plants, animals, and other organisms died, their remains piled up. Layers of sand, rock, and mud buried the remains. Over time, heat and the pressure of the layers changed the remains into other substances. **Fossil fuels** are the energy-rich substances formed from the remains. ⟶ **The three major fossil fuels are coal, oil, and natural gas.**

Fossil fuels are made of hydrocarbons. **Hydrocarbons** are chemical compounds that contain carbon and hydrogen atoms. When the fossil fuels are burned, the atoms react. They combine with oxygen to form new molecules. These reactions release energy in the forms of heat and light.

Burning fossil fuels provides more energy per kilogram than burning other fuels. One kilogram of coal, for example, can provide twice as much energy as one kilogram of wood. Oil and natural gas can provide three times as much energy as an equal mass of wood.

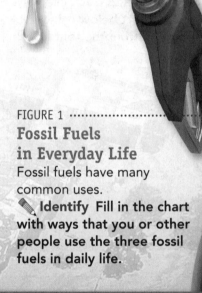

FIGURE 1 ·····················

Fossil Fuels in Everyday Life

Fossil fuels have many common uses.

✎ Identify Fill in the chart with ways that you or other people use the three fossil fuels in daily life.

Fossil Fuel	Common Uses	Uses in Your Life
Coal	• Used to generate half of all U.S. electricity • Used to make products like fertilizer and medicine • When heated, used to make steel	
Oil	• As gasoline and diesel fuels, used to power vehicles • Used to heat homes • Used to make plastics and other petroleum products	
Natural gas	• Used to generate electricity • Used to cook food • Used to heat homes	

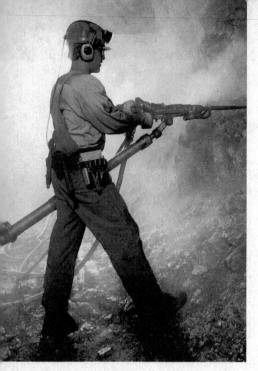

Coal

People have burned coal to produce heat for thousands of years. For much of that time, wood was more convenient and cheaper than coal for most people. But during the 1800s, the huge energy needs of growing industries made it worthwhile to find, mine, and transport coal. Today, coal makes up about 22 percent of the fuel used in the United States. Most of that coal fuels electrical power plants.

Before coal can be used to produce energy, it has to be removed from the ground. Miners use machines to chop the coal into chunks and lift it to the surface. Coal mining can be a dangerous job. Thousands of miners have been killed or injured in mining accidents. Many more suffer from lung diseases. Fortunately, modern safety procedures and better equipment have made coal mining safer, although it is still very dangerous.

Coal is the most plentiful fossil fuel in the United States. It is fairly easy to transport and provides a lot of energy when burned. But coal also has some disadvantages. Coal mining can increase erosion. Runoff from coal mines can cause water pollution. Burning most types of coal results in more air pollution than using other fossil fuels. See **Figure 2.**

Figure 3 shows how plant remains build up over time and form coal.

FIGURE 2 ·····························

Pros and Cons of Coal Use
Coal mining, shown above, is a dangerous job.

✎ **Compare and Contrast**
Fill in the chart below using information from the text.

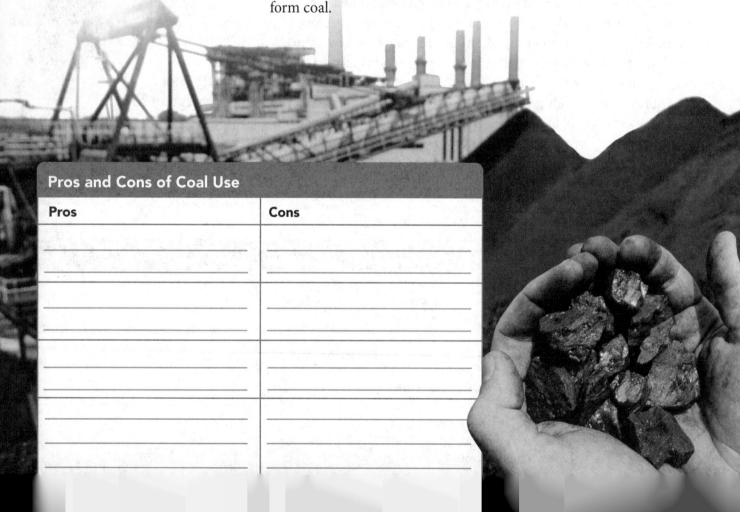

Pros and Cons of Coal Use	
Pros	**Cons**
_____	_____
_____	_____
_____	_____
_____	_____
_____	_____
_____	_____
_____	_____

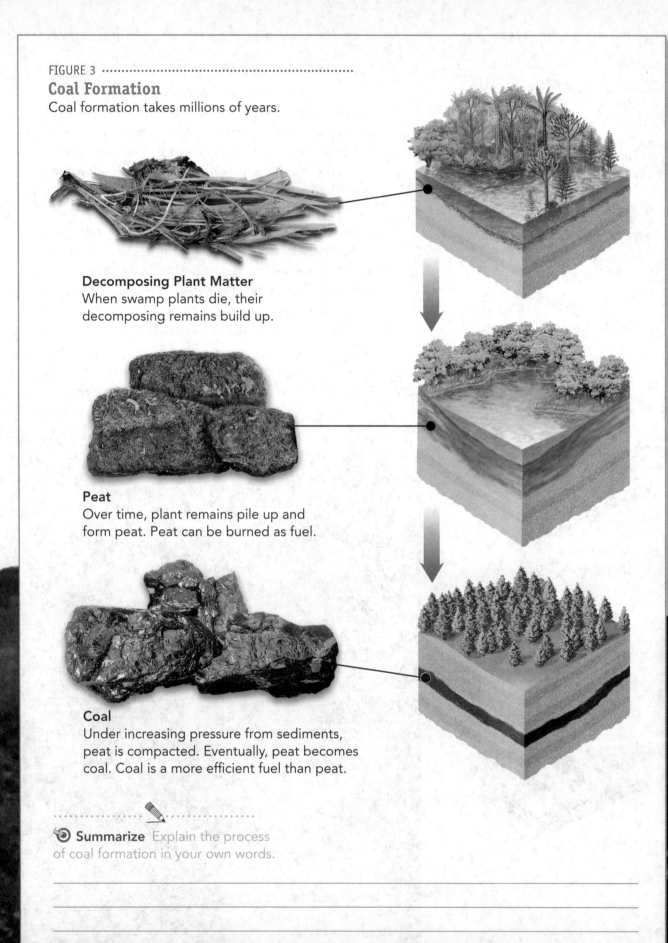

FIGURE 3 ···

Coal Formation

Coal formation takes millions of years.

Decomposing Plant Matter
When swamp plants die, their decomposing remains build up.

Peat
Over time, plant remains pile up and form peat. Peat can be burned as fuel.

Coal
Under increasing pressure from sediments, peat is compacted. Eventually, peat becomes coal. Coal is a more efficient fuel than peat.

Summarize Explain the process of coal formation in your own words.

_____

_____

_____

FIGURE 4 ·······················

▶ ART IN MOTION Oil Formation

Oil is formed in a process similar to coal.

✎ **Interpret Diagrams** Use what you know to fill in the steps of oil formation in the diagrams below.

300–400 million years ago

_____

_____

_____

50–100 million years ago

_____

_____

_____

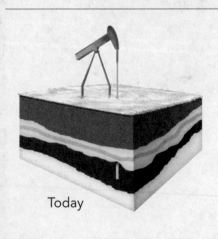

Today

_____

_____

_____

Oil Oil is a thick, black, liquid fossil fuel. It formed from the remains of small animals, algae, and other organisms that lived in oceans and shallow inland seas hundreds of millions of years ago. **Petroleum** is another name for oil. Petroleum comes from the Latin words *petra* (rock) and *oleum* (oil). Petroleum accounts for more than one third of the energy produced in the world. Fuel for most cars, airplanes, trains, and ships comes from petroleum. Many homes are heated by oil as well.

Most oil deposits are located underground in tiny holes in sandstone or limestone. **Figure 4** shows how oil is formed. The oil fills the holes somewhat like the way water fills the holes of a sponge. Because oil deposits are usually located deep below the surface, finding oil is difficult. Scientists can use sound waves to test an area for oil. Even using this technique, scientists may not always locate wells that will produce a usable amount of oil.

FIGURE 5 ························
Oil Pipeline
Workers build an oil pipeline in Russia.

When oil is first pumped out of the ground, it is called crude oil. To be made into useful products, crude oil must undergo a process called refining. A factory in which crude oil is heated and separated into fuels and other products is called a **refinery.** Many of the products that you use every day are made from crude oil. **Petrochemicals** are compounds that are made from oil. Petrochemicals are used to make plastics, paints, medicines, and cosmetics.

apply it!

Over 2,500 species of plants and animals live in Lake Baikal, in Russia. Eighty percent of these species live nowhere else on Earth. One of those species is the Baikal seal—one of only three freshwater seal species on Earth. The seal and other species were threatened when oil companies planned to build the world's longest oil pipeline within 800 meters of the lake's shore. The pipeline would bring oil from Russia's interior to China and ports along the Pacific Ocean. Citizens were concerned that oil leaks and spills would damage the lake. They worked together to convince the oil companies to move the pipeline 40 kilometers to the north. The design of the new pipeline protects the lake and also delivers oil to places that need it.

Communicate An oil pipeline is proposed in your area near a body of water you think is important. Using Lake Baikal as an example, write a letter to the editor of your local paper explaining what you think should be done about the pipeline and why. Give your letter a headline.

_____

_____

_____

_____

_____

_____

_____

_____

_____

_____

_____

_____

_____

_____

_____

_____

_____

_____

Natural Gas Natural gas is a mixture of methane and other gases. Natural gas forms from some of the same organisms as oil. Because it is less dense than oil, natural gas often rises above an oil deposit, forming a pocket of gas in the rock.

Pipelines transport natural gas from its source to the places where it is used. If all the gas pipelines in the United States were connected, they would reach to the moon and back—three times! Natural gas can also be compressed into a liquid and stored in tanks as fuel for trucks and buses.

Natural gas has several benefits. It produces large amounts of energy, but has lower levels of many air pollutants compared to coal or oil. It is also easy to transport once pipelines are built. One cost of natural gas is that it is highly flammable. A gas leak can cause explosions and fires. If you use natural gas in your home, you probably are familiar with the "gas" smell alerting you when there is unburned gas in the air. You may be surprised to learn that natural gas actually has no odor. What causes the strong smell? Gas companies add a chemical with a distinct smell to the gas so that people can detect a gas leak.

FIGURE 6 ·······························
Natural Gas
A gas-top burner uses natural gas to cook food.

✎ **Analyze Costs and Benefits** Fill in the boxes with some costs and benefits of natural gas.

Costs of Natural Gas
_____
_____
_____
_____
_____
_____

Benefits of Natural Gas
_____
_____
_____
_____
_____
_____

Lab® **zone** Do the Quick Lab *Observing Oil's Consistency.*

🔑 Assess Your Understanding

1a. Define What are petrochemicals?

_____

_____

_____

b. Make Judgments Should the federal government decide where to build oil or natural gas pipelines? Explain.

_____

_____

_____

got**it?** ··

○ **I get it!** Now I know that the three major fossil fuels are_____

○ I need extra help with _____

Go to MY SCIENCE ⬢ⁱ COACH online for help with this subject.

Why Are Fossil Fuels Nonrenewable Resources?

The many advantages of using fossil fuels as an energy source have made them essential to modern life. **Since fossil fuels take hundreds of millions of years to form, they are considered nonrenewable resources.** Earth's known oil reserves, or the amount of oil that can currently be used, took 500 million years to form. Fossil fuels will run out if they are used faster than they are formed.

Many nations that consume large amounts of fossil fuels have very small reserves or supplies. They have to buy oil, natural gas, and coal from nations with large supplies to make up the difference. The United States, for example, uses about one quarter of all the oil produced in the world. But only two percent of the world's oil supply is located in this country. The uneven distribution of fossil fuel reserves has often been a cause of political problems in the world.

do the math!

Use the graph to answer the questions below.

1 Read Graphs Which energy source generates the most electricity in the United States? _____

2 Calculate What percentage of the fuels in the graph are fossil fuels? _____

3 CHALLENGE How might this graph look in 50 years? Give reasons to support your answer. _____
_____
_____

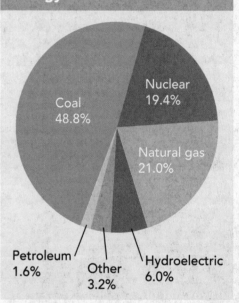

Recent Electricity Production in the United States by Energy Source

- Coal 48.8%
- Nuclear 19.4%
- Natural gas 21.0%
- Petroleum 1.6%
- Other 3.2%
- Hydroelectric 6.0%

Lab zone Do the Quick Lab *Fossil Fuels.*

Assess Your Understanding

got it? . . . .

○ **I get it!** Now I know that fossil fuels are nonrenewable because_____
_____

○ I need extra help with _____
Go to MY SCIENCE COACH online for help with this subject.

Renewable Sources of Energy

UNLOCK THE BIG ?

🔑 **What Are Some Renewable Sources of Energy?**

🔑 **How Does a Nuclear Power Plant Produce Electricity?**

my planet Diary

An Unlikely Decision

T. Boone Pickens's family taught him the value of hard work during the Great Depression of the 1930s. At 11, he delivered newspapers. By 26, he founded his own oil and gas company and became rich. In 2007, T. Boone Pickens surprised everyone by announcing plans to build the world's largest wind farm. He insisted the country must replace oil with wind and solar power. Even though he still promotes oil, he was one of the first oil businessmen to admit a change was needed. "I've been an oil man all my life," Pickens said, "but this is one emergency we can't drill our way out of."

BIOGRAPHY

Communicate Discuss these questions with a group of classmates. Write your answers below.

1. Why do you think Pickens's decision was so surprising?

_____

_____

2. Do you think more focus should be put on finding sources of energy other than oil? Why or why not?

_____

_____

> **PLANET DIARY** Go to **Planet Diary** to learn more about renewable energy.

 Lab zone Do the Inquiry Warm-Up *Can You Capture Solar Energy?*

What Are Some Renewable Sources of Energy?

Coal, oil, and natural gas are not the only energy options available on Earth. 🔑 **Renewable sources of energy include sunlight, water, wind, biomass fuels, and geothermal energy.** Other energy options include nuclear power and hydrogen. Scientists are trying to put these energy resources to work.

Vocabulary

- solar energy • hydroelectric power • biomass fuel
- gasohol • geothermal energy • nuclear fission
- reactor vessel • fuel rod • control rod

Skills

↻ Reading: Relate Cause and Effect
△ Inquiry: Infer

Solar Energy The warmth you feel on a sunny day is **solar energy,** or energy from the sun. The sun constantly gives off energy in the forms of light and heat. Solar energy is the source, directly or indirectly, of most other renewable energy resources. In one hour, Earth receives enough solar energy to meet the energy needs of the world for an entire year. Solar energy does not cause pollution. It will not run out for billions of years.

So why hasn't solar energy replaced energy from fossil fuels? One reason is that solar energy is only available when the sun is shining. Another problem is that the energy Earth receives from the sun is very spread out. To obtain a useful amount of power, it is necessary to collect solar energy from a large area.

Solar Power Plants One way to capture the sun's energy involves using giant mirrors. In a solar power plant, rows of mirrors focus the sun's rays to heat a tank of water. The water boils. This creates steam. The steam can then be used to generate electricity.

Solar Cells Solar energy can be converted directly into electricity in a solar cell. When light hits the cell, an electric current is produced. Solar cells power some calculators, lights, and other small devices.

↻ **Relate Cause and Effect**
Underline one way solar energy is collected and circle the way it is used.

did you
know?

Photovoltaic cells, or solar cells, are named for the Greek word for light, *photo*, and electricity pioneer Alessandro Volta.

FIGURE 1 ·······
Everyday Solar Power

Many objects, including calculators, street lights, and even backpacks that charge electronic devices, can be powered by the sun.

✎ **Describe** What object in your everyday life would you like to run on solar power? Would you want the sun to be its only power source? Why?

_____

_____

_____

_____

_____

301

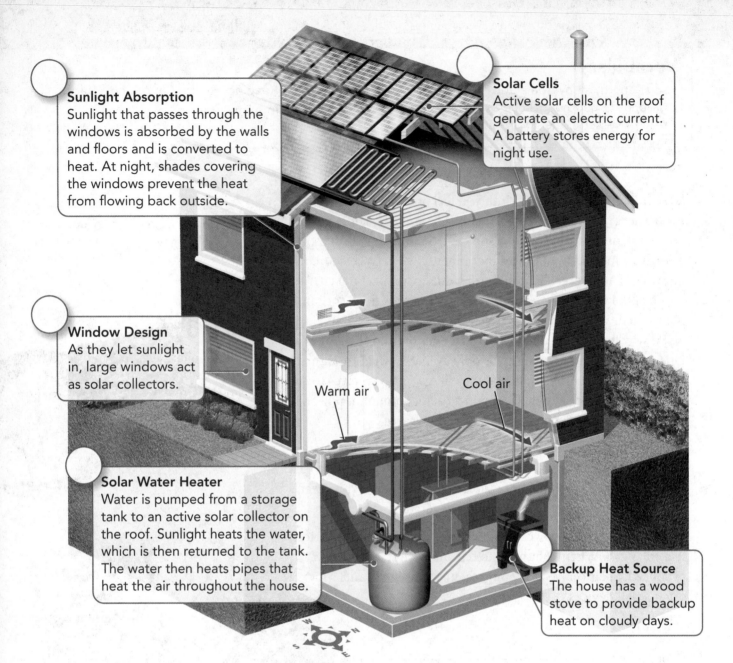

Sunlight Absorption
Sunlight that passes through the windows is absorbed by the walls and floors and is converted to heat. At night, shades covering the windows prevent the heat from flowing back outside.

Solar Cells
Active solar cells on the roof generate an electric current. A battery stores energy for night use.

Window Design
As they let sunlight in, large windows act as solar collectors.

Warm air

Cool air

Solar Water Heater
Water is pumped from a storage tank to an active solar collector on the roof. Sunlight heats the water, which is then returned to the tank. The water then heats pipes that heat the air throughout the house.

Backup Heat Source
The house has a wood stove to provide backup heat on cloudy days.

FIGURE 2 ·······················
Solar-Powered House
This house takes advantage of active and passive solar heating.
▲ **Infer** Draw a checkmark in the blank circles on the passive sources of solar energy. Draw a star in the blank circles on the active sources.

Passive Solar Heating Solar energy can be used to heat buildings with passive solar systems. A passive solar system converts sunlight into heat, or thermal energy. The heat is then distributed without using pumps or fans. Passive solar heating is what occurs in a parked car on a sunny day. Solar energy passes through the car's windows and heats the seats and other car parts. These parts transfer heat to the air, warming the inside of the car. The same principle can be used to heat a home.

Active Solar Heating An active solar system captures the sun's energy, and then uses pumps and fans to distribute the heat. First, light strikes the dark metal surface of a solar collector. There, it is converted to thermal energy. Water is pumped through pipes in the solar collector to absorb the thermal energy. The heated water then flows to a storage tank. Finally, pumps and fans distribute the heat throughout the building. Refer to **Figure 2.**

Hydroelectric Power

Solar energy is the indirect source of water power. In the water cycle, energy from the sun heats water on Earth's surface. The heat turns the water into water vapor. The vapor condenses and falls back to Earth as rain, sleet, hail, or snow. As the water flows over land, it provides another source of energy.

Hydroelectric power is electricity produced by flowing water. A dam across a river blocks the flow of water, creating a body of water called a reservoir. When a dam's gates are opened, water flows through tunnels at the bottom of the dam. As the water moves through the tunnels, it turns turbines (like a fan's blades). The turbines are connected to a generator. Once a dam is built, generating electricity is inexpensive. But dams can prevent some fish species from breeding. They can also damage aquatic habitats.

Capturing the Wind

Like water power, wind energy is also an indirect form of solar energy. The sun heats Earth's surface unevenly. As a result, different areas of the atmosphere have different temperatures and air pressures. The differences in pressure cause winds to form as air moves from one area to another.

Wind can be used to turn a turbine and generate electricity. Wind farms consist of many wind turbines. Together, the wind turbines generate large amounts of power. Wind is the fastest-growing energy source in the world. Wind energy does not cause pollution. In places where fuels are difficult to transport, wind energy is the major source of power if it is available.

Nuclear Power

Like water and wind power, nuclear power does not produce air pollution since no fuel is burned. Instead, the energy released from the splitting of atoms is used to create steam that turns turbines. This process can be dangerous and even cause explosions if too much energy is released. Wastes generated by nuclear plants can be dangerous if disposed of improperly.

FIGURE 3 ·····················

Hydroelectric and Wind Power

Hydroelectric and wind power do not rely on fossil fuels.

✎ **Compare and Contrast**
List similarities and differences between water and wind power in the Venn diagram.

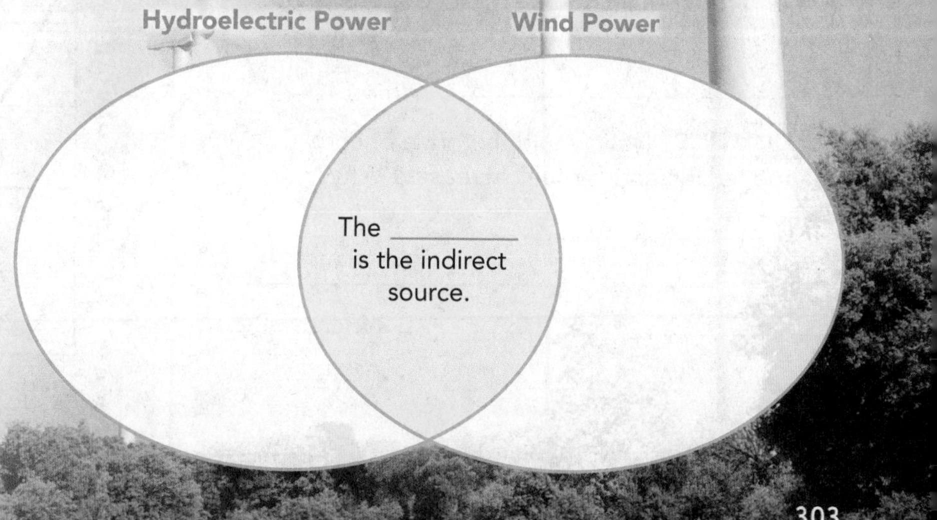

Hydroelectric Power   Wind Power

The _____ is the indirect source.

303

Biomass Fuels Wood was probably the first fuel ever used for heat and light. Wood belongs to a group of fuels called **biomass fuels.** Biomass fuels are made from living things. Other biomass fuels include leaves, food wastes, and even manure. As fossil fuel supplies shrink, people are taking a closer look at biomass fuels. For example, when oil prices rose in the early 1970s, Hawaiian farmers began burning sugar cane wastes to generate electricity.

In addition to being burned as fuel, biomass materials can be converted into other fuels. For example, corn, sugar cane, and other crops can be used to make alcohol. Adding alcohol to gasoline forms **gasohol.** Gasohol can be used as fuel for cars. Bacteria can produce methane gas by decomposing biomass materials in landfills. That methane can be used to heat buildings. And some crops, such as soybeans, can produce oil. The oil can be used as fuel, which is called biodiesel fuel.

Biomass fuels are renewable resources. But it takes time for new trees to replace those that have been cut down. And it is expensive to produce alcohol and methane in large quantities. As a result, biomass fuels are not widely used today in the United States. But as fossil fuels become scarcer, biomass fuels may provide another source for meeting energy needs.

FIGURE 4

Corn Power
Biomass fuels come from living things, such as corn. It takes about 11.84 kilograms of corn to make one gallon of fuel!

apply it!

What can happen when a food crop is used for fuel? The relationship is plotted with two curves on the graph.

❶ Interpret Graphs According to the graph, as demand for corn increases, what happens to the supply?

_____

❷ CHALLENGE How would the price of corn change as demand for fuel increases? Why?

_____
_____
_____

Supply and Demand for Food and Fuel Crops

Amount of Corn

— Demand
— Supply

Increasing Time ⟶

Tapping Earth's Energy Below Earth's surface are pockets of very hot liquid rock called magma. In some places, magma is very close to the surface. The intense heat from Earth's interior that warms the magma is called **geothermal energy.**

In certain regions, such as Iceland and New Zealand, magma heats underground water to the boiling point. In these places, the hot water and steam can be valuable sources of energy. For example, in Reykjavík, Iceland, 90 percent of the homes are heated by water warmed underground in this way. Geothermal energy can also be used to generate electricity, as shown in **Figure 5.**

Geothermal energy does have disadvantages. There are only a few places where Earth's crust is thin enough for magma to come close to the surface. Elsewhere, very deep wells would be needed to tap this energy. Drilling deep wells is very expensive. Even so, geothermal energy is likely to become a good method for meeting energy needs for some locations in the future.

FIGURE 5 ·····························

Geothermal Power in Iceland

Geothermal power plants like the one shown here use heat from Earth's interior to generate electricity.

✎ **Infer** On the diagram below, draw Earth's crust and show where magma might be located in relation to Iceland's surface.

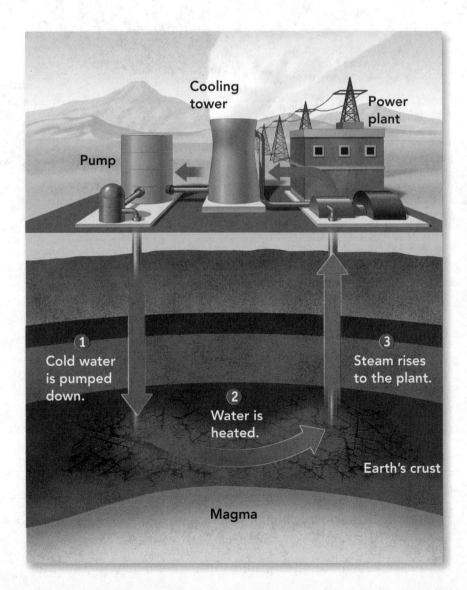

Cooling tower

Power plant

Pump

① Cold water is pumped down.

② Water is heated.

③ Steam rises to the plant.

Earth's crust

Magma

Earth's crust

Magma

305

The Energy Around Us

What are some of Earth's energy sources?

FIGURE 6

> INTERACTIVE ART People use many energy sources in their daily lives. Each source has its pros and cons.

✎ **Analyze Costs and Benefits** In the boxes, write one pro and one con about each energy source pictured.

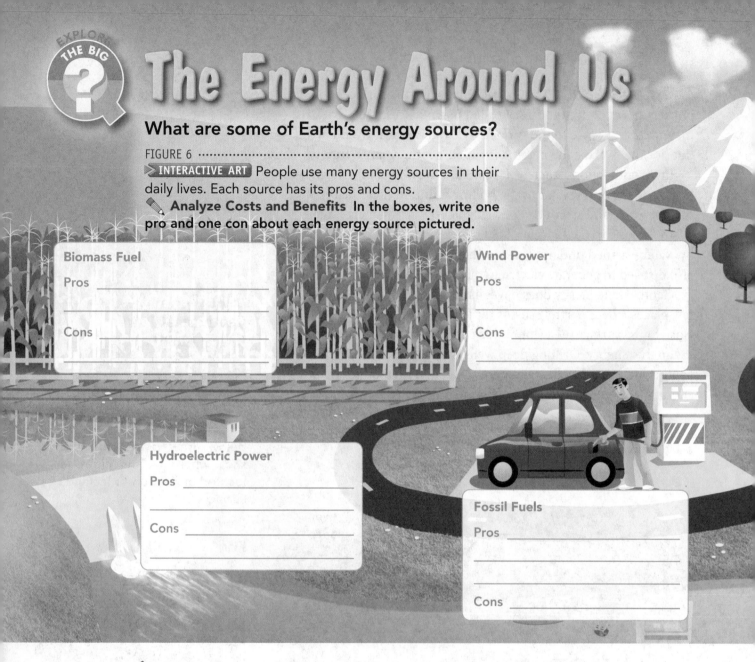

Biomass Fuel

Pros _____

_____

Cons _____

_____

Wind Power

Pros _____

_____

Cons _____

_____

Hydroelectric Power

Pros _____

_____

Cons _____

_____

Fossil Fuels

Pros _____

_____

Cons _____

_____

Vocabulary High-Use Academic Words The word *emit* means "to give off." What do vehicles that run on hydrogen fuel cells emit?

_____

_____

_____

_____

Electric Cars and Hydrogen Fuel Cells

You may have heard about or even seen battery-powered electric cars. But what about cars that use hydrogen fuel cells? Both technologies, battery-powered electric cars and hydrogen fuel cells, have been developed to use renewable energy. See **Figure 6.**

Electric cars run entirely on batteries, and you plug them into an outlet to recharge them. The electricity used can be generated by power plants that use hydroelectric or solar energy. Some electric cars have adaptors that let you recharge them in minutes.

Some cars can run on hydrogen. They have tanks called hydrogen fuel cells that hold hydrogen instead of gasoline. Many power plants can use excess energy to break water molecules apart to make hydrogen. This hydrogen can then be pumped into cars. Cars that run on hydrogen fuel cells emit water vapor, not exhaust.

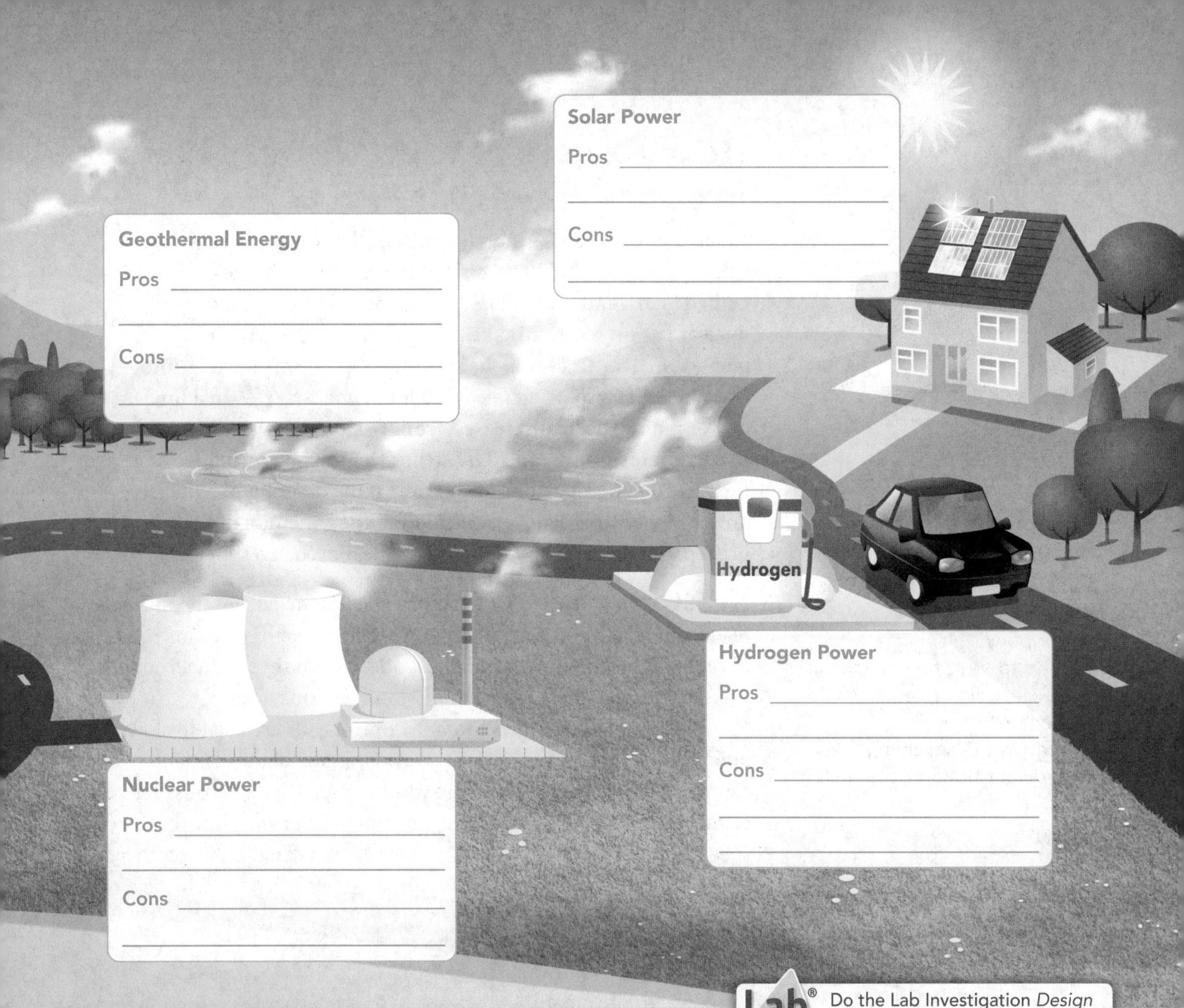

Geothermal Energy

Pros _____

_____

Cons _____

_____

Solar Power

Pros _____

_____

Cons _____

_____

Hydrogen

Hydrogen Power

Pros _____

_____

Cons _____

_____

_____

Nuclear Power

Pros _____

_____

Cons _____

_____

Lab zone® Do the Lab Investigation *Design and Build a Solar Cooker.*

🔑 Assess Your Understanding

1a. Review What forms of energy are provided by the sun?_____

b. Explain Are biomass fuels renewable? Why?_____

_____

c. ANSWER THE BIG ❓ What are some of Earth's energy sources?

_____

_____

_____

_____

got it? ....

○ **I get it!** Now I know that alternative energy sources include_____

_____

○ I need extra help with _____

Go to MY SCIENCE ⑤ COACH *online for help with this subject.*

How Does a Nuclear Power Plant Produce Electricity?

Nuclear power plants generate much of the world's electricity. They generate about 20 percent of the electricity in the United States and more than 70 percent in France. Controlled nuclear fission reactions take place inside nuclear power plants. **Nuclear fission** is the splitting of an atom's nucleus into two nuclei. The splitting releases a lot of energy. 🔑 **In a nuclear power plant, the heat released from fission reactions is used to turn water into steam. The steam then turns the blades of a turbine to generate electricity.** Look at the diagram of a nuclear power plant in **Figure 7**. In addition to the generator, it has two main parts: the reactor vessel and the heat exchanger.

Reactor Vessel The **reactor vessel** is the part of the nuclear reactor in which nuclear fission occurs. The reactor contains rods of radioactive uranium called **fuel rods.** When several fuel rods are placed close together, a series of fission reactions occurs.

If the reactor vessel gets too hot, control rods are used to slow down the chain reactions. **Control rods,** made of the elements cadmium, boron or hafnium, are inserted near the fuel rods. The elements absorb particles released during fission and slow the speed of the chain reactions. The control rods can then be removed to speed up the chain reactions again.

FIGURE 7 ·······················

> **INTERACTIVE ART** **Nuclear Power Plants**
Nuclear power plants are designed to turn the energy from nuclear fission reactions into electricity.

✎ **Interpret Diagrams** Where does nuclear fission occur in the plant?

_____

_____

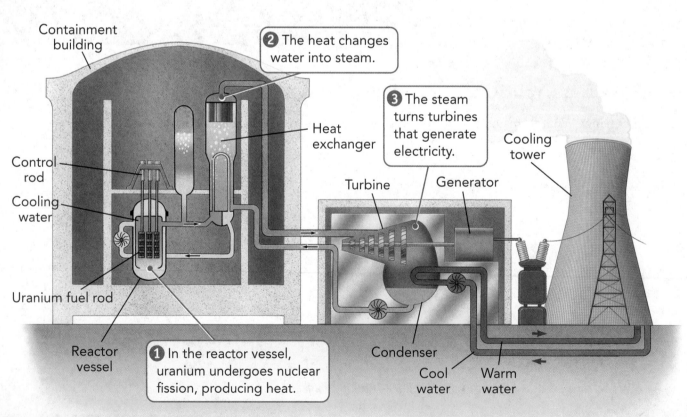

Containment building

❷ The heat changes water into steam.

Heat exchanger

❸ The steam turns turbines that generate electricity.

Cooling tower

Control rod

Cooling water

Turbine   Generator

Uranium fuel rod

Reactor vessel

❶ In the reactor vessel, uranium undergoes nuclear fission, producing heat.

Condenser

Cool water   Warm water

Heat Exchanger Heat is removed from the reactor vessel by water or another fluid that is pumped through the reactor. This fluid passes through a heat exchanger. There, the fluid boils water to produce steam. The steam runs the electrical generator. The steam is condensed again and pumped back to the heat exchanger.

The Risks of Nuclear Power At first, people thought that nuclear fission would provide an almost unlimited source of clean, safe energy. But accidents at nuclear power plants have led to safety concerns. In 1986, the reactor vessel in a nuclear power plant in Chernobyl, Ukraine, overheated. The fuel rods generated so much heat that they started to melt. This condition is called a meltdown. The excess heat caused a series of explosions, which injured or killed dozens of people immediately. In addition, radioactive materials escaped into the environment and killed many more people.

Plant operators can avoid accidents at nuclear facilities through careful planning and by improving safety features. A more difficult problem is the disposal of radioactive wastes. Radioactive wastes remain dangerous for many thousands of years. Scientists must find ways to store these wastes safely for very long periods of time.

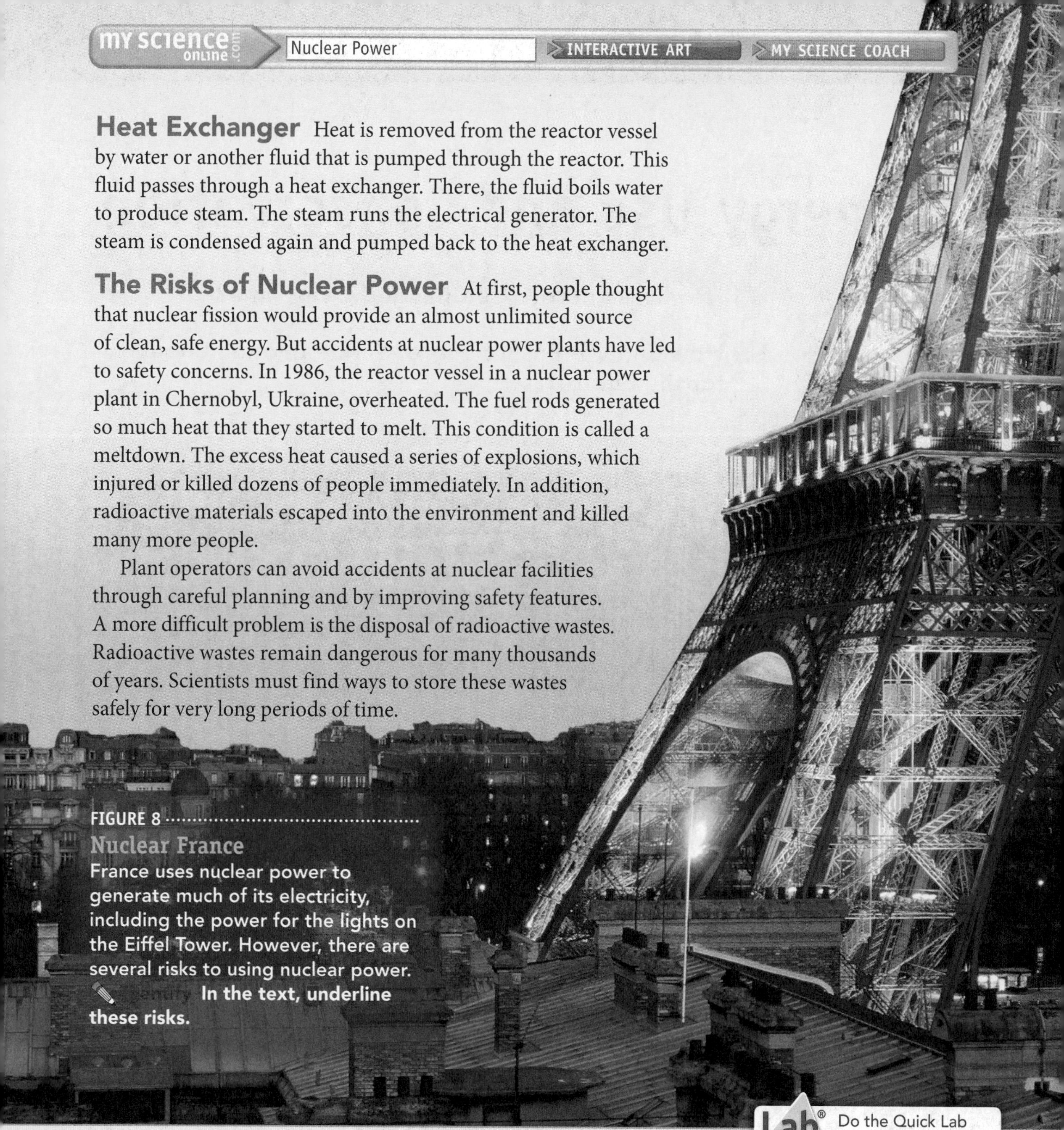

FIGURE 8
Nuclear France
France uses nuclear power to generate much of its electricity, including the power for the lights on the Eiffel Tower. However, there are several risks to using nuclear power. **In the text, underline these risks.**

Lab zone ® Do the Quick Lab *Producing Electricity.*

Assess Your Understanding

got it?

○ **I get it!** Now I know that nuclear power plants produce energy by _____

_____

○ I need extra help with _____

Go to **my science** COACH *online for help with this subject.*

LESSON
3 Energy Use and Conservation

UNLOCK THE BIG Q?

🔑 How Has Energy Use Changed Over Time?

🔑 How Can We Ensure There Will Be Enough Energy for the Future?

my planet Diary

TECHNOLOGY

House of Straw

What was that first little pig thinking? Was he just lazy—building a house of straw as quickly as he could without much thought? Or was he helping the environment? It turns out that straw is one of the best materials for keeping warm air inside in cold weather and keeping hot air outside in hot weather. Builders place stacks of straw along the exterior walls of a building and then seal the straw with mud. Bales of straw are natural and cheap, since straw is left over after grain is harvested. It's no wonder that more and more people are using straw to insulate their homes!

Communicate Write your answers below.

1. How does using straw for insulation save energy?

_____

_____

_____

2. Why is using straw for insulation good for the environment?

_____

_____

_____

▷ **PLANET DIARY** Go to **Planet Diary** to learn more about energy use and conservation.

Lab zone® Do the Inquiry Warm-Up *Which Bulb Is More Efficient?*

Vocabulary
- efficiency • insulation
- energy conservation

Skills
- ➲ Reading: Identify the Main Idea
- ⚠ Inquiry: Observe

How Has Energy Use Changed Over Time?

Energy, beyond using your own muscle power, is essential to the way most people live. The methods people use to obtain energy have changed, especially in the last 200 years.  **For most of human history, people burned wood for energy. Only recently have fossil fuels become the main energy source.**

Eventually, people harnessed the power of other renewable resources. Ships used tall sails to capture wind energy. Flowing water turned wheels connected to stones that ground grain into flour.

Wood, wind, and water were also the main sources of energy in the United States until the nineteenth century. Coal gained in popularity as a fuel during the westward expansion of the railroads. Coal remained the dominant fuel until 1951, when it was replaced by oil and natural gas.

Today, scientists are continually looking for new and better fuels to meet the world's energy needs. As fossil fuel supplies continue to decrease, the interest in renewable energy sources has increased. With more focus on protecting the environment, scientists are working to meet our energy needs while reducing and eliminating many sources of pollution.

➲ **Identify the Main Idea**
Energy use has changed over time. On the timeline, label and shade the periods in which coal and oil were the dominant fuel sources in the United States.

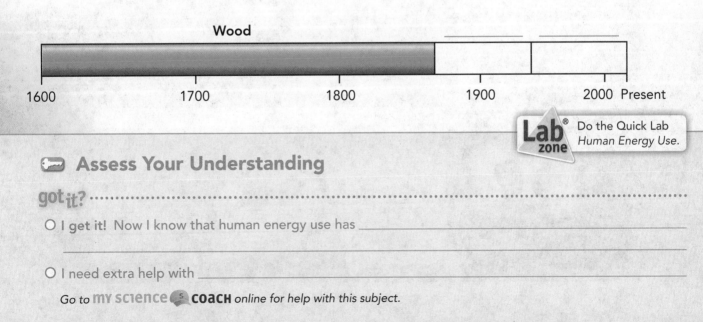

Wood					
1600	1700	1800	1900	2000	Present

Lab zone | Do the Quick Lab
Human Energy Use.

🗝 Assess Your Understanding

got it? ....

○ **I get it!** Now I know that human energy use has _____

_____

○ I need extra help with _____

Go to MY SCIENCE ⑤ COACH online for help with this subject.

How Can We Ensure There Will Be Enough Energy for the Future?

What would happen if the world ran out of fossil fuels today? The heating and cooling systems in most buildings would stop functioning. Forests would disappear as people began to burn wood for heating and cooking. Cars, buses, and trains would be stranded wherever they ran out of fuel. About 70 percent of the world's electric power would disappear. Since televisions, computers, and telephones depend on electricity, communication would be greatly reduced. Lights and most home appliances would no longer work.

Although fossil fuels won't run out immediately, they also won't last forever. Most people think that it makes sense to use fuels more wisely now to avoid fuel shortages in the future. **One way to preserve our current energy resources is to increase the efficiency of our energy use. Another way is to conserve energy whenever possible.** Refer to **Figure 1**.

FIGURE 1 ··················

> **REAL-WORLD INQUIRY** **Wasting Energy**

Many things, such as lights and appliances, use energy. If people do not use these things properly, energy can be wasted.

Observe Circle everything in this scene that is wasting energy.

Energy Efficiency One way to make energy resources last longer is to use fuels more efficiently. **Efficiency** is the percentage of energy that is actually used to perform work. The rest of the energy is "lost" to the surroundings, usually as heat. People have developed many ways to increase energy efficiency.

Heating and Cooling One method of increasing the efficiency of heating and cooling systems is insulation. **Insulation** is a layer of material that traps air. This helps block the transfer of heat between the air inside and outside a building. You have probably seen insulation made of fiberglass. It looks like pink cotton candy. A layer of fiberglass 15 centimeters thick insulates a room as well as a brick wall 2 meters thick!

Trapped air can act as insulation in windows too. Many windows consist of two panes of glass with space in between them. The air between the panes of glass acts as insulation.

Lighting Much of the electricity used for home lighting is wasted. For example, less than 10 percent of the electricity that an incandescent light bulb uses is converted into light. The rest is given off as heat. In contrast, compact fluorescent bulbs use about one fourth as much energy to provide the same amount of light.

FIGURE 2 ....

Solutions to Wasting Energy
There are many ways to save energy in a home.
✎ **Explain** Pick at least three of the things you circled in the scene and explain what people could do to stop wasting energy.

Ways to Conserve Energy

_____

_____

_____

_____

_____

_____

_____

_____

_____

_____

_____

_____

Transportation Engineers have improved the energy efficiency of cars by designing better engines and batteries. For instance, many new cars use high-efficiency hybrid engines that go twice as far on a tank of fuel than other cars. Buses in some cities are now entirely electric, running on high-power rechargeable batteries. New kinds of batteries allow some electric cars to drive hundreds of kilometers before recharging.

Another way to save energy is to reduce the number of cars on the road. In many communities, public transit systems provide an alternative to driving. Other cities encourage carpooling and bicycling. Many cities now set aside lanes for cars containing two or more people.

apply it!

1 You have been put in charge of designing an ad campaign for your area to get more people to use public transportation. Design a poster that will get people's attention and inform them about their choices. On your poster, list at least three reasons why people should use public transportation. Give your poster a title.

2 Describe Where would you want to display your poster? Why?

_____

_____

3 CHALLENGE How else could you increase awareness about public transportation?

_____

_____

_____

Energy Conservation Another approach to making energy resources last longer is conservation. **Energy conservation** means reducing energy use.

You can reduce your personal energy use by changing your behavior in some simple ways. For example, if you walk to the store instead of getting a ride, you are conserving the gasoline it would take to drive to the store.

While these suggestions seem like small things, multiplied by millions of people they add up to a lot of energy saved for the future.

FIGURE 3 ·······················
Energy Conservation in Your Everyday Life
Even students like you can conserve energy.
✎ **Communicate** With a partner, think of ways you can conserve energy in your daily life. Write your answers in the notebook.

 Do the Quick Lab *Future Energy Use.*

🔑 Assess Your Understanding

1a. Define What does it mean to say that something is "energy efficient"?

_____

_____

_____

_____

b. Solve Problems What are some strategies a city could use to increase energy conservation?

_____

_____

_____

_____

got it? ·······························

○ **I get it!** Now I know that ensuring that the future has enough energy requires _____

_____

○ **I need extra help with** _____

Go to MY SCIENCE ⬤ⁱ COACH *online for help with this subject.*

315

Study Guide

Earth has many energy sources, including _____ such as coal; the sun, which can be used for _____; and flowing water, which can be used for hydroelectric power.

LESSON 1 Fossil Fuels

🔑 The three major fossil fuels are coal, oil, and natural gas.

🔑 Since fossil fuels take hundreds of millions of years to form, they are considered nonrenewable resources.

Vocabulary
• fuel   • fossil fuel
• hydrocarbon
• petroleum   • refinery
• petrochemical

LESSON 2 Renewable Sources of Energy

🔑 Renewable sources of energy include sunlight, water, wind, biomass fuels, and geothermal energy.

🔑 In a nuclear power plant, the heat released from fission reactions is used to change water into steam. The steam then turns the blades of a turbine to generate electricity.

Vocabulary
• solar energy   • hydroelectric power   • biomass fuel   • gasohol
• geothermal energy   • nuclear fission
• reactor vessel   • fuel rod   • control rod

LESSON 3 Energy Use and Conservation

🔑 For most of human history, the main fuel source was wood. Only recently have fossil fuels become the main energy source.

🔑 One way to preserve our current energy resources is to increase the efficiency of our energy use. Another way is to conserve energy whenever possible.

Vocabulary
• efficiency   • insulation   • energy conservation

Review and Assessment

LESSON 1 Fossil Fuels

1. What is one similarity among oil, coal, and natural gas?

   a. They are all petrochemicals.

   b. They all must be processed in a refinery.

   c. They are all gases at room temperature.

   d. They are all formed from the remains of dead organisms.

2. Fossil fuels take hundreds of millions of years to form, and therefore are considered _____ energy sources.

3. Compare and Contrast Describe one main use for each fuel: coal, oil, and natural gas.

_____

_____

_____

_____

_____

_____

4. Sequence How does coal form?

_____

_____

_____

_____

_____

_____

_____

5. 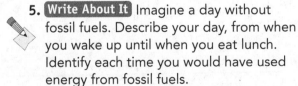 **Write About It** Imagine a day without fossil fuels. Describe your day, from when you wake up until when you eat lunch. Identify each time you would have used energy from fossil fuels.

LESSON 2 Renewable Sources of Energy

6. Which of the following is not a biomass fuel?

   a. gasohol   **b.** methane from landfills

   c. hydrogen   **d.** sugar cane wastes

7. Running water can be used as an energy source to produce _____ power.

8. Apply Concepts Fill in the boxes with two benefits and two costs of hydrogen power.

Benefits	Costs
_____	_____
_____	_____
_____	_____
_____	_____

9. Interpret Photos Explain how a nuclear power plant, like the one pictured below, produces energy.

_____

_____

_____

_____

Energy Use and Conservation

10. What is efficiency?

    a. the percentage of energy that is lost to the environment as heat

    b. the percentage of energy that is used to perform work

    c. the percentage of energy that is conserved when work is done

    d. the percentage of energy that is wasted when electronics are left on

11. _____

involves using less energy, helping energy

resources last longer.

12. Draw Conclusions How is energy use today different from energy use 200 years ago?

_____

_____

_____

_____

_____

_____

_____

_____

13. Solve Problems Describe three actions a person can take to conserve energy.

_____

_____

_____

_____

_____

_____

_____

APPLY THE BIG ? **What are some of Earth's energy sources?**

14. Earth's energy sources include both renewable and nonrenewable resources. Name at least three sources of energy that could be used in a classroom like the one below. Then describe the ideal energy source for generating most of your school's electricity and explain why you chose this source.

_____

_____

_____

_____

_____

_____

_____

_____

_____

_____

_____

_____

_____

_____

Standardized Test Prep

Multiple Choice

Circle the letter of the best answer.

1. Which statement is best supported by the table below?

2007 Global Oil Production and Use		
Country	Oil production global rank	Oil use global rank
United States	3	1
Russia	1	6
China	5	3
Brazil	15	8

   A Brazil produces more oil than China.

   B Russia produces the most oil.

   C China consumes the most oil.

   D The United States consumes and produces the most oil in the world.

2. Which of the following is not a fossil fuel?

   A oil

   B coal

   C natural gas

   D wood

3. The interior of a car heats up on a sunny day because of

   A solar cells.

   B active solar heating.

   C passive solar heating.

   D direct solar heating.

4. Which explains why systems that transform energy are not completely efficient?

   A Increasing energy resources increases efficiency.

   B Doing less work gives off more heat.

   C Some energy is converted to heat that flows to surrounding material.

   D An increase in the amount of energy is needed to generate electricity.

5. How does a nuclear power plant produce energy?

   A with solar panels

   B through nuclear fission reactions

   C with geothermal heat

   D through nuclear meltdown reactions

Constructed Response

Use the diagram below and your knowledge of science to help you answer Question 6. Write your answer on a separate sheet of paper.

6. Describe how energy is produced in the diagram above. Then, describe one advantage and one disadvantage of this source.

How Low Is Low Impact?

▲ This electric car is charged by attaching an electric cord to an outlet. However, the source of the electricity may be a fossil fuel-based power plant.

Hybrid engines, windmills, low-impact this, alternative-energy that—everywhere you look, people are trying to find ways to create energy by using renewable resources. Sometimes, a technology seems to conserve energy, but in reality it has hidden costs. For example, electric cars do not release air pollutants during use, but the method that is used to generate the electricity for the car may cause pollution. Is the electricity really "clean"?

Evaluating the costs and benefits of different technologies is an important scientific skill. Use the following questions to sharpen your decision-making skills.

What is the source? What materials are used to create or power the technology? How are they obtained?

What are the products? What is produced when the technology is created or used? How do these products affect the environment? How are these products stored, recycled, or disposed of?

How does it affect our lives? Does using a technology encourage people to use more energy? If it does, do the benefits of the technology outweigh the environmental costs?

Every technology has costs and benefits. However, it is important to be able to evaluate new technologies to find out if the benefits outweigh the costs!

Write About It In a group, discuss the questions listed above. Can you think of ways to add to them or to change them? Then, create an Environmental Decision-Making Guide and use it to evaluate two of the energy technologies described in this chapter.

Life on an Oil Rig

OFFSHORE PETROLEUM ENGINEER

This professional's office is on a huge steel platform that is half the area of a football field, surrounded by water. With much of Earth's oil located under the ocean floor, petroleum engineers must go where the oil is. Many of them work on offshore oil rigs—large drilling platforms that extract oil from under the ocean floor.

Conditions far out in the the ocean can be harsh or dangerous. Large equipment, fires, and even hurricanes threaten workers' safety. However, far out in the ocean, workers on oil rigs can see sharks, manta rays, and other marine life.

Petroleum engineers study geology, physics, and chemistry to understand the properties of rock formations that contain oil. They use high-tech remote sensing equipment to find oil and computer modeling software to figure out how to get the oil out of the ocean's floor.

Write About It Find out more about life on an offshore oil rig. Then, write a diary or blog entry that describes a week in the life of an offshore petroleum engineer.

▲ The Petronius platform is located in the Gulf of Mexico.

Hydrokinetic Energy

Whirlpool! Maelstrom! Vortex! Do these words make you think of a rushing spiral of water, sucking fish and boats into its center? Not all vortexes sink ships. Fish and whales cause little vortexes when they swim. As the animals move, they create turbulence in the water. Turbulent water moves away from the animal and gives it a little push.

An engineer named Michael Bernitsas has developed a device that uses this effect to generate electricity. As currents push water around a cylindrical device, a vortex forms. As the vortex moves away from the device, the cylinder moves up and down. The device then converts that mechanical energy into electrical energy. Bernitsas has even improved the device by adding mechanical "fish tails" to the generators! Bernitsas is still testing his system, but he hopes that it can someday Be used to help meet society's needs for a renewable source of energy.

Design It Find out more about how fish swim. Then, design a model that shows how the body of a fish moves in the water. In your model, show where a vortex would form as the fish swims.

WHERE IS THIS WATER GOING?

THE BIG ? How does fresh water cycle on Earth?

Watch out below! This river is carrying the kayaker straight down. But where did the water come from in the first place? Where is it going? And why is water important?

✎ Develop Hypotheses Explain where you think the water in the river came from and where it will go next.

_____

_____

_____

_____

_____

_____

_____

▶ UNTAMED SCIENCE Watch the **Untamed Science** video to learn more about water on Earth.

CHAPTER

Water 10

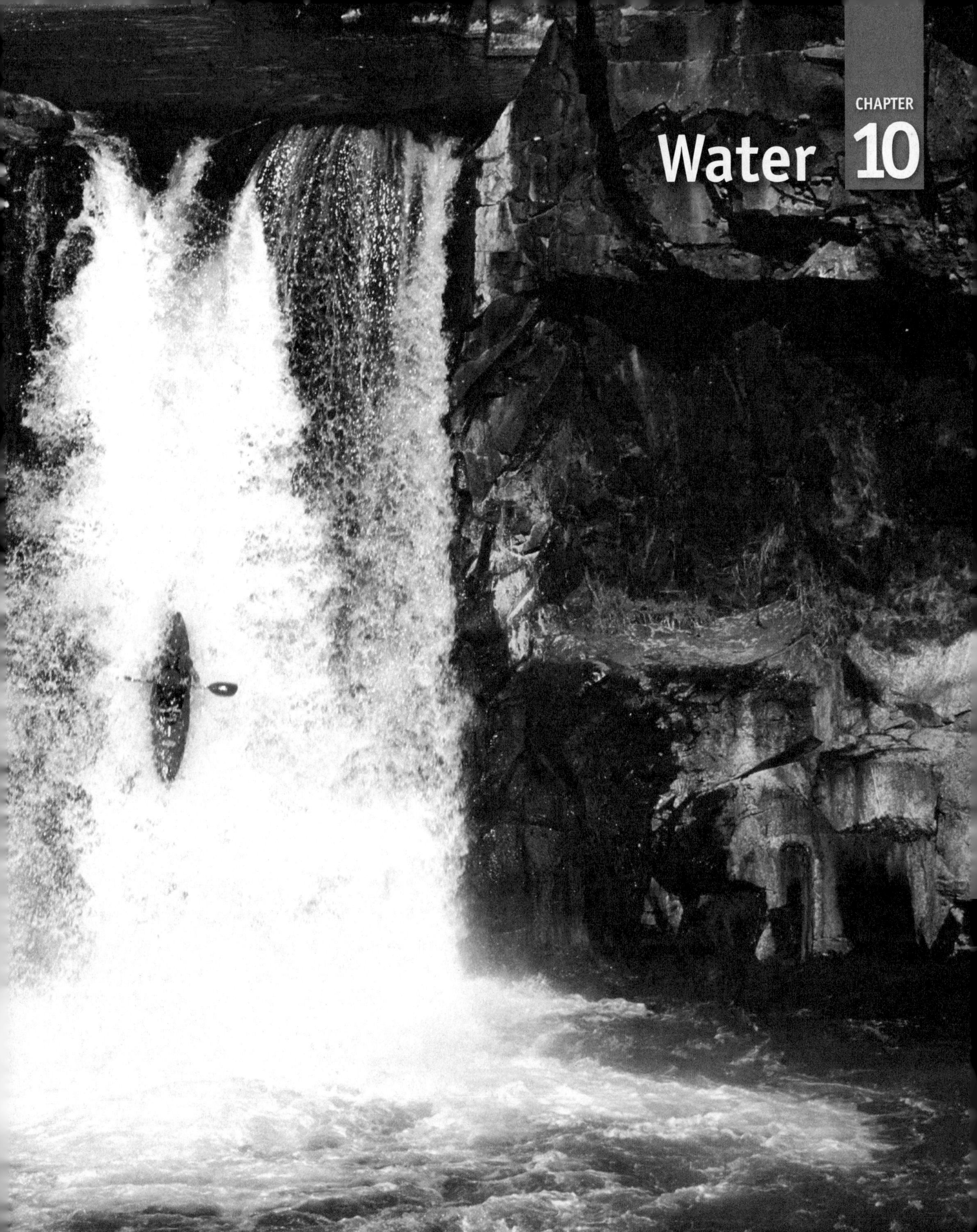

10 Getting Started

Check Your Understanding

1. Background Read the paragraph below and then answer the question.

Have you ever sat at a window on a misty day? You might see **condensation** as drops of water form on the glass. These drops form when **water vapor** in the air cools and turns into a liquid. **Gravity** pulls the drops down the windowpane toward Earth's surface.

> **Condensation** occurs when a substance changes from a gas to a liquid.
>
> **Water vapor** is water in the gaseous state.
>
> **Gravity** is a force that attracts all objects toward each other.

• How do water drops form on the window?

_____

_____

> **MY READING WEB** If you had trouble completing the question above, visit **My Reading Web** and type in *Fresh Water.*

Vocabulary Skill

Latin Word Origins Many science words come to English from Latin. In this chapter you will learn the term *permeable*. *Permeable* comes from the Latin word parts *per-*, meaning "through"; *meare*, meaning "to go" or "to pass"; and *-bilis*, meaning "capable of."

$$\underset{\text{through}}{per\text{-}} + \underset{\text{go or pass}}{meare} + \underset{\text{capable of}}{\text{-}bilis} = \underset{\text{capable of going through}}{permeable}$$

Learn these Latin word parts to help you remember the vocabulary terms.

Latin Origin	Meaning	Example
trans-	across	transpiration, *n.*
spirare	to breathe	transpiration, *n.*
vapor	steam	evaporation, *n.*
videre	to separate	divide, *v.*

2. Quick Check Use the table to answer the question.
• Based on the table, predict the meaning of *transpiration*.

_____

groundwater

water cycle

wave

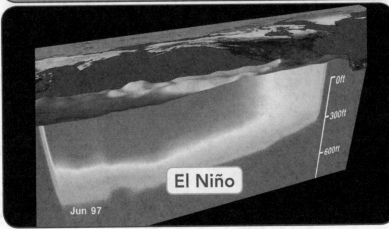

El Niño

Jun 97

0ft
300ft
600ft

Chapter Preview

LESSON 1
- habitat   • groundwater
- water cycle   • evaporation
- transpiration   • precipitation
- Identify the Main Idea
- Observe

LESSON 2
- tributary   • watershed
- divide   • reservoir
- eutrophication
- Sequence
- Form Operational Definitions

LESSON 3
- permeable   • impermeable
- unsaturated zone
- saturated zone   • water table
- aquifer   • artesian well
- Relate Cause and Effect
- Predict

LESSON 4
- salinity   • sonar   • seamount
- trench   • continental slope
- continental shelf   • abyssal plain
- mid-ocean ridge
- Identify the Main Idea
- Interpret Data

LESSON 5
- wave   • wavelength   • frequency
- wave height   • tsunami
- longshore drift   • rip current
- groin
- Relate Cause and Effect
- Form Operational Definitions

LESSON 6
- current   • Coriolis effect
- climate   • El Niño   • La Niña
- Compare and Contrast
- Infer

> VOCAB FLASH CARDS For extra help with vocabulary, visit **Vocab Flash Cards** and type in *Water*.

Water on Earth

UNLOCK THE BIG ?

🔑 **Why Is Water Important?**

🔑 **Where Is Water Found?**

🔑 **What Is the Water Cycle?**

my planeT DiaRY

SCIENCE STATS

How Much Water Do You Use?

You take a shower. You brush your teeth. You take a big drink after soccer practice. All day long, you need water! How much water do you use in a day? How much do you think your whole state uses? The graph shows the water used per person in the ten states of the United States with the largest populations. The data include the water used for all purposes, including farming, industry, and electric power.

Water Use per Person per Day

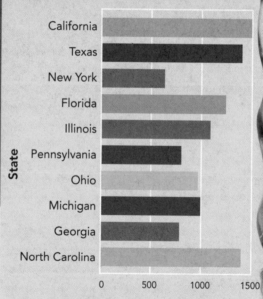

Gallons Used per Person per Day

Study the graph. Then answer the questions below.

1. In which state is the water use per person greatest? In which state is it least?

_____

_____

2. What do you think might explain the difference in water use between states?

_____

_____

> PLANET DIARY   Go to **Planet Diary** to learn more about fresh water on Earth.

 Lab zone® Do the Inquiry Warm-Up *Where Does the Water Come From?*

Vocabulary

- habitat • groundwater • water cycle • evaporation
- transpiration • precipitation

Skills

↻ Reading: Identify the Main Idea

△ Inquiry: Observe

Why Is Water Important?

What do you and an apple have in common? You both consist mostly of water! Water makes up nearly two thirds of your body's mass. That water is necessary to keep your body functioning. **All living things need water in order to carry out their body processes. In addition, many living things live in water.**

Body Processes Without water, neither you nor an apple could survive. Water allows organisms to break down food, grow, reproduce, and get and use materials they need from their environments. Animals obtain water by drinking it or by eating foods that contain water. Most animals cannot survive more than a few days without water.

Plants and other organisms that make their own food also need water. Algae and plants use water, along with carbon dioxide and energy from the sun, to make their own food in a process called photosynthesis (foh toh SIN thuh sis). Other organisms get food by eating the plants, or by eating organisms that eat the plants.

Habitats Water provides habitats for many living things. An organism's **habitat** is the place where it lives and obtains all the things it needs to survive. Some organisms cannot live out of water. You are probably familiar with large water-dwelling organisms such as sharks. But most such organisms are microscopic. In fact, aquatic, or water, habitats contain more types of organisms than land habitats do.

FIGURE 1 ....
The Need for Water
✎ **Predict** Underline the sentence that explains why these animals need the water hole. What would happen if the water hole dried up?

_____

_____

_____

_____

Lab zone ® Do the Quick Lab
Water, Water, Everywhere.

Assess Your Understanding

got it? ....

○ I get it! Now I know that living things use water _____

_____

○ I need extra help with _____

Go to **my science** ⓢ **coach** *online for help with this subject.*

327

Where Is Water Found?

When you turn on the tap, it might seem that an endless supply of fresh water comes out! But Earth's freshwater supply is very limited. 🔑 **Most of Earth's surface water—roughly 97 percent—is salt water found in oceans. Only 3 percent is fresh water.**

Of that 3 percent, about two thirds is frozen in huge masses of ice near the North and South poles. About a third of the fresh water is underground. A tiny fraction of fresh water occurs in lakes and rivers. An even tinier fraction is found in the atmosphere, most of it in the form of invisible water vapor, the gaseous form of water.

Oceans Find the oceans on the map in **Figure 2.** Pacific, Atlantic, Indian, and Arctic are the names used for the different parts of the ocean. (Some scientists call the area around Antarctica the Southern Ocean.) But the waters are really all interconnected, making up one big ocean. The Pacific Ocean is the largest, covering an area greater than all the land on Earth. The Atlantic Ocean is next largest, though the Indian Ocean is deeper. The Arctic Ocean surrounds the North Pole. Smaller saltwater bodies are called seas.

Ice Much of Earth's fresh water is frozen into sheets of ice. Massive ice sheets cover most of Greenland and Antarctica. Icebergs are floating chunks of ice made of fresh water that break off from ice sheets. You could also find icebergs in the Arctic Ocean and in the North Atlantic.

🔄 **Identify the Main Idea**
Underline the main idea in each paragraph on this page.

do the math!

Analyzing Data

These graphs show how much of Earth's water is found in different forms.

❶ **Read Graphs** Where is most water on Earth found? _____

❷ **Read Graphs** About what fraction of Earth's fresh water is in the form of ice? _____

❸ **Interpret Data** How does the total amount of groundwater compare to the total amount of ice?

_____
_____
_____

Salt water in oceans and salt lakes **97%**

Fresh water **3%**

Water vapor **0.04%**

Ice **69%**

Groundwater **30%**

Lakes and rivers **0.26%**

Rivers and Lakes Look at **Figure 2**. All the rivers and lakes marked on the map contain fresh water, as do many other smaller rivers and lakes. North America's five Great Lakes contain about 20 percent of all the water in the world's freshwater lakes.

Groundwater To find some of the fresh water on Earth, you have to look underground. When it rains or snows, most water that doesn't evaporate soaks into the ground. This water trickles through spaces between particles of soil and rock. Water that fills the cracks and spaces in underground soil and rock layers is called **groundwater.** Far more fresh water is located underground than in all of Earth's rivers and lakes.

FIGURE 2 · · · · · · · · · · · · · · · ·

Earth's Major Waterways
The map shows Earth's oceans and some major freshwater sources.

✎ **Classify** Circle the names of three saltwater sources. Underline the names of three freshwater sources.

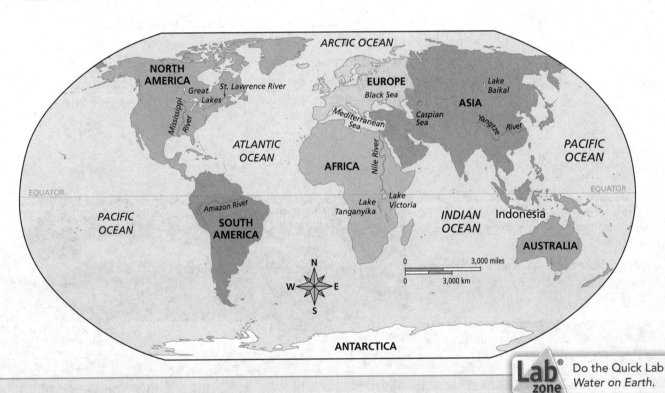

Lab zone® Do the Quick Lab
Water on Earth.

🔑 **Assess Your Understanding**

1a. List What are the four main sources of fresh water on Earth?

_____

_____

b. Make Judgments Which freshwater source do you think is most important to people? Why?

_____

_____

_____

got it? ·

○ **I get it!** Now I know that Earth's water is found in _____

_____

○ **I need extra help with** _____

Go to MY SCIENCE ⑤ COACH online for help with this subject.

What Is the Water Cycle?

Earth has its own built-in water recycling system: the water cycle. The **water cycle** is the continuous process by which water moves from Earth's surface to the atmosphere and back, driven by energy from the sun and gravity. 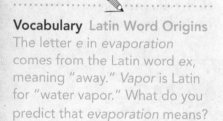 **In the water cycle, water moves between land, living things, bodies of water on Earth's surface, and the atmosphere.**

Water Evaporates Where does the water in a puddle go when it disappears? It evaporates, becoming water vapor. **Evaporation** is the process by which molecules at the surface of a liquid absorb enough energy to change to a gaseous state. Water constantly evaporates from the surfaces of bodies of water such as oceans and lakes, as well as from soil and your skin. Plants play a role, too, in this step of the water cycle. Plants draw in water from the soil through their roots. Eventually the water is given off through the leaves as water vapor in a process called **transpiration**.

FIGURE 3 ·····················

> INTERACTIVE ART The Water Cycle

The diagram below shows the processes of the water cycle.

Apply Concepts As you read these two pages, label each process shown in the diagram.

Condensation Forms Clouds
After a water molecule evaporates, warm air can carry the water molecule upward. Air tends to become colder as it rises. Water vapor condenses more easily at lower temperatures, so some water vapor cools and condenses into liquid water. Droplets of liquid water clump around solid particles in the air, forming clouds.

Water Falls as Precipitation
As more water vapor condenses, the water droplets grow larger. Eventually, they become so heavy that they fall back to Earth. Water that falls to Earth as rain, snow, hail, or sleet is called **precipitation.**

Most precipitation falls directly into the ocean. Of the precipitation that falls on land, most evaporates. A small amount of the remaining water runs off the surface into streams and lakes in a process called runoff, but most of it seeps into groundwater. After a long time, this groundwater may flow down to the ocean and evaporate again.

Precipitation is the source of almost all fresh water on and below Earth's surface. For millions of years, the total amount of water cycling through the Earth system has remained fairly constant—the rates of evaporation and precipitation are balanced.

apply it!

1 ☐ **Observe** What water cycle process can you observe here?

_____

2 CHALLENGE What other process or processes can you infer are also taking place?

_____

3 Give an example of a water cycle process you have seen.

_____

_____

 Lab zone Do the Lab Investigation *Water From Trees.*

🔑 Assess Your Understanding

2a. Identify What are the three major steps in the water cycle?

_____

_____

b. Sequence Start with a puddle on a sunny day. How might water move through the water cycle and eventually fall as rain?

_____

_____

_____

_____

_____

got it? ....

○ **I get it!** Now I know that the water cycle

is _____

_____

_____

○ **I need extra help with** _____

Go to MY SCIENCE 🔍 COACH *online for help with this subject.*

Surface Water

🔑 **What Is a River System?**

🔑 **What Are Ponds and Lakes?**

🔑 **How Can Lakes Change?**

my planet diary

FUN FACT

So Near, So Far

In Colorado's mountains, some rain seeps into the Fryingpan River. That river flows into the Colorado River and, more than 2,000 kilometers later, into the Gulf of California. Less than 15 kilometers away, rain seeps into the Arkansas River, which flows 2,350 kilometers until it joins the Mississippi River. Eventually, the Mississippi flows into the Gulf of Mexico. Water that fell less than 15 kilometers apart ends up almost 3,000 kilometers apart, in different oceans!

Use the map and your knowledge of science to answer the following question.

Why do you think the two rivers that start so close together flow to such different locations?

_____

_____

_____

▶ PLANET DIARY Go to **Planet Diary** to learn more about water on Earth's surface.

Royal Gorge

Pueblo

KANSAS

PACIFIC OCEAN

GULF OF MEXICO

John Martin Reservoir

Great Bend

Wichita

COLORADO

Lab zone® Do the Inquiry Warm-Up *Mapping Surface Waters.*

Vocabulary
- tributary • watershed • divide • reservoir
- eutrophication

Skills
- Reading: Sequence
- Inquiry: Form Operational Definitions

What Is a River System?

If you were hiking near the beginning of the Fryingpan and Arkansas rivers, you could observe tiny streams of water from melted snow. Gravity causes these tiny streams to flow downhill. As you follow one small stream, you would notice that the stream reaches another stream and joins it, forming a larger stream. That larger stream joins other streams until a small river forms.

Tributaries As you continue following the small river downhill, you might notice more streams joining the river. Eventually, the small river itself flows into a larger river. This river grows as more small rivers flow into it, before finally spilling into the ocean. The streams and smaller rivers that feed into a main river are called **tributaries.** Tributaries flow downward toward the main river, pulled by the force of gravity. 🔑 **A river and all the streams and smaller rivers that flow into it together make up a river system.**

Why is the Arkansas River considered a tributary of the Mississippi River?

_____

_____

_____

FIGURE 1 ·····························

The Arkansas River

✎ **Make Judgments** Put a *K* on the map where you might go kayaking. Put an *F* where you might get water for farming. Put an *M* where you might build a manufacturing plant. Explain why you chose the locations you did.

_____

_____

_____

Kaw Lake · Tulsa · Lake Dardanelle · ARKANSAS · Little Rock · Mississippi River · OKLAHOMA

Watersheds Just as all the water in a bathtub flows toward the drain, all the water in a river system drains into a main river. The land area that supplies water to a river system is called a **watershed.** Watersheds are sometimes known as drainage basins.

As you can see in **Figure 2,** the Missouri and Ohio rivers are quite long. Yet they flow into the Mississippi River. When rivers join another river system, the areas they drain become part of the largest river's watershed. The watershed of the Mississippi River covers nearly one third of the United States!

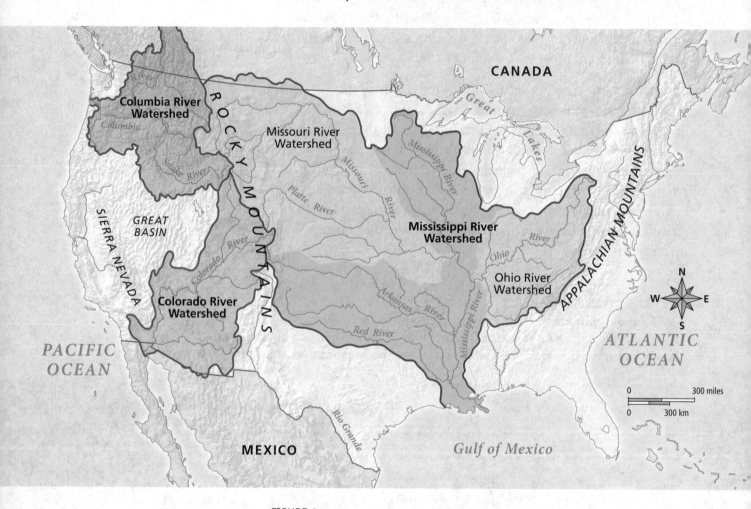

FIGURE 2 ··

Major Watersheds of the United States

This map shows watersheds of several large rivers in the United States. ✎ **Interpret Maps** Draw the path that water would take from the Platte River's source to the ocean. Which watersheds would the water pass through?

_____

_____

_____

Divides What keeps watersheds separate? One watershed is separated from another by a ridge of land called a **divide**. Streams on each side of the divide flow in different directions. The Great Divide (also called the Continental Divide) is the longest divide in North America. It follows the line of the Rocky Mountains. West of this divide, water flows toward the Pacific Ocean. Some water is trapped between the Rockies and the Sierra Nevadas, in the Great Basin. Between the Rocky and Appalachian mountains, water flows toward the Mississippi River and into the Gulf of Mexico.

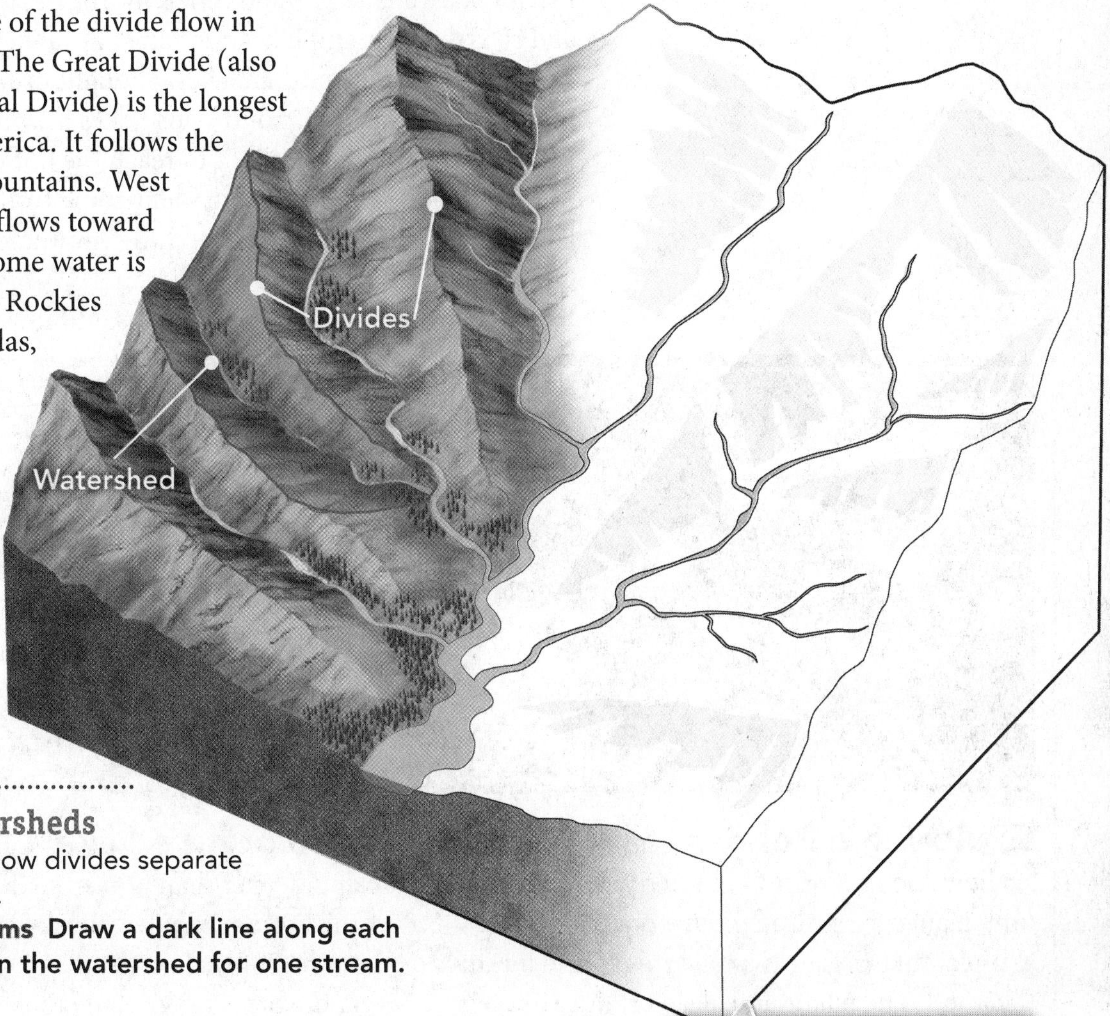

FIGURE 3 ·······················
Divides and Watersheds
The diagram shows how divides separate land into watersheds.

✏️ **Interpret Diagrams** Draw a dark line along each divide. Then shade in the watershed for one stream.

Divides

Watershed

Lab ® Do the Quick Lab
zone *What Is a Watershed?*

🔑 **Assess Your Understanding**

1a. Identify A (divide/tributary) separates two watersheds.

b. Summarize How is a watershed related to a river system? _____

_____

_____

c. Make Generalizations How can a stream be part of more than one watershed?

_____

_____

_____

_____

_____

_____

got it? ··

○ **I get it!** Now I know that a river system is _____

_____

○ I need extra help with _____

Go to MY SCIENCE 🄢 COACH online for help with this subject.

335

What Are Ponds and Lakes?

What makes a lake or pond different from a river? Unlike streams and rivers, ponds and lakes contain still water. In general, ponds are smaller and shallower than lakes. Sunlight usually reaches to the bottom of all parts of a pond. Most lakes have areas where the water is too deep for much sunlight to reach the bottom.

Where does pond and lake water come from? Some ponds and lakes are supplied by rainfall, melting snow and ice, and runoff. Others are fed by rivers or groundwater. 🔑 **Ponds and lakes form when water collects in hollows and low-lying areas of land.**

Exploring a Pond Because the water is shallow enough for sunlight to reach the bottom, plants grow throughout a pond. Bacteria and plantlike organisms called algae also live in the pond. The plants and algae produce oxygen as they use sunlight to make food. Fish and other animals in the pond use the oxygen and food provided by plants and algae. Some animals also use these plants for shelter.

Exploring a Lake Lakes are usually larger and deeper than ponds, so little sunlight reaches the bottom of a deep lake. Fewer plants can live in in the chilly, dark depths of such a lake. Mollusks and worms move along the lake's sandy or rocky bottom. They eat food particles that drift down from the surface. Young bony fishes such as pike and sturgeon eat the tiny bottom-dwellers, while the adult fish eat other fish.

apply it!

❶ Complete the Venn diagram to compare and contrast characteristics of lakes and ponds.

❷ △ **Form Operational Definitions** Based on your answers, write an operational definition for *lake*.

_____

_____

_____

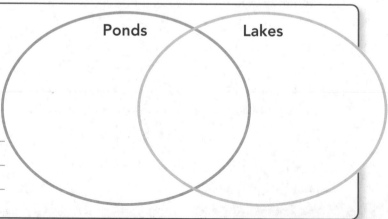

Ponds   Lakes

Lake Formation
Lakes can form through several natural processes. A river, for example, may bend and loop as it encounters obstacles in its path. Eventually, a new channel might form, cutting off a loop. The cutoff loop may become an oxbow lake.

Some lakes, such as the Great Lakes, formed in depressions created by ice sheets that melted at the end of the Ice Age. Other lakes were created by movements of Earth's crust that formed long, deep valleys called rift valleys. In Africa, Lake Tanganyika lies in a rift valley. Volcanoes can also form lakes. Lava or mud from a volcano can block a river, forming a lake. Lakes can also form in the empty craters of volcanoes.

People can create a lake by building a dam. A lake that stores water for human use is called a **reservoir.**

FIGURE 4 ·······························

Types of Lakes
The photos show examples of glacial, volcanic, and rift valley lakes. ✎ **Classify** Write **G** on the glacial lake, **V** on the volcanic lake, and **R** on the rift valley lake.

Lab zone® Do the Quick Lab Modeling How a Lake Forms.

🔑 Assess Your Understanding

2a. Explain What is one major difference between a lake and a pond?

_____

_____

b. Compare and Contrast How is a reservoir different from other kinds of lakes?

_____

_____

_____

got it?

○ I get it! Now I know that lakes and ponds are ___

_____

_____

_____

_____

○ I need extra help with _____

Go to MY SCIENCE ⬤s COACH online for help with this subject.

337

How Can Lakes Change?

If you watch a lake or pond over many years, you will see it change. In time, the lake may shrink and become shallower. **Natural processes and human activities can cause lakes to disappear.**

Eutrophication As lake organisms die, bacteria break down the bodies and release nutrients into the water. These nutrients, such as nitrogen and phosphorus, are chemicals that other organisms need. Over time, nutrients can build up in the lake in a process called **eutrophication** (yoo troh fih KAY shun). Algae use these nutrients and spread, forming a layer on the lake's surface.

Figure 5 shows how eutrophication can change a lake. When the algae layer becomes so thick that it blocks sunlight, plants cannot carry out photosynthesis, and they die. Without food and oxygen from the plants, animals die. Decaying material from dead organisms piles up on the bottom, making the lake shallower. As the area fills in, land plants grow in the mud. Eventually, the area fills with plants, and a meadow replaces the former lake.

The Human Role Though eutrophication occurs naturally, human activities can also cause or increase it. For example, fertilizer from farms runs off into ponds and lakes, providing extra nutrients to the algae. The extra nutrients speed up the growth of algae, leading to faster eutrophication.

Sequence Which of the following processes occurs first during eutrophication?
○ Nutrients build up in a lake.
○ A lake is replaced by a meadow.
○ Plants stop carrying out photosynthesis.

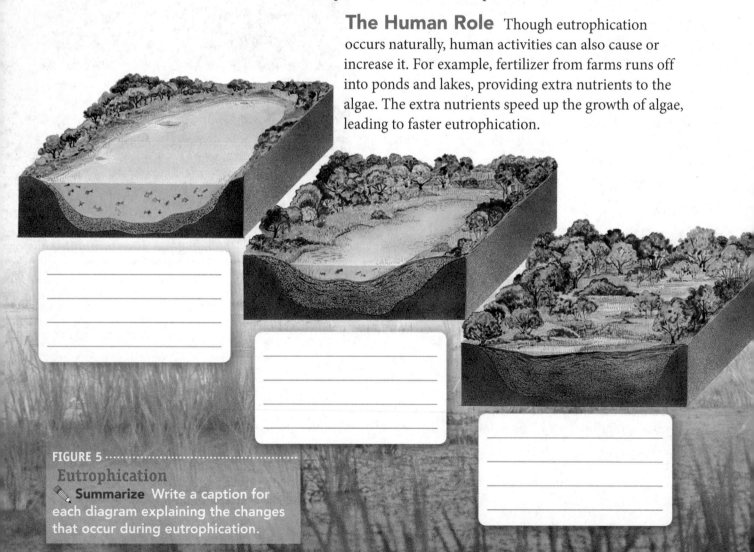

FIGURE 5
Eutrophication
Summarize Write a caption for each diagram explaining the changes that occur during eutrophication.

An Endless Cycle

How does fresh water cycle on Earth?

FIGURE 6 ....

> **REAL-WORLD INQUIRY** Make a cycle diagram to show how water cycles. Include the processes listed below.

Processes

Evaporation

Condensation

Transpiration

Precipitation

Runoff

Include examples of:
a river system
a lake or pond
an ocean
groundwater

Lab zone® Do the Quick Lab How Can Algal Growth Affect Pond Life?

Assess Your Understanding

3a. Explain Eutrophication occurs when algae block sunlight in a lake or pond and plants cannot _____

b. ANSWER THE BIG ? How does fresh water cycle on Earth?

_____
_____
_____
_____
_____
_____

got it?

○ **I get it!** Now I know that lakes can change due to _____
_____
_____
_____
_____

○ **I need extra help with** _____
_____

Go to **my science COACH** *online for help with this subject.*

339

Water Underground

🔑 How Does Water Move Underground?

🔑 How Do People Use Groundwater?

my planeT DiaRY   CAREER

Looking for Water

How do you know where the water you drink comes from? Saskia Oosting could help you find out! Ms. Oosting works for a company that locates and protects groundwater supplies. She is a project manager, which means she coordinates the work of many other people.

One of her company's jobs is figuring out where the water in a particular well comes from. Scientists and engineers drill other wells near the well they're observing. Then they pump water out of the first well and watch the others to see where the level of groundwater drops. Once they've found the area that contributes water to the well, the company can help people who use that water keep the supply clean.

✎ **Communicate** With a partner, discuss your answers to these questions.

1. How do engineers find out where the water in a well comes from?

_____

_____

_____

_____

2. What kinds of science skills do you think Ms. Oosting needs to do her job?

_____

_____

_____

_____

▷ PLANET DIARY Go to **Planet Diary** to learn more about groundwater.

 Lab zone® Do the Inquiry Warm-Up *Where Does the Water Go?*

Vocabulary
- permeable • impermeable
- unsaturated zone • saturated zone
- water table • aquifer • artesian well

Skills
 Reading: Relate Cause and Effect
 Inquiry: Predict

How Does Water Move Underground?

Where does underground water come from? Like surface water, underground water generally comes from precipitation. Some precipitation soaks into the ground, pulled by gravity.

If you pour water into a glass full of pebbles, the water flows down around the pebbles until it reaches the bottom of the glass. Then the water begins to fill up the spaces between the pebbles. **In the same way, water underground trickles down between particles of soil and through cracks and spaces in layers of rock.**

Effects of Different Materials Different types of rock and soil have different-sized spaces, or pores, between their particles, as shown in **Figure 1.** The size of the pores and the connections between them determine how easily water moves. Because they have large and connected pores, materials such as sand and gravel allow water to pass through, or permeate. They are thus known as **permeable** (PUR mee uh bul) materials.

Other materials have few or no pores or cracks, or the pores are very small. Clay has very small pores and is less permeable than sand. Unless it is cracked, granite is **impermeable,** meaning that water cannot pass through easily.

FIGURE 1 ·······················

Permeable and Impermeable Materials
Compare how water moves in clay (left) and gravel (right).
✎ **Compare and Contrast Which material is more permeable?** (gravel/clay) **Why?**

_____
_____
_____
_____

Water Zones Water from precipitation soaks down through permeable rock and soil layers. These layers contain air as well as water, so they are not saturated, or filled, with water. This top layer is thus called the **unsaturated zone.**

However, at some depth, the water reaches a level where the pores in the ground are saturated with water, called the **saturated zone.** The top of the saturated zone is the **water table.** If you know the depth of the water table in your area, you can tell how deep you must dig to reach groundwater.

The saturated zone often reaches deep into Earth, even though the rock becomes less permeable the deeper you go. Sometimes the direction of the water's flow is changed by impermeable layers, which the water has a harder time flowing through.

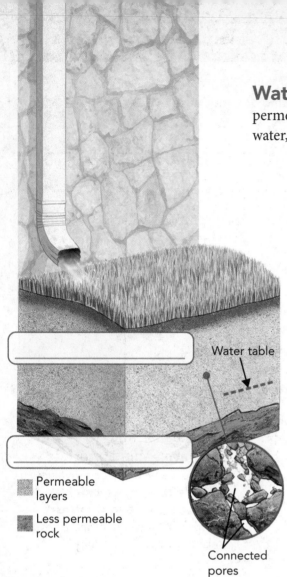

Water table

Permeable layers

Less permeable rock

Connected pores

FIGURE 2 ·······································

> **ART IN MOTION** **Groundwater Formation**
Upper areas of the soil contain both air and water, while lower areas, including less permeable rock, are saturated with water.
✎ **Interpret Diagrams** Label the saturated and unsaturated zones. Shade in the area where water will collect.

Do the Quick Lab
Soil Percolation.

🔑 Assess Your Understanding

1a. Review Water slows down when it reaches (permeable/impermeable) material.

b. Explain What is the water table?

_____

_____

c. Infer The rock deep within the saturated zone most likely has (large/small) and (connected/unconnected) pores. Explain your answer.

_____

_____

_____

_____

got it? ···

○ **I get it!** Now I know that water moves through soil by _____

_____

○ I need extra help with _____

Go to MY SCIENCE ⬢ COACH online for help with this subject.

How Do People Use Groundwater?

Suppose you live far from a river, lake, or pond. How could you reach groundwater for your needs? You might be in luck: The water table in your area might be only a few meters underground. In fact, in some places the water table actually meets the surface. Springs can form as groundwater bubbles or flows out of cracks in the rock.

Aquifers Any underground layer of permeable rock or sediment that holds water and allows it to flow is called an **aquifer.** Aquifers can range in size from a small patch to an area the size of several states. The huge Ogallala aquifer lies beneath the plains of the Midwest, from South Dakota to Texas. This aquifer provides water for millions of people, as well as for crops and livestock.

Aquifers are not unlimited sources of water. If people take water from the aquifer faster than the aquifer refills, the level of the aquifer will drop. As you'll see on the next page, this will make it more difficult to reach water in the future.

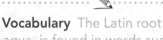

Vocabulary The Latin root *aqua-* is found in words such as *aquarium* and *aquatic* as well as *aquifer.* What do you think this root means?

_____

do the math!

Uses of Water

The graph shows water use in the United States. Use the graph to answer the questions below.

1 **Read Graphs** What would be a good title for this graph? _____

2 **Interpret Data** The two largest categories combine to make up about what percentage of the total water used in the United States? _____

3 **Predict** How would an increase in the amount of land used for farms affect this graph?

_____

_____

4 **Calculate** If the total daily usage of water in the United States is 1,280 billion liters, about how many liters are used by power plants?

_____

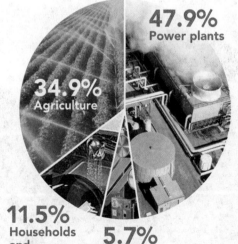

47.9%
Power plants

34.9%
Agriculture

11.5%
Households and businesses

5.7%
Industries and mining

know?

Deep underground, water in some areas experiences great heat and pressure. The pressure forces boiling-hot water and steam to the surface, creating bubbling hot springs and erupting geysers. More than half the known geysers in the world are found in Yellowstone National Park.

Movement in Aquifers Do you picture groundwater as a large, still pool beneath Earth's surface? In fact, the water is moving, seeping through layers of rock or soil. The rate of motion depends largely on the slope of the water table and the permeability of the rocks. Some groundwater moves only a few centimeters a day. At that rate, the water moves about 10 meters a year. Groundwater may travel hundreds of kilometers and stay in an aquifer for thousands of years before coming to the surface again.

Wells The depth and level of a water table can vary greatly over a small area. Generally, the level of a water table follows the shape of the surface of the land, as shown in **Figure 3**. The level can rise during heavy rains or snow melts, and fall in times of dry weather.

Since ancient times, people have brought groundwater to the surface for drinking and other everyday uses. **People can obtain groundwater from an aquifer by drilling a well below the water table.** When the bottom of the well is in a saturated zone, the well contains water. If the water table drops below the bottom of the well, the well will run dry and water cannot be obtained from it.

FIGURE 3

Springs and Wells

Suppose you are a farmer looking for water sources.

✎ **Make Judgments** Draw lines showing where you would drill a regular well and an artesian well. Explain why you chose those locations.

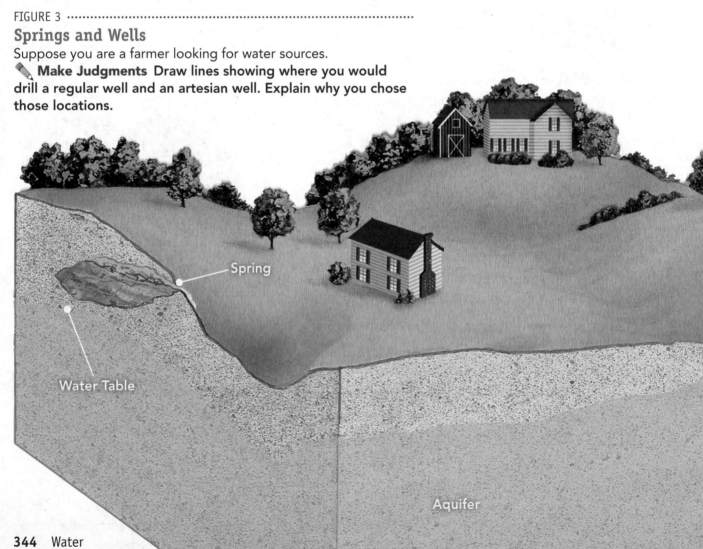

Spring

Water Table

Aquifer

344 Water

Using Pumps

Long ago, people dug wells by hand. They used a bucket to bring up the water. People may also have used simple pumps. Today, however, most wells are dug with well-drilling equipment. Mechanical pumps bring up the groundwater.

Pumping water out of an aquifer lowers the water level near the well. If too much water is pumped out too fast, a well may run dry. The owners of the well will have to dig deeper to reach the lowered water table, or wait for rainfall to refill the aquifer.

Relying on Pressure

Another option for bringing up groundwater is an artesian well. In an **artesian well** (ahr TEE zhun), water rises on its own because of pressure within an aquifer.

In some aquifers, groundwater becomes trapped between two layers of impermeable rock or sediment. This water is under great pressure from the water extending back up the aquifer. If the top layer of rock is punctured, the pressure sends water spurting up through the hole. No pump is necessary—in an artesian well, water pressure does the job.

Relate Cause and Effect
If the water table near a well is (raised/lowered), the well may run dry.

Do the Quick Lab
An Artesian Well.

Assess Your Understanding

2a. Describe What are three ways people can get water from an aquifer?

_____

_____

_____

b. Infer Use **Figure 3** as a guide. Why is it important to know the depth of an aquifer before drilling a well?

_____

_____

_____

c. Solve Problems During the winter, you draw your water from a well. Every summer, the well dries up. What might be the reason for the change?

_____

_____

_____

_____

got it? ....

○ I get it! Now I know that people reach

underground water by _____

_____

○ I need extra help with _____

Go to MY SCIENCE ⓢ COACH *online for help with this subject.*

Exploring the Ocean

🔑 How Do Conditions Vary in Earth's Oceans?

🔑 What Are Some Features of the Ocean Floor?

my planet Diary · SCIENCE AND TECHNOLOGY

Deep-Sea Escape

You've heard of how parachutes are used for escapes. But have you heard of a special suit that allows people to escape from a submarine 183 meters under water? The suit is designed to help sailors survive very cold temperatures and very high pressure. In an emergency, sailors put on this suit and enter a water-filled rescue chamber. Then the sailors shoot out, rising at two to three meters per second. If the suit tears, they have to exhale all the way to the surface so their lungs don't explode. At the surface, part of the suit inflates to become a life raft.

Discuss these questions with a classmate and write your answers below.

1. What technology was developed to help sailors escape a submarine accident?

_____

_____

_____

2. What would it feel like to escape from a submarine deep under water? How would you help your body adjust to the changing pressure?

_____

_____

> PLANET DIARY Go to **Planet Diary** to learn more about characteristics of the ocean.

 Lab zone Do the Inquiry Warm-Up
What Can You Learn Without Seeing?

How Do Conditions Vary in Earth's Oceans?

People have explored the ocean since ancient times. For centuries, the ocean has provided food and served as a route for trade and travel. Modern scientists have studied the characteristics of the ocean's waters and the ocean floor. 🔑 **The water in Earth's oceans varies in salinity, temperature, and depth.**

Vocabulary

- salinity • sonar • seamount • trench
- continental slope • continental shelf • abyssal plain
- mid-ocean ridge

Skills

Reading: Identify the Main Idea

Inquiry: Interpret Data

Salinity If you've ever swallowed a mouthful of water while you were swimming in the ocean, you know it's pretty salty. But just how salty? If you boiled a kilogram of ocean water in a pot until the water was gone, there would be about 35 grams of salt left in the pot. That's about two tablespoons of salt. **Salinity** is the total amount of dissolved salts in a sample of water. In most parts of the ocean, the salinity is between 34 and 37 parts per thousand.

The substance you know as table salt is sodium chloride. This salt is present in the greatest amount in ocean water. When sodium chloride dissolves in water, it separates into sodium and chloride particles called ions. Ocean water also contains smaller amounts of more than a dozen ions, including magnesium and calcium.

Near the ocean's surface, rain, snow, and melting ice add fresh water, lowering the salinity. Evaporation, on the other hand, increases salinity. Salt is left behind as the water evaporates. Salinity can also be higher near the poles. As the surface water freezes into ice, the salt is left behind in the remaining water.

Effects of Salinity

Salinity affects ocean water in different ways. For instance, fresh water freezes at 0°C. But ocean water doesn't freeze until the temperature drops to about −1.9°C. The salt acts as a kind of antifreeze by interfering with the formation of ice. Salt water also has a higher density than fresh water. That means that the mass of one liter of salt water is greater than the mass of one liter of fresh water. Because its density is greater, seawater lifts, or buoys up, less dense objects floating in it.

> **Vocabulary** **Suffixes** Circle the correct word to complete the sentence below.
>
> Ocean water has a higher (salinity/saline) than fresh water.

Composition of Ocean Water

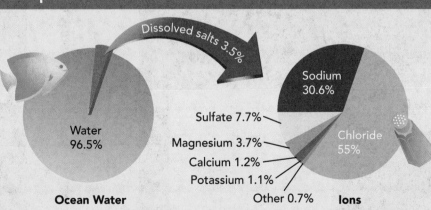

Dissolved salts 3.5%

Water 96.5%

Ocean Water

Sodium 30.6%

Sulfate 7.7%

Magnesium 3.7%

Calcium 1.2%

Potassium 1.1%

Chloride 55%

Other 0.7%

Ions

FIGURE 1 ···

> VIRTUAL LAB **Composition of Ocean Water**

When salts dissolve, they separate into particles called ions.

Read Graphs In ocean water, which ion is most common? Which salt?

_____

_____

_____

⊃ **Identify the Main Idea**
Underline the two changes that happen with depth.

Depth

Temperature The broad surface of the ocean absorbs energy from the sun. ⊂━ **Like temperatures on land, temperatures at the surface of the ocean vary with location and the seasons.** Near the equator, surface ocean temperatures often reach 25°C, about room temperature. The temperatures drop as you travel away from the equator. Warm water is less dense than cold water, so it doesn't sink. Warm water forms only a thin layer on the ocean surface.

Depth If you could swim from the surface of the ocean to the ocean floor, you would pass through a vertical section of the ocean. This section, shown in **Figure 2,** is referred to as the water column. ⊂━ **As you descend through the ocean, the water temperature decreases.** There are three temperature zones in the water column. The surface zone is the warmest. It typically extends from the surface to between 100 and 500 meters. The average temperature worldwide for this zone is 16.1°C. Next is the transition zone, which extends from the bottom of the surface zone to about 1 kilometer. Temperatures in the transition zone drop very quickly to about 4°C. Below the transition zone is the deep zone. Average temperatures there are 3.5°C in most of the ocean.

Water pressure, the force exerted by the weight of water, also changes with depth. ⊂━ **In the ocean, pressure increases by 1 bar, the air pressure at sea level, with each 10 meters of depth.** Due to the high pressure in the deep ocean, divers can descend safely only to about 40 meters without specialized equipment. To observe the deep ocean, scientists can use a submersible, an underwater vehicle built of materials that resist pressure.

FIGURE 2 ·······························
Changes With Depth
✎ Relate Text and Visuals The conditions in Earth's oceans change with depth.

1. Shade in each temperature zone in the depth bar and make a key.
2. Fill in the blank in the pressure bar to identify what happens to pressure with depth.

Key

☐ _____

☐ _____

☐ _____

0.5 km

1.0 km

1.5 km

2.0 km

2.5 km

3.0 km

3.5 km

4.0 km

Pressure _____ with depth.

apply it!

Each panel of dials provides information about conditions at various depths in the ocean.

1 Interpret Data Find the incorrect dial in each panel and correct its reading.

2 Label where in the ocean you might find each set of readings: surface zone, transition zone, or deep zone.

Depth (m)   Temperature   Pressure

_____

3 CHALLENGE Based on the information in the panels, where is the most dense water in the ocean?

_____

_____

_____

_____

know?

The Deep Flight Super Falcon is the first winged submersible available to the public. It can "fly" quickly and easily to depths of more than 100 meters.

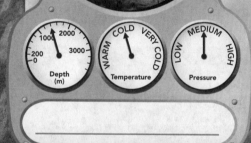

Depth (m)   Temperature   Pressure

_____

Depth (m)   Temperature   Pressure

_____

Lab zone Do the Quick Lab *Ocean Conditions.*

🔑 Assess Your Understanding

got it?

○ **I get it!** Now I know that the water in Earth's oceans varies in _____

_____

○ **I need extra help with** _____

Go to **MY SCIENCE COACH** online for help with this subject.

What Are Some Features of the Ocean Floor?

The ocean is very deep—3.8 kilometers deep on average. That's more than twice as deep as the Grand Canyon. Humans can't survive the darkness, cold temperatures, and extreme pressure of the deep ocean. So scientists have developed technology to study the ocean floor. A major advance in ocean-floor mapping was **sonar**, SOund NAvigation and Ranging. This system uses sound waves to calculate the distance to an object. A ship's sonar system sends out pulses of sound that bounce off the ocean floor. The equipment then measures how quickly the sound waves return to the ship.

Once scientists mapped the ocean floor, they discovered that the deep waters hid mountain ranges bigger than any on land, as well as deep canyons. 🔑 **Major ocean floor features include trenches, the continental shelf, the continental slope, the abyssal plain, and the mid-ocean ridge. These features have all been formed by the interaction of Earth's plates.** You can see these feaures in **Figure 3**.

FIGURE 3 ·······························
Ocean Floor
✏️ **Relate Text and Visuals**
Match the descriptions below with the ocean floor features in the image. Write the number for each description in the corresponding circles.
(Image not to scale. To show major ocean floor features, thousands of kilometers have been squeezed into one illustration.)

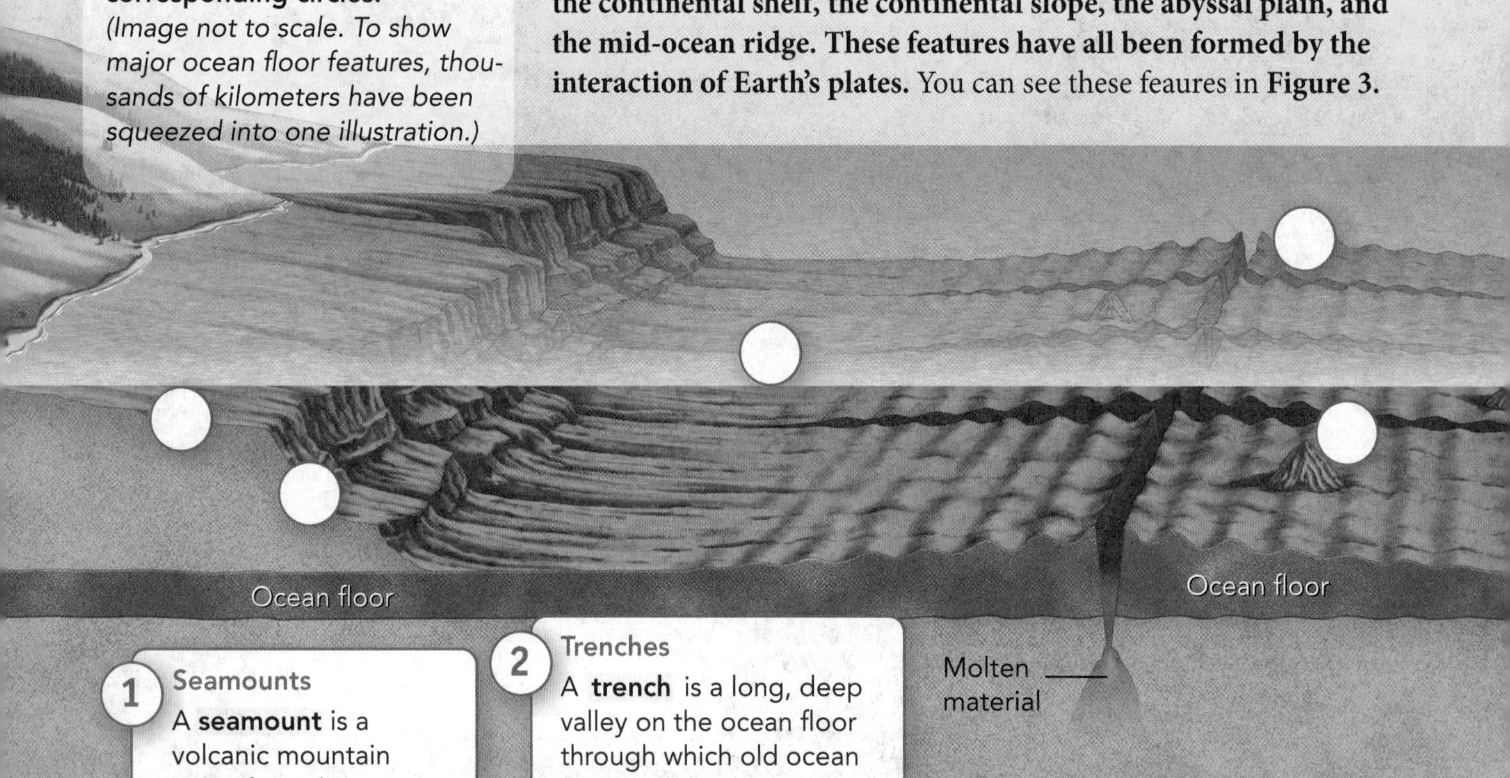

Ocean floor

Ocean floor

Molten _____ material

1 Seamounts
A **seamount** is a volcanic mountain rising from the ocean floor that doesn't reach the surface. Seamounts often form near mid-ocean ridges. Some seamounts were once volcanic islands. But they slowly sank because of the movement of the ocean floor toward a trench.

2 Trenches
A **trench** is a long, deep valley on the ocean floor through which old ocean floor sinks back toward the mantle. The Marianas Trench in the Pacific Ocean is 11 kilometers deep.

3 Continental Slope
At 130 meters down, the slope of the ocean floor gets steeper. The steep edge of the continental shelf is called the **continental slope.**

4 Continental Shelf
The **continental shelf** is a gently sloping, shallow area that extends outward from the edge of each continent. Its width varies from a few kilometers to as much as 1,300 kilometers.

LOST AT SEA

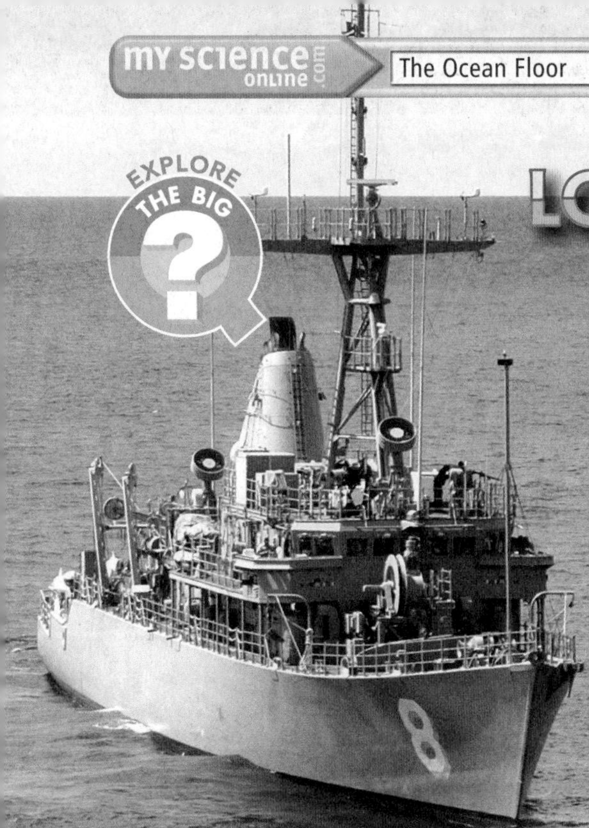

FIGURE 4 ....

> INTERACTIVE ART **What are some characteristics of Earth's oceans?**

✎ **Predict** Your ship has been radioed by a submarine that has lost the use of its navigation instruments. Based on the information in their last transmission, where might the vessel be? What might the conditions of the water be at this depth? Discuss your prediction with a partner.

Last transmission from sub: "Depth reading 3,000 meters; passed over a flat plain...sonar returned waves quickly; possibly approaching mountains."

_____
_____
_____
_____
_____
_____
_____
_____
_____

Lab zone ® Do the Quick Lab *The Shape of the Ocean Floor.*

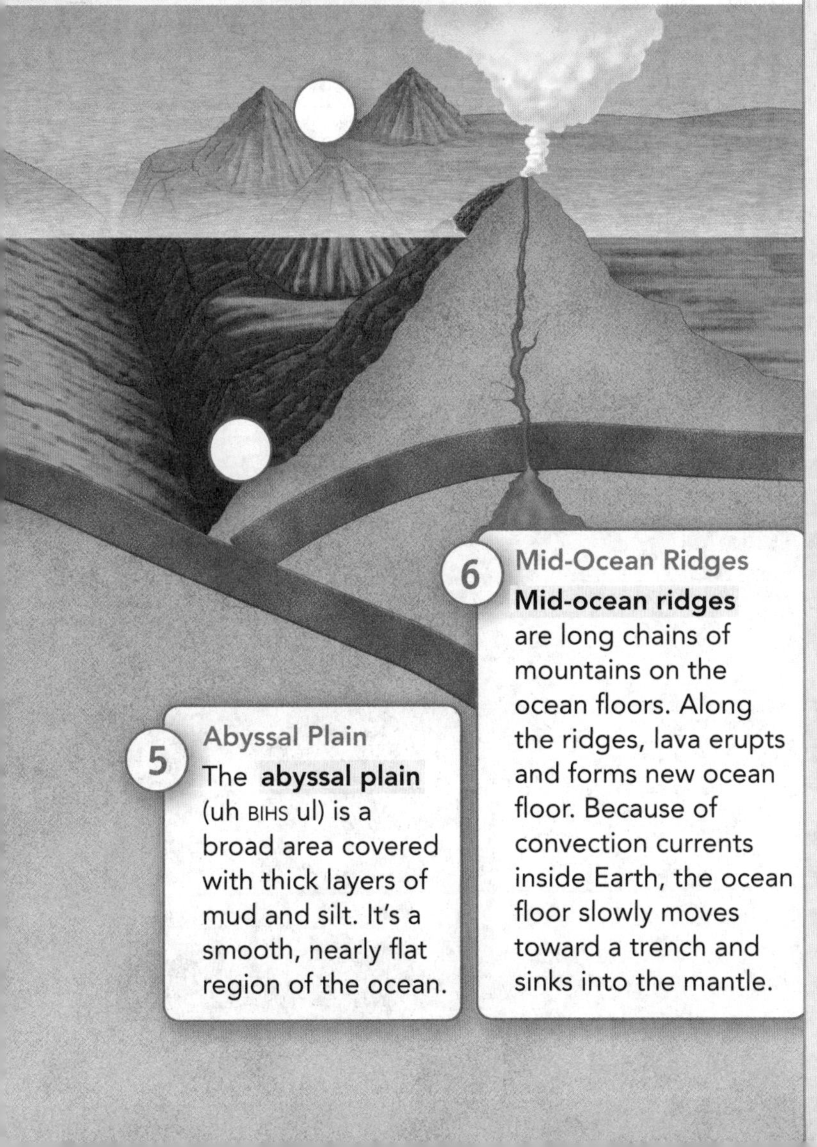

🔖 Assess Your Understanding

1a. List What are four features of the ocean floor?

_____
_____

b. Explain Why has investigation of the ocean been difficult?

_____

c. What are some characteristics of Earth's oceans?

_____
_____

got it?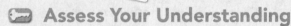

○ **I get it!** Now I know that the ocean floor has many different features formed by _____

_____
_____

○ **I need extra help with** _____

Go to my science COACH *online for help with this subject.*

---

6 Mid-Ocean Ridges

Mid-ocean ridges are long chains of mountains on the ocean floors. Along the ridges, lava erupts and forms new ocean floor. Because of convection currents inside Earth, the ocean floor slowly moves toward a trench and sinks into the mantle.

5 Abyssal Plain

The **abyssal plain** (uh BIHS ul) is a broad area covered with thick layers of mud and silt. It's a smooth, nearly flat region of the ocean.

Wave Action

UNLOCK THE BIG ?

🗝 **How Do Waves Form and Change?**

🗝 **How Do Waves Affect the Shore?**

my planeτ Diary

DISASTER

Rogue Waves

For hundreds of years, sailors have returned from the sea to tell of 30-meter-high waves that appeared out of nowhere. These waves, they said, plunged the largest ships into the ocean depths. For hundreds of years, these tales were taken no more seriously than the Scottish legend of the Loch Ness monster. Ships were sunk, scientists said, in storms.

Then, in 1995, an oil rig in the North Sea was struck by a rogue wave. Instruments on board measured the wave's height at 26 meters. As a result, the European Union set up a project to study these rogue waves using satellites. What the scientists found was shocking. Within three weeks, they tracked ten different giant waves.

Discuss these questions with a classmate and write your answers below.

1. Why did people begin to believe in rogue waves?

_____

_____

_____

2. How might you track a rogue wave?

_____

_____

> PLANET DIARY Go to **Planet Diary** to learn more about wave action.

Lab zone Do the Inquiry Warm-Up *How Do Waves Change a Beach?*

Vocabulary
- wave • wavelength • frequency • wave height
- tsunami • longshore drift • rip current • groin

Skills
- Reading: Relate Cause and Effect
- Inquiry: Form Operational Definitions

How Do Waves Form and Change?

When you watch a surfer's wave crash onto a beach, you are seeing the last step in the development of a wave. A **wave** is the movement of energy through a body of water. Wave development usually begins with wind. Without the energy of wind, the surface of the ocean would be as smooth as a mirror. **Most waves form when winds blowing across the water's surface transmit their energy to the water.**

The size of a wave depends on the strength of the wind and on the length of time it blows. A gentle breeze creates small ripples on the surface of the water. Stronger winds create larger waves. The size of a wave also depends on the distance over which the wind blows. Winds blowing across longer distances build up bigger waves. That's why small ponds have ripples but the Great Lakes have waves you can surf!

FIGURE 1 ....

Wave Formation

✎ **Predict** Using what you've learned about wave size, circle the surfer who might ride the biggest waves. Explain your prediction.

353

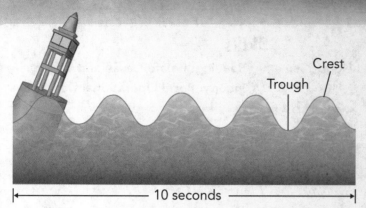

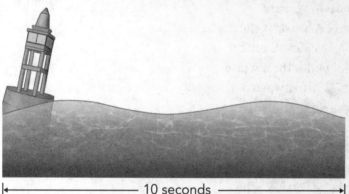

Crest
Trough

| 10 seconds |

| 10 seconds |

FIGURE 2

Wave Characteristics Scientists have a vocabulary to describe the characteristics of waves. The name for the highest part of a wave is the crest. The horizontal distance between crests is the **wavelength.** Long, rolling waves with lots of space between crests have long wavelengths. Short, choppy waves have shorter wavelengths. Waves are also measured by their **frequency,** the number of waves that pass a point in a certain amount of time.

As you can see in **Figure 2,** the lowest part of a wave is the trough. The vertical distance from the crest to the trough is the **wave height.** The energy and strength of a wave depend mainly on its wave height. In the open ocean, most waves are between 2 and 5 meters high. During storms, waves can grow much higher and more powerful.

Wave Characteristics

There are many different types of waves, but they have similar characteristics.

✎ **Read the text and complete the activity.**

1. **Identify** Find and label wavelength, wave height, crest, and trough on the diagrams. *Hint:* One diagram is started.

2. **Compare and Contrast** How does the frequency of the waves compare in the two diagrams?

_____

_____

_____

apply it!

Conditions at sea are constantly changing.

❶ Use the scientific vocabulary you learned above to describe the conditions at sea in the photo.

_____

_____

_____

_____

❷ **Form Operational Definitions** Write your own definition for one of the scientific terms you used above.

_____

_____

Wave Energy

Waves may appear to carry water toward shore, but water doesn't actually move forward in deep water. If it did, ocean water would eventually pile up on the coasts of every continent! The energy of the wave moves toward shore, but the water itself remains in place. You can test this by floating a cork in a bowl of water. Use a spoon to make a wave in the bowl. As the wave passes, the cork lurches forward a little; then it bobs backward. It ends up in almost the same spot where it started.

Water Motion

What happens to the water as a wave travels along? Notice in **Figure 3** that as the wave passes, water particles move in a circular path. They swing forward and down with the energy of the wave, then back up to their original position. Deeper water particles move in smaller circles than those near the surface. At a depth equal to about one half the wavelength, water particles are not affected by the surface wave.

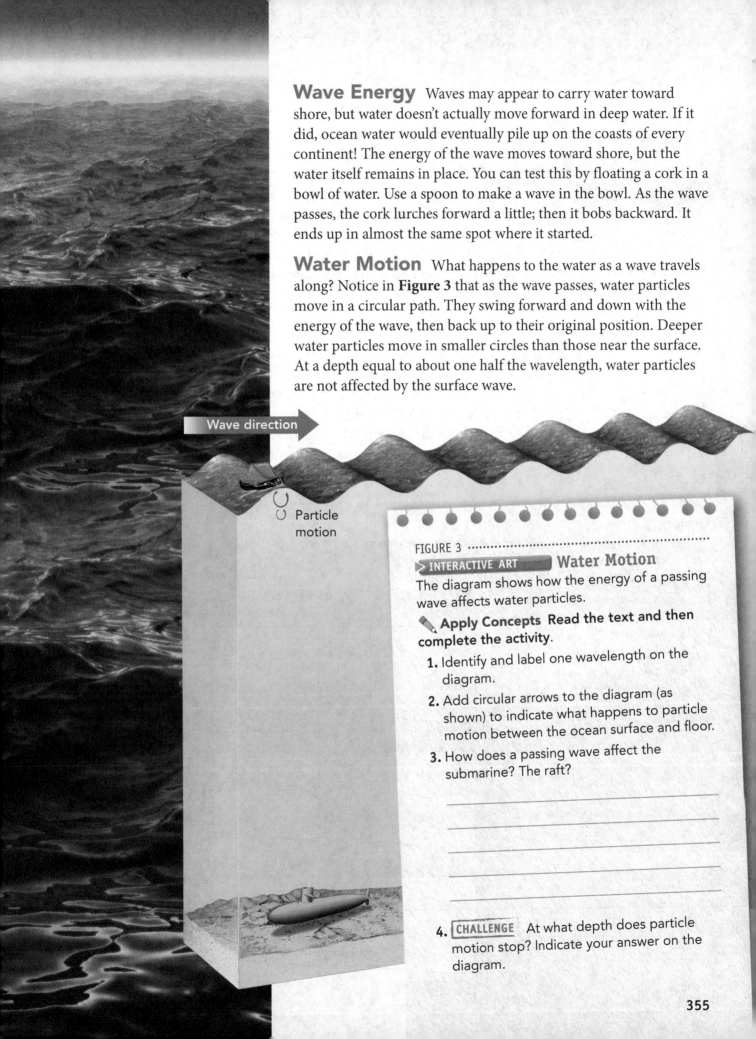

Wave direction

Particle motion

FIGURE 3 ·······························

> INTERACTIVE ART   **Water Motion**

The diagram shows how the energy of a passing wave affects water particles.

✎ **Apply Concepts** Read the text and then complete the activity.

1. Identify and label one wavelength on the diagram.
2. Add circular arrows to the diagram (as shown) to indicate what happens to particle motion between the ocean surface and floor.
3. How does a passing wave affect the submarine? The raft?

_____

_____

_____

_____

4. [CHALLENGE] At what depth does particle motion stop? Indicate your answer on the diagram.

Breakers

The white-capped waves that crash onto shore are often called "breakers." In deep water, these waves usually travel as long, low waves called swells. As the waves approach the shore, the water becomes shallower. The bottoms of the waves begin to touch the sloping ocean floor. Friction between the ocean floor and the water causes the waves to slow down. As the speed of the waves decreases, their shapes change. **Near shore, wave height increases and wavelength decreases.** When a wave reaches a certain height, the crest of the wave topples. The wave breaks onto the shore, forming surf.

As the wave breaks, it continues to move forward. At first the breaker surges up the beach. But gravity soon slows it down, eventually stopping it. The water that has rushed up the beach then flows back out to sea. Have you ever stood at the water's edge and felt the pull of the water rushing back out to the ocean? This pull, often called an undertow, carries shells, seaweed, and sand away from the beach. A strong undertow can be dangerous to swimmers.

✏️ **Relate Cause and Effect**
Read the text. Then, underline the cause of breakers and circle the effect.

FIGURE 4 ···

Breakers

✏️ **After you read about breakers, do the activity to show how waves change shape as they get closer to shore.**

1. **Interpret Diagrams** Shade in one drawing in each column to show the sequence of how a wave forms.

2. **Summarize** How does the wave change as it approaches shore?

_____

_____

_____

_____

_____

_____

_____

_____

_____

_____

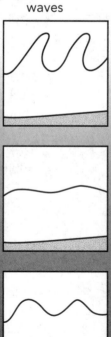

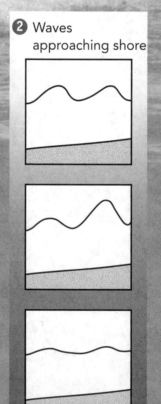
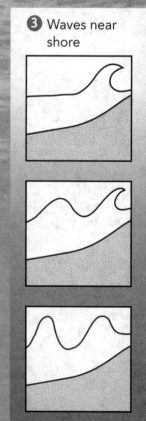

❶ Deep-water waves

❷ Waves approaching shore

❸ Waves near shore

Tsunami So far you've been reading about waves that are caused by the wind. But another kind of wave forms far below the ocean surface. This type of wave, called a **tsunami,** is usually caused by an earthquake beneath the ocean floor. The ocean floor's abrupt movement sends pulses of energy through the water, shown in the diagram below.

Despite the huge amount of energy a tsunami carries, people on a ship at sea may not even realize a tsunami is passing. How is this possible? A tsunami in deep water may have a wavelength of 200 kilometers or more, but a wave height of less than a meter. When the tsunami reaches shallow water near the coast, friction with the ocean floor causes the long wavelength to decrease suddenly. The wave height increases as the water "piles up." Some tsunamis have reached heights of 20 meters or more—taller than a five-story building!

Tsunamis are most common in the Pacific Ocean, often striking Alaska, Hawaii, and Japan. In response, nations in the Pacific have developed a warning system, which can alert them if a tsunami forms. On March 11, 2011, an enormous Tsunami devastated Japan. But not all tsunamis occur in the Pacific Ocean. On December 26, 2004, a major earthquake in the Indian Ocean caused tremendous tsunamis that hit 11 nations. Tragically, these tsunamis took the lives of more than 230,000 people. Several nations are now developing a warning system for the Indian Ocean.

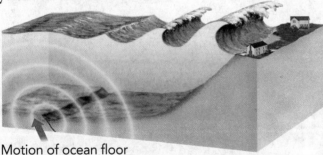

Motion of ocean floor

FIGURE 5 ·······················

Tsunami

✎ **Communicate** Use the diagram below, showing how a tsunami forms, to help you develop a tsunami warning system. Include how you would warn people living in remote areas.

_____

_____

_____

_____

_____

_____

_____

An Indonesian village hit by the 2004 tsunami

Lab zone Do the Quick Lab
Making Waves.

🗝 **Assess Your Understanding**

got it? ···

○ **I get it!** Now I know that waves change as they approach shore because _____

_____

○ I need extra help with _____

Go to MY SCIENCE COACH online for help with this subject.

How Do Waves Affect the Shore?

As waves approach and crash onto the shore, the beach can change. Wave direction at sea is determined by the wind. Waves usually roll toward shore at an angle. But as they touch bottom, the shallower water slows the shoreward side of the wave first. The rows of waves gradually turn and become more nearly parallel to the shore.

Longshore Drift As waves come into shore, water washes up the beach at an angle, carrying sand grains, as shown in **Figure 6**. The water and sand then run down the beach. This movement of sand along the beach is called **longshore drift**. 🔑 **As the waves slow down, they deposit the sand they are carrying on the shallow, underwater slope, forming a long ridge called a sandbar.**

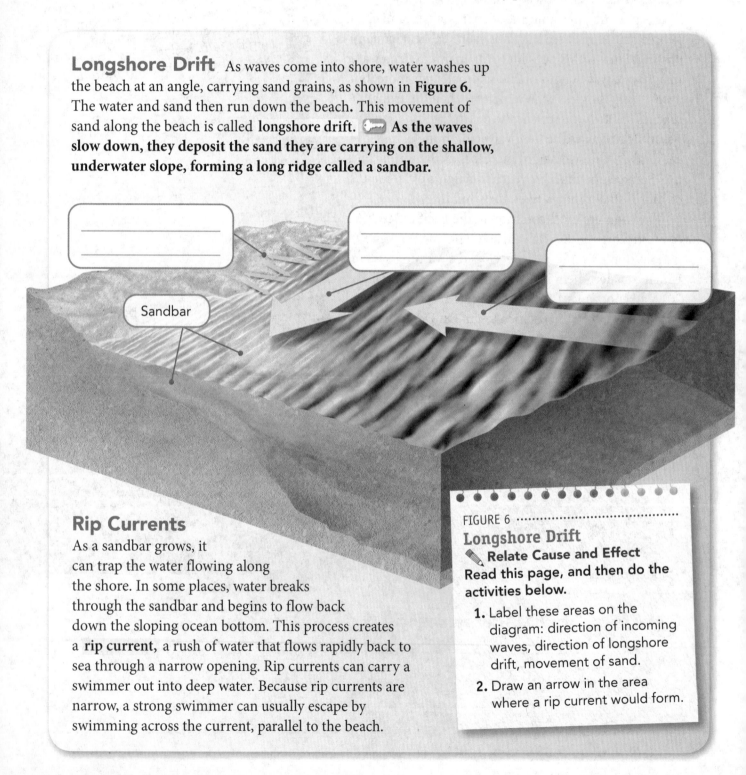

Sandbar

Rip Currents

As a sandbar grows, it can trap the water flowing along the shore. In some places, water breaks through the sandbar and begins to flow back down the sloping ocean bottom. This process creates a **rip current**, a rush of water that flows rapidly back to sea through a narrow opening. Rip currents can carry a swimmer out into deep water. Because rip currents are narrow, a strong swimmer can usually escape by swimming across the current, parallel to the beach.

FIGURE 6 ················
Longshore Drift
✏️ **Relate Cause and Effect**
Read this page, and then do the activities below.

1. Label these areas on the diagram: direction of incoming waves, direction of longshore drift, movement of sand.

2. Draw an arrow in the area where a rip current would form.

Beach Erosion If you walk on the same beach every day, you might not notice that it's changing. But if you visit a beach just once each year, you might be startled by the changes you see. ⚊ **Waves shape a beach by eroding the shore in some places and building it up in others.**

Barrier Beaches Long sand deposits called barrier beaches form parallel to the shore and are separated from the mainland by a shallow lagoon. Waves break against the barrier beach, protecting the mainland from erosion. For this reason, people are working to preserve barrier beaches along the Atlantic coast from Georgia to Massachusetts.

Sand Dunes Hills of windblown sand, called sand dunes, can make a beach more stable and protect the shore from erosion. The strong roots of dune plants hold the sand in place and help slow erosion. Without them, sand dunes can be easily washed away by wave action.

Groins Many people like to live near the ocean, but erosion can threaten buildings near the beach. One way to reduce beach erosion is to build a wall of rocks or concrete, called a **groin**, outward from the beach. Sand carried by the water piles up on one side of the groin instead of moving down shore. However, groins increase erosion farther down the beach.

FIGURE 7 ·····················
Beach Erosion
✎ **Evaluate the Impact on Society** Your community planning board wants to limit beach erosion. Do you vote to protect the dunes from being built on or to construct a groin instead? Why?

_____
_____
_____
_____
_____
_____
_____

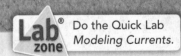

Lab zone Do the Quick Lab
Modeling Currents.

⚊ **Assess Your Understanding**

got it? ···

○ I get it! Now I know that waves shape the beach by _____
_____

○ I need extra help with _____

Go to **my science** ⑤ **coach** online for help with this subject.

Currents and Climate

UNLOCK
THE BIG

🔑 **What Causes Surface Currents?**

🔑 **What Causes Deep Currents?**

my planet Diary

EVERYDAY SCIENCE

Ducky Overboard

What happens when a ship loses its cargo at sea? Is it gone forever? You might think so. One ship traveling from Hong Kong to Tacoma, Washington, lost 29,000 plastic toys. They fell overboard in a storm and were considered lost at sea. But when hundreds of the toys began washing up on distant shores, scientists got excited.

One way scientists study ocean currents is by releasing empty bottles into the ocean. But of 500 to 1,000 bottles released, scientists might only recover 10. That doesn't give them much data. The large number of floating toys could give scientists better data from more data points.

The first toys were spotted off the coast of Alaska. Then beachcombers began finding them in Canada, in Washington, and even as far away as Scotland.

Discuss these questions with a classmate and write your answers below.

1. Why was the plastic toy spill so helpful to scientists studying ocean currents?

_____

_____

_____

2. Have you ever found objects on the beach? What data would scientists need from you for their research?

_____

_____

_____

Lab zone® Do the Inquiry Warm-Up *Bottom to Top.*

> PLANET DIARY Go to **Planet Diary** to learn more about ocean currents.

Vocabulary
- current
- climate
- Coriolis effect
- El Niño
- La Niña

Skills
- ↻ Reading: Compare and Contrast
- △ Inquiry: Infer

What Causes Surface Currents?

A **current** is a large stream of moving water that flows through the oceans. Unlike waves, currents carry water from one place to another. Some currents move water at the surface of the ocean. Other currents move water deep in the ocean.

🔑 **Surface currents affect water to a depth of several hundred meters. They are driven mainly by winds.** Surface currents follow Earth's major wind patterns. They move in circular patterns in the five major oceans. Most of the currents flow east or west, then double back to complete the circle, as shown in **Figure 1**.

Coriolis Effect Why do the currents move in these circular patterns? If Earth were standing still, winds and currents would flow in more direct paths between the poles and the equator. But as Earth rotates, the paths of the winds and currents curve. This effect of Earth's rotation on the direction of winds and currents is called the **Coriolis effect** (kawr ee OH lis). In the Northern Hemisphere, the Coriolis effect causes the currents to curve clockwise. In the Southern Hemisphere, the Coriolis effect causes the currents to curve counterclockwise.

FIGURE 1 ·······················
Surface Currents
✏ **Infer** The toys that fell overboard washed up in many places. Two of the locations are marked with ducks below. Circle the currents that you think moved the toys to these spots. Discuss your answer with a classmate.

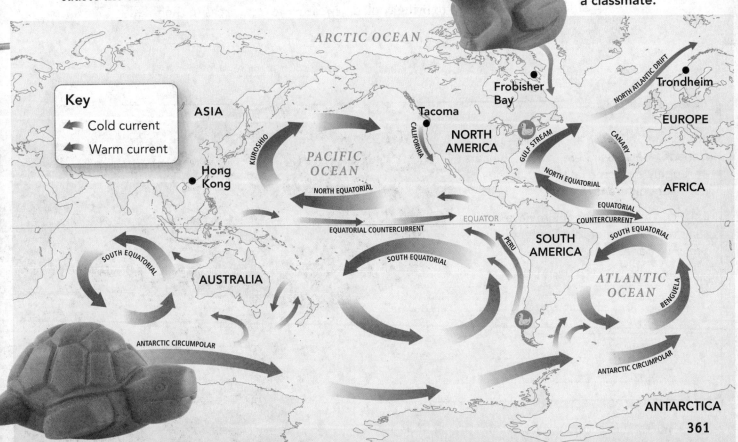

Key
- ◀ Cold current
- ◀ Warm current

ARCTIC OCEAN

ASIA
KUROSHIO
Hong Kong
PACIFIC OCEAN
NORTH EQUATORIAL
EQUATORIAL COUNTERCURRENT
EQUATOR
SOUTH EQUATORIAL
AUSTRALIA
ANTARCTIC CIRCUMPOLAR

Tacoma
CALIFORNIA
NORTH AMERICA
Frobisher Bay
GULF STREAM
NORTH EQUATORIAL
PERU
SOUTH AMERICA
SOUTH EQUATORIAL

NORTH ATLANTIC DRIFT
Trondheim
EUROPE
CANARY
EQUATORIAL COUNTERCURRENT
SOUTH EQUATORIAL
AFRICA
ATLANTIC OCEAN
BENGUELA
ANTARCTIC CIRCUMPOLAR
ANTARCTICA

361

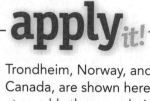

Compare and Contrast Use the space below to compare and contrast the effects of warm and cold currents on climate.

_____

_____

_____

_____

_____

_____

_____

_____

_____

_____

_____

Gulf Stream

The Gulf Stream is the largest and most powerful surface current in the North Atlantic Ocean. This current is caused by strong winds from the west. It is more than 30 kilometers wide and 300 meters deep. The Gulf Stream moves warm water from the Gulf of Mexico to the Caribbean Sea. It then continues northward along the east coast of the United States. Near Cape Hatteras, North Carolina, it curves eastward across the Atlantic, as a result of the Coriolis effect. When the Gulf Stream crosses the Atlantic it becomes the North Atlantic Drift.

Effects on Climate

The Gulf Stream has a warming effect on the climate of nearby land areas. **Climate** is the pattern of temperature and precipitation typical of an area over a long period of time. The mid-Atlantic region of the United States, including North Carolina and Virginia, has a more moderate climate because of the Gulf Stream. Winters are very mild and summers are humid.

Currents affect climate by moving cold and warm water around the globe. Currents generally move warm water from the tropics toward the poles and bring cold water back toward the equator. **A surface current warms or cools the air above it. This affects the climate of land near the coast.** Winds pick up moisture as they blow across warm-water currents. This explains why the warm Kuroshio Current brings mild, rainy weather to the southern islands of Japan. Cold-water currents cool the air above them. Cold air holds less moisture than warm air. So cold currents tend to bring cool, dry weather to land areas in their path.

apply it!

Trondheim, Norway, and Frobisher Bay, Canada, are shown here in July. They are at roughly the same latitude, but they have very different climates.

Infer Why does Trondheim have a mild climate? *Hint:* Refer to the map on the previous page.

_____

_____

_____

Trondheim, Norway

Frobisher Bay, Canada

El Niño Changes in wind patterns and currents can have a major impact on the oceans and nearby land. One example of such changes is **El Niño,** a climate event that occurs every two to seven years in the Pacific Ocean. El Niño begins when an unusual pattern of winds forms over the western Pacific. This causes a vast sheet of warm water to move east toward the South American coast, as shown in **Figure 2.** This warm water prevents the cold deep water from moving to the surface. El Niño conditions can last for one to two years before the usual winds and currents return.

El Niño causes shifts in weather patterns. This leads to unusual and often severe conditions in different areas. A major El Niño occurred between 1997 and 1998. It caused an especially warm winter in the northeastern United States. It was also responsible for heavy rains, flooding, and mudslides in California, as well as a string of deadly tornadoes in Florida.

La Niña When surface waters in the eastern Pacific are colder than normal, a climate event known as **La Niña** occurs. A La Niña event is the opposite of an El Niño event. La Niña events typically bring colder than normal winters and greater precipitation to the Pacific Northwest and the north central United States.

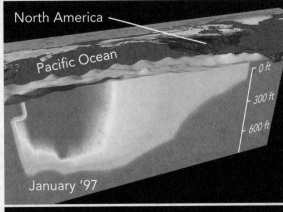

North America

Pacific Ocean

0 ft
300 ft
600 ft

January '97

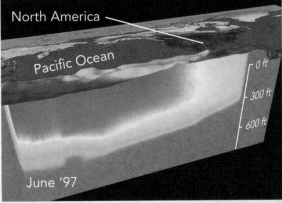

North America

Pacific Ocean

0 ft
300 ft
600 ft

June '97

FIGURE 2 ··

> ART IN MOTION **Warming Sea Temperature**
The images show what happens to temperature below the surface of the ocean during an El Niño event. Red indicates a warmer sea surface temperature.

✎ **Draw Conclusions** What happened to the the water temperature over six months?

_____

_____

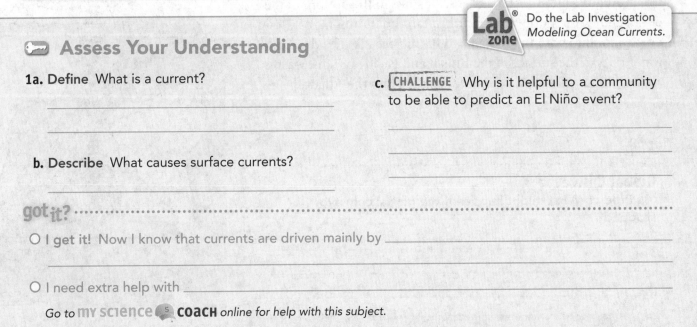

Lab® Do the Lab Investigation
zone *Modeling Ocean Currents.*

🔑 **Assess Your Understanding**

1a. Define What is a current?

_____

_____

b. Describe What causes surface currents?

_____

c. CHALLENGE Why is it helpful to a community to be able to predict an El Niño event?

_____

_____

_____

_____

got it? ···

○ **I get it!** Now I know that currents are driven mainly by _____

_____

○ I need extra help with _____

Go to my science ⑤ **COACH** *online for help with this subject.*

What Causes Deep Currents?

Deep below the ocean surface, another type of current causes chilly waters to creep slowly across the ocean floor. 🗝 **Deep currents are caused by differences in the density of ocean water.** Recall that cold water is more dense than warm water.

Salinity When a warm surface current moves from the equator toward one of the poles, it gradually cools. As ice forms near the poles, the salinity of the water increases from the salt left behind during freezing. As the water's temperature decreases and its salinity increases, the water becomes denser and sinks. Then, the cold water flows back along the ocean floor as a deep current. Deep currents are affected by the Coriolis effect, which causes them to curve.

🗝 **Deep currents move and mix water around the world. They carry cold water from the poles toward the equator.** Deep currents flow slowly. They may take as long as 1,000 years to circulate between the oceans back to where they started.

Global Ocean Conveyor The simplified pattern of ocean currents in **Figure 3** looks like a conveyor belt, moving water between the oceans. This pattern of ocean currents results from density differences due to temperature and salinity. The currents bring oxygen into the deep ocean that is needed for marine life.

The ocean's deep currents mostly start as cold water in the North Atlantic Ocean. This is the same water that moved north across the Atlantic as part of the Gulf Stream. This cold, salty water, called the North Atlantic Deep Water, is dense. It sinks to the bottom of the ocean and flows southward toward Antarctica. From there it flows northward into both the Indian and Pacific oceans. The deep cold water rises to the surface in the Indian and Pacific oceans, warms, and eventually flows back along the surface into the Atlantic.

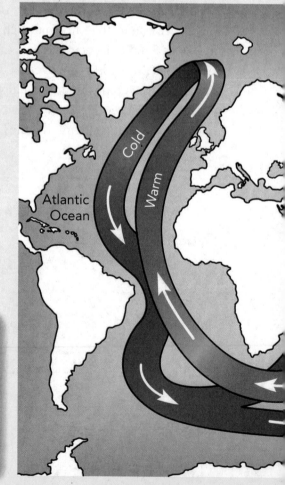

FIGURE 3 ···
Global Conveyor
✎ **Predict** What might happen if the global conveyor stopped?

_____

_____

_____

do the math! Analyzing Data

Calculating Density

Temperature affects the density of ocean water. To calculate the density of a substance, divide the mass of the substance by its volume.

$$\text{Density} = \frac{\text{Mass}}{\text{Volume}}$$

···················· Practice Problem ····················

Calculate Find the density of the following 1-L samples of ocean water. Sample A has a mass of 1.01 kg; Sample B has a mass of 1.06 kg. Which sample is likely to have the higher salinity? Why?

_____

_____

_____

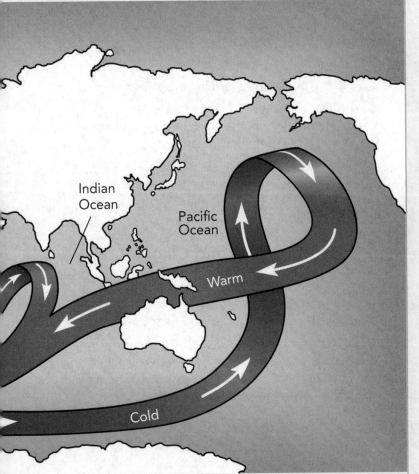

Indian Ocean

Pacific Ocean

Warm

Cold

Lab® zone Do the Quick Lab *Deep Currents.*

🔑 Assess Your Understanding

2a. Review What causes deep currents?

_____

_____

b. Explain How does the temperature of ocean water affect its density?

_____

_____

_____

_____

got it? ···

○ **I get it!** Now I know how the global ocean

conveyor moves: _____

_____

_____

_____

○ **I need extra help with** _____

Go to my science ⓢ coach *online for help with this subject.*

10 Study Guide

Fresh water on Earth cycles between _____, _____, and the atmosphere.

LESSON 1 Water on Earth

🔑 All living things need water in order to carry out their body processes.

🔑 Most of Earth's surface water—roughly 97 percent—is salt water found in oceans. Only 3 percent is fresh water.

🔑 In the water cycle, water moves between land, living things, bodies of water on Earth's surface, and the atmosphere.

Vocabulary
• habitat • groundwater • water cycle
• evaporation • transpiration • precipitation

LESSON 2 Surface Water

🔑 A river and all the streams and smaller rivers that flow into it together make up a river system.

🔑 Ponds and lakes form when water collects in hollows and low-lying areas of land.

🔑 Natural processes and human activities can cause lakes to disappear.

Vocabulary
• tributary • watershed • divide
• reservoir • eutrophication

LESSON 3 Water Underground

🔑 Water underground trickles down between particles of soil and through cracks and spaces in layers of rock.

🔑 People can obtain groundwater from an aquifer by drilling a well below the water table.

Vocabulary
• permeable • impermeable
• unsaturated zone • saturated zone
• water table • aquifer • artesian well

LESSON 4 Exploring the Ocean

🔑 The water in Earth's oceans varies in salinity, temperature, and depth.

🔑 Ocean surface temperatures vary with location and the seasons. The water temperature decreases with increasing depth.

🔑 In the ocean, pressure increases with depth.

🔑 Major ocean floor features include trenches, the continental shelf, the continental slope, the abyssal plain, and the mid-ocean ridge.

Vocabulary
• salinity • sonar • seamount • trench
• continental slope • continental shelf
• abyssal plain • mid-ocean ridge

LESSON 5 Wave Action

🔑 Most waves form when winds blowing across the water's surface transmit energy to the water.

🔑 Near shore, wave height increases and wavelength decreases.

🔑 Waves shape a beach by eroding the shore in some places and building it up in others.

Vocabulary
• wave • wavelength • frequency • wave height
• tsunami • longshore drift • rip current • groin

LESSON 6 Currents and Climate

🔑 Surface currents are driven mainly by winds. A surface current warms or cools the air above it, affecting the climate of the land near the coast.

🔑 Deep currents are caused by differences in the density of ocean water. They move and mix water around the world and carry cold water from the poles toward the equator.

Vocabulary
• current • Coriolis effect • climate
• El Niño • La Niña

Review and Assessment

LESSON 1 Water on Earth

1. Where is most of Earth's total water supply found?

a. atmosphere   b. groundwater

c. ice sheets   d. oceans

2. Apply Concepts Why is so little of Earth's water available for human use?

_____

_____

_____

_____

_____

3. math! About 3 percent of Earth's water is fresh water. Of that 3 percent, about 69 percent is ice. About what percent of Earth's total water supply is ice?

_____

_____

LESSON 2 Surface Water

4. What is the area that supplies water to a river system called?

a. reservoir   b. tributary

c. watershed   d. wetland

5. Two watersheds are separated by a(n)

_____

6. Classify How can a large river also be a tributary?

_____

_____

_____

_____

_____

LESSON 3 Water Underground

7. The top of the saturated zone forms the

a. artesian well.   b. impermeable rock.

c. unsaturated zone.   d. water table.

8. Water can flow through pores or cracks in a _____ material.

Use the diagram to answer Questions 9–11.

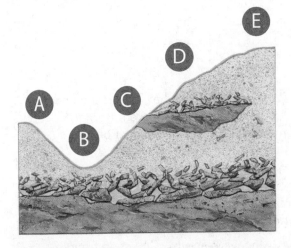

9. Make Judgments Would location D or E be a better place to dig a well? Explain.

_____

_____

_____

_____

10. Infer At which location could you obtain water without using a pump? What is this called?

_____

11. Predict What changes would you expect to see in this area during a very rainy season?

_____

_____

_____

_____

Exploring the Ocean

12. Why is ocean water more dense than fresh water at the same temperature?

    a. circular winds   **b.** less pressure

    c. deep currents   **d.** higher salinity

13. Relate Cause and Effect Name two properties of ocean water affected by depth. How does depth affect each?

_____

_____

_____

_____

14. **Write About It** In what ways is the ocean at 1,000 meters deep different from the ocean at the surface in the same location?

Wave Action

15. Which describes rolling waves with a large horizontal distance between crests?

    a. long wavelength   **b.** deep trough

    c. great wave height   **d.** high frequency

16. Interpret Diagrams Where will sand pile up against the groins shown in the diagram? Explain.

_____

_____

_____

_____

_____

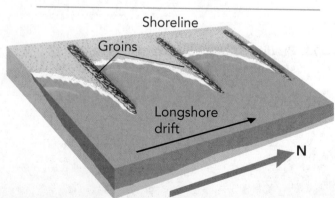

Shoreline

Groins

Longshore drift

N

Currents and Climate

17. What makes winds and currents move in curved paths?

    a. Coriolis effect   **b.** wave height

    c. longshore drift   **d.** ocean trenches

18. Flooding is common during an El Niño, which is _____

_____

_____

19. Compare and Contrast What causes surface currents? Deep currents?

_____

_____

_____

APPLY THE BIG ? How does fresh water cycle on Earth?

20. In a process called cloud seeding, small particles of chemicals such as dry ice are spread into clouds from airplanes. The goal is to provide a place for condensation, causing raindrops to form and fall as precipitation. How would increased condensation affect the other processes of the water cycle?

_____

_____

_____

_____

_____

_____

_____

Standardized Test Prep

Multiple Choice

Circle the letter of the best answer.

1. Use the diagram to answer the question.

Which of the following is a process that occurs in the water cycle?

A condensation   B evaporation

C precipitation   D all of the above

2. How do waves shape beaches?

A by preventing beach erosion

B by counteracting longshore drift

C by compacting the sand into permanent position

D by eroding the shore in some places and building it up in others

3. For a science project, you must build a model of an aquifer. What material would be **best** to use for the layer where the water will accumulate?

A clay

B granite

C gravel

D bedrock

4. What is a watershed?

A the land area that supplies a river system

B the amount of oxygen in a lake

C the total water supply within a lake

D sediment from streams that fills up lakes

5. A major warm ocean surface current flows along a coastal area. What type of climate would you most likely find in the area influenced by the current?

A cool and dry

B very cool and wet

C mild and wet

D very hot and dry

Constructed Response

Use the graph and your knowledge of science to answer Question 6. Write your answer on a separate sheet of paper.

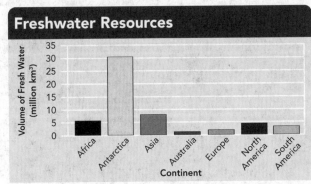

6. The graph shows the total amount of fresh water in all forms found on each continent. Why is so much of Earth's fresh water located in Antarctica? Is that water usable by humans? Explain your answer.

A Pearl of a Solution

▲ Oysters filter nutrients and pollutants from the water in which they feed.

It's hard to say who are the bigger heroes in the Chesapeake Bay—the scientists or the oysters.

The Chesapeake Bay is the world's third-largest estuary. More than 17 million people live within the Chesapeake watershed. For many years, fishing has been an important industry for people in the area. People depend on the bay for food and work. Pollution and habitat loss in the watershed have dramatically reduced marine life in the bay, and people who live and work there have found it more difficult to find food or earn a living.

Now, scientists and volunteers are using oysters to help clean the bay's waters. Oysters get their food by filtering plankton and other nutrients from the water. In this way, oysters help remove pollutants from the water. The oyster population has fallen sharply in recent years, and there are not enough oysters to keep up with the pollution. The Chesapeake Bay Foundation is hoping to restock the bay with 31 million oysters in the next 10 years. If they succeed, other marine life may also return to the bay.

Research It Make a map that shows the Chesapeake Bay watershed and the major rivers that drain into it. On the map, indicate how freshwater pollutants, such as excess fertilizer, enter the bay. Write a paragraph explaining the impact on society if the pollution is allowed

What Was Fort Miami?

Ohio's 2,000-Year-Old Aqueduct

▲ Archaeologists use computer-generated images to show what the 2,000-year-old irrigation system might have looked like when it was built.

Archaeologists from the University of Cincinnati have made a startling discovery. They had thought that a 2,000-year-old ruin on a hilltop in southwestern Ohio was a fort used by the Shawnee people native to the region to defend their lands from attack. Recently, however, archaeologists have found evidence that the ruin was actually a complex system of dams and canals, stretching almost 6 kilometers! At one spot, the Shawnee constructed a dam nearly 61 meters high!

The Shawnee built the system to collect water from a series of springs and to transport it to farmland, so that they could grow enough food to support their society. Climate records suggest that 2,000 years ago, when the Shawnee built the system, the region was colder and drier than it is now. So moving water from its source to where it was needed for farming would have helped the Shawnee survive.

Design It Find out more about water management systems used by ancient civilizations such as the Maya. Make a presentation that compares how two different civilizations used natural resources. Explain how the climate each group faced may have affected its

▲ Archaeologists sift carefully

WHAT KEEPS THIS HANG GLIDER FLYING?

THE BIG ?

How does the sun's energy affect Earth's atmosphere?

Imagine yourself lazily soaring like a bird above Earth. The quiet, gentle winds and warm sun are so relaxing. No noisy engine, no flapping wings, but wait, what's keeping you aloft? Everyone knows that humans can't fly. ▶ Develop Hypotheses **How does this hang glider fly?**

_____

_____

_____

_____

_____

_____

▶ UNTAMED SCIENCE   Watch the **Untamed Science** video to learn more about Earth's atmosphere.

The Atmosphere

11 Getting Started

Check Your Understanding

1. **Background** Read the paragraph below and then answer the question.

Helen blows up a balloon. She adds it to a large garbage bag already full of balloons. Its low **weight** makes the bag easy to carry, but its large **volume** might be a problem fitting it in the car. Capturing air in a balloon makes it easier to understand that air has **mass**.

Weight is a measure of the force of gravity on an object.

Volume is the amount of space that matter occupies.

Mass is the amount of matter in an object.

- How could the bag's volume make it difficult to fit in the car?

_____

_____

> MY READING WEB If you had trouble completing the question above, visit **My Reading Web** and type in *The Atmosphere.*

Vocabulary Skill

Word Origins Many words come to English from other languages. Learning a few common Greek word parts can help you understand new science words.

Greek Word Part	Meaning	Example
-meter	measure	barometer, *n.* an instrument that measures air pressure
thermo-	heat	thermosphere, *n.* the outer layer of Earth's atmosphere

2. **Quick Check** Use the Greek word parts above to write a definition of a thermometer.

_____

_____

atmosphere

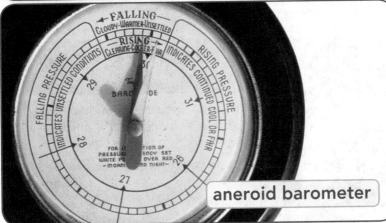

aneroid barometer

troposphere

wind

Chapter Preview

LESSON 1
- weather • atmosphere
- water vapor

  ↻ **Summarize**
  △ Infer

LESSON 2
- density • air pressure
- barometer • mercury barometer
- aneroid barometer • altitude

  ↻ **Relate Cause and Effect**
  △ Develop Hypotheses

LESSON 3
- troposphere • stratosphere
- mesosphere • thermosphere
- ionosphere • exosphere

  ↻ **Identify Supporting Evidence**
  △ Interpret Data

LESSON 4
- electromagnetic waves
- radiation • infrared radiation
- ultraviolet radiation • scattering
- greenhouse effect

  ↻ **Ask Questions**
  △ Graph

LESSON 5
- temperature • thermal energy
- thermometer • heat
- convection • conduction
- convection currents

  ↻ **Identify the Main Idea**
  △ Infer

LESSON 6
- wind • anemometer
- windchill factor • local winds
- sea breeze • land breeze
- global winds • Coriolis effect
- latitude

  ↻ **Identify Supporting Evidence**
  △ Draw Conclusions

The Air Around You

UNLOCK
THE BIG
?

🔑 **What Is the Composition of Earth's Atmosphere?**

🔑 **How Is the Atmosphere a System?**

my planeT DiARY

VOICES FROM HISTORY

Antoine Lavoisier

French chemist Antoine Lavoisier was determined to solve a puzzle: How could a metal burned to a powder weigh more than the original metal? In his 1772 lab notes he observed, "Sulphur, in burning . . . gains weight." So did mercury. Lavoisier thought a gas in the air was combining with the mercury as it burned, making it heavier. Then he heated the mercury powder to a higher temperature. It turned back to liquid mercury and a gas. Lavoisier observed that a mouse exposed to the gas could breathe it. He named the gas *principe oxygine*. Today we call it oxygen.

Discuss Lavoisier's experiment with a partner and answer the question below.

Why do you think Lavoisier exposed a mouse to the gas he collected from the mercury?

_____

_____

_____

> PLANET DIARY Go to **Planet Diary** to learn more about air.

Lab ® Do the Inquiry Warm-Up *How*
zone *Long Will the Candle Burn?*

What Is the Composition of Earth's Atmosphere?

The sun disappears behind thick, dark clouds. In the distance you see a bright flash. Then you hear a crack of thunder. You make it home just as the downpour begins. The weather changed quickly—that was close!

Weather is the condition of Earth's atmosphere at a particular time and place. But what is the atmosphere? Earth's **atmosphere** (AT muh sfeer) is the envelope of gases that surrounds the planet. 🔑 **Earth's atmosphere consists of nitrogen, oxygen, carbon dioxide, water vapor, and other gases, as well as particles of liquids and solids.**

Vocabulary
- weather • atmosphere
- water vapor

Skills
- Reading: Summarize
- Inquiry: Infer

Nitrogen The most abundant gas in the atmosphere is nitrogen. It makes up a little more than three fourths of the air we breathe. Nitrogen occurs in all living things and makes up about 3 percent of the weight of the human body.

Oxygen Although oxygen is the second most abundant gas in the atmosphere, it makes up only about 21 percent of the volume. Plants and animals take oxygen directly from the air and use it to release energy from their food.

Oxygen is also involved in many other processes. A fire uses oxygen rapidly as it burns. Without oxygen, a fire will go out. Some processes use oxygen more slowly. Steel in cars and other objects reacts slowly with oxygen to form iron oxide, or rust.

Carbon Dioxide Carbon dioxide makes up much less than 1 percent of the atmosphere, but it is essential to life. Plants must have carbon dioxide to produce food. The cells of animals break down food and give off carbon dioxide as a waste product.

When fuels like coal and gasoline are burned, they also release carbon dioxide. Burning these fuels increases the amount of carbon dioxide in the atmosphere.

Other Gases Oxygen and nitrogen together make up 99 percent of dry air. Argon makes up most of the other 1 percent. The remaining gases are called trace gases because only small amounts of them are present.

FIGURE 1 ·····························

Gases in the Air
The atmosphere is a thin layer of gases.

Graph **Identify which circle graph shows the correct percentage of gases in the atmosphere. Shade in the key and the graph. Give your graph a title.**

Key
☐ Nitrogen
☐ Oxygen
☐ Other gases

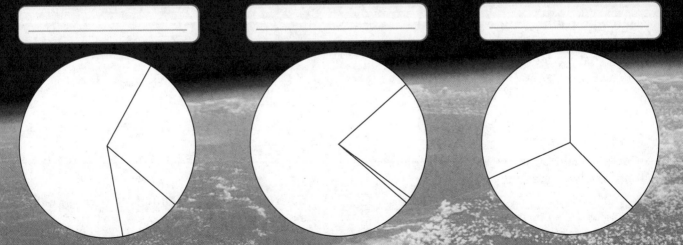

The amount of water vapor in the air can differ from place to place.

1 There is more water vapor in the (desert/rain forest) than in the (desert/rain forest).

2 Infer What evidence do you see for your answer to Question 1?

_____

_____

_____

3 CHALLENGE What factors might affect the amount of water vapor in the air?

_____

_____

_____

Water Vapor

So far, we've discussed the composition of dry air. But in reality, air is not dry. Air contains **water vapor** —water in the form of a gas. Water vapor is invisible. It is not the same thing as steam, which is made up of tiny droplets of liquid water.

The amount of water vapor in the air varies greatly from place to place and from time to time. Water vapor plays an important role in Earth's weather. Clouds form when water vapor condenses out of the air to form tiny droplets of liquid water or crystals of ice. If these droplets or crystals become heavy enough, they fall as rain or snow.

Particles

Pure air contains only gases. But pure air exists only in laboratories. In the real world, air contains tiny solid and liquid particles of dust, smoke, salt, and chemicals. You can see some of these particles in the air around you, but most of them are too small to see.

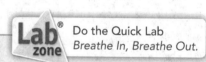

Do the Quick Lab
Breathe In, Breathe Out.

🔑 Assess Your Understanding

1a. Define The _____ is the envelope of _____ that surrounds Earth.

b. List What are the four most common gases in dry air?

_____

_____

c. Compare and Contrast What is the difference between wet air and dry air?

_____

_____

got it?

○ **I get it!** Now I know that the atmosphere is made up of _____

_____

_____

_____

○ **I need extra help with** _____

_____

Go to **my science** 🌐 **coach** *online for help with this subject.*

How Is the Atmosphere a System?

The atmosphere is a system that interacts with other Earth systems, such as the ocean. The atmosphere has many different parts. Some of these parts you can actually see, such as clouds. But most parts of the atmosphere—like air, wind, and energy—you can't see. Instead, you might feel a wind when it blows on you. Or you might feel energy from the sun warming your face on a cool winter day.

At first, the wind that blows and the heat you feel may seem unrelated. But as you'll learn, the different parts of the atmosphere interact with one another. **Events in one part of the atmosphere affect other parts of the atmosphere.**

Energy from the sun drives the motions in the atmosphere. A storm such as the hurricane in **Figure 2** involves a tremendous amount of energy. The spiraling shape of a hurricane is due in part to forces resulting from Earth's rotation. A hurricane also gains energy from warm ocean water. Since the ocean water is warmed by the sun, a hurricane's energy comes mostly from the sun.

Summarize Write a short summary of the third paragraph.

_____

_____

_____

_____

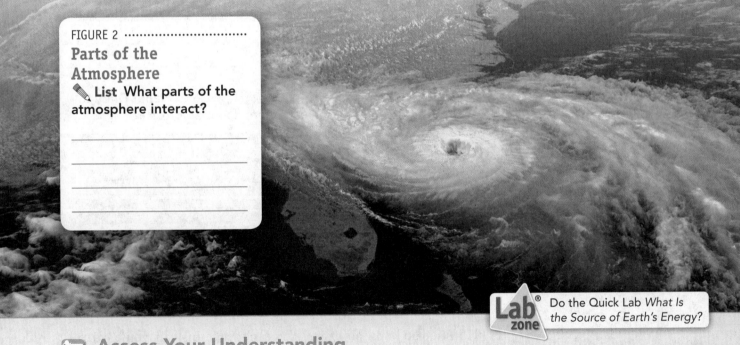

FIGURE 2 ....

Parts of the Atmosphere

✎ **List** What parts of the atmosphere interact?

_____

_____

_____

_____

Lab zone® Do the Quick Lab *What Is the Source of Earth's Energy?*

🔑 Assess Your Understanding

got it? ....

○ **I get it!** Now I know that events in one part of the atmosphere _____

_____

○ **I need extra help with** _____

Go to my science 🔎 coach *online for help with this subject.*

Air Pressure

UNLOCK
THE BIG

🔑 **What Are Some Properties of Air?**

🔑 **What Instruments Measure Air Pressure?**

🔑 **How Does Altitude Affect Air Pressure and Density?**

my planeT DiaRY

DISCOVERY

Flying High

Astronauts aren't the only people who go into space. High-altitude pilots who fly above 15,250 meters are in a zone with conditions similar to deep space. At these heights, air pressure is so low that blood can boil. A pilot can also pass out in less than a minute from lack of oxygen. To survive, pilots wear pressure suits. These suits weigh about 16 kilograms and are custom-built for each pilot. They inflate in an emergency, keeping air pressure stable for the pilot. The suits are "very, very restrictive," says pilot David Wright. "But it saves your life, so you're able to put up with that."

Discuss your answer with a classmate.
Pilots wear pressure suits in addition to flying in a pressurized plane. Why do you think this is so?

_____

_____

_____

▶ PLANET DIARY Go to **Planet Diary** to learn more about air pressure.

Lab® Do the Inquiry Warm-Up
zone *Does Air Have Mass?*

What Are Some Properties of Air?

How do you know air exists? You can't see it. Instead, you have to understand what air does. It may seem to you that air has no mass. But the air in the atmosphere consists of atoms and molecules, which have mass. 🔑 **Because air has mass, it also has other properties, including density and pressure.**

Vocabulary
- density • air pressure
- barometer • mercury barometer
- aneroid barometer • altitude

Skills
- Reading: Relate Cause and Effect
- Inquiry: Develop Hypotheses

Density The amount of mass in a given volume of air is its **density.** You calculate the density of a substance by dividing its mass by its volume. If there are more molecules in a given volume, the density is greater. If there are fewer molecules, the density is less.

Pressure The atmosphere is heavy. Its weight exerts a force on surfaces like you. The force pushing on an area or surface is called pressure. **Air pressure** is the result of the weight of a column of air pushing on an area.

As **Figure 1** shows, there is a column of air above you that extends all the way up through the entire atmosphere. In fact, the weight of the column of air above your desk is about the same as the weight of a large school bus. So why doesn't air pressure crush your desk? The reason is that the molecules in air push in all directions—down, up, and sideways. The air pushing down on top of your desk is balanced by the air pushing up on the bottom of your desk.

AIR COLUMN

FIGURE 1 ·······························
Air Column
The weight of the column of air above you puts pressure on you.

✎ **Answer the questions below.**

1. **Describe** What's an air column?

_____

_____

2. **Apply Concepts** Add arrows to the diagram below to indicate how the pressure from air molecules keeps you from being crushed.

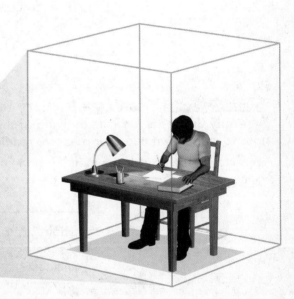

Lab zone® Do the Quick Lab *Properties of Air.*

🗝 Assess Your Understanding

got it? ··

○ I get it! Now I know that air has properties such as _____

_____

○ I need extra help with _____

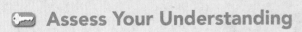

Go to **my science** COACH *online for help with this subject.*

What Instruments Measure Air Pressure?

Air pressure can change daily. A denser substance has more mass per unit volume than a less dense one. So denser air exerts more pressure than less dense air. A **barometer** (buh RAHM uh tur) is an instrument that is used to measure air pressure. 🗝️ **The two common kinds of barometers are mercury barometers and aneroid barometers.**

Mercury Barometers Look at **Figure 2** to see a mercury barometer model. A **mercury barometer** consists of a long glass tube that is closed at one end and open at the other. The open end of the tube rests in a dish of mercury. The closed end of the tube is almost a vacuum—the space above the mercury contains very little air. The air pressing down on the surface of the mercury in the dish is equal to the pressure exerted by the weight of the column of mercury in the tube. When the air pressure increases, it presses down more on the surface of the mercury. Greater air pressure forces the column of mercury higher. So, the level of the mercury in the tube shows you the pressure of the air that day.

Vocabulary Greek Word Origins
The Greek word part *baro-* means "weight." How would it relate to the word part *-meter*?

_____

_____

_____

FIGURE 2 ···

> INTERACTIVE ART **Reading a Mercury Barometer**
✏️ **Apply Concepts** Use the drawing of the barometer on the right to show what a low air pressure reading looks like.

1. Shade in the level of the mercury in the tube and in the dish.

2. Describe what is happening.

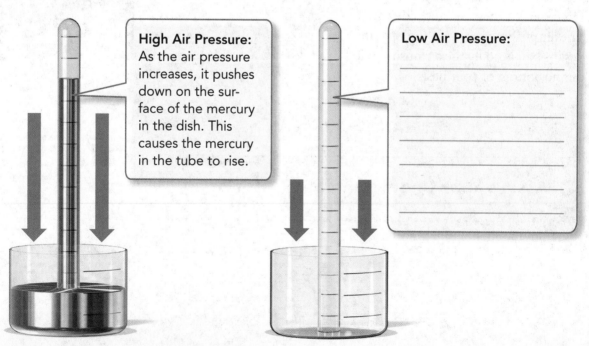

High Air Pressure:
As the air pressure increases, it pushes down on the surface of the mercury in the dish. This causes the mercury in the tube to rise.

Low Air Pressure:

_____

_____

_____

_____

_____

_____

_____

Aneroid Barometers

If you have a barometer at home, it's probably an aneroid barometer. The word *aneroid* means "without liquid." An **aneroid barometer** (AN uh royd) has an airtight metal chamber, as shown in **Figure 3**. The metal chamber is sensitive to changes in air pressure. When air pressure increases, the thin walls of the chamber are pushed in. When the pressure drops, the walls bulge out. The chamber is connected to a dial by a series of springs and levers. As the shape of the chamber changes, the needle on the dial moves.

Units of Air Pressure

Weather reports use several different units for air pressure. Most weather reports for the general public use inches of mercury. For example, if the column of mercury in a mercury barometer is 30 inches high, the air pressure is "30 inches of mercury" or "30 inches."

National Weather Service maps indicate air pressure in millibars. The pressure of the atmosphere is equal to one bar. One inch of mercury is about 33.86 millibars, so 30 inches of mercury is equal to about 1,016 millibars.

FIGURE 3 ·······························

Inside an Aneroid Barometer

An aneroid barometer has an airtight metal chamber, shown in red, below.

✎ **Identify** Label the diagram that shows the aneroid barometer under high pressure and the diagram that shows it under low pressure.

_____   _____

Lab zone Do the Quick Lab
Soda Bottle Barometer.

🗝 Assess Your Understanding

1a. Name What two instruments are commonly used to measure air pressure?

_____

_____

b. Identify What units are used to measure air pressure?

_____

_____

c. CHALLENGE How many millibars are equal to 27.23 inches of mercury?

_____

got it? ·······························

○ **I get it!** Now I know that air pressure can

be measured _____

_____

○ **I need extra help with** _____

Go to MY SCIENCE ⓢ COACH online for help with this subject.

How Does Altitude Affect Air Pressure and Density?

The higher you hike on a mountain, the more changes you'll notice. The temperature will drop, and the plants will get smaller. But you might not notice another change that is happening. At the top of the mountain, the air pressure is less than the air pressure at sea level—the average level of the oceans. **Altitude,** or elevation, is the distance above sea level. **Air pressure decreases as altitude increases. As air pressure decreases, so does density.**

Altitude Affects Air Pressure Suppose you have a stack of books. Which book has more weight on it, the second book from the top or the book at the bottom? The second book from the top has the weight of only one book on top of it. The book at the bottom of the stack has the weight of all the books pressing on it.

Air at sea level is like the bottom book. Sea-level air has the weight of the whole atmosphere pressing on it. Air near the top of the atmosphere is like the second book from the top. There, the air has less weight pressing on it and thus has lower air pressure.

apply it!

You're back from a high-altitude hike. As you empty your bag, you notice that the two empty bottles you carried down from the mountain look different.

1 Observe What observations can you make about the bottles?

_____

_____

_____

2 Develop Hypotheses What's a possible explanation for your observations?

_____

_____

_____

_____

_____

_____

_____

_____

6 km

5 km

4 km

3 km

2 km

Which hiker has the least pressure on him/her?

_____

1 km

Sea level

Altitude Also Affects Density
As you go up through the atmosphere, the density of the air decreases. This means the gas molecules that make up the atmosphere are farther apart at high altitudes than they are at sea level. If you were near the top of a tall mountain and tried to run, you would quickly get out of breath. Why? The air contains 21 percent oxygen, whether you are at sea level or on top of a mountain. However, since the air is less dense at a high altitude, each cubic meter of air you breathe has fewer oxygen molecules than at sea level. So you would become short of breath more quickly at a high altitude.

⟳ Relate Cause and Effect
Underline the sentence that explains how altitude can make you short of breath.

FIGURE 4 ·····················
> VIRTUAL LAB **Effect of Altitude on Pressure and Density**
✎ **Complete the activities below.**

1. **Relate Evidence and Explanation** Draw the air column above each hiker on the mountain. Then answer the question below the hikers.

2. **Make Models** In the empty circles below, draw how densely packed you think the molecules would be at the altitudes shown.

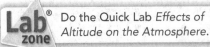

Lab zone ® Do the Quick Lab *Effects of Altitude on the Atmosphere.*

⚷ Assess Your Understanding

2a. Define What is altitude?

_____

b. Summarize How does air pressure change as altitude increases?

_____

c. Predict What changes in air pressure would you expect if you carried a barometer down a mine shaft?

_____
_____
_____
_____

got it? ·····················

○ I get it! Now I know the properties of air
_____

○ I need extra help with _____

Go to my science ⑤ **COACH** *online for help with this subject.*

385

Layers of the Atmosphere

UNLOCK
THE BIG

🔑 **What Are the Four Main Layers of the Atmosphere?**

🔑 **What Are the Characteristics of the Atmosphere's Layers?**

my pLaneT DiaRY

MISCONCEPTION

Earth's Atmosphere

Misconception: The blanket of gases that makes up Earth's atmosphere is thick.

Fact: Earth's atmosphere extends far out into space, at least as far again as the radius of Earth. However, most of the atmosphere is so thin that it would be hard to tell it apart from the vacuum of space. Most of the gas in the atmosphere is found close to Earth's surface. In fact, half of the gas in the atmosphere is found in the bottom 5.5 kilometers—the height of a tall mountain! The rest of the gas extends thinly out into space for thousands of kilometers.

Evidence: The mass of the atmosphere is surprisingly small. In fact, a thin column of air 1 cm² extending out into space for thousands of kilometers has about the same mass as a 1-liter bottle of water.

Talk about these questions with a classmate and then record your answers.

1. Where is most of the gas in the atmosphere found?

_____

_____

_____

2. Why do you think that people think of the atmosphere as a thick layer around Earth?

_____

_____

> PLANET DIARY Go to **Planet Diary** to learn more about layers of the atmosphere.

Lab
zone® Do the Inquiry Warm-Up
Is Air There?

Vocabulary
- troposphere   • stratosphere
- mesosphere   • thermosphere
- ionosphere   • exosphere

Skills
Reading: Identify Supporting Evidence
Inquiry: Interpret Data

What Are the Four Main Layers of the Atmosphere?

Imagine taking a trip upward into the atmosphere in a hot-air balloon. You begin on a warm beach near the ocean, at an altitude of 0 kilometers above sea level.

You hear a roar as the balloon's pilot turns up the burner to heat the air in the balloon. The balloon begins to rise, and Earth's surface gets farther away. As the balloon reaches an altitude of 3 kilometers, you realize the air is getting colder. At 6 kilometers you begin to have trouble breathing. The air is becoming less dense. It's time to go back down.

Six kilometers is pretty high. In fact, it's higher than all but the very tallest mountains. But there are still hundreds of kilometers of atmosphere above you. It may seem as though air is the same from the ground to the edge of space. But air pressure and temperature change with altitude. **Scientists divide Earth's atmosphere into four main layers classified according to changes in temperature. These layers are the troposphere, the stratosphere, the mesosphere, and the thermosphere.**

Identify Supporting Evidence
Underline the evidence in the text above that explains how the atmosphere changes as you go up in a hot-air balloon.

Lab zone
Do the Quick Lab *Layers of the Atmosphere.*

Assess Your Understanding

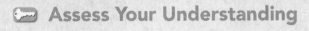

got it? ....

○ I get it! Now I know that the atmosphere has four main layers: _____

_____

○ I need extra help with _____

Go to my science COACH online for help with this subject.

What Are the Characteristics of the Atmosphere's Layers?

Unless you become an astronaut, you won't make a trip to the upper atmosphere. But if you could make that journey, what would you see? Read on to learn more about the conditions you would experience in each layer of the atmosphere.

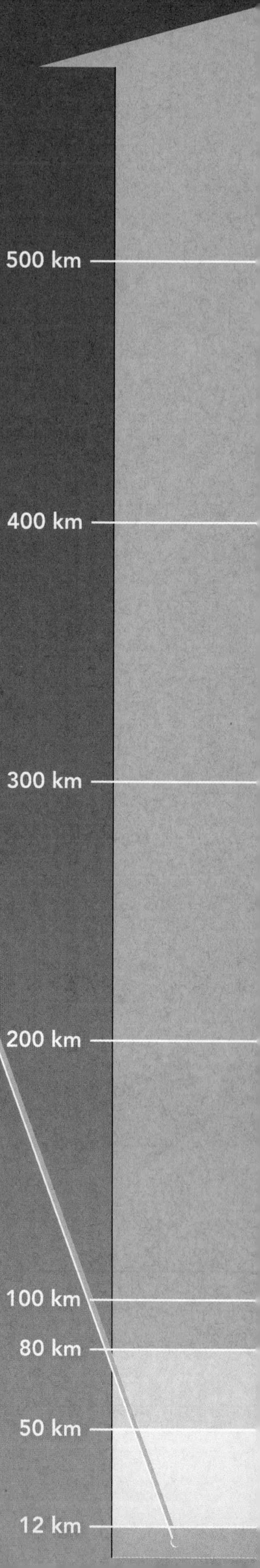

The Troposphere You live in the inner, or lowest, layer of Earth's atmosphere, the **troposphere** (TROH puh sfeer). *Tropo-* means "turning" or "changing." Conditions in the troposphere are more variable than in the other layers. 🔑 **The troposphere is the layer of the atmosphere in which Earth's weather occurs.** The troposphere is about 12 kilometers thick, as you can see in **Figure 1.** However, it varies from 16 kilometers thick above the equator to less than 9 kilometers thick above the North and South poles. Although it's the shallowest layer, the troposphere is the most dense. It contains almost all the mass of the atmosphere.

As altitude increases in the troposphere, the temperature decreases. On average, for every 1-kilometer increase in altitude, the air gets about 6.5°C cooler. At the top of the troposphere, the temperature stops decreasing and stays at about –60°C. Water here forms thin, feathery clouds of ice.

FIGURE 1 ·······························
The Atmosphere Layers
✎ **Observe** Use the journal pages in this lesson to record your observations of the layers of the atmosphere.

Altitude _____

Temperature _____
_____

Observations _____
_____
_____
_____

500 km ——

400 km ——

300 km ——

200 km ——

100 km ——
80 km ——

50 km ——

12 km ——

500 km

400 km

300 km

200 km

100 km

80 km

50 km

12 km

The Stratosphere

The **stratosphere** extends from the top of the troposphere to about 50 kilometers above Earth's surface. *Strato-* means "layer" or "spread out." **The stratosphere is the second layer of the atmosphere and contains the ozone layer.**

The lower stratosphere is cold, about –60°C. Surprisingly, the upper stratosphere is warmer than the lower stratosphere. Why is this? The middle portion of the stratosphere has a layer of air where there is much more ozone than in the rest of the atmosphere. Ozone is a form of oxygen that has three atoms in each molecule instead of the usual two. When ozone absorbs energy from the sun, the energy is converted into heat, warming the air. The ozone layer protects living things from ultraviolet radiation from the sun.

Altitude _____

Temperature _____

Observations _____

_____

do the math!

Changing Temperatures

The graph shows how temperatures in the atmosphere change with altitude. Use it to answer the questions below.

❶ **Read Graphs** What is the temperature at the bottom of the stratosphere?

_____

❷ **Interpret Data** What layer of the atmosphere has the lowest temperature?

_____

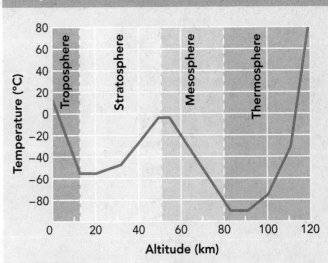

Temperature in the Atmosphere

Troposphere   Stratosphere   Mesosphere   Thermosphere

Temperature (°C): 80, 60, 40, 20, 0, –20, –40, –60, –80

Altitude (km): 0, 20, 40, 60, 80, 100, 120

❸ **CHALLENGE** How does temperature change with altitude in the troposphere?

_____

_____

389

The Mesosphere Above the stratosphere, a drop in temperature marks the beginning of the next layer, the **mesosphere**. *Meso-* means "middle," so the mesosphere is the middle layer of the atmosphere. The mesosphere begins 50 kilometers above Earth's surface and ends at an altitude of 80 kilometers. In the upper mesosphere, temperatures approach −90°C.

The mesosphere is the layer of the atmosphere that protects Earth's surface from being hit by most meteoroids. Meteoroids are chunks of stone and metal from space. What you see as a shooting star, or meteor, is the trail of hot, glowing gases the meteoroid leaves behind in the mesosphere as it burns up.

Altitude _____

Temperature _____
_____

Observations _____
_____
_____
_____
_____
_____
_____

500 km ———

400 km ———

300 km ———

200 km ———

100 km ———

80 km ———

50 km ———

12 km ———

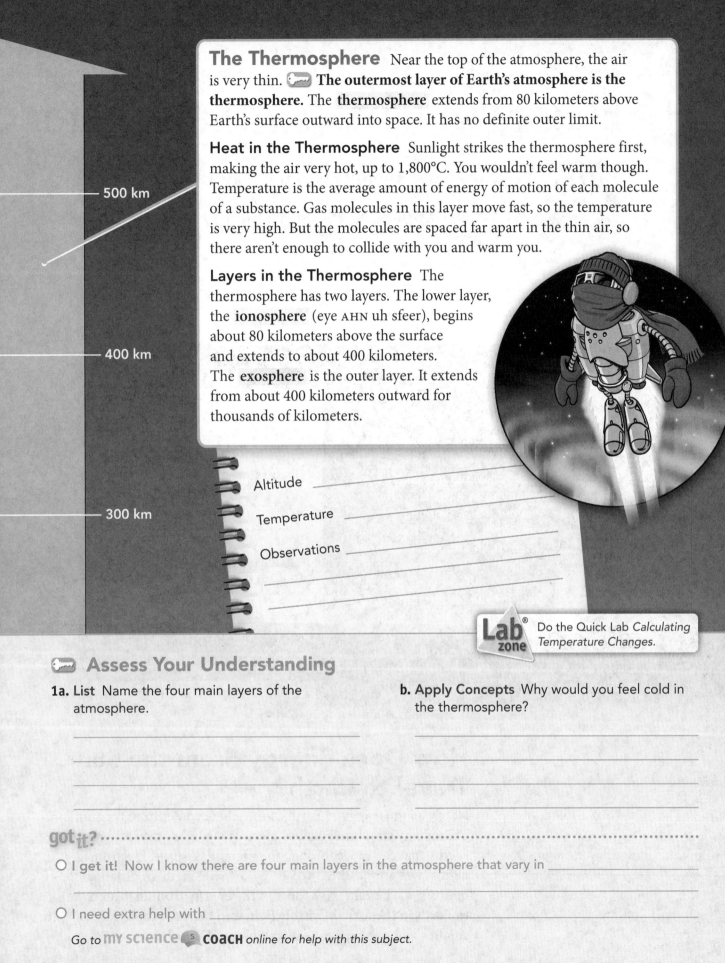

The Thermosphere Near the top of the atmosphere, the air is very thin. 🔑 **The outermost layer of Earth's atmosphere is the thermosphere.** The **thermosphere** extends from 80 kilometers above Earth's surface outward into space. It has no definite outer limit.

Heat in the Thermosphere Sunlight strikes the thermosphere first, making the air very hot, up to 1,800°C. You wouldn't feel warm though. Temperature is the average amount of energy of motion of each molecule of a substance. Gas molecules in this layer move fast, so the temperature is very high. But the molecules are spaced far apart in the thin air, so there aren't enough to collide with you and warm you.

Layers in the Thermosphere The thermosphere has two layers. The lower layer, the **ionosphere** (eye AHN uh sfeer), begins about 80 kilometers above the surface and extends to about 400 kilometers. The **exosphere** is the outer layer. It extends from about 400 kilometers outward for thousands of kilometers.

500 km

400 km

300 km

Altitude _____

Temperature _____

Observations _____

_____

_____

Lab ® Do the Quick Lab *Calculating*
zone *Temperature Changes.*

🔑 **Assess Your Understanding**

1a. List Name the four main layers of the atmosphere.

_____

_____

_____

_____

b. Apply Concepts Why would you feel cold in the thermosphere?

_____

_____

_____

_____

got it? ....

○ **I get it!** Now I know there are four main layers in the atmosphere that vary in _____

_____

○ **I need extra help with** _____

Go to MY SCIENCE ⑤ COACH *online for help with this subject.*

Energy in Earth's Atmosphere

- 🔑 How Does Energy From the Sun Travel to Earth?

- 🔑 What Happens to the Sun's Energy When It Reaches Earth?

my planet diary

BLOG

Posted by: Amanda

Location: Hastings, New York

I love to swim. One time I was swimming at a beach in the summer. I was swimming for a long time. I got out to eat and dried off in about half an hour. Then I went swimming again, and it clouded over. I got out, and it took about an hour to dry off this time. The sun was behind clouds, so it took longer for me to dry off. I found it very interesting.

Read the blog and answer the question.

Why did it take Amanda longer to dry off the second time?

_____

_____

> PLANET DIARY Go to **Planet Diary** to learn more about the sun's energy.

Do the Inquiry Warm-Up
Does a Plastic Bag Trap Heat?

How Does Energy From the Sun Travel to Earth?

Nearly all the energy in Earth's atmosphere comes from the sun. This energy travels to Earth as **electromagnetic waves,** a form of energy that can move through the vacuum of space. Electromagnetic waves are classified according to wavelength, or distance between wave peaks. 🔑 **Most of the energy from the sun travels to Earth in the form of visible light and infrared radiation. A smaller amount arrives as ultraviolet radiation.**

Vocabulary

- electromagnetic waves
- radiation
- infrared radiation
- ultraviolet radiation
- scattering
- greenhouse effect

Skills

- Reading: Ask Questions
- Inquiry: Graph

Visible Light Visible light includes all of the colors that you see in a rainbow: red, orange, yellow, green, blue, and violet. The different colors are the result of different wavelengths. Red and orange light have the longest wavelengths, while blue and violet light have the shortest wavelengths, as shown in **Figure 1.**

Nonvisible Radiation The direct transfer of energy by electromagnetic waves is called **radiation.** One form of electromagnetic energy, **infrared radiation,** has wavelengths that are longer than wavelengths for red light. Infrared radiation is not visible by humans, but can be felt as heat. The sun also gives off **ultraviolet radiation,** which is an invisible form of energy with wavelengths that are shorter than wavelengths for violet light. Ultraviolet radiation can cause sunburns.

FIGURE 1 ·····················

Radiation From the Sun
Energy travels to Earth as electromagnetic waves.
✏ **Identify** Label the types of electromagnetic radiation in the diagram.

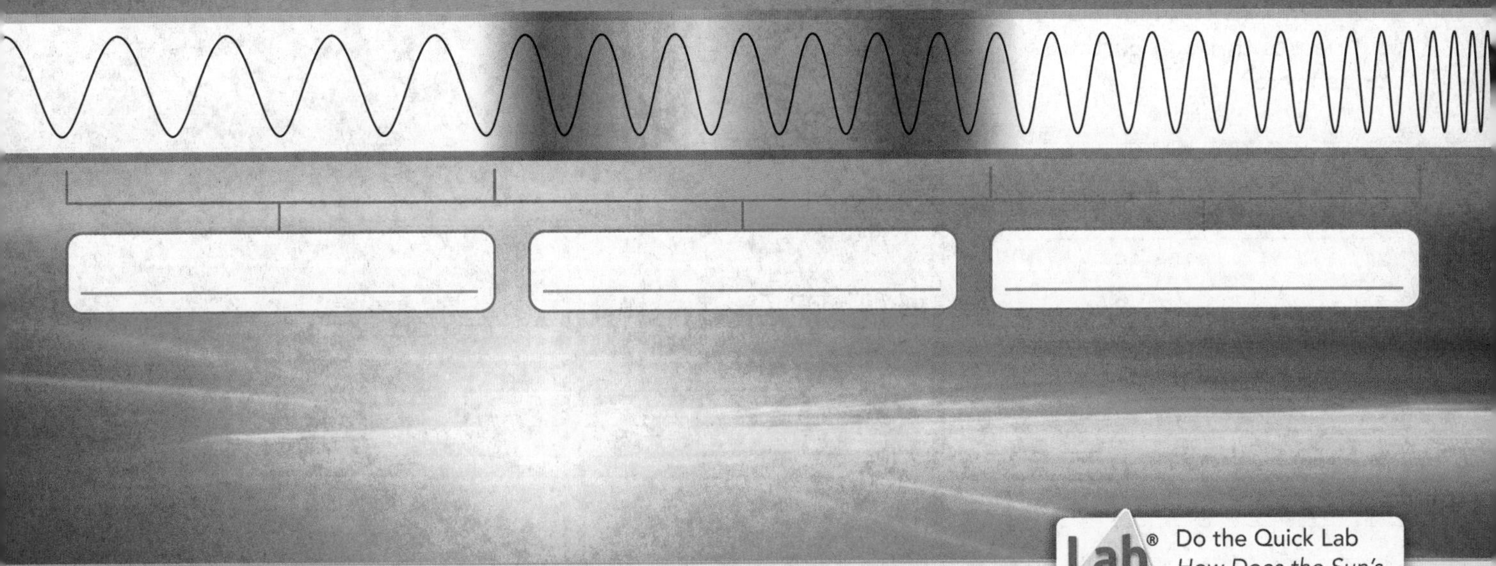

Lab zone® Do the Quick Lab *How Does the Sun's Energy Reach Earth?*

🔑 Assess Your Understanding

got it? ·······················

O **I get it!** Now I know energy from the sun reaches Earth as _____

_____

O **I need extra help with** _____

Go to **my science** COACH online for help with this subject.

393

What Happens to the Sun's Energy When It Reaches Earth?

Sunlight must pass through the atmosphere before it reaches Earth's surface. The path of the sun's rays is shown in **Figure 2**. 🔑 **Some sunlight is absorbed or reflected by the atmosphere before it can reach the surface. The rest passes through the atmosphere to the surface.**

Upper Atmosphere Different wavelengths of radiation are absorbed by different layers in the atmosphere. For example, some ultraviolet radiation is absorbed by the ozone layer in the stratosphere. Infrared radiation penetrates farther into the atmosphere before some of it is absorbed by water vapor and carbon dioxide.

FIGURE 2 ··································

Energy in the Atmosphere
Some wavelengths reach Earth's surface. Other wavelengths are completely or partially absorbed in the atmosphere.

✎ **Compare and Contrast**
What happens to the radiation as it passes through Earth's atmosphere?

_____

_____

_____

_____

_____

_____

_____

_____

_____

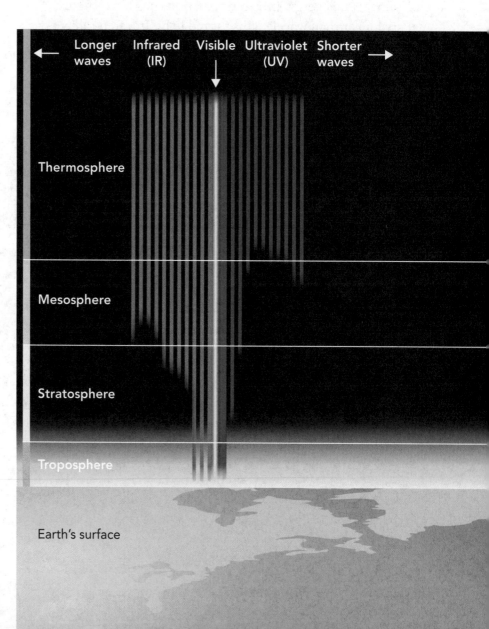

Troposphere

Clouds act as mirrors, reflecting sunlight back into space. Dust-size particles and gases in the atmosphere disperse light in all directions, a process called **scattering.** When you look at the sky, the light you see has been scattered by gas molecules in the atmosphere. Gas molecules scatter short wavelengths of visible light (blue and violet) more than long wavelengths (red and orange). Scattered light looks bluer than ordinary sunlight. That's why the clear daytime sky looks blue.

Earth's Surface

It may seem like a lot of the sun's energy is absorbed by gases in the atmosphere or reflected by clouds and particles. However, about 50 percent of the energy that reaches Earth's surface is absorbed by land and water and changed into heat. Look at **Figure 3** to see what happens to incoming sunlight at Earth's surface.

Ask Questions Before you read, preview the headings on these two pages. Ask a question you'd like to have answered. After you read, answer your question.

_____
_____
_____
_____
_____
_____

apply it!

The materials at Earth's surface shown below reflect different amounts of energy.

❶ **Graph** Use the higher percentages below to draw a bar graph. Give it a title.

❷ Based on your graph, which material reflects the most sunlight? Which absorbs the most?

_____

❸ CHALLENGE Predict what might happen if a forested area was replaced with an asphalt parking lot.

_____
_____

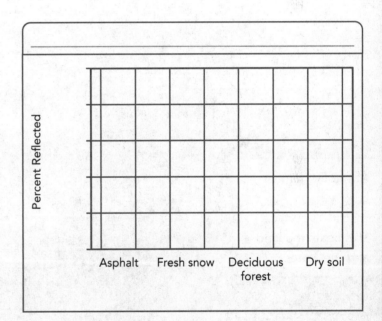

Percent Reflected

Asphalt   Fresh snow   Deciduous forest   Dry soil

Asphalt
5–10% reflected

Fresh snow
80–90% reflected

Deciduous forest
15–20% reflected

Dry soil
20–25% reflected

FIGURE 3 ·······························

Energy at Earth's Surface

✎ **Identify** What's happening to energy in the lower atmosphere and at Earth's surface? Find out by using the words in the word bank below to complete each sentence.

Word Bank

reflected   absorbed   radiated

Words may be used more than once.

✎ **Draw Conclusions** Using the diagram below, draw a conclusion about energy at Earth's surface.

_____

_____

_____

About 25 percent of incoming sunlight is _____ by clouds, dust, and gases in the atmosphere.

About 50 percent is _____ by Earth's surface. This heats the land and the water.

About 20 percent is _____ by gases and particles in the atmosphere.

Some absorbed energy is _____ back into the atmosphere.

About 5 percent is _____ by the surface back into the atmosphere.

Earth's Energy Budget What happens to the energy that heats the land and water? 🔑 **Earth's surface radiates some energy back into the atmosphere as infrared radiation.** Much of this infrared radiation doesn't immediately travel all the way back into space. Instead, it's absorbed by water vapor, carbon dioxide, methane, and other gases in the air. The energy from the absorbed radiation heats the gases in the air. These gases in turn hold heat in Earth's atmosphere in a process called the **greenhouse effect.**

The greenhouse effect, shown in **Figure 4,** is a natural process. It keeps Earth's atmosphere at a temperature that is comfortable for most living things. Over time, the amount of energy absorbed by the atmosphere and Earth's surface is in balance with the amount of energy radiated into space. In this way, Earth's average temperatures remain fairly constant. But scientists have evidence that human activities may be altering this process.

FIGURE 4 ....
▷**ART IN MOTION** **Greenhouse Effect**
The greenhouse effect is a natural heat-trapping process.

✎ **Sequence** Number each step in the diagram to show how the greenhouse effect takes place. Discuss the diagram with a partner.

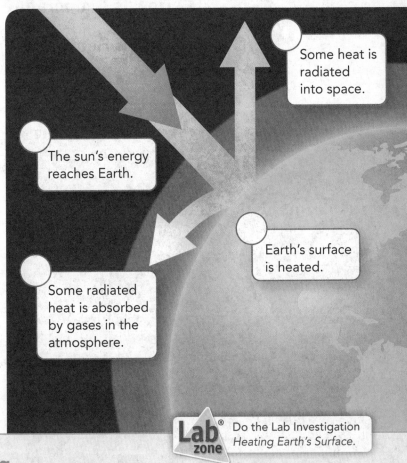

Some heat is radiated into space.

The sun's energy reaches Earth.

Earth's surface is heated.

Some radiated heat is absorbed by gases in the atmosphere.

Lab zone® Do the Lab Investigation
Heating Earth's Surface.

🔑 Assess Your Understanding

1a. Summarize What happens to most of the sunlight that reaches Earth?

_____
_____

b. Interpret Diagrams In **Figure 3,** what percentage of incoming sunlight is reflected by clouds, dust, and gases in the atmosphere?

_____
_____

c. Predict How might conditions on Earth be different without the greenhouse effect?

_____
_____
_____
_____

got**it?** ....

○ I get it! Now I know some energy _____
_____

○ I need extra help with _____

Go to MY SCIENCE ⬤ COACH online for help with this subject.

Heat Transfer

UNLOCK THE BIG Q?

🔑 **How Is Temperature Measured?**

🔑 **How Is Heat Transferred?**

my pLaneT DiaRY

SCIENCE IN THE KITCHEN

From the Freezer to the Table

French fries are on many restaurant menus. But have you ever wondered how they get from the freezer to the table? It takes a little science in the kitchen to make it happen.

First, you heat oil in a fryer until it's around 340°F. Then, the frozen potato slices are dropped in. Hot oil moves from the bottom of the fryer and begins to heat the potatoes. Exposure to so much heat causes the water in the potatoes to boil. This is indicated by bubbles rising to the surface of the oil. As the outside of the potato heats up, it transfers heat to the inside of the potato slice. In a matter of minutes it's crunchy on the outside and soft on the inside.

Answer the following question and discuss it with a partner.

Explain in your own words what happens when the potatoes are exposed to heat.

_____

_____

_____

▸ PLANET DIARY Go to **Planet Diary** to learn more about heat transfer.

Lab® zone Do the Inquiry Warm-Up *What Happens When Air Is Heated?*

How Is Temperature Measured?

All substances are made up of tiny particles (atoms and molecules) that are constantly moving. The faster the particles are moving, the more energy they have. **Temperature** is the *average* amount of energy of motion of each particle of a substance. In **Figure 1,** the hot tea in the teapot is the same temperature as the hot tea in the teacup. But do they have the same thermal energy?

Vocabulary

- temperature
- thermal energy
- thermometer
- heat
- convection
- conduction
- convection currents

Skills

- Reading: Identify the Main Idea
- Inquiry: Infer

Thermal energy measures the *total* energy of motion in the particles of a substance. This means that the tea in the pot has more thermal energy than the tea in the cup because it has more mass.

Measuring Temperature

Temperature is an important factor affecting weather. 🔑 **Air temperature is usually measured with a thermometer.** A **thermometer** is a device that measures temperature. Some thermometers have a thin glass tube with a bulb on one end that holds liquid mercury or colored alcohol. When the air temperature increases, the temperature of the liquid in the bulb increases. This causes the liquid to expand and rise up the column.

Temperature Scales

Temperature is measured in units called degrees. Two temperature scales are the Celsius scale and the Fahrenheit scale. On the Celsius scale at sea level, the freezing point of water is 0°C, while the boiling point is 100°C. On the Fahrenheit scale at sea level, the freezing point of water is 32°F and the boiling point is 212°F. To convert from Farenheit to Celsius, you would use the following formula:

$$\frac{Fahrenheit - 32}{1.8} = Celsius$$

FIGURE 1

Measuring Temperature

✎ Read and then answer the questions.

1. **Review** Circle the correct word in this sentence: The tea in the cup has (the same/less/more) thermal energy than the tea in the pot.

2. **Calculate** If the tea in the cup cooled to 70°F, what would a Celsius thermometer read?

_____

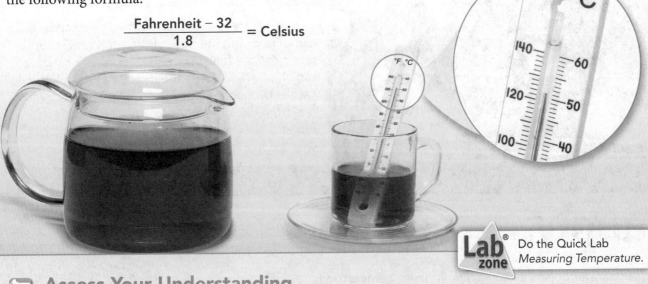

Lab zone Do the Quick Lab *Measuring Temperature*.

🔑 Assess Your Understanding

got it? ···

O **I get it!** Now I know that temperature and thermal energy are different because _____

_____

O **I need extra help with** _____

Go to my science ⓢ COACH *online for help with this subject.*

How Is Heat Transferred?

Heat is thermal energy that is transferred from a hotter object to a cooler one. 🔑 Heat is transferred in three ways: convection, conduction, and radiation.

1 Convection In fluids (liquids and gases), atoms and molecules can move easily from one place to another. As they move, their energy moves along with them. The transfer of heat by the movement of a fluid is called **convection.**

2 Conduction The transfer of heat between two substances that are in direct contact is called **conduction.** In **Figure 2,** heat is being conducted between the pot and the grate and between the pot and the liquid. When a fast-moving molecule bumps into a slower-moving molecule, the faster molecule transfers some of its energy to the slower one. The closer together the molecules are in a substance, the better they conduct heat. Conduction works well in some solids, such as metals, but not as well in liquids and gases. Air and water do not conduct heat well.

3 Radiation Have you ever warmed yourself by a campfire or felt the heat of the sun's rays on your face? You are feeling the transfer of energy by radiation. Radiation is the direct transfer of energy by electromagnetic waves. Most of the heat you feel from the sun travels to you as infrared radiation. You cannot see infrared radiation, but you can feel it as heat.

FIGURE 2 ....

Heat Transfer
✏ Use the numbers provided in the text to identify each type of heat transfer in the photo.

apply it!

Heat transfer occurs when a warm radiator heats a room.

🔺**Infer** What type of heat transfer could keep the paper in the air? Draw arrows on the image to indicate your answer and explain below.

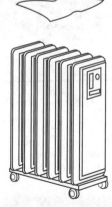

_____

_____

_____

Heating the Troposphere

Heating the Troposphere Radiation, conduction, and convection work together to heat the troposphere. Notice in **Figure 3** how the sun's radiation heats Earth's surface during the day. The land gets warmer than the air. Air doesn't conduct heat well. So only the first few meters of the troposphere are heated by conduction. When ground-level air warms up, its molecules move more rapidly. As they bump into each other they move farther apart, making the air less dense. Cooler, denser air sinks toward the surface, forcing the warmer air to rise. The upward movement of warm air and the downward movement of cool air form convection currents. **Heat is transferred mostly by convection within the troposphere.**

> **Identify the Main Idea**
> Underline the main idea in the paragraph at the left.

> FIGURE 3
> **Heating the Troposphere**
> **Summarize** Describe the process of heat transfer taking place in the diagram at the left.
> _____
> _____
> _____
> _____
> _____
> _____
> _____
> _____
> _____
> _____

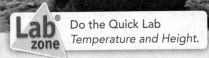
Do the Quick Lab
Temperature and Height.

Assess Your Understanding

1a. Explain Why is convection more important than conduction in the troposphere?

_____
_____
_____

b. Apply Concepts Explain how a convection current can enable a hawk or eagle to soar upward without flapping its wings.

_____
_____
_____

got it?

○ **I get it!** Now I know that heat transfer happens in three ways in the atmosphere: _____
_____

○ **I need extra help with** _____

Go to my science COACH online for help with this subject.

Winds

UNLOCK
THE BIG
?

🔑 **What Causes Winds?**

🔑 **How Do Local Winds and Global Winds Differ?**

my planet diary

EXTREME SPORTS

Windsurfing

Imagine being able to ride a wave at almost 81 km/h—not in a boat powered by a motor but on a board powered only by the wind. That's what windsurfing is all about.

Windsurfers stand on a sailboard, which is similar to a surfboard. But the sailboard has a mast and a sail that the surfer can control with his or her hands. It uses a sail to capture wind and move the surfer along the surface of the water. Jim Drake, one of the first inventors of windsurfing, points out:

"It's the simplicity of standing up so you can adjust your weight and move quickly, as well as actively participate in transmitting the sail's forces to the board."

Discuss these questions with a classmate. Write your answers below.

1. How does wind move the sail?

_____

_____

_____

2. How have you experienced the effects of wind?

_____

_____

_____

▶ PLANET DIARY Go to **Planet Diary** to learn more about winds.

Lab®
zone

Do the Inquiry Warm-Up
Does the Wind Turn?

Vocabulary

- wind • anemometer • windchill factor
- local winds • sea breeze • land breeze
- global winds • Coriolis effect • latitude

Skills

- Reading: Identify Supporting Evidence
- Inquiry: Draw Conclusions

What Causes Winds?

Air is a fluid, so it can move easily from place to place. But how does it do that? **Differences in air pressure cause the air to move. Wind** is the movement of air parallel to Earth's surface. Winds move from areas of high pressure to areas of lower pressure.

Most differences in air pressure are caused by the unequal heating of the atmosphere. Recall that convection currents form when an area of Earth's surface is heated by the sun's rays. Air over the heated surface expands and becomes less dense. As the air becomes less dense, its air pressure decreases. If a nearby area is not heated as much, the air above the less-heated area will be cooler and denser. The cool, dense air with a higher pressure flows underneath the warm, less dense air. This forces the warm air to rise.

FIGURE 1 ....

Moving Air

Windsurfers need wind in order to move across the water. **Explain** How do differences in air pressure cause wind?

_____

_____

_____

_____

WIND

Measuring Wind

Winds are described by their direction and speed. Winds can blow from all directions: north, south, east, and west. Wind direction is determined with a wind vane. The wind swings the wind vane so that one end points into the wind. The name of a wind tells you where the wind is coming from. For example, a south wind blows from the south toward the north. A north wind blows to the south.

Wind speed can be measured with an **anemometer** (an uh MAHM uh tur). An anemometer has three or four cups mounted at the ends of spokes that spin on an axle. The force of the wind against the cups turns the axle. A meter connected to the axle shows the wind speed. **Figure 2** shows a wind vane and an anemometer.

Windchill Factor

On a warm day, a cool breeze can be refreshing. But during the winter, the same breeze can make you feel uncomfortably cold. The wind blowing over your skin removes body heat. The stronger the wind, the colder you feel. The increased cooling that a wind can cause is called the **windchill factor.** A weather report may say, "The temperature outside is 20 degrees Fahrenheit. But with a wind speed of 30 miles per hour, the windchill factor makes it feel like 1 degree above zero."

FIGURE 2 ·······························

Wind Direction and Speed

✎ **Identify** Based on the direction of the wind vane, which direction would your kite be flying? Indicate your answer by shading in your kite.

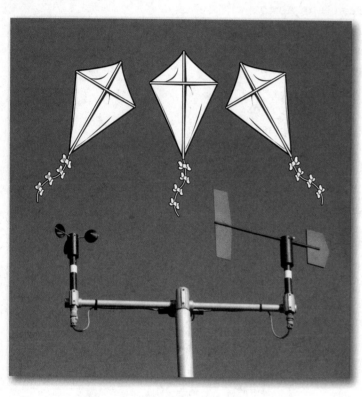

Lab® zone Do the Quick Lab
Build a Wind Vane.

🔑 Assess Your Understanding

1a. Define What is wind?

_____

_____

_____

b. Relate Cause and Effect How is wind related to air pressure and temperature?

_____

_____

_____

got it? ···

○ **I get it!** Now I know that wind is _____

_____

○ I need extra help with _____

Go to MY SCIENCE ⬛s COACH online for help with this subject.

How Do Local Winds and Global Winds Differ?

Have you ever noticed a breeze at the beach on a hot summer day? Even if there is no wind inland, there may be a cool breeze blowing in from the water. This breeze is an example of a local wind.

Local Winds Winds that blow over short distances are called local winds. 🔑 **The unequal heating of Earth's surface within a small area causes local winds.** These winds form only when large-scale winds are weak. Two types of local winds are sea breezes and land breezes, as shown in **Figure 3.**

FIGURE 3 ....

Local Winds

✎ **Relate Text and Visuals** Read about sea breezes. Add arrows to the bottom diagram to indicate how a land breeze develops. Then summarize the process.

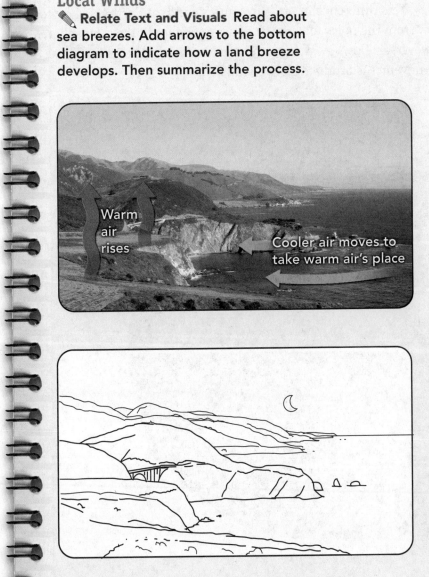

Warm air rises

Cooler air moves to take warm air's place

Sea Breeze During the day, the land warms up faster than the water. The air over the land gets warmer than the air over the water. This warm air is less dense. It expands and rises, creating a low-pressure area. Cool air blows inland from over the water and moves underneath the warm air, causing a sea breeze. A **sea breeze** or a lake breeze is a local wind that blows from an ocean or lake.

Land Breeze At night, the process is reversed. The flow of air from land to a body of water forms a **land breeze.**

_____

_____

_____

_____

_____

405

Global Winds

Global winds are winds that blow steadily from specific directions over long distances. 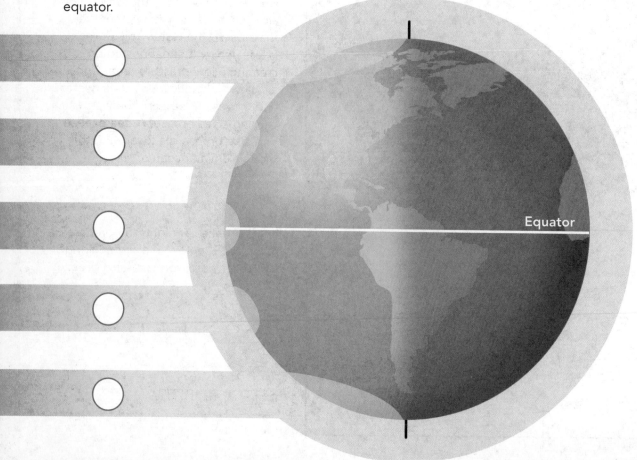 **Like local winds, global winds are created by the unequal heating of Earth's surface. But unlike local winds, global winds occur over a large area.** In **Figure 4,** you can see how the sun's radiation strikes Earth. In the middle of the day near the equator, the sun is almost directly overhead. The direct rays from the sun heat Earth's surface intensely. Near the poles, the sun's rays strike Earth's surface at a lower angle. The sun's energy is spread out over a larger area, so it heats the surface less. As a result, temperatures near the poles are much lower than they are near the equator.

Global Convection Currents

How do global winds develop? Temperature differences between the equator and the poles produce giant convection currents in the atmosphere. Warm air rises at the equator, and cold air sinks at the poles. Therefore air pressure tends to be lower near the equator and greater near the poles. This difference in pressure causes winds at Earth's surface to blow from the poles toward the equator. Higher in the atmosphere, however, air flows away from the equator toward the poles. Those air movements produce global winds.

FIGURE 4 ·······························

Heating of Earth's Surface

✎ **Interpret Diagrams** The angle of the sun's rays causes temperature differences at Earth's surface.

1. Label the areas where the sun hits Earth most directly (M) and least directly (L).

2. **CHALLENGE** Draw a convection current in the atmosphere north of the equator.

Equator

The Coriolis Effect If Earth did not rotate, global winds would blow in a straight line from the poles toward the equator. Because Earth is rotating, however, global winds do not follow a straight path. As the winds blow, Earth rotates from west to east underneath them, making it seem as if the winds have curved. The way Earth's rotation makes winds curve is called the **Coriolis effect** (kawr ee OH lis). Because of the Coriolis effect, global winds in the Northern Hemisphere gradually turn toward the right. A wind blowing toward the south gradually turns toward the southwest. In the Southern Hemisphere, winds curve toward the left.

⊙ **Identify Supporting Evidence** Underline the text that describes how winds blow due to the Coriolis effect.

apply it!

The Coriolis effect determines the direction of global winds.

1 Look at the globe on the left. Shade in the arrows that show the direction the global winds would blow without the Coriolis effect.

2 Look at the globe on the right. Shade in the arrows that show the direction the global winds blow as a result of the Coriolis effect.

3 ⚠ **Draw Conclusions** Based on your last answer, what direction do global winds blow in the Northern Hemisphere? In the Southern Hemisphere?

_____

_____

_____

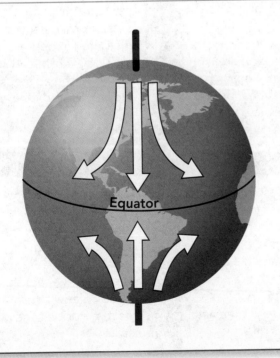

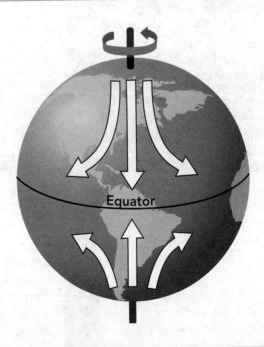

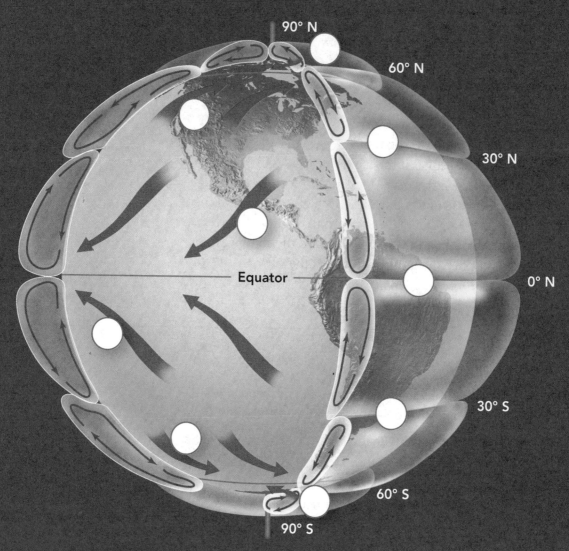

90° N

60° N

30° N

0° N

30° S

60° S

90° S

Equator

FIGURE 5 ·································

▶ INTERACTIVE ART

Global Wind Belts

The Coriolis effect and other factors combine to produce a pattern of wind belts and calm areas around Earth.

✎ Relate Text and Visuals
Match the descriptions of the global winds with their location on the globe.

A **Doldrums** are a calm area where warm air rises. They occur at the equator where the sun heats the surface strongly. Warm air rises steadily, creating an area of low pressure. Cool air moves into the area, but is warmed rapidly and rises before it moves very far.

B **Horse Latitudes** are two calm areas of sinking air. **Latitude** is the distance from the equator, measured in degrees. At about 30° north and south latitudes, the air stops moving toward the poles and sinks.

C **Trade Winds** blow from the horse latitudes toward the equator. As cold air over the horse latitudes sinks, it forms a region of high pressure. This causes surface winds to blow. The winds that blow toward the equator are turned west by the Coriolis effect.

D **Prevailing Westerlies** blow from west to east, away from the horse latitudes. In the mid-latitudes, between 30° and 60° north and south, winds that blow toward the poles are turned toward the east by the Coriolis effect.

E **Polar Easterlies** blow cold air away from the poles. Air near the poles sinks and flows back toward lower latitudes. The Coriolis effect shifts these polar winds to the west, producing the polar easterlies.

Parts of the Atmosphere

How does the sun's energy affect Earth's atmosphere?

FIGURE 6 ···
Earth's atmosphere is a system made up of many different parts.

✎ **Communicate** In the space below, draw a picture or a diagram that helps you understand the relationship between the concepts in the word bank. Explain your diagram to a classmate.

Word Bank	
atmosphere	air pressure
convection	radiation
global winds	

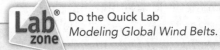

Lab® zone

Do the Quick Lab
Modeling Global Wind Belts.

🔑 Assess Your Understanding

2a. Summarize What causes local winds?

_____

_____

b. Identify What is a global wind?

_____

_____

c. ANSWER THE BIG ? How does the sun's energy affect Earth's atmosphere?

_____

_____

_____

_____

_____

got it? ···

○ **I get it!** Now I know that winds blow locally and globally due to _____

_____

○ **I need extra help with** _____

Go to MY SCIENCE ⬤ᔆ COACH *online for help with this subject.*

The sun's energy affects Earth's atmosphere by _____ Earth's surface, causing differences in _____ that result in _____.

LESSON 1 The Air Around You

🔑 Earth's atmosphere consists of nitrogen, oxygen, carbon dioxide, water vapor, and other gases, as well as particles of liquids and solids.

🔑 Events in one part of the atmosphere affect other parts of the atmosphere.

Vocabulary
• weather
• atmosphere
• water vapor

LESSON 2 Air Pressure

🔑 Because air has mass, it also has other properties, including density and pressure.

🔑 Two common kinds of barometers are mercury barometers and aneroid barometers.

🔑 Air pressure decreases as altitude increases. As air pressure decreases, so does density.

Vocabulary
• density • air pressure • barometer
• mercury barometer • aneroid barometer
• altitude

LESSON 3 Layers of the Atmosphere

🔑 Scientists divide Earth's atmosphere into four main layers according to changes in temperature.

🔑 Earth's weather occurs in the troposphere. The stratosphere contains the ozone layer.

🔑 The mesosphere protects Earth from meteoroids. The thermosphere is the outermost layer of Earth's atmosphere.

Vocabulary
• troposphere • stratosphere • mesosphere
• thermosphere • ionosphere • exosphere

LESSON 4 Energy in Earth's Atmosphere

🔑 The sun's energy travels to Earth as visible light, infrared radiation, and ultraviolet radiation.

🔑 Some sunlight is absorbed or reflected by the atmosphere. Some of the energy Earth absorbs is radiated back out as infrared radiation.

Vocabulary
• electromagnetic waves • radiation
• infrared radiation • ultraviolet radiation
• scattering • greenhouse effect

LESSON 5 Heat Transfer

🔑 Air temperature is usually measured with a thermometer.

🔑 Heat is transferred in three ways: convection, conduction, and radiation.

🔑 Heat is transferred mostly by convection within the troposphere.

Vocabulary
• temperature • thermal energy • thermometer
• heat • convection • conduction
• convection currents

LESSON 6 Winds

🔑 Winds are caused by differences in air pressure.

🔑 The unequal heating of Earth's surface within a small area causes local winds.

🔑 Global winds are caused by the unequal heating of Earth's surface over a large area.

Vocabulary
• wind • anemometer • windchill factor
• local winds • sea breeze • land breeze
• global winds • Coriolis effect • latitude

Review and Assessment

LESSON 1   The Air Around You

1. Which gas forms less than one percent of the atmosphere, but is essential to life?

   a. carbon dioxide   **b.** oxygen

   c. hydrogen   **d.** nitrogen

2. Weather occurs in Earth's troposphere, which is _____

_____

3. Draw Conclusions Why is it difficult to include water vapor in a graph of the percentages of various gases in the atmosphere? How could you solve the problem?

_____

_____

_____

_____

LESSON 2   Air Pressure

4. When density increases, the number of molecules in a volume

   a. increases.   **b.** decreases.

   c. stays the same.   **d.** varies.

5. One force affecting an object is air pressure, which is _____

_____

6. Apply Concepts Why can an aneroid barometer measure elevation as well as air pressure?

_____

_____

7. **Write About It** Suppose you're on a hot-air balloon flight. Describe how air pressure and the amount of oxygen would change during your trip. What would the changes feel like?

LESSON 3   Layers of the Atmosphere

8. The layers of the atmosphere are classified according to changes in

   a. altitude.   **b.** air pressure.

   c. distance.   **d.** temperature.

9. Sequence List the layers of the atmosphere in order, moving up from Earth's surface.

_____

_____

10. The ozone layer is important because

_____

_____

_____

11. Infer Why are clouds at the top of the troposphere made of ice crystals rather than drops of water?

_____

_____

12. Compare and Contrast How are the upper and lower parts of the stratosphere different?

_____

_____

_____

13. Calculate The table shows the temperature at various altitudes above Omaha, Nebraska, on a January day. Suppose an airplane was 6.8 kilometers above Omaha. What is the approximate temperature at this height?

_____

Altitude (kilometers)	0	1.6	3.2	4.8	6.4	7.2
Temperature (°C)	0	−4	−9	−21	−32	−40

411

11 Review and Assessment

LESSON 4 Energy in Earth's Atmosphere

14. How does most of the energy from the sun travel to Earth's surface?

a. convection   b. conduction

c. radiation   d. scattering

15. What are three forms of radiation that come from the sun?

_____

16. Relate Cause and Effect Why do people need to wear sunscreen at the beach?

_____
_____
_____
_____

LESSON 5 Heat Transfer

17. What is the main way heat is transferred in the troposphere?

a. radiation currents   b. reflection currents

c. conduction currents   d. convection currents

18. Compare and Contrast A pail of lake water is the same temperature as a lake. Compare the thermal energy of the pail of water with the thermal energy of the lake.

_____
_____
_____
_____
_____

19. Write About It Describe an example of heat transfer in your daily life.

LESSON 6 Winds

20. The calm areas near the equator where warm air rises are

a. horse latitudes.   b. trade winds.

c. doldrums.   d. polar easterlies.

21. Nights often feature land breezes, which blow

_____

22. Relate Cause and Effect How does the movement of hot air at the equator and cold air at the poles produce global wind patterns?

_____
_____
_____
_____
_____

APPLY THE BIG Q How does the sun's energy affect Earth's atmosphere?

23. Imagine you are sailing around the world. What winds would you expect to find on different parts of your route? Explain the role of the sun's energy in creating those winds.

_____
_____
_____
_____
_____
_____
_____
_____
_____

Standardized Test Prep

Multiple Choice

Circle the letter of the best answer.

1. Which of the following determines the movement of global winds?

   A   humidity and temperature

   B   infrared and ultraviolet radiation

   C   prevailing winds and upper air currents

   D   convection currents in the atmosphere and the Coriolis effect

2. What is the most abundant gas in the atmosphere?

   A   ozone

   B   water vapor

   C   oxygen

   D   nitrogen

3. What happens to air with increased altitude?

   A   temperature increases

   B   pressure decreases

   C   pressure increases

   D   wind speed decreases

4. Which layer of the atmosphere protects Earth from meteoroids?

   A   mesosphere

   B   troposphere

   C   ionosphere

   D   stratosphere

5. Uneven heating of Earth's atmosphere causes which of the following?

   A   global temperature increase

   B   infrared radiation

   C   the greenhouse effect

   D   local and global winds

Constructed Response

Use the diagram and your knowledge of science to answer Question 6. Write your answer on another sheet of paper.

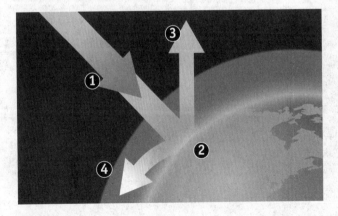

6. Describe the process that results in the greenhouse effect. How does it affect Earth's atmosphere?

Everyday Science

When someone mentions the National Aeronautics and Space Administration (NASA), you might think of missions to Mars or Pluto. However, many of NASA's missions help us understand our own planet. In 2004, NASA launched *Aura*, the third satellite in its Earth Observing System (EOS) program. *Aura* helps scientists study the chemistry of the atmosphere.

The *Aura* mission seeks to answer three questions about our atmosphere.

1. Is the ozone layer recovering? *Aura* helps scientists monitor atmospheric gases, such as chlorofluorocarbons (CFCs), that affect the ozone layer. If the ozone layer does not recover, scientists predict that we will need to learn to better protect ourselves from the sun. In the next 10 years, will we need SPF 100 sunscreen?

2. How do pollutants affect air quality? *Aura* monitors levels of ozone, particulate matter, carbon monoxide, nitrogen dioxide, and sulfur dioxide. The data help scientists understand—and predict—the movement of air pollutants. Are attempts to reduce air pollution working?

3. How is Earth's climate changing? *Aura* checks levels of greenhouse gases in the atmosphere to help scientists build more accurate models of climate change. This way, we will have a better idea of how to plan for long-term climate change. Will you need to invest in a really good raincoat?

Research It Research NASA's EOS program. What are the major satellites in this program? Which Earth systems are they designed to monitor? What discoveries has the EOS program made? Make a display with information and pictures to show what you find out.

Up, Up, and Away!

Bobbing along in the sky, hot air balloons look like a fun way to spend a day. Before the invention of satellites or airplanes, though, scientists used hot air balloons to study the atmosphere. Riding in their balloons, scientists recorded air temperatures and humidity, and even gathered information about cosmic rays. For more than 150 years, balloons were cutting-edge atmospheric observatories.

Research It Find out more about the history of ballooning. How did scientific research using balloons contribute to early space missions? Make a timeline showing balloonists' discoveries.

PLUGGING INTO THE JET STREAM

It's windy up there! About 10 kilometers above Earth's surface, the jet stream winds blow constantly. The winds average 80 to 160 km/h, and they can reach 400 km/h. If we could harness just a small fraction of the wind's energy, we could meet the electricity needs of everyone on Earth!

Scientists are testing designs for high-altitude wind farms. They propose that kite-like wind generators flying above Earth could generate electricity. Cables could then transfer the electricity to Earth.

Design It Research the proposed designs for wind farms in the sky. Make a graphic organizer to show the proposed designs, the risks, and the ways scientists are addressing these risks.

WHAT CLUES CAN PREDICT A STORM?

THE BIG

How do meteorologists predict the weather?

This tornado bearing down on this home in Kansas in June of 2004 reached wind speeds of 254–331 km/h. The state of Kansas had 124 tornadoes that year. Although tornadoes can occur anywhere, the United States leads the world with more than 1,000 tornadoes per year. **Observe** How could you predict a tornado was coming?

_____

_____

_____

_____

_____

_____

▶ **UNTAMED SCIENCE** Watch the **Untamed Science** video to learn more about weather.

12 Getting Started

Check Your Understanding

1. **Background** Read the paragraph below and then answer the question.

"Is that smoke over the baseball field?" Eddie asked Cara in the park. "No," she replied. "It's **fog**." "Ah, water **vapor**," Eddie said. "No," Cara said. "If you can see it, it's water droplets suspended in the **atmosphere**. Water vapor is an invisible gas and can't be seen."

> **Fog** is made up of clouds that form near the ground.
>
> **Vapor** is water in the form of a gas.
>
> The **atmosphere** is the envelope of gases surrounding Earth.

• What does water vapor in the atmosphere look like?

_____

_____

> **MY READING WEB** If you had trouble completing the question above, visit **My Reading Web** and type in *Weather.*

Vocabulary Skill

Prefixes A prefix is a word part that is added at the beginning of a word to change its meaning. For example, the prefix *anti-* means "against" or "opposed to" and is used frequently in science. In the word *antivenom*, the prefix *anti-* is added to the word *venom* to form *antivenom*, meaning "against poison."

Prefix	Meaning	Example
psychro-	cold	psychrometer, *n.*
alto-	high	altocumulus, *n.*; altostratus, *n.*
anti-	against or opposed to	anticyclone, *n.*

2. **Quick Check** Review the prefixes above. Then predict what the word *altocumulus* means using what you know about the prefix *alto-*. After reading the chapter, revise your definition as needed.

_____

_____

_____

_____

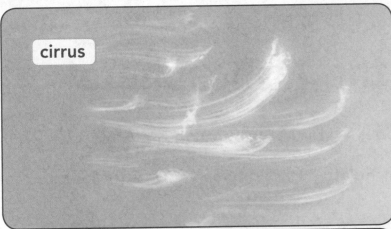

cirrus

precipitation

front

tornado

Chapter Preview

LESSON 1
- water cycle • evaporation
- condensation • humidity
- relative humidity • psychrometer

↻ **Sequence**
△ **Interpret Data**

LESSON 2
- dew point • cirrus • cumulus
- stratus

↻ **Summarize**
△ **Predict**

LESSON 3
- precipitation • rain gauge
- flood • drought

↻ **Relate Cause and Effect**
△ **Calculate**

LESSON 4
- air mass • tropical • polar
- maritime • continental
- jet stream • front • occluded
- cyclone • anticyclone

↻ **Relate Text and Visuals**
△ **Classify**

LESSON 5
- storm • thunderstorm • lightning
- hurricane • storm surge
- tornado • evacuate

↻ **Outline**
△ **Infer**

LESSON 6
- meteorologist • isobar
- isotherm

↻ **Compare and Contrast**
△ **Predict**

▶ **VOCAB FLASH CARDS** For extra help with vocabulary, visit **Vocab Flash Cards** and type in *Weather.*

Water in the Atmosphere

🔑 How Does Water Move Through the Atmosphere?

🔑 What Is Relative Humidity and How Is It Measured?

MY PLANET DIARY

Chile
Uruguay
Argentina
Pacific Ocean
Atlantic Ocean

The Driest Place on Earth

The Atacama Desert in Chile is so dry that there are places where humans have never measured a single drop of rain. But even the Atacama has some moisture in the air. A dense fog along the coastline, known as *camanchaca*, often flows inland from the Pacific Ocean. At one point, the people of the fishing village Chungungo set up nets above the mountains to catch the fog. Water condensed on the nets and then was collected and sent through pipes that brought the water to the village.

 Do the Inquiry Warm-Up *Where Did the Water Go?*

FUN FACT

Write your answers to each question below. Then discuss your answers with a partner.

1. Why did the people of Chungungo need to use nets to catch moisture in the air?

_____

_____

2. What would be one way of collecting water where you live?

_____

> PLANET DIARY Go to **Planet Diary** to learn more about water in the atmosphere.

How Does Water Move Through the Atmosphere?

During a rainstorm, the air feels moist. On a clear, cloudless day, the air may feel dry. As the sun heats the land and oceans, the sun provides energy to change the amount of water in the atmosphere. Water is always moving between Earth's atmosphere and surface.

The movement of water through Earth's systems, powered by the sun's energy, is the **water cycle.** 🔑 **In the water cycle, water vapor enters the atmosphere by evaporation from the oceans and other bodies of water and leaves by condensation. Evaporation** is the process by which molecules of liquid water escape into the air after becoming water vapor. **Condensation** is the process by which water vapor becomes liquid water.

Vocabulary
- water cycle • evaporation • condensation
- humidity • relative humidity • psychrometer

Skills
- ↻ Reading: Sequence
- △ Inquiry: Interpret Data

Water vapor is also added to the air by living things. Water enters the roots of plants, rises to the leaves, and is released into the air as water vapor. Animals also release water vapor into the air every time they exhale.

As part of the water cycle, shown in **Figure 1,** some of the water vapor in the atmosphere condenses to form clouds. Rain and snow fall from the clouds toward the surface as precipitation. The water then runs off the surface or moves through the ground, back into lakes, streams, and eventually the oceans. Then the water cycle starts all over again with evaporation.

↻ **Sequence** Starting with precipitation, list the order of the steps of the water cycle.

_____

_____

_____

_____

FIGURE 1 ·····················

▷ **INTERACTIVE ART** **The Water Cycle**

In the water cycle, water moves from plants, lakes, rivers, and oceans into the atmosphere and then falls back to Earth.

✎ **Summarize** Use the word bank to label the parts of the water cycle.

Word Bank

Condensation

Evaporation

Precipitation

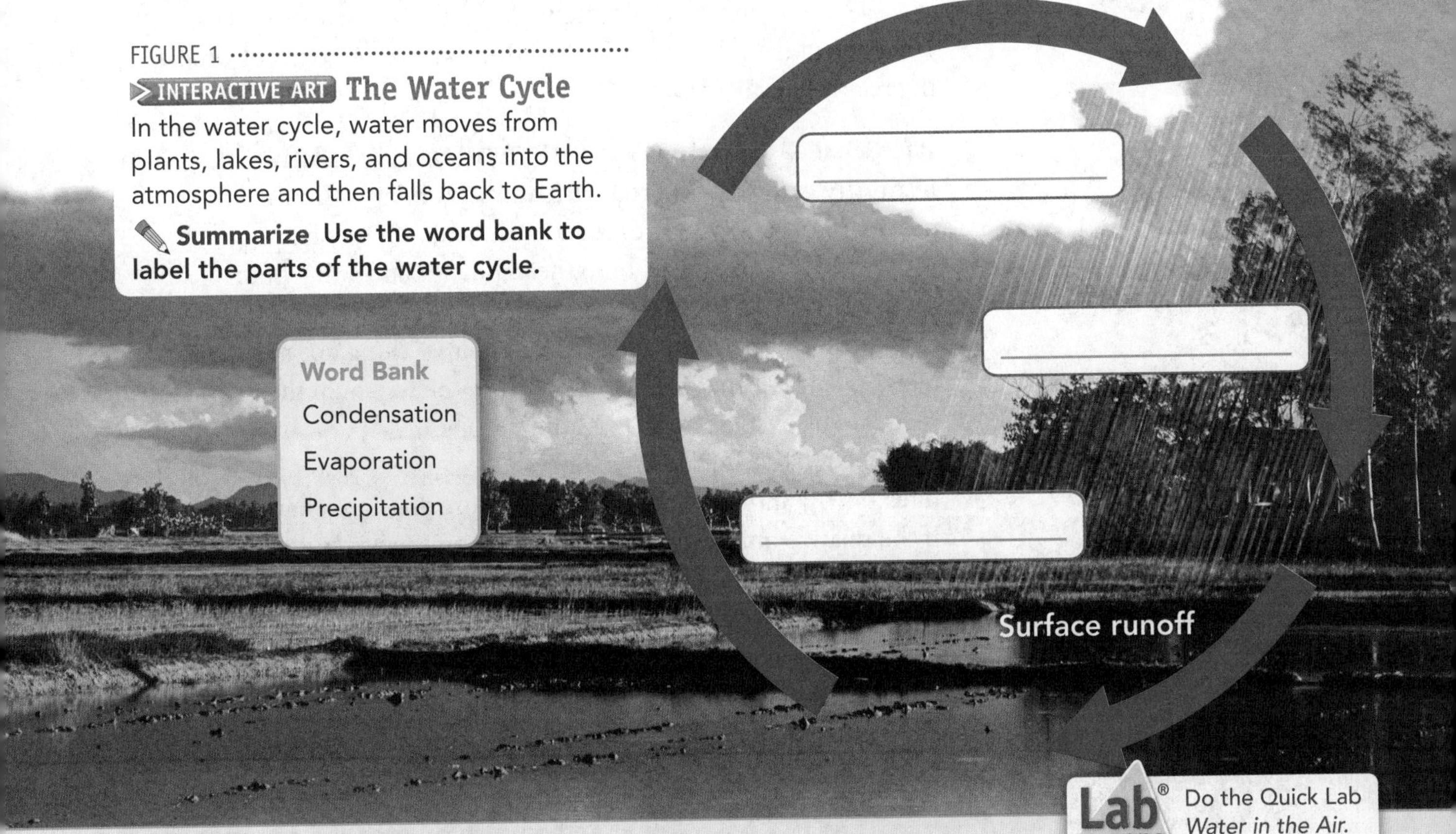

Surface runoff

Lab zone ® Do the Quick Lab *Water in the Air.*

🔑 Assess Your Understanding

got it? ·····························

○ **I get it!** Now I know that in the water cycle_____

_____

○ **I need extra help with** _____

Go to **MY SCIENCE** Ⓢ **COACH** *online for help with this subject.*

421

What Is Relative Humidity and How Is It Measured?

How is the quantity of water vapor in the atmosphere measured? **Humidity** is a measure of the amount of water vapor in the air. The ability of air to hold water vapor depends on its temperature. Warm air can hold more water vapor than cool air.

Relative Humidity

Weather reports usually refer to the water vapor in the air as relative humidity. **Relative humidity** is the percentage of water vapor that is actually in the air compared to the maximum amount of water vapor the air can hold at a particular temperature. For example, at 10°C, 1 cubic meter of air can hold at most 8 grams of water vapor. If there were 8 grams of water vapor in the air, then the relative humidity of the air would be 100 percent. Air with a relative humidity of 100 percent is said to be saturated. If the air had 4 grams of vapor, the relative humidity would be 50 percent.

Measuring Relative Humidity

Relative humidity can be measured with an instrument called a psychrometer. A **psychrometer** (sy KRAHM uh tur) has two thermometers, a wet-bulb thermometer and a dry-bulb thermometer. As shown in **Figure 2,** the wet bulb is covered by a moist cloth. When the psychrometer is "slung," or spun, air blows over both thermometers. Because the wet-bulb thermometer is cooled by evaporation, its reading drops.

If the relative humidity is high, the water on the wet bulb evaporates slowly, and the wet-bulb temperature does not change much. If the relative humidity is low, the water on the wet bulb evaporates rapidly, and the wet-bulb temperature drops by a large amount. The relative humidity can be found by comparing the temperatures of the wet-bulb and dry-bulb thermometers.

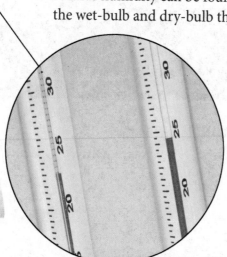

Wet bulb

Dry bulb

FIGURE 2 ·······················

Sling Psychrometer

✎ **Relate Text and Visuals** Read the psychrometer and compare the two Celsius temperatures. Is the relative humidity low or high? How do you know?

_____

_____

_____

_____

do the math!

Relative Humidity

Relative humidity is affected by temperature. Use the data table to answer the questions below. First, find the dry-bulb temperature in the left column of the table. Then find the difference between the wet- and dry-bulb temperatures across the top of the table. The number in the table where these two readings intersect indicates the percentage of relative humidity.

Relative Humidity					
Dry-Bulb Reading (°C)	Difference Between Wet- and Dry-Bulb Readings (°C)				
	1	2	3	4	5
10	88	76	65	54	43
12	88	78	67	57	48
14	89	79	69	60	50
16	90	80	71	62	54
18	91	81	72	64	56
20	91	82	74	66	58
22	92	83	75	68	60

1 Interpret Data At noon the readings on a sling psychrometer are 18°C for the dry bulb and 14°C for the wet bulb. What is the relative humidity?

_____

2 Interpret Data At 5 P.M. the reading on the dry bulb is 12°C and the reading on the wet bulb is 11°C. Determine the new relative humidity.

_____

3 CHALLENGE What was the difference in relative humidity between noon and 5 P.M.? How was the relative humidity affected by air temperature?

_____
_____

Lab zone® Do the Quick Lab Measuring to Find the Dew Point.

🔑 Assess Your Understanding

1a. Review What is humidity?

_____
_____

b. Calculate Suppose a sample of air can hold at most 10 grams of water vapor. If the sample actually has 2 grams of water vapor, what is its relative humidity?

_____

c. Compare and Contrast How are humidity and relative humidity different?

_____
_____
_____
_____
_____
_____

got it? ....

O **I get it!** Now I know that relative humidity is _____

_____ and it can be measured with _____

O **I need extra help with** _____

Go to MY SCIENCE ⓢ COACH online for help with this subject.

Clauds

UNLOCK
THE BIG
?

🗝️ **How Do Clouds Form?**

🗝️ **What Are the Three Main Types of Clouds?**

MY PLANET DIARY

BLOG

Posted by: Chase

Location: Marshfield, Massachusetts

The first time I flew to visit my grandparents, I learned something that really surprised me. When we got above the clouds, I was amazed that something as big as a cloud could float in the sky! I was gazing at the clouds when I asked my mom what they were made of. I was shocked to discover that clouds were mostly fog and mist! I thought they looked like giant piles of mashed potatoes.

Communicate Write your answers to each question below. Then discuss your answers with a partner.

1. Why do you think large clouds can float in the sky?

_____

_____

_____

2. How might you describe what clouds look like?

_____

_____

▷ PLANET DIARY Go to **Planet Diary** to learn more about clouds.

Lab zone® Do the Inquiry Warm-Up *How Does Fog Form?*

How Do Clouds Form?

When you look at a cloud, you are seeing millions of tiny water droplets or ice crystals. 🗝️ **Clouds form when water vapor in the air condenses to form liquid water or ice crystals.** Molecules of water vapor in the air become liquid water in a process called condensation. How does water in the atmosphere condense? Two conditions are required for condensation: cooling of the air and the presence of particles in the air.

Vocabulary
- dew point • cirrus
- cumulus • stratus

Skills
- Reading: Summarize
- Inquiry: Predict

The Role of Cooling
As you have learned, cold air holds less water vapor than warm air. As air cools, the amount of water vapor it can hold decreases. The water vapor condenses into tiny droplets of water or ice crystals. The temperature at which condensation begins is called the **dew point.** If the dew point is above freezing, the water vapor forms droplets. If the dew point is below freezing, the water vapor may change directly into ice crystals.

The Role of Particles
For water vapor to condense and form clouds, tiny particles must be present in the atmosphere so that the water has a surface on which to condense. Most of these particles are salt crystals, dust from soil, or smoke. Water vapor also condenses on solid surfaces, such as blades of grass or window panes. Liquid water that condenses from the air onto a cooler surface is called dew. Ice deposited on a surface that is below freezing is called frost.

Summarize What is the difference between dew and frost?

_____

3 Water vapor condenses on tiny _____ in the air.

FIGURE 1

How Clouds Form
Clouds form when warm, moist air rises and cools.

Interpret Diagrams Fill in the blanks to complete the sentences about cloud formation.

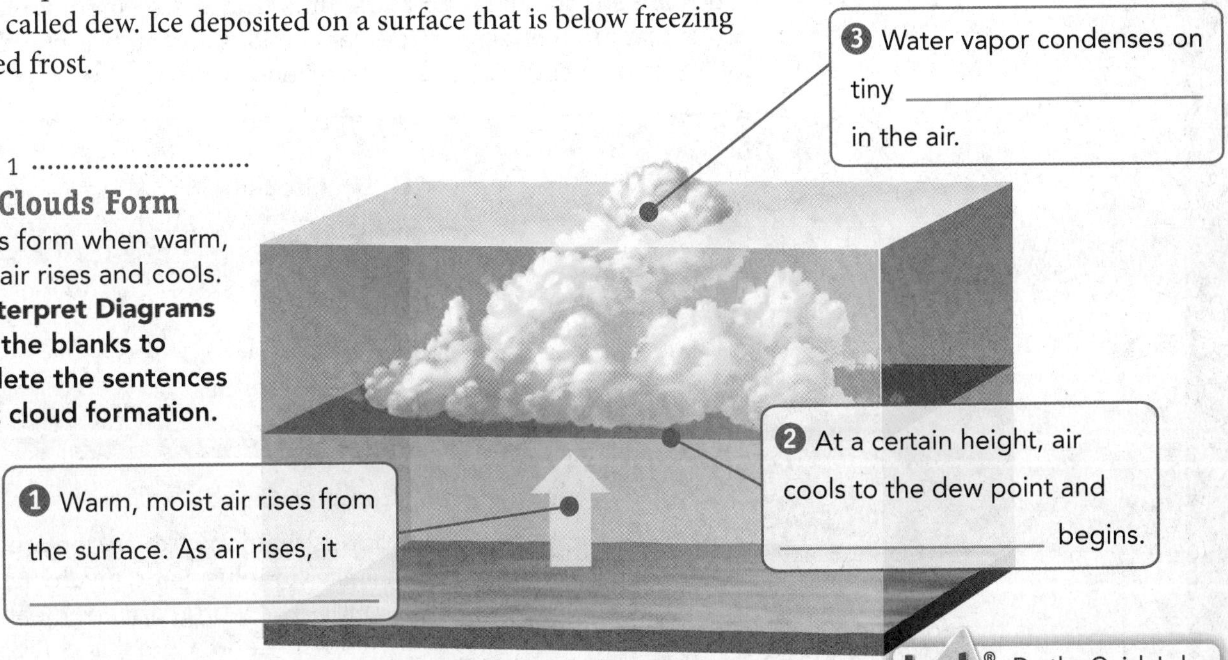

1 Warm, moist air rises from the surface. As air rises, it _____

2 At a certain height, air cools to the dew point and _____ begins.

Lab zone Do the Quick Lab _How Clouds Form._

Assess Your Understanding

got it? ....

O I get it! Now I know that clouds form when _____

O I need extra help with _____

Go to MY SCIENCE COACH online for help with this subject.

What Are the Three Main Types of Clouds?

🔑 **Scientists classify clouds into three main types based on their shape: cirrus, cumulus, and stratus. Clouds are further classified by their altitude.** Each type of cloud is associated with a different type of weather.

(km)

13 —

12 —

11 —

10 —

9 —

8 —

7 —

6 —

5 —

4 —

3 —

2 —

1 —

Cirrus

Cumulonimbus

Altocumulus

Altostratus

Cumulus

Fog

Cirrus Clouds

Wispy, feathery clouds are called **cirrus** (SEER us) clouds. *Cirrus* comes from a word meaning "a curl." Cirrus clouds form at high altitudes, usually above 6 km, and at low temperatures. They are made of ice crystals and indicate fair weather.

Altocumulus and Altostratus

Clouds that form between 2 and 6 km above Earth's surface have the prefix *alto-*, which means "high." The two main types of these clouds are altocumulus and altostratus. These are "medium-level" clouds that are higher than regular cumulus and stratus clouds, but lower than cirrus clouds. These clouds indicate precipitation.

Cumulus Clouds

Clouds that look like cotton are called **cumulus** (KYOO myuh lus) clouds. The word *cumulus* means "heap" in Latin. Cumulus clouds form less than 2 km above the ground, but they may extend upward as much as 18 km. Short cumulus clouds usually indicate fair weather. Towering clouds with flat tops, or cumulonimbus clouds, often produce thunderstorms. The suffix *-nimbus* means "rain."

Fog

Clouds that form near the ground are called fog. Fog can form when the ground cools at night after a humid day.

CHALLENGE What happens to fog after sunrise?

FIGURE 2 ·····················

Cloud Types

There are many different types of clouds.

△Predict **Read about clouds in the text. Then fill in the table to predict the weather that you would expect with each type of cloud.**

Cloud	Weather
Cirrus	
Cirrocumulus	
Cumulus	
Cumulonimbus	
Stratus	
Nimbostratus	

Cirrocumulus

Cirrocumulus Clouds

Cirrocumulus clouds, which look like cotton balls, often indicate that a storm is on its way.

Stratus Clouds

Clouds that form in flat layers are known as **stratus** (STRAT us) clouds, from the Latin word *strato*, meaning "spread out." Stratus clouds usually cover all or most of the sky and are a dull, gray color. As stratus clouds thicken, they may produce drizzle, rain, or snow. They are then called *nimbostratus* clouds.

Nimbostratus   **Stratus**

apply it!

❶ **Observe** Look out your window and identify the clouds you see. What kind of clouds are they? Circle a cloud on the page that looks most like one of the clouds you see.

_____

_____

❷ △Predict From what you know about this type of cloud, what sort of weather would you expect over the next 24 hours? Why?

_____

_____

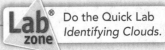

Lab zone® Do the Quick Lab *Identifying Clouds.*

🔑 Assess Your Understanding

1a. Describe Briefly describe the shapes of the three main types of clouds.

_____

_____

_____

b. Classify Classify each of the following cloud types as low-level, medium-level, or high-level.

Altocumulus _____

Altostratus _____

Cirrocumulus _____

Cirrus _____

Cumulus _____

Nimbostratus _____

Stratus _____

got it? ·····························

○ **I get it!** Now I know that the three main

types of clouds are _____

_____

○ I need extra help with _____

Go to my science ⁵ coach *online for help with this subject.*

427

3 Precipitation

UNLOCK THE BIG Q?

🔑 **What Are the Common Types of Precipitation?**

🔑 **What Are the Causes and Effects of Floods and Droughts?**

MY PLANET DIARY

Cloud Seeding

Is that a space weapon you see in this photo? Not at all. This scientist in China is launching tiny crystals of silver iodide into the air to make rain. Clouds often contain water droplets that have cooled below 0°C. But the droplets do not freeze unless they can condense onto solid particles. When the silver iodide crystals reach the clouds, the droplets can condense onto them. Once that happens, the droplets can fall as rain.

Some scientists think that cloud seeding can increase rainfall by 10 percent. Others think that this is unlikely. In the United States, several western states are trying cloud seeding. Dry states, such as Wyoming and Utah, need as much rainfall as they can get.

TECHNOLOGY

Write your answer to each question below. Then discuss your answers with a partner.

1. Why would scientists want to find a way to make it rain?

_____

_____

_____

_____

2. Name a situation when you would want it to rain.

_____

_____

▶ PLANET DIARY Go to **Planet Diary** to learn more about precipitation.

Lab zone® Do the Inquiry Warm-Up *How Can You Make Hail?*

Vocabulary
- precipitation   • rain gauge
- flood   • drought

Skills
⤴ Reading: Relate Cause and Effect
△ Inquiry: Calculate

What Are the Common Types of Precipitation?

Suppose you could control the weather. If you wanted it to rain, you would have to get the water from somewhere.

Water evaporates from every water surface on Earth and eventually falls back to the surface. **Precipitation** is any form of water that falls from clouds and reaches Earth's surface. It is a vital part of the water cycle. In warm climates, precipitation is almost always rain. In colder regions, it may fall as snow or ice. ⌫ **Common types of precipitation include rain, sleet, freezing rain, snow, and hail.**

Rain   The most common kind of precipitation is rain. As shown in **Figure 1,** drops of water are called rain if they are at least 0.5 millimeters in diameter. Precipitation made up of smaller drops of water is called drizzle. Precipitation of even smaller drops is called mist.

Measuring Rain   What if scientists need to measure how much rain has fallen? An open-ended tube that collects rain is called a **rain gauge.** The amount of rain is measured by dipping a ruler into the water or by reading a scale. For rainfall to be measured more accurately, a rain gauge may have a funnel at the top that collects ten times as much rain as the tube alone would without it. The depth is easier to measure. To get the actual depth of rain, it is necessary to divide by ten.

FIGURE 2 ·····················
Rain Gauge
The rain gauge, measuring in centimeters, collects ten times the actual depth of rain that falls.
✏ △ Calculate How much rain has fallen so far?

_____

FIGURE 1 ·····················
Water Droplets
Cloud droplets condense to become larger droplets.
✏ △ Calculate Determine how many times larger the diameter of a large (5 mm) raindrop is than the diameter of a cloud droplet.

_____

_____

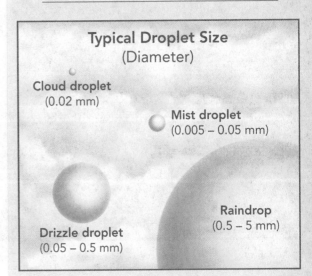

Typical Droplet Size
(Diameter)

Cloud droplet
(0.02 mm)

Mist droplet
(0.005 – 0.05 mm)

Drizzle droplet
(0.05 – 0.5 mm)

Raindrop
(0.5 – 5 mm)

Freezing Rain

On a cold day, raindrops can sometimes fall as liquid water but freeze when they touch a cold surface. This kind of precipitation is called freezing rain.

Snow

You probably know that snow-flakes have an endless number of different shapes and patterns, many with six sides or branches. A snowflake forms when water vapor in a cloud is converted directly into ice crystals. Snow-flakes often join together into large clumps of snow in which the crystals are hard to see.

FIGURE 3 ·

ART IN MOTION Freezing Precipitation

There are four types of freezing precipitation: freezing rain, snow, sleet, and hail.

Review Circle the temperature range in the air and on the ground for which you would expect each kind of precipitation. In some cases, more than one choice may be correct.

Precipitation	Air Temperature	Ground Temperature
Rain	Above 0 °C / At or below 0 °C	Above 0 °C / At or below 0 °C
Freezing rain	Above 0 °C / At or below 0 °C	Above 0 °C / At or below 0 °C
Sleet	Above 0 °C / At or below 0 °C	Above 0 °C / At or below 0 °C
Snow	Above 0 °C / At or below 0 °C	Above 0 °C / At or below 0 °C
Hail	Above 0 °C / At or below 0 °C	Above 0 °C / At or below 0 °C

Hail

A hailstone is a round pellet of ice larger than 5 millimeters in diameter. If you cut a hailstone in half, you would see layers of ice, like the layers of an onion. Hail forms only inside cumulonimbus clouds during thunderstorms. A hailstone starts as an ice pellet inside a cold region of a cloud. Strong updrafts carry the hailstone up through the cold region many times. Each time the hailstone goes through the cold region, a new layer of ice forms around it. Eventually the hailstone becomes heavy enough to fall to the ground. Because hailstones can grow large, hail can cause damage to crops, buildings, and vehicles.

Sleet

Sometimes raindrops fall through a layer of air that is below 0°C, the freezing point of water. As they fall, the raindrops freeze into solid particles of ice. Ice particles smaller than 5 millimeters in diameter are called sleet.

Measuring Snow Rain is not the only kind of precipitation meteorologists measure. Have you ever walked through a large snowstorm and wanted to know exactly how much snow had fallen?

Snowfall is usually measured in two ways: by using a simple measuring stick or by melting collected snow and measuring the depth of water it produces. On average, 10 centimeters of snow contains about the same amount of water as 1 centimeter of rain. However, light, fluffy snow contains far less water than heavy, wet snow does.

apply it!

A rain gauge with a wide funnel collects ten times the actual depth of rain that falls. After the rain ends, the water level is at 15 centimeters.

1 How much rain actually fell?

_____

2 Calculate If snow had fallen instead, how deep would that snow have been?

_____

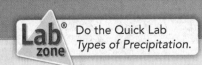

Lab ® Do the Quick Lab
zone *Types of Precipitation.*

🔑 Assess Your Understanding

1a. Define What is precipitation?

_____

_____

_____

b. Draw Conclusions What factors determine if precipitation falls as freezing rain or as sleet?

_____

_____

_____

got it? ....

O **I get it!** Now I know that the common types of precipitation are _____

_____

O **I need extra help with** _____

Go to MY SCIENCE ⓢ COACH *online for help with this subject.*

What Are the Causes and Effects of Floods and Droughts?

In September 2008, just three years after Hurricane Katrina, Hurricane Gustav blasted the coasts of Louisiana and Mississippi. Lakes and rivers overflowed. The result was severe flooding.

Floods A **flood** is an overflowing of water in a normally dry area. The floods caused by Gustav fortunately were not as devastating as those caused by Katrina. Because of the flooding caused by Katrina, more than 100,000 homes and businesses were destroyed, along with many bridges and highways.

Causes and Effects of Floods Not all floods are as severe as those caused by a hurricane.  **Small or large, many floods occur when the volume of water in a river increases so much that the river overflows its channel.** As rain and melting snow add more water, a river gains speed and strength. A flooding river can uproot trees and pluck boulders from the ground. It can even wash away bridges and buildings.

People who live near rivers try to control floods with dams and levees. A dam is a barrier across a river that may redirect the flow of the river to other channels or store floodwaters so they can be released slowly. A levee is an embankment built along a river to prevent flooding of the surrounding land. People sometimes strengthen levees with sandbags or stones and concrete. But powerful floodwaters can sometimes break through dams and levees.

FIGURE 4 ·······

Flooding Caused by Hurricane Gustav
Hurricane Gustav hit the Gulf Coast in September 2008, causing severe flooding. ✎ **Answer the questions below.**

1. **Infer** What sort of damage would you expect to your home if this flood took place in the area where you live?

_____

_____

2. CHALLENGE A "100-year flood" is the flooding elevation that has a 1% chance of happening each year. Why is the name misleading?

_____

_____

Relate Cause and Effect
What causes a flood? A drought?

FIGURE 5
Drought in Texas
In July 1998, a drought hit Wharton County, Texas. This farmer lost about 50 percent of his normal cereal crop to the drought.

Droughts
If you went away for a month and no one was around to water your plants, what would happen to them? They would probably die from lack of water. A long period of scarce rainfall or dry weather is known as a **drought** (drowt). A drought reduces the supplies of groundwater and surface water. A drought can result in a shortage of water for homes and businesses.

Causes and Effects of Droughts
Droughts are usually caused by dry weather systems that remain in one place for weeks or months at a time. Long-term droughts can devastate a region. Droughts can cause crop failure. A drought can even cause famine in places where people must grow their own food. Streams and ponds dry up, and people and animals suffer.

People can prepare for droughts in several ways. When dry conditions first occur, people can begin conserving water. Farmers can grow drought-resistant plants that have been bred to withstand dry conditions. By practicing water and soil conservation, people can ensure that when droughts do occur, people will be prepared for their effects.

Lab zone — Do the Quick Lab *Floods and Droughts.*

Assess Your Understanding

2a. Explain What are two ways to help reduce the dangers of floods?

_____

b. Make Judgments Your community is considering building a dam on a nearby river to reduce flooding. Would you support this proposal? Explain.

_____
_____
_____
_____
_____
_____
_____

got it? ....

○ I get it! Now I know that floods are caused

by _____

and droughts are caused by _____

_____

○ I need extra help with _____

Go to MY SCIENCE ⑤ COACH *online for help with this subject.*

433

Air Masses

UNLOCK THE BIG ?

🔑 What Are the Major Air Masses?

🔑 What Are the Main Types of Fronts?

🔑 What Weather Do Cyclones and Anticyclones Bring?

my planet diary

MISCONCEPTION

Cyclones and Tornadoes

Misconception: A cyclone is another name for tornado.

Fact: Both cyclones and tornadoes are spinning storm systems. Both rotate around an area of low pressure. However, tornadoes cover a much smaller area than cyclones do. And tornado winds reach much higher speeds.

Evidence: Outside the tropics, cyclones can be 1,000 to 4,000 kilometers across. Tropical cyclones, which are powerful hurricanes, are smaller, ranging from 100 to 1,000 kilometers across. But tornadoes are smaller still. Tornadoes range in size from a few meters to 1,600 meters across. Tornado winds are the fastest known winds on Earth. They can reach speeds of 480 km/h, but are usually much slower. Cyclone winds are strong, but do not move as fast as the fastest tornado winds. Tropical cyclone winds rarely reach more than 320 km/h.

Think about the cyclones and tornadoes you have heard about as you answer the following questions.

1. Which kind of storm do you think would cause damage over a larger area, a cyclone or a tornado? Why?

_____

_____

_____

2. Have you ever seen water swirl down a drain? How is it related to a tornado?

_____

_____

▷ PLANET DIARY Go to **Planet Diary** to learn more about violent weather.

Lab zone® Do the Inquiry Warm-Up *How Do Fluids of Different Densities Move?*

Vocabulary
- air mass • tropical • polar • maritime
- continental • jet stream • front
- occluded • cyclone • anticyclone

Skills
↻ Reading: Relate Text and Visuals
△ Inquiry: Classify

What Are the Major Air Masses?

When you have a certain type of weather taking place outside, that's because a certain type of air mass is influencing the weather. An **air mass** is a huge body of air in the lower atmosphere that has similar temperature, humidity, and air pressure at any given height. Scientists classify air masses according to temperature and humidity. ⌐**Four major types of air masses influence the weather in North America: maritime tropical, continental tropical, maritime polar, and continental polar.**

As shown in **Figure 1,** the characteristics of an air mass depend on the temperatures and moisture content of the region over which the air mass forms. Remember that temperature affects air pressure. Cold, dense air has a higher pressure, while warm, less-dense air has a lower pressure. **Tropical,** or warm, air masses form in the tropics and have low air pressure. **Polar,** or cold, air masses form north of 50° north latitude and south of 50° south latitude. Polar air masses have high air pressure.

Whether an air mass is humid or dry depends on whether it forms over water or land. **Maritime** air masses form over oceans. Water evaporates from the oceans, so the air can become very humid. **Continental** air masses form over land. Continental air masses have less exposure to large amounts of moisture from bodies of water. Therefore, continental air masses are drier than maritime air masses.

FIGURE 1 ·····························

Types of Air Masses
Air masses can be classified according to temperature and humidity.

✎ △ Classify Fill in the table. Classify each type of air mass as *maritime* or *continental* and as *tropical* or *polar*.

	Wet	Dry
Warm		
	_____	_____
Cool		
	_____	_____

FIGURE 2 ....

North American Air Masses

Air masses can be warm or cold, and humid or dry. **Classify** Identify the two unlabeled air masses on the page by their descriptions.

Maritime Polar

Cool, humid air masses form over the icy cold North Atlantic ocean. These air masses are often pushed out to sea by westerly winds.

Continental Polar

Large air masses form over Canada and Alaska and can bring bitterly cold weather with low humidity. Storms may occur when these air masses move south and collide with maritime tropical air masses moving north.

Cool, humid air masses form over the icy cold North Pacific ocean. Even in summer, these air masses often cool the West Coast.

🖊 **Type of air mass:** _____

PACIFIC OCEAN

ATLANTIC OCEAN

Gulf of Mexico

Warm, humid air masses form over the Gulf of Mexico and the Atlantic Ocean. They can bring thunderstorms, heavy rain, or snow.

🖊 **Type of air mass:** _____

Continental Tropical

Hot, dry air masses form mostly in summer over dry areas of the Southwest and northern Mexico. They can bring hot, dry weather to the southern Great Plains.

Maritime Tropical

Warm, humid air masses form over the Pacific Ocean. In summer, they usually bring hot, humid weather, summer showers, and thunderstorms. In winter, they can bring heavy rain or snow.

↻ **Relate Text and Visuals** According to the map and the text, which two of the following air masses form over water?

○ Maritime tropical
○ Maritime polar
○ Continental tropical
○ Continental polar

How Air Masses Move

When an air mass moves into an area and interacts with other air masses, it causes the weather to change, sometimes drastically. In the continental United States, air masses are commonly moved by the prevailing westerlies and jet streams.

Prevailing Westerlies The prevailing westerlies, the major wind belts over the continental United States, generally push air masses from west to east. For example, maritime polar air masses from the Pacific Ocean are blown onto the West Coast, bringing low clouds and showers.

Jet Streams Embedded within the prevailing westerlies are jet streams. **Jet streams** are bands of high-speed winds about 10 kilometers above Earth's surface. As jet streams generally blow from west to east, air masses are carried along their tracks.

Fronts As huge masses of air move across the land and the oceans, they collide with each other, but do not easily mix. Think about a bottle of oil and water. The less-dense oil floats on top. Something similar happens when two air masses of different temperature and humidity collide. They do not easily mix. The boundary where the air masses meet becomes a **front.** Storms and changeable weather often develop along fronts like the one in **Figure 3.**

FIGURE 3 ··

How a Front Forms

The boundary where unlike air masses meet is called a front. A front may be 15 to 600 km wide and extend high into the troposphere. ⟳ **Relate Text and Visuals** What kind of weather would develop along the front shown in the photo?

_____

_____

Direction of moving front

Warm air mass

Cold air mass

Do the Quick Lab
Tracking Air Masses.

🔑 Assess Your Understanding

1a. Review What two characteristics are used to classify air masses?

_____

_____

b. Apply Concepts What type of air mass would form over the northern Atlantic Ocean?

_____

c. Classify Classify the four major types of air masses according to moisture content.

_____

_____

_____

_____

got it? ···

○ **I get it!** Now I know that the four major types of air masses are _____

_____

○ **I need extra help with** _____

Go to **my science COACH** *online for help with this subject.*

What Are the Main Types of Fronts?

When you leave school in the afternoon, you may find that the weather is different from when you arrived in the morning. That might be because a front has just recently passed through the area. 🔑 **Colliding air masses can form four types of fronts: cold fronts, warm fronts, stationary fronts, and occluded fronts.** The kind of front that develops depends on the characteristics of the air masses and the direction in which they move.

FIGURE 4 ·······························

▶ INTERACTIVE ART **Types of Fronts**

✏️ **Infer** Identify the type of weather brought by each front as it passes through an area.

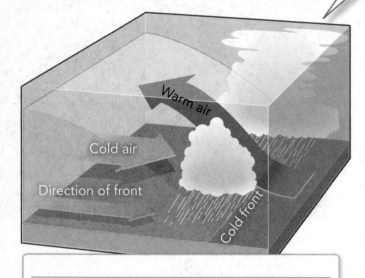

Cold Fronts

Cold air is dense and tends to sink. Warm air is less dense and tends to rise. When a faster cold air mass runs into a slower warm air mass, the denser cold air slides under the lighter warm air. The warm air is pushed upward along the leading edge of the colder air. A cold front forms.

As the warm air rises, it expands and cools. The rising air soon reaches the dew point, the temperature at which water vapor in the air condenses. Clouds form. Heavy rain or snow may fall.

Cold fronts tend to arrive quickly, because their leading edges move along the ground. They can cause abrupt weather changes, including thunderstorms. After a cold front passes, colder, drier air moves in, often bringing clear skies, a shift in wind direction, and lower temperatures.

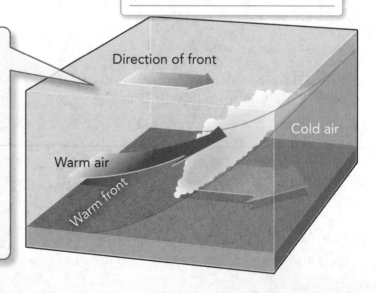

Warm Fronts

Clouds and precipitation also accompany warm fronts. At a warm front, a fast-moving warm air mass overtakes a slower cold air mass. Because cold air is denser than warm air, the warm air moves over the cold air. If the warm air is humid, light rain or snow falls along the front. If the air is dry, scattered clouds form. Because warm fronts arrive slowly, the weather may be rainy or cloudy for several days. After a warm front passes, the weather tends to be warmer and humid.

Occluded Fronts

The most complex weather situation occurs at an occluded front, where a warm air mass is caught between two cooler air masses. The denser cool air masses move underneath the less dense warm air mass and push the warm air upward. The two cooler air masses meet in the middle and may mix. The temperature near the ground becomes cooler. The warm air mass is cut off, or **occluded,** from the ground. As the warm air cools and its water vapor condenses, the weather may turn cloudy and rain or snow may fall.

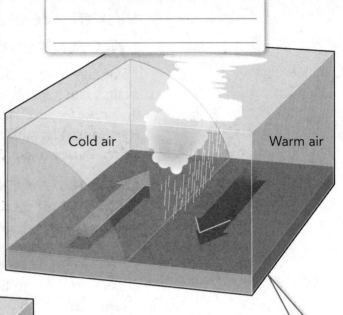

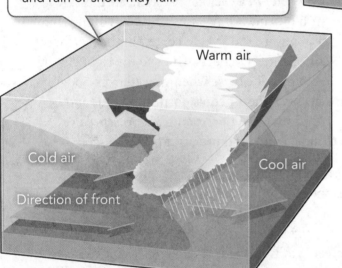

Stationary Fronts

Sometimes cold and warm air masses meet, but neither one can move the other. In this case, the front is called a stationary front. Where the warm and cool air meet, water vapor in the warm air condenses into rain, snow, fog, or clouds. But if a stationary front stalls, it may bring many days of clouds and precipitation.

Do the Quick Lab
Weather Fronts.

🔑 Assess Your Understanding

2a. Define What is a front?

_____

_____

b. Describe What type of weather occurs as a warm front moves through an area?

_____

_____

c. Classify What types of fronts would cause several days of rain and clouds?

_____

_____

got it?

○ **I get it!** Now I know that the four main types

of fronts are _____

_____

_____

○ I need extra help with _____

_____

Go to MY SCIENCE ⬤ COACH online for help with
this subject.

What Weather Do Cyclones and Anticyclones Bring?

As air masses collide to form fronts, the boundary between the fronts sometimes becomes distorted. This distortion can be caused by surface features, such as mountains, or strong winds, such as the jet stream. When this happens, the air begins to swirl. The swirling air can cause a low-pressure center to form.

Cyclones
A circled *L* on a weather map stands for "low," and indicates an area of relatively low air pressure. A swirling center of low air pressure is a **cyclone,** from a Greek word meaning "wheel." You can see a cyclone in **Figure 5.**

As warm air at the center of a cyclone rises, the air pressure decreases. Cooler air blows inward from nearby areas of higher air pressure. Winds spiral inward toward the center. In the Northern Hemisphere, the Coriolis effect deflects winds to the right. So the cyclone winds spin counterclockwise when viewed from above.

As air rises in a cyclone, the air cools, forming clouds and precipitation. 🔑 **Cyclones and decreasing air pressure are associated with clouds, wind, and precipitation.**

Anticyclones
As its name suggests, an anticyclone is the opposite of a cyclone. **Anticyclones** are high-pressure centers of dry air, shown by an *H* on a weather map. Winds spiral outward from the center, moving toward areas of lower pressure. Because of the Coriolis effect, winds in an anticyclone spin clockwise in the Northern Hemisphere. As air moves out from the center, cool air moves downward from higher in the troposphere. The cool air warms up, so its relative humidity drops. 🔑 **The descending air in an anticyclone generally causes dry, clear weather.**

Vocabulary Prefixes How does knowing the meaning of the prefix *anti-* help you remember how an anticyclone spins?

_____

_____

_____

_____

FIGURE 5 ·······························

Cyclones and Anticyclones
✎ **Interpret Diagrams** Label each diagram as either a cyclone or an anticyclone. In each circle, draw an arrow to show the direction of air motion for the system as it would be seen from above.

apply it!

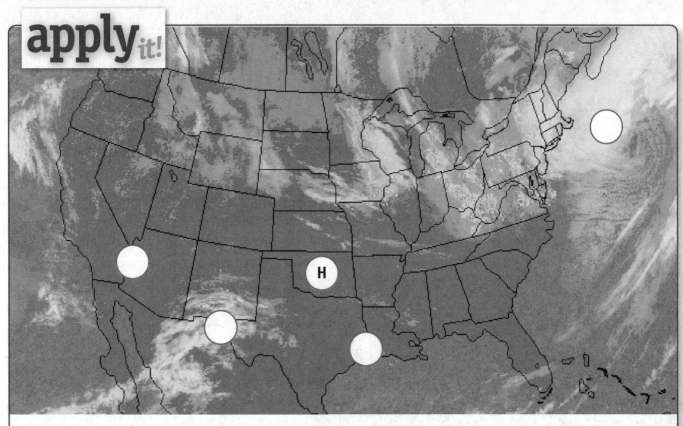

❶ Classify Fill in the empty circles with either *L* for a low-pressure center or *H* for a high-pressure center.

❷ CHALLENGE What information on the map helped you decide if an area's air pressure was low or high?

_____

_____

_____

 Do the Quick Lab *Cyclones and Anticyclones.*

🔑 Assess Your Understanding

3a. Identify What is a cyclone?

_____

b. 🔄 Relate Text and Visuals How does air move in a cyclone?

_____

_____

c. Compare and Contrast What kind of weather is associated with a cyclone? What kind of weather is associated with an anticyclone?

_____

_____

_____

got it? ....

○ I get it! Now I know that cyclones cause _____

and anticyclones cause _____

○ I need extra help with _____

Go to my science ⓢ COACH online for help with this subject.

Storms

UNLOCK THE BIG

🔑 **How Do the Different Types of Storms Form?**

🔑 **How Can You Stay Safe in a Storm?**

my planet DiaRY

DISASTERS

The Blizzard of 1978

In February 1978, a huge blizzard hit the northeastern United States. Weather stations recorded hurricane-force winds, and many cities received record-breaking amounts of snow. The storm hovered over New England, and heavy snow fell for almost 33 hours without letting up.

In Massachusetts, people driving on highways abandoned their cars when the snow became too deep to drive through. Rescuers used cross-country skis and snowmobiles to help evacuate the roads. Stranded drivers returned home any way they could. The governor of Massachusetts declared a state of emergency. He called in the National Guard to clear the roads of snow. It took almost a week until the roads opened again.

Communicate Write your answers to each question below. Then discuss your answers with a partner.

1. What do you think made the blizzard so dangerous?

_____

_____

_____

2. Besides the hurricane-force winds and the roads filling with snow, what other hazards do you think the blizzard caused?

_____

_____

▷ PLANET DIARY Go to **Planet Diary** to learn more about strong storms.

Lab zone® Do the Inquiry Warm-Up *Can You Make a Tornado?*

Vocabulary
- storm • thunderstorm • lightning
- hurricane • storm surge • tornado • evacuate

Skills
- Reading: Outline
- Inquiry: Infer

How Do the Different Types of Storms Form?

The Blizzard of 1978 was one of the most intense storms ever to hit the northeastern United States. A **storm** is a violent disturbance in the atmosphere. Storms involve sudden changes in air pressure, which cause rapid air movements. There are several types of severe storms: winter storms, thunderstorms, hurricanes, and tornadoes.

Winter Storms In the winter in the northern United States, a large amount of precipitation falls as snow. **All year round, most precipitation begins in clouds as snow. If the air is colder than 0°C all the way to the ground, the precipitation falls as snow.** Heavy snow can block roads, trapping people in their homes and delaying emergency vehicles. Extreme cold can damage crops and cause water pipes to burst.

Some places, including Buffalo and Rochester in upstate New York, get a lot more snow than others. In an average winter, nearly three meters of snow fall on these cities due to lake-effect snow, as shown in **Figure 1.** Buffalo is located east of Lake Erie. Rochester is located south of Lake Ontario. In the fall and winter, the land near these lakes cools much more rapidly than the water in the lakes. When a cold, dry air mass moves southeast across one of the lakes, it picks up water vapor and heat. As soon as the air mass reaches the other side of the lake, the air rises and cools again. The water vapor condenses and falls as snow.

FIGURE 1 ·······························
Lake-Effect Snow
As cold, dry air moves across the warmer water, it becomes more humid as water vapor evaporates from the lake surface. When the air reaches land and cools, lake-effect snow falls.

✎ **Interpret Maps** Circle the cities that receive lake-effect snow. In the box on the map, name a city that does not get it and explain why.

Key
Areas of lake-effect snow
0   100 miles
0   100 km

Cold, dry air
Lake Huron
Lake Ontario
Lake Michigan
Lake Erie
Rochester
Buffalo
Erie
Detroit
Cleveland
Chicago

443

did you know?

A fulgurite forms when lightning strikes sand or sandy soil. The temperature of the lightning is so high that it melts the sand and forms a tube made of glass.

Thunderstorms Do you find thunderstorms frightening? Exciting? As you watch the brilliant flashes of lightning and listen to long rolls of thunder, you may wonder what causes them.

How Thunderstorms Form A **thunderstorm** is a small storm often accompanied by heavy precipitation and frequent thunder and lightning. 🔑 **Thunderstorms form in large cumulonimbus clouds, also known as thunderheads.** Most cumulonimbus clouds form on hot, humid afternoons or evenings. They also form when warm air is forced upward along a cold front. In both cases, the warm, humid air rises rapidly, as shown in **Figure 2.** The air cools, forming dense thunderheads with water condensing into rain droplets. Heavy rain falls, sometimes along with hail. Within the thunderhead are strong upward and downward winds known as updrafts and downdrafts. Many thunderstorms form in the spring and summer in southern states or on the western plains.

FIGURE 2 ⋯⋯⋯⋯⋯⋯⋯⋯⋯⋯⋯⋯⋯⋯⋯⋯
How Thunderstorms Form
A thunderstorm forms when warm, humid air rises rapidly within a cumulonimbus cloud.
✏️ **Interpret Diagrams** Fill in the captions noting the direction of the warm, humid air and the cold air.

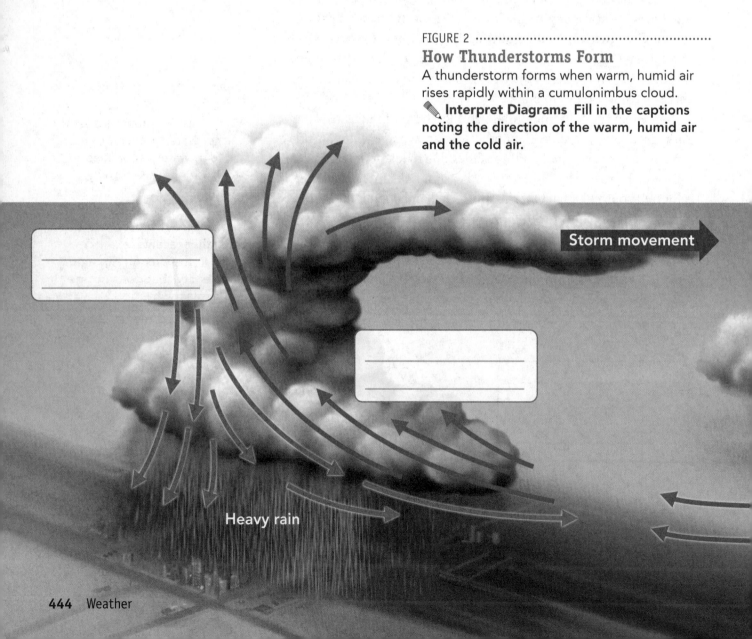

Storm movement

Heavy rain

Lightning and Thunder During a thunderstorm, areas of positive and negative electrical charges build up in the storm clouds. **Lightning** is a sudden spark, or electrical discharge, as these charges jump between parts of a cloud, between nearby clouds, or between a cloud and the ground. Lightning is similar to the shocks you sometimes feel when you touch a metal object on a very dry day. Because lightning is electricity, it is easily conducted by metal.

What causes thunder? A lightning bolt can heat the air near it to as much as 30,000°C, much hotter than the sun's surface. The rapidly heated air expands explosively. Thunder is the sound of the explosion. Because light travels faster than sound, you see lightning before you hear thunder.

Thunderstorm Damage Thunderstorms can cause severe damage. The heavy rains associated with thunderstorms can flood low-lying areas. Lightning can also cause damage. When lightning strikes the ground, the hot, expanding air can shatter tree trunks or start forest fires. When lightning strikes people or animals, it acts like a powerful electric shock. Lightning can cause unconsciousness, serious burns, and heart failure.

Floods A major danger during severe thunderstorms is flooding. Some floods occur when so much water pours into a stream or river that its banks overflow, covering the surrounding land with water. In urban areas, floods can occur when the ground is already saturated by heavy rains. The water can't soak into the water-logged ground or the many areas covered with buildings, roads, and parking lots. A flash flood is a sudden, violent flood that occurs shortly after a storm.

FIGURE 3 ·······························
Lightning Damage
Lightning can cause fires, serious damage, and injuries. ✏️ ◣ **Infer Which is more likely to be hit by lightning, a metal or a wooden boat? Why?**

✏️

Outline After reading the text on this page, complete the outline by adding details about how a hurricane forms.

I. Hurricanes

  A. How a Hurricane Forms

    1._____

    _____

    _____

    _____

    2._____

    _____

    _____

    3._____

    _____

    _____

Hurricanes

Hurricanes A **hurricane** is a tropical cyclone with winds of 119 km/h or higher. A typical hurricane is about 600 kilometers across. Hurricanes form in the Atlantic, Pacific, and Indian oceans. In the western Pacific, they are called typhoons. In the Indian ocean, they are simply called cyclones.

How Hurricanes Form A typical hurricane that strikes the United States forms in the Atlantic Ocean north of the equator in August, September, or October. 🔑 **A hurricane begins over warm ocean water as a low-pressure area, or tropical disturbance.** If the tropical disturbance grows in size and strength, it becomes a tropical storm, which may then become a hurricane.

Look at **Figure 4** to see how a hurricane forms. A hurricane draws its energy from the warm, humid air at the ocean's surface. As this air rises and forms clouds, more air is drawn into the system. Inside the storm are bands of very high winds and heavy rains. Winds spiral inward toward the area of lowest pressure at the center. The lower the air pressure at the center of a storm, the faster the winds blow toward the center. Hurricane winds may be as strong as 320 km/h.

Hurricane winds are strongest in a narrow band around the storm's center. At the center is a ring of clouds, called the eyewall, that encloses a quiet "eye." The wind gets stronger as the eye approaches. When the eye arrives, the weather changes suddenly. The air grows calm and the sky may clear. After the eye passes, the storm resumes, but the wind blows from the opposite direction.

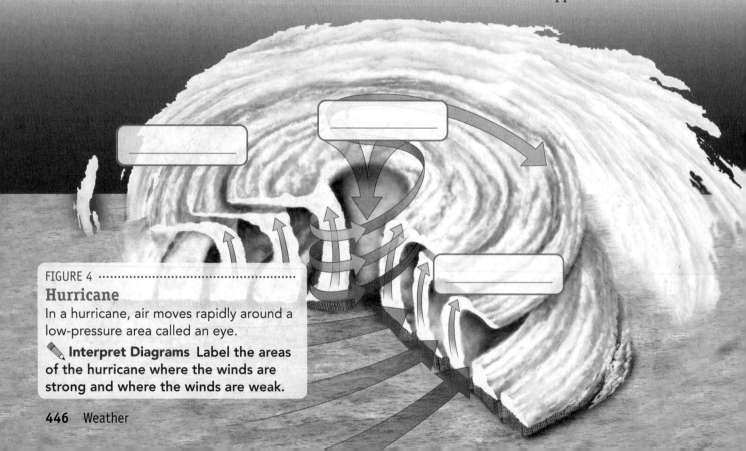

FIGURE 4 ·······

Hurricane

In a hurricane, air moves rapidly around a low-pressure area called an eye.

✏️ **Interpret Diagrams** Label the areas of the hurricane where the winds are strong and where the winds are weak.

August 24, 2005: Katrina approaches Florida.

August 26, 2005: Hurricane Katrina picks up strength over the Gulf of Mexico.

August 29, 2005: Hurricane Katrina hits the Gulf Coast.

How Hurricanes Move Hurricanes can last longer than other storms—a week or more. During that period, they can travel thousands of kilometers. Hurricanes that form in the Atlantic Ocean are steered by easterly trade winds toward the Caribbean islands and the southeastern United States. After a hurricane passes over land, it no longer has warm, moist air to draw energy from. The hurricane gradually weakens, although heavy rainfall may continue for several days.

Hurricane Damage When a hurricane comes ashore, it brings high waves and severe flooding, as well as wind damage. The low pressure and high winds of the hurricane over the ocean raise the level of the water as much as 6 meters above normal sea level. The result is a **storm surge,** a "dome" of water that sweeps across the coast where the hurricane lands. Storm surges can cause great damage, washing away beaches, destroying coastal buildings, and eroding the coastline.

FIGURE 5 ···

Hurricane Katrina

The picture shows the path of Hurricane Katrina.

✏ **Predict** On the picture, draw lines showing the possible paths the hurricane could have taken after reaching land. What happens to a hurricane after it reaches land?

447

Tornadoes

A tornado is one of the most frightening and intense types of storms. A **tornado** is a rapidly whirling, funnel-shaped cloud that reaches down from a thunderstorm to touch Earth's surface. If a tornado occurs over a lake or ocean, the storm is called a waterspout. Tornadoes are usually brief, but can be deadly. They may touch the ground for 15 minutes or less and be only a few hundred meters across. But an intense tornado's wind speed may approach 500 km/h.

How Tornadoes Form Tornadoes can form in any situation involving severe weather. 🔑 **Tornadoes most commonly develop in thick cumulonimbus clouds—the same clouds that bring thunderstorms.** Tornadoes often occur when thunderstorms are likely—in spring and early summer, late in the afternoon when the ground is warm.

Tornado Alley Tornadoes occur in nearly every part of the United States. However, the Great Plains often have the kind of weather pattern that is likely to create tornadoes: A warm, humid air mass moves north from the Gulf of Mexico into the lower Great Plains, and a cold, dry air mass moves south from Canada. When the air masses meet, the cold air moves under the warm air, forcing it to rise. A line of thunderstorms called a squall line is likely to form, with storms traveling northeast. A single squall line can produce ten or more tornadoes.

FIGURE 6 ·····················

> INTERACTIVE ART **Tornado Formation**
About 1,200 tornadoes occur in the United States every year. Weather patterns on the Great Plains result in a "tornado alley."

✎ **Interpret Maps** Pick a state on the map (or your home state) and indicate whether its risk of tornadoes is low or high.

_____

_____

_____

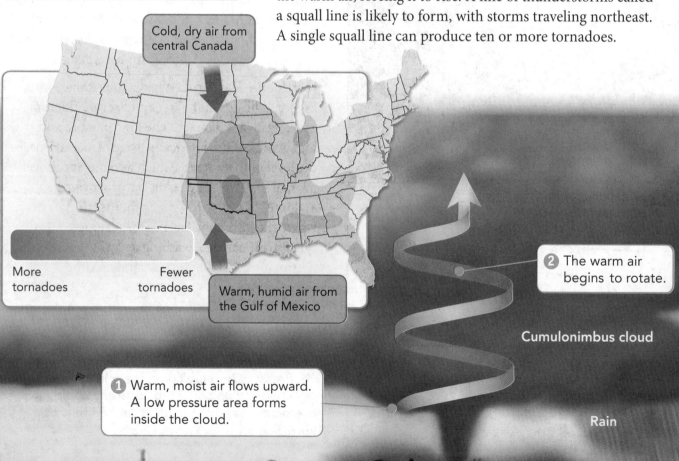

Cold, dry air from central Canada

More tornadoes   Fewer tornadoes

Warm, humid air from the Gulf of Mexico

1 Warm, moist air flows upward. A low pressure area forms inside the cloud.

2 The warm air begins to rotate.

Cumulonimbus cloud

Rain

Tornado Damage Tornado damage comes from both strong winds and flying debris. The low pressure inside the tornado sucks objects into the funnel. Tornadoes can move large objects and scatter debris many miles away. One tornado tore a sign off in Oklahoma and dropped it 50 km away in Arkansas! A tornado can level houses on one street but leave neighboring houses standing.

Tornadoes are ranked on the Enhanced Fujita scale by the amount of damage they cause. The scale was named for the scientist who devised the original scale, Dr. T. Theodore Fujita. As shown in **Figure 7,** the scale goes from light damage (EF0) to extreme damage (EF5). Only about one percent of tornadoes are ranked as EF4 or EF5.

FIGURE 7 ··

Tornado Damage

✎ [CHALLENGE] **How would you rank this tornado damage on the Enhanced Fujita scale? Why?**

_____

_____

_____

Enhanced Fujita Scale	Types of Damage
EF0	Branches broken off trees
EF1	Mobile homes overturned
EF2	Trees uprooted
EF3	Roofs and walls torn down
EF4	Houses leveled
EF5	Houses carried away

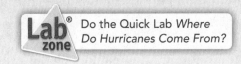

Do the Quick Lab *Where Do Hurricanes Come From?*

🔑 Assess Your Understanding

1a. Identify What is a hurricane?

_____

_____

_____

_____

b. Explain How do hurricanes form?

_____

_____

_____

c. Compare and Contrast How do hurricanes differ from tornadoes?

_____

_____

_____

_____

_____

_____

_____

_____

got it? ···

○ **I get it!** Now I know that the main kinds of storms are _____

_____

_____

○ I need extra help with _____

_____

_____

Go to MY SCIENCE 🔊 COACH *online for help with this subject.*

449

How Can You Stay Safe in a Storm?

A winter storm or a thunderstorm can be fun to watch if you're in a safe place. But you don't want to be near a hurricane or tornado if you can avoid it.

Winter Storm Safety Imagine being caught in a snowstorm when the wind suddenly picks up. High winds can blow falling snow sideways or pick up snow from the ground and suspend it in the air. This situation can be dangerous because the blowing snow limits your vision and makes it easy to get lost. Also, strong winds cool a person's body rapidly. **If you are caught in a snowstorm, try to find shelter from the wind.** Cover exposed parts of your body and try to stay dry. If you are in a car, keep the engine running only if the exhaust pipe is clear of snow.

Thunderstorm Safety The safest place to be during a thunderstorm is indoors. Avoid touching telephones, electrical appliances, or plumbing fixtures. It is usually safe to stay in a car. The electricity will move along the metal skin of the car and jump to the ground. However, do not touch any metal inside the car. **During thunderstorms, avoid places where lightning may strike. Also, avoid objects that can conduct electricity, such as metal objects and bodies of water.**

How can you remain safe if you are caught outside during a thunderstorm? Do not seek shelter under a tree, because lightning may strike the tree. Instead, find a low area away from trees, fences, and poles. Crouch with your head down. If you are swimming or in a boat, get to shore and find shelter away from the water.

Hurricane Safety Today, weather satellites can track the paths of hurricanes. So people now receive a warning well in advance of an approaching hurricane. A "hurricane watch" indicates that hurricane conditions are possible in an area within the next 36 hours. You should be prepared to **evacuate** (ee VAK yoo ayt), or move away temporarily. A "hurricane warning" means that hurricane conditions are expected within the next 24 hours. **If you hear a hurricane warning and are told to evacuate, leave the area immediately.**

FIGURE 8 ·······················

Evacuation Site
In September 2005, the city of Dallas opened up shelters such as the Reunion Arena for people who fled Hurricane Katrina.

Explain What is the difference between a hurricane watch and a hurricane warning?

_____

_____

_____

_____

_____

_____

_____

apply it!

EVACUATION ROUTE

The two signs in the pictures show warnings about possible storms.

1 **Infer** Match each safety sign to the appropriate storm.

2 In the space to the right, draw a sign to show how one could stay safe in a thunderstorm or winter storm.

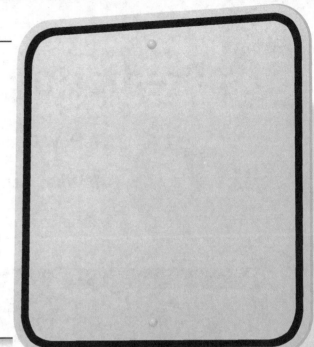

Tornado Safety A "tornado watch" is an announcement that tornadoes are possible in your area. A "tornado warning" is an announcement that a tornado has been seen in the sky or on weather radar. If you hear a tornado warning, move to a safe area as soon as you can. Do not wait until you actually see the tornado.

The safest place to be during a tornado is in a storm shelter or a basement. If there is no basement, move to the middle of the ground floor. Stay away from windows and doors. Lie under a sturdy piece of furniture. If you are outdoors, lie flat in a ditch.

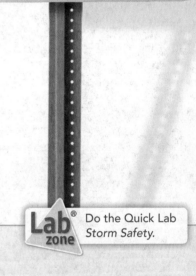

Do the Quick Lab *Storm Safety.*

Assess Your Understanding

2a. List Based on the safety steps, list the four storms from least to most dangerous.

_____

_____

_____

_____

b. Solve Problems How can a community make sure people stay safe in a storm?

_____

_____

_____

_____

got it?

○ **I get it!** Now I know that to stay safe in a storm I should either _____

or, in the case of a hurricane, I should _____

○ **I need extra help with** _____

Go to my science ⓢ coach *online for help with this subject.*

Predicting the Weather

UNLOCK
THE BIG
?

🔑 How Do You Predict the Weather?

🔑 What Can You Learn From Weather Maps?

MY PLANET DIARY

CAREERS

Meteorologist Mish Michaels

Mish Michaels uses computers in her work every day to sort data from weather satellites, radar, and weather stations from all over the world. Then she shares her weather forecasts with Boston television viewers.

Michaels became interested in weather while in kindergarten in Maryland. She watched a tornado damage her family's apartment complex. Since then, she has been fascinated by storms. Michaels went on to major in meteorology at Cornell University.

Michaels is devoted to educating others about weather. She supports the WINS program (Women in the Natural Sciences) of Blue Hill Weather Observatory in Milton, Massachusetts. The program inspires girls to pursue careers in math, science, and technology.

Communicate After you read about Mish Michaels, answer these questions with a partner.

1. Why do you think that meteorologists depend so heavily on computers?

_____

_____

_____

2. What subjects do you think future meteorologists need to study in school?

_____

_____

▷ PLANET DIARY Go to **Planet Diary** to learn more about predicting the weather.

Lab® zone

Do the Inquiry Warm-Up *Predicting Weather.*

Vocabulary
- meteorologist
- isobar
- isotherm

Skills
- Reading: Compare and Contrast
- Inquiry: Predict

How Do You Predict the Weather?

The first step in weather forecasting is to collect data, either from direct observations or through the use of instruments. For example, if a barometer shows that the air pressure is falling, you can expect an approaching low-pressure area, possibly bringing rain or snow.

Making Simple Observations You can read weather signs in the clouds, too. Cumulus clouds often form on warm days. If they grow larger and taller, they can become cumulonimbus clouds, which may produce a thunderstorm. If you can see thin cirrus clouds high in the sky, a warm front may be approaching.

Even careful weather observers often turn to meteorologists for weather information. **Meteorologists** (mee tee uh RAHL uh jists) are scientists who study and try to predict weather.

Interpreting Complex Data Meteorologists interpret information from a variety of sources. **Meteorologists use maps, charts, computers, and other technology to analyze weather data and to prepare weather forecasts.**

Weather reporters get their information from the National Weather Service, which uses balloons, satellites, radar, and surface instruments to gather data.

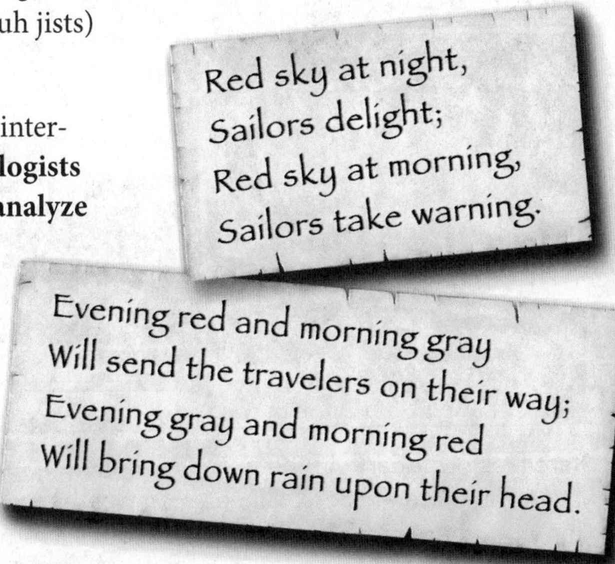

FIGURE 1
Red Sky
Many people have their own weather sayings. Many of these sayings are based on long-term observations.

✎ **Write your own weather poem in the space below.**

Red sky at night,
Sailors delight;
Red sky at morning,
Sailors take warning.

Evening red and morning gray
Will send the travelers on their way;
Evening gray and morning red
Will bring down rain upon their head.

Using Technology Techniques for predicting weather have changed dramatically in recent years. Short-range forecasts—forecasts for up to five days—are now fairly reliable. Meteorologists can also make somewhat accurate long-range predictions. Technological improvements in gathering weather data and using computers have improved the accuracy of weather forecasts.

FIGURE 2 ·······················
Weather Technology

✎ **Explain** why better technology leads to improved weather forecasting.

_____

_____

_____

Automated Weather Stations

Weather stations gather data from surface locations for temperature, air pressure, relative humidity, rainfall, and wind speed and direction. The National Weather Service has established a network of more than 1,700 surface weather observation sites.

Weather Balloons

Weather balloons carry instruments into the troposphere and lower stratosphere. The instruments measure temperature, air pressure, and humidity.

Weather Satellites

Satellites orbit Earth in the exosphere, the uppermost layer of the atmosphere. Cameras on weather satellites can make images of Earth's surface, clouds, storms, and snow cover. Satellites also collect data on temperature, humidity, solar radiation, and wind speed and direction.

Computer Forecasts

Computers process weather data quickly to help forecasters make predictions. The computer works through thousands of calculations using equations from weather models to make forecasts.

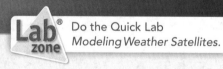

Lab® zone Do the Quick Lab
Modeling Weather Satellites.

⚷ Assess Your Understanding

got it? ··

○ **I get it!** Now I know that meteorologists prepare weather forecasts using _____

_____

○ I need extra help with _____

Go to MY SCIENCE ⬤ COACH online for help with this subject.

What Can You Learn From Weather Maps?

A weather map is a "snapshot" of conditions at a particular time over a large area. There are many types of weather maps.

Weather Service Maps Data from many local weather stations all over the country are assembled into weather maps at the National Weather Service. The way maps display data is shown in the Apply It feature below. The simplified weather map at the end of this lesson includes a key that shows weather station symbols.

On some weather maps you see curved lines. These lines connect places with similar conditions of temperature or air pressure. **Isobars** are lines joining places on the map that have the same air pressure. (*Iso* means "equal" and *bar* means "weight.") The numbers on the isobars are the pressure readings. These readings may be given in inches of mercury or in millibars.

Isotherms are lines joining places that have the same temperature. The isotherm may be labeled with the temperature in degrees Fahrenheit, degrees Celsius, or both.

Compare and Contrast How are isobars and isotherms alike? How do they differ?

_____

apply it!

The tables below show what various weather symbols represent.

❶ **Apply Concepts** According to the weather map symbol below, what are the amount of cloud cover and the wind speed?

_____

❷ **Predict** Would you expect precipitation in an area marked by this weather symbol? Why?

_____

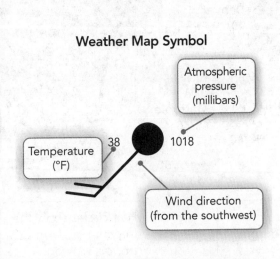

Weather Map Symbol

Cloud Cover (%)	Symbol
0	○
10	◐
20–30	◕
40	◑
50	◑
60	◒
70–80	◕
90	◑
100	●

Wind Speed (mi/h)	Symbol
1–2	
3–8	
9–14	
15–20	
21–25	
26–31	
32–37	
38–43	
44–49	
50–54	
55–60	
61–66	
67–71	
72–77	

Atmospheric pressure (millibars)

Temperature (°F)

38 1018

Wind direction (from the southwest)

FIGURE 3 ....

Newspaper Weather Map

The symbols on this map show fronts, high- and low-pressure areas, the high and low temperature readings for different cities, and precipitation. The color bands indicate different temperature ranges.

✎ **Answer the questions below.**

1. **Interpret Maps** Identify the weather that will occur in Denver according to this map.

_____

_____

2. **CHALLENGE** Can you predict the weather in Denver a week later? Explain.

_____

_____

Newspaper Weather Maps Maps in newspapers are simplified versions of maps produced by the National Weather Service. **Figure 3** shows a typical newspaper weather map. From what you have learned in this lesson, you can probably interpret most symbols on this map. 🗝 **Standard symbols on weather maps show fronts, areas of high and low pressure, types of precipitation, and temperatures.** Note that the high and low temperatures are given in degrees Fahrenheit instead of Celsius.

Limits of Weather Forecasts As computers have grown more powerful, and new satellites and radar technologies have been developed, scientists have been able to make better forecasts. But even with extremely powerful computers, it is unlikely that forecasters will ever be able to predict the weather accurately a month in advance. This has to do with the so-called "butterfly effect." The atmosphere works in such a way that a small change in the weather today can mean a larger change in the weather a week later! The name refers to a scientist's suggestion that even the flapping of a butterfly's wings causes a tiny disturbance in the atmosphere. A tiny event might cause a larger disturbance that could—eventually—grow into a large storm.

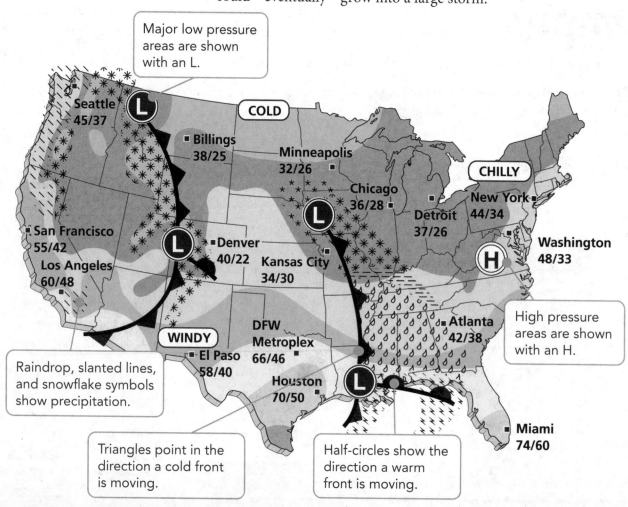

Major low pressure areas are shown with an L.

High pressure areas are shown with an H.

Raindrop, slanted lines, and snowflake symbols show precipitation.

Triangles point in the direction a cold front is moving.

Half-circles show the direction a warm front is moving.

Seattle 45/37 · Billings 38/25 · Minneapolis 32/26 · Chicago 36/28 · Detroit 37/26 · New York 44/34 · San Francisco 55/42 · Denver 40/22 · Kansas City 34/30 · Washington 48/33 · Los Angeles 60/48 · DFW Metroplex 66/46 · El Paso 58/40 · Atlanta 42/38 · Houston 70/50 · Miami 74/60

COLD · CHILLY · WINDY

Predicting the Weather
How do meteorologists predict the weather?

FIGURE 4 ....

> **REAL-WORLD INQUIRY** **Using a Weather Map**

✏️ What would you tell the people of Miami, Kansas City, and Seattle about tomorrow's weather? Explain why.

_____

_____

_____

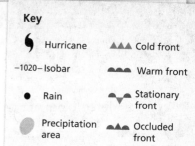

Key

🌀 Hurricane   ▲▲▲ Cold front

—1020— Isobar   ⌢⌢⌢ Warm front

● Rain   Stationary front

⬤ Precipitation area   Occluded front

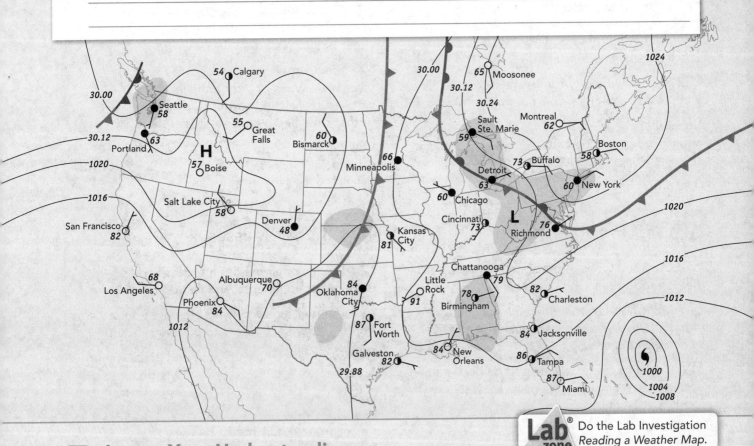

Do the Lab Investigation
Reading a Weather Map.

🔑 **Assess Your Understanding**

1a. Explain What is a weather map?

_____

_____

_____

_____

b. How do meteorologists predict the weather?

_____

_____

_____

_____

_____

got it? ....

⭕ **I get it!** Now I know that standard symbols on weather maps show _____

_____

⭕ **I need extra help with** _____

Go to MY SCIENCE COACH online for help with this subject.

457

12 Study Guide

Meteorologists predict the weather by collecting data about _____,
_____ , _____ , and _____ .

LESSON 1 Water in the Atmosphere

🔑 In the water cycle, water vapor enters the atmosphere by evaporation from the oceans and other bodies of water and leaves by condensation.

🔑 Relative humidity can be measured with an instrument called a psychrometer.

Vocabulary
- water cycle
- evaporation
- condensation
- humidity
- relative humidity
- psychrometer

LESSON 2 Clouds

🔑 Clouds form when water vapor in the air condenses to form liquid water or ice crystals.

🔑 Scientists classify clouds into three main types based on their shape: cirrus, cumulus, and stratus. Clouds are further classified by their altitude.

Vocabulary
- dew point
- cirrus
- cumulus
- stratus

LESSON 3 Precipitation

🔑 Common types of precipitation include rain, sleet, freezing rain, snow, and hail.

🔑 Many floods occur when the volume of water in a river increases so much that the river overflows its channel.

🔑 Droughts are usually caused by dry weather systems that remain in one place for weeks or months at a time.

Vocabulary
- precipitation
- rain gauge
- flood
- drought

LESSON 4 Air Masses

🔑 The major air masses are classified as maritime or continental and as tropical or polar.

🔑 The four types of fronts are cold fronts, warm fronts, stationary fronts, and occluded fronts.

🔑 Cyclones come with wind and precipitation. An anticyclone causes dry, clear weather.

Vocabulary
- air mass
- tropical
- polar
- maritime
- continental
- jet stream
- front
- occluded
- cyclone
- anticyclone

LESSON 5 Storms

🔑 Most precipitation begins in clouds as snow.

🔑 Thunderstorms and tornadoes form in cumulonimbus clouds.

🔑 A hurricane begins over warm ocean water as a low-pressure area, or tropical disturbance.

🔑 Always find proper shelter from storms.

Vocabulary
- storm
- thunderstorm
- lightning
- hurricane
- storm surge
- tornado
- evacuate

LESSON 6 Predicting the Weather

🔑 Meteorologists use maps, charts, computers, and other technology to prepare weather forecasts.

🔑 Standard symbols on weather maps show fronts, air pressure, precipitation, and temperature.

Vocabulary
- meteorologist
- isobar
- isotherm

Review and Assessment

Water in the Atmosphere

1. Infer What is the energy source for the water cycle?

_____

2. math! At 3 P.M., a dry-bulb thermometer reading is 66°F. The wet-bulb reading is 66°F. What is the relative humidity? Explain.

_____
_____
_____
_____
_____
_____
_____

Clouds

3. What type of cloud forms at high altitudes and appears wispy and feathery?

 a. stratus   **b.** altocumulus

 c. cumulus   **d.** cirrus

4. One type of cloud is a nimbostratus, which is

_____
_____
_____

5. Infer Why do clouds usually form high in the air instead of near Earth's surface?

_____
_____
_____
_____

Precipitation

6. What is the name for raindrops that freeze as they fall through the air?

 a. dew   **b.** sleet

 c. hail   **d.** frost

7. Rain and hail are both precipitation, which is

_____
_____
_____
_____

8. [**Write About It**] It is winter where Jenna lives. It's been snowing all day, but now the snow has changed to sleet and then to freezing rain. What is happening to cause these changes? In your answer, explain how snow, sleet, and freezing rain form.

Air Masses

9. What do you call a hot air mass that forms over land?

_____

10. Predict What type of weather is most likely to form at the front shown below?

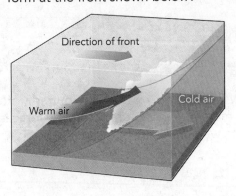

_____
_____
_____

CHAPTER
12 Review and Assessment

LESSON 5 Storms

11. What are very large tropical cyclones with high winds called?

    a. storm surges   **b.** tornadoes

    c. hurricanes   **d.** thunderstorms

12. Thunderstorms usually contain lightning,

which is _____

_____

_____

_____

13. Make Judgments What do you think is the most important thing people should do to reduce the dangers of storms?

_____

_____

_____

_____

LESSON 6 Predicting the Weather

14. On a weather map, lines joining places with the same temperature are called

    a. low-pressure systems.   **b.** isotherms.

    c. high-pressure systems.   **d.** isobars.

15. To predict weather, meteorologists use

_____

_____

_____

_____

16. Apply Concepts How does the butterfly effect keep meteorologists from accurately forecasting the weather a month in advance?

_____

_____

_____

_____

_____

 APPLY THE BIG ? **How do meteorologists predict the weather?**

17. Meteorologists use information from many sources to make predictions about the weather. The weather map shows that right now it is sunny in Cincinnati, but the weather report for tomorrow shows a major snowstorm. Using the map, explain how a meteorologist is able to make this prediction. Include details on weather technology used and the atmospheric conditions that lead to a snowstorm. Make sure to discuss clouds, air masses, fronts, temperature, and pressure.

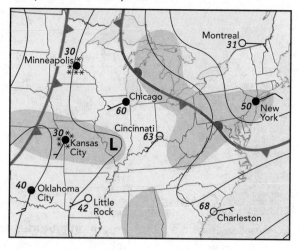

_____

_____

_____

_____

_____

_____

_____

_____

_____

_____

_____

_____

_____

_____

_____

Standardized Test Prep

Multiple Choice

Circle the letter of the best answer.

1. The table below shows the amount of rainfall in different months.

Average Monthly Rainfall			
Month	**Rainfall**	**Month**	**Rainfall**
January	1 cm	July	49 cm
February	1 cm	August	57 cm
March	1 cm	September	40 cm
April	2 cm	October	20 cm
May	25 cm	November	4 cm
June	52 cm	December	1 cm

Which two months had the most rainfall?

A June and August   **B** January and March

C June and July   **D** August and May

2. When the temperature equals the dew point, what is the relative humidity?

A zero   **B** 10%

C 50%   **D** 100%

3. How does the jet stream influence weather?

A by elevating temperature and pressure

B by lowering pressure and humidity

C by reducing temperature and density

D by moving air masses to produce fronts

4. Low pressure over warm ocean water may produce which of the following conditions?

A fair weather

B a thunderstorm

C a hurricane

D a tornado

5. Which of the following map symbols identifies a place likely to experience fair weather?

A isobars

B H for *high pressure*

C isotherms

D H for *high temperature*

Constructed Response

Use the diagram below and your knowledge of science to help you answer Question 6. Write your answer on a separate piece of paper.

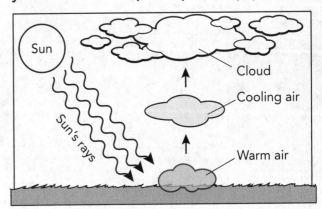

6. Describe the process by which a cloud forms. What two conditions are necessary for this process to occur? How does this process compare to the process by which dew or frost form?

461

The S'COOL Project

Schools around the world are teaming up to help scientists at the National Aeronautics and Space Administration (NASA). Since 1998, students have been helping NASA check satellite observations through a project called Students' Cloud Observations On-Line (S'COOL).

NASA tells schools in the program the date and time when the project satellites will be passing over different regions of the world. When a satellite passes over their school, students observe the clouds in the sky. Students can also measure weather data such as temperature and relative humidity. These observations are uploaded to the project Web site. Then NASA scientists compare the satellite data with the students' observations. This process, called ground truthing, helps scientists determine how accurate the satellite data are.

◄ Students' observations are compared to data collected by satellites like this one.

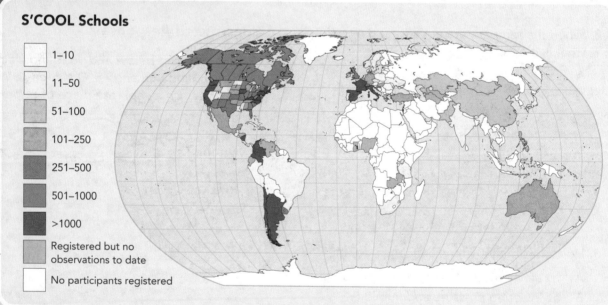

S'COOL Schools

- 1–10
- 11–50
- 51–100
- 101–250
- 251–500
- 501–1000
- >1000
- Registered but no observations to date
- No participants registered

▲ Schools around the world participate in the S'COOL program. The map above shows where they are. If you had to recruit schools to help NASA get complete data, where would you look for schools?

Research It Make a record book. Use it to keep a weeklong log of cloud formations and weather conditions, including photos or sketches, at a specific time each day.

Tracking Hurricanes
with Latitude and Longitude

Do you understand the important bulletin on the computer screen? Lines of latitude and longitude are imaginary lines that crisscross Earth's surface. Because the lines cross, they can help you describe any location on Earth, including the location of hurricanes. A location's latitude is always written before its longitude.

Hurricane Hilda is located in the Atlantic Ocean off the southeastern coast of the United States.

Write About It Assume that Hurricane Hilda is following a straight path. Using the information in the bulletin and the map, try to predict the path the hurricane will take to reach land, and how long it will take to get there. Compare your predicted path with the path of a real hurricane. Evaluate your prediction. Does the bulletin provide enough information for you to make a precise prediction? Write a paragraph explaining why or why not.

ATTENTION

HURRICANE HILDA IS CURRENTLY
LOCATED AT 30°N, 74°W.
IT IS MOVING 21 KM/H NW.
ALL RESIDENTS OF NEARBY
COASTAL AREAS ARE ADVISED
TO EVACUATE IMMEDIATELY.

Hurricane Hilda is currently located at 30° N, 74° W. You can plot the hurricane's location on a map. What information do you need to predict where it will reach land? ▶

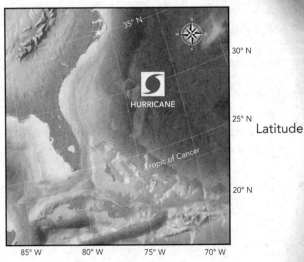

463

HOW IS THIS CLIMATE DIFFERENT FROM YOURS?

What factors affect Earth's climate?

On this icy, frozen island in Svalbard, Norway, the sun shines all day and night from mid-April to mid-August. Winter is long and cold, with three months of complete darkness. The average winter temperature is −12°C. But the average annual precipitation, mainly snow, is only about 20 centimeters. The island is located above the Arctic Circle, and scientists study glaciers, the environment, and meteorology there to detect climate changes.

Develop Hypotheses How might this island climate in Norway be different from your climate?

_____

_____

_____

_____

> **UNTAMED SCIENCE** Watch the **Untamed Science** video to learn more about Earth's climate.

Climate and
Climate Change

13 Getting Started

Check Your Understanding

1. **Background** Read the paragraph below and then answer the question.

Derek walks steadily up the path. As he climbs to a higher **altitude,** the air changes. He can feel the **temperature** get cooler. Soon, he puts up his hood to stay dry. At first the **precipitation** is rain, but as Derek gets higher up the mountain, it changes to snow.

- Why does the precipitation change to snow as Derek gets higher up the mountain?

_____

_____

> **Altitude** is the height of a place above sea level.
>
> **Temperature** is a measure of how hot or cold an object is compared to a reference point.
>
> **Precipitation** is any form of water that falls from clouds and reaches Earth's surface.

> **MY READING WEB** If you had trouble completing the question above, visit **My Reading Web** and type in *Climate and Climate Change.*

Vocabulary Skill

High-Use Academic Words Learning high-use words will help you understand, discuss, and write about the science content in this chapter. These words differ from key terms because they appear in many other subject areas.

Word	Definition	Example
affect	*v.* to produce a change in or have an effect on	The actions of humans *affect* the environment.
distinct	*adj.* different; not the same	Each type of cloud is *distinct.*

2. **Quick Check** Choose the best word from the table to complete each sentence.

- Trees in the rain forest form several _____ layers.

- If you are high up on a mountain, the altitude can _____ how you breathe.

climate

aerosol

greenhouse gas

fossil fuel

Chapter Preview

LESSON 1
- climate
- tropical zone
- polar zone
- temperate zone
- marine climate
- continental climate
- windward
- leeward
- monsoon

↻ **Summarize**
△ **Infer**

LESSON 2
- rain forest
- savanna
- steppe
- desert
- humid subtropical
- subarctic
- tundra
- permafrost

↻ **Identify the Main Idea**
△ **Communicate**

LESSON 3
- ice age
- aerosol
- sunspot

↻ **Identify Supporting Evidence**
△ **Interpret Data**

LESSON 4
- greenhouse gas
- fossil fuel
- global warming

↻ **Ask Questions**
△ **Make Models**

⟩ VOCAB FLASH CARDS For extra help with vocabulary, visit **Vocab Flash Cards** and type in *Climate and Climate Change.*

What Causes Climate?

UNLOCK
THE BIG
?

🔑 **What Factors Affect Temperature?**

🔑 **What Factors Affect Precipitation?**

my planet Diary

MISCONCEPTION

Changes in Climate

Misconception: Only changes in the atmosphere can affect climate.

Fact: As air moves, it's affected by sunlight, cloud cover, oceans, and even landforms such as mountains.

Evidence: The ocean plays a big role in shaping climate. For example, rain that falls in the mountains eventually runs into rivers and oceans. Then water evaporates from the oceans and forms clouds. Water in the oceans also absorbs heat. Ocean currents transfer thermal energy from the equator to cooler areas in the Northern and Southern hemispheres.

Think about your own observations of Earth's climate. Then answer these questions with a partner.

1. How does the ocean affect Earth's climate?

_____

_____

2. How do you think the climate in coastal areas differs from the climate farther inland?

_____

_____

▷ **PLANET DIARY** Go to **Planet Diary** to learn more about climate.

Lab zone®

Do the Inquiry Warm-Up *How Does Latitude Affect Climate?*

Vocabulary
- climate • tropical zone • polar zone • temperate zone
- marine climate • continental climate • windward
- leeward • monsoon

Skills
↻ Reading: Summarize
△ Inquiry: Infer

What Factors Affect Temperature?

No matter where you live, the weather changes every day. In some areas, the change might be as small as a 1-degree drop in temperature from one day to the next. In other areas, it can mean a cold, rainy day followed by a warm, sunny one. Climate, on the other hand, is the long-term weather pattern in an area. Specifically, **climate** refers to the average, year-after-year conditions of temperature, precipitation, wind, and clouds in an area. Both weather and climate depend on the transfer of thermal energy and water into and out of the atmosphere.

Temperature changes cause evaporation and precipitation. The water cycle determines climate patterns. For example, in California's Mojave Desert, shown in **Figure 1,** there is more evaporation than precipitation. The climate there is hot and dry. If you moved west from the Mojave desert toward California's coast, you'd notice a different climate. It would be cooler and more humid. How is this possible? ⌧ **Temperature is affected by latitude, altitude, distance from large bodies of water, and ocean currents.**

FIGURE 1 ···

Climate

✎ **List** Make a short list of words comparing the climate of the Mojave with the climate of the area in which you live.

Mojave's Climate:	Your Climate:

✏ Summarize Read about latitude. Then summarize in your own words how latitude affects temperature.

_____

_____

_____

_____

_____

_____

_____

Latitude
In general, areas near the equator have warmer climates than areas far from the equator. The reason is that the sun's rays hit Earth's surface more directly at the equator than at the poles. At the poles, the same amount of solar radiation is spread over a larger area, which brings less warmth.

Recall that latitude is the distance from the equator, measured in degrees, as shown in **Figure 2**. Based on latitude, Earth's surface can be divided into three types of temperature zones.

The **tropical zone** is the area near the equator, between about 23.5° north latitude and 23.5° south latitude. It receives direct or nearly direct sunlight all year, making climates there warm.

In contrast, the sun's rays always strike at a lower angle near the North and South poles, making climates there cold. These **polar zones** extend from about 66.5° to 90° north and 66.5° to 90° south latitudes.

Between the tropical zones and the polar zones are the **temperate zones.** In summer, the sun's rays strike the temperate zones more directly. In winter, the sun's rays strike at a lower angle. As a result, the weather in the temperate zones ranges from warm or hot in summer to cool or cold in winter.

Key

☐ _____

☐ _____

☐ _____

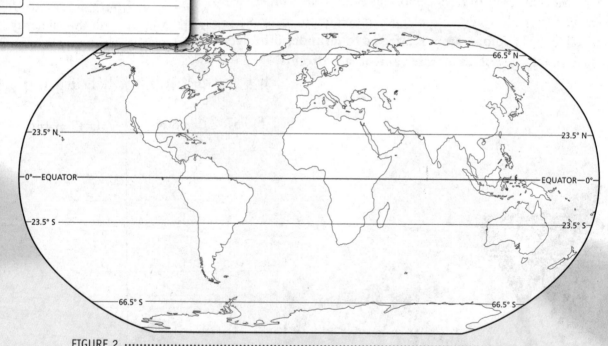

FIGURE 2 ·······························

Latitude and Temperature
✏ **Use the map above to complete the activity.**

1. **Relate Text and Visuals** Shade in the three temperature zones differently on the map and complete the key.

2. **Observe** In which temperature zone is most of the United States located?

_____

Altitude Standing at 6,309 meters high, Mount Chimborazo is Ecuador's tallest mountain. Its peak is covered in glaciers year-round, as shown in **Figure 3.** But at 1° south latitude, Chimborazo is located very close to the equator. How does the top of this mountain stay so cold?

In the case of high mountains, altitude is a more important climate factor than latitude. In the troposphere, temperature decreases about 6.5°C for every 1-kilometer increase in altitude. As a result, many mountainous areas have cooler climates than the lower areas around them. Chimborazo is just over 6 kilometers high. The air at the top of this mountain is about 39°C colder than the air at sea level at the same latitude.

did you

know?................

A species of *Polylepsis* tree in Bolivia grows at the highest altitude of any tree in the world—up to 5,200 m.

FIGURE 3 ··

▶ VIRUAL LAB **Altitude and Temperature**

🖉 **Read about altitude and answer these questions.**

1. **Name** Use **Figure 2** to identify the temperature zone in which Ecuador is located. (*Hint:* Ecuador is in northwestern South America.)

_____

2. **Calculate** If it was 30°C at the base of Mount Chimborazo, about how cold would it be at the peak?

_____

3. **Interpret Photos** Use the photo below to compare the conditions at the base of Mount Chimborazo with the conditions at the peak.

_____

_____

_____

_____

Vocabulary High-Use Academic Words Complete the sentence to show you understand the meaning of the word *affect*. The ocean is too far from the middle of North America to _____

Distance From Large Bodies of Water

Oceans or large lakes can also affect temperatures. Oceans greatly moderate, or make less extreme, the temperatures of nearby land. Water heats up about five times more slowly than land. It also cools down more slowly. Therefore, winds off the ocean often prevent extremes of hot and cold in coastal regions. Much of the west coasts of North America, South America, and Europe have **marine climates.** These climates have relatively mild winters and cool summers.

The centers of North America and Asia are too far inland to be warmed or cooled by the ocean. Most of Canada, Russia, and the central United States have **continental climates.** These climates reach more extreme temperatures than marine climates. Winters are cold, while summers are warm or hot.

apply it!

Alaska is about twice the size of Texas. Factors influencing temperature, such as distance from large bodies of water, affect this big state in different ways.

1 Observe Where are Juneau and Fairbanks located in relation to each other?

_____

_____

_____

2 Infer Which climate data do you think describe Juneau, A or B? Which describe Fairbanks, A or B? Why?

_____

_____

_____

_____

_____

_____

_____

_____

	City A	City B	City C
Average Number of Days Below −17°C (0°F)	113	6	168
Average Number of Days Above 18°C (65°F)	82	40	2

3 CHALLENGE Which city on the map do you think represents the set of data for City C? Why?

_____

_____

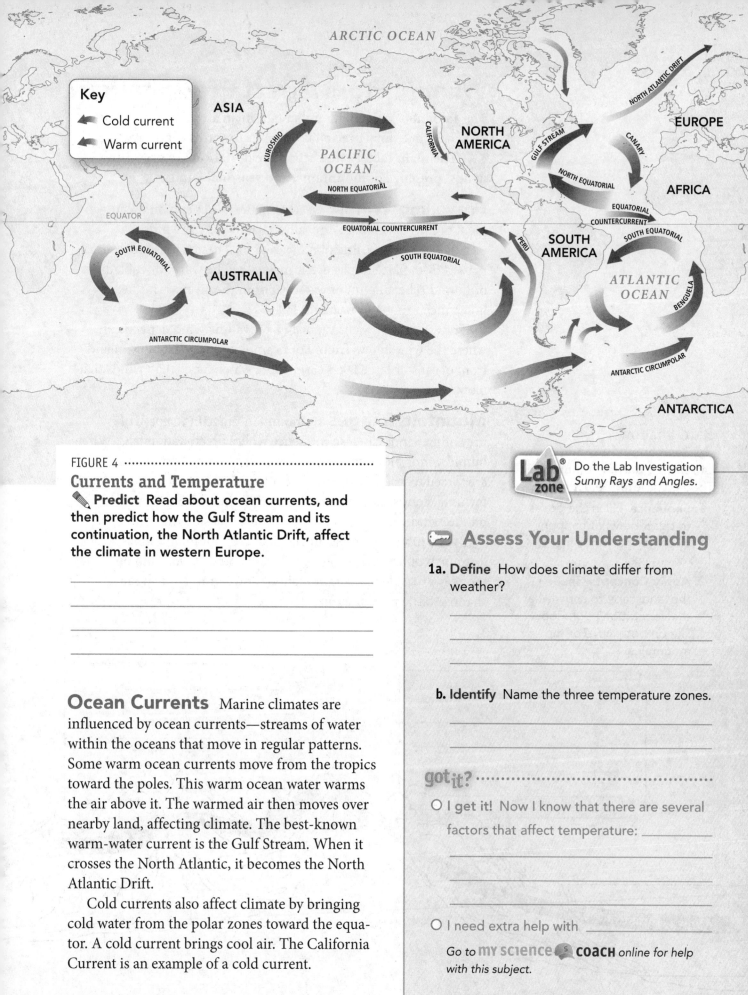

Key
← Cold current
← Warm current

ASIA

KUROSHIO

PACIFIC OCEAN

CALIFORNIA

NORTH AMERICA

GULF STREAM

NORTH ATLANTIC DRIFT

EUROPE

CANARY

NORTH EQUATORIAL

NORTH EQUATORIAL

AFRICA

EQUATOR

EQUATORIAL COUNTERCURRENT

EQUATORIAL COUNTERCURRENT

SOUTH EQUATORIAL

AUSTRALIA

SOUTH EQUATORIAL

PERU

SOUTH AMERICA

SOUTH EQUATORIAL

ATLANTIC OCEAN

BENGUELA

ANTARCTIC CIRCUMPOLAR

ANTARCTIC CIRCUMPOLAR

ANTARCTICA

FIGURE 4 ·······················

Currents and Temperature

✎ **Predict** Read about ocean currents, and then predict how the Gulf Stream and its continuation, the North Atlantic Drift, affect the climate in western Europe.

_____
_____
_____
_____

Ocean Currents
Marine climates are influenced by ocean currents—streams of water within the oceans that move in regular patterns. Some warm ocean currents move from the tropics toward the poles. This warm ocean water warms the air above it. The warmed air then moves over nearby land, affecting climate. The best-known warm-water current is the Gulf Stream. When it crosses the North Atlantic, it becomes the North Atlantic Drift.

Cold currents also affect climate by bringing cold water from the polar zones toward the equator. A cold current brings cool air. The California Current is an example of a cold current.

Lab zone ® Do the Lab Investigation *Sunny Rays and Angles.*

🔑 Assess Your Understanding

1a. Define How does climate differ from weather?

_____
_____
_____

b. Identify Name the three temperature zones.

_____
_____

got it? ·······························

○ **I get it!** Now I know that there are several factors that affect temperature: _____

_____
_____

○ **I need extra help with** _____

Go to MY SCIENCE ᷂ˢ COACH *online for help with this subject.*

What Factors Affect Precipitation?

The amount of precipitation that falls in an area can vary yearly. But, over time, total precipitation tends toward a yearly average. 🔑 **The main factors that affect precipitation are prevailing winds, presence of mountains, and seasonal winds.**

Prevailing Winds Weather patterns depend on the movement of huge air masses. Prevailing winds are the winds that usually blow in one direction in a region. These winds move air masses from place to place. Air masses can be warm or cool, dry or humid. The amount of water vapor in the air mass influences how much rain or snow might fall.

The amount of water vapor in a prevailing wind depends on where the wind blows from. For example, winds that blow inland from oceans or large lakes carry more water vapor than winds that blow from over land.

Mountain Ranges A mountain range in the path of prevailing winds can also influence where precipitation falls. When humid winds blow from the ocean toward coastal mountains, they are forced to rise. The rising air cools and its water vapor condenses, forming clouds, as shown in **Figure 5**. Rain or snow falls on the **windward** side of the mountains, the side the wind hits.

By the time the air has moved over the mountains, it has lost much of its water vapor, so it's cool and dry. The land on the **leeward** side of the mountains—downwind—is in a rain shadow. Little precipitation falls there.

FIGURE 5 ·······················

Rain Shadow

✎ **Read about how mountains can form a barrier to humid air. Then complete the activity.**

1. **Sequence** Fill in the boxes to describe what happens as prevailing winds meet mountains.

2. **Apply Concepts** Shade in the landscape to show what the vegetation might look like on both sides of the mountains.

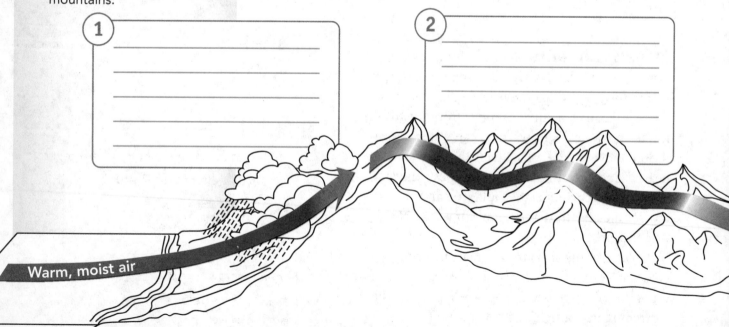

Warm, moist air

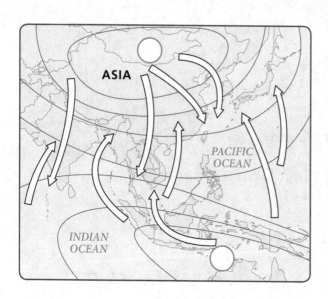

FIGURE 6

Monsoons

Monsoons are seasonal winds that bring drastic changes in precipitation.

✎ **Read about seasonal winds below, and then complete the activity.**

1. **Relate Cause and Effect** Shade in the arrows that indicate a summer monsoon.

2. **Identify** Write an *H* or *L* in the circles on the map to indicate the areas of high pressure and low pressure during the summer monsoon.

Seasonal Winds In some parts of the world, a seasonal change in wind patterns can affect precipitation. Sea and land breezes over a large region that change direction with the seasons are called **monsoons.** What produces a monsoon? In the summer in South and Southeast Asia, the land gradually gets warmer than the ocean. A wind blows inland from the ocean all summer, even at night. Winds blow from areas of high pressure to areas of low pressure. The air blowing from the ocean during this season is very warm and humid. As the humid air rises over the land, the air cools. This cooling air causes water vapor to condense into clouds, producing heavy rains. In winter, the land becomes colder than the ocean. A wind blows from the land to the ocean. These winds carry little moisture.

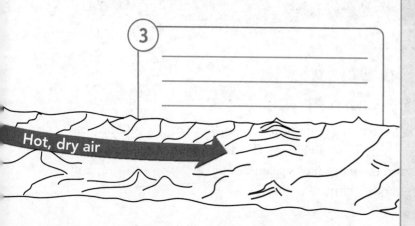

Lab zone Do the Quick Lab *Inferring United States Precipitation Patterns.*

🔑 Assess Your Understanding

2a. Define What is the leeward side of a mountain?

_____

b. Summarize How do prevailing winds affect precipitation?

_____

got it?

I get it! Now I know three factors affect precipitation: _____

I need extra help with _____

Go to **my science COACH** *online for help with this subject.*

475

Climate Regions

How Do Scientists Classify Climates?

What Are the Six Main Climate Regions?

MY PLANET DIARY

Rain, Rain Every Day

When you think of Hawaii, warm, sunny days spent surfing monster waves are probably the first thing that comes to mind. But Hawaii gets its fair share of rain, too. In fact, it's home to one of the wettest places on Earth—Mount Waialeale.

A lush mountain on the island of Kauai, Waialeale gets an average of 1,143 centimeters, or 450 inches, of rain every year. That's more than an inch of rain every day! Yet nearby parts of Kauai get only 10 inches of rain per year.

FUN FACT

Read about one of the rainiest places in the world and answer the questions.

1. Why do you think Mount Waialeale gets so much rain?

_____

_____

2. How much rain does your area get compared with Mount Waialeale?

_____

_____

_____

> PLANET DIARY Go to **Planet Diary** to learn more about climate regions.

 Do the Inquiry Warm-Up *How Do Climates Differ?*

How Do Scientists Classify Climates?

Suppose you lived at the equator for an entire year. It would be very different from where you live now. The daily weather, the amount of sunlight, and the pattern of seasons would all be new to you. You would be in another climate region.

Vocabulary

- rain forest • savanna • steppe • desert
- humid subtropical • subarctic • tundra
- permafrost

Skills

⟳ **Reading:** Identify the Main Idea

△ **Inquiry:** Communicate

🔑 **Scientists classify climates according to two major factors: temperature and precipitation.** They use a system developed around 1900 by Wladimir Köppen (KEP un). Besides temperature and precipitation, Köppen also looked at the distinct vegetation in different areas. This system identifies broad climate regions, each of which has smaller subdivisions.

FIGURE 1 ....

Reading Climate Graphs

✏ **Interpret Graphs** A graph of temperature can be combined with a graph of precipitation to form a climate graph. The graphs below show climate data for Makindu, Kenya.

1. Look at the first graph. What is the average temperature in July?

_____

2. Look at the second graph. What is the average precipitation in July?

_____

3. Look at the climate graph. How much rain does Makindu get in its hottest month?

_____

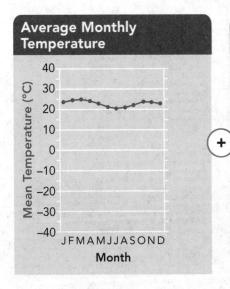

Average Monthly Temperature

+

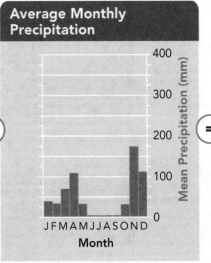

Average Monthly Precipitation

=

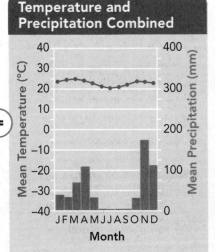

Temperature and Precipitation Combined

Lab zone Do the Quick Lab *Classifying Climates.*

🔑 Assess Your Understanding

got it? ....

○ **I get it!** Now I know that climates are classified using _____

_____

○ **I need extra help with** _____

Go to my science s **COACH** *online for help with this subject.*

477

What Are the Six Main Climate Regions?

Maps can show boundaries between climate regions. But generally, in the real world, no clear boundaries mark where one climate region ends and another begins. In most cases, each region blends gradually into the next. 🔑 **The six main climate regions are tropical rainy, dry, temperate marine, temperate continental, polar, and highlands.** These climate regions are shown in **Figure 2**.

Key

Tropical Rainy: Temperature always 18°C or above
- Tropical wet
- Tropical wet-and-dry

Dry: Occurs wherever potential evaporation is greater than precipitation; may be hot or cold
- Semiarid
- Arid

Temperate Marine: Averages 10°C or above in warmest month, between –3°C and 18°C in the coldest month
- Mediterranean
- Humid subtropical
- Marine west coast

Temperate Continental: Average temperature 10°C or above in the warmest month, –3°C or below in the coldest month
- Humid continental
- Subarctic

Polar: Average temperature below 10°C in the warmest month
- Tundra
- Ice cap

Highlands: Generally cooler and wetter than nearby lowlands; temperature decreasing with altitude
- Highlands

FIGURE 2 ·······························

Climate Regions

✎ **Identify** You've been selected by an Olympic committee to visit six cities this July and to choose one to host the next summer games.

1. On the map, draw a line connecting the stops on your itinerary.
2. List each city and its climate region.

1. Location: _____
   Climate Region: _____
2. Location: _____
   Climate Region: _____
3. Location: _____
   Climate Region: _____
4. Location: _____
   Climate Region: _____
5. Location: _____
   Climate Region: _____
   6. Location: _____
      Climate Region: _____

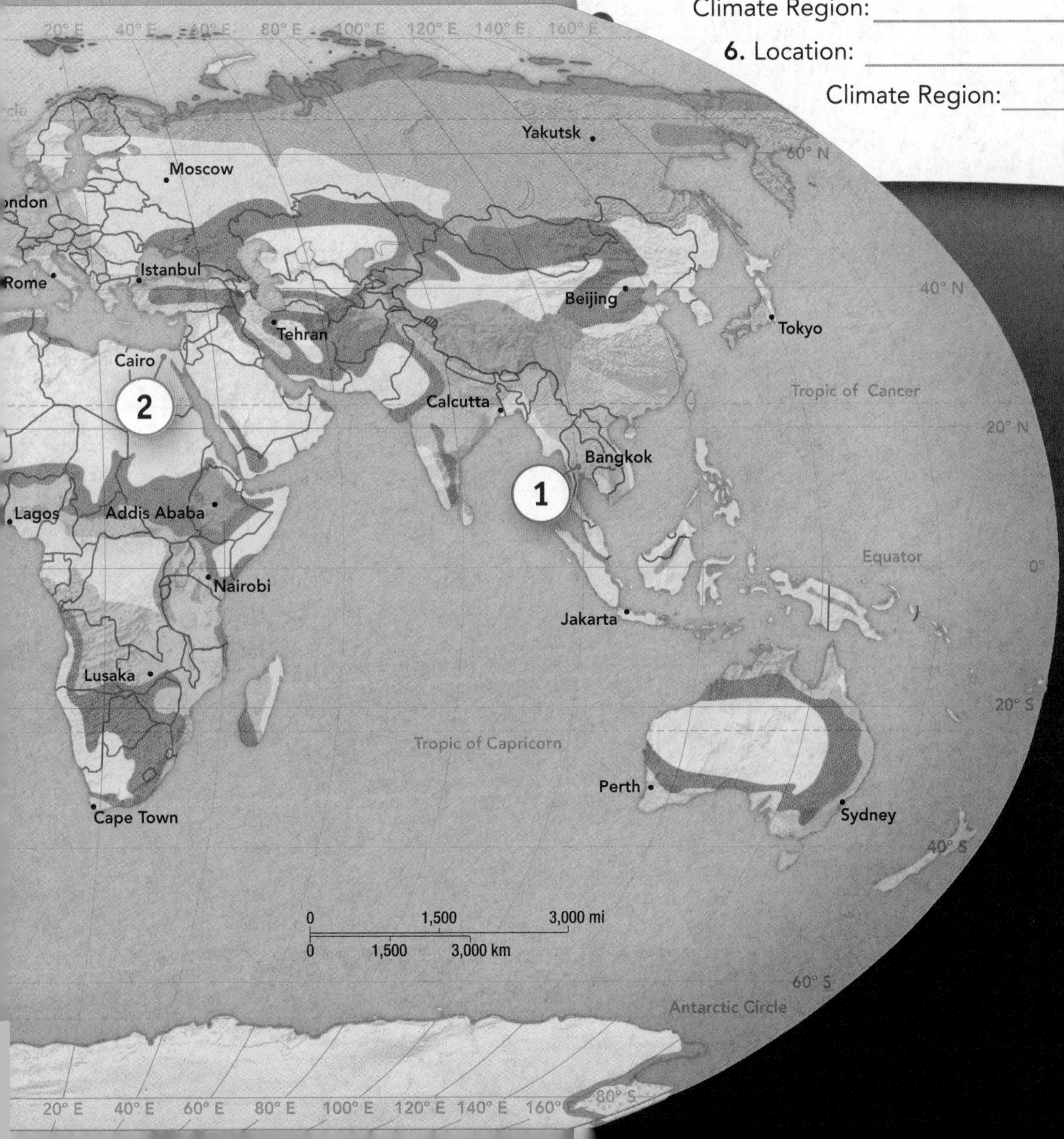

Identify the Main Idea
As you read, underline the main idea about tropical wet regions.

Tropical Rainy Climates Travel to Manaus, Brazil, or Bangkok, Thailand, and there's a good chance you might see some rain on your trip. Although continents apart, these two cities are both in the tropics. 🔑 **The tropics are an area that have two types of rainy climates: tropical wet and tropical wet-and-dry.**

❶ **Tropical Wet** A tropical wet climate has many rainy days and frequent afternoon thunderstorms. These thunderstorms are triggered by midday heating. The trade winds also bring moisture from the oceans to some tropical wet areas. With year-round heat and heavy rainfall, vegetation grows lush and green. **Rain forests**—forests in which large amounts of rain fall year-round—are common. In the United States, only the windward sides of the Hawaiian Islands have a tropical wet climate.

❷ **Tropical Wet-and-Dry** Areas with tropical wet-and-dry climates get slightly less rain than areas with tropical wet climates. They also have distinct dry and rainy seasons. Instead of rain forests, these climates have tropical grasslands called **savannas.** Scattered clumps of trees that can survive the dry season stand in the coarse grasses. Only a small part of the United States—the southern tip of Florida—has a tropical wet-and-dry climate.

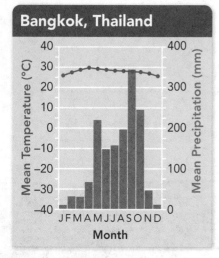

Bangkok, Thailand

Subject: _____

_____

July Temp.: _____ July Precip.: _____

FIGURE 3
Bangkok, Thailand
It's July—time to travel! You'll be updating a Web page on your trip. Be sure to record the climate data for July during each stop on your itinerary. ✎ *Explain* **In the box, write a blog entry that explains how you packed for Bangkok's climate and why you packed that way.**

Dry Climates A climate is dry if the amount of precipitation that falls is less than the amount of water that could potentially evaporate. 🔑 **Dry climates include semiarid and arid climates.**

❶ Semiarid Large semiarid areas are usually located on the edges of deserts. These semiarid areas are called steppes. A **steppe** is dry, but it gets enough rainfall for short grasses and low bushes to grow. For this reason, a steppe may also be called a prairie or grassland. The Great Plains are the steppe region in the United States.

❷ Arid When you think about **deserts,** or arid regions, you may picture blazing heat and drifting sand dunes. But deserts can actually be cold and rocky, too. On average, arid regions get less than 25 centimeters of rain a year. Some years may bring no rain at all. Only specialized plants such as cactus and yucca can survive the desert's dryness and extreme temperatures. In the United States there are arid climates in parts of California and the Southwest.

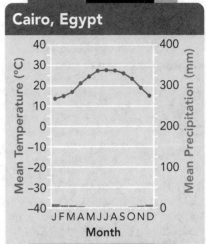

Cairo, Egypt

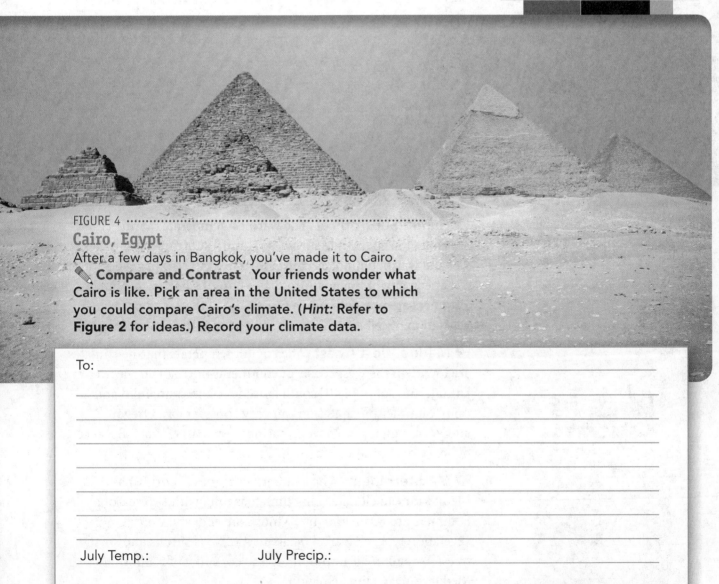

FIGURE 4 ···

Cairo, Egypt
After a few days in Bangkok, you've made it to Cairo.
✎ **Compare and Contrast** Your friends wonder what Cairo is like. Pick an area in the United States to which you could compare Cairo's climate. (*Hint:* Refer to **Figure 2** for ideas.) Record your climate data.

To: _____

_____

_____

_____

_____

_____

_____

July Temp.: _____   July Precip.: _____

481

Temperate Marine Climates Along the coasts of continents in the temperate zones, you can find the third main climate region, temperate marine. 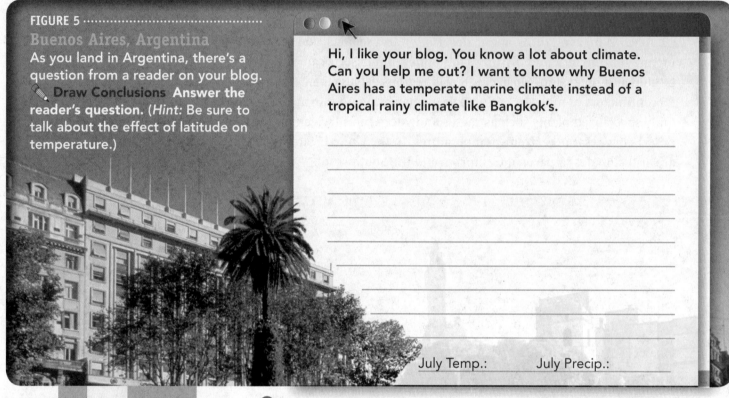 **There are three kinds of temperate marine climates: humid subtropical, marine west coast, and Mediterranean.** Because of the moderating influence of oceans, all three are humid and have mild winters.

FIGURE 5

Buenos Aires, Argentina
As you land in Argentina, there's a question from a reader on your blog.
✎ Draw Conclusions **Answer the reader's question.** (*Hint:* Be sure to talk about the effect of latitude on temperature.)

Hi, I like your blog. You know a lot about climate. Can you help me out? I want to know why Buenos Aires has a temperate marine climate instead of a tropical rainy climate like Bangkok's.

_____

_____

_____

_____

_____

_____

July Temp.: _____ July Precip.: _____

Buenos Aires, Argentina

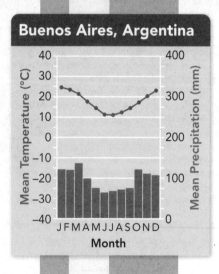

❶ **Humid Subtropical** The warmest temperate marine climates are along the edges of the tropics. **Humid subtropical** climates are wet and warm, but not as constantly hot as the tropics. The South American city of Buenos Aires has a humid subtropical climate. Summers are hot, with much more rainfall than winters. Mixed vegetation of ceiba trees, rushes, and passionflowers grow here.

❷ **Marine West Coast** The coolest temperate marine climates are found on the west coasts of continents north of 40° north latitude and south of 40° south latitude. Winters are mild and rainy. Summer precipitation can vary considerably. Oregon and Washington both have a marine west coast climate. Because of heavy precipitation, thick forests of tall trees grow in these areas.

❸ **Mediterranean** The southern coast of California has a Mediterranean climate. This climate is mild with two seasons. Summers are warm and dry; winters are cool and rainy. One vegetation type, chaparral (shap uh RAL), has shrubs and small trees. Agriculture is important to the economy of California's Mediterranean climate region.

Temperate Continental Climates

Temperate continental climates are not influenced very much by oceans, so they commonly have extremes of temperature. 🔑 **Temperate continental climates are only found on continents in the Northern Hemisphere, and include humid continental and subarctic.** In the Southern Hemisphere there are no large land areas at the right latitude for this climate to occur.

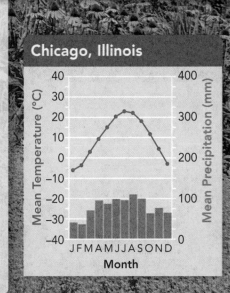

FIGURE 6 ···

Chicago, Illinois, U.S.

✏️ **Observe** One of your pen pals wants a picture of Illinois. But your digital camera is broken. Use the space below to draw a picture showing what the climate and vegetation of the Midwest look like in July. (*Hint:* Consult your climate graph.)

July Temp.: _____   July Precip.: _____

❶ **Humid Continental** Shifting tropical and polar air masses bring constantly changing weather to humid continental climates. In winter, continental polar air masses move south, bringing bitterly cold weather. In summer, tropical air masses move north, bringing heat and high humidity. In the United States, the eastern part of the climate region is the Northeast. There is a mixture of forest types in this area. Much of the western part of this climate region—the Midwest—was once tall grasslands, but is now farmland.

❷ **Subarctic** The **subarctic** climates lie north of the humid continental climates. Summers in the subarctic are short and cool. Winters are long and bitterly cold. In North America, coniferous trees such as spruce and fir make up a huge northern forest that stretches from Alaska to eastern Canada.

Polar Climates

Polar Climates Most polar climates are relatively dry, because the cold air contains little moisture. **The polar climate is the coldest climate region and includes the tundra and ice cap climates.**

❶ Tundra The **tundra** climate region stretches across northern Alaska, Canada, and Russia. Short, cool summers follow bitterly cold winters. Because of the cold, some layers of tundra soil are always frozen. This permanently frozen soil is called **permafrost.** Because of the permafrost, water can't drain away, so the soil is wet and boggy in summer. It's too cold for trees to grow, but mosses, grasses, wildflowers, and shrubs grow during summer.

❷ Ice Cap With average temperatures always at or below freezing, the land in ice cap climate regions is covered with ice and snow. Intense cold makes the air dry. Lichens and a few low plants may grow on the rocks. Ice cap climates are found mainly in Greenland and Antarctica.

FIGURE 7 ....
Godthåb, Greenland
Your flight from Chicago to Greenland takes you to Godthåb, a city in the tundra. ✎ **Identify Record the climate data for July.**

Temperature: _____ Precipitation: _____

Highlands

Highlands Why are highlands a distinct climate region? **Temperature falls as altitude increases, so highland regions are colder than the regions that surround them.** Increasing altitude produces climate changes similar to the climate changes you would expect with increasing latitude.

The climate on the lower slopes of a mountain range is like that of the surrounding countryside. The Rocky Mountain foothills, for instance, share the semiarid climate of the Great Plains. But higher up into the mountains, temperatures become lower and precipitation increases. Climbing 1,000 meters up in elevation is like traveling 1,200 kilometers toward one of the poles. The climate high in the mountains is like the subarctic: cool with coniferous trees.

FIGURE 8 ....
Mexico City, Mexico
Finally, you've reached your last stop: Mexico City, Mexico. The surrounding highlands are very different from the tundra.

✎ **Identify Record the climate data for July.**

Temperature: _____ Precipitation: _____

apply it!

You're home from your travel assignment. It's time to send your recommendation to the Olympic committee.

1 Graph Use the climate data you gathered for July to build a bar graph.

2 Communicate Write a letter to the committee explaining your choice of location. To support your answer, be sure to include information about the climate in the city you chose.

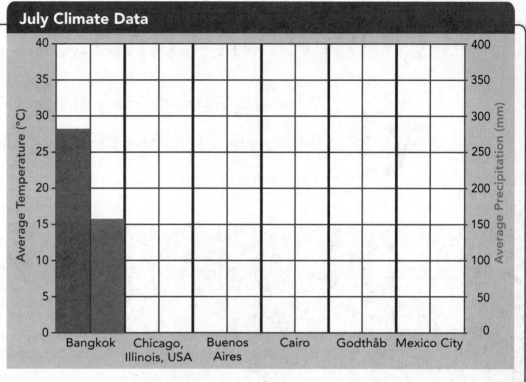

July Climate Data

_____
_____
_____
_____
_____

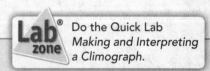 Do the Quick Lab *Making and Interpreting a Climograph.*

🔑 Assess Your Understanding

1a. Sequence Place these climates in order from coldest to warmest: tundra, subarctic, humid continental, and ice cap.

_____
_____

b. CHALLENGE What place would have more severe winters: central Russia or the west coast of France?

_____
_____

got it?

○ I get it! Now I know where climate regions are found _____

I also know they change with latitude

and _____

○ I need extra help with _____

_____

Go to MY SCIENCE 🔑 COACH *online for help with this subject.*

Changes in Climate

UNLOCK
THE BIG
?

🔑 **How Do Scientists Study Ancient Climates?**

🔑 **What Natural Factors Can Cause Climate Change?**

my planeT DiaRY

DISCOVERY

Ötzi the Ice Man

Have you ever seen something so bizarre that you stopped right in your tracks? That's just what happened to a pair of hikers in 1991. During a hike in the Alps, they came across something strange. It was the 5,000-year-old mummified body of a man emerging from a melting glacier.

Archaelogists named the mummy Ötzi. After removing him from the ice, they began to study his weapons, clothes, and tools. What they found surprised them. There was evidence that early humans knew how to make warm, waterproof clothing. Ötzi's shoes were very complex. They had bearskin soles, top panels made of deerhide, and netting made of tree bark to give them traction on snow. Soft grass inside the shoes acted like a warm sock.

Read about the ice man and answer the questions below.

1. What does the discovery of Ötzi tell you about today's climate?

_____

_____

_____

2. What does Ötzi's clothing tell you about the climate during his time?

_____

_____

_____

_____

> PLANET DIARY Go to **Planet Diary** to learn more about ancient climates.

Lab zone® Do the Inquiry Warm-Up
What Story Can Tree Rings Tell?

Vocabulary
- ice age
- aerosol
- sunspot

Skills
- Reading: Identify Supporting Evidence
- Inquiry: Interpret Data

How Do Scientists Study Ancient Climates?

Think about a weather forecast that you've seen or heard. This forecast is a prediction about changes in upcoming weather. This prediction can help you plan your day. However, long-term changes in climate happen more slowly, and may not be apparent for years. Yet regardless of how slowly climate changes, the consequences can be great.

Take Greenland, for example. Today this large island is mostly covered by an ice cap. But 80 million years ago Greenland had a warm, moist climate. Fossils of magnolias and palm trees found in Greenland provide evidence for this climate change. Today magnolias and palm trees are native to warm, moist climates, like Florida. Scientists assume that the ancestors of these trees required similar conditions. **In studying ancient climates, scientists follow an important principle: If plants or animals today need certain conditions to live, then similar plants and animals in the past also required those conditions.**

FIGURE 1 ·······················

Climate Change
Changes in climate happen gradually, but they have big effects on conditions in an area.

✎ **Develop Hypotheses** Why do you think Greenland's climate changed?

_____
_____
_____
_____
_____
_____
_____
_____
_____
_____
_____

Greetings from GREENLAND

Pollen One source of information about ancient climates is pollen records. Each type of plant has a particular type of pollen. Some lake bottoms have accumulated thick layers of mud and plant material, including pollen, over thousands of years. Scientists can drill down into these layers and bring up samples to examine. Using a microscope to look at the pollen in each layer, scientists can tell what types of plants lived there.

Tree Rings Tree rings also tell a story about ancient climates. Each summer, a tree grows a new layer of wood just under its bark. These layers form rings, as shown in **Figure 2.** Wide rings indicate a good growing season that was long or wet. Narrow rings indicate a dry year or a short growing season. Scientists study the patterns of thick or thin tree rings. From these data they can see if previous years were wet or dry, warm or cool.

Ice Cores Imagine drilling three kilometers down into ice and removing an ice core almost eight times longer than the Empire State Building! Ice cores have a layer for each year, just like tree rings. Scientists study these layers to find out about Earth's climate record. They can also analyze what's in the layers of ice, such as pollen and dust.

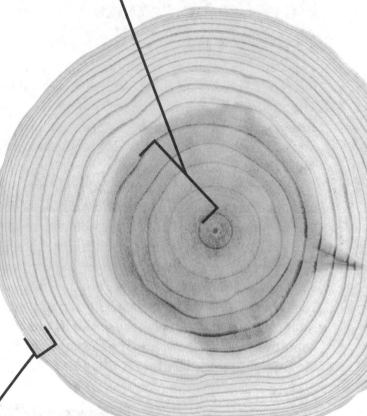

1. What was the climate like when the tree was young?

_____

_____

_____

_____

2. What was the climate like when the tree was older? How did the climate change over time?

_____

_____

_____

_____

FIGURE 2 ···

Evidence of Climate Change
Inner tree rings hold clues about a tree's early years. Outer rings hold clues about a tree's later years.

✎ **Infer** Look at the two sets of tree rings above, and answer the questions.

Do the Quick Lab
Climate Clues.

What Natural Factors Can Cause Climate Change?

Why do climates change? 🔑 **Possible explanations for major climate changes include movement of the continents, variations in the position of Earth relative to the sun, major volcanic eruptions, and changes in the sun's energy output.**

Movement of Continents The continents have not always been located where they are now. Look at **Figure 3.** About 200 million years ago, most of the land on Earth was part of a single continent called Pangaea (pan JEE uh). At that time, most continents were far from their present positions. Continents that are now in the polar zones were once near the equator. This movement explains how tropical plants such as magnolias and palm trees could once have been native to Greenland.

The movements of continents over time changed the locations of land and sea. These changes affected the global patterns of winds and ocean currents, which slowly changed climates. As the continents continue to move, their climates will continue to change.

FIGURE 3 ·······························

⟩ INTERACTIVE ART **Moving Continents**

✎ **Use the maps to determine how continental movement has affected climate.**

1. **Interpret Maps** Look at the two maps. What happened to the location of Greenland over time?

_____

_____

_____

2. **Infer** How do you think the breakup of Pangaea affected Greenland's climate?

_____

_____

_____

_____

_____

_____

_____

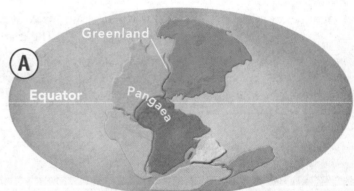

Earth 200 Million Years Ago

Earth Today

489

◑ **Identify Supporting Evidence** Underline the changes in Earth's position that cause ice ages.

Earth's Position and Ice Ages

The angle of Earth's axis and the shape of Earth's orbit affect Earth's climate. Earth travels in an elliptical orbit around the sun. But the shape of this ellipse varies over a period of about 100,000 years. When Earth's orbit is more elliptical, less sunlight reaches Earth during the year. This change causes Earth to experience an **ice age,** a period of glacial advance. Earth warms when its orbit is more circular. The angle at which Earth's axis tilts and the direction of the axis change over time as well. These changes in Earth's position affect the severity of ice ages. Altogether, these changes cause repeating 100,000-year cycles of ice ages interrupted by warm periods.

🔑 **During each ice age, huge sheets of ice called continental glaciers covered large parts of Earth's surface.** Glaciers transformed the landscape. They carved grooves in solid rock and deposited piles of sediment. They also moved huge boulders hundreds of kilometers. From this evidence, scientists have concluded that there were about 20 major ice ages in the last two million years. Brief, warm periods called interglacials occur between long, cold ice ages. The last ice age ended only about 10,000 years ago.

FIGURE 4 ··

Glaciers in North America

The map shows the parts of North America that were covered by glaciers 18,000 years ago.

✎ **Observe Find and shade in your state. Was it covered with ice during the ice age?** _____

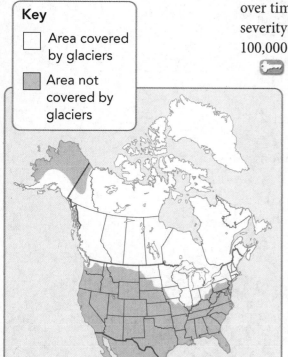

Key
- ☐ Area covered by glaciers
- ▨ Area not covered by glaciers

do the math!

Ice Ages and Temperature

The estimated average worldwide temperature for the past 350,000 years was about 14°C. Cold glacial periods have alternated with warm interglacial periods.

① Interpret Data Explain the pattern you see in these data.

_____

_____

_____

② CHALLENGE Based on the pattern in the graph, how might global temperature change in the future?

_____

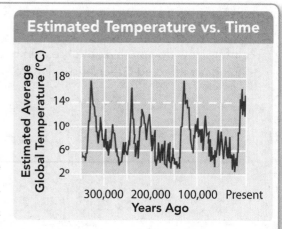

Estimated Temperature vs. Time

Estimated Average Global Temperature (°C): 18°, 14°, 10°, 6°, 2°

Years Ago: 300,000 200,000 100,000 Present

FIGURE 5 ·······························

Volcanic Activity and Climate

The year 1816 is often called "the year without summer." A volcanic eruption in 1815 affected climates around the world.

✏️ **Relate Cause and Effect** Write captions for the two photos to help tell the story of that summer.

Volcanic Activity

Major volcanic eruptions release huge quantities of ash and aerosols into the atmosphere. **Aerosols** are solid particles or liquid drops in gas. Aerosols and ash can stay in the upper atmosphere for months or years. Scientists think that aerosols and ash reflect away some of the incoming solar radiation, and may lower temperatures. For example, the eruption of Mount Tambora in Indonesia in 1815 blasted about 100 cubic kilometers of ash into the atmosphere. Climates worldwide were dramatically colder the next few years, as shown in **Figure 5.**

Solar Energy

Short-term changes in climate have been linked to changes in the amount of light given off by the sun. This amount changes over a regular 11-year cycle. It can also change over hundreds of years. The Little Ice Age was a period of cooling between about 1600 and 1850. It was caused by a decrease in the sun's energy output. The number of **sunspots,** dark, cooler regions on the surface of the sun, increases when the sun gives off more light. They can be used to measure solar output over the past 400 years.

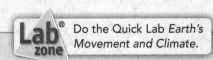 Do the Quick Lab *Earth's Movement and Climate.*

🔑 Assess Your Understanding

1a. Review What principle do scientists follow when studying ancient climates?

_____

_____

_____

b. Relate Cause and Effect How does a volcanic eruption affect climate?

_____

_____

got it?

○ **I get it!** Now I know that natural factors such as _____

_____

can cause climate change.

○ **I need extra help with** _____

Go to MY SCIENCE ⓢ **COACH** online for help with this subject.

491

Human Activities and Climate Change

🗝️ How Are Human Activities Affecting Earth's Climate?

my planet Diary

EVERYDAY SCIENCE

How Big Is Your Footprint?

Today people are measuring their effect on the environment by looking at their carbon footprint. Carbon is found in two of the greenhouse gases most responsible for warming Earth's climate. Your carbon footprint measures the total amount of greenhouse gases you emit directly and indirectly. Cars, factories, and home heating all rely on fuels that release carbon into the atmosphere. The manufacturing of products you use, like food and clothing, does, too. When people know how big their carbon footprints are, they can make changes that improve their own lives and the environment.

Brainstorm with a classmate and answer the questions below.

What activities affect your carbon footprint? How big is your carbon footprint?

_____

_____

_____

_____

_____

_____

> PLANET DIARY Go to **Planet Diary** to learn more about global warming.

 Lab® zone Do the Inquiry Warm-Up
What Is the Greenhouse Effect?

How Are Human Activities Affecting Earth's Climate?

You may not realize it, but you are a powerful geologic force. Humans change the land, air, and water of Earth's surface faster than most geologic processes. In fact, human activities are causing a major change in the temperature of Earth's atmosphere. It's important to understand this impact because the atmosphere controls our climate and weather.

Vocabulary
- greenhouse gas
- fossil fuel
- global warming

Skills
- Reading: Ask Questions
- Inquiry: Make Models

Greenhouse Effect Outer space is incredibly cold: −270°C. If you were in a spaceship, you would rely on the insulated walls of the ship to keep you from freezing to death. Now think of Earth as a spaceship, moving through space as it orbits the sun. Earth's atmosphere is like the walls of the ship. It insulates us from the cold of space. How does it do this? The atmosphere keeps Earth's surface warm through a process called the greenhouse effect, as shown in **Figure 1.**

When the sun warms Earth's surface, this heat is radiated back to space as infrared waves. The infrared waves pass easily through nitrogen and oxygen, which make up 99 percent of Earth's atmosphere. However, **greenhouse gases,** such as water vapor, carbon dioxide, and methane, absorb the heat leaving Earth's surface. These gases then radiate some energy back toward Earth, trapping heat in the lower atmosphere. Greenhouse gases make up less than 1 percent of the atmosphere. But as you can see, it only takes a small amount of them to absorb heat, keeping Earth warm.

Ask Questions What questions do you have about the greenhouse effect? Before you read about it, write one question below. Try to answer your question after you read.

_____

_____

_____

_____

_____

FIGURE 1 ....

> ART IN MOTION **Greenhouse Effect**

Communicate Use the word bank to fill in the blanks. Then talk about the steps in the greenhouse effect with a classmate.

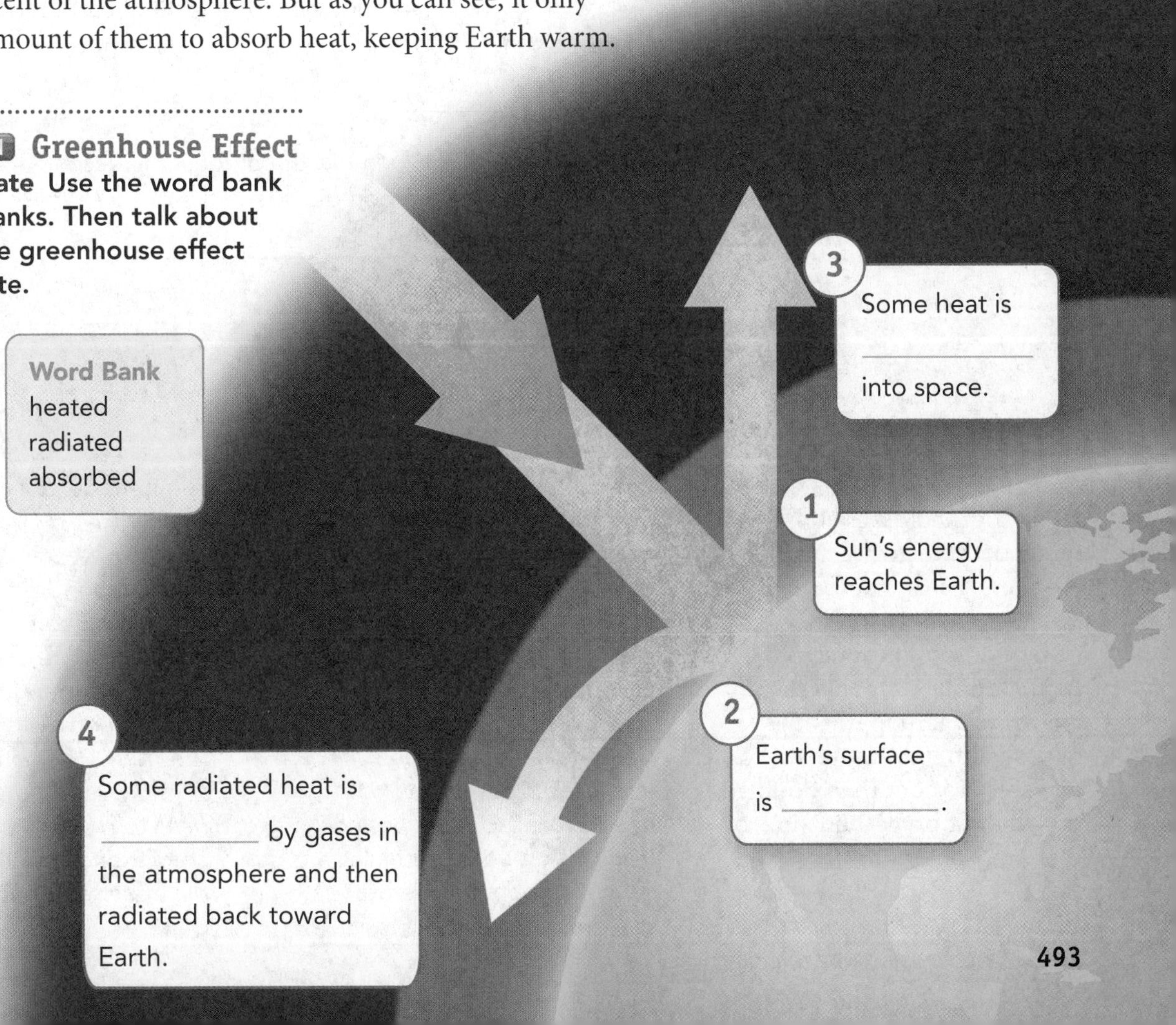

Word Bank
heated
radiated
absorbed

3 Some heat is _____ into space.

1 Sun's energy reaches Earth.

2 Earth's surface is _____.

4 Some radiated heat is _____ by gases in the atmosphere and then radiated back toward Earth.

Levels of Greenhouse Gases
We need the greenhouse effect, but you can have too much of a good thing. 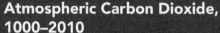 **Many human activities are increasing the level of greenhouse gases in the atmosphere and producing changes in climate worldwide. This increase is causing global temperatures to rise.** This conclusion is based on our observations and measurements of the greenhouse gases humans release. It's also based on an understanding of how greenhouse gases affect the temperature at Earth's surface.

FIGURE 2 ·················

Carbon Dioxide Levels
The graph shows the levels of carbon dioxide in the atmosphere over time.

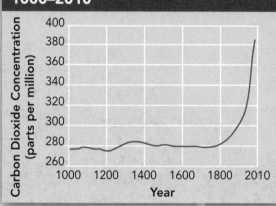

Atmospheric Carbon Dioxide, 1000–2010

Carbon Dioxide One of the most abundant greenhouse gases is carbon dioxide. Humans release billions of tons of it into the atmosphere each year. Most of this carbon dioxide is released by burning **fossil fuels**—energy-rich substances formed from the remains of organisms. Humans burn fossil fuels such as coal, natural gas, and gasoline to generate electricity, heat homes, and power cars.

· ·

✎ **Read Graphs Study the graph and answer the questions below.**

1. Describe what the level of carbon dioxide was like about 500 years ago.

   _____

2. When did the biggest increase in carbon dioxide levels occur? Why?

   _____

   _____

Methane

Human activities increase the amount of the greenhouse gas methane. Livestock emit methane. Large numbers of livestock, such as cattle, are raised for food production. As the population of livestock increases, more methane is released. In past centuries, this activity has more than doubled the amount of methane in the atmosphere.

Temperature Increase

Over the last 120 years, the average temperature of the troposphere has increased by about 0.7°C. This gradual increase in the temperature of Earth's atmosphere is called **global warming.** The effect is the same as it would be if the heat from the sun increased by about half of one percent. But increasing levels of greenhouse gases are causing global temperatures to rise more quickly than before.

Climate Models

Some models of climate change predict that global temperatures may rise several degrees over the next hundred years. Climate models are complex computer programs. They use data to predict temperature, precipitation, and other atmospheric conditions. Scientists are trying to improve climate models. They want to make more specific predictions about how warming will affect different regions.

Effects of Global Warming

Over the past 800,000 years, global temperatures have gone up and down. Scientists look at past events to predict the possible effects of global warming. **The effects of global warming include melting glaciers, rising sea levels, drought, desertification, changes to the biosphere, and regional changes in temperature. Global warming is part of a larger set of changes to Earth's climate that together are called climate change.**

FIGURE 3 ·············

Sea Level Rise

This satellite image shows how sea level rise could affect the eastern United States.

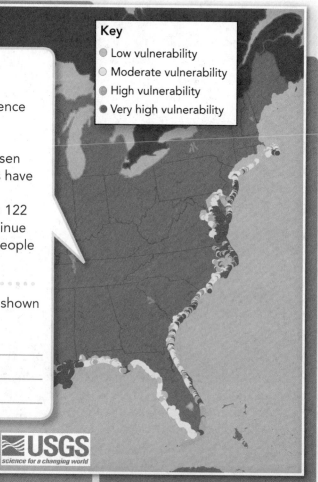

Key
- Low vulnerability
- Moderate vulnerability
- High vulnerability
- Very high vulnerability

USGS
science for a changing world

Melting Glaciers and Rising Sea Levels

Over the last century, scientists have observed glaciers retreating in many mountain regions. Now there is evidence that mountain glaciers are melting worldwide.

Records also indicate that temperatures in parts of Antarctica, which is covered by a thick ice sheet, have risen 6 degrees over 50 years. In fact, several giant ice sheets have collapsed and tumbled into the sea.

Since the end of the last ice age, sea levels have risen 122 meters. As glaciers continue to melt, sea levels will continue to rise. This rise poses a threat to the large number of people who live near the ocean.

✎ **Interpret Data** How would the sea level prediction shown here affect people in the eastern United States?

_____

_____

_____

Droughts and Desertification

When global temperatures rise, some regions get very warm and dry. This can lead to water shortages or periods of drought. Today the southwestern United States is experiencing a severe drought at a time when global temperatures are warming. Severe droughts also cause some lands to become deserts. This process of desertification can lead to food shortages.

Changes to the Biosphere

Each climate region has its own communities of living organisms that are adapted to that climate. As global climates warm, organisms are often pushed to new locations to find familiar climates. Organisms that can't adapt may become extinct. Species that can adapt to warmer conditions will survive.

Regional Changes in Temperature

Global temperature changes affect regions differently. During the twentieth century, global temperatures increased by an average of less than one degree. Yet some parts of the world got warmer by more than five degrees, while others got cooler. In some areas, temperature changes have led to longer growing seasons.

Limiting Global Warming Scientists think human activities that release greenhouse gases are responsible for our recent episode of global warming. The solution might sound simple: Reduce greenhouse gas emissions. But how do we do that? ⟸ **Solutions for limiting global warming and climate change include finding clean, renewable sources of energy, being more energy efficient, and removing carbon from fossil fuel emissions.**

Clean Energy Sources

Clean energy refers to energy sources that release very small amounts of greenhouse gases. Solar, wind, hydroelectric, geothermal, nuclear, and tidal energy are clean energy sources.

Solar energy might be the most important future energy source. The sun provides a continuous and nearly unlimited supply of energy. In one hour, Earth receives as much energy from the sun as all humans use in one year. Solar energy drives the water cycle behind hydroelectric power and the air motions behind wind power.

Efficient Energy

One of the best ways to reduce global warming is to develop more energy-efficient technologies. Clean energy power plants can power electric and hydrogen fuel cell cars. And factories can run on steam from power plants. People can also practice energy-efficient habits. They can turn off lights when they leave a room or use public transportation.

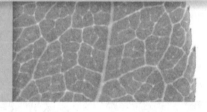

Carbon Capture

When fossil fuels are burned, they release exhaust. Technologies are being developed to remove carbon dioxide from exhaust. The carbon dioxide could then be buried underground. This process takes more energy and is a bit more expensive, but the result is that fewer greenhouse gases are released.

apply it!

Make Models How can you help limit global warming? Pick one item from your home. Come up with a plan to make it more energy efficient. Use the space provided to draw or explain your idea.

EXPLORE
THE BIG
?

CLIMATE IN THE MEDIA

What factors affect Earth's climate?

FIGURE 4 ···

> INTERACTIVE ART ✎ **Evaluate Science in the Media** Working with a group, choose at least three different media sources. Spend a week collecting stories about climate change from these sources. Discuss the stories with your group. Evaluate how they cover the topic of climate change. Present your findings to the class.

Lab® zone   Do the Quick Lab *Greenhouse Gases and Global Warming.*

🔑 Assess Your Understanding

1a. Define What is a greenhouse gas?

_____

_____

b. List What are some solutions for reducing greenhouse gases?

_____

ANSWER
THE BIG
?

c. What factors affect Earth's climate?

_____

_____

_____

_____

_____

got it? ···

O **I get it!** Now I know that human activities can affect Earth's climate by _____

_____

O I need extra help with _____

Go to MY SCIENCE ⑤ COACH *online for help with this subject.*

13 Study Guide

Some factors that affect Earth's climate are _____, altitude, _____
_____, ocean currents, prevailing and
_____ winds, and _____ .

LESSON 1 What Causes Climate?

🔑 Temperature is affected by latitude, altitude, distance from large bodies of water, and ocean currents.

🔑 Precipitation is affected by prevailing winds, presence of mountains, and seasonal winds.

Vocabulary
• climate • tropical zone • polar zone
• temperate zone • marine climate
• continental climate • windward
• leeward • monsoon

LESSON 2 Climate Regions

🔑 Scientists classify climates according to two major factors: temperature and precipitation.

🔑 The six main climate regions are tropical rainy, dry, temperate marine, temperate continental, polar, and highlands.

Vocabulary
• rain forest • savanna • steppe
• desert • humid subtropical • subarctic
• tundra • permafrost

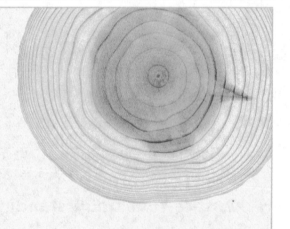

LESSON 3 Changes in Climate

🔑 In studying ancient climates, scientists follow an important principle: If plants and animals today need certain conditions to live, then similar plants and animals in the past also required those conditions.

🔑 Possible explanations for major climate changes include movement of continents, variations in the position of Earth relative to the sun, major volcanic eruptions, and changes in the sun's energy output.

Vocabulary
• ice age • aerosol • sunspot

LESSON 4 Human Activities and Climate Change

🔑 Many human activities are increasing the level of greenhouse gases in the atmosphere, causing global temperatures to rise.

🔑 The effects of global warming include melting glaciers, rising sea levels, drought, desertification, changes in the biosphere, and regional changes in temperature.

🔑 Solutions for limiting global warming include finding clean, renewable sources of energy, being more energy efficient, and removing carbon from fossil fuel emissions.

Vocabulary
• greenhouse gas • fossil fuel • global warming

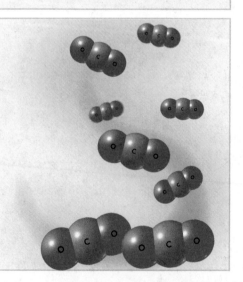

Review and Assessment

What Causes Climate?

1. In which area do temperatures range from warm or hot summers to cool or cold winters?

   a. polar zone   **b.** temperate zone

   c. tropical zone   **d.** tundra zone

2. The long-term weather in an area is its climate, which includes _____

_____

Use the map of world temperature zones to answer Question 3.

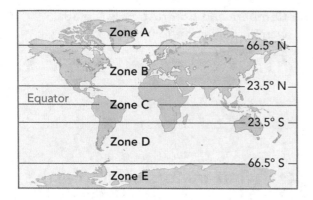

3. Interpret Maps Which zone has the highest average temperatures all year? Why?

_____

4. Relate Cause and Effect Explain how distance from large bodies of water can affect the temperature of nearby land areas.

_____

_____

_____

5. Compare and Contrast How are summer monsoons different from winter monsoons?

_____

_____

Climate Regions

6. What do we call a climate region that is semiarid with short grasses and low bushes?

   a. tundra   **b.** savanna

   c. desert   **d.** steppe

7. Rain forests are common in tropical wet regions because _____

_____

_____

_____

8. Explain Why are highland regions considered a climate region?

_____

_____

_____

_____

_____

_____

_____

9. Calculate Suppose a city receives an average of 35 centimeters of precipitation in November. If an average of 140 centimeters of precipitation falls there in a year, what percentage falls in November?

_____

_____

10. **Write About It** Suppose you live in Location A, a part of the United States with a semiarid climate. You travel to Location B, which is in a neighboring area. There you find a humid continental climate. In which direction is Location B likely to be, relative to Location A? What is the best explanation for the difference? (*Hint:* Read the section on humid continental climates.)

LESSON 3 Changes in Climate

11. Which of the following is probably the main cause of ice ages?

  a. Earth's orbit

  b. volcanic activity

  c. continental movement

  d. solar energy

12. Define Some climate changes are correlated with sunspots, which are _____

_____

13. Relate Cause and Effect How does the movement of continents explain changes in climate over millions of years?

_____

_____

_____

_____

_____

14. Infer How is Earth's climate affected by major volcanic eruptions?

_____

_____

_____

_____

15. Draw Conclusions Thick tree rings in a cool climate suggest a longer warm season. Thick tree rings in a dry climate suggest a rainier wet season. What conclusions can you draw about the effect of climate on tree growth?

_____

_____

_____

LESSON 4 Human Activities and Climate Change

16. Which change in the atmosphere appears to contribute to global warming?

  a. decreased moisture

  b. decreased heat

  c. increased oxygen

  d. increased carbon dioxide

17. Identify Greenhouse gases absorb _____

_____

18. Compare and Contrast How is global warming different from earlier changes in Earth's climate?

_____

_____

APPLY THE BIG ? What factors affect Earth's climate?

19. You've been asked to give a report about global warming at your next school meeting. As you prepare your report, be sure to mention what you think the town can do to reduce its carbon footprint.

_____

_____

_____

_____

_____

_____

_____

_____

Standardized Test Prep

Multiple Choice

Circle the letter of the best answer.

The graph below shows average monthly precipitation for a location in Arizona. Use the graph to answer Question 1.

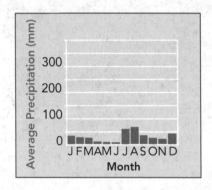

1. During which period does this location get the most precipitation?

A   January–March   C   July–September

B   April–June   D   October–December

2. What kind of climate would you expect to find in an area with these features: interior of a large continent, east side of a major mountain range, and winds usually from west to east?

A   polar

B   temperate marine

C   tropical rainy

D   dry

3. What two major factors are usually used to classify climate?

A   altitude and precipitation

B   precipitation and temperature

C   air pressure and humidity

D   temperature and air pressure

4. Which of the following factors contribute to global warming?

A   volcanic dust and industrial pollution

B   falling sea levels and ozone depletion

C   decreased coastal flooding and drought

D   spreading glaciers and acid rain

5. Which climate is warm, wet, and located on the edges of the tropics?

A   humid continental

B   subarctic

C   semiarid

D   humid subtropical

Constructed Response

Use the map and your knowledge of science to answer Question 6. Write your answer on a separate piece of paper.

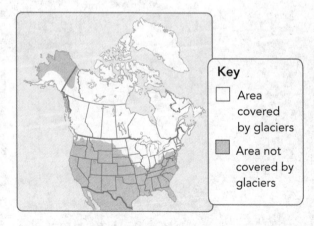

Key
☐ Area covered by glaciers
▨ Area not covered by glaciers

6. Ice ages have occurred at several times during Earth's history. What is an ice age, and how does it affect the land surface and the oceans?

TRACKING EARTH'S GASES FROM SPACE

Our planet has gas. In fact, it is surrounded by gas. Satellites help us measure this gassy envelope.

Specifically, these satellites measure greenhouse gases. The Japanese satellite GOSAT was launched on January 23, 2009. Its main job is to measure the levels of two major greenhouse gases—carbon dioxide (CO_2) and methane (CH_4). Watching changes in the concentrations of these gases all over the world will help scientists learn about climate change.

Scientists already use 282 land-based observation sites, but GOSAT will gather data from 56,000 locations! In 44 orbits, GOSAT will map all of Earth every three days. GOSAT will also record greenhouse gas concentrations over remote areas like the ocean and help every country keep track of its greenhouse gas emissions.

As Earth gets gassier, satellites are helping us get a clearer picture.

The GOSAT satellite's mission is to record the concentration of greenhouse gases on Earth. ▼

Research It The levels of CO_2 have been increasing, but not all scientists agree on the best solutions for reducing CO_2 emissions. Research different ways of reducing or combating greenhouse gas emissions, and participate in a class debate about the costs and benefits of different approaches.

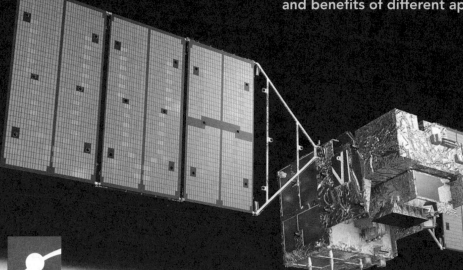

Museum of Science

Bacterial RAINMAKERS

Could bacteria influence the weather? Some scientists think that some bacteria can! Researchers have found rainmaking bacteria in samples of rainwater throughout the world. These bacteria are also found in the clouds that produce rain.

The cycle that carries bacteria from Earth to the clouds and back, known as bioprecipitation, begins at Earth's surface. The bacteria reproduce on the leaves of plants, often damaging their hosts. Then wind currents carry the bacteria high into the atmosphere. If conditions are right, water vapor freezes on the bacteria, forming rain. Rain carries the bacteria back to Earth's surface and the bioprecipitation cycle repeats.

Understanding the role of bacteria in weather patterns could be important for predicting or even preventing droughts. In the future, scientists may be able to increase the chance of rain by seeding clouds with rainmaking bacteria.

Research It Find out more about bioprecipitation. Make a presentation that shows how rainmaking bacteria may influence weather patterns as part of their life cycle.

▲ Rainmaking bacteria, carried into the atmosphere by Earth's winds, may play a role in Earth's patterns of rain and drought.

WHAT'S HAPPENING TO THE MOON?

How do Earth, the moon, and the sun interact?

This photograph shows a series of images of the moon taken over the course of an evening. Why do you think the moon looks different in each image? Develop Hypotheses Explain what you think happened during the period of time shown in the photograph.

> UNTAMED SCIENCE Watch the **Untamed Science** video to learn more about the moon.

_____

_____

_____

_____

_____

_____

_____

_____

_____

14 Getting Started

Check Your Understanding

1. **Background** Read the paragraph below and then answer the question.

Santiago is studying a globe. He sees that Earth has North and South poles. The globe rotates around a line through its center between the two poles. Another line called the equator divides Earth into two halves, the Northern Hemisphere and the Southern Hemisphere.

> To **rotate** is to spin in place around a central line, or axis.
>
> The **equator** is the imaginary line that divides Earth into two halves, the **Northern Hemisphere** and the **Southern Hemisphere.**

• Where is the equator found?

_____

_____

> MY READING WEB If you had trouble answering the question above, visit **My Reading Web** and type in *Earth, Moon, and Sun.*

Vocabulary Skill

Identify Multiple Meanings Words you use every day may have different meanings in science. Look at the different meanings of the words below.

Word	Everyday Meaning	Scientific Meaning
weight	*n.* a heavy object used for exercise **Example:** The athlete lifted *weights* to build strength.	*n.* a measure of the force of gravity on an object **Example:** The object's *weight* was 10 newtons.
force	*v.* to use power to make someone do something **Example:** She had to *force* herself to get up early.	*n.* a push or pull exerted on an object **Example:** You exert *force* when you open and close a door.

2. **Quick Check** Circle the sentence below that uses the scientific meaning of *force.*

• The *force* of gravity holds objects in their orbits.

• Her parents are trying to *force* her to get a job.

solstice

Chapter Preview

LESSON 1
- satellite • planet • meteor
- comet • star • constellation

⟳ **Identify the Main Idea**
△ **Predict**

LESSON 2
- axis • rotation • revolution
- orbit • calendar • solstice
- equinox

⟳ **Sequence**
△ **Infer**

inertia

LESSON 3
- force • gravity
- law of universal gravitation
- mass • weight • inertia
- Newton's first law of motion

⟳ **Ask Questions**
△ **Draw Conclusions**

LESSON 4
- phase • eclipse • solar eclipse
- umbra • penumbra
- lunar eclipse

⟳ **Relate Text and Visuals**
△ **Make Models**

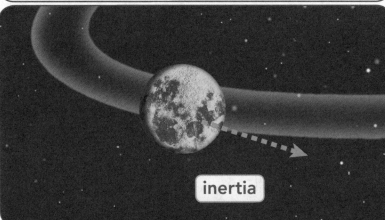

phase

LESSON 5
- tide • spring tide • neap tide

⟳ **Relate Cause and Effect**
△ **Observe**

LESSON 6
- maria • crater • meteoroid

⟳ **Compare and Contrast**
△ **Develop Hypotheses**

> **VOCAB FLASH CARDS** For extra help with vocabulary, visit **Vocab Flash Cards** and type in *Earth, Moon, and Sun.*

solar eclipse

The Sky From Earth

🔑 **What Can You See in the Night Sky?**

🔑 **How Do Objects in the Sky Appear to Move?**

my planet Diary

BIOGRAPHY

Watching the Stars

When you look up at the night sky, what questions do you ask yourself? Do you wonder why the stars seem to move, or why the moon shines? Aryabhata (ar yah BAH tah) was an early Indian astronomer who thought about these questions. He was born in India in A.D. 476.

Many historians think that Aryabhata realized that the stars appear to move from east to west because Earth rotates from west to east. He also wrote that the moon and the planets shine because they reflect light from the sun. And he made all these inferences using just his eyes and his mind. The first telescopes wouldn't come along for more than a thousand years!

Communicate Discuss Aryabhata's discoveries with a partner. Then answer the questions below.

1. What did Aryabhata infer about the motion of Earth?

_____

_____

_____

2. What questions do you think about when you look at stars, the moon, or the planets?

_____

_____

_____

▶ **PLANET DIARY** Go to **Planet Diary** to learn more about the night sky.

Lab zone® Do the Inquiry Warm-Up *Earth's Sky.*

Vocabulary
• satellite • planet • meteor
• comet • star • constellation

Skills
🔁 Reading: Identify the Main Idea
⚠ Inquiry: Predict

What Can You See in the Night Sky?

Depending on how dark the sky is where you are, you might see 2,000 or 3,000 stars using just your eyes. 🔑 On a clear night, you may see stars, the moon, planets, meteors, and comets.

Moon About half of every month, Earth's moon outshines everything else in the night sky. The moon is Earth's only natural satellite. A **satellite** is a body that orbits a planet.

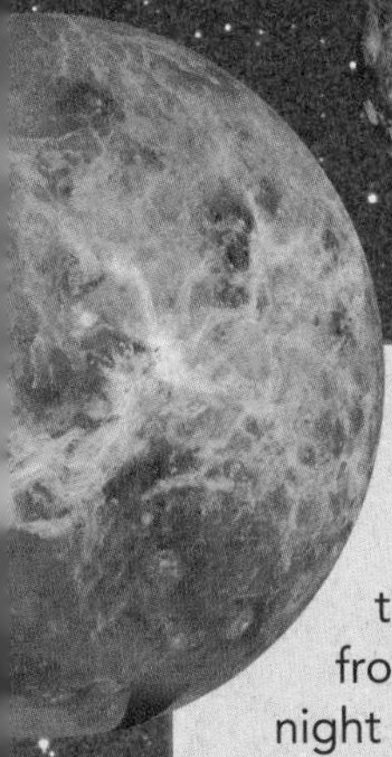

Planets You may see objects that move from night to night against the background stars. These are planets. A **planet** is an object that orbits the sun, is large enough to have become rounded by its own gravity, and has cleared the area of its orbit. There are eight planets in the solar system. Five are visible from Earth without a telescope: Mercury, Venus, Mars, Jupiter, and Saturn.

Meteors and Comets Have you ever seen a "shooting star"? These sudden bright streaks are called **meteors**. A meteor is the streak of light produced when a small object burns up entering Earth's atmosphere. You can see a meteor on almost any night. Comets are rarer. A **comet** is a cold mixture of dust and ice that gives off a long trail of light as it approaches the sun.

Stars Stars appear as tiny points of light. However, scientists infer that a **star** is a giant ball of hot gas, mainly composed of hydrogen and helium. As seen from Earth, the positions of stars relative to each other do not seem to change.

FIGURE 1 ·······································
These photos show examples of stars, planets, and other objects.

✏ **Observe** What can you observe about the objects shown on this page? Include at least two different objects.

_____
_____
_____
_____
_____

509

Constellations For thousands of years humans have seen patterns in groups of stars and given names to them. 🔑 **A constellation is a pattern or group of stars that people imagined to represent a figure, animal, or object.** Astronomers also use the word *constellation* for an area of the sky and all the objects in that area.

Different cultures have identified different constellations. In Western culture, there are 88 constellations. Most constellation names used today come from the ancient Greeks, who probably took them from the Egyptians and Mesopotamians.

Some constellations' names come from Latin. The constellation Leo, for example, is named from the Latin word meaning "lion." Some constellations are named for people or animals in Greek myths. You may have read some of these myths in school. Do the names *Pegasus* or *Perseus* sound familiar? They are mythological characters and also constellations.

FIGURE 2 ···

> **INTERACTIVE ART** **How to Use a Star Chart**
To use a star chart at night, follow these steps.

1. Choose the chart that fits your location and season. This is a summer chart for the Northern Hemisphere. (There are charts for the other seasons in the Appendix.)

2. Hold the chart upright in front of you. Turn the chart so the label at the bottom matches the direction you face. (*Hint:* If you are looking at the Big Dipper, you are looking north.)

3. Hold the chart at eye level. Compare the figures on the bottom half of the chart to the sky in front of you.

Eastern Horizon

Southern Horizon

CASSIOPEIA
CEPHEUS
Deneb
DRACO
DELPHINUS
CYGNUS
LYRA
Vega
HERCULES
CORONA BOREALIS
Altair
AQUILA
SERPENS CAPUT
SERPENS CAUDA
OPHIUCHUS
SAGITTARIUS
SCORPIUS
Antares
LIBRA

apply it!

❶ Interpret Diagrams Find these constellations in **Figure 2**. Then write each constellation's name by its picture.

❷ CHALLENGE Choose another constellation from **Figure 2**. What does it represent? Do research to find out.

_____

_____

_____

Northern Horizon

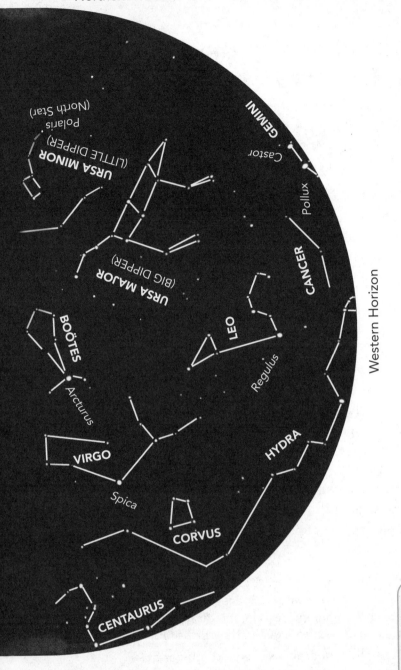

Polaris (North Star)

URSA MINOR (LITTLE DIPPER)

GEMINI

Castor

Pollux

URSA MAJOR (BIG DIPPER)

CANCER

BOÖTES

LEO

Arcturus

Regulus

Western Horizon

VIRGO

HYDRA

Spica

CORVUS

CENTAURUS

Finding Constellations

A star chart, like the one shown in **Figure 2**, can help you find constellations in the night sky. Read the instructions for how to use the chart. It may seem a little! strange at first, but with some practice, these charts are easy to use. Here is one tip to help you get started.

You can probably recognize the Big Dipper. This group of stars is actually not a constellation itself. It is part of the constellation Ursa Major, or the Great Bear. The two stars at the end of the dipper's "bowl" are called the Pointers.

Picture an imaginary line between those two stars. If you continue it away from the "bowl," the first fairly bright star you'll reach is called Polaris (po LA ris). Polaris is commonly called the North Star. It is located close to the sky's North Pole.

In the Appendix, you can find star charts for all four seasons. Take one outside on a clear night and see what you can find!

Lab zone ® Do the Quick Lab *Observing the Night Sky.*

🗝 Assess Your Understanding

got it? •••••••••••••••••••••••••••••••••••••••

O **I get it!** Now I know that objects visible in the night sky include _____

_____

_____

_____

O **I need extra help with** _____

_____

Go to MY SCIENCE 🄢 COACH *online for help with this subject.*

511

How Do Objects in the Sky Appear to Move?

Stars, planets, and other objects appear to move over time. They do move in space, but those actual motions and their apparent, or visible, motions may be very different. 🔑 **The apparent motion of objects in the sky depends on the motions of Earth.**

Star Motions

Stars generally appear to move from east to west through the night. As Aryabhata thought, this apparent motion is actually caused by Earth turning from west to east. The sun's apparent motion during the day is also caused by Earth's motion. **Figure 3** shows how this kind of apparent motion occurs.

Seasonal Changes

Constellations and star patterns remain the same year after year, but which ones you can see varies from season to season. For example, you can find Orion in the eastern sky on winter evenings. But by spring, you'll see Orion in the west, disappearing below the horizon shortly after sunset.

These seasonal changes are caused by Earth's orbit around the sun. Each night, the position of most stars shifts slightly to the west. Soon you no longer see stars once visible in the west, and other stars appear in the east.

There are a few constellations that you can see all year long. These are the ones closest to the North Star. As Earth rotates, these constellations never appear to rise or set.

🔄 **Identify the Main Idea**
Underline the main idea in the paragraph called Star Motions.

FIGURE 3 ···

Opposite Motions

The restaurant on top of Seattle's Space Needle rotates much as Earth does. The restaurant turns in one direction, which makes objects outside appear to move in the opposite direction.

⚠️ **Predict** Draw the mountain as it would appear at each time shown.

Motion of restaurant | 6:00 P.M. | 6:35 P.M. | 7:20 P.M.

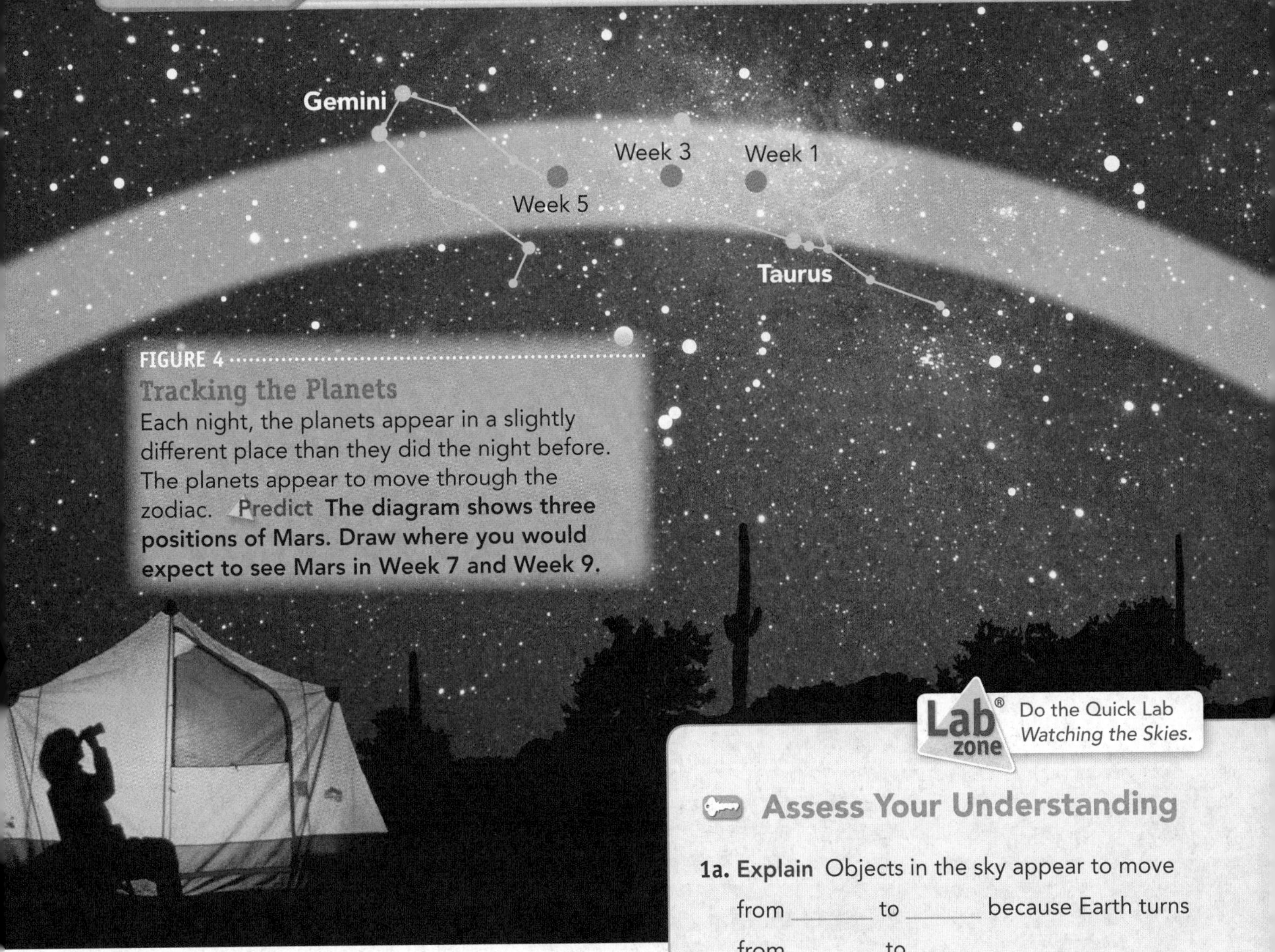

Gemini

Week 3   Week 1

Week 5

Taurus

FIGURE 4 ··········

Tracking the Planets

Each night, the planets appear in a slightly different place than they did the night before. The planets appear to move through the zodiac. *Predict* **The diagram shows three positions of Mars. Draw where you would expect to see Mars in Week 7 and Week 9.**

 Do the Quick Lab
Watching the Skies.

Planets Planets appear to move against the background of stars, as shown in **Figure 4.** Because the planets all orbit the sun in about the same plane, they appear to move through a narrow band in the sky. This band is called the zodiac. It includes constellations such as Taurus, Leo, and Virgo.

Some planets, when they are visible, can be seen all night long. Mars, Jupiter, and Saturn are all farther from the sun than Earth is. Sometimes, Earth passes between them and the sun. When this occurs, the planets are visible after sunset, once the sun's bright light no longer blocks the view.

You can see Venus and Mercury only in the evening or morning. They are closer to the sun than Earth, and so they always appear close to the sun. Venus is the brightest object in the night sky, other than the moon. Mercury appears low in the sky and is visible for a limited time around sunrise or sunset.

🔑 Assess Your Understanding

1a. Explain Objects in the sky appear to move from _____ to _____ because Earth turns from _____ to _____

b. Make Generalizations What determines whether a planet is visible all night long?

_____

_____

_____

_____

got it? ·····························

○ I get it! Now I know that objects in the sky appear to move _____

_____

_____

○ I need extra help with _____

Go to MY SCIENCE ⁵ COACH *online for help with this subject.*

513

Earth in Space

🔑 **How Does Earth Move?**

🔑 **What Causes Seasons?**

my pLaneT DiaRy

The Seasons

Misconception: The seasons change because Earth's distance from the sun changes.

Fact: Seasons are the result of Earth's tilted axis.

Evidence: Earth's distance from the sun does change, but that's not why Earth has seasons. If that were the cause, people in the Northern and Southern hemispheres would have the same seasons at the same time. Instead, seasons in the Northern and Southern hemispheres are reversed. As Earth moves around the sun, sometimes the Northern Hemisphere is tilted toward the sun. At other times the Southern Hemisphere is tilted toward the sun.

January
21
where are you and what are you doing today?

MISCONCEPTION

Before you read the rest of this lesson, answer the questions below.

1. Why are summers generally warmer than winters?

   _____
   _____
   _____
   _____

2. Where on Earth is the tilt of Earth least likely to affect seasons? Why?

   _____
   _____
   _____
   _____

▶ **PLANET DIARY** Go to **Planet Diary** to learn more about Earth's motions.

Lab zone
Do the Inquiry Warm-Up
What Causes Day and Night?

Vocabulary
- axis • rotation • revolution • orbit
- calendar • solstice • equinox

Skills
○ Reading: Sequence
△ Inquiry: Infer

How Does Earth Move?

Until a few hundred years ago, most people thought that Earth stood still and the sun, moon, and stars moved around it. But today, scientists know that Earth itself moves and that objects seem to move across the sky because of Earth's motion. **Earth moves in space in two major ways: rotation and revolution.**

Rotation The imaginary line that passes through Earth's center and the North and South poles is Earth's **axis.** The spinning of Earth on its axis is called **rotation.**

Earth's rotation causes day and night, as you can see in **Figure 1.** As Earth rotates eastward, the sun appears to move west across the sky. As Earth continues to turn to the east, the sun appears to set in the west. Sunlight can't reach the side of Earth facing away from the sun, so it is night there. It takes Earth about 24 hours to rotate once. As you know, each 24-hour cycle of day and night is called a day.

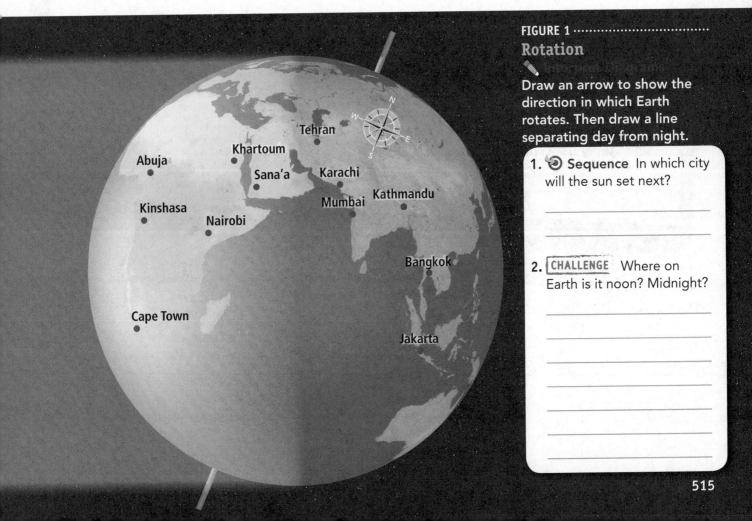

FIGURE 1 ·······················
Rotation
✏ *Interpret Diagrams*
Draw an arrow to show the direction in which Earth rotates. Then draw a line separating day from night.

1. ○ **Sequence** In which city will the sun set next?

_____

_____

2. [CHALLENGE] Where on Earth is it noon? Midnight?

_____

_____

_____

_____

_____

515

Revolution In addition to rotating, Earth travels around the sun. **Revolution** is the movement of one object around another. One revolution of Earth around the sun is called a year. Earth's path, or **orbit,** is a slightly elongated circle, or ellipse. Earth's orbit brings the planet closest to the sun in January.

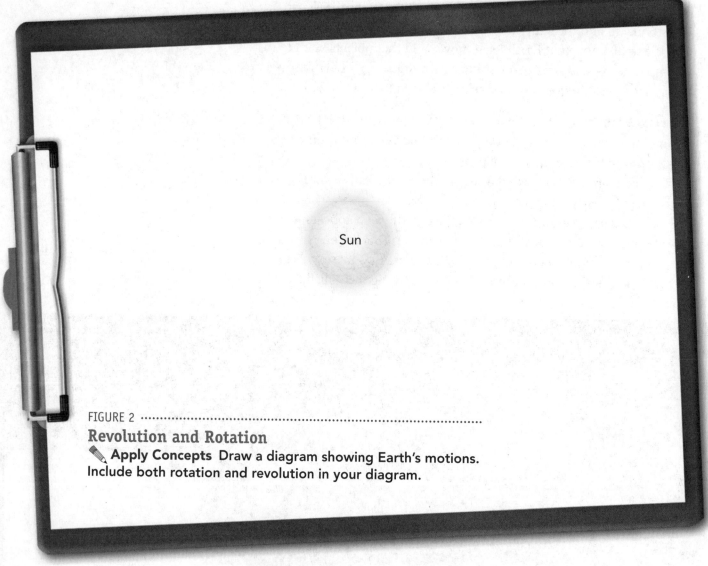

Sun

FIGURE 2 ·

Revolution and Rotation
✎ **Apply Concepts** Draw a diagram showing Earth's motions. Include both rotation and revolution in your diagram.

⊙ **Sequence** Which calendar discussed in this section was developed most recently?

Calendars People of many cultures have divided time based on the motions of Earth and the moon. They have used the motions to establish calendars. A **calendar** is a system of organizing time that defines the beginning, length, and divisions of a year.

The most common calendar today is divided into years, months, and days. One year equals the time it takes Earth to complete one orbit. One day equals the time it takes Earth to turn once on its axis. People also divide the year into months based on the moon's cycle. The time from one full moon to another is about 29 days, though modern months do not match the moon's cycle exactly.

The History of the Calendar

Egyptian

The ancient Egyptians created one of the first calendars. Based on star motions, they calculated that the year was about 365 days long. They divided the year into 12 months of 30 days each, with an extra 5 days at the end.

Roman

The Romans borrowed the Egyptian calendar. But Earth's orbit actually takes about 365¼ days. The Romans adjusted the Egyptian calendar by adding one day every four years. You know this fourth year as "leap year," when February is given 29 days instead of its usual 28. Using leap years helps to ensure that annual events, such as the beginning of summer, occur on the same date each year.

Gregorian

The Roman calendar was off by a little more than 11 minutes a year. Over the centuries, these minutes added up. By the 1500s, the beginning of spring was about ten days too early. To straighten things out, Pope Gregory XIII dropped ten days from the year 1582. He also made some other minor changes to the Roman system to form the calendar that we use today.

Lab zone ® Do the Quick Lab *Sun Shadows.*

🔑 Assess Your Understanding

1a. Identify What are the two major motions of Earth as it travels through space?

_____

b. Explain Which motion causes day and night?

_____

c. ⚠ Infer Why do people use Earth's motions to determine units of time?

_____
_____
_____

got it? ....

○ **I get it!** Now I know that Earth moves by _____
_____

○ **I need extra help with** _____

Go to **MY SCIENCE 🄢 COACH** online for help with this subject.

What Causes Seasons?

Many places that are far from Earth's equator and its poles have four distinct seasons: winter, spring, summer, and autumn. But there are differences in temperature from place to place. For instance, it is generally warmer near the equator than near the poles. Why?

How Sunlight Hits Earth
Figure 3 shows how sunlight strikes Earth's surface. Notice that, near the equator, sunlight hits Earth's surface from almost overhead. Near the poles, sunlight arrives at a steep angle. As a result, it is spread out over a greater area. That's why it is warmer near the equator than near the poles.

Earth's Tilted Axis
If Earth's axis were straight up and down relative to its orbit, temperatures in an area would remain fairly constant year-round. There would be no seasons. **Earth has seasons because its axis is tilted as it revolves around the sun.**

Notice in **Figure 4** that Earth's axis is always tilted at an angle of 23.5° from the vertical. The North Pole always points in the same direction. As Earth revolves around the sun, the north end of its axis is tilted away from the sun for part of the year and toward the sun for part of the year. Summer and winter are caused by Earth's tilt as it revolves around the sun.

FIGURE 3 ·······························

Sunlight on Earth
The diagram shows how Earth's tilted axis affects the strength of sunlight in different places.

△ **Infer** Draw a circle around the area where sunlight is most direct. Mark an X on the places that sunlight reaches, but where it is less direct.

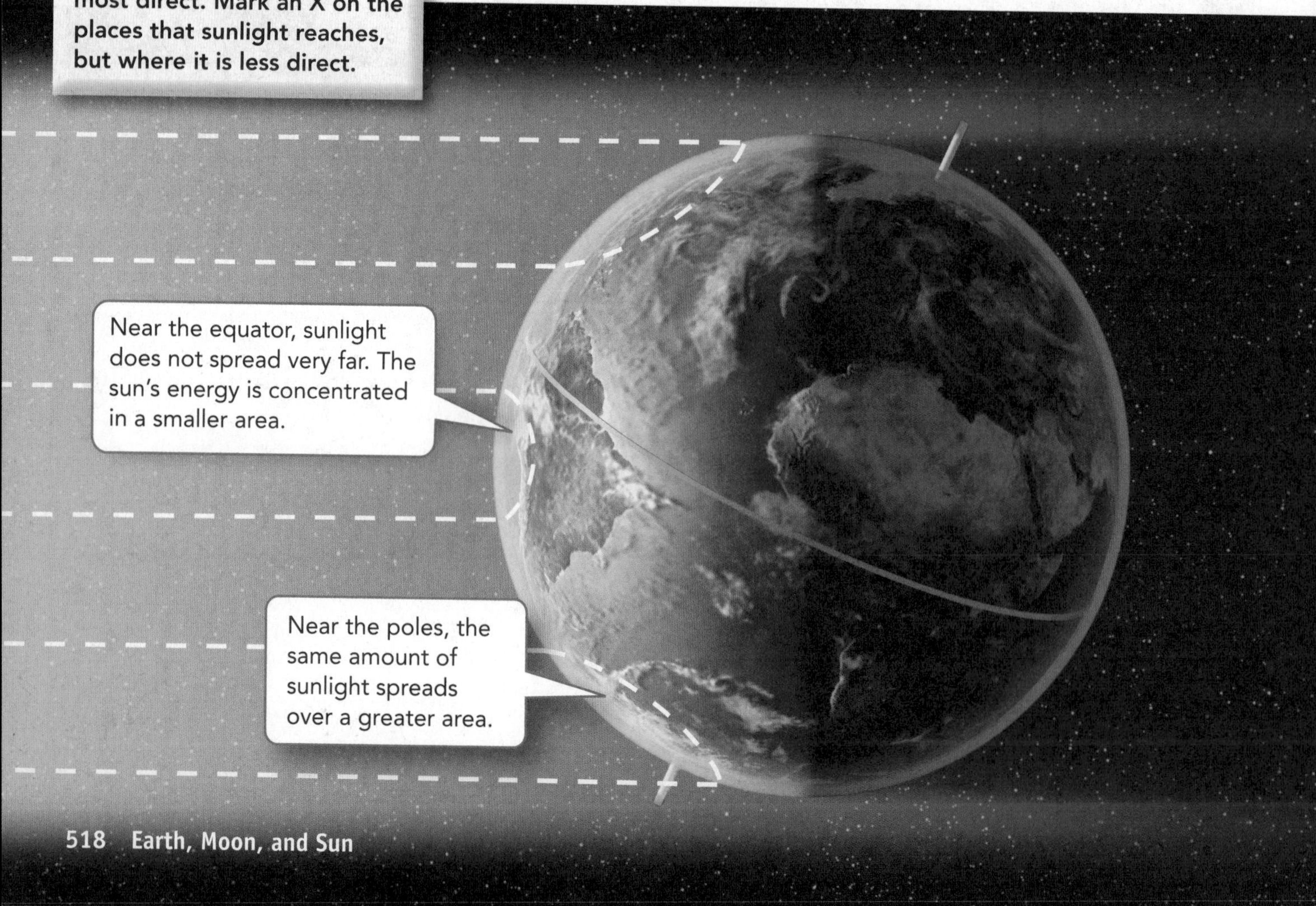

Near the equator, sunlight does not spread very far. The sun's energy is concentrated in a smaller area.

Near the poles, the same amount of sunlight spreads over a greater area.

June In June, the north end of Earth's axis is tilted toward the sun. In the Northern Hemisphere, the noon sun is high in the sky and there are more hours of daylight than darkness. The sun's rays are concentrated. It is summer in the Northern Hemisphere.

At the same time south of the equator, the sun's energy is spread over a larger area. The sun is low in the sky and days are shorter than nights. It is winter in the Southern Hemisphere.

December In December, people in the Southern Hemisphere receive the most direct sunlight, so it is summer. At the same time, the sun's rays in the Northern Hemisphere are more slanted and there are fewer hours of daylight. So it is winter in the Northern Hemisphere.

March

June

December

September

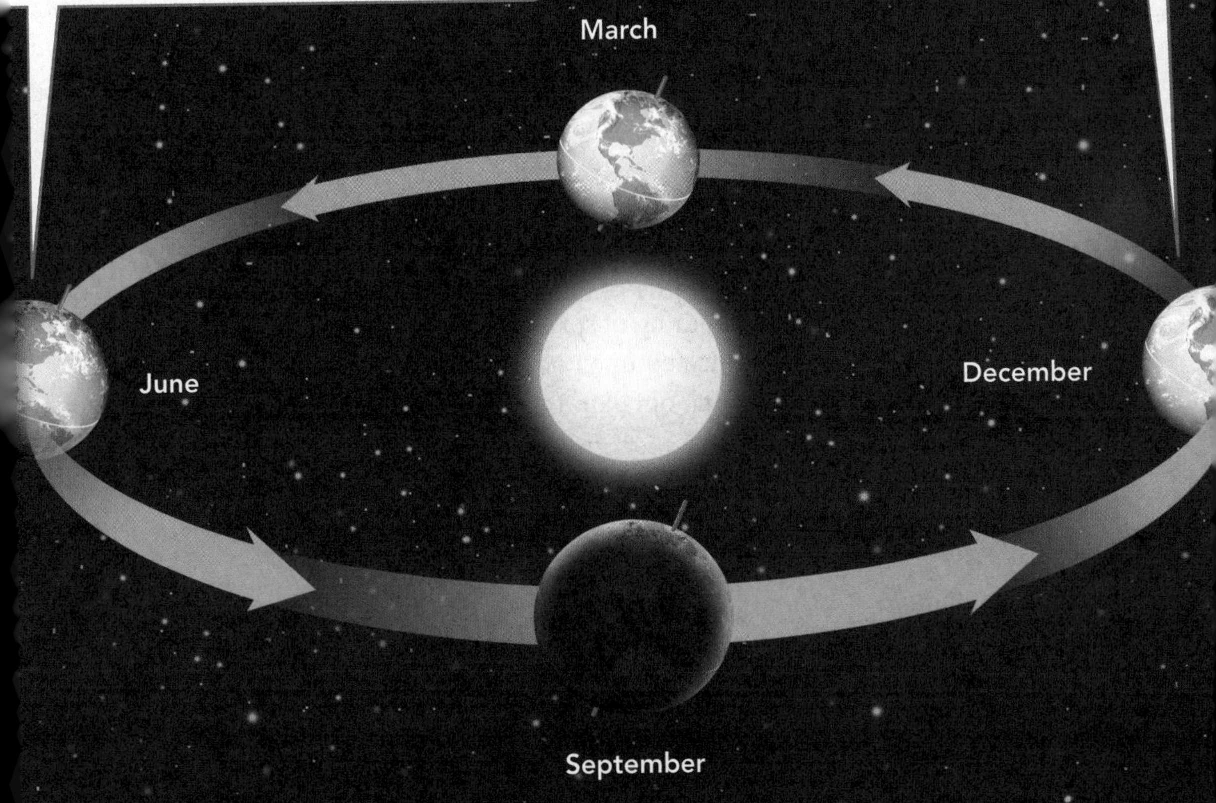

FIGURE 4 ·····························
> INTERACTIVE ART **Seasons**
The diagram shows how Earth moves during the year. It is not drawn to scale.

✎ **Make Generalizations** Describe the weather and sunlight in the Northern and Southern hemispheres in March and September.

_____
_____
_____
_____
_____
_____
_____
_____
_____

Solstices

The sun appears farthest north of the equator once each year and farthest south once each year. Each of these days is known as a **solstice** (SOHL stis). The day when the sun appears farthest north is the summer solstice in the Northern Hemisphere and the winter solstice in the Southern Hemisphere. This solstice occurs around June 21 each year. It is the longest day of the year in the Northern Hemisphere and the shortest day in the Southern Hemisphere. As you can see in **Figure 5,** the sun rises to the northeast and sets to the northwest.

Similarly, around December 21, the sun appears farthest south. This is the winter solstice in the Northern Hemisphere and the summer solstice in the Southern Hemisphere. The sun rises to the southeast and sets to the southwest.

Equinoxes

Halfway between the solstices, neither hemisphere is tilted toward the sun. The noon sun is directly overhead at the equator, rises due east, and sets due west. Each of these days is known as an **equinox,** which means "equal night." During an equinox, day and night are each about 12 hours long everywhere. The vernal (spring) equinox occurs around March 21 and marks the beginning of spring in the Northern Hemisphere. The fall, or autumnal, equinox occurs around September 22. It marks the beginning of fall in the Northern Hemisphere.

FIGURE 5 ·······························

Solstices and Equinoxes

The diagrams show the apparent path of the sun at the solstices and equinoxes in the Northern Hemisphere. The sun rises and sets farthest north at the June solstice and farthest south at the December solstice.

✎ **Apply Concepts** Draw the sun's path at the equinoxes and the December solstice for the Southern Hemisphere.

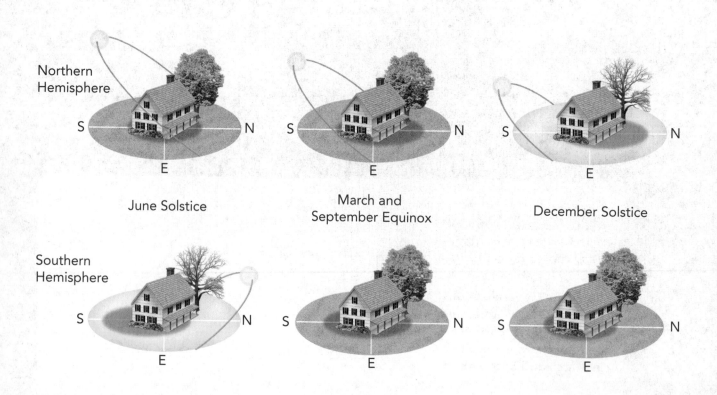

Northern Hemisphere

June Solstice

March and September Equinox

December Solstice

Southern Hemisphere

do the math! Sample Problem

Calculating Percents

The table shows the number of hours of sunlight in three cities at different times of year. What percentage of a 24-hour day has sunlight in Guadalajara on January 1?

STEP 1 Divide the number of hours of sunlight by the total number of hours.

$$\frac{\text{Hours of sunlight}}{\text{Total hours}} = \frac{10.90 \text{ hours}}{24 \text{ hours}} = 0.45$$

STEP 2 Multiply by 100 to find the percent.

$$0.45 \times 100 = 45\%$$

In Guadalajara, 45% of a 24-hour day has sunlight on January 1.

1 Calculate What percentage of a day has sunlight in Helsinki on July 1?

2 Calculate What is the difference in the percentage of the day that has sunlight in Helsinki and in Philadelphia on January 1?

3 Infer What percentage of the day would you expect to have sunlight at the equator in January? In June?

City	Approximate Latitude	Hours of Daylight			
		January 1	April 1	July 1	October 1
Helsinki, Finland	60°N	5.98	13.33	18.80	11.45
Philadelphia, United States	40°N	9.38	12.68	14.95	11.77
Guadalajara, Mexico	20°N	10.90	12.37	13.37	11.95

Lab zone® Do the Lab Investigation
Reasons for the Seasons.

Assess Your Understanding

2a. Define The noon sun is directly overhead at the equator during (a solstice/an equinox).

b. Relate Cause and Effect What causes the seasons? _____

_____

_____

c. Predict How would the seasons be different if Earth were not tilted on its axis? Explain.

_____

_____

_____

_____

_____

got it?

○ **I get it!** Now I know that Earth's seasons are caused by _____

_____

○ **I need extra help with** _____

Go to MY SCIENCE COACH *online for help with this subject.*

Gravity and Motion

🔑 **What Determines Gravity?**

🔑 **What Keeps Objects in Orbit?**

my planeT DiaRY

Gravity Assists

You might think that gravity only brings objects down. But gravity can also speed things up and send them flying! If a space probe comes close to a planet, the planet's gravity changes the probe's path. Engineers plan space missions to take advantage of these "gravity assists." A gravity assist can shorten the probe's interplanetary trip by many years. The diagram shows how the probe *Voyager 2* used gravity assists to visit all four outer planets!

Path of spacecraft

TECHNOLOGY

Use what you know about gravity to answer this question.

How does a planet's gravity change the path of a space probe?

_____

_____

_____

▶ **PLANET DIARY** Go to **Planet Diary** to learn more about gravity.

Lab zone® Do the Inquiry Warm-Up *What Factors Affect Gravity?*

What Determines Gravity?

Earth revolves around the sun in a nearly circular orbit. The moon orbits Earth in the same way. But what keeps Earth and the moon in orbit? Why don't they just fly off into space?

The first person to answer these questions was the English scientist Isaac Newton. In the 1600s, Newton realized that there must be a force acting between Earth and the moon that kept the moon in orbit. A force is a push or a pull.

Vocabulary
- force • gravity • law of universal gravitation
- mass • weight • inertia • Newton's first law of motion

Skills
⟳ Reading: Ask Questions
△ Inquiry: Draw Conclusions

Gravity Newton hypothesized that the force that pulls an apple to the ground also pulls the moon toward Earth, keeping it in orbit. This force, called **gravity,** attracts all objects toward each other. Newton's **law of universal gravitation** states that every object in the universe attracts every other object. 🔑 **The strength of the force of gravity between two objects depends on two factors: the masses of the objects and the distance between them.**

Gravity, Mass, and Weight The strength of gravity depends in part on the masses of each of the objects. **Mass** is the amount of matter in an object. Because Earth is so massive, it exerts a much greater force on you than this book does.

The measure of the force of gravity on an object is called **weight.** Mass doesn't change, but an object's weight can change depending on its location. On the moon, you would weigh about one sixth as much as on Earth. This is because the moon has less mass than Earth, so the pull of the moon's gravity on you would also be less.

Gravity and Distance Gravity is also affected by the distance between two objects. The force of gravity decreases rapidly as distance increases. If the distance between two objects doubles, the force of gravity decreases to one fourth of its original value.

did you know?

You could say we owe our understanding of gravity to disease! In 1665, Isaac Newton was a student. Then a disease called plague shut down the university for 18 months. Newton had to go home. While he was there, he thought of the ideas that led to his theory. (But it may not be true that he got the idea when an apple fell from a tree.)

FIGURE 1 ·······················

▷ VIRTUAL LAB **Gravity, Mass, and Distance**

✎ **Compare and Contrast** Draw arrows showing the force of gravity in the second and third pictures.

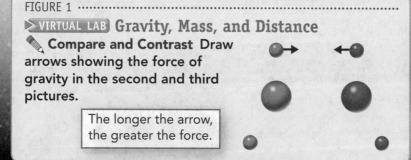

The longer the arrow, the greater the force.

Lab zone® Do the Quick Lab *What's Doing the Pulling?*

🔑 **Assess Your Understanding**

got it? ·······················

○ **I get it!** Now I know that the force of gravity depends on _____

_____

○ **I need extra help with** _____

Go to my science COACH *online for help with this subject.*

What Keeps Objects in Orbit?

If the sun and Earth are constantly pulling on one another because of gravity, why doesn't Earth fall into the sun? Similarly, why doesn't the moon crash into Earth? The fact that such collisions have not occurred shows that there must be another factor at work. That factor is called inertia.

Inertia The tendency of an object to resist a change in motion is **inertia.** You feel the effects of inertia every day. When you are riding in a car and it stops suddenly, you keep moving forward. If you didn't have a seat belt on, your inertia could cause you to bump into the car's windshield or the seat in front of you. The more mass an object has, the greater its inertia. An object with greater inertia is more difficult to start or stop.

Isaac Newton stated his ideas about inertia as a scientific law. **Newton's first law of motion** says that an object at rest will stay at rest and an object in motion will stay in motion with a constant speed and direction unless acted on by a force.

Orbital Motion Why do Earth and the moon remain in orbit? 🔑 **Newton concluded that inertia and gravity combine to keep Earth in orbit around the sun and the moon in orbit around Earth.** You can see how this occurs in **Figure 2.**

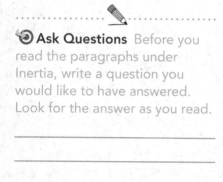

Ask Questions Before you read the paragraphs under Inertia, write a question you would like to have answered. Look for the answer as you read.

_____

_____

_____

_____

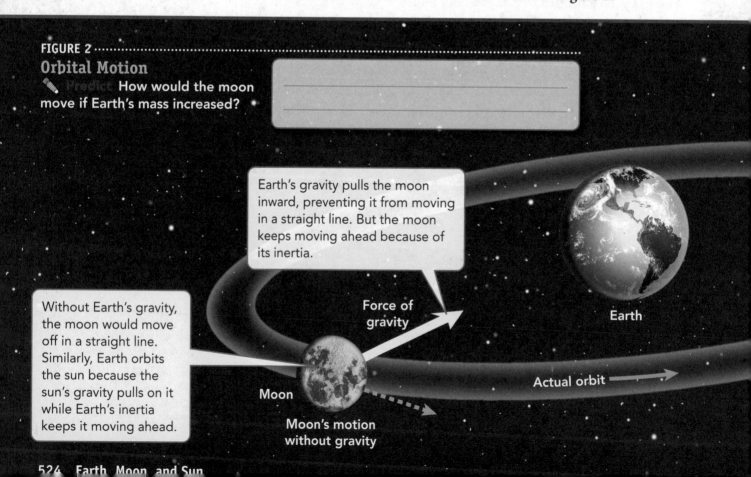

FIGURE 2 ··
Orbital Motion
✎ Predict How would the moon move if Earth's mass increased?

Earth's gravity pulls the moon inward, preventing it from moving in a straight line. But the moon keeps moving ahead because of its inertia.

Without Earth's gravity, the moon would move off in a straight line. Similarly, Earth orbits the sun because the sun's gravity pulls on it while Earth's inertia keeps it moving ahead.

Force of gravity

Earth

Moon

Actual orbit

Moon's motion without gravity

do the math! Analyzing Data

Gravity Versus Distance

As a rocket leaves a planet's surface, the force of gravity between the rocket and the planet changes. Use the graph to answer the questions below.

1 Read Graphs The variables being graphed

are _____

and _____

2 Read Graphs What is the force of gravity on the rocket at the planet's surface?

_____

3 Read Graphs What is the force of gravity on the rocket at two units (twice the planet's radius from its center)?

_____

4 Make Generalizations In general, how does the force of gravity on the rocket change as its distance from the planet increases?

_____

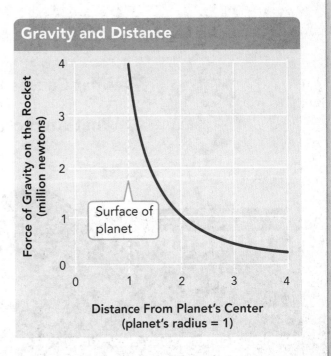

Gravity and Distance

Force of Gravity on the Rocket (million newtons)

Surface of planet

Distance From Planet's Center (planet's radius = 1)

Lab zone® Do the Quick Lab *Around and Around We Go.*

🔑 Assess Your Understanding

1a. Identify What two factors keep a planet in orbit around the sun?

_____

b. Draw Conclusions What keeps Earth from falling into the sun?

_____

c. CHALLENGE How would a planet move if the sun suddenly disappeared? Explain.

_____

_____

_____

got it? . . . .

O **I get it!** Now I know that objects are kept in orbit by _____

_____

O **I need extra help with** _____

Go to MY SCIENCE ⓢ COACH online for help with this subject.

Phases and Eclipses

🔑 **What Causes the Moon's Phases?**

🔑 **What Are Eclipses?**

my planet diary

BLOG

Posted by: Nicole

Location: Bernhard's Bay, New York

One night, my mom, dad, and I were coming home from eating dinner. When we got out of the car, we saw that the moon was turning red. We looked at the moon for a while. Then our neighbor called and said that it was a lunar eclipse. It was an amazing sight.

Think about your own experiences as you answer the question below.

What is the most interesting or unusual event you have ever seen in the sky?

_____

_____

_____

_____

_____

▷ PLANET DIARY Go to **Planet Diary** to learn more about eclipses.

 Do the Inquiry Warm-Up *How Does the Moon Move?*

What Causes the Moon's Phases?

Have you ever been kept awake by bright moonlight? The light streaming through your window actually comes from the sun! The moon does not shine with its own light. Instead, it reflects light from the sun. When the moon is full, this light may be bright enough to read by! But at other times, the moon is just a thin crescent in the sky. The different shapes of the moon you see from Earth are called **phases.** Phases are caused by the motions of the moon around Earth.

Vocabulary
- phase
- eclipse
- solar eclipse
- umbra
- penumbra
- lunar eclipse

Skills
- Reading: Relate Text and Visuals
- Inquiry: Make Models

Motions of the Moon When you look up at the moon, you may see what looks like a face. What you are really seeing is a pattern of light-colored and dark-colored areas on the moon's surface that just happens to look like a face. Oddly, this pattern never seems to move. The same side of the moon, the "near side," always faces Earth. The "far side" of the moon always faces away from Earth. Why? The answer has to do with the moon's motions.

Like Earth, the moon moves through space in two ways. The moon revolves around Earth and also rotates on its own axis. The moon rotates once on its axis in the same time that it takes to revolve once around Earth. Thus, a "day" on the moon is the same length as a month on Earth. For this reason, the same side of the moon always faces Earth, as you can see in **Figure 1.**

As the moon orbits Earth, the relative positions of the moon, Earth, and sun change. **The changing relative positions of the moon, Earth, and sun cause the phases of the moon.**

Vocabulary Identify Multiple Meanings Which sentence uses the scientific meaning of *phase*?

○ The doctor told the parent that the child was just going through a phase.

○ The moon goes through a cycle of phases every month.

FIGURE 1

The Moon's Motion
The diagram shows the moon's rotation and revolution. ✎ **Infer** Find the face on the rightmost view of the moon. Draw the face as it would appear on each view.

CHALLENGE How would the moon appear from Earth if the moon did not rotate?

_____

_____

527

Phases of the Moon Half the moon is almost always in sunlight. But since the moon orbits Earth, you see the moon from different angles. The phase of the moon you see depends on how much of the sunlit side of the moon faces Earth.

During the new moon phase, the side of the moon facing Earth is not lit. As the moon revolves around Earth, you see more of the lit side of the moon, until you see all of the lit side. As the month continues, you see less of the lit side. You can see these changes in Figure 2. About 29.5 days after the last new moon, a new moon occurs again.

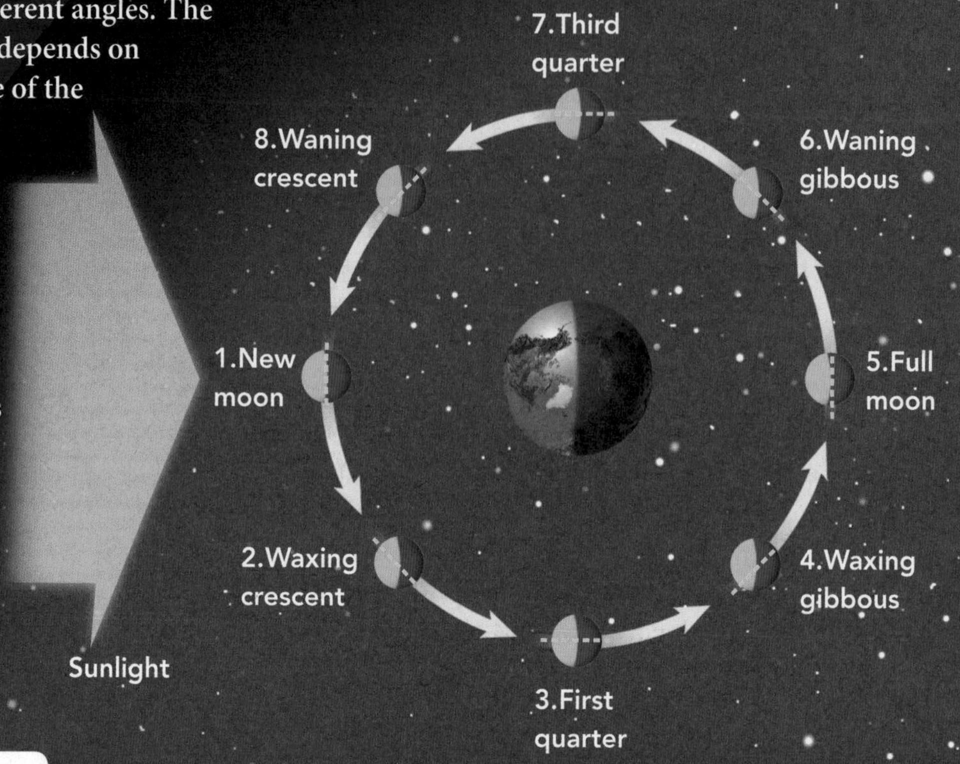

7. Third quarter

8. Waning crescent

6. Waning gibbous

1. New moon

5. Full moon

2. Waxing crescent

4. Waxing gibbous

Sunlight

3. First quarter

apply it!

⚠ **Make Models** Describe a way to model the moon's phases using items you might have at home.

_____
_____
_____
_____
_____
_____

FIGURE 2 ·······················
Moon Phases
As the moon revolves around Earth, the amount of the moon's surface that is lit remains the same. The part of the lit surface that can be seen from Earth changes.

✏ Interpret Diagrams **Match each photo to its phase shown on the diagram. Write the number of the phase.**

Lab zone® Do the Quick Lab Moon Phases.

🔑 Assess Your Understanding

got it? ···

○ **I get it!** Now I know that moon phases are caused by _____
_____

○ I need extra help with _____

Go to MY SCIENCE ⑤ COACH online for help with this subject.

What Are Eclipses?

The moon's orbit around Earth is slightly tilted with respect to Earth's orbit around the sun. As a result, the moon travels above and below Earth's orbit. But on rare occasions, Earth, the moon, and the sun line up.

When an object in space comes between the sun and a third object, it casts a shadow on that object, causing an **eclipse** (ih KLIPS) to take place. There are two types of eclipses: solar eclipses and lunar eclipses. (The words *solar* and *lunar* come from the Latin words for "sun" and "moon.")

Solar Eclipses During a new moon, the moon lies between Earth and the sun. ⟜ A solar eclipse occurs when the moon passes directly between Earth and the sun, blocking sunlight from Earth. The moon's shadow then hits Earth.

Total Solar Eclipses The very darkest part of the moon's shadow is the umbra (UM bruh). You can see how the umbra strikes Earth in **Figure 3**. Within the umbra, the sun's light is completely blocked. Only people within the umbra experience a total solar eclipse. During a total solar eclipse, the sky grows as dark as night. The air gets cool and the sky becomes an eerie color. You can see the stars and the solar corona, which is the faint outer atmosphere of the sun.

Partial Solar Eclipses The moon casts another part of its shadow that is less dark than the umbra. This larger part of the shadow is called the penumbra (peh NUM bruh). In the penumbra, part of the sun is visible from Earth. During a solar eclipse, people in the penumbra see only a partial eclipse.

FIGURE 3 ·······························

Solar Eclipse
The diagram shows the moon's penumbra and umbra during an eclipse. It is not drawn to scale.

↩ Relate Text and Visuals
Mark an X to show where a total solar eclipse would be visible. Circle the area in which a partial solar eclipse would be visible.

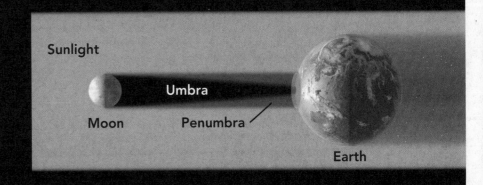

Sunlight

Umbra

Moon

Penumbra

Earth

Lunar Eclipses During most months, the moon moves near Earth's shadow but not quite into it. A lunar eclipse occurs at a full moon when Earth is directly between the moon and the sun. You can see a lunar eclipse in Figure 4. 🔑 During a lunar eclipse, Earth blocks sunlight from reaching the moon. Lunar eclipses occur only when there is a full moon because the moon is closest to Earth's shadow at that time.

✏️ Relate Text and Visuals
Mark an X on the photograph above that shows a total eclipse.

Total Lunar Eclipses Like the moon's shadow in a solar eclipse, Earth's shadow has an umbra and a penumbra. When the moon is in Earth's umbra, you see a total lunar eclipse. Unlike a total solar eclipse, a total lunar eclipse can be seen anywhere on Earth that the moon is visible. So you are more likely to see a total lunar eclipse than a total solar eclipse.

Partial Lunar Eclipses For most lunar eclipses, Earth, the moon, and the sun are not quite in line, and only a partial lunar eclipse results. A partial lunar eclipse occurs when the moon passes partly into the umbra of Earth's shadow. The edge of the umbra appears blurry, and you can watch it pass across the moon for two or three hours.

FIGURE 4 ·······························
Lunar Eclipse
As the moon moves through Earth's shadow, total and partial eclipses occur. This diagram is not to scale.

✏️ Infer Draw a circle labeled *T* to show where the moon would be during a total eclipse. Draw two circles labeled *P* to show two places the moon could be during a partial eclipse.

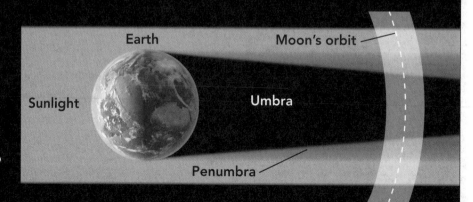

Earth

Moon's orbit

Sunlight

Umbra

Penumbra

Seasons and Shadows

How do Earth, the moon, and the sun interact?

FIGURE 5 ··

▶ INTERACTIVE ART Look at the diagram below. (The diagram is not to scale.) Identify what season it is in the Northern Hemisphere, what the phase of the moon is, and what kind of eclipse, if any, could occur.

Season

_____

Moon Phase

_____

Eclipse

_____

Use the above diagram as a model. Draw the arrangement of Earth, the moon, and the sun during a total lunar eclipse in December.

Do the Quick Lab
Eclipses.

🗝 Assess Your Understanding

1a. Explain A (solar/lunar) eclipse occurs when the moon passes into Earth's shadow. A (solar/lunar) eclipse occurs when Earth passes into the moon's shadow.

b. ANSWER THE BIG ❓ How do Earth, the moon, and the sun interact? _____

_____

_____

_____

got it? ··

○ **I get it!** Now I know that eclipses occur when _____

_____

○ **I need extra help with** _____

Go to my science ⬛ COACH online for help with this subject.

🔑 What Are Tides?

UNLOCK
THE BIG
?

my planeT DiaRY

FUN FACT

A River in Reverse

If you were visiting New Brunswick in Canada, you might see the Saint John River flowing into the ocean. But six hours later, you might find that the river changed direction while you were gone! How could this happen? The Saint John River really does reverse course twice a day. At low tide, it empties into the Bay of Fundy, shown below. At high tide, the Bay of Fundy's tide pushes into the river, forcing the river to run in the opposite direction. The Bay of Fundy's tides are among the highest in the world.

Use your experience to answer the questions.

1. Why does the Saint John River change direction?

_____

_____

_____

2. Have you ever seen a natural event that surprised you? Why was it surprising?

_____

_____

_____

 PLANET DIARY Go to **Planet Diary** to learn more about tides.

Lab® zone Do the Inquiry Warm-Up *When Is High Tide?*

High tide

Low tide

Vocabulary
- tide
- spring tide
- neap tide

Skills
- Reading: Relate Cause and Effect
- Inquiry: Observe

What Are Tides?

The reversing Saint John River is caused by ocean **tides,** the rise and fall of ocean water that occurs every 12.5 hours or so. The water rises for about six hours, then falls for about six hours.

The Tide Cycle The force of gravity pulls the moon and Earth (including the water on Earth's surface) toward each other. 🔑 **Tides are caused mainly by differences in how much gravity from the moon and the sun pulls on different parts of Earth.**

At any one time on Earth, there are two places with high tides and two places with low tides. As Earth rotates, one high tide occurs on the side of Earth that faces the moon. The second high tide occurs on the opposite side of Earth. **Figure 1** explains why.

✎ **Relate Cause and Effect** As you read **Figure 1,** underline the causes of high and low tides.

FIGURE 1 ·······

> **ART IN MOTION** **Tides**

You can think of Earth as a ball surrounded by a layer of water, as shown here. The layer is really much thinner than this, but is drawn thicker so it is easier to see.

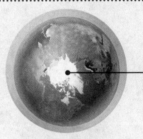

— North Pole

The Near Side The moon's gravity pulls a little more strongly on the water on the side closest to the moon than on Earth as a whole. This difference causes a bulge of water on the side of Earth closest to the moon. This bulge causes high tide.

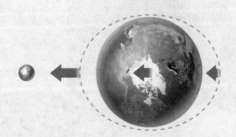

The Far Side The moon's gravity pulls more weakly on the water on the far side of Earth than on Earth as a whole. Since Earth is pulled more strongly, the water is "left behind." Water flows toward the far side, causing high tide. Halfway between the high tides, water flows toward the high tides, causing low tide.

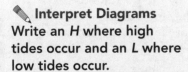
✎ **Interpret Diagrams** Write an *H* where high tides occur and an *L* where low tides occur.

The Sun's Role Even though the sun is about 150 million kilometers from Earth, it is so massive that its gravity affects the tides. The sun pulls the water on Earth's surface toward it. 🔑 Changes in the positions of Earth, the moon, and the sun affect the heights of the tides during a month.

New Moon

The sun, the moon, and Earth are nearly in a line during a new moon. The gravity of the sun and the moon pull in the same direction. Their combined forces produce a tide with the greatest difference between consecutive low and high tides, called a **spring tide.** The term "spring tide" comes from an Old English word, *springen,* meaning "to jump."

First Quarter

During the moon's first-quarter phase, the line between Earth and the sun is at right angles to the line between Earth and the moon. The sun's pull is at right angles to the moon's pull. This arrangement produces a **neap tide,** a tide with the least difference between consecutive low and high tides. Neap tides occur twice a month.

Full Moon

At full moon, the moon and the sun are on opposite sides of Earth. Since there are high tides on both sides of Earth, a spring tide is also produced. It doesn't matter in which order the sun, Earth, and the moon line up.

Third Quarter

✎ **Infer** Draw the position of the moon and the tide bulges at third quarter. What kind of tide occurs?

_____

apply it!

The table shows high and low tides at four times in May 2008, in St. John, New Brunswick. St. John is on the Bay of Fundy.

① Interpret Data Spring tides occurred at two of the times shown. Which two? How do you know?

_____

_____

_____

② CHALLENGE Would the tide be higher when the moon is on the same side of Earth as New Brunswick or on the opposite side? Why?

_____

_____

_____

_____

_____

High and Low Tides at St. John, New Brunswick

Date	High Tide (meters)	Low Tide (meters)
May 6–7	8.7	0.0
May 13–14	7.1	1.7
May 21	7.5	1.2
May 26	6.9	2.0

Vocabulary Identify Multiple Meanings Does a spring tide always happen in the season of spring? Explain your answer.

_____

_____

_____

_____

_____

_____

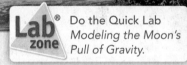

Lab zone® Do the Quick Lab Modeling the Moon's Pull of Gravity.

🔑 Assess Your Understanding

1a. Review Most coastal areas have _____ high tides and _____ low tides each day.

b. 🔄 Relate Cause and Effect What causes tides?

_____

_____

_____

c. Observe Look at the diagrams on the previous page. What is the angle formed by the sun, Earth, and the moon during a neap tide? A spring tide?

_____

_____

_____

got it?

○ **I get it!** Now I know that tides are _____

_____

○ **I need extra help with** _____

Go to MY SCIENCE ⑤ COACH online for help with this subject.

Earth's Moon

UNLOCK THE BIG

🔑 **What Is the Moon Like?**

MY PLANET DIARY

VOICES FROM HISTORY

Galileo Galilei

In 1609, the Italian astronomer Galileo Galilei turned a new tool—the telescope—toward the moon. What he saw amazed him: wide dark areas and strange spots and ridges.

I have been led to that opinion... that I feel sure that the surface of the Moon is not perfectly smooth...but that, on the contrary, it is ... just like the surface of the Earth itself, which is varied everywhere by high mountains and deep valleys.

Today, scientists know that Galileo was right. Powerful telescopes have shown the mountains and craters on the moon, and astronauts have walked and driven over the moon's surface.

✏️ **Communicate** Discuss Galileo's observations with a partner. Then answer the questions below.

1. What conclusions did Galileo draw about the moon?

_____

_____

2. How do you think it would feel to make an observation that no one had made before?

_____

_____

_____

▶ PLANET DIARY Go to **Planet Diary** to learn more about Earth's moon.

Lab zone® Do the Inquiry Warm-Up *Why Do Craters Look Different From Each Other?*

Vocabulary
- maria • crater
- meteoroid

Skills
- Reading: Compare and Contrast
- Inquiry: Develop Hypotheses

What Is the Moon Like?

For thousands of years, people could see the moon, but didn't know much about it. Galileo's observations were some of the first to show details on the moon's surface. Scientists have since learned more about the moon's features. **The moon is dry and airless and has an irregular surface. Compared to Earth, the moon is small and has large variations in its surface temperature.**

Surface Features As **Figure 1** shows, the moon has many unusual structures, including maria, craters, and highlands.

Maria Dark, flat areas, called **maria** (MAH ree uh), are hardened rock formed from huge lava flows that occurred 3–4 billion years ago. The singular form of *maria* is *mare* (MAH ray).

Craters Large round pits called **craters** can be hundreds of kilometers across. These craters were caused by the impacts of **meteoroids,** chunks of rock or dust from space. Maria have relatively few craters. This means that most of the moon's craters formed from impacts early in its history, before maria formed.

Highlands Some of the light-colored features you can see on the moon's surface are highlands, or mountains. The peaks of the lunar highlands and the rims of the craters cast dark shadows. The highlands cover most of the moon's surface.

FIGURE 1 ·······················

Moon Features
This photograph shows the features of the northern part of the side of the moon that you can see from Earth.

✏ **Relate Diagrams and Photos** How is the photograph different from Galileo's drawing on the previous page?

_____

_____

_____

_____

FIGURE 2

Different Worlds
This photo of Earth, taken from orbit around the moon, clearly shows the contrast between the barren moon and water-covered Earth.

✎ Compare and Contrast
Complete the table below to compare and contrast Earth and the moon.

Size and Density
The moon is 3,476 kilometers across, a little less than the distance across the United States. This is about one fourth of Earth's diameter. However, the moon has only one eightieth as much mass as Earth. Though Earth has a very dense core, its outer layers are less dense. The moon's average density is similar to the density of Earth's outer layers. Its gravity is about one sixth of Earth's.

Temperature
At the moon's equator, temperatures range from a torrid 130°C in direct sunlight to a frigid −170°C at night. Temperatures at the poles are even colder. Temperatures vary so much because the moon does not have an atmosphere. The moon's surface gravity is so weak that gases can easily escape into space.

Water
For many years, people thought the moon had no water, except for small amounts of ice. In 2009, scientists using data from several space probes determined that a thin layer of water exists in the moon's soil. The total amount of water is very small, but it is found in many places on the moon's surface.

Origins of the Moon
Scientists have suggested many possible theories for how the moon formed. The theory that seems to best fit the evidence is called the collision-ring theory. About 4.5 billion years ago, when Earth was very young, the solar system was full of rocky debris. Scientists theorize that a planet-sized object collided with Earth. Material from the object and Earth's outer layers was ejected into orbit around Earth, where it formed a ring. Gravity caused this material to clump together to form the moon.

	Density	Temperatures	Atmosphere	Water
Earth				
Moon				

apply it!

Within your lifetime, tourists may be able to travel to the moon. If you were taking a trip to the moon, what would you pack? Remember that the moon is dry, has almost no liquid water, and has no atmosphere.

1 Solve Problems On the packing list to the right, list five items you would need on the moon.

2 CHALLENGE List two items that you could not use on the moon. Why would they not work?

_____
_____
_____
_____
_____
_____
_____

Things to Pack

1. _____
2. _____
3. _____
4. _____
5. _____

Lab zone® Do the Quick Lab Moonwatching.

🔑 Assess Your Understanding

1a. List What are the three main surface features on the moon?

_____

b. 🔄 Compare and Contrast How does the moon's gravity compare with Earth's?

_____

c. Develop Hypotheses Write a hypothesis explaining why the moon has very little liquid water.

_____
_____
_____

got it? ....

O **I get it!** Now I know that the characteristics of Earth's moon are _____

_____

O **I need extra help with** _____

Go to MY SCIENCE ⬤ COACH online for help with this subject.

14 Study Guide

 Interactions between Earth, the moon, and the sun cause _____, _____, _____, and _____.

LESSON 1 The Sky From Earth

🔑 On a clear night, you may see stars, the moon, planets, meteors, and comets.

🔑 A constellation is a pattern or grouping of stars imagined by people to represent figures.

🔑 The apparent motion of objects in the sky depends on the motions of Earth.

Vocabulary
- satellite • planet • meteor • comet
- star • constellation

LESSON 2 Earth in Space

🔑 Earth moves in space in two major ways: rotation and revolution.

🔑 Earth has seasons because its axis is tilted as it revolves around the sun.

Vocabulary
- axis • rotation
- revolution
- orbit • calendar
- solstice • equinox

LESSON 3 Gravity and Motion

🔑 The strength of the force of gravity between two objects depends on two factors: the masses of the objects and the distance between them.

🔑 Newton concluded that inertia and gravity combine to keep Earth in orbit around the sun and the moon in orbit around Earth.

Vocabulary
- force • gravity • law of universal gravitation
- mass • weight • inertia
- Newton's first law of motion

LESSON 4 Phases and Eclipses

🔑 The changing relative positions of the moon, Earth, and sun cause the phases of the moon.

🔑 A solar eclipse occurs when the moon passes directly between Earth and the sun, blocking sunlight from Earth. During a lunar eclipse, Earth blocks sunlight from reaching the moon.

Vocabulary
- phase • eclipse • solar eclipse • umbra
- penumbra • lunar eclipse

LESSON 5 Tides

🔑 Tides are caused by differences in how much gravity from the moon and the sun pulls on different parts of Earth.

🔑 Changes in the positions of Earth, the moon, and the sun affect the heights of the tides during a month.

Vocabulary
- tide • spring tide • neap tide

LESSON 6 Earth's Moon

🔑 The moon is dry and airless and has an irregular surface. Compared to Earth, the moon is small and has large variations in its surface temperature.

Vocabulary
- maria • crater
- meteoroid

Review and Assessment

LESSON 1 The Sky From Earth

1. Which of the following objects is found in Earth's atmosphere?

a. comet **b.** meteor

c. moon **d.** planet

2. Over time, people have given names to groups of stars, called _____

3. Predict The constellation Orion appears in the eastern sky in December. Where would you expect it to appear in March? Why?

_____

_____

 4. Write About It Suppose you were camping on a summer night. Describe what objects you might see in the sky and how the sky would change throughout the night.

LESSON 2 Earth in Space

5. What is Earth's annual motion around the sun called?

a. month **b.** revolution

c. rotation **d.** seasons

6. The _____ occurs when the sun is farthest north of the equator.

7. Infer Mars's axis is tilted at about the same angle as Earth's axis. Do you think Mars has seasons? Explain your answer.

_____

_____

 8. Write About It Write a guide for younger children explaining how Earth's motions are related to the lengths of days and years.

LESSON 3 Gravity and Motion

9. The tendency of an object to resist a change in motion is called

a. force. **b.** gravity.

c. inertia. **d.** weight.

10. An object is kept in orbit by _____ and _____

11. Relate Cause and Effect If you move two objects farther apart, how does the force of gravity between the two objects change?

_____

12. Compare and Contrast How are weight and mass different? _____

_____

_____

13. Explain Explain Newton's first law of motion in your own words. _____

_____

_____

_____

_____

Use this illustration to answer Question 14.

450 N

14. math! How much would the person above weigh on the moon? _____

LESSON 4 Phases and Eclipses

15. The moon's shadow falling on Earth causes a

    a. full moon.   **b.** lunar eclipse.

    c. phase.   **d.** solar eclipse.

16. The darkest part of the moon's shadow is the

_____

17. Relate Cause and Effect Why does the moon have phases? _____

_____

_____

18. Make Generalizations Which occurs more often, a partial or a total lunar eclipse? Why?

_____

_____

_____

LESSON 5 Tides

19. About how long passes between high tides?

    a. 6 hours   **b.** 12 hours

    c. 24 hours   **d.** 48 hours

20. The least difference between high and low tides occurs during a _____

Use the diagram to answer Question 21.

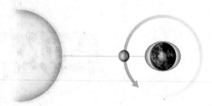

21. Interpret Diagrams Does the diagram show a spring or a neap tide? How do you know?

_____

_____

LESSON 6 Earth's Moon

22. What caused the moon's craters?

    a. maria   **b.** meteoroids

    c. tides   **d.** volcanoes

23. The moon's light-colored highlands are

_____

24. Explain Why do temperatures vary so much on the moon? _____

_____

_____

_____

25. 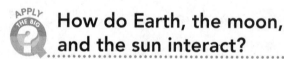 **Write About It** Suppose you were hired to design a spacesuit for use on the moon. What characteristics of the moon would be important for you to consider? Explain.

How do Earth, the moon, and the sun interact?

26. Can more people see a total solar eclipse or a total lunar eclipse? Explain your answer.

_____

_____

_____

_____

_____

_____

_____

_____

_____

_____

_____

Standardized Test Prep

Multiple Choice

Circle the letter of the best answer.

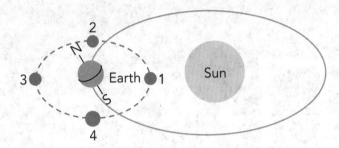

1. Which of the following can occur when the moon is at location 1?

   A only a lunar eclipse

   B only a solar eclipse

   C both a solar and a lunar eclipse

   D neither a solar nor a lunar eclipse

2. On what does the force of gravity between two objects depend?

   A mass and weight

   B speed and distance

   C weight and speed

   D mass and distance

3. What happens at a spring tide?

   A There is only one high tide each day.

   B There is only one low tide each day.

   C There is the most difference between consecutive high and low tides.

   D There is the least difference between consecutive high and low tides.

4. Which motion does Earth complete every 365 days?

   A eclipse

   B equinox

   C revolution

   D rotation

5. The calendar we use is based on

   A the time it takes the moon to rotate once on its axis.

   B the time it takes Earth to complete one orbit.

   C the occurrence of a solar eclipse.

   D the length of each season.

Constructed Response

Use the diagram below to answer the question.

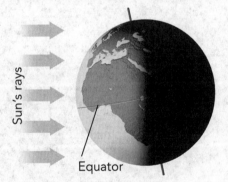

6. In the Northern Hemisphere, is it the summer solstice, winter solstice, or one of the equinoxes? Explain how you know.

KEEPING TRACK OF TIME

▲ This sun stone is sometimes called the Aztec calendar. It shows the 20 days in the Aztec month. The Aztec calendar was a solar calendar, with a total of 365 days in a year.

What day of the week is your birthday this year? Better check the calendar.

Calendars were invented to keep track of important events, such as planting schedules and festivals.

Early people noticed certain patterns in nature. The seasons change. The sun rises and sets. The moon changes phases. These patterns became the basis for calendars even before people understood that Earth rotates on an axis and revolves around the sun or that the moon revolves around Earth.

Calendars were lunar (based on the moon), solar (based on the sun), or lunisolar (based on a combination). But none was completely accurate—important events shifted around from one year to the next.

The Gregorian calendar, introduced in 1582, is the standard calendar in use today. It is more accurate than most calendars, but even it requires some tinkering. We add an extra day almost every four years, giving us a leap year. Century years (like 2000) are not leap years unless they are divisible by 400.

Research It There are about 40 different kinds of calendars in use today. Pick one and research it. Write an essay describing the calendar and how it is different from the Gregorian calendar. What does the calendar tell you about the society that uses it?

SPACE SPINOFFS

Do you have any space gadgets in your home? You almost certainly do. The scientists and engineers who have worked on the space program have developed thousands of new materials and devices for use in space. Many of those items are useful on Earth as well. An item that has uses on Earth but was originally developed for use in space is called a space spinoff.

Space spinoffs include many new materials, as well as devices used in consumer products and medical technology. Here are some examples:

Space Technology	Spinoff Use
Joystick controllers	Wheelchairs and video games
Scratch-resistant lenses	Eyeglasses
Freeze-dried foods	Camping provisions
Shock-absorbing helmets	Bicycle helmets
Composite materials	Tennis rackets and golf clubs
Memory metals	Flexible eyeglass frames
Clear ceramics	Dental braces
Shielding material	Houses, cars, and trucks
Computer-aided imaging	Hospital diagnosis techniques
Lasers	Surgical techniques
Longer-life batteries	Pacemakers for hearts

Research It Research space spinoffs developed throughout the history of the space program. Design an illustrated timeline that displays the five spinoffs that you think are the most useful. Display your timeline and defend your choices in class.

▲ Game controllers are an example of space spinoffs.

545

WHAT MIGHT SATURN'S RINGS BE MADE OF?

Why are objects in the solar system different from each other?

This photograph from the *Cassini* space probe shows Saturn and part of its magnificent system of rings. Space probes such as *Cassini* have helped scientists learn more about the objects in the solar system.

△**Infer** What do you think Saturn's rings are made of? How might they have formed?

_____
_____
_____
_____
_____
_____

> **UNTAMED SCIENCE** Watch the **Untamed Science** video to learn more about the solar system.

The Solar System

15 Getting Started

Check Your Understanding

1. **Background** Read the paragraph below and then answer the question.

> Tyrone is watching a movie. He sees astronauts explore a planet that **revolves** around a star. As the astronauts travel, they notice that the planet **rotates**. Tyrone knows that **gravity** holds the planet in orbit around the star.

Revolution is the motion of one object around another.

An object **rotates** when it spins around a central axis.

Gravity is the force that attracts all objects toward each other.

• What causes day and night on a planet?

_____

_____

> **MY READING WEB** If you had trouble completing the question above, visit **My Reading Web** and type in *The Solar System.*

Vocabulary Skill

Greek Word Origins Many science words come to English from Greek. In this chapter, you will learn the term *geocentric. Geocentric* comes from the Greek word parts *ge,* meaning "Earth," and *kentron,* meaning "center."

$$\underset{\text{Earth}}{ge} + \underset{\text{center}}{kentron} = \underset{\text{having Earth at the center}}{geocentric}$$

Learn these Greek word parts to help you remember the vocabulary terms.

Greek Word	Meaning	Example
helios	sun	heliocentric, *adj.*
chromas	color	chromosphere, *n.*
sphaira	sphere	photosphere, *n.*

2. **Quick Check** Predict the meaning of *heliocentric.*

_____

_____

planet

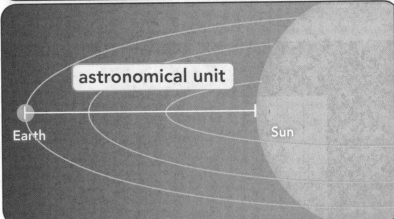

astronomical unit

Earth   Sun

solar system

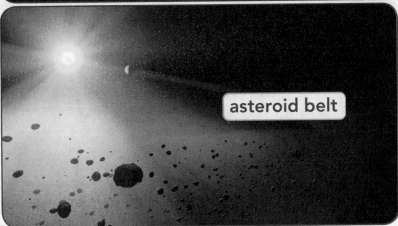

asteroid belt

Chapter Preview

LESSON 1
- geocentric • heliocentric
- ellipse
- ↻ Sequence
- △ Make Models

LESSON 2
- solar system • astronomical unit
- planet • dwarf planet
- planetesimal
- ↻ Identify Supporting Evidence
- △ Calculate

LESSON 3
- core • nuclear fusion
- radiation zone • convection zone
- photosphere • chromosphere
- corona • solar wind • sunspot
- prominence • solar flare
- ↻ Relate Cause and Effect
- △ Interpret Data

LESSON 4
- terrestrial planet
- greenhouse effect
- ↻ Compare and Contrast
- △ Communicate

LESSON 5
- gas giant • ring
- ↻ Outline
- △ Pose Questions

LESSON 6
- asteroid belt • Kuiper belt
- Oort cloud • comet
- coma • nucleus • asteroid
- meteoroid • meteor • meteorite
- ↻ Summarize
- △ Classify

> **VOCAB FLASH CARDS** For extra help
with vocabulary, visit **Vocab Flash
Cards** and type in *The Solar System.*

Models of the Solar System

UNLOCK THE BIG Q?

🔑 **What Was the Geocentric Model?**

🔑 **How Did the Heliocentric Model Develop?**

my planet Diary

Picturing the Solar System

When Walter Myers was seven years old, he found a book with drawings of astronauts walking on the moons of Saturn. Ever since, he's been making space pictures himself. At first, he used pencil. Today, he works on computers. He likes using computers because he can create images that are more like photographs, such as the ones below.

As an artist, Mr. Myers can show scenes that haven't been photographed, such as ideas for future spacecraft and the views from another planet's moons. Mr. Myers especially likes creating views of what human visitors to other planets might see. His work has appeared in books, magazines, Web sites, and even on television!

Use what you have read to answer these questions.

1. What tool does Walter Myers use?

_____

2. Why do people use art or other models to show objects in the solar system?

_____

_____

_____

▶ PLANET DIARY Go to **Planet Diary** to learn more about models of the solar system.

Lab zone® Do the Inquiry Warm-Up *What Is at the Center?*

Vocabulary
- geocentric
- heliocentric
- ellipse

Skills
- Reading: Sequence
- Inquiry: Make Models

What Was the Geocentric Model?

From here on Earth, it seems as if our planet is stationary and that the sun, moon, and stars are moving around Earth. But is the sky really moving above you? Centuries ago, before there were space shuttles or even telescopes, people had no easy way to find out.

Ancient Observations Ancient observers, including the Greeks, Chinese, and Mayans, noticed that the patterns of the stars didn't change over time. Although the stars seemed to move, they stayed in the same position relative to one another. These people also observed planets, which moved among the stars.

Many early observers thought Earth was at the center of the universe. Some Chinese observers thought Earth was under a dome of stars. Many Greek astronomers thought that Earth was inside rotating spheres nested inside each other. These spheres contained the stars and planets. Since *ge* is the Greek word for "Earth," an Earth-centered model is known as a **geocentric** (jee oh SEN trik) model. **In a geocentric model, Earth is at the center of the revolving planets and stars.**

Ptolemy's Model About A.D. 140, the Greek astronomer Ptolemy (TAHL uh mee) further developed the geocentric model. Like the earlier Greeks, Ptolemy thought that Earth was at the center of the universe. In Ptolemy's model, however, the planets moved in small circles carried along in bigger circles.

Ptolemy's geocentric model explained the motions observed in the sky fairly accurately. As a result, the geocentric model of the universe was widely accepted for nearly 1,500 years after Ptolemy.

apply it!

Critique Scientific Explanations and Models Describe an experience from everyday life that appears to support the geocentric model.

_____
_____
_____
_____
_____
_____

Lab zone Do the Quick Lab *Going Around in Circles.*

Assess Your Understanding

got it? ....

O I get it! Now I know that the geocentric model is _____

_____

O I need extra help with _____

Go to my science COACH online for help with this subject.

How Did the Heliocentric Model Develop?

Not everybody believed in the geocentric system. An ancient Greek scientist named Aristarchus developed a sun-centered model called a heliocentric (hee lee oh SEN trik) system. *Helios* is Greek for "sun." In a heliocentric system, Earth and the other planets revolve around the sun. This model was not well received in ancient times, however, because people could not accept that Earth was not at the center of the universe.

FIGURE 1 ···

Changing Models

⚠ Make Models Draw each model of the solar system. Include the sun, Earth, the moon, and Jupiter. Include Jupiter's moons in Galileo's model.

CHALLENGE   Why might people not have believed Galileo's discoveries?

_____

_____

A.D.   1500   1550

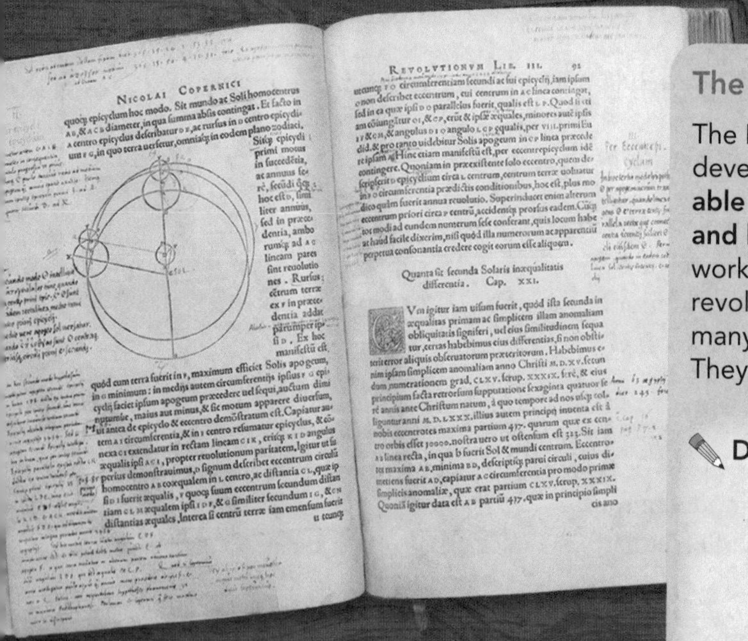

The Copernican Revolution

The Polish astronomer Nicolaus Copernicus further developed the heliocentric model. 🔑 **Copernicus was able to work out the arrangement of the known planets and how they move around the sun.** He published his work in 1543. Copernicus's theory would eventually revolutionize the science of astronomy. But at first many people were unwilling to accept his theory. They needed more evidence to be convinced.

✏️ Draw Copernicus's model.

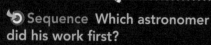

↺ Sequence Which astronomer did his work first?
- Tycho Brahe
- Nicolaus Copernicus
- Galileo Galilei
- Johannes Kepler

Brahe and Kepler

Ptolemy and Copernicus both assumed that planets moved in perfect circles. Their models fit existing observations fairly well. But in the late 1500s, the Dutch astronomer Tycho Brahe (TEE koh BRAH uh) made much more accurate observations. Brahe's assistant, Johannes Kepler, used the observations to figure out the shape of the planets' orbits. When he used circular orbits, his calculations did not fit the observations. **After years of detailed calculations, Kepler found that the orbit of each planet is an ellipse. An ellipse is an oval shape.**

Tycho Brahe's Observatory

1600   1650

✏️ **Draw Kepler's model.**

Galileo's Evidence

In the 1500s and early 1600s, most people still believed in the geocentric model. **However, evidence collected by the Italian scientist Galileo Galilei gradually convinced others that the heliocentric model was correct.** In 1610, Galileo used a telescope to discover four moons around Jupiter. These moons proved that not everything in the sky revolves around Earth. Galileo also discovered that Venus goes through a series of phases similar to the moon's. But Venus would not have a full set of phases if both it and the sun circled around Earth. Therefore, Galileo reasoned, the geocentric model must be incorrect.

✏️ **Draw Galileo's model.**

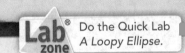
Lab zone Do the Quick Lab A Loopy Ellipse.

🔑 Assess Your Understanding

1a. Review (Kepler/Copernicus) discovered that planets move in ellipses.

b. Relate Evidence and Explanation What discoveries by Galileo support the heliocentric model?

_____

_____

got it?

○ **I get it!** Now I know that the heliocentric model was developed _____

_____

○ **I need extra help with** _____

Go to MY SCIENCE COACH online for help with this subject.

2 Introducing the Solar System

UNLOCK THE BIG ?

🔑 **What Makes Up the Solar System?**

🔑 **How Did the Solar System Form?**

my planet Diary

Extreme Conditions

Imagine a place where the sun shines 11 times brighter than it does on Earth. How could you keep anything cool there? Engineers had to solve just that problem when designing the Mercury *MESSENGER* spacecraft. In 2008, this spacecraft began to visit Mercury, where temperatures can reach up to 370°C. Engineers designed a sunshade to protect *MESSENGER*'s instruments. It's made from ceramic fabric! The fabric, made of elements such as silicon, aluminum, and boron, is resistant to heat. It reflects most of the sun's heat away from the *MESSENGER* spacecraft, keeping all the instruments at a comfortable room temperature (about 20°C).

TECHNOLOGY

Use what you have read to answer the questions below.

1. Why did engineers need to design a sunshade for Mercury *MESSENGER*?

_____

_____

_____

2. What other challenges do you think there would be for engineers designing a spacecraft to travel to Mercury?

_____

_____

_____

▶ PLANET DIARY Go to **Planet Diary** to learn more about the solar system.

Lab® zone Do the Inquiry Warm-Up *How Big Is Earth?*

Vocabulary
- solar system • astronomical unit
- planet • dwarf planet
- planetesimal

Skills
Reading: Identify Supporting Evidence
Inquiry: Calculate

What Makes Up the Solar System?

Mercury is just one of many objects that make up the solar system. **Our solar system consists of the sun, the planets, their moons, and a variety of smaller objects.** The sun is at the center of the solar system, with other objects orbiting around it. The force of gravity holds the solar system together.

Distances in the Solar System Distances within the solar system are so large that they cannot be easily measured in meters or kilometers. Instead, scientists often use a unit called the astronomical unit. One **astronomical unit** (AU) equals the average distance between Earth and the sun, about 150,000,000 kilometers. The solar system extends more than 100,000 AU from the sun.

do the math!

Converting Units

To convert from astronomical units (AU) to kilometers (km), you can multiply the number of AU by 150,000,000.

1 Calculate Mars is 1.52 AU from the sun. About how many kilometers is Mars from the sun? _____

2 Apply Concepts If you know an object's distance from the sun in kilometers, how can you find its distance in AU? _____
_____

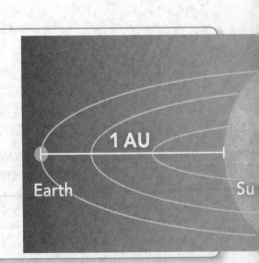

1 AU

Earth   Su

The Sun At the center of our solar system is the sun. The sun is much larger than anything else in the solar system. About 99.85 percent of the mass of the solar system is contained within the sun. Despite being more than a million times the volume of Earth, our sun is actually a very ordinary mid-sized star. Using telescopes, we see stars that have volumes a thousand times greater than the sun's! This turns out to be a very good thing for us. Large stars burn out and die quickly, but our sun will last for five billion more years.

Identify Supporting Evidence Underline a sentence that supports the statement, "The sun is much larger than anything else in the solar system."

FIGURE 1 ···

> INTERACTIVE ART **The Solar System**

The planets' sizes are shown to scale, but their distances from the sun are not.

✎ **Mark the position of each planet on the distance scale above.**

1. **Interpret Data** Where is the largest gap between planets?

_____

2. CHALLENGE Could you show the planets' relative sizes and distances from the sun in the same diagram on one page? Why or why not?

_____

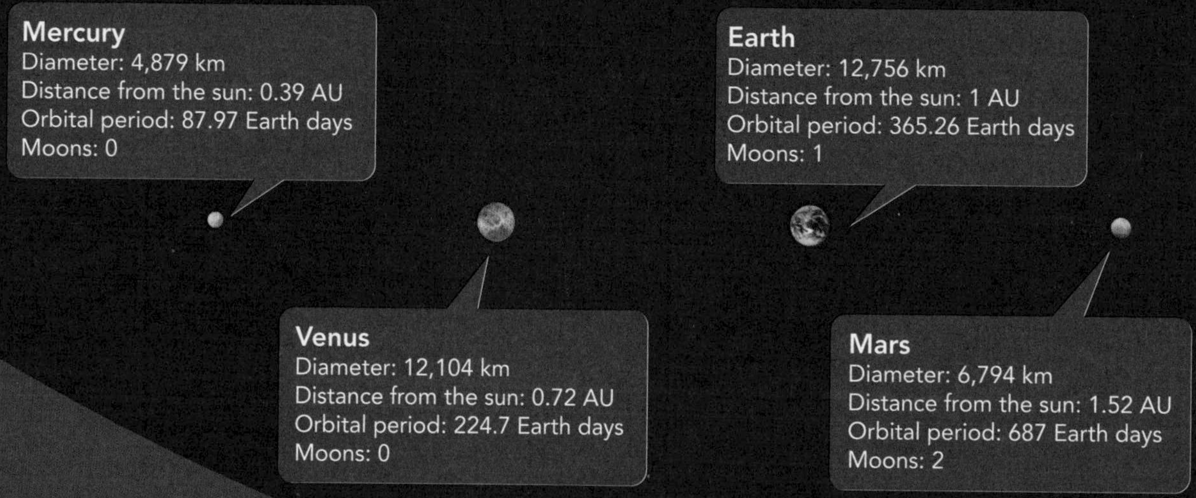

Mercury
Diameter: 4,879 km
Distance from the sun: 0.39 AU
Orbital period: 87.97 Earth days
Moons: 0

Earth
Diameter: 12,756 km
Distance from the sun: 1 AU
Orbital period: 365.26 Earth days
Moons: 1

Venus
Diameter: 12,104 km
Distance from the sun: 0.72 AU
Orbital period: 224.7 Earth days
Moons: 0

Mars
Diameter: 6,794 km
Distance from the sun: 1.52 AU
Orbital period: 687 Earth days
Moons: 2

Planets

There are many different objects in the solar system. How do you decide what is a planet and what isn't? In 2006, astronomers decided that a planet must be round, orbit the sun, and have cleared out the region of the solar system along its orbit. The first four planets are small and are mostly made of rock and metal. The last four planets are very large and are mostly made of gas and liquid. Like Earth, each planet has a "day" and a "year." Its day is the time it takes to rotate on its axis. Its year is the time it takes to orbit the sun. **Figure 1** shows some basic facts about the planets.

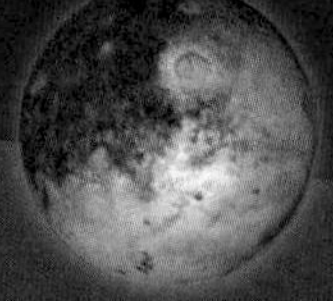

Dwarf Planets

For many years, Pluto was considered the ninth planet in the solar system. But Pluto shares the area of its orbit with other objects. Pluto is now considered a dwarf planet. A dwarf planet is an object that orbits the sun and has enough gravity to be spherical, but has not cleared the area of its orbit. There are five known dwarf planets in our solar system: Pluto, Eris, Ceres, Makemake (MAH keh MAH keh), and Haumea (how MAY uh). As scientists observe more distant objects, the number of dwarf planets might grow.

Satellites

Except for Mercury and Venus, every planet in the solar system has at least one natural satellite, or moon. Earth has the fewest moons, with just one. Jupiter and Saturn each have more than 60! Some dwarf planets also have satellites.

Smaller Objects

The solar system also includes many smaller objects that orbit the sun. Some, called asteroids, are small, mostly rocky bodies. Many asteroids are found in an area between the orbits of Mars and Jupiter. Comets are another large group of solar system objects. Comets are loose balls of ice and rock that usually have very long, narrow orbits.

Saturn
Diameter: 120,536 km
Distance from the sun: 9.54 AU
Orbital period: 29.47 Earth years
Moons: 60+

Neptune
Diameter: 49,258 km
Distance from the sun: 30.07 AU
Orbital period: 163.72 Earth years
Moons: 13+

Uranus
Diameter: 51,118 km
Distance from the sun: 19.19 AU
Orbital period: 83.75 Earth years
Moons: 20+

Jupiter
Diameter: 142,984 km
Distance from the sun: 5.20 AU
Orbital period: 11.86 Earth years
Moons: 60+

 Lab zone® Do the Lab Investigation *Speeding Around the Sun.*

Assess Your Understanding

1a. Sequence List the planets in order of increasing distance from the sun.

_____

b. Make Generalizations What is the relationship between a planet's distance from the sun and the length of its year?

_____

got it?

○ I get it! Now I know that the solar system includes _____

○ I need extra help with _____

Go to MY SCIENCE COACH *online for help with this subject.*

557

How Did the Solar System Form?

Where did the objects in the solar system come from? ▭ **Scientists think the solar system formed about 4.6 billion years ago from a cloud of hydrogen, helium, rock, ice, and other materials pulled together by gravity.**

A Spinning Disk The process began as gravity pulled the cloud's material together. The cloud collapsed and started to rotate, forming a disk. Most of the material was pulled to the center. As this material became tightly packed, it got hotter and the pressure on it increased.

Eventually, the temperature and pressure became so high that hydrogen atoms were pressed together to form helium. This process, called nuclear fusion, releases large amounts of energy. Once nuclear fusion began, the sun gave off light and became a stable star. Sunlight is one form of the energy produced by fusion.

The Planets Form Away from the sun, planets began to form as gravity pulled rock, ice, and gas together. The rock and ice formed small bodies called **planetesimals** (pla nuh TE suh muhlz). Over time, planetesimals collided and stuck together, eventually combining to form all the other objects in the solar system.

Inner Planets Close to the sun, the solar system was very hot. Most water evaporated, preventing ice from forming. The bodies that formed in this region were comparatively low in mass. Their gravity was too weak to hold on to light gases such as hydrogen and helium. This is why the inner planets are small and rocky.

Outer Planets At greater distances from the sun, temperatures were cooler. Ice formed, adding mass to the planets that formed at these distances. As the planets grew, their gravity was strong enough to hold hydrogen and helium, forming the gas giant planets. Beyond the gas giants, temperatures were even lower. Ice and other materials produced comets and dwarf planets.

FIGURE 2 ···

> **ART IN MOTION** **Formation of the Solar System**

✎ **Sequence** Write the numbers 1 through 4 in the circles to put the images in order.

EXPLORE THE BIG ?

Solve THE SOLAR SYSTEM

Why are objects in the solar system different from each other?

FIGURE 3 ·······················
Use the clues to complete the puzzle.
Then answer the question.

ACROSS

3 The planet farthest from the sun
4 A loose, icy body with a long, narrow orbit
6 A gas giant planet that is smaller than Jupiter but larger than Neptune
7 The smallest planet in the solar system
8 An object that orbits a planet

DOWN

1 The largest planet in the solar system
2 A planet that formed closer to the sun than Earth but not closest to the sun
5 A small rocky body that orbits the sun

Why are the objects in clues 2 and 6 so different?

_____

_____

_____

Lab zone ® Do the Quick Lab *Clumping Planets.*

🔑 Assess Your Understanding

2a. Explain What force formed the solar system?

_____

b. **ANSWER THE BIG ?** Why are objects in the solar system different from each other?

_____

_____

_____

got it?

○ **I get it!** Now I know that the solar system formed when _____

_____

_____

○ **I need extra help with** _____

Go to **my science 🔊 COACH** online for help with this subject.

The Sun

UNLOCK
THE BIG
?

🔑 **What Is the Structure of the Sun?**

🔑 **What Features Can You See on the Sun?**

MY PLANET DIARY

Left in the Dark

On March 13, 1989, a flood of electric particles from the sun reached Earth, causing a magnetic storm. Bright streamers of color filled the sky as far south as Jamaica. But in Quebec, Canada, the storm brought problems. At 2:45 A.M., the entire electric power system collapsed. People woke up with no heat or light. Traffic snarled as traffic lights and subways stopped working.

How could particles from the sun take out a power system? The magnetic storm caused an electrical surge through the power lines. Electric stations couldn't handle the extra electricity, and they blew out, taking the power system with them.

✏️ **Communicate** Discuss the Quebec blackout with a partner. Then answer the questions below.

1. What caused the Quebec blackout of 1989?

_____

_____

2. How would your life be affected if a magnetic storm shut down electricity in your area?

_____

_____

_____

▷ PLANET DIARY Go to **Planet Diary** to learn more about the sun.

Lab
zone®

Do the Inquiry Warm-Up
*How Can You Safely
Observe the Sun?*

Vocabulary

- core • nuclear fusion • radiation zone
- convection zone • photosphere • chromosphere
- corona • solar wind • sunspot • prominence
- solar flare

Skills

- Reading: Relate Cause and Effect
- Inquiry: Interpret Data

What Is the Structure of the Sun?

Unlike Earth, the sun has no solid surface. About three fourths of the sun's mass is hydrogen, and about one fourth is helium. There are tiny amounts of other elements. **The sun has an interior and an atmosphere. The interior includes the core, the radiation zone, and the convection zone. Figure 1** shows the sun's interior.

FIGURE 1 ....

Layers of the Sun

The diagram shows the layers of the sun's interior.

✎ **Apply Concepts** Draw arrows to show energy as it passes from the sun's core through the radiation and convection zones. Underline clues in the text that help you determine the path.

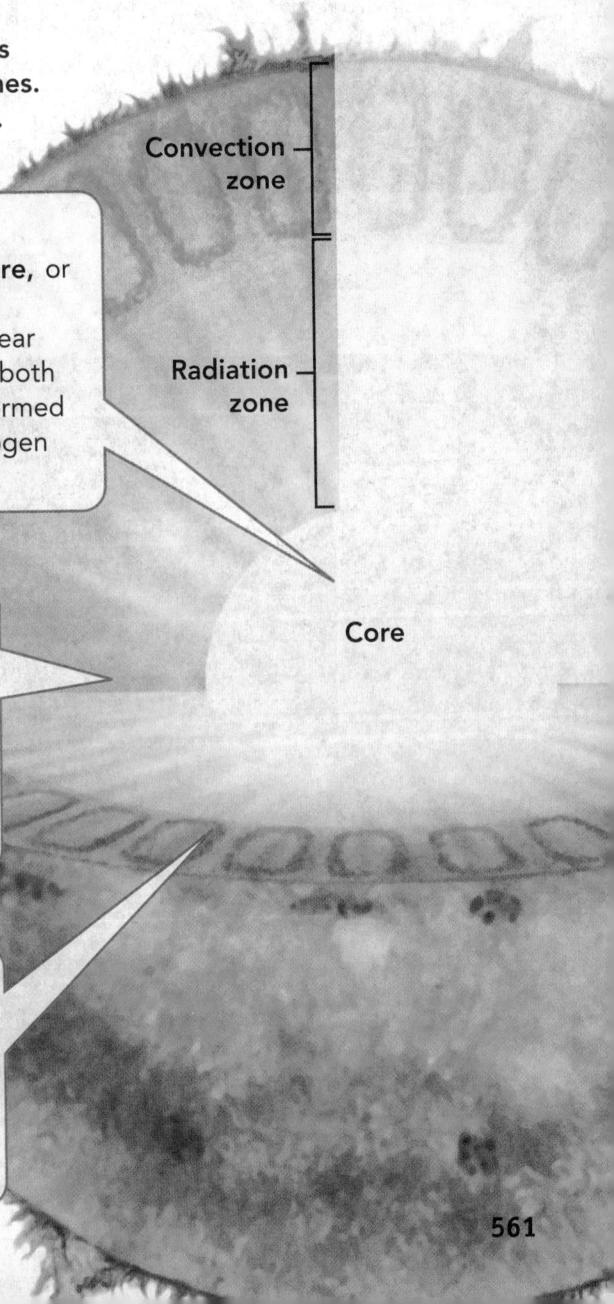

The Core

The sun produces an enormous amount of energy in its **core,** or central region, through nuclear fusion. In the process of **nuclear fusion,** hydrogen atoms join to form helium. Nuclear fusion requires extremely high temperature and pressure, both of which are found in the core. The total mass of helium formed by nuclear fusion is slightly less than the mass of the hydrogen that goes into it. The remaining mass becomes energy.

The Radiation Zone

The energy produced in the sun's core moves outward through the radiation zone. The **radiation zone** is a region of very tightly packed gas where energy moves mainly in the form of electromagnetic radiation. Because the radiation zone is so dense, energy can take more than 100,000 years to move through it.

The Convection Zone

The **convection zone** is the outermost layer of the sun's interior. Hot gases rise from the bottom of the convection zone and gradually cool as they approach the top. Cooler gases sink, forming loops of gas that move energy toward the sun's surface.

Convection zone

Radiation zone

Core

Vocabulary Greek Word Origins
The Greek word *photos* means "light." What does *photosphere* mean?

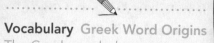

The Sun's Atmosphere

The sun has an atmosphere that stretches far into space, as you can see in Figure 2. The layers of the atmosphere become less dense the farther they are from the radiation zone. Like the sun's interior, the atmosphere is primarily composed of hydrogen and helium. **The sun's atmosphere includes the photosphere, the chromosphere, and the corona. Each layer has unique properties.**

FIGURE 2

INTERACTIVE ART **The Sun's Atmosphere**

This image is a combination of two photographs of the sun. One shows the sun's surface and was taken through a special filter that shows the sun's features. The other shows the corona and was taken during an eclipse.

Relate Text and Visuals On the photograph, label the photosphere and corona. Shade in the area of the chromosphere.

CHALLENGE Why can the chromosphere and corona only be seen from Earth during an eclipse?

The Photosphere

The inner layer of the sun's atmosphere is called the **photosphere** (FOH tuh sfeer). The sun does not have a solid surface, but the gases of the photosphere are thick enough to be visible. When you look at an image of the sun, you are looking at the photosphere. It is considered to be the sun's surface layer.

The Chromosphere

At the start and end of a total eclipse, a reddish glow is visible just around the photosphere. This glow comes from the middle layer of the sun's atmosphere, the **chromosphere** (KROH muh sfeer). The Greek word *chroma* means "color," so the chromosphere is the "color sphere."

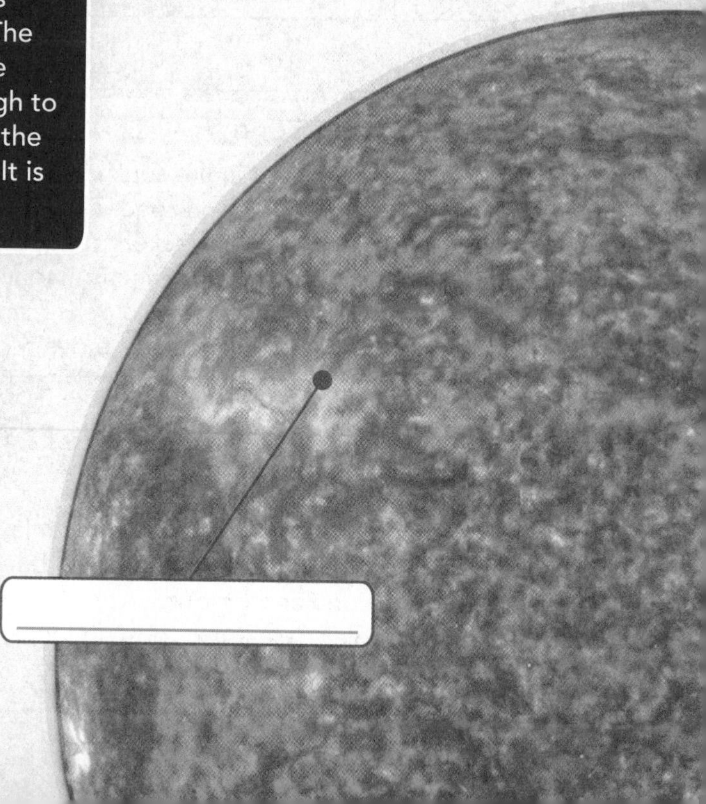

do the math! Analyzing Data

Solar Temperature

Use the table to answer the questions.

Layer	Temperature (°C)
Core	About 15,000,000
Radiation and Convection Zones	About 4,000,000
Photosphere	About 6,000
Inner Chromosphere	About 4,300
Outer Chromosphere	About 8,300
Corona	About 1,000,000

1 ⚠ **Interpret Data** Which layer is hottest?

_____

2 **Compare and Contrast** How does the temperature change in the sun's atmosphere differ from the temperature change in the sun's interior?

_____

_____

The Corona

During a total solar eclipse, an even fainter layer of the sun becomes visible, as you can see in **Figure 2.** This outer layer, which looks like a white halo around the sun, is called the **corona,** which means "crown" in Latin. The corona extends into space for millions of kilometers. It gradually thins into streams of electrically charged particles called the **solar wind.**

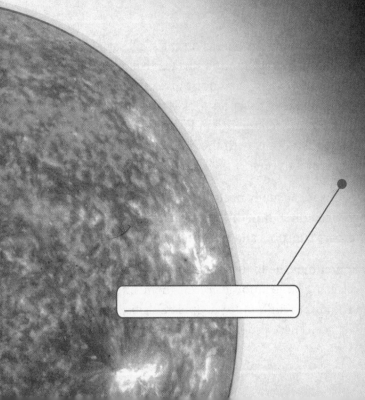

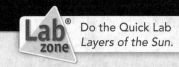

Do the Quick Lab
Layers of the Sun.

🔑 Assess Your Understanding

1a. List List the layers of the sun's interior and atmosphere, starting from the center.

_____

_____

_____

b. Compare and Contrast What is one key difference between the radiation and convection zones?

_____

_____

_____

_____

got it? •

○ **I get it!** Now I know that the sun's structure includes _____

_____

○ **I need extra help with** _____

_____

Go to MY SCIENCE ⓢ COACH *online for help with this subject.*

563

What Features Can You See on the Sun?

For hundreds of years, scientists have used special telescopes to study the sun. They have spotted a variety of features on the sun's surface. 🔑 **Features on or just above the sun's surface include sunspots, prominences, and solar flares.**

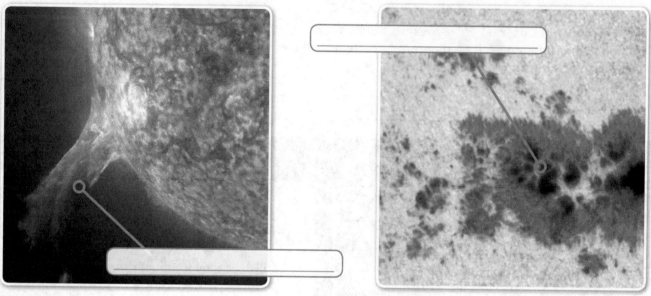

FIGURE 3 ··

Sunspots and Prominences

Sunspots look dark in regular photographs. Some photos of the sun are taken with special filters that show the sun's structure. Sunspots may appear white in these photos. Sunspots are visible in both of the photos above. ✎ **Classify Label a prominence and a sunspot in the photos.**

Relate Cause and Effect
When prominences join, they cause (sunspots/solar flares).

Sunspots Photographs show dark areas on the sun's surface. These **sunspots** are areas of gas on the sun's surface that are cooler than the gases around them. Cooler gases don't give off as much light as hotter gases, which is why sunspots look dark. Sunspots look small, but in fact they can be larger than Earth. The number of sunspots varies in a regular cycle, with the most sunspots appearing about once every 11 years.

Prominences Sunspots usually occur in groups. Huge loops of gas called **prominences** often link different parts of sunspot regions. You can compare sunspots and prominences in **Figure 3.**

Solar Flares Sometimes the loops in sunspot regions suddenly connect, releasing large amounts of magnetic energy. The energy heats gas on the sun to millions of degrees Celsius, causing the gas to erupt into space. These eruptions are called **solar flares.**

Solar Wind The solar wind is made up of electrical particles from the sun. Solar flares can greatly increase the solar wind, which means that more particles reach Earth's upper atmosphere. Earth's atmosphere and magnetic field normally block these particles. But near the North and South poles, the particles can enter Earth's atmosphere. There, they create powerful electric currents that cause gas molecules in the atmosphere to glow. These particles cause auroras near the poles. They can also cause magnetic storms like the one that caused the blackout in Quebec in 1989. **Figure 4** shows how the solar wind interacts with Earth's magnetic field.

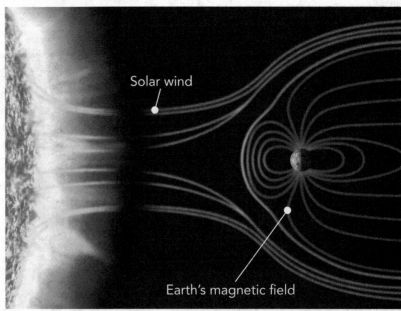

FIGURE 4 ·······························

Solar Wind
Particles from the solar wind spread through the solar system. When they reach Earth, they interact with Earth's magnetic field. (Note: The diagram is not to scale.)

✎ **Make Generalizations** The corona is the least dense layer of the sun's atmosphere. How do you think the density of the solar wind compares to the density of the corona?

_____

_____

_____

Lab® Do the Quick Lab
zone *Viewing Sunspots.*

🔑 **Assess Your Understanding**

2a. Define (Prominences/sunspots) are loops of gas that extend from the sun's surface.

b. Explain Why do sunspots look darker than the rest of the sun's photosphere?

_____

_____

_____

c. 🔄 **Relate Cause and Effect** How is the solar wind related to magnetic storms on Earth?

_____

_____

_____

_____

_____

got it? ···

○ **I get it!** Now I know that features on the sun include _____

_____

○ **I need extra help with** _____

Go to my science 🔵 coach *online for help with this subject.*

The Inner Planets

🔑 What Do the Inner Planets Have in Common?

🔑 What Are the Characteristics of the Inner Planets?

MY PLANET DIARY

What's in a Name?

Where in the solar system could you find Lewis and Clark's guide Sacagawea, artist Frida Kahlo, writer Helen Keller, and abolitionist Sojourner Truth all in the same place? On Venus! In fact, almost every feature on Venus is named for a real, fictional, or mythological woman.

In general, the person or people who discover an object or feature in the solar system get to choose its name. But scientists have agreed on some guidelines. Features on Mercury are named for authors, artists, and musicians. Many craters on Mars are named for towns on Earth. And most of the craters on Earth's moon are named for astronomers, physicists, and mathematicians.

FUN FACT

After you read the information to the left, answer the questions below.

1. Who decides what to name a newly discovered feature in the solar system?

_____

_____

2. If you discovered a new planet, how would you decide what to name its features?

_____

_____

_____

> PLANET DIARY Go to **Planet Diary** to learn more about the inner planets.

Lab ® Do the Inquiry Warm-Up
zone *Ring Around the Sun.*

Vocabulary
- terrestrial planet
- greenhouse effect

Skills
- Reading: Compare and Contrast
- Inquiry: Communicate

What Do the Inner Planets Have in Common?

Earth, Mercury, Venus, and Mars are more like each other than they are like the outer planets. **The inner planets are small and dense and have rocky surfaces.** The inner planets are often called the **terrestrial planets,** from the Latin word *terra,* which means "Earth." **Figure 1** summarizes data about the inner planets.

The terrestrial planets all have relatively high densities. They are rich in rocky and metallic materials, including iron and silicon. Each has a solid surface. All except Mercury have atmospheres.

FIGURE 1 ....

INTERACTIVE ART

The Inner Planets

Interpret Data Use the table to answer the questions below.

1. Which planet is largest?

_____

2. Which planet has the most moons?

_____

3. Which planet is most similar to Earth in size?

_____

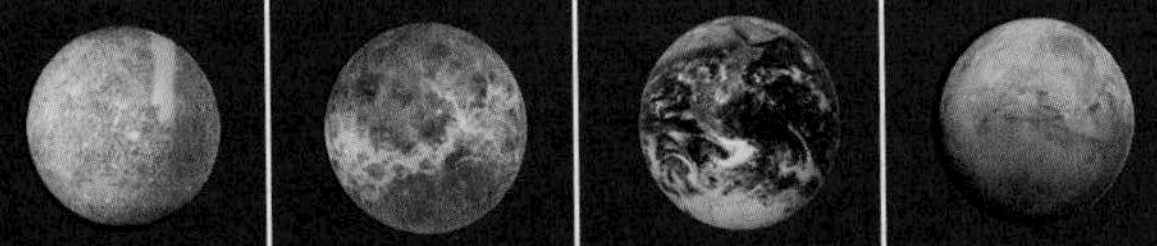

Planet	Mercury	Venus	Earth	Mars
Diameter (km)	4,879	12,104	12,756	6,794
Period of rotation (Earth days)	58.9	244	1.0	1.03
Average distance from sun (AU)	0.39	0.72	1.0	1.52
Period of revolution (Earth days)	88	224.7	365.2	687
Number of moons	0	0	1	2

Note: Planets are not shown to scale.

Lab zone Do the Quick Lab *Characteristics of the Inner Planets.*

Assess Your Understanding

got it?

○ **I get it!** Now I know that the inner planets are _____

_____

○ **I need extra help with** _____

Go to my science COACH online for help with this subject.

What Are the Characteristics of the Inner Planets?

Though the four inner planets have many features in common, they differ in size and composition as well as distance from the sun.

Mercury Would you like to visit a place where the temperature can range from 430°C to below −170°C? 🔑 **Mercury is the smallest terrestrial planet and the planet closest to the sun.** Mercury is not much larger than Earth's moon. The interior of Mercury is probably made up mainly of the dense metal iron.

Mercury's Surface As you can see in **Figure 2,** Mercury has flat plains and craters on its surface. Most of these craters formed early in the history of the solar system. Since Mercury has no water and not much atmosphere, the craters have not worn away over time.

Mercury's Atmosphere Mercury has virtually no atmosphere. Because Mercury's mass is small, its gravity is weak. Gas particles can easily escape into space. However, astronomers have detected small amounts of sodium and other gases around Mercury.

During the day, the side of Mercury facing the sun can reach temperatures of 430°C. Because there is so little atmosphere, the planet's heat escapes at night. Then the temperature drops below −170°C.

Exploring Mercury Much of what astronomers know about Mercury has come from space probes. *Mariner 10* flew by Mercury three times in 1974 and 1975. *Mercury MESSENGER* has passed Mercury several times, and will begin orbiting Mercury in 2011.

Size of Mercury compared to Earth

I'm visiting the planets! As you read this lesson and the next one, keep track of how far I've traveled.

TOTAL AU:

SOL 8 TOURS

INTERPLANETARY FREQUENT TRAVELER REWARDS PROGRAM

SPF 1000000

FIGURE 2 ···

Mercury

The photo shows Mercury's cratered surface.

✏️ **Answer the questions below.**

1. Solve Problems List three things a visitor to Mercury would need to bring.

_____

_____

2. CHALLENGE Refer to **Figure 1.** How many Mercury days are there in a Mercury year?

_____

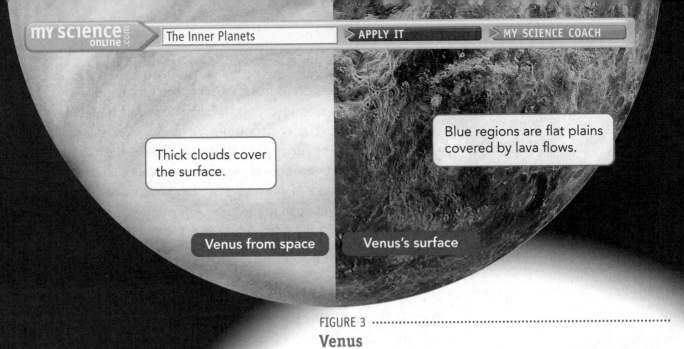

Thick clouds cover the surface.

Blue regions are flat plains covered by lava flows.

Venus from space

Venus's surface

FIGURE 3 ....

Venus

This figure combines images of Venus taken from space with a camera (left) and radar (right). Radar is able to penetrate Venus's thick clouds to reveal the surface. The colors in both images are altered to show more details.

✎ **Infer** Why do scientists need to use radar to study Venus's surface?

_____

_____

Size of Venus compared to Earth

Venus Venus is so similar in size and mass to Earth that it is sometimes called "Earth's twin." Venus's density and internal structure are similar to Earth's. But in other ways Venus and Earth are very different. ⚷ **Venus has a thick atmosphere, an unusual pattern of rotation, and the hottest surface of any planet.**

Venus's Atmosphere Venus's atmosphere is so thick that it is always cloudy. As you can see in **Figure 3,** astronomers can see only a smooth cloud cover over Venus. The thick clouds are made mostly of droplets of sulfuric acid.

At Venus's surface, you would quickly be crushed by the weight of its atmosphere. The pressure of Venus's atmosphere is 90 times greater than the pressure of Earth's atmosphere. You couldn't breathe on Venus because its atmosphere is mostly carbon dioxide.

Venus's Rotation Venus takes about 7.5 Earth months to revolve around the sun. It takes about 8 months for Venus to rotate once on its axis. Thus, Venus rotates so slowly that its day is longer than its year! Oddly, Venus rotates from east to west, the opposite direction from most other planets and moons. Astronomers hypothesize that this unusual rotation was caused by a very large object that struck Venus billions of years ago. Such a collision could have caused the planet to change its direction of rotation. Another hypothesis is that Venus's thick atmosphere could have somehow altered its rotation.

569

⤺ Compare and Contrast
List one feature Venus has in common with Earth and one feature that is different.

In common: _____

_____

Different: _____

_____

_____

A Hot Planet Because Venus is closer to the sun than Earth is, it receives more solar energy than Earth does. Much of this radiation is reflected by Venus's atmosphere. However, some radiation reaches the surface and is later given off as heat. The carbon dioxide in Venus's atmosphere traps heat so well that Venus has the hottest surface of any planet. At 460°C, its average surface temperature is hot enough to melt lead. This trapping of heat by the atmosphere is called the **greenhouse effect. Figure 4** shows how the greenhouse effect occurs.

Exploring Venus The first probe to land on Venus's surface and send back data, *Venera 7*, landed in 1970. It survived for only a few minutes because of the high temperature and pressure. Later probes were more durable and sent images and data back to Earth.

The *Magellan* probe reached Venus in 1990, carrying radar instruments. Radar works through clouds, so *Magellan* was able to map nearly the entire surface. The *Magellan* data confirmed that Venus is covered with rock. Venus's surface has more than 10,000 volcanoes. Lava flows from these volcanoes have formed plains.

More recent probes have included *Venus Express,* from the European Space Agency, as well as brief visits by space probes headed for other planets. Images from *Venus Express* have helped scientists understand how Venus's clouds form and change.

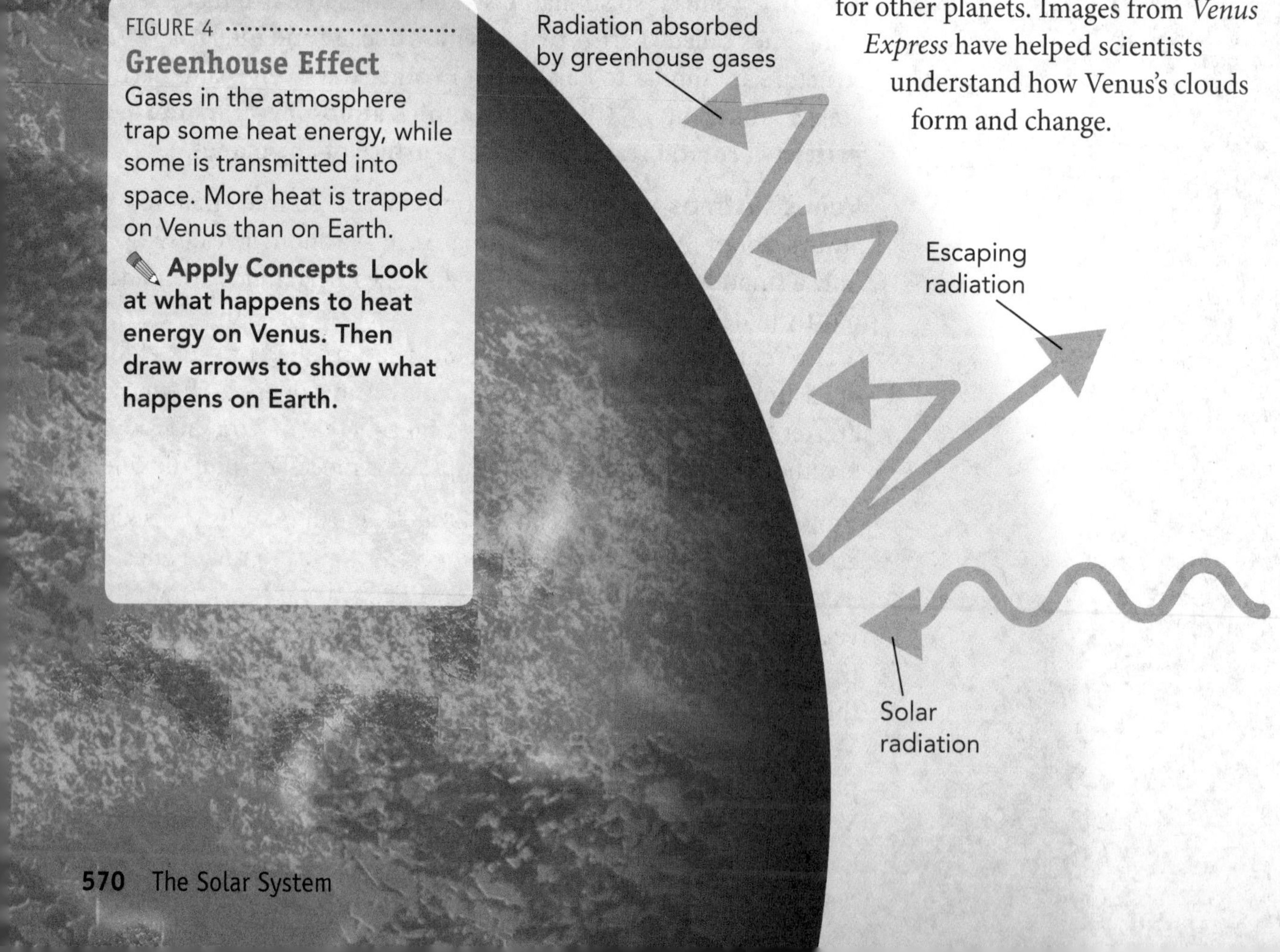

FIGURE 4 ·······························
Greenhouse Effect
Gases in the atmosphere trap some heat energy, while some is transmitted into space. More heat is trapped on Venus than on Earth.

✐ **Apply Concepts** Look at what happens to heat energy on Venus. Then draw arrows to show what happens on Earth.

Radiation absorbed by greenhouse gases

Escaping radiation

Solar radiation

Earth There's only one planet in the solar system where you could live easily: Earth. 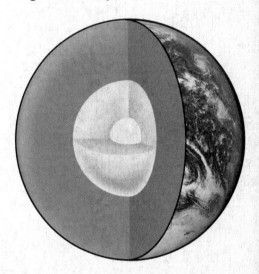 **Earth has liquid water and a suitable temperature range and atmosphere for living things to survive.**

The Water Planet Earth is unique in our solar system in having liquid water on its surface. In fact, most of Earth's surface, about 70 percent, is covered with water.

Earth's Temperature Scientists sometimes speak of Earth as having "Goldilocks" conditions—in other words, Earth is "just right" for life as we know it. Earth is not too hot and not too cold. If Earth were a little closer to the sun, it would be so hot that liquid water would evaporate. If it were a little farther away and colder, water would always be solid ice.

Earth's Atmosphere Earth has enough gravity to hold on to most gases. These gases make up Earth's atmosphere. Earth is the only planet with an atmosphere that is rich in oxygen. Oxygen makes up about 20 percent of Earth's atmosphere. Nearly all the rest is nitrogen, with small amounts of other gases such as argon, carbon dioxide, and water vapor.

Like Venus, Earth experiences a greenhouse effect. Earth's atmosphere traps heat, though less heat than Venus's atmosphere does. Without the atmosphere, Earth would be much colder.

FIGURE 5 ···

Earth's Structure
Earth has three main layers—a crust, a mantle, and a core. The crust includes the solid, rocky surface. Under the crust is the mantle, a layer of hot rock. Earth has a dense core made mainly of iron and nickel.

✎ **Relate Text and Visuals** Label the layer of Earth with the highest density.

Solar radiation

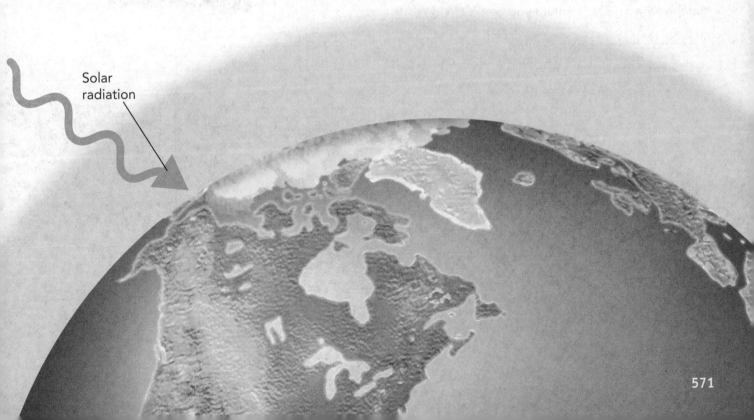

Size of Mars
compared to Earth

Mars

Mars is called the "red planet." **Figure 6** shows why. This reddish color is due to the breakdown of iron-rich rocks, leaving a rusty dust behind. 🔑 **Though Mars is mostly too cold for liquid water, it does have water ice now and shows evidence of intermittent seasonal flowing water today as well as liquid water in the past.**

Mars's Atmosphere

The atmosphere of Mars is more than 95 percent carbon dioxide. You could walk around on Mars, but you would have to wear an airtight suit and carry your own oxygen. Mars has few clouds, and they are very thin compared to clouds on Earth. Temperatures on the surface range from −140°C to 20°C.

Water and Ice

Images of Mars taken from space show a variety of features that look as if they were made by ancient streams, lakes, or floods. Scientists think that more liquid water flowed on Mars's surface in the distant past. Scientists infer that Mars must have been much warmer and had a thicker atmosphere at that time.

Today, Mars's atmosphere is so thin that most liquid water would quickly turn into a gas. Some water is located in the planet's two polar ice caps, which are almost entirely made of frozen water. Observations from the *Mars Reconnaissance Orbiter* in 2015 found evidence of flowing water in warmer areas today.

FIGURE 6 ···

The Red Planet

Remote-controlled landers such as *Phoenix*, *Spirit*, and *Opportunity* have sent back pictures of the surface of Mars.

✎ **Design a Solution** If you were designing a lander to work on Mars, where on Earth would you test it? Why?

_____

_____

_____

apply *it!*

▲ **Communicate** Choose one of the inner planets other than Earth. Describe an alien that could live there. Include at least three features of your alien that make it well suited for the planet you chose. Draw your alien to the right.

_____

_____

_____

_____

_____

FIGURE 7 ·····························

Olympus Mons

This computer-generated image is based on data from the *Mars Global Surveyor* mission.

Volcanoes Some regions of Mars have giant volcanoes. There are signs that lava flowed from the volcanoes in the past, but the volcanoes are rarely active today. Olympus Mons, shown in **Figure 7,** is the largest volcano in the solar system. It is as large as Missouri and is nearly three times as tall as Mount Everest!

Mars's Moons Mars has two very small moons. Phobos, the larger moon, is about 22 kilometers across. Deimos is even smaller, about 13 kilometers across. Like Earth's moon, Phobos and Deimos are covered with craters.

Exploring Mars Many space probes have visited Mars, looking for signs of water and possible life. Rovers called *Spirit* and *Opportunity* found traces of salts and minerals that form in the presence of water. The *Phoenix* mission found frozen water near the north polar cap, and the *Mars Reconnaissance Orbiter* found evidence of flowing water in warmer areas. *Mars Express* detected methane gas in Mars's atmosphere. This gas might be a clue that microscopic life forms exist on Mars, even today!

Lab® Do the Quick Lab
zone *Greenhouse Effect.*

🔑 Assess Your Understanding

1a. Name Which inner planet has the thickest

atmosphere? _____

b. Relate Cause and Effect Why is Venus hotter

than Mercury? _____

_____

_____

got *it?*

○ **I get it!** Now I know that the inner planets

differ in _____

_____

○ **I need extra help with** _____

Go to **MY SCIENCE** ⓢ **COACH** *online for help with this subject.*

The Outer Planets

🔑 **What Do the Outer Planets Have in Common?**

🔑 **What Are the Characteristics of Each Outer Planet?**

my planeT DiaRY

Predicting a Planet

In the 1840s, astronomers were puzzled. Uranus didn't move as expected, based on the theory of gravity. Astronomers John Couch Adams and Urbain Leverrier independently hypothesized that Uranus was being affected by another planet's gravity. They calculated where this planet should be. Another astronomer, Johann Galle, aimed his telescope at the place Leverrier predicted. On September 23, 1846, he discovered the new planet—Neptune.

DISCOVERY

✎ **Communicate Work with a partner to answer the question.**

What science skills did the astronomers use when they discovered Neptune?

_____

_____

_____

_____

▷ **PLANET DIARY** Go to **Planet Diary** to learn more about the outer planets.

Lab zone Do the Inquiry Warm-Up *How Big Are the Planets?*

What Do the Outer Planets Have in Common?

If you could visit the outer planets, you wouldn't have a solid place to stand! **The four outer planets are much larger and more massive than Earth, and they do not have solid surfaces.** Because these four planets are so large, they are often called **gas giants**. **Figure 1** summarizes some basic facts about the gas giants.

Composition Jupiter and Saturn are composed mainly of hydrogen and helium. Uranus and Neptune contain some of these gases, but also ices of ammonia and methane. Because they are so massive, the gas giants exert a very strong gravitational force. This gravity keeps gases from escaping, forming thick atmospheres.

Vocabulary
- gas giant
- ring

Skills
- Reading: Outline
- Inquiry: Pose Questions

Despite the name "gas giant," much of the material in these planets is actually liquid because the pressure inside the planets is so high. The outer layers are extremely cold because they are far from the sun. Temperatures increase greatly within the planets.

Moons and Rings
All the gas giants have many moons, ranging from 13 around Neptune to more than 60 around Jupiter! These moons vary from tiny balls of rock and ice barely a kilometer across to moons larger than Mercury. Some of these moons even have their own atmospheres!

In addition, each of the gas giants is surrounded by a set of rings. A **ring** is a thin disk of small particles of ice and rock. Saturn's rings are the largest and most complex.

As you visit each planet, don't forget to keep track of how many AU you've collected!

TOTAL AU:

SOL TOURS
INTERPLANETARY FREQUENT TRAVELER REWARDS PROGRAM

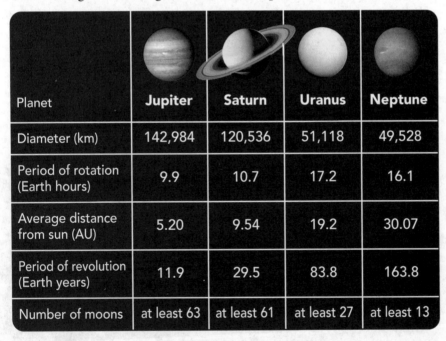

Planet	Jupiter	Saturn	Uranus	Neptune
Diameter (km)	142,984	120,536	51,118	49,528
Period of rotation (Earth hours)	9.9	10.7	17.2	16.1
Average distance from sun (AU)	5.20	9.54	19.2	30.07
Period of revolution (Earth years)	11.9	29.5	83.8	163.8
Number of moons	at least 63	at least 61	at least 27	at least 13

Note: Planets are not shown to scale.

FIGURE 1 ·····························
> INTERACTIVE ART
The Outer Planets
The table summarizes data about the outer planets.

✏ **Estimate** Earth's diameter is about 12,750 km. About how many times larger is Jupiter's diameter than Earth's?

_____

Lab® Do the Quick Lab
zone Density Mystery.

🔑 Assess Your Understanding

got it? ·······························

○ **I get it!** Now I know that the gas giants all _____

_____

○ I need extra help with _____

Go to my science ⓢ coACH online for help with this subject.

What Are the Characteristics of Each Outer Planet?

Since telescopes were first invented, scientists have studied the features of the outer planets and their moons. Today, space-based telescopes and space probes including the *Voyager, Galileo,* and *Cassini* missions have revealed many details of these planets that are not visible from Earth. Scientists are constantly discovering new information about these planets and their moons.

Jupiter

Jupiter is the largest and most massive planet. Jupiter's enormous mass dwarfs the other planets. In fact, its mass is about $2\frac{1}{2}$ times that of all the other planets combined!

Jupiter's Atmosphere Like all of the gas giants, Jupiter has a thick atmosphere made up mainly of hydrogen and helium. One notable feature of Jupiter's atmosphere is its Great Red Spot, a storm that is larger than Earth! The storm's swirling winds are similar to a hurricane, as you can see in **Figure 2.** Unlike hurricanes on Earth, however, the Great Red Spot shows no signs of going away.

Jupiter's Structure Astronomers think that Jupiter probably has a dense core of rock and iron at its center. A thick mantle of liquid hydrogen and helium surrounds this core. Because of the weight of Jupiter's atmosphere, the pressure at Jupiter's core is estimated to be about 30 million times greater than the pressure at Earth's surface.

Size of Jupiter compared to Earth

Outline As you read, make an outline about Jupiter.

I. Atmosphere

  A. _____

    _____

  B. _____

    _____

II. Structure

  A. _____

    _____

  B. _____

    _____

  C. _____

    _____

FIGURE 2
The Great Red Spot

This storm is about 20,000 km long and 12,000 km wide. The largest tropical storm on Earth was 2,200 km across.

Calculate Think of the storm on Earth as a square and the Great Red Spot as a rectangle. About how many Earth storms would fit inside the Great Red Spot?

Jupiter's Moons The Italian astronomer Galileo Galilei discovered Jupiter's largest moons in 1610. These moons, shown in **Figure 3,** are named Io, Europa, Ganymede, and Callisto. Since Galileo's time, astronomers have discovered dozens of additional moons orbiting Jupiter. Many of these are small moons that have been found in the last few years thanks to improved technology.

FIGURE 3 ⋯⋯⋯⋯⋯⋯⋯⋯⋯

The Moons of Jupiter

Jupiter's four largest moons are larger than Earth's moon. Each has characteristics that set it apart from the others.

✎ **Relate Text and Visuals** Based on the photograph, match each description below to its moon.

1 Ganymede is Jupiter's largest moon. It is larger than Mercury! Its surface is divided into dark and bright areas.

2 Callisto is second to Ganymede in size, but has less ice. It has the most craters of any of Jupiter's moons.

3 Io is not icy, unlike most of Jupiter's moons. It may have as many as 300 active volcanoes. The eruptions from those volcanoes constantly change the moon's surface.

4 Europa is covered with ice. There may be liquid water below the ice—and if there's water, there might be life!

Titan This giant moon has a thick atmosphere.

TOTAL AU:

SOL 8 TOURS

INTERPLANETARY
FREQUENT TRAVELER
REWARDS PROGRAM

FIGURE 4 ·······

The Saturn System
Recent space probes have shown details of Saturn and its moons.

🖊 **Answer the questions below.**

1. **Make Judgments** Would it be easier to build a space colony on Saturn or on one of its moons? Why?

   _____

   _____

2. CHALLENGE Look at the photographs of Mimas and Tethys. What can you infer about the history of these moons?

   _____

   _____

Mimas A giant impact nearly broke Mimas apart, leaving the enormous crater shown here.

Iapetus This moon has light and dark areas.

🖊 **Develop Hypotheses** What might the light areas be?

Saturn The second-largest planet in the solar system is Saturn. Saturn, like Jupiter, has a thick atmosphere made up mainly of hydrogen and helium. Saturn's atmosphere also contains clouds and storms, but they are less dramatic than those on Jupiter. The *Cassini* space probe found unusual six-sided cloud patterns around Saturn's north pole. Scientists aren't sure what causes these patterns.

Saturn's Rings Saturn has the most spectacular rings of any planet. These rings are made of chunks of ice and rock, each traveling in its own orbit around Saturn. From Earth, it looks as though Saturn has only a few rings and that they are divided from each other by narrow, dark regions. Space probes have shown that each of these obvious rings is divided into many thinner rings. Saturn's rings are broad and thin, like a compact disc. Some rings are kept in place by gravity from tiny moons that orbit on either side of the ring.

Saturn's Moons Saturn's largest moon, Titan, is larger than the planet Mercury. It is also the only moon in the solar system that has a thick atmosphere. The atmosphere is composed mostly of nitrogen and methane. Some of these gases break down high in the atmosphere, forming a haze that is somewhat like smog on Earth. In 2005, the *Huygens* probe landed on Titan's surface. Photos from *Huygens* show features that may have been formed by flowing liquid. A few scientists think that Titan might support life.

Scientists have learned a great deal about Saturn's moons from the *Cassini* space probe. Giant craters and trenches cut cross Mimas (MY mus) and Tethys (TEE this). Ice and water erupt in geysers from the surface of Enceladus (en SEL uh dus). In 2009, scientists discovered a ring of material that may come from the outermost moon, Phoebe (FEE bee). **Figure 4** shows some of the members of the Saturn system.

Size of Saturn compared to Earth

did you **know**?

Saturn has the lowest density of any planet. If you could build a bathtub big enough, Saturn would float!

Tethys In this photo, you can just see a group of canyons that circle this moon.

Enceladus This photo shows faint bluish plumes erupting from the surface of Enceladus.

✎ **Make Generalizations** Eruptions from Enceladus form one of Saturn's rings. What is that ring most likely made of?

Size of Uranus
compared to Earth

Uranus Although the gas giant Uranus (YOOR uh nus) is about four times the diameter of Earth, it is still much smaller than Jupiter and Saturn. Uranus is twice as far from the sun as Saturn, so it is much colder. Uranus looks blue-green because of traces of methane in its atmosphere. Like the other gas giants, Uranus is surrounded by a group of thin, flat rings, although they are much darker than Saturn's rings.

Uranus's Moons Photographs from *Voyager 2* show that Uranus's five largest moons have icy, cratered surfaces. The craters show that rocks from space have hit the moons. Uranus's moons also have lava flows on their surfaces, suggesting that material has erupted from inside each moon. *Voyager 2* images revealed 10 moons that had never been seen before. Recently, astronomers discovered several more moons, for a total of at least 27.

A Tilted Planet Uranus's axis of rotation is tilted at an angle of about 90 degrees from the vertical. Viewed from Earth, Uranus rotates from top to bottom instead of from side to side, as other planets do. You can see the tilt in **Figure 5.** Uranus's rings and moons rotate around this tilted axis. Astronomers think that billions of years ago, an object hit Uranus and knocked it on its side. Images from the *Voyager 2* space probe allowed scientists to determine that Uranus rotates in about 17 hours.

FIGURE 5 ....
A Sideways Planet
✎ **Compare and Contrast** How do day and night at Uranus's equator change as Uranus revolves around the sun?

_____

_____

_____

_____

_____

_____

_____

_____

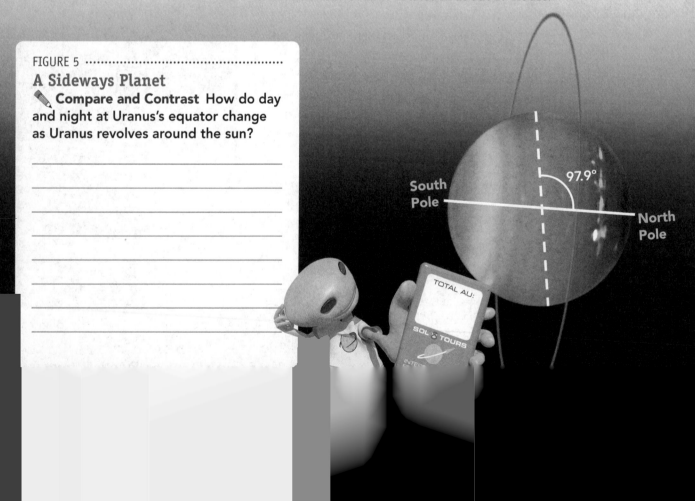

South Pole

97.9°

North Pole

TOTAL AU:

SOL TOURS

Neptune

Neptune is similar in size and color to Uranus.  **Neptune is a cold, blue planet. Its atmosphere contains visible clouds.** The color comes from methane in the atmosphere. Neptune's interior is hot due to energy left over from its formation. As this energy rises, it produces clouds and storms in the atmosphere.

Neptune's Atmosphere In 1989, *Voyager 2* flew by Neptune and photographed a Great Dark Spot about the size of Earth. Like the Great Red Spot on Jupiter, the Great Dark Spot was probably a giant storm. But it didn't last long. Images taken five years later showed that the spot was gone.

Neptune's Moons Astronomers have discovered at least 13 moons orbiting Neptune. The largest moon is Triton, which has a thin atmosphere. *Voyager 2* images show that the area of Triton's south pole is covered by nitrogen ice.

Size of Neptune compared to Earth

FIGURE 6 ....

Changing Neptune

The photograph above was taken in 1989. The photograph below was taken in 2002.

✏ **Interpret Photos** How did Neptune change?

_____

_____

_____

_____

apply it!

Congratulations! You've earned enough AU in your travels to qualify for a free mission to one planet or moon of your choice!

1 Make Judgments Which planet or moon do you choose? List three reasons for your choice.

_____

_____

2 Pose Questions What is one question you would want your mission to answer?

_____

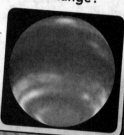

Lab zone Do the Quick Lab *Make a Model of Saturn.*

🔑 Assess Your Understanding

1. **Describe** Describe one feature of each outer planet that distinguishes it from the others.

_____

_____

_____

got it?

○ **I get it!** Now I know that the outer planets differ in _____

_____

○ **I need extra help with** _____

Go to MY SCIENCE ⓢ COACH *online for help with this subject.*

581

Small Solar System Objects

UNLOCK
THE BIG
?

🔑 **How Do Scientists Classify Small Objects in the Solar System?**

my planet Diary

BLOG

Posted by: Haley

Location: Constantia, New York

During the summer my dad and I go outside when it gets dark. We like to go stargazing. I have even seen shooting stars! Shooting stars are very hard to spot. You have to stare at the sky and sometimes you will see one shoot by. They only stick around for one split second, but it is really amazing to see one. This is my favorite thing to do when it gets dark during the summer!

✏️ **Communicate** Discuss your answers to these questions with a partner.

1. What do you think shooting stars are?

_____

_____

_____

_____

2. What do you like to observe in the night sky?

_____

_____

_____

> PLANET DIARY Go to **Planet Diary** to learn more about small solar system objects.

 Do the Inquiry Warm-Up
Collecting Micrometeorites.

Vocabulary

- asteroid belt • Kuiper belt • Oort cloud
- comet • coma • nucleus • asteroid
- meteoroid • meteor • meteorite

Skills

⟳ Reading: Summarize

△ Inquiry: Classify

How Do Scientists Classify Small Objects in the Solar System?

The solar system contains many small objects that, like the planets, orbit the sun. 🔑 **Scientists classify these objects based on their sizes, shapes, compositions, and orbits. The major categories include dwarf planets, comets, asteroids, and meteoroids.**

Areas of the Solar System Most of the small objects in the solar system are found in three areas: the asteroid belt, the Kuiper belt, and the Oort cloud. The **asteroid belt** is a region of the solar system between Mars and Jupiter. Beyond Neptune's orbit is a region called the **Kuiper belt** (KY per) which extends to about 100 times Earth's distance from the sun. Beyond the Kuiper belt, the **Oort cloud** (ort) stretches out more than 1,000 times the distance between the sun and Neptune. **Figure 1** shows these areas.

FIGURE 1 ....

Areas of the Solar System

The diagram below shows the relative positions of the asteroid belt, the Kuiper belt, and the Oort cloud.

✎ **Relate Text and Visuals** As you read this lesson, write a C to show where a comet would most likely come from. Write a P to show where you would expect to find a plutoid. Write an A to show where you would expect to find an asteroid.

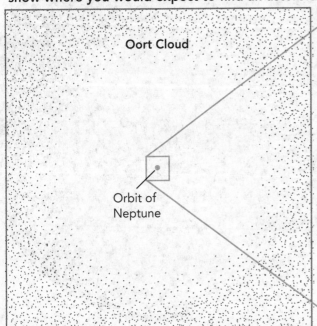

Oort Cloud

Orbit of Neptune

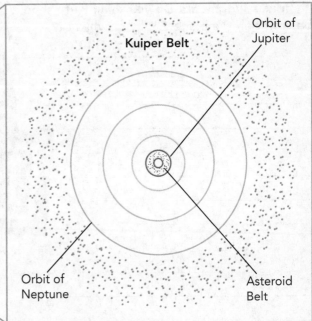

Kuiper Belt

Orbit of Jupiter

Orbit of Neptune

Asteroid Belt

Vocabulary Greek Word Origins The word *comet* comes from the Greek word *kometes,* meaning "long hair." Why do you think this word is used?

_____

_____

_____

Dwarf Planets "What happened to Pluto?" You may have found yourself asking this question as you have learned about the solar system. For many years, Pluto was considered a planet. But then scientists discovered other objects that were at least Pluto's size. Some were even farther away than Pluto. Scientists began debating how to define a planet.

Defining Dwarf Planets In 2006, astronomers developed a new category of objects, called dwarf planets. These objects orbit the sun and have enough gravity to pull themselves into spheres, but they have other objects in the area of their orbits. As of 2009, scientists had identified five dwarf planets: Pluto, Eris, Makemake, Haumea, and Ceres. Eris is believed to be the largest dwarf planet so far. There are at least a dozen more objects that may turn out to be dwarf planets, once scientists are able to study them.

   Like planets, dwarf planets can have moons. Pluto has three moons: Charon, Nix, and Hydra. Haumea has two and Eris has one.

Kuiper Belt Objects All the known dwarf planets except Ceres orbit beyond Neptune. (Ceres orbits in the asteroid belt.) A dwarf planet that orbits beyond Neptune is also called a plutoid. Most plutoids orbit the sun in the Kuiper belt, though Eris may be beyond it. The Kuiper belt also includes many other objects that are too small to be considered dwarf planets.

FIGURE 2 ·······························
> VIRTUAL LAB **Planet or Not?**
This figure shows one artist's idea of what the surface of Pluto looks like.

   Make Judgments Do you think Pluto should be considered a planet? Why or why not?

_____

_____

_____

_____

_____

_____

_____

_____

Comets A comet is one of the most dramatic objects you can see in the night sky. On a dark night, you can see its fuzzy white head and long, streaming tails. **Comets** are loose collections of ice, dust, and small rocky particles whose orbits can be very long, narrow ellipses. Some comets have smaller orbits that bring them near Earth regularly. Most comets originate in the Oort cloud.

A Comet's Head When a comet gets close to the sun, the energy in sunlight turns the ice into gas, releasing gas and dust. Clouds of gas and dust form a fuzzy outer layer called a **coma**. **Figure 3** shows the coma and the **nucleus,** the solid inner core of a comet. The nucleus is usually only a few kilometers across.

A Comet's Tail As a comet approaches the sun, it heats up and starts to glow. Some of its gas and dust stream outward, forming a tail. Most comets have two tails—a gas tail and a dust tail. The gas tail points away from the sun and the dust tail points along the path the comet has taken. A comet's tail can be more than 100 million kilometers long and from Earth, appears to stretch across most of the sky. The material is stretched out very thinly, however.

⟳ **Summarize** Write a few sentences to summarize the structure of a comet.

_____

_____

_____

_____

_____

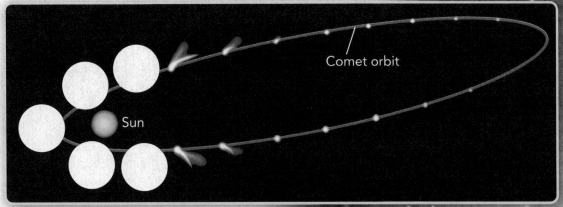

FIGURE 3 ·······························

A Comet's Orbit
Comets, as shown here, have long, narrow orbits. Their tails tend to grow longer as they approach the sun.
✎ **Apply Concepts** Complete the diagram above by adding the comet's tails.

Comet orbit

Sun

Gas tail

Nucleus

Dust tail

Coma

Asteroids Hundreds of small, irregular, rocky objects orbit the sun. These **asteroids** are rocky objects, most of which are too small and too numerous to be considered planets or dwarf planets. Astronomers have discovered more than 100,000 asteroids, and they are constantly finding more.

Small Bodies Most asteroids are small—less than a kilometer in diameter. Only Ceres, Pallas, Vesta, and Hygiea are more than 300 kilometers across. (Ceres is both a dwarf planet and the largest asteroid.) Most asteroids are not spherical. Scientists hypothesize that asteroids are leftover pieces of the early solar system that never came together to form a planet.

Asteroid Orbits Most asteroids orbit the sun in the asteroid belt. Some, however, have very elliptical orbits that bring them closer to the sun than Earth's orbit. Someday, an asteroid will hit Earth. One or more large asteroids did hit Earth about 65 million years ago, filling the atmosphere with dust and smoke and blocking out sunlight around the world. Scientists hypothesize that many species of organisms, including the dinosaurs, became extinct as a result.

apply it!

Classify For each description below, classify the object as a dwarf planet, comet, asteroid, or meteoroid.

❶ This object is slightly smaller than Pluto. It orbits the sun beyond Neptune and is spherical. _____

❷ This object is irregularly shaped. It orbits the sun just outside the orbit of Mars. _____

❸ This object is a chunk of rock and metal. It was once part of another object that orbited the sun. _____

❹ This object is composed of ice and rock. It orbits the sun in an elongated orbit, taking many years to complete one orbit.

_____

❺ [CHALLENGE] Which two types of objects are hardest to tell apart? Why? _____

_____

_____

Meteoroids Chunks of rock or dust smaller than asteroids are called **meteoroids.** Meteoroids are generally less than 10 meters across. Some meteoroids form when asteroids collide. Others form when comets break up, creating dust clouds.

Meteors and Meteorites When a meteoroid enters Earth's atmosphere, friction with the air creates heat and produces a streak of light. This streak is a **meteor.** (People often call meteors shooting stars, but they are not stars.) Most meteors come from tiny bits of rock or dust that burn up completely. But some larger meteoroids do not burn up. Meteoroids that pass through the atmosphere and are found on Earth's surface are called **meteorites.** Meteorite impacts can leave craters, such as the one shown in **Figure 4.**

Meteor Showers Meteor showers occur when Earth passes through an area with many meteoroids. Some of these groups of meteoroids are bits of comets that broke up. These meteor showers occur every year as Earth passes through the same areas. Meteor showers are often named for the constellation from which they appear to come. The Perseids, Geminids, and Orionids are examples of meteor showers.

FIGURE 4 ···

Meteor Crater

Meteor Crater in Arizona formed about 50,000 years ago from the impact of a meteorite 50–100 meters wide. ✎ **Predict How would a large meteorite impact affect Earth today?**

_____

_____

_____

Approximate size of meteorite relative to crater

Do the Quick Lab
Changing Orbits.

🔑 **Assess Your Understanding**

1a. Review (Comets/Asteroids) are rocky, while (comets/asteroids) are made of ice and dust.

b. Compare and Contrast What is the difference between a dwarf planet and an asteroid?

_____

_____

_____

c. Relate Cause and Effect How and why does a comet change as it approaches the sun?

_____

_____

_____

_____

got**it?** ···

○ **I get it!** Now I know that small solar system objects include _____

_____

_____

○ **I need extra help with** _____

  Go to my science ⑤ coach *online for help with this subject.*

587

15 Study Guide

REVIEW THE BIG ?

Objects in the solar system are different because they formed _____

LESSON 1 Models of the Solar System

🔑 In a geocentric model, Earth is at the center.

🔑 Copernicus worked out the arrangement of the known planets and how they orbit the sun.

🔑 Kepler found that planets' orbits are ellipses.

🔑 Evidence from Galileo Galilei convinced others that the heliocentric model was correct.

Vocabulary
• geocentric • heliocentric • ellipse

LESSON 2 Introducing the Solar System

🔑 Our solar system consists of the sun, the planets, their moons, and smaller objects.

🔑 The solar system formed about 4.6 billion years ago from a cloud of hydrogen, helium, rock, ice, and other materials pulled together by gravity.

Vocabulary
• solar system • astronomical unit • planet
• dwarf planet • planetesimal

LESSON 3 The Sun

🔑 The sun's interior consists of the core, the radiation zone, and the convection zone. The sun's atmosphere includes the photosphere, the chromosphere, and the corona.

🔑 Features on or just above the sun's surface include sunspots, prominences, and solar flares.

Vocabulary
• core • nuclear fusion • radiation zone
• convection zone • photosphere
• chromosphere • corona • solar wind
• sunspot • prominence • solar flare

LESSON 4 The Inner Planets

🔑 The inner planets are small and dense and have rocky surfaces.

🔑 Mercury is the smallest terrestrial planet and the planet closest to the sun. Venus has a thick atmosphere and the hottest surface of any planet. Earth has a suitable temperature range and atmosphere for living things to survive. Mars has ice and evidence of flowing liquid water.

Vocabulary
• terrestrial planet • greenhouse effect

LESSON 5 The Outer Planets

🔑 The outer planets are much larger than Earth and do not have solid surfaces.

🔑 Jupiter is the largest and most massive planet. Saturn has the most spectacular rings of any planet. Uranus's axis of rotation is tilted at an angle of about 90 degrees from the vertical. Neptune is a cold, blue planet with visible clouds.

Vocabulary
• gas giant • ring

LESSON 6 Small Solar System Objects

🔑 Scientists classify small objects based on their sizes, shapes, compositions, and orbits. The major categories include dwarf planets, comets, asteroids, and meteoroids.

Vocabulary
• asteroid belt • Kuiper belt • Oort cloud
• comet • coma • nucleus • asteroid
• meteoroid • meteor • meteorite

Review and Assessment

LESSON 1 Models of the Solar System

1. What object is at the center of a geocentric system?

  a. Earth   **b.** the moon

  c. a star   **d.** the sun

2. Kepler discovered that planets move in

_____

3. **Relate Cause and Effect** How did Tycho Brahe's work contribute to the development of the heliocentric model?

_____

_____

_____

4. **Write About It** Suppose you lived at the time of Copernicus. Write a letter to a scientific journal supporting the heliocentric model.

LESSON 2 Introducing the Solar System

5. Pluto is an example of a(n)

  a. dwarf planet.   **b.** inner planet.

  c. outer planet.   **d.** planetesimal.

6. An astronomical unit is equal to _____

_____

7. **Compare and Contrast** Compare the conditions that led to the formation of the inner planets with those that led to the formation of the outer planets.

_____

_____

_____

_____

LESSON 3 The Sun

8. In which part of the sun does nuclear fusion take place?

  a. chromosphere   **b.** convection layer

  c. core   **d.** corona

9. Relatively cool areas on the sun's surface are called _____

10. **Explain** How can the solar wind affect life on Earth? _____

_____

_____

11. **math!** The density of the sun's core is about 160 g/cm^3. The density of Earth's core is about 13.0 g/cm^3. About how many times denser is the sun's core than Earth's?

_____

LESSON 4 The Inner Planets

12. What feature is shared by all the inner planets?

  a. thick atmosphere   **b.** rocky surface

  c. ring system   **d.** liquid water

13. The inner planets are also called _____

_____

14. **Apply Concepts** Explain why Venus has the hottest surface of any planet.

_____

_____

_____

_____

15. **Write About It** Choose one inner planet. Write a news article describing a visit to that planet's surface. Include descriptive details.

LESSON 5 **The Outer Planets**

16. Which planet's orbit is farthest from Earth's?

a. Jupiter b. Neptune

c. Saturn d. Uranus

17. All the gas giants are surrounded by _____ _____

Use the illustration to answer Question 18.

18. Interpret Diagrams What planet is shown above? What is unusual about it? What do scientists think caused that unusual feature?

_____
_____
_____
_____
_____

19. Predict Do you think astronomers have found all the moons of the outer planets? Explain.

_____
_____
_____
_____
_____
_____

LESSON 6 **Small Solar System Objects**

20. Where are most dwarf planets found?

a. asteroid belt b. Kuiper belt

c. Oort cloud d. plutoid belt

21. A _____ is a meteoroid that reaches Earth's surface.

22. Compare and Contrast Compare and contrast asteroids, comets, and meteoroids.

_____
_____
_____
_____

23. **Write About It** Suppose you could witness a large meteorite or asteroid striking Earth. Write a news report explaining the event.

APPLY THE BIG ? **Why are objects in the solar system different from each other?**

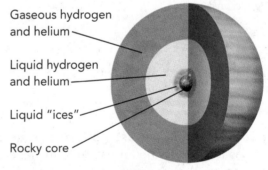

Gaseous hydrogen and helium

Liquid hydrogen and helium

Liquid "ices"

Rocky core

24. What type of planet is shown? Under what conditions would it most likely have formed?

_____
_____
_____
_____

Standardized Test Prep

Multiple Choice

Circle the letter of the best answer.

1. The table below shows data for five planets.

Planet	Period of Rotation (Earth days)	Period of Revolution (Earth years)	Average Distance from the Sun (million km)
Mars	1.03	1.9	228
Jupiter	0.41	12	779
Saturn	0.45	29	1,434
Uranus	0.72	84	2,873
Neptune	0.67	164	4,495

According to the table, which planet has a "day" that is most similar in length to a day on Earth?

A Mars
B Jupiter
C Neptune
D Uranus

2. What characteristic do all of the outer planets share?

A They have rocky surfaces.
B They are larger than the sun.
C They have many moons.
D They have thin atmospheres.

3. Which is the best description of our sun?

A a small star
B a mid-sized star
C a large star
D a supergiant star

4. Mercury has a daytime temperature of about 430°C and a nighttime temperature below −170°C. What is the *best* explanation for this?

A Mercury has a greenhouse effect.
B Mercury is the closest planet to the sun.
C Mercury has little to no atmosphere.
D Mercury has no liquid water.

5. From what region do *most* comets come?

A asteroid belt
B inner solar system
C Kuiper belt
D Oort cloud

Constructed Response

Use the diagram below to answer Question 6.

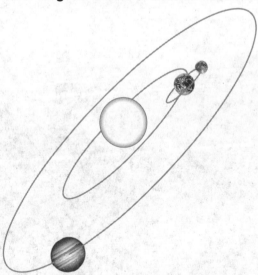

6. What model of the solar system is shown above? Give at least two pieces of evidence that support the model.

Mars Rovers

High school students came up with the names—*Spirit* and *Opportunity*—and scientists at the National Aeronautics and Space Administration (NASA) came up with the plan. Mars is too far away for humans to explore directly. So robot rovers would be dropped onto the surface of Mars and do the exploring for us. The rovers landed on Mars in January 2004. Their assignment was to collect images that would help answer the question: Was there ever water on Mars and could there have been life?

Chemical and physical data from the rovers suggested that there once was water on Mars. The rovers found evidence of erosion as well as of chemicals that would exist in an acidic lake or hot springs. Then, in 2015, NASA's *Mars Reconnaissance Orbiter* found evidence of flowing liquid water on Mars even today. It is still impossible to know for sure whether life ever existed on Mars.

Organize It Find three articles about the rover mission. Organize the information in the articles into a two-column chart. In one column, list any data about Mars described in the articles. In the second column, list any conclusions that scientists made about Mars based on that evidence. Circle any conclusions that were confirmed by later Mars missions.

Elliptical, Predictable Orbits

Even the planets flying through the solar system have to obey the law! Gravitational forces determine the ways in which objects move throughout the solar system. In the early 1600s, Johannes Kepler proposed three laws to describe how these forces affect the motion of the planets in orbit around the sun. Kepler's first law of planetary motion states that all planets orbit the sun in a path that resembles an ellipse, with the sun located at one of the ellipse's two foci.

Kepler's second law uses a mathematical formula to describe the speed at which planets orbit the sun. Planets travel fastest when they are moving along the sun side of the ellipse. They travel more slowly along the opposite side of the ellipse. In his third law, Kepler was able to demonstrate that by knowing a planet's period of revolution, the planet's distance from the sun can be calculated. The formulas in Kepler's laws are still used to describe the motion of planets and other satellites.

▲ *The two foci that anchor Earth's elliptical path are almost directly on top of each other. This makes Earth's orbit almost circular. The orbits of the outer planets are more strongly elliptical.*

Model It You can make an ellipse using a pencil, a string, a sheet of paper, two pushpins, and a piece of cardboard. First, use two pushpins to fasten the sheet of paper to the cardboard. Next, tie the string into a loose loop around the two pins. The loop should have plenty of slack. Pull the string tight with your pencil tip. The string should form a triangle with the pencil and pins at its three corners. Then, trace out a path with the pencil, pulling the string along the farthest possible path from the pins. The resulting shape will be an ellipse.

HOW CAN YOU GAZE DEEP INTO SPACE?

How do astronomers learn about distant objects in the universe?

Two galaxies are colliding! It all started 40 million years ago and will take millions more for these two spiral galaxies to actually combine. Astronomers know that the galaxy on the left, NGC 2207, and the galaxy on the right, IC 2163, are 140 million light-years from Earth. A light-year is the distance light travels in one year, or 9.46 trillion kilometers. That makes these galaxies about 1,320,000,000,000,000,000,000 kilometers away. ⚠ Infer **How can astronomers see so far into space?**

_____

_____

_____

_____

> UNTAMED SCIENCE Watch the **Untamed Science** video to learn more about the universe.

Stars, Galaxies, and the Universe

16

Getting Started

Check Your Understanding

1. Background Read the paragraph below and then answer the question.

The children all held onto the edge of the giant parachute and shook it. The fabric moved up and down as a **wave** moved across it. "There's **energy** traveling across the fabric," their teacher said. "If we shake the edge quickly, the **distance** between the tops of the waves will get smaller."

> A **wave** is a disturbance that transfers energy from place to place.
>
> **Energy** is the ability to do work or cause change.
>
> **Distance** is the length of a path between two points.

• What will happen if the students shake the parachute more slowly?

_____

_____

> **MY READING WEB** If you had trouble completing the question above, visit **My Reading Web** and type in *Stars, Galaxies, and the Universe*.

Vocabulary Skill

Suffixes A suffix is a letter or group of letters added to the end of a word to form a new word with a slightly different meaning. Adding a suffix to a word often changes its part of speech.

Suffix	Meaning	Part of Speech	Example
-tion/-ion	Process of, action of	Noun	scientific nota*tion*
-ory	Place or thing connected with or used for	Noun	observa*tory*

2. Quick Check Use the information in the chart to suggest a meaning for each vocabulary term below.

• observatory: _____

_____

• scientific notation: _____

radio telescope

supernova

spiral galaxy

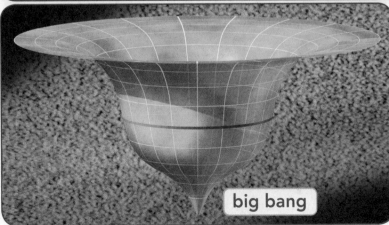

big bang

Chapter Preview

LESSON 1
- electromagnetic radiation
- visible light • wavelength
- spectrum • telescope
- optical telescope
- refracting telescope • convex lens
- reflecting telescope • observatory
- radio telescope

↻ **Ask Questions**
△ **Infer**

LESSON 2
- parallax • universe
- light-year • scientific notation

↻ **Summarize**
△ **Calculate**

LESSON 3
- spectrograph
- apparent brightness
- absolute brightness
- Hertzsprung-Russell diagram
- main sequence

↻ **Identify the Main Idea**
△ **Interpret Data**

LESSON 4
- nebula • protostar • white dwarf
- supernova • neutron star
- pulsar • black hole

↻ **Compare and Contrast**
△ **Predict**

LESSON 5
- binary star • eclipsing binary
- open cluster • globular cluster
- galaxy • spiral galaxy
- elliptical galaxy • irregular galaxy
- quasar

↻ **Relate Cause and Effect**
△ **Draw Conclusions**

LESSON 6
- big bang • Hubble's law
- cosmic background radiation
- dark matter • dark energy

↻ **Identify Supporting Evidence**
△ **Make Models**

597

LESSON 1

Telescopes

UNLOCK THE BIG Q?

🔑 **What Are the Regions of the Electromagnetic Spectrum?**

🔑 **What Are Telescopes and How Do They Work?**

MY PLANET DiARY

TECHNOLOGY

Infrared Goggles

Suppose you're a spy on a dark street, hoping to spot another spy. How would you see the other spy in the dark? Wear a pair of infrared goggles.

All objects give off radiation that you can't see. The glowing coils of an electric heater give off infrared radiation, which you feel as heat. Human beings also glow infrared, and with the infrared goggles you can see a green outline of a person in the dark. Some objects in space also give off invisible radiation that we can detect with special telescopes.

Communicate Answer the following question. Then discuss your answer with a partner.

In what other situations might you want to use infrared goggles?

_____

_____

_____

_____

_____

> **PLANET DIARY** Go to **Planet Diary** to learn more about telescopes.

Lab zone Do the Inquiry Warm-Up *How Does Distance Affect an Image?*

What Are the Regions of the Electromagnetic Spectrum?

To understand how telescopes work, it's useful to understand **electromagnetic radiation** (ih LEK troh mag NET ik), or energy that can travel through space in the form of waves.

Scientists call the light you can see **visible light.** Visible light is just one of many types of electromagnetic radiation. Many objects give off radiation that you can't see. Objects in space give off all types of electromagnetic radiation.

Vocabulary

- electromagnetic radiation • visible light • wavelength • spectrum
- telescope • optical telescope • refracting telescope • convex lens
- reflecting telescope • observatory • radio telescope

Skills

↻ Reading: Ask Questions

△ Inquiry: Infer

The distance between the crest of one wave and the crest of the next wave is called the **wavelength.** Visible light has very short wavelengths, less than one millionth of a meter. There are some electromagnetic waves that have even shorter wavelengths. Other waves have much longer wavelengths, even several meters long.

If you shine white light through a prism, the light spreads out to make a range of different colors with different wavelengths, called a **spectrum.** The spectrum of visible light is made of the colors red, orange, yellow, green, blue, and violet. 🔑 **The electromagnetic spectrum includes the entire range of radio waves, infrared radiation, visible light, ultraviolet radiation, X-rays, and gamma rays.** Look at **Figure 1** to see the spectrum.

Flower seen in visible light

FIGURE 1 ·············

The Electromagnetic Spectrum

Humans see visible light, but bees can see ultraviolet light, so flowers look different to a bee.

✏️ CHALLENGE **What advantage does having ultraviolet vision give bees?**

_____

_____

_____

_____

Flower seen in ultraviolet light

Lab zone® Do the Quick Lab *Observing a Continuous Spectrum.*

🔑 Assess Your Understanding

got it? ·····················

○ I get it! Now I know that the electromagnetic spectrum includes _____

_____

○ I need extra help with _____

Go to my science 🔍 coach online for help with this subject.

What Are Telescopes and How Do They Work?

On a clear night, your eyes can see at most a few thousand stars. But with a telescope, you can see many millions. Why? The light from stars spreads out as it moves through space and your eyes are too small to gather much light.

🔑 **Telescopes are instruments that collect and focus light and other forms of electromagnetic radiation.** Telescopes make distant objects appear larger and brighter. A telescope that uses lenses or mirrors to collect and focus visible light is called an **optical telescope.** There are also nonoptical telescopes. These telescopes collect and focus different types of electromagnetic radiation, just as optical telescopes collect visible light.

Optical Telescopes The two major types of optical telescopes are refracting telescopes and reflecting telescopes.

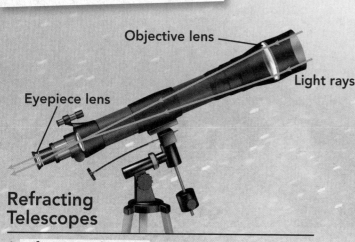

Objective lens

Eyepiece lens

Light rays

Refracting Telescopes

A **refracting telescope** is a telescope that uses convex lenses to gather and focus light. A **convex lens** is a piece of glass that is curved, so the middle is thicker than the edges.

A simple refracting telescope has two convex lenses, one at each end of a long tube. Light enters the telescope through the large objective lens at the top. The objective lens focuses the light at a certain distance from the lens. This distance is the focal length of the lens. A larger objective lens means that the telescope can collect more light. This makes it easier for astronomers to see faint objects, or objects that are far away.

The smaller lens at the lower end of a refracting telescope is the eyepiece lens. The eyepiece lens magnifies the image produced by the objective lens. A magnified image can be easier to study.

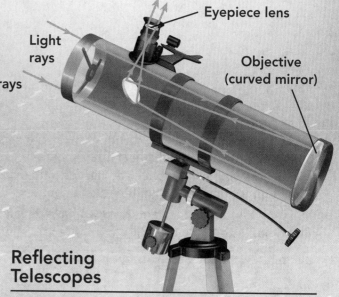

Eyepiece lens

Light rays

Objective (curved mirror)

Reflecting Telescopes

In 1668, Isaac Newton built the first reflecting telescope. A **reflecting telescope** uses a curved mirror to collect and focus light. Like the objective lens in a refracting telescope, the curved mirror in a reflecting telescope focuses a large amount of light onto a small area. A larger mirror means that the telescope can collect more light. The largest optical telescopes today are all reflecting telescopes.

Why are the largest optical telescopes reflecting telescopes? Because the mirror can be supported from below. But the lens of a refracting telescope must be supported from the edges, so light can pass through it.

FIGURE 2 ·····························

> INTERACTIVE ART **Refracting and Reflecting Telescopes**
A refracting telescope uses convex lenses to focus light.
A reflecting telescope uses a curved mirror to focus light.

✎ Compare and Contrast **After reading about refracting and reflecting telescopes, circle the correct answers in the table showing the similarities and differences between the two.**

TELESCOPE	Objective	Eyepiece	Typical size	Light collection
Refracting	Lens / Mirror	Lens / Mirror	Smaller / Larger	Less / More
Reflecting	Lens / Mirror	Lens / Mirror	Smaller / Larger	Less / More

The Hubble telescope

The glowing shell of a supernova remnant

The Cone Nebula

FIGURE 3 ·····························
The Hubble Space Telescope
The Hubble telescope is a reflecting telescope with a mirror 2.4 meters in diameter. The Hubble telescope orbits Earth above the atmosphere. As a result, it produces very detailed images in visible light. It also collects ultraviolet and infrared radiation. Images such as the ones shown here have changed the way astronomers view the universe.

A supernova remnant in the Large Magellanic Cloud

The Sombrero Galaxy

did you know?

Astronomers are concerned about "light pollution," artificial lighting that makes it hard to see the skies at night. Some cities have replaced their street lamps with ones that point down. With these lamps, light isn't beamed into the night sky and people can once again see the stars.

🔄 **Ask Questions** Write a question you would like answered about telescopes.

_____

_____

_____

_____

Other Telescopes Telescopes are usually located in observatories. An **observatory** is a building that contains one or more telescopes. Many large observatories are located on the tops of mountains or in space. Why? Earth's atmosphere makes objects in space look blurry. The sky on some mountaintops is clearer than at sea level and is not brightened by city lights.

- **Radio telescopes** detect radio waves from objects in space. Most radio telescopes have curved, reflecting surfaces. These surfaces focus faint radio waves the way the mirror in a reflecting telescope focuses light waves. Radio telescopes need to be large to collect and focus more radio waves, because radio waves have long wavelengths. Some radio telescopes, like the one in **Figure 4**, are placed in valleys.
- The Spitzer Space Telescope, launched in 2003, produces images in the infrared portion of the spectrum.
- Very hot objects in space give off X-rays. The Chandra X-ray Observatory produces images in the X-ray portion of the spectrum. X-rays are blocked by Earth's atmosphere, so this telescope is located in outer space.

Some new telescopes are equipped with computer systems that correct images for problems such as telescope movement and changes in air temperature or mirror shape.

FIGURE 4

Arecibo Radio Telescope
The Arecibo telescope in Puerto Rico is 305 meters in diameter.

✏️ **Evaluate the Design** Why are radio telescopes so large?

_____

_____

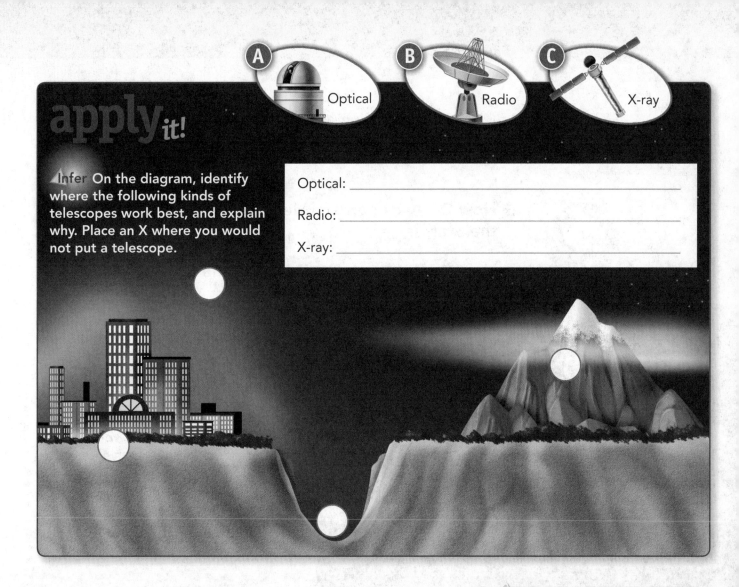

apply it!

Infer On the diagram, identify where the following kinds of telescopes work best, and explain why. Place an X where you would not put a telescope.

Optical: _____

Radio: _____

X-ray: _____

A Optical

B Radio

C X-ray

Lab zone® Do the Lab Investigation
Design and Build a Telescope.

🔑 Assess Your Understanding

1a. Sequence List the electromagnetic waves, from longest to shortest wavelength.

_____

_____

_____

_____

_____

b. Identify Faulty Reasoning A student of astronomy suggests locating a radio telescope near a radio station. Is this a good idea? Why or why not?

_____

_____

_____

_____

_____

got it? ....

○ **I get it!** Now I know that telescopes are _____

_____

○ **I need extra help with** _____

Go to **MY SCIENCE ⓢ COACH** *online for help with this subject.*

The Scale of the Universe

UNLOCK
THE BIG
?

🔑 **How Do Astronomers Measure Distances to the Stars?**

🔑 **How Do Astronomers Describe the Scale of the Universe?**

my planeT DiaRY

FUN FACT

Voyager Golden Record

Sixteen billion kilometers away flies a gold-plated copper disk with a voice saying "Hello from the children of planet Earth." The disk is carried aboard *Voyager 1*, a spacecraft launched in 1977 that once sent back information about the planets of the outer solar system. The disk is filled with images and sounds of Earth. One day, aliens might find *Voyager 1* and learn all about us!

Communicate Discuss the Voyager Record with a partner. Then answer the question below.

What images and sounds would you put on a recording for aliens?

_____

_____

_____

_____

▷ PLANET DIARY Go to **Planet Diary** to learn more about the scale of the universe.

Lab ® Do the Inquiry Warm-Up
zone *Stringing Along.*

How Do Astronomers Measure Distances to the Stars?

Standing on Earth looking up at the sky, it may seem as if there is no way to tell how far away the stars are. However, astronomers have found ways to measure those distances. 🔑 **Astronomers often use parallax to measure distances to nearby stars.**

Parallax is the apparent change in position of an object when you look at it from different places. Astronomers can measure the parallax of nearby stars to determine their distances.

Vocabulary
- parallax
- light-year
- universe
- scientific notation

Skills
- Reading: Summarize
- Inquiry: Calculate

FIGURE 1 ···

Parallax of Stars

The apparent movement of a star when seen from a different position is called parallax. Note that the diagram is not to scale.

CHALLENGE Hold a finger about half an arm's length away from your face, as shown in the picture below. Switch back and forth between closing your left and right eye and watch how your finger appears to move against the background. Why does your finger seem to move? How is this related to the parallax of stars?

_____
_____
_____
_____
_____
_____
_____
_____

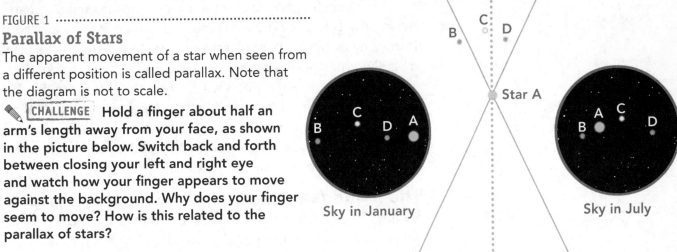

Sky in January

Sky in July

Star A

January

July

As shown in **Figure 1,** astronomers look at a nearby star when Earth is on one side of the sun. Then they look at the same star again six months later, when Earth is on the opposite side of the sun. Astronomers measure how much the nearby star appears to move against a background of stars that are much farther away. They can then use this measurement to calculate the distance to the nearby star. The less the nearby star appears to move, the farther away it is.

Astronomers can use parallax to measure distances up to a few hundred light-years from Earth. The parallax of any star that is farther away is too small to measure accurately.

Lab zone Do the Quick Lab
How Far Is That Star?

🔑 Assess Your Understanding

got it? ···

○ **I get it!** Now I know that astronomers often measure the distances to nearby stars using _____, which is _____

_____
_____
_____

○ **I need extra help with** _____
_____

_Go to_ **my science** ⓢ **coach** _online for help with this subject._

How Do Astronomers Describe the Scale of the Universe?

Astronomers define the **universe** as all of space and everything in it. The universe is enormous, almost beyond imagination. Astronomers study objects as close as the moon and as far away as quasars. They study incredibly large objects, such as clusters of galaxies that are millions of light-years across. They also study the behavior of tiny particles, such as the atoms within the stars. 🔑 **Since the numbers astronomers use are often very large or very small, they frequently use scientific notation to describe sizes and distances in the universe. They use a unit called the light-year to measure distances between the stars.**

The Light-Year
Distances to the stars are so large that meters are not very practical units. In space, light travels at a speed of about 300,000,000 meters per second. A **light-year** is the distance that light travels in one year, about 9.46 trillion kilometers.

The light-year is a unit of distance, not time. To understand this better, consider an example. If you bicycle at 10 kilometers per hour, it would take you 1 hour to go to a mall 10 kilometers away. You could say that the mall is "1 bicycle-hour" away.

Scientific Notation
Scientific notation uses powers of ten to write very large or very small numbers in shorter form. Each number is written as the product of a number between 1 and 10 and a power of 10. For example: 1,200 is written as 1.2×10^3.

One light-year is about 9,460,000,000,000,000 meters. To express this number in scientific notation, first insert a decimal point in the original number so that you have a number between one and ten. In this case, the rounded number is 9.5. To determine the power of ten, count the number of places that the decimal point moved. Since there are 15 digits after the first digit, in scientific notation this number can now be written as 9.5×10^{15} meters.

The Immensity of Space
The objects in the universe vary greatly in their distance from Earth. To understand the scale of these distances, imagine that you are going on a journey through the universe. Refer to **Figure 2** as you take your imaginary trip. Start on Earth. Now shift to the right and change the scale by 100,000,000,000, or 10^{11}. You're now close to the sun, which is located 1.5×10^{11} meters away. As you move from left to right across **Figure 2**, the distance increases. The nearest star to our sun, Alpha Centauri, is 4.2×10^{16} meters or 4.3 light-years away. The nearest galaxy to the Milky Way, the Andromeda galaxy, is about 2.4×10^{22} meters away.

✏️ **Summarize** Explain why astronomers use scientific notation to describe sizes.

_____

_____

_____

do the math!

Scientific Notation

To express a number in scientific notation, first insert a decimal point in the original number so you have a number between one and ten. Then count the number of places that the decimal point moved. That gives you the power of ten.

1 Calculate The sun takes about 220,000,000 years to revolve once around the center of the galaxy. Express this length of time in scientific notation.

_____

_____

2 Calculate The distant star Deneb is thought by some astronomers to be 3,230 light-years away. Write this distance in scientific notation.

_____

_____

FIGURE 2 ··································

> INTERACTIVE ART **Scale of the Universe**

Scientists often use scientific notation to help describe the vast distances in space. The sun is 1.5×10^{11} m away from Earth, but the next star, Alpha Centauri, is 4.2×10^{16} m away, almost 300,000 times as far.

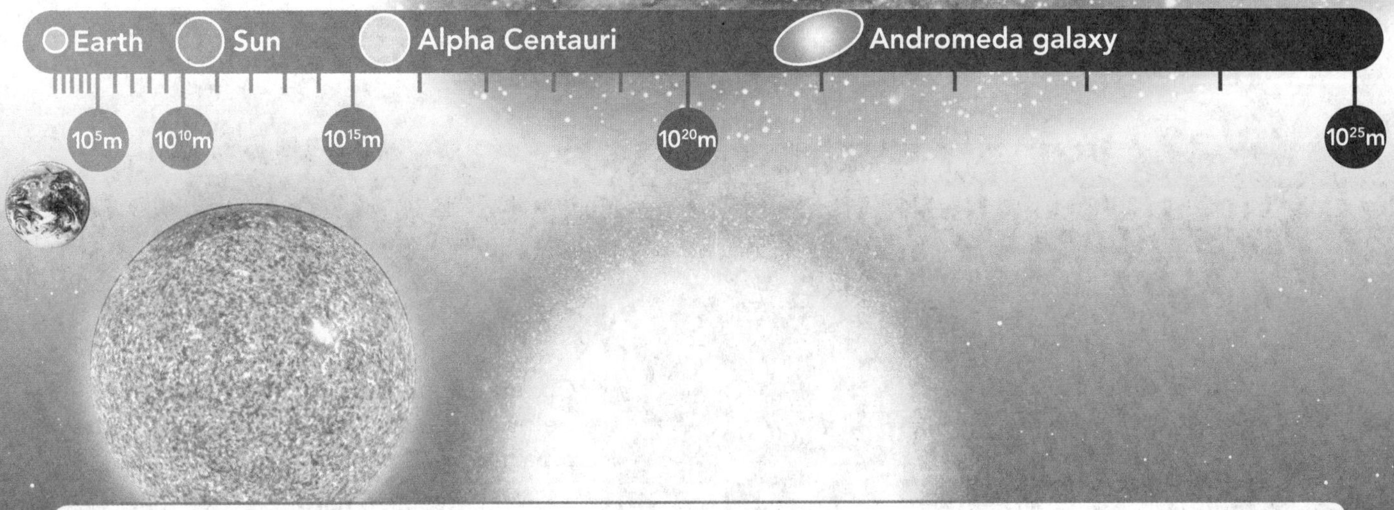

◯ Earth   ◯ Sun   ◯ Alpha Centauri   Andromeda galaxy

10^5m 10^{10}m 10^{15}m 10^{20}m 10^{25}m

Calculate Express the distances to the sun and Alpha Centauri in meters by writing out all the zeroes in the number.

Sun: _____

Alpha Centauri: _____

Lab zone® Do the Quick Lab *Measuring the Universe.*

🔑 Assess Your Understanding

1a. Review What is scientific notation?

_____
_____
_____
_____

b. Explain How is scientific notation useful to astronomers?

_____
_____
_____
_____

c. Calculate The Andromeda galaxy is 2,200,000 light-years away. Write that measurement using scientific notation.

_____

got it? ···

◯ **I get it!** Now I know that to describe the scale

of the universe, astronomers use _____

_____

◯ **I need extra help with** _____

Go to MY SCIENCE ⬢ᔆ **COACH** *online for help with this subject.*

3 Characteristics of Stars

UNLOCK THE BIG **?**

🔑 **How Are Stars Classified?**

🔑 **What Is an H-R Diagram and How Do Astronomers Use It?**

MY PLANET DIARY

CAREERS

Black Holes

If you were an astronomer, you might study some of the strangest objects in the universe. For almost 100 years, scientists believed that some stars became black holes when they died. But a black hole is an object with gravity so strong that not even light can escape. So scientists couldn't prove that black holes existed because they couldn't see them. Eventually, astronomers discovered a way to prove black holes exist. They realized that they could detect the matter being pulled into the black hole. That matter reaches such high temperatures that it releases X-rays. In the 1960s, astronomers launched a rocket to record X-rays from outer space. On this first mission, they found evidence for black holes!

Communicate Answer the questions below. Then discuss your answers with a partner.

1. Why was it so hard to prove that black holes exist?

_____

_____

_____

_____

2. What subjects, other than astronomy, would astronomers have to study in order to discover black holes?

_____

_____

_____

▶ PLANET DIARY Go to **Planet Diary** to learn more about characteristics of stars.

 Do the Inquiry Warm-Up *How Stars Differ.*

Vocabulary
- spectrograph
- absolute brightness
- main sequence
- apparent brightness
- Hertzsprung-Russell diagram

Skills
- Reading: Identify the Main Idea
- Inquiry: Interpret Data

How Are Stars Classified?

All stars are huge spheres of glowing gas. Made up mostly of hydrogen, stars produce energy through the process of nuclear fusion. Astronomers classify stars according to their physical characteristics. 🗝 **Characteristics used to classify stars include color, temperature, size, composition, and brightness.**

Color and Temperature If you look at the night sky, you can see slight differences in the colors of the stars. Some stars look reddish. Others are yellow or blue-white, as shown in **Figure 1.**

A star's color reveals its surface temperature. The coolest stars— with a surface temperature of about 3,200°C—appear red. Our yellow sun has a surface temperature of about 5,500°C. The hottest stars, with surface temperatures of over 20,000°C, appear bluish.

Size When you look at stars in the sky, they all appear to be points of light of the same size. Many stars are actually about the size of the sun. However, some stars are much larger than the sun. Very large stars are called giant stars or supergiant stars.

Most stars are smaller than the sun. White dwarf stars are about the size of Earth. Neutron stars are even smaller, about 20 kilometers in diameter.

✏ **Identify the Main Idea**
Write a sentence that says what the color of a star indicates.

_____

_____

_____

_____

FIGURE 1 ·······················
Star Color and Temperature
Stars vary in size, color, and temperature.
✎ **Draw Conclusions** Which of the four stars shown has the highest temperature? Why?

_____

_____

_____

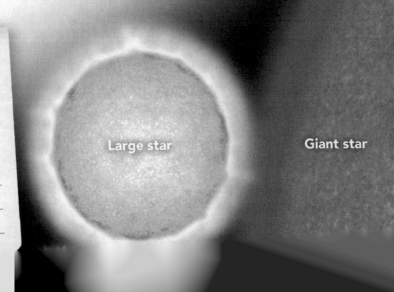

Large star

Giant star

Chemical Composition

Stars vary in their chemical composition. The chemical composition of most stars is about 73 percent hydrogen, 25 percent helium, and 2 percent other elements by mass. This is close to the composition of the sun.

Astronomers use spectrographs to determine the elements found in stars. A **spectrograph** (SPEK truh graf) is a device that breaks light into colors and produces an image of the resulting spectrum. Today, most large telescopes have spectrographs to analyze light.

The gases in a star's atmosphere absorb some wavelengths of light produced within the star. When the star's light is seen through a spectrograph, each absorbed wavelength is shown as a dark line on a spectrum. Each chemical element absorbs light at particular wavelengths. Just as each person has a unique set of fingerprints, each element has a unique set of spectral lines for a given temperature.

Alnitak
approximately
800
light-years away

Alnilam
approximately
1,300
light-years away

apply it!

The lines on the spectrums below are from four different elements. By comparing a star's spectrum with the spectrums of known elements, astronomers can infer each element found in the star. Each star's spectrum is an overlap of the spectrums from the individual elements.

△ **Interpret Data** Identify the elements with the strongest lines in Stars A, B, and C.

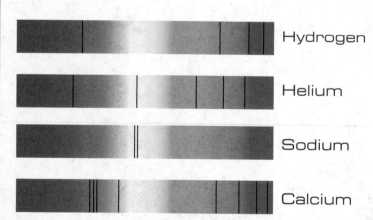

Hydrogen

Helium

Sodium

Calcium

A

B

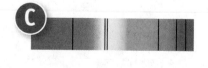

C

Brightness of Stars

Stars also differ in brightness, the amount of light they give off. 🔑 **The brightness of a star depends upon both its size and temperature.** A larger star tends to be brighter than a smaller star. A hotter star tends to be brighter than a cooler star.

How bright a star appears depends on both its distance from Earth and how bright the star truly is. Because of these two factors, the brightness of a star is described in two ways: apparent brightness and absolute brightness.

Apparent Brightness A star's **apparent brightness** is its brightness as seen from Earth. Astronomers can measure apparent brightness fairly easily using electronic devices. However, astronomers can't tell how much light a star gives off just from the star's apparent brightness. Just as a flashlight looks brighter the closer it is to you, a star looks brighter the closer it is to Earth. For example, the sun looks very bright. This does not mean that the sun gives off more light than all other stars. The sun looks so bright simply because it is so close.

Absolute Brightness A star's **absolute brightness** is the brightness the star would have if it were at a standard distance from Earth. Finding absolute brightness is more complex than finding its apparent brightness. An astronomer must first find out both the star's apparent brightness and its distance from Earth. The astronomer can then calculate the star's absolute brightness.

Astronomers have found that the absolute brightness of stars can vary tremendously. The brightest stars are more than a billion times brighter than the dimmest stars!

> ▶ VIRTUAL LAB FIGURE 2 ·························
>
> ### Apparent and Absolute Brightness
> The three stars Alnitak, Alnilam, and Mintaka in the constellation Orion all seem to have the same apparent brightness from Earth. But Alnilam is actually farther away than the other two stars.
>
> ✏️ CHALLENGE **Which star has the greatest absolute brightness? How do you know?**
>
> _____
> _____
> _____
> _____

Mintaka
approximately
900
light-years away

Lab zone Do the Quick Lab *Star Bright.*

🔑 **Assess Your Understanding**

got it? ···································

○ **I get it!** Now I know that stars are classified by _____

_____

_____

○ **I need extra help with** _____

_____

Go to MY SCIENCE 🔊 COACH *online for help with this subject.*

611

What Is an H-R Diagram and How Do Astronomers Use It?

About 100 years ago, two scientists working independently made the same discovery. Both Ejnar Hertzsprung (EYE nahr HURT sprung) in Denmark and Henry Norris Russell in the United States made graphs to find out if the temperature and the absolute brightness of stars are related. They plotted the surface temperatures of stars on the *x*-axis and their absolute brightness on the *y*-axis. The points formed a pattern. The graph they made is still used by astronomers today. It is called the **Hertzsprung-Russell diagram,** or H-R diagram.

FIGURE 3

Hertzsprung-Russell Diagram
The H-R diagram shows the relationship between surface temperature and absolute brightness of stars.

✎ **Interpret Diagrams** Place the stars listed in the table on the diagram, and note on the table the classification of each star.

H-R DIAGRAM

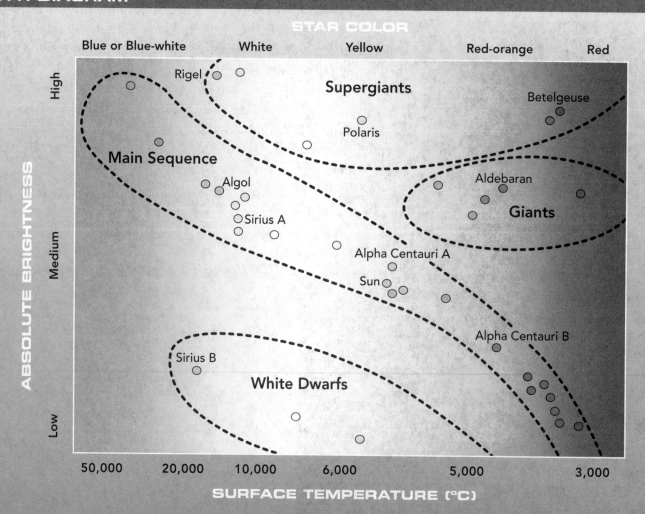

Astronomers use H-R diagrams to classify stars and to understand how stars change over time. As shown in **Figure 3,** most of the stars in the H-R diagram form a diagonal area called the **main sequence.** More than 90 percent of all stars, including the sun, are main-sequence stars. Within the main sequence, the surface temperature increases as absolute brightness increases. Thus, hot bluish stars are located at the left of an H-R diagram and cooler reddish stars are located at the right of the diagram.

The brightest stars are located near the top of an H-R diagram, while the dimmest stars are located at the bottom. Giant and supergiant stars are very bright. They can be found near the top center and right of the diagram. White dwarfs are hot, but not very bright, so they appear at either the bottom left or bottom center of the diagram.

STAR A

Color	Red-orange
Temperature	5,000°C
Brightness	High
Type	

STAR B

Color	Yellow
Temperature	6,000°C
Brightness	Medium
Type	

STAR C

Color	White
Temperature	10,000°C
Brightness	Low
Type	

Lab zone® Do the Quick Lab
Interpreting the H-R Diagram.

Assess Your Understanding

1a. Review What two characteristics of stars are shown in an H-R diagram?

_____

_____

_____

b. Explain What is the relationship between brightness and temperature shown within the main sequence?

_____

_____

_____

_____

c. Interpret Diagrams The star Procyon B has a surface temperature of 7,500°C and a low absolute brightness. What type of star is it?

_____

_____

got it?..

○ I get it! Now I know that astronomers use H-R diagrams to _____

_____

_____

○ I need extra help with _____

_____

Go to my science ⊙s coach
online for help with this subject.

Lives of Stars

🔑 How Does a Star Form and What Determines Its Life Span?

🔑 What Happens to a Star When It Runs Out of Fuel?

MY PLANET DIARY

DISCOVERY

The Supernova of 1054

In the summer of 1054, some Chinese astronomers noticed a "guest star" in the night sky. The star was so bright people could see it during the day! The star remained visible for almost two years. How did these ancient astronomers interpret it? Was it a sign that the emperor would be visited by an important guest? People from around the world recorded and interpreted the event differently. Almost 1,000 years later, scientists realized the "guest star" was the explosion of a giant star 4,000 light-years away. So powerful was the explosion that all life within about 50 light-years would have been wiped out. Now called Supernova 1054, its remains are known as the Crab Nebula.

Communicate Discuss the supernova with a partner and answer the questions below.

1. Why was Supernova 1054 so notable?

_____

_____

_____

_____

2. How do you think ancient astronomers might have interpreted the event differently than astronomers today?

_____

_____

_____

 Do the Inquiry Warm-Up *What Determines How Long Stars Live?*

> PLANET DIARY Go to **Planet Diary** to learn more about stars.

Vocabulary
- nebula • protostar • white dwarf • supernova
- neutron star • pulsar • black hole

Skills
- Reading: Compare and Contrast
- Inquiry: Predict

How Does a Star Form and What Determines Its Life Span?

Stars do not last forever. Each star is born, goes through its life cycle, and eventually dies. (Of course, stars are not really alive. The words *born, live,* and *die* are just helpful comparisons.) **A star is born when the contracting gas and dust from a nebula become so dense and hot that nuclear fusion starts. How long a star lives depends on its mass.**

A Star Is Born All stars begin their lives as parts of nebulas, such as the one in **Figure 1.** A **nebula** is a large cloud of gas and dust spread out in an immense volume. A star, on the other hand, is made up of a large amount of gas in a relatively small volume.

In the densest part of a nebula, gravity pulls gas and dust together. A contracting cloud of gas and dust with enough mass to form a star is called a **protostar.** *Proto-* means "earliest" in Greek, so a protostar is the earliest stage of a star's life.

Recall that nuclear fusion is the process by which atoms combine to form heavier atoms. In the sun, for example, hydrogen atoms combine to form helium. During nuclear fusion, enormous amounts of energy are released. Nuclear fusion begins in a protostar.

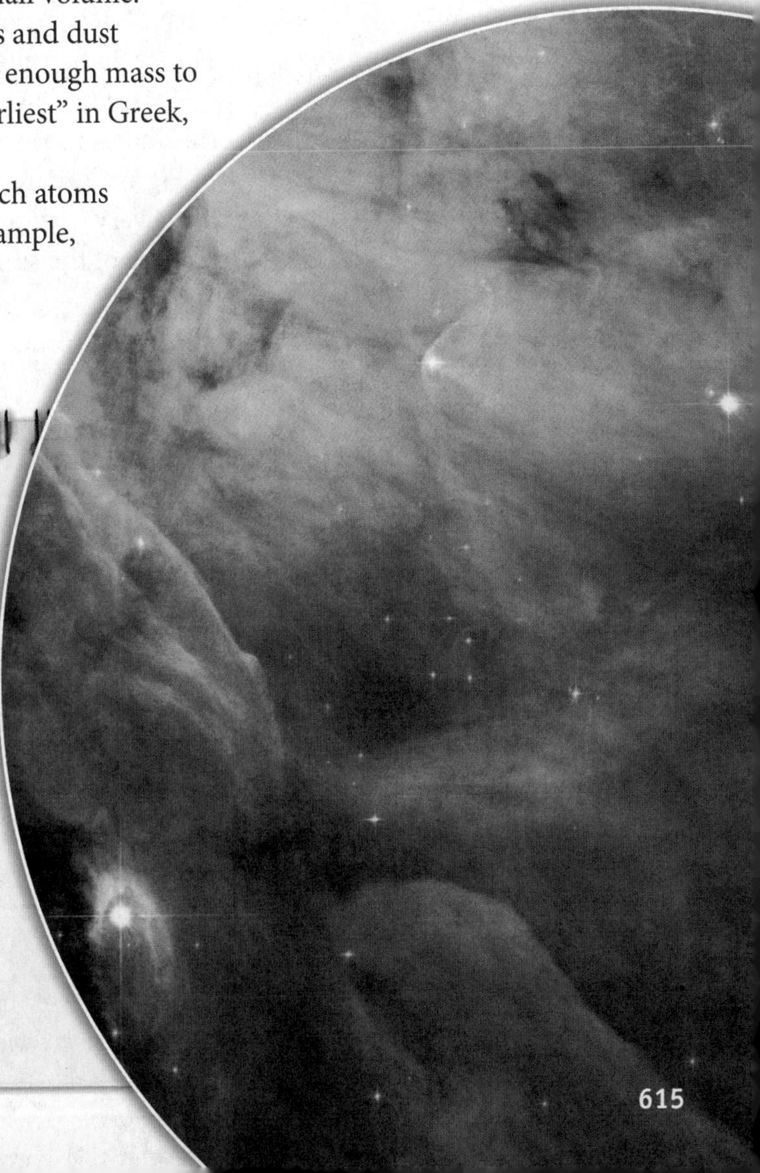

FIGURE 1 ·············
A Stellar Nursery
New stars are forming in the nebula.

✎ **Summarize** Describe the process of star formation.

_____

_____

_____

_____

_____

_____

_____

615

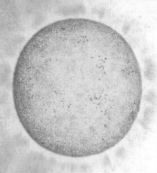

FIGURE 2 ·······················

Life of a Star
A star's lifetime depends on its mass.

✎ **Explain** The yellow star has much less mass than the blue star and so will live longer. Explain why.

_____

_____

_____

_____

Lifetimes of Stars How long a star lives depends on the star's mass. You might think that stars with more mass would last longer than stars with less mass. But the reverse is true. You can think of stars as being like cars. A small car has a small gas tank, but it also has a small engine that burns gas slowly. A large car has a larger gas tank, but it also has a larger engine that burns gas rapidly. So the small car can travel farther on a tank of gas than the larger car. Small-mass stars use up their fuel more slowly than large-mass stars, so they have much longer lives.

Generally, stars that have less mass than the sun use their fuel slowly, and can live for up to 200 billion years. A medium-mass star like the sun will live for about 10 billion years. The sun is about 4.6 billion years old, so it is about halfway through its lifetime. In **Figure 2**, the yellow star is similar to the sun.

Stars that have more mass than the sun have shorter lifetimes. A star that is more massive than the sun, such as the blue star shown in **Figure 2,** may live only about 10 million years. That may seem like a very long time, but it is only one tenth of one percent of the lifetime of the sun.

Lab zone® Do the Quick Lab
Life Cycle of Stars.

🔑 Assess Your Understanding

1a. Review How does a star form from a nebula?

_____

_____

_____

_____

b. Summarize What factor determines how long a star lives?

_____

_____

c. Predict A star is twice as massive as the sun. How will its lifespan compare?

_____

_____

got it? ··

○ **I get it!** Now I know that stars are born when _____

_____

and how long a star lives depends on _____

○ **I need extra help with** _____

Go to **MY SCIENCE** ⑤ **COACH** online for help with this subject.

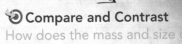

What Happens to a Star When It Runs Out of Fuel?

When a star begins to run out of fuel, its core shrinks and its outer portion expands. Depending on its mass, the star becomes either a red giant or a supergiant. Red giants and supergiants evolve in very different ways. **After a star runs out of fuel, it becomes a white dwarf, a neutron star, or a black hole.**

White Dwarfs Low-mass stars and medium-mass stars like the sun take billions of years to use up their nuclear fuel. As they start to run out of fuel, their outer layers expand, and they become red giants. Eventually, the outer parts grow larger still and drift out into space, forming a glowing cloud of gas called a planetary nebula. The blue-white core of the star that is left behind cools and becomes a **white dwarf.**

White dwarfs are about the size of Earth, but they have about as much mass as the sun. A white dwarf is about one million times as dense as the sun. White dwarfs have no fuel, but they glow faintly from leftover energy. After billions of years, a white dwarf stops glowing. Then it is called a black dwarf.

Supernovas The life cycle of a high-mass star is quite different. These stars quickly evolve into brilliant supergiants. When a supergiant runs out of fuel, it can explode suddenly. Within hours, the star blazes millions of times brighter. The explosion is called a **supernova.** After a supernova, some of the material from the star expands into space. This material may become part of a nebula. This nebula can then contract to form a new, partly recycled star. Recall that nuclear fusion creates heavy elements. A supernova provides enough energy to create the heaviest elements. Astronomers think that the matter in the sun and the planets around it came from a gigantic supernova. If so, this means that the matter all around you was created in a star, and all matter on Earth is a form of stardust.

Compare and Contrast
How does the mass and size of a white dwarf compare with the mass and size of the sun?

○ Same mass; greater size

○ Less mass; greater size

○ Same mass; smaller size

○ Less mass; smaller size

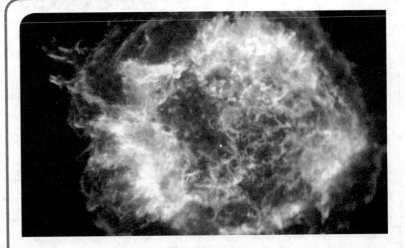

FIGURE 3 ·······························

Supernova Remnant Cassiopeia A
Cassiopeia A is the remnant of a once-massive star that died in a supernova explosion seen 325 years ago.

CHALLENGE Explain the connection between your body and a supernova.

_____

_____

_____

617

FIGURE 4 ···

> INTERACTIVE ART **Lives of Stars**
✎ **Relate Text and Visuals** Fill in the missing stages on the diagram. Now, think about where the sun fits on the diagram. On the lines below, describe what will happen to the sun when it runs out of fuel.

_____

_____

_____

_____

_____

_____

_____

_____

_____

_____

Protostar

Low- or medium-mass star

High-mass star

apply it!

⚠ **Predict** An alien civilization is in orbit around a high-mass supergiant star. Should they stay or should they go elsewhere? Why?

_____

_____

_____

_____

_____

Neutron Stars After a supergiant explodes, some of the material from the star is left behind. This material may form a neutron star. **Neutron stars** are the remains of high-mass stars. They are even smaller and denser than white dwarfs. A neutron star may contain as much as three times the mass of the sun but be only about 25 kilometers in diameter, the size of a city.

In 1967, Jocelyn Bell, a British astronomy student working with Antony Hewish, detected an object in space that appeared to give off regular pulses of radio waves. Some astronomers thought the pulses might be signals from an extraterrestrial civilization. At first, astronomers even named the source LGM, for the "Little Green Men" in early science-fiction stories. Soon, however, astronomers concluded that the source of the radio waves was really a rapidly spinning neutron star. Spinning neutron stars are called **pulsars,** short for pulsating radio sources. Some pulsars spin hundreds of times per second!

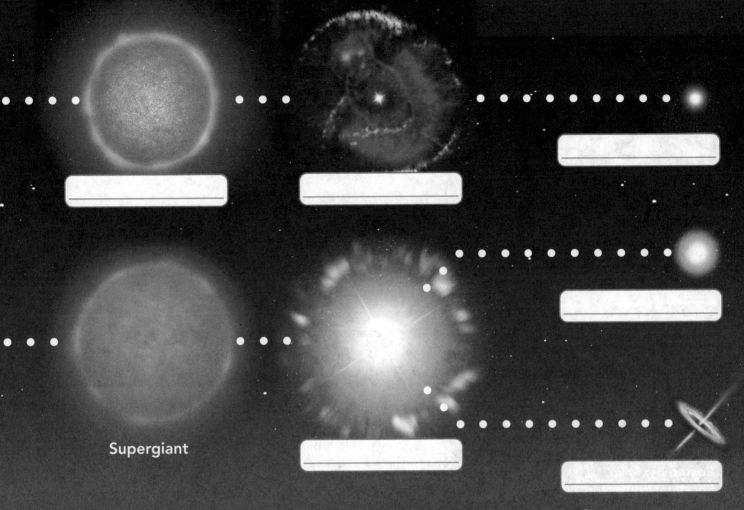

Supergiant

Black Holes

The most massive stars—those that have more than 10 times the mass of the sun—may become black holes when they die. A **black hole** is an object with gravity so strong that nothing, not even light, can escape. After a very massive star dies in a supernova explosion, more than five times the mass of the sun may be left. The gravity of this mass is so strong that the gas is pulled inward, packing the gas into a smaller and smaller space. The star's gas becomes squeezed so hard that the star converts into a black hole, and its intense gravity will not allow even light to escape.

No light, radio waves, or any other form of radiation can ever get out of a black hole, so it is not possible to detect directly. But astronomers can detect black holes indirectly. For example, gas near a black hole is pulled so strongly that it revolves faster and faster around the black hole. Friction heats the gas up. Astronomers can detect X-rays coming from the hot gas and infer that a black hole is present.

Lab zone® Do the Quick Lab *Death of a Star.*

Assess Your Understanding

2a. Review What determines if a star becomes a white dwarf, neutron star, or black hole?

_____

b. Predict Which will the sun become: a white dwarf, neutron star, or a black hole? Why?

_____

_____

got it? ....

○ **I get it!** Now I know that after a star runs out of fuel, it becomes _____

_____

_____

○ **I need extra help with** _____

Go to MY SCIENCE 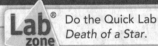 COACH *online for help with this subject.*

619

Star Systems and Galaxies

UNLOCK
THE BIG

🔑 **What Is a Star System?**

🔑 **What Are the Major Types of Galaxies?**

MY PLANET DIARY

BLOG

Posted by: Mike
Location: Brewerton, New York

When I was ten, I went to visit a friend in the Adirondack Mountains. We were outside on a clear, dark night until 2:00 A.M., and we saw the Milky Way. It was a big, white stream in the sky. The Milky Way was filled with stars.

Communicate Answer these questions. Discuss your answers with a partner.

1. Why would it be easier to see the Milky Way from the mountains?

_____

_____

2. Why does the Milky Way appear more like a white stream than separate stars?

_____

_____

_____

_____

▶ PLANET DIARY Go to **Planet Diary** to learn more about galaxies.

 ® Do the Inquiry Warm-Up *Why Does the Milky Way Look Hazy?*

What Is a Star System?

Our solar system has only one star: the sun. But this is not a common situation for stars. 🔑 **Most stars are members of groups of two or more stars, called star systems.** If you were on a planet in one of these star systems, at times you might see two or more suns in the sky! At other times, one or more of these suns might be below the horizon.

Vocabulary

- binary star • eclipsing binary • open cluster
- globular cluster • galaxy • spiral galaxy
- elliptical galaxy • irregular galaxy • quasar

Skills

- Reading: Relate Cause and Effect
- Inquiry: Draw Conclusions

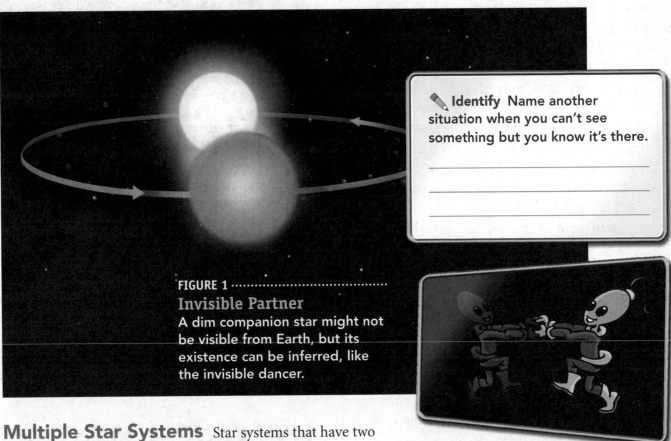

FIGURE 1
Invisible Partner
A dim companion star might not be visible from Earth, but its existence can be inferred, like the invisible dancer.

✎ **Identify** Name another situation when you can't see something but you know it's there.

_____

_____

_____

Multiple Star Systems

Star systems that have two stars are called double stars or **binary stars.** (The prefix *bi-* means "two.") Those with three stars are called triple stars.

Often one star in a binary star is much brighter and more massive than the other. Astronomers can sometimes detect a binary star even if only one of the stars can be seen from Earth. Astronomers can often tell that there is a dim star in a binary system by observing the effects of its gravity. As the dim companion star revolves around a bright star, the dim star's gravity causes the bright star to wobble. Imagine watching a pair of dancers who are twirling each other around, as shown in **Figure 1**. Even if one dancer were invisible, you could tell the invisible dancer was there from the motion of the visible dancer.

Eclipsing Binaries

A wobble is not the only clue that a star has a dim companion. A dim star in a binary star may pass in front of a brighter star and eclipse it. From Earth, the bright star would suddenly look much dimmer. A system in which one star blocks the light from another periodically is called an **eclipsing binary.**

⟳ **Relate Cause and Effect**
What causes a binary star to wobble back and forth?
○ Gravity of another star
○ Eclipsing by another star

621

Planets Around Other Stars In 1995, astronomers first discovered a planet revolving around another ordinary star. They used a method similar to the one used in studying binary stars. The astronomers observed that the star was moving slightly toward and then away from us. They knew that the invisible object causing the movement didn't have enough mass to be a star. They inferred that it must be a planet.

Since then, astronomers have discovered more than 300 planets around other stars, and new ones are being discovered all of the time. Most of these new planets are very large, with at least half of the mass of Jupiter. A small planet would be hard to detect because it would have little gravitational effect on the star it orbited.

Could there be life on planets in other solar systems? Some scientists think it is possible. A few astronomers are using radio telescopes to search for signals that could not have come from natural sources. Such signals might be evidence that an alien civilization was sending out radio waves.

Star Clusters Many stars belong to larger groupings called star clusters. All of the stars in a particular cluster formed from the same nebula at about the same time and are about the same distance from Earth.

There are two major types of star clusters: open clusters and globular clusters. **Open clusters** have a loose, disorganized appearance as shown in **Figure 3** and contain up to a few thousand stars. They often contain many bright supergiants and much gas and dust. In contrast, **globular clusters** are large groupings of older stars. Globular clusters are round and packed with stars. Some may contain more than a million stars.

FIGURE 3 ·····················
Star Cluster Pleiades
✎ CHALLENGE Why did some ancient astronomers call the Pleiades the "seven sisters"?

_____

_____

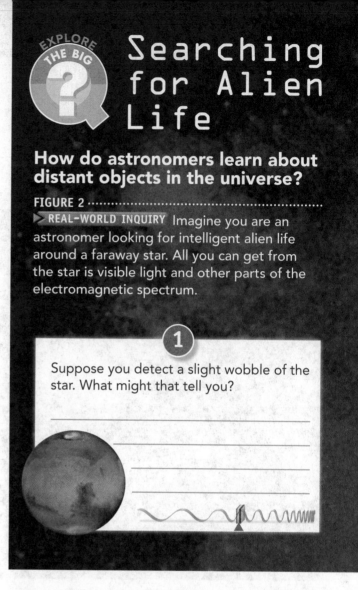

Searching for Alien Life

EXPLORE THE BIG ?

How do astronomers learn about distant objects in the universe?

FIGURE 2 ·······················
▶ REAL-WORLD INQUIRY Imagine you are an astronomer looking for intelligent alien life around a faraway star. All you can get from the star is visible light and other parts of the electromagnetic spectrum.

1 Suppose you detect a slight wobble of the star. What might that tell you?

_____

_____

_____

_____

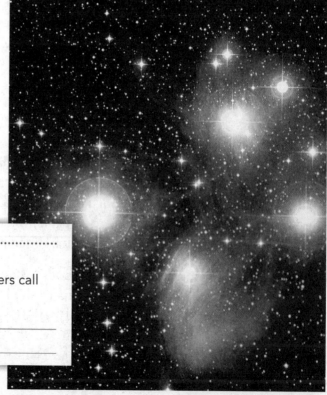

2

This artist's conception of a planet orbiting another star is based on an infrared picture from the Spitzer space telescope.

3

What might you infer if you picked up a regular radio signal from the star system?

_____
_____
_____
_____
_____
_____
_____

4

✎ Apply Concepts Explain what information we can get from light, and how that tells us about things that are far away.

_____
_____
_____
_____
_____
_____
_____
_____
_____

Lab zone® Do the Quick Lab *Planets Around Other Stars.*

🔑 Assess Your Understanding

1a. Define What is a binary star?

_____

b. Apply Concepts In what two ways can we tell if a star is a binary star?

_____
_____
_____

c. ANSWER THE BIG ? How do astronomers learn about distant objects in the universe?

_____
_____
_____
_____
_____

got it? ....

○ I get it! Now I know that star systems are _____

○ I need extra help with _____

Go to MY SCIENCE ⬤ COACH online for help with this subject.

623

What Are the Major Types of Galaxies?

A **galaxy** is a huge group of single stars, star systems, star clusters, dust, and gas bound together by gravity. There are billions of galaxies in the universe. The largest galaxies have more than a trillion stars. ⟜ **Astronomers classify most galaxies into the following types: spiral, elliptical, and irregular.**

① Spiral Galaxies

Some galaxies appear to have a bulge in the middle and arms that spiral outward, like pinwheels. These galaxies are spiral galaxies. The arms contain gas, dust, and many bright, young stars. Most new stars in spiral galaxies form in these arms. Barred-spiral galaxies have a bar-shaped area of stars and gas that passes through the center.

② Elliptical Galaxies

Not all galaxies have spiral arms. Elliptical galaxies look like round or flattened balls. These galaxies contain billions of stars but have little gas and dust between the stars. Because there is little gas or dust, stars are no longer forming. Most elliptical galaxies contain only old stars.

③ Irregular Galaxies

Some galaxies do not have regular shapes. These are known as irregular galaxies. Irregular galaxies are typically smaller than other types of galaxies. They generally have many bright, young stars and lots of gas and dust to form new stars.

④ Quasars

Astronomers in the 1960s discovered distant, extremely bright objects that looked like stars. Since *quasi* means "something like" in Latin, these objects were called quasi-stellar objects, or quasars. Quasars are active young galaxies with huge black holes at their centers. Gas spins around the black hole, heats up, and glows.

FIGURE 4 ···
Types of Galaxies
✎ Relate Text and Visuals Identify the four galaxies shown on these pages and explain.

Ⓐ _____
_____
Ⓑ _____
_____
Ⓒ _____
_____
Ⓓ _____
_____

A
○ Spiral   ○ Elliptical
○ Irregular   ○ Quasar

apply it!

Our solar system is located in a galaxy called the Milky Way. From the side, the Milky Way would look like a narrow disk with a large bulge in the middle. But from the top or bottom, the Milky Way would have a pinwheel shape. You can't see the shape of the Milky Way from Earth because our solar system is inside one of the arms.

When you see the Milky Way at night during the summer, you are looking toward the center of our galaxy. The center of the galaxy is about 25,000 light-years away, but it is hidden from view by large clouds of dust and gas. But astronomers can study the center using X-rays, infrared radiation, and radio waves.

Draw Conclusions What kind of galaxy is the Milky Way? Explain why and draw a sketch of what the Milky Way might look like from outside.

_____

_____

_____

B
○ Spiral   ○ Elliptical
○ Irregular ○ Quasar

C
○ Spiral   ○ Elliptical
○ Irregular ○ Quasar

D
○ Spiral   ○ Elliptical
○ Irregular ○ Quasar

Lab zone Do the Quick Lab *A Spiral Galaxy*.

🔑 Assess Your Understanding

got it? ....

○ **I get it!** Now I know that astronomers classify most galaxies into one of the following three types: _____

_____

_____

○ **I need extra help with** _____

_____

Go to my science ⓢ coach *online for help with this subject.*

The Expanding Universe

UNLOCK THE BIG

What Does the Big Bang Theory Say About the Universe?

my planeT DiaRY

BLOG

Posted by: David
Location: Bowie, Maryland

On Sunday, March 15, 2009, I flew to Orlando, Florida, to see the launch of *Discovery* in Cape Canaveral, the first launch I ever saw. At 5 seconds, the engines ignited and at 0 seconds, *Discovery* went into the sky. I could feel the vibrations. *Discovery* looked like a ball of fire the color of autumn leaves, and it left a trail of smoke.

Communicate Write your answer to the question below. Then discuss your answer with a partner.

What would you want scientists to learn about the universe from a space shuttle mission?

_____

_____

_____

_____

_____

▶ PLANET DIARY Go to **Planet Diary** to learn more about the universe.

Lab zone® Do the Inquiry Warm-Up *How Does the Universe Expand?*

What Does the Big Bang Theory Say About the Universe?

Astronomers have learned a lot about the universe. They theorize that the universe began 13.7 billion years ago. At that time, the part of the universe we can see was no larger than the period at the end of this sentence. This tiny universe was incredibly hot and dense. The universe then exploded in what astronomers call the **big bang**.

Vocabulary
- big bang • Hubble's law
- cosmic background radiation
- dark matter • dark energy

Skills
- ↪ Reading: Identify Supporting Evidence
- △ Inquiry: Make Models

🔑 **According to the big bang theory, the universe formed in an instant, billions of years ago, in an enormous explosion. New observations lead many astronomers to conclude that the universe will likely expand forever.** Since the big bang, the size of the universe has been increasing. The universe is immensely larger now than it once was.

As the universe expanded, it gradually cooled. After a few hundred thousand years, atoms formed. Within about the first 500 million years after the big bang, the first stars and galaxies formed.

Moving Galaxies In the 1920s, an American astronomer, Edwin Hubble, discovered important evidence that led to the big bang theory. Hubble studied the spectrums of many galaxies at various distances from Earth. By examining a galaxy's spectrum, Hubble could tell how fast the galaxy was moving and whether it was moving toward our galaxy or away from it.

Hubble discovered that almost all galaxies are moving away from us and from each other. Hubble found the relationship between the distance to a galaxy and its speed. **Hubble's law** states that the farther away a galaxy is, the faster it is moving away from us. Hubble's law strongly supports the big bang theory.

Cosmic Background Radiation Another piece of evidence for the big bang was discovered by accident. In 1965, two American physicists, Arno Penzias and Robert Wilson, detected faint radiation on their radio telescope coming from all directions. Scientists later concluded that this **cosmic background radiation** is the leftover thermal energy from the big bang. This energy was distributed in every direction as the universe expanded.

↪ **Identify Supporting Evidence** Underline the main evidence Hubble found that the universe is expanding.

apply it!

The galaxies in the universe are like raisins in rising bread dough.
△ **Make Models** Draw the raisins in their new positions on the bottom picture. Explain why the raisins are like galaxies.

_____

_____

_____

_____

_____

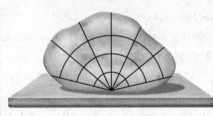

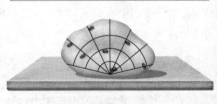

FIGURE 1 ·······································
Age of the Universe
By measuring how fast the universe is expanding, astronomers can infer how long it has been expanding. The COBE satellite shown measured the cosmic background radiation, which also gave clues to the age of the universe.

The Big Bang and the Future of the Universe

What will happen to the universe in the future? One possibility is that the universe will continue to expand. All of the stars will eventually run out of fuel and burn out, and the universe will be cold and dark. Another possibility is that the force of gravity will begin to pull the galaxies back together, as shown in **Figure 2**. The result would be a reverse big bang, or "big crunch." The universe would be crushed in an enormous black hole.

FIGURE 2 ··

The Big Crunch
The small diagram represents the expansion of the universe until now. The big bang is at the bottom.

✎ CHALLENGE **On the top part of the diagram, draw a sketch of the universe collapsing to a big crunch. Explain your drawing.**

_____

_____

_____

_____

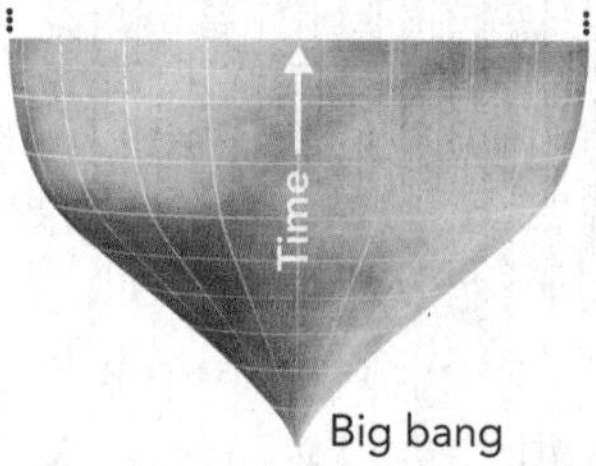

Time

Big bang

Which of these possibilities is more likely? Recent discoveries have produced a surprising new view of the universe that is still not well understood. But many astronomers conclude that the universe will likely expand forever.

Dark Matter Until recently, astronomers assumed that the universe consisted solely of the matter they could observe directly. But this idea was disproved by American astronomer Vera Rubin. Rubin studied the rotation of spiral galaxies. She discovered that the matter that astronomers can see makes up as little as ten percent of the mass in galaxies. The rest exists in the form of dark matter.

Dark matter is matter that does not give off electromagnetic radiation. It cannot be seen directly. However, its presence can be inferred by observing the effect of its gravity on visible objects.

An Accelerating Expansion In the late 1990s, astronomers observed that the expansion of the universe appeared to be accelerating. That is, galaxies seemed to be moving apart at a faster rate than in the past. This observation was puzzling, as no known force could account for it. Astronomers infer that a mysterious new force, which they call **dark energy,** is causing the expansion of the universe to accelerate, as shown in **Figure 3**.

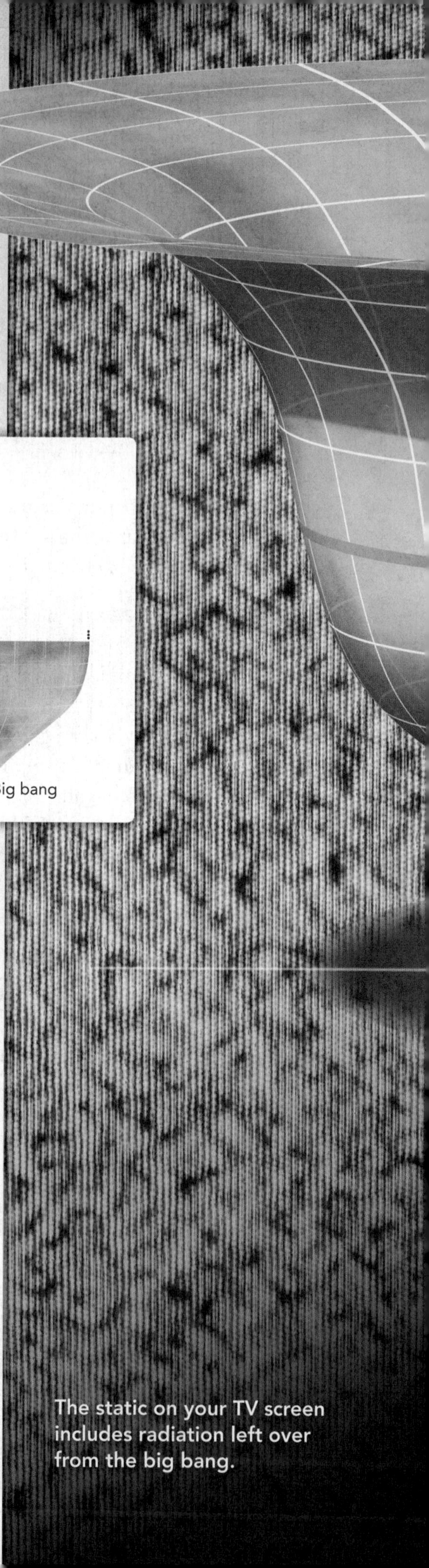

The static on your TV screen includes radiation left over from the big bang.

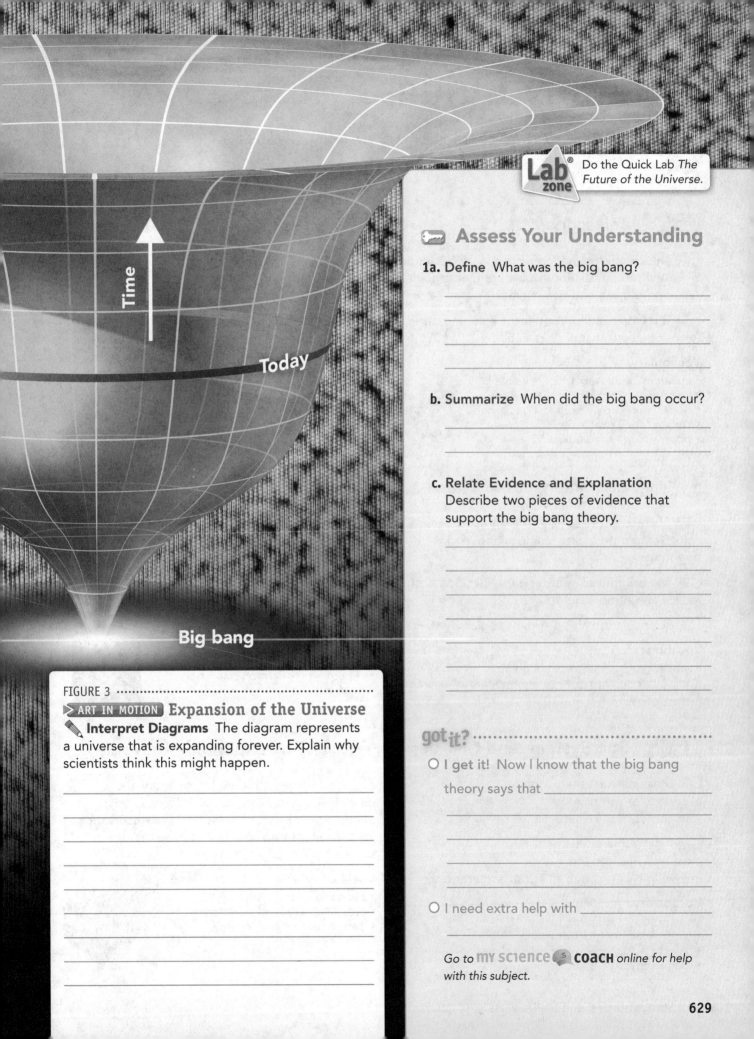

Time

Today

Big bang

FIGURE 3 ·····················

> ART IN MOTION Expansion of the Universe

✎ Interpret Diagrams The diagram represents a universe that is expanding forever. Explain why scientists think this might happen.

_____

_____

_____

_____

_____

_____

_____

Lab® Do the Quick Lab *The Future of the Universe.*

🔑 **Assess Your Understanding**

1a. Define What was the big bang?

_____

_____

_____

_____

b. Summarize When did the big bang occur?

_____

_____

c. Relate Evidence and Explanation Describe two pieces of evidence that support the big bang theory.

_____

_____

_____

_____

_____

_____

_____

_____

got it? ···

○ **I get it!** Now I know that the big bang theory says that _____

_____

_____

○ **I need extra help with** _____

_____

Go to MY SCIENCE ⓢ COACH online for help with this subject.

16 Study Guide

Astronomers learn about distant objects in the universe by studying _____

LESSON 1 Telescopes

🔑 The electromagnetic spectrum includes radio waves, infrared radiation, visible light, ultraviolet radiation, X-rays, and gamma rays.

🔑 Telescopes collect and focus light and other forms of electromagnetic radiation.

Vocabulary
- electromagnetic radiation • visible light
- wavelength • spectrum • telescope
- optical telescope • refracting telescope
- convex lens • reflecting telescope
- observatory • radio telescope

LESSON 2 The Scale of the Universe

🔑 Astronomers often use parallax to measure distances to nearby stars.

🔑 Since the numbers astronomers use are often very large or very small, they frequently use scientific notation to describe sizes and distances in the universe. They use a unit called the light-year to measure distances between the stars.

Vocabulary
- parallax • universe
- light-year • scientific notation

LESSON 3 Characteristics of Stars

🔑 Characteristics used to classify stars include color, temperature, size, composition, and brightness.

🔑 The brightness of a star depends upon both its size and temperature.

🔑 Scientists use H-R diagrams to classify stars.

Vocabulary
- spectrograph • apparent brightness
- absolute brightness • Hertzsprung-Russell diagram
- main sequence

LESSON 4 Lives of Stars

🔑 A star is born when the contracting gas and dust from a nebula becomes so dense and hot that nuclear fusion starts. How long a star lives depends on its mass.

🔑 After a star runs out of fuel, it becomes a white dwarf, a neutron star, or a black hole.

Vocabulary
- nebula • protostar • white dwarf
- supernova • neutron star • pulsar
- black hole

LESSON 5 Star Systems and Galaxies

🔑 Most stars are members of groups of two or more stars, called star systems.

🔑 Astronomers classify most galaxies into the following types: spiral, elliptical, and irregular.

Vocabulary
- binary star • eclipsing binary
- open cluster • globular cluster
- galaxy • spiral galaxy • elliptical galaxy
- irregular galaxy • quasar

LESSON 6 The Expanding Universe

🔑 According to the big bang theory, the universe formed in an instant, billions of years ago, in an enormous explosion. New observations lead many astronomers to conclude that the universe will expand forever.

Vocabulary
- big bang • Hubble's law
- cosmic background radiation
- dark matter • dark energy

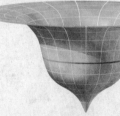

Review and Assessment

LESSON 1 Telescopes

1. What is visible light?

a. gamma rays and X-rays

b. the spectrum of rays

c. a particular wavelength

d. a form of electromagnetic radiation

2. Explain An optical telescope works by

_____

_____

_____

3. Draw Conclusions What advantage might there be in placing a telescope on the moon?

_____

_____

_____

_____

LESSON 2 The Scale of the Universe

4. Which type of numbers does scientific notation best describe?

a. very small or very large

b. very large only

c. very small only

d. large and small combined

5. Develop Hypotheses Why can't astronomers measure the parallax of a star that is a million light-years away?

_____

_____

_____

6. math! The star Antares is about 604 light-years from Earth. Write this distance in scientific notation.

_____

LESSON 3 Characteristics of Stars

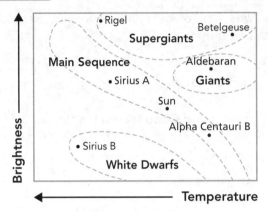

Use the diagram to answer the questions below.

7. Interpret Diagrams On the diagram, circle the star that has a greater absolute brightness: Aldebaran or Sirius B.

8. Apply Concepts On the diagram, underline the star that is most likely to be red: Rigel, Sirius B, or Betelgeuse.

LESSON 4 Lives of Stars

9. Relate Cause and Effect How does a star's mass affect its lifetime?

_____

_____

_____

_____

10. Sequence Explain how a black hole forms.

_____

_____

_____

_____

_____

_____

LESSON 5 Star Systems and Galaxies

11. In what kind of star system does one star block the light from another?

    a. open cluster   **b.** binary star system

    c. quasar system   **d.** eclipsing binary

12. Compare and Contrast How is the number of stars different in an open cluster than in a globular cluster?

_____

_____

_____

_____

_____

13. Write About It Describe the "life story" of a star in a spiral galaxy. Explain where it was born and what it was like there.

LESSON 6 The Expanding Universe

14. What is the name of the explosion that began the universe?

    a. solar nebula   **b.** big bang

    c. dark matter   **d.** supernova

15. Classify Radio telescopes are able to detect cosmic background radiation, which is

_____

_____

16. Compare and Contrast Explain the difference between a big crunch and an ever-expanding universe.

_____

_____

_____

_____

APPLY THE BIG Q How do astronomers learn about distant objects in the universe?

17. Write the introduction of a manual for young astronomers. Briefly describe different tools astronomers have for learning about distant objects in the universe. Tell what kind of information each tool can provide.

_____

_____

_____

_____

_____

_____

_____

_____

_____

_____

_____

_____

_____

_____

_____

_____

_____

_____

_____

_____

_____

_____

_____

_____

Standardized Test Prep

Multiple Choice

Circle the letter of the best answer.

1. The table below gives an estimate of star distribution in the Milky Way galaxy. According to the table, what is the most common type of star in the Milky Way?

Type of Star	Percentage of Total
Main sequence	90.75 %
Red giant	0.50 %
Supergiant	< 0.0001 %
White dwarf	8.75 %

A   main-sequence star
B   red giant
C   supergiant
D   white dwarf

2. What is the main factor that affects the evolution of a star?

A   color   B   brightness
C   mass   D   parallax

3. Which describes the volume of the sun in relation to the volume of Earth?

A   more than ten times greater
B   more than a hundred times greater
C   more than a thousand times greater
D   more than a million times greater

4. Which of the following best describes a reflecting telescope?

A   Isaac Newton invention
B   has an objective lens
C   is the smallest telescope
D   has a mirror lens

5. What is one example of electromagnetic energy?

A   electricity
B   heat
C   infrared light
D   sound waves

Constructed Response

Use the diagram below and your knowledge of science to help you answer Question 6. Write your answer on a separate sheet of paper.

Milky Way Side View
Sun   Center   Bulge

6. Describe the appearance of the Milky Way as you would see it both from Earth and from a point directly above the galaxy. Why does the galaxy look different from different places?

BLACK HOLES

Scientists can't see them, but they keep studying them. For years, astronomers have known that black holes exist. The extreme gravity of a black hole allows nothing to escape, not even light. So astronomers need to use some pretty high-powered tools to study them.

Astronomers use data from space telescopes to measure the visible light, X-rays, and radio waves emitted from objects near a black hole. Astronomers have used this data to learn a lot about black holes. They know that black holes come in two main sizes—stellar-sized, formed when massive stars collapse inward, and supermassive.

Supermassive black holes are found in the center of galaxies. The gravity from the black hole helps bind the stars, star systems, star clusters, dust, and gas into a galaxy.

Evaluate It Black holes are often described in movies and science fiction novels. Find one example of a black hole in a novel, graphic novel, TV show, or movie. Write an essay that explains how the black hole is described in your sources. Evaluate the source's scientific accuracy, and correct any inaccurate information.

◄ This image of two galaxies colliding was taken by the Hubble Space Telescope in 2008. Astronomers believe that supermassive black holes are at the center of galaxies.

APPRENTICE ASTRONOMERS

Kids in the Boston area have their heads in the stars. At least the lucky ones do. They're part of the Youth Astronomy Apprenticeship (YAA) program run by four astronomical and educational institutions in the area.

The goal of YAA is to give urban kids more exposure to astronomers and astronomy. In after-school programs, apprentices learn many things, including how to understand and interpret images from a network of telescopes students control online, and how to prepare the images to illustrate their own research. In Stage 2 of the program, apprentices can go on to a summer apprentice program. In the summer program, participants are paid to help make museum exhibits and perform science and astronomy plays. Participants also help teach other people about the universe. Some students go on to become youth assistants, teaching the next group of young stargazers.

Are the apprentices "star-struck"? The YAA program hopes they are.

Design It Choose a topic in astronomy that interests you. Working with a partner, prepare an exhibit about that topic. Present your exhibit to members of your school community.

HOW IS THIS HOUSE SAVING OUR PLANET?

What can people do to use resources wisely?

Have you ever thought of ways to reuse something you would normally throw away? This home is made from the shipping containers you see transporting goods on ships and trucks. These containers would have been thrown away but an architect thought of a new way to use them.

Infer How can reusing shipping containers and other objects help our planet?

_____

_____

_____

_____

_____

> UNTAMED SCIENCE Watch the **Untamed Science** video to learn more about reusing resources.

Land, Air, and Water Resources

17 Getting Started

Check Your Understanding

1. Background Read the paragraph below and then answer the question.

On a lazy summer day, Mia pours water on the hot sidewalk and imagines where the water will go as it travels through the **water cycle.** After the water **evaporates,** it may float through the **atmosphere** and fall as rain in faraway lands or the ocean.

- What makes the water cycle a *cycle*?

_____

_____

The **water cycle** is the continuous process by which water moves from Earth's surface to the atmosphere and back.

Evaporation is the process by which molecules of liquid water absorb energy and change to a gas.

The **atmosphere** is the envelope of gases that surrounds the planet.

> **MY READING WEB** If you had trouble answering the question above, visit **My Reading Web** and type in *Land, Air, and Water Resources.*

Vocabulary Skill

Prefixes Some words can be divided into parts. A root is the part of the word that carries the basic meaning. A prefix is a word part placed in front of the root to change the word's meaning. The prefixes below will help you understand some of the vocabulary in this chapter.

Prefix	Meaning	Example
bio-	life	biodegradable, *adj.* describes a material that can be broken down and recycled by bacteria and other decomposers
photo-	light	photochemical, *adj.* describes a chemical reaction that occurs in the presence of light

2. Quick Check In the definitions of the example words in the table, circle the part that includes the prefix meaning.

nonrenewable resource

exponential growth

topsoil

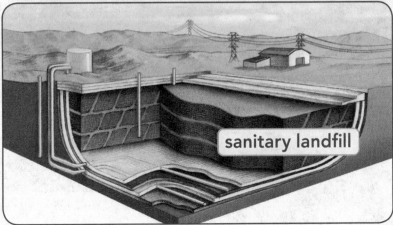

sanitary landfill

Chapter Preview

LESSON 1
- natural resource • pollution
- point source • nonpoint source
- environmental science

🔄 Relate Cause and Effect
△ Draw Conclusions

LESSON 2
- renewable resource
- nonrenewable resource
- sustainable use
- ecological footprint
- conservation

🔄 Relate Text and Visuals
△ Calculate

LESSON 3
- litter • topsoil • subsoil
- bedrock • erosion
- nutrient depletion • fertilizer
- desertification • drought
- land reclamation

🔄 Relate Cause and Effect
△ Infer

LESSON 4
- municipal solid waste
- incineration • pollutant
- leachate • sanitary landfill
- recycling • biodegradable
- hazardous waste

🔄 Compare and Contrast
△ Graph

LESSON 5
- emissions • photochemical smog
- ozone • temperature inversion
- acid rain • radon • ozone layer
- chlorofluorocarbon

🔄 Relate Text and Visuals
△ Communicate

LESSON 6
- groundwater • pesticide
- sewage • sediment

🔄 Outline
△ Design Experiments

▶ VOCAB FLASH CARDS For extra help with vocabulary, visit **Vocab Flash Cards** and type in *Land, Air, and Water Resources.*

639

Introduction to Environmental Issues

🔑 **What Are the Types of Environmental Issues?**

🔑 **How Are Environmental Decisions Made?**

my pLaneT DiaRY

CAREER

How Do You Feel About Nature?

You have probably heard of scientists who study animals, plants, rocks, and everything else in an ecosystem. Social scientists study an often-overlooked but very important part of any ecosystem—the people who use it! These scientists study how people value nature. They study how much people would be willing to pay to preserve nature. They also study how different age groups, genders, races, and social groups use nature. For example, a scuba diver wants coral reefs to remain beautiful and full of all kinds of organisms to enjoy in future dives. A commercial fisherman cares more about a coral reef supporting the kind of fish he wants to catch. You might care about coral reefs because you want to visit one someday.

Communicate Discuss the question with a group of classmates. Then write your answer below.

Do you think it is important to consider how people value nature? Explain.

_____

_____

_____

_____

_____

_____

_____

▶ **PLANET DIARY** Go to **Planet Diary** to learn more about environmental issues.

Lab zone Do the Inquiry Warm-Up *How Do You Decide?*

Vocabulary
- natural resource • pollution • point source
- nonpoint source • environmental science

Skills
- Reading: Relate Cause and Effect
- Inquiry: Draw Conclusions

What Are the Types of Environmental Issues?

Here is a riddle for you: what place is bigger than the United States and Mexico combined? This place is covered with ice more than two kilometers thick. It is a habitat for many animals and is a source of oil, coal, and iron. Stumped? The answer is Antarctica. Some people think of Antarctica as a useless, icy wasteland, but there are unique wildlife habitats in Antarctica. There are also valuable minerals beneath its thick ice.

What is the best use of Antarctica? Many people want access to its rich deposits of minerals and oil. Others worry that mining will harm its delicate ecosystems. Some people propose building hotels, parks, and ski resorts. Others think that Antarctica should remain undeveloped. Who should decide Antarctica's fate?

In 1998, 26 nations agreed to ban mining and oil exploration in Antarctica for at least 50 years. As resources become more scarce elsewhere in the world, the debate will surely continue.

Antarctica's future is just one environmental issue that people face today. **Environmental issues fall into three general categories: population growth, resource use, and pollution.** Because these three types of issues are interconnected, they are very difficult to study and resolve.

FIGURE 1 ·····················

Arguing Over Antarctica
Some people want to leave Antarctica wild. Others want it developed.

✎ **Summarize** Fill in the boxes with points outlining each argument.

Argument One: Keep Antarctica Wild	Argument Two: Develop Antarctica

641

Population Growth

The human population grew very slowly until about A.D. 1650. Around that time, improvements in medicine, agriculture, and waste disposal led to people living longer. The human population has been growing faster and faster since then.

When a population grows, the demand for resources also grows. Has your town or city ever experienced a water shortage? If so, you might have noticed that people have been asked to restrict their water use. This sometimes happens in areas with fast-growing populations. The water supplies in such areas were designed to serve fewer people than they now do, so shortages can occur during unusually dry weather.

Resource Use

Earth provides many materials people use throughout their lives. Anything that occurs naturally in the environment and is used by people is called a **natural resource.** Natural resources include trees, water, oil, coal, and other things. However, people do not use resources in the same way. In some areas of the world, people use a wide variety of resources. In other areas, people have little or no access to certain natural resources. For example, people in central Asia live too far away from ocean waters that provide fish and other resources. Conflict arises when a natural resource is scarce or used in a way that people feel is unfair.

Vocabulary Identify Related Word Forms The word *conflict* means a disagreement between people, ideas, or interests. What causes conflicting opinions about natural resource use?

_____

_____

_____

_____

_____

_____

FIGURE 2

Everyday Natural Resources

We use natural resources many times a day without even realizing it! A trip to the beach uses land, water, fuel, and many other resources.

✎ **List** On the journal page, list all the ways you have used natural resources so far today. For example, this book is made of paper that started as a tree.

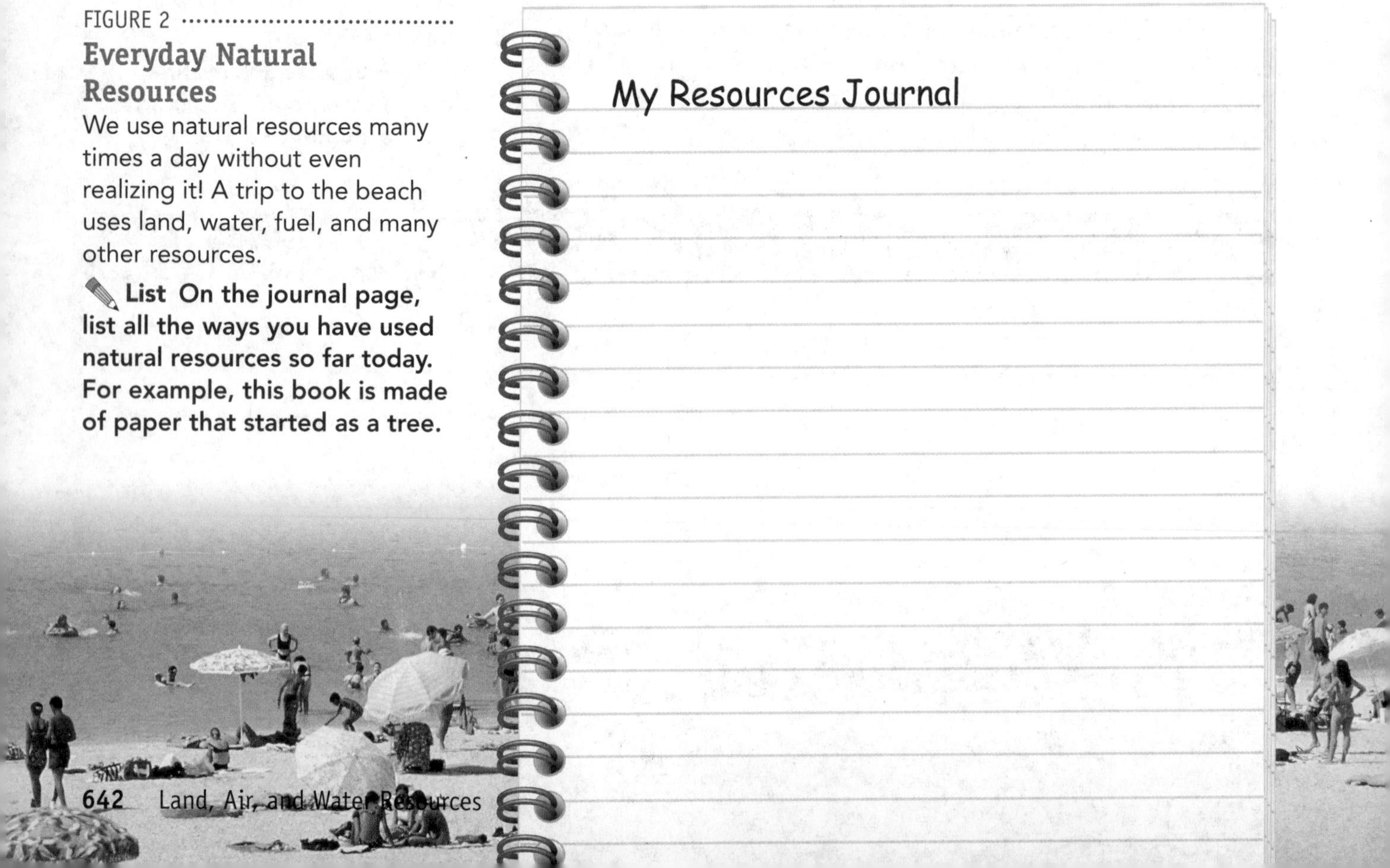

My Resources Journal

Pollution Many environmental factors can contribute to less than ideal conditions on Earth for people or other organisms. The contamination of Earth's land, water, or air is called **pollution.** Pollution can be caused by wastes, chemicals, noise, heat, light, and other sources. Pollution can destroy wildlife and cause human health problems.

Pollution is usually related to population growth and resource use. As you probably know, the burning of gasoline releases pollutants into the air. With more cars on the road, more gasoline is used, so more pollutants are released into the air. As populations grow and more people need to be fed, more fertilizers and other chemicals may be used to produce that food. As these chemicals run off the land, they can pollute bodies of water.

Pollution sources can be grouped into two categories. A **point source** is a specific pollution source that can be identified. A pipe gushing polluted water into a river is an example of a point source. A nonpoint source of pollution is not as easy to identify. A **nonpoint source** is widely spread and cannot be tied to a specific origin. For example, the polluted air that can hang over urban areas comes from vehicles, factories, and other polluters. The pollution cannot be tied to any one car or factory.

🖉 **Relate Cause and Effect**
Use what you have read about pollution so far to fill in the boxes below.

Some Causes of Pollution
_____
_____
_____
_____
_____
_____

Some Effects of Pollution
_____
_____
_____
_____
_____
_____

Lab **zone** Do the Quick Lab
Environmental Issues.

🔑 **Assess Your Understanding**

1a. Define What is a natural resource?
_____
_____
_____
_____

b. Make Generalizations How is population growth related to resource use and pollution?
_____
_____
_____
_____

got**it?** ....

○ **I get it!** Now I know that the types of environmental issues are_____
_____

○ I need extra help with _____

Go to MY SCIENCE 💬 COACH *online for help with this subject.*

How Are Environmental Decisions Made?

Dealing with environmental issues means making decisions. Decisions can be made at many levels. Your decision to walk to your friend's house rather than ride in a car is made at a personal level. A town's decision about how to dispose of its trash is made at a local level. A decision about whether the United States should allow oil drilling in a wildlife refuge is made on a national level. Decisions about how to protect Earth's atmosphere are made on a global level. Your personal decisions have a small impact. But when the personal decisions of millions of people are combined, they have a huge impact on the environment.

Balancing Different Needs Lawmakers work with many groups to make environmental decisions. One such group is environmental scientists. **Environmental science** is the study of natural processes in the environment and how humans can affect them. Data provided by environmental scientists are only part of the decision-making process. Environmental decision making requires a balance between the needs of the environment and the needs of people. **To help balance the different opinions on an environmental issue, decision makers weigh the costs and benefits of a proposal for change before making a decision.**

apply it!

Suppose you are a member of a city planning board. A company wants to buy a piece of land outside the city and build a factory on it. When you go into work one day, you are met by protesters demanding that the land be turned into a wildlife park.

1 Solve Problems How should you decide what to do with the land?

_____

_____

_____

2 CHALLENGE What are some ways you could find out people's opinions about the issue?

_____

_____

_____

Types of Costs and Benefits
Costs and benefits are often economic. Will a proposal provide jobs? Will it cost too much money? Costs and benefits are not measured only in terms of money. For example, suppose a state must decide whether to allow logging in a certain area. Removing trees changes the ecosystem, which is an ecological cost. However, the wood and jobs provided by the logging are economic benefits.

It is also important to consider the short-term and long-term costs and benefits of an environmental decision. A plan's short-term costs might be outweighed by its long-term benefits.

Costs of Offshore Drilling	Benefits of Offshore Drilling
• Setting up sites is expensive.	• Creates jobs
• Transporting the oil is risky and expensive.	• A larger oil supply lowers oil prices.
• Oil supply is limited and will not meet energy demands.	• Provides new oil supply to fight shortages
• Oil spills and leaks harm marine organisms and the environment.	• Reduces dependence on foreign oil

FIGURE 3 ....
> INTERACTIVE ART Weighing Costs and Benefits
Once you have identified the potential costs and benefits of a decision, you must analyze them.
Draw Conclusions Read the chart. Based on these costs and benefits, write a brief letter to your senator explaining your opinion either in favor of or against offshore drilling.

Lab zone® Do the Quick Lab Comparing Costs and Benefits.

Assess Your Understanding

got it? ....

○ I get it! Now I know that environmental decisions are made by _____

○ I need extra help with _____

Go to my science COACH online for help with this subject.

Introduction to Natural Resources

UNLOCK THE BIG ?

🔑 What Are Natural Resources?

🔑 Why Are Natural Resources Important?

my planet Diary

VOICES FROM HISTORY

"It was a spring without voices. On the mornings that had once throbbed with the dawn chorus of robins . . . there was now no sound; only silence lay over the fields and woods and marsh."

—Rachel Carson

In the twentieth century, farmers began to use chemicals to fight insects that killed their crops. People didn't realize that these chemicals were hurting other animals as well. Rachel Carson, born in 1907, was a scientist who wrote about sea life and nature. Carson began to worry about these chemicals. In 1962, she wrote the book *Silent Spring*. She explained what was happening to animals on land, in the air, and in the sea. Today, people are more careful to protect living things.

Write your answers below.

1. What dangers did Rachel Carson warn people about?

_____

_____

_____

2. Do you think the spring Carson wrote about would look different now that some harmful chemicals are banned? Why or why not?

_____

_____

_____

_____

_____

_____

▶ PLANET DIARY Go to **Planet Diary** to learn more about natural resources.

 Lab zone

Do the Inquiry Warm-Up *Using Resources.*

Vocabulary
- renewable resource • nonrenewable resource
- sustainable use • ecological footprint • conservation

Skills
- Reading: Relate Text and Visuals
- Inquiry: Calculate

What Are Natural Resources?

Did you turn on a light or use an alarm clock today? Flush a toilet or take a shower? Ride in a car or bus? Eat some food? Use any paper—other than this page that you are reading right now? All of these things—and so much more—depend on Earth's resources.

Recall that anything that occurs naturally in the environment and is used by people is called a natural resource. **Natural resources include organisms, water, sunlight, minerals, and oil.**

Renewable Resources A **renewable resource** is either always available or is naturally replaced in a relatively short time. Some renewable resources, like wind and sunlight, are almost always available. Other renewable resources, like water and trees, are renewable only if they are replaced as fast as they are used.

Original trees on land

Trees after first harvest

Trees after replanting

✏️

Relate Text and Visuals The trees in the first diagram are being harvested for wood. The landowner tells you the trees are a renewable resource. Based on the number of trees being harvested and replanted, is the landowner right? Why?

_____

_____

_____

_____

_____

_____

_____

_____

_____

_____

Nonrenewable Resources Over millions of years, natural processes changed the remains of organisms into the substances now called oil and coal. Today's world is powered by these fuels. Humans use these resources much faster than they are naturally replaced. Resources that are not replaced in a useful time frame are **nonrenewable resources.** Metals and minerals are also nonrenewable. Remember that some resources, such as trees, may be renewable or nonrenewable, depending on how quickly they are replaced.

FIGURE 1 ·······················

Categorizing Resources

Resources are grouped into two main categories: renewable and nonrenewable. Gold, shown above, is nonrenewable.

✎ **Summarize** Use what you have read to fill in the table comparing renewable and nonrenewable resources.

Renewable Resources	Nonrenewable Resources	Both
Replaced in a short time or always available	Not replaced in a useful time frame	Fits both natural resource categories
Examples:_____ _____ _____ _____ _____	Examples:_____ _____ _____ _____ _____	Examples:_____ _____ _____ _____ _____

Do the Quick Lab
Natural Resources.

🔑 Assess Your Understanding

1a. Define What is a renewable resource?

_____

_____

_____

_____

b. Compare and Contrast Sunlight and trees are both natural resources. How are they different?

_____

_____

_____

_____

got it? ···

○ **I get it!** Now I know that natural resources include _____

_____

○ I need extra help with _____

Go to **MY SCIENCE COACH** online for help with this subject.

Why Are Natural Resources Important?

Humans cannot live without some natural resources, such as sunlight and fresh water. Others, such as metals, are necessary to sustain modern life. **Humans depend on Earth's natural resources for survival and for development.**

How People Use Resources Around the world, people rely on natural resources for the same basic needs. Not all resources are equally available in all parts of the world. In some areas, there is a plentiful supply of clean fresh water. In other areas, water is scarce. In some places, pollution threatens the water supply.

Globally, fuels are used for cooking, heating, and power. Different fuels are common in different parts of the world. Coal is plentiful in some areas of the world and oil is plentiful in others. See **Figure 2.** In some areas, wood is the main fuel, not coal or oil.

FIGURE 2 ·······················

Resources Around the World

People use natural resources in different ways around the world.

✎ **Describe** In the blank box below, draw or describe one way you use natural resources.

In Sierra Leone, entire communities get their drinking water from a main well.

In China, coal is delivered to homes by bicycle to be burned for heat.

In Iceland, most homes get hot water and heat from the energy of the hot, liquidlike rock under Earth's surface.

649

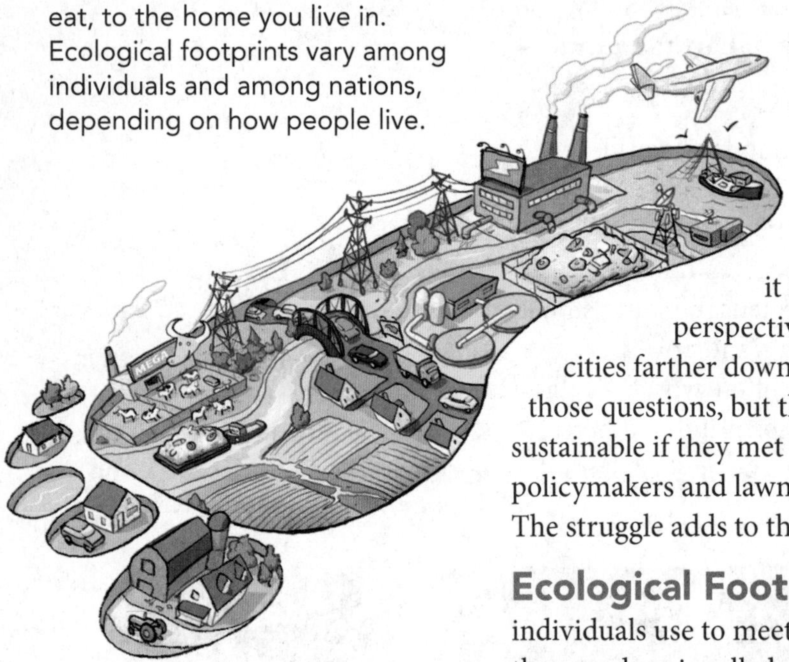

FIGURE 3

Ecological Footprint

Everything you do contributes to your ecological footprint, from how you travel, to the food you eat, to the home you live in. Ecological footprints vary among individuals and among nations, depending on how people live.

Sustainable Use How long a resource lasts depends on how people use it. **Sustainable use** of a resource means using it in ways that maintain the resource at a certain quality for a certain period of time. For example, a city may want to manage a river. Does the city want the water to be clean enough to drink or clean enough to swim in? Does the city want the water to be clean for fifty years, two hundred years, or indefinitely? The answers to these questions define what would be considered sustainable use of the river. However, it may not be sustainable from an ecological perspective even if it meets human needs. Other cities farther down the river may have different answers to those questions, but their plans could also be considered sustainable if they met their goals. Because of these differences, policymakers and lawmakers struggle to define sustainable use. The struggle adds to the challenge of regulating resources.

Ecological Footprint The amount of land and water that individuals use to meet their resource needs and absorb the waste they produce is called an **ecological footprint.** A high level of resource use means a larger footprint. A low level of resource use means a smaller footprint. Refer to **Figure 3.**

apply it!

The chart below gives the average ecological footprints for the people of several countries. It also gives the footprint for each country as a whole. Ecological footprints are measured in global hectares. A global hectare (gha) is a unit of area. It is adjusted to compare how much life different places on Earth can support.

Country	Average Ecological Footprint (gha/person)	Total Ecological Footprint (million gha)
United States	9.6	2,819
United Kingdom	5.6	333
Germany	4.5	375
Mexico	2.6	265
China	1.6	2,152

❶ **Interpret Tables** Which country has the largest ecological footprint? _____

❷ **Calculate** About how many times larger is the average ecological footprint per person in the United States than per person in Mexico?

_____

❸ CHALLENGE China has a smaller ecological footprint per person than the United Kingdom, but a much larger total ecological footprint. Why?

_____

_____

_____

_____

_____

Conservation While we cannot avoid using resources, there are better ways to use them. Resource **conservation** is the practice of managing the use of resources wisely so the resources last longer. Conservation cannot make resources last forever, but it can make resources last longer.

Governments and industries greatly affect resource conservation. Even individuals can make a difference. Walking, riding a bike, or riding the bus conserves fuel resources. People can also conserve resources when they turn off lights and unplug equipment that they are not using. Taking shorter showers saves water. When many people make small changes, the results can be huge.

did you **know?**

If everyone on Earth lived like the average American, it would take the resources of five planets to support us!

Resource Conservation at My School

_____
_____
_____
_____
_____
_____
_____
_____

FIGURE 4 ·······················

Conserving Resources at School
Students like you can take action to conserve natural resources.

✎ **List** On the notebook paper, write ways your school can conserve resources.

Lab® Do the Lab Investigation
zone *Recycling Paper.*

🔑 Assess Your Understanding

2a. Review Resources (are/are not) equally available around the world.

b. Summarize What two factors determine whether or not a resource is being used sustainably?

_____

c. Evaluate the Impact on Society As the human population continues to grow, how do you think it will affect the use of natural resources?

_____
_____
_____

got it? ··

○ **I get it!** Now I know that natural resources are important because_____
_____

○ I need extra help with _____

Go to **my science** ⬢ **coach** online for help with this subject.

Conserving Land and Soil

UNLOCK THE BIG Q?

🔑 How Do People Use Land?

🔑 Why Is Soil Management Important?

my planet DiaRY   VOICES FROM HISTORY

Land Inspiration

Conservation is a state of harmony between men and land.
            —Aldo Leopold

Aldo Leopold spent his life in beautiful landscapes. He was so inspired by what he saw that he sought to better understand it. Leopold realized that land and all it contains—living and nonliving—are connected. He believed people should use land in a way that protects it for all living things as well as for future generations. Leopold called his idea the "land ethic." He wrote several books on conservation using this philosophy, including his most famous book, *A Sand County Almanac*.

Communicate Discuss this question with a group of classmates. Write your answer below.

How do you think land should be used?

_____

_____

_____

_____

_____

▶ PLANET DIARY   Go to **Planet Diary** to learn more about conserving land and soil.

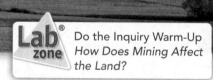

Lab zone Do the Inquiry Warm-Up
How Does Mining Affect the Land?

How Do People Use Land?

Less than a quarter of Earth's surface is dry, ice-free land. All people on Earth must share this limited amount of land to produce their food, build shelter, and obtain resources. As the American author Mark Twain once said about land, "They don't make it anymore."

People use land in many ways. 🔑 **Three uses that change the land are agriculture, mining, and development.** See **Figure 1.**

Vocabulary
- litter • topsoil • subsoil • bedrock • erosion
- nutrient depletion • fertilizer • desertification
- drought • land reclamation

Skills
↻ Reading: Relate Cause and Effect
△ Inquiry: Infer

Agriculture

Strip Mining

Development

Agriculture Land provides most of the food that people eat. Crops such as wheat require lots of fertile land, but less than a third of Earth's land can be farmed. The rest is too dry, too salty, or too mountainous. New farmland is created by clearing forests, draining wetlands, and irrigating deserts. Land can also be used to grow food for animals, to provide grazing for livestock, or to grow crops such as cotton.

Mining Mining is the removal of nonrenewable resources from the land. Resources just below the surface are strip mined. Strip mining removes a strip of land to obtain minerals. The strip is then replaced. Strip mining exposes soil, which can then be blown or washed away. The area may remain barren for years. Resources can also be removed from deeper underground by digging tunnels to bring the minerals to the surface.

Development People settled in areas that had good soil near fresh water. As populations grew, the settlements became towns and cities. People developed the land by constructing buildings, bridges, and roads. In the United States, an area half the size of New Jersey is developed each year.

FIGURE 1 ....
Land Use
The ways that people use land vary greatly. For example, about 93 percent of land in Nebraska is used for agriculture, while only 10 percent of land in Massachusetts is used for agriculture.

✎ **Describe** How is land used in your area?

_____

_____

Lab zone Do the Quick Lab
Land Use.

🔑 Assess Your Understanding
got it? ....

O **I get it!** Now I know the ways people use and change land include _____

O **I need extra help with** _____

Go to my science ⓢ COACH online for help with this subject.

Why Is Soil Management Important?

To understand why soil management is important, you need to know about the structure and function of fertile soil. It can take hundreds of years to form just a few centimeters of new soil. Soil contains the minerals and nutrients that plants need to grow. Soil also absorbs, stores, and filters water. Bacteria, fungi, and other organisms in soil break down the wastes and remains of living things. See **Figure 2.**

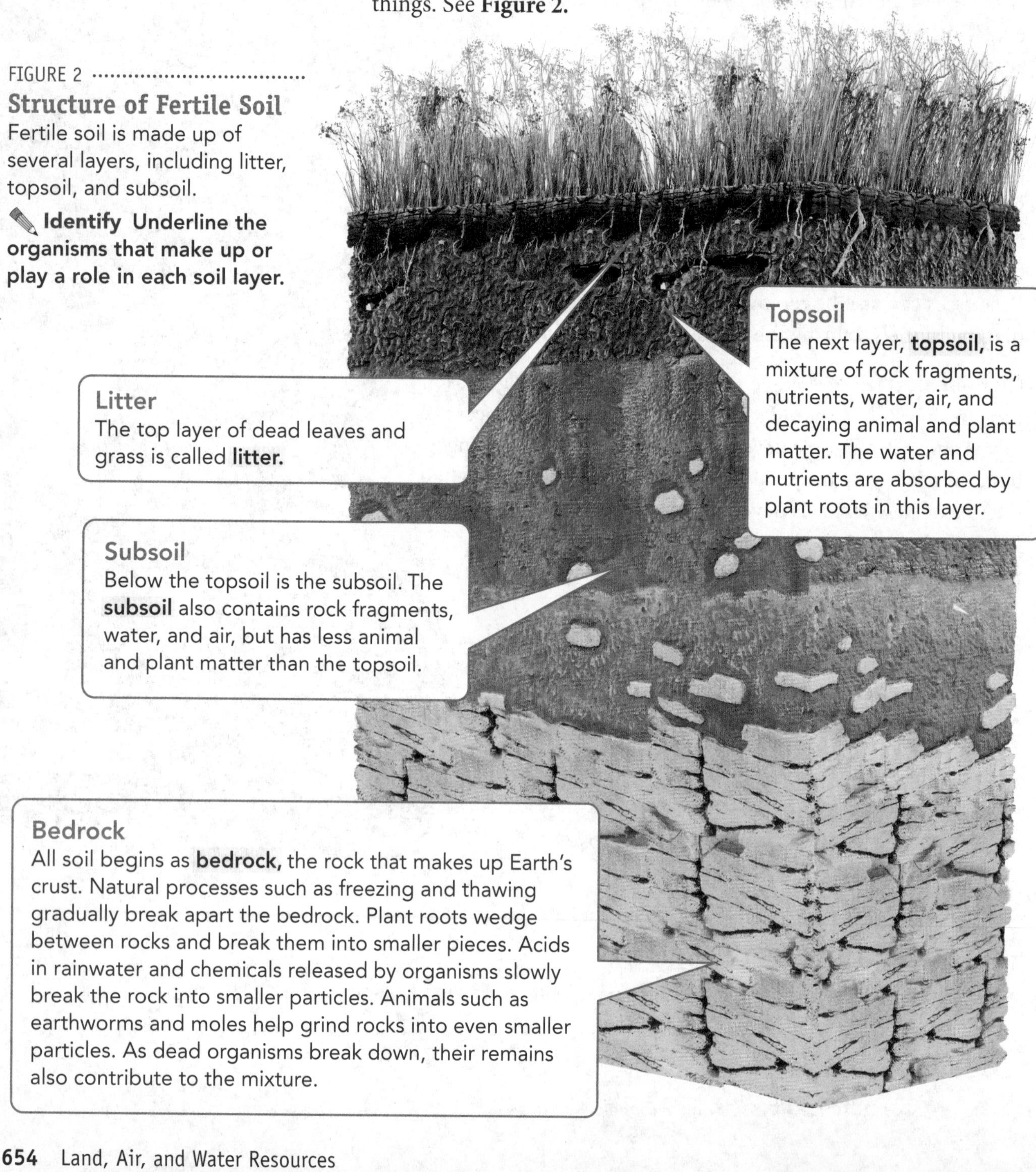

FIGURE 2 ....

Structure of Fertile Soil

Fertile soil is made up of several layers, including litter, topsoil, and subsoil.

✎ **Identify** Underline the organisms that make up or play a role in each soil layer.

Litter
The top layer of dead leaves and grass is called **litter.**

Topsoil
The next layer, **topsoil,** is a mixture of rock fragments, nutrients, water, air, and decaying animal and plant matter. The water and nutrients are absorbed by plant roots in this layer.

Subsoil
Below the topsoil is the subsoil. The **subsoil** also contains rock fragments, water, and air, but has less animal and plant matter than the topsoil.

Bedrock
All soil begins as **bedrock,** the rock that makes up Earth's crust. Natural processes such as freezing and thawing gradually break apart the bedrock. Plant roots wedge between rocks and break them into smaller pieces. Acids in rainwater and chemicals released by organisms slowly break the rock into smaller particles. Animals such as earthworms and moles help grind rocks into even smaller particles. As dead organisms break down, their remains also contribute to the mixture.

Soil Use Problems Because rich topsoil takes so long to form, it is important to protect Earth's soil. ▱ **Without soil, most life on land could not exist. Poor soil management can result in three problems: erosion, nutrient depletion, and desertification.** Fortunately, damaged soil can sometimes be restored.

Erosion Normally, plant roots hold soil in place. But when plants are removed during logging, mining, or farming, the soil is exposed and soil particles can easily move. The process by which water, wind, or ice moves particles of rocks or soil is called **erosion.** Terracing, one farming method that helps reduce erosion, is shown in **Figure 3.**

✎ **Relate Cause and Effect** In the text, underline the causes and circle the effects of two soil use problems.

Nutrient Depletion Plants make their own food through photosynthesis. Plants also need nutrients such as the nitrogen, potassium, and phosphorus found in soil to grow. Decomposers supply these nutrients to the soil as they break down the wastes and remains of organisms. But if a farmer plants the same crops in a field every year, the crops may use more nutrients than the decomposers can supply. The soil becomes less fertile, a situation called **nutrient depletion.**

When soil becomes depleted, farmers usually apply **fertilizers,** which include nutrients that help crops grow better. Farmers may choose other methods of soil management, too. They may periodically leave fields unplanted. The unused parts of crops, such as cornstalks, can be left in fields to decompose, adding nutrients to the soil. Farmers also can alternate crops that use many nutrients with crops that use fewer nutrients.

FIGURE 3 ....
Terracing
✎ A terrace is a leveled section of a hill used to grow crops and prevent erosion. The flat surfaces allow crops to absorb water before the water flows downhill.

1. **Interpret Photos** Draw the path of water down the first hill and the terraced hill.

2. **Infer** Why do you think terracing helps prevent erosion?

_____

_____

_____

655

Desertification If the soil in a once-fertile area becomes depleted of moisture and nutrients, the area can become a desert. The advance of desertlike conditions into areas that previously were fertile is called **desertification** (dih zurt uh fih KAY shun).

One cause of desertification is climate. For example, a **drought** is a period when less rain than normal falls in an area. During droughts, crops fail. Without plant cover, the exposed soil easily blows away. Overgrazing of grasslands by cattle and sheep and cutting down trees for firewood can cause desertification, too.

Desertification is a serious problem. People cannot grow crops and graze livestock where desertification has occurred. As a result, people may face famine and starvation. Desertification is severe in central Africa. Millions of rural people there are moving to the cities because they can no longer support themselves on the land.

apply it!

Desertification affects many areas around the world.

❶ **Name** Which continent has the most existing desert?

_____

❷ **Interpret Maps** Where in the United States is the greatest risk of desertification?

_____

❸ **Infer** Is desertification a threat only in areas where there is existing desert? Explain. Circle an area on the map to support your answer.

_____
_____

❹ [CHALLENGE] If an area is facing desertification, what are some things people could do to possibly limit its effects?

_____
_____

Key

Existing desert
High-risk area
Moderate-risk area

Land Reclamation Fortunately, it is possible to replace land damaged by erosion or mining. The process of restoring an area of land to a more productive state is called **land reclamation.** In addition to restoring land for agriculture, land reclamation can restore habitats for wildlife. Many different types of land reclamation projects are currently underway all over the world. But it is generally more difficult and expensive to restore damaged land and soil than it is to protect those resources in the first place. In some cases, the land may not return to its original state.

FIGURE 4 ·······················

Land Reclamation
These pictures show land before and after it was mined.

✎ **Communicate** Below the pictures, write a story about what happened to the land.

_____
_____
_____

 Do the Quick Lab
Modeling Soil Conservation.

Assess Your Understanding

1a. Review Subsoil has (less/more) plant and animal matter than topsoil.

b. Explain What can happen to soil if plants are removed?

_____
_____
_____

c. Apply Concepts What are some problems that could prevent people from supporting land reclamation?

_____
_____
_____
_____
_____

got it? ···

○ **I get it!** Now I know that soil management is important because _____

_____
_____

○ **I need extra help with** _____

Go to MY SCIENCE ⓢ COACH *online for help with this subject.*

Waste Disposal and Recycling

What Are Three Solid Waste Disposal Methods?

What Are the Major Categories of Recycling?

How Are Hazardous Wastes Safely Disposed Of?

my planet diary

Trash Talk

Here are some interesting facts about trash:

• Every hour, people throw away 2.5 million plastic bottles.

• Recycling one aluminum can saves enough energy to run a TV for three hours.

• Americans create two kilograms of trash per day. That trash could fill 63,000 garbage trucks each day!

• In 2005 the U.S. government recorded the first-ever drop in the amount of trash produced from the previous year. Trash declined by 1.5 million metric tons from 2004 to 2005, partly due to an increase in recycling.

SCIENCE STATS

Communicate Discuss these questions with a group of classmates. Write your answers below.

1. Do you think the amount of trash we produce will increase or decrease in the future? Explain.

_____

_____

_____

2. What can you do to reduce the amount of trash you create?

_____

_____

_____

> PLANET DIARY Go to **Planet Diary** to learn more about waste disposal and recycling.

 Do the Inquiry Warm-Up *What's in the Trash?*

Vocabulary
- municipal solid waste
- incineration
- pollutant
- leachate
- sanitary landfill
- recycling
- biodegradable
- hazardous waste

Skills
- Reading: Compare and Contrast
- Inquiry: Graph

What Are Three Solid Waste Disposal Methods?

People generate many types of waste, including empty packaging, paper, and food scraps. The wastes produced in homes, businesses, schools, and in the community are called **municipal solid waste.** Other sources of solid waste include construction debris, agricultural wastes, and industrial wastes. ⚙ **Three methods of handling solid waste are burning, burying, and recycling.** Each method has its advantages and disadvantages.

Incineration The burning of solid waste is called **incineration** (in sin ur AY shun). The burning facilities, or incinerators, do not take up much space. They do not directly pollute groundwater. The heat produced by burning solid waste can be used to produce electricity. Incinerators supply electricity to many homes.

Unfortunately, incinerators do have drawbacks. Even the best incinerators create some air pollution. Although incinerators reduce the volume of waste by as much as 90 percent, some waste still remains and needs to be disposed of somewhere. Incinerators are also expensive to build.

apply it!

What happens to all the trash?

1 △ **Graph** Use the data in the table and the key to fill in the bar graph. The graph represents the methods of municipal waste disposal in the United States in 2007. Give the graph a title.

Disposal Method	Waste (Percent)
Incineration	13%
Landfills	54%
Recycling	33%

2 CHALLENGE Why do you think incineration is the least popular method of solid waste disposal?

_____

_____

_____

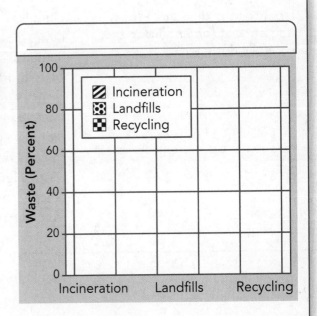

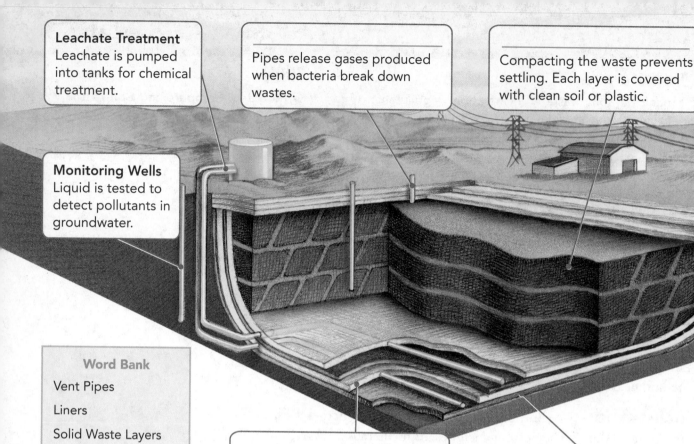

Leachate Treatment
Leachate is pumped into tanks for chemical treatment.

Pipes release gases produced when bacteria break down wastes.

Compacting the waste prevents settling. Each layer is covered with clean soil or plastic.

Monitoring Wells
Liquid is tested to detect pollutants in groundwater.

Word Bank
Vent Pipes
Liners
Solid Waste Layers

Leachate Collection
Water moving through the landfill dissolves wastes, forming leachate.

Clay and plastic liners prevent liquids from reaching the soil.

FIGURE 1 ·····························

Sanitary Landfill Design
Sanitary landfills are designed to protect the surrounding area.

✎ **Interpret Diagrams** Use the terms listed in the word bank to fill in the missing labels on the diagram. Why is it important for landfills to be carefully designed?

_____

_____

_____

_____

_____

Landfills Until fairly recently, people disposed of waste in open holes in the ground called dumps. Some of this waste polluted the environment. Any substance that causes pollution is a **pollutant.** Dumps were dangerous and unsightly. Rainwater falling on a dump dissolved chemicals from the wastes, forming a polluted liquid called **leachate.** Leachate could run off into streams and lakes, or trickle down into the groundwater.

In 1976, the government banned open dumps. Now much solid waste is buried in landfills that are built to hold the wastes more safely. A **sanitary landfill** holds municipal solid waste, construction debris, and some types of agricultural and industrial waste. **Figure 1** shows the parts of a well-designed sanitary landfill. Once a landfill is full, it is covered with a clay cap to keep rainwater from entering the waste.

Even well-designed landfills can pollute groundwater. Capped landfills can be reused as parks and sites for sports arenas. They cannot be used for housing or agriculture.

Recycling You may have heard of the "three R's"—reduce, reuse, and recycle. *Reduce* refers to creating less waste from the beginning, such as using cloth shopping bags rather than disposable ones. *Reuse* refers to finding another use for an object rather than discarding it, such as refilling reusable bottles with drinking water instead of buying new bottled water.

The process of reclaiming raw materials and reusing them to create new products is called **recycling.** You can recycle at home and encourage others to recycle. You can buy products made from recycled materials. Your purchase makes it more profitable for companies to use recycled materials in products.

Another way to reduce solid waste is to start a compost pile. The moist, dark conditions in a compost pile allow natural decomposers to break down grass clippings, leaves, and some food wastes. Compost is an excellent natural fertilizer for plants.

🔁 **Compare and Contrast**
In the table below, write one pro and one con for each of the three solid waste disposal methods.

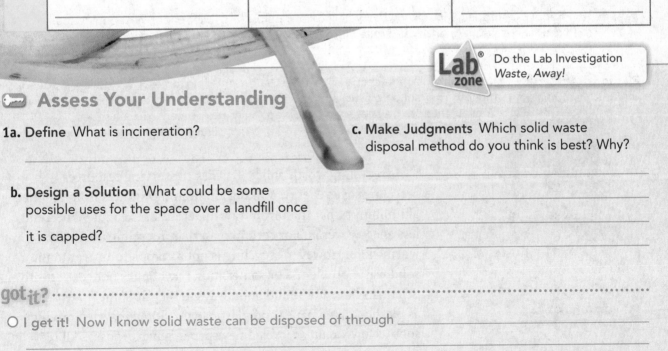

	Incineration	Sanitary Landfills	Recycling
Pro			
Con			

Lab zone Do the Lab Investigation *Waste, Away!*

🗝 Assess Your Understanding

1a. Define What is incineration?

_____

b. Design a Solution What could be some possible uses for the space over a landfill once it is capped? _____

_____

c. Make Judgments Which solid waste disposal method do you think is best? Why?

_____
_____
_____
_____

got it? ···

O **I get it!** Now I know solid waste can be disposed of through _____
_____

O I need extra help with _____

Go to **MY SCIENCE** ⬤ **COACH** online for help with this subject.

What Are the Major Categories of Recycling?

Recycling reduces the volume of solid waste by reusing materials. Recycling uses energy, but it also saves the energy that would be needed to obtain, transport, and process raw materials. Recycling is also cheaper than making new materials. Additionally, recycling conserves nonrenewable resources and limits the environmental damage caused by mining for raw materials.

Materials that can be broken down and recycled by bacteria and other decomposers are **biodegradable** (by oh dih GRAY duh bul). Many products people use today are not biodegradable, such as plastic containers, metal cans, rubber tires, and glass jars. Instead, people have developed different ways to recycle the raw materials in these products.

A wide range of materials can be recycled. ⊂━ **Most recycling focuses on four major categories of products: metal, glass, paper, and plastic.**

Vocabulary Prefixes The prefix *bio-* means "life." A material is biodegradable if it can be broken down and recycled by living things such as

_____

_____

Material	Recycling Process	Products Made From Recycling
Metal	Metals are melted in furnaces and rolled into sheets.	Cars, cans, bicycles, jewelry, office supplies, house siding
Glass	Glass pieces are melted in furnaces and cast into new glass.	Bottles, floor tiles, countertops, jewelry, jars
Paper	Paper is shredded and mixed with water to form pulp. The pulp is washed, dried, and rolled into new sheets.	Toilet paper, notebook paper, paper cups, paper plates, napkins, envelopes
Plastic	Plastic containers are chopped, washed, and melted. The molten plastic is turned into pellets that can be heated and molded.	Picnic tables, park benches, speed bumps, recycling bins, playground equipment, deck lumber, fleece (see girl's jacket at left)

Is recycling worthwhile? Besides conserving resources, recycling saves energy. Making aluminum products from recycled aluminum rather than from raw materials uses about 90 percent less energy overall. For certain materials, recycling is usually worthwhile. However, recycling is not a complete answer to the solid waste problem. For some cities, recycling is not cost-effective. Scientists have not found good ways to recycle some materials, such as plastic-coated paper and plastic foam. Some recycled products, such as low-quality recycled newspaper, have few uses. All recycling processes require energy and create pollution. The value of recycling must be judged on a case-by-case basis.

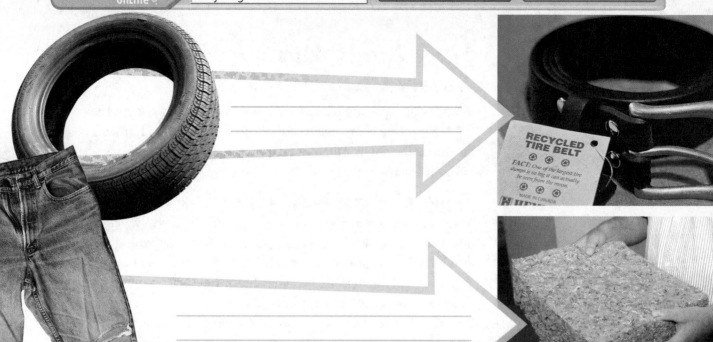

RECYCLED TIRE BELT

FACT: One of the largest tire dumps is so big it can actually be seen from the moon.

MADE IN CANADA

recycled

FIGURE 2 ···

> INTERACTIVE ART **Like New**

Did you know that old tires can be made into belts? Or jeans into insulation?

✎ **Apply Concepts** Besides the examples shown, name other objects that could be made from these recyclables.

Lab® Do the Quick Lab
zone *It's in the Numbers.*

🔑 **Assess Your Understanding**

2a. Explain How does recycling save energy?

_____

_____

_____

_____

b. Solve Problems How could your community solve its solid waste problem?

_____

_____

_____

_____

got it?

○ **I get it!** Now I know recyclable

materials are categorized as _____

_____

_____

_____

○ **I need extra help with** _____

_____

Go to **MY SCIENCE** 🔍 **COACH** *online for help with this subject.*

How Are Hazardous Wastes Safely Disposed Of?

Many people picture hazardous wastes as bubbling chemicals or oozing slime. Any material that can be harmful to human health or the environment if it is not properly disposed of is a **hazardous waste.**

Types of Hazardous Wastes Toxic wastes can damage the health of humans and other organisms. Explosive wastes can react very quickly when exposed to air or water, or explode when dropped. Flammable wastes easily catch fire. Corrosive wastes can dissolve many materials. Everyday hazardous wastes include electronic devices, batteries, and paint.

Other wastes that require special disposal are radioactive wastes. Radioactive wastes give off radiation that can cause cancer and other diseases. Some radioactive waste can remain dangerous for millions of years.

Health Effects A person can be exposed to hazardous wastes by breathing, eating, drinking, or touching them. Even short-term exposure to hazardous wastes can cause problems such as skin irritation or breathing difficulties. Long-term exposure can cause diseases such as cancer, damage to body organs, or death.

FIGURE 3 ·······················

Sort It Out!
Wastes can be thrown away, recycled, or disposed of as hazardous waste.

✏ **Summarize** Draw a line from each object to its appropriate disposal container.

Disposal Methods
It is difficult to safely dispose of hazardous wastes. Hazardous wastes are most often disposed of in carefully designed landfills. The landfills are lined and covered with clay and plastic. These materials prevent chemicals from leaking into the soil and groundwater. **Hazardous wastes that are not disposed of in carefully designed landfills may be incinerated or broken down by organisms. Liquid wastes may be stored in deep rock layers.**

Scientists are still searching for methods that will provide safe and permanent disposal of radioactive wastes. Some wastes are currently stored in vaults dug hundreds of meters underground or in concrete and steel containers above ground.

Disposal Sites
It is a challenge to decide where to build hazardous waste disposal facilities. In general, people would prefer to have a single large facility located in an area where few people live. However, it may be safer, cheaper, and easier to transport wastes to small local facilities instead.

Reducing Hazardous Waste
The best way to manage hazardous wastes is to produce less of them in the first place. Industries are eager to develop safe alternatives to harmful chemicals. At home, you can find substitutes for some hazardous household chemicals. For example, you could use citronella candles instead of insect spray to repel insects.

FIGURE 4

Hazardous Wastes
Hazardous waste can be harmful if improperly handled.

✎ **Review** What is the best way to manage hazardous wastes?

○ Store waste in small facilities.
○ Produce less waste to start.
○ Incinerate waste.

Do the Quick Lab Half-Life.

Assess Your Understanding

3a. Name What are some negative health effects of exposure to hazardous wastes?

_____

b. Make Judgments Do you think hazardous wastes should be disposed of at one large central facility? Explain.

_____

got it?

○ I get it! Now I know that hazardous wastes are disposed of by_____

○ I need extra help with _____
Go to MY SCIENCE COACH online for help with this subject.

Air Pollution and Solutions

🔑 **What Causes Outdoor and Indoor Air Pollution?**

🔑 **What Causes Damage to the Ozone Layer?**

🔑 **How Can Air Pollution Be Reduced?**

my planet Diary

PROFILE

Drawing for a Difference

Some people may think that kids can't help the environment. Kids in the San Joaquin Valley of California know better! Each year, students enter their drawings into a contest for a Clean Air Kids Calendar sponsored by the San Joaquin Valley Air Pollution Control District. Lisa Huang (bottom right drawing) and Saira Delgada (bottom left drawing) are two middle school students whose work was chosen to be a part of the 2008 calendar. Their drawings show people why healthy air is important. Every time people looked at the calendar, the drawings reminded them of the simple ways they can help the planet.

Communicate Discuss the question with a group of classmates. Then, write your answer below.

How could you raise awareness about air pollution in your community?

_____

_____

_____

_____

> PLANET DIARY Go to **Planet Diary** to learn more about air pollution and solutions.

 Lab zone Do the Inquiry Warm-Up *How Does the Scent Spread?*

Vocabulary

- emissions
- photochemical smog
- ozone
- temperature inversion
- acid rain
- radon
- ozone layer
- chlorofluorocarbon

Skills

↻ Reading: Relate Text and Visuals
△ Inquiry: Communicate

What Causes Outdoor and Indoor Air Pollution?

You can't usually see it, taste it, or smell it, but you are surrounded by air. Air is a mixture of nitrogen, oxygen, carbon dioxide, water vapor, and other gases. Almost all living things depend on these gases to survive. Recall that these gases cycle between living things and the atmosphere. These cycles guarantee that the air supply will not run out, but they don't guarantee that the air will be clean.

Outdoor Air Pollution What causes air pollution? Until the mid-1900s in the United States, factories and power plants that burned coal produced most of the pollutants, or **emissions,** that were released into the air. 🔑 **Today, a large source of emissions resulting in air pollution outdoors comes from motor vehicles such as cars and trucks.** There are also some natural causes of air pollution. Methane released from animals such as cows also sends pollutants into the atmosphere.

Air pollution sources can be grouped as point or nonpoint sources. A point source is a specific source of pollution that is easy to identify, such as a smokestack. A nonpoint source is a source that is widely spread and cannot be tied to a specific origin, such as vehicle emissions. So the pollution cannot be traced to any specific vehicle.

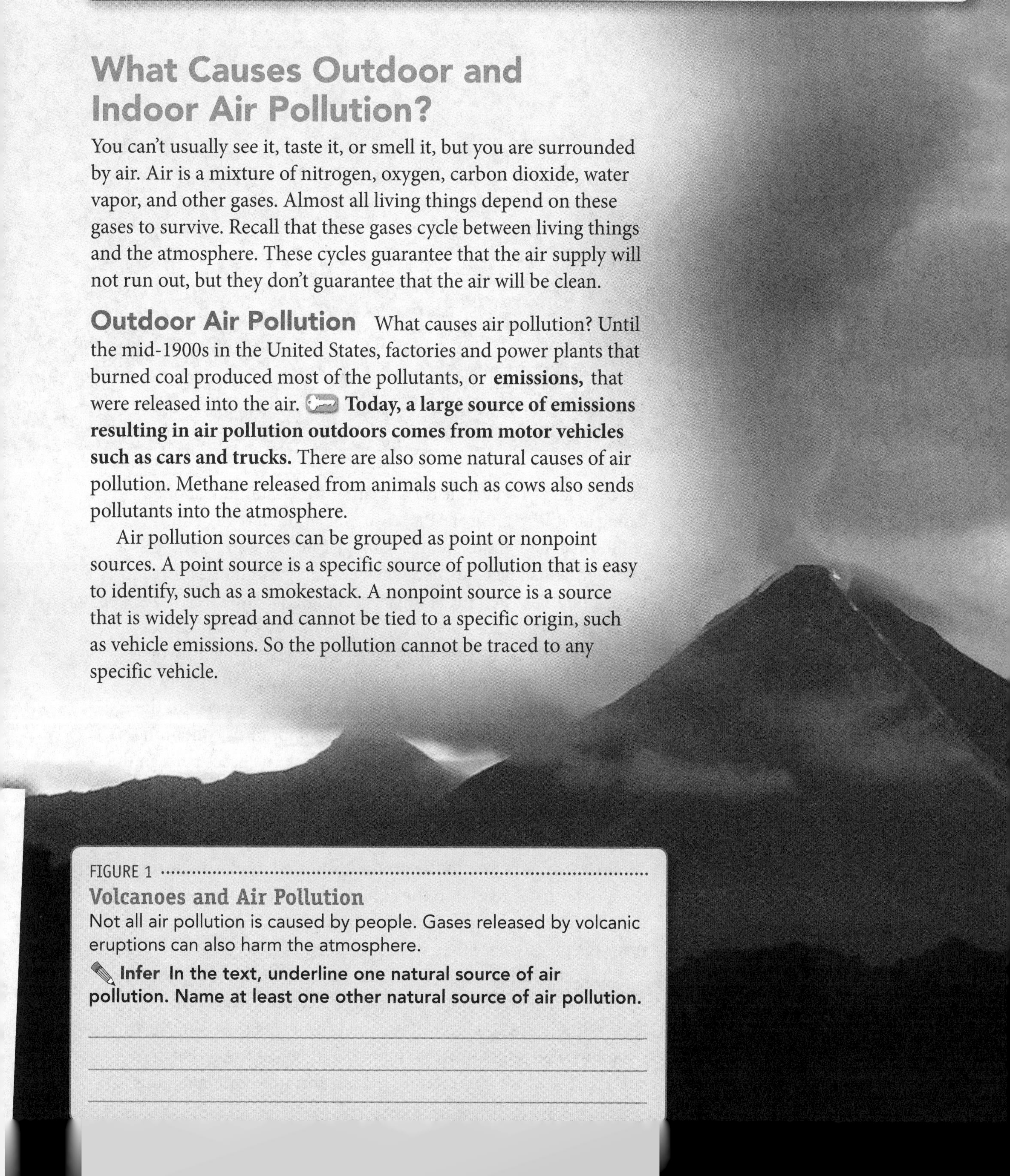

FIGURE 1 ···

Volcanoes and Air Pollution

Not all air pollution is caused by people. Gases released by volcanic eruptions can also harm the atmosphere.

✏ **Infer** In the text, underline one natural source of air pollution. Name at least one other natural source of air pollution.

_____

_____

_____

_____

_____

_____

FIGURE 2 ·················

Temperature Inversion
Normally, pollutants rise into the atmosphere and blow away. During a temperature inversion, warm air traps the pollution close to the ground.

✎ **Interpret Photos** On the photo above, label the warm air, cool air, and polluted air.

Smog Have you ever heard a weather forecaster talk about a "smog alert"? A smog alert is a warning about a type of air pollution called photochemical smog. **Photochemical smog** is a thick, brownish haze formed when certain gases in the air react with sunlight. When the smog level is high, it settles as a haze over a city. Smog can cause breathing problems and eye and throat irritation. Exercising outdoors can make these problems worse.

The major sources of smog are the gases emitted by cars and trucks. Burning gasoline in a car engine releases gases into the air. These gases include hydrocarbons (compounds containing hydrogen and carbon) and nitrogen oxides. The gases react in the sunlight and produce a form of oxygen called **ozone.** Ozone, which is toxic, is the major chemical found in smog. Ozone can cause lung infections and damage the body's defenses against infection.

Normally, air close to the ground is heated by Earth's surface. As the air warms, it rises into the cooler air above it. Any pollutants in the air are carried higher into the atmosphere and are blown away from the place where they were produced.

Certain weather conditions can cause a condition known as a temperature inversion. During a **temperature inversion,** as shown in **Figure 2,** a layer of warm air prevents the rising air from escaping. The polluted air is trapped and held close to Earth's surface. The smog becomes more concentrated and dangerous.

FIGURE 3 ·······················

Acid Rain
Acid rain harms plants, animals, buildings, and statues.

✎ **Review** In the text, underline the cause of acid rain.

Acid Rain Precipitation that is more acidic than normal because of air pollution is called **acid rain.** Acid rain can also take the form of snow, sleet, or fog. Acid rain is caused by the emissions from power plants and factories that burn coal and oil. These fuels produce nitrogen oxides and sulfur oxides when they are burned. The gases that are released react with water vapor in the air, forming nitric acid and sulfuric acid. The acids dissolve in precipitation and return to Earth's surface.

As you can imagine, acid falling from the sky has some negative effects. When acid rain falls into a pond or lake, it changes the conditions there. Many fish, particularly their eggs, cannot survive in more acidic water. When acid rain falls on plants, it can damage their leaves and stems. Acid rain that falls on the ground can also damage plants by affecting the nutrient levels in the soil. Whole forests have been destroyed by acid rain. Fortunately, some of the effects of acid rain are reversible. Badly damaged lakes have been restored by adding lime or other substances that neutralize the acid.

Acid rain doesn't just affect living things. The acid reacts with stone and metal in buildings and statues. Statues and stonework damaged by acid rain may look as if they are melting, as seen in **Figure 3.** Automobiles rust more quickly in areas with acid rain. These effects are not reversible and the damage can be costly.

apply it!

You are a scientist called to testify before Congress about acid rain. The government is proposing putting limits on emissions that lead to acid rain.

❶ ⚠ **Communicate** Some of the members of Congress do not think acid rain causes real damage. What do you tell them?

_____

_____

❷ **Explain** Is rain the only form of precipitation you would identify as being potentially acidic? Explain.

_____

❸ CHALLENGE What could you tell a company that was unwilling to reduce its emissions because the initial cost was high?

_____

_____

_____

FIGURE 4

Indoor Air Pollution

Indoor air pollution has many sources. ✏ **Identify** Circle the sources of indoor air pollution in this room.

Indoor Air Pollution You might think that you can avoid air pollution by staying inside. The air inside buildings can be polluted, too. 🔑 **Some substances that cause indoor air pollution, such as dust and pet hair, bother only those people who are sensitive to them. Other indoor air pollutants, such as toxic chemicals, can affect anyone.** Glues and cleaning supplies may give off toxic fumes. Cigarette smoke, even from another person's cigarette, can damage the lungs and heart. **Figure 4** shows some sources of air pollution that can be found in homes.

Carbon Monoxide One particularly dangerous indoor air pollutant is carbon monoxide. Carbon monoxide is a colorless and odorless gas that forms when fuels are not completely burned. When carbon monoxide builds up in an enclosed space, like a house, it can be deadly. Any home heated by wood, coal, oil, or gas needs a carbon monoxide detector.

Radon Another indoor air pollutant that is difficult to detect is radon. **Radon** is a colorless, odorless gas that is radioactive. It is formed naturally by certain rocks underground. Radon can enter homes through cracks in basement walls or floors. Breathing radon gas over many years may cause lung cancer and other health problems. Homeowners can install ventilation systems to prevent radon from building up in their homes.

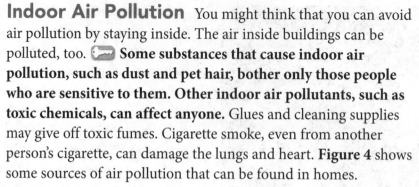

Lab zone® Do the Quick Lab *How Acid Is Your Rain?*

🔑 **Assess Your Understanding**

1a. Name (Photochemical smog/Methane) is a thick, brownish haze formed when gases in the air are exposed to sunlight.

b. Make Judgments Do you think the government should regulate sources of air pollution such as factory and car emissions? Explain.

_____

_____

_____

_____

_____

got it? ....

○ **I get it!** Now I know outdoor air pollution is

caused by _____

_____

and indoor air pollution is caused by _____

_____

○ **I need extra help with** _____

_____

_____

Go to **my science 🅂 coach** online for help with this subject.

What Causes Damage to the Ozone Layer?

If you have ever had a sunburn, you have experienced the painful effects of the sun's ultraviolet radiation. But did you know that sunburns would be even worse without the protection of the ozone layer? The **ozone layer** is a layer of the upper atmosphere about 15 to 30 kilometers above Earth's surface. The amount of ozone in this layer is very small. Yet even this small amount of ozone in the ozone layer protects people from the effects of too much ultraviolet radiation. These effects include sunburn, eye diseases, and skin cancer.

Because you read earlier that ozone is a pollutant, the fact that ozone can be helpful may sound confusing. The difference between ozone as a pollutant and ozone as a helpful gas is its location in the atmosphere. Ozone close to Earth's surface in the form of smog is harmful. Ozone higher in the atmosphere, where people cannot breathe it, protects us from too much ultraviolet radiation.

The Source of Ozone Ozone is constantly being made and destroyed. See **Figure 5.** When sunlight strikes an ozone molecule, the energy of the ultraviolet radiation is partly absorbed. This energy causes the ozone molecule to break apart into an oxygen molecule and an oxygen atom. The oxygen atom soon collides with another oxygen molecule. They react to form a new ozone molecule. Each time this cycle occurs, some energy is absorbed. That energy does not reach Earth's surface.

FIGURE 5 ·····················

Ozone Cycle
The ozone cycle prevents harmful ultraviolet radiation from reaching Earth's surface.

✎ **Sequence Explain the ozone cycle in your own words.**

_____

_____

_____

_____

_____

_____

_____

_____

_____

_____

_____

_____

_____

_____

_____

_____

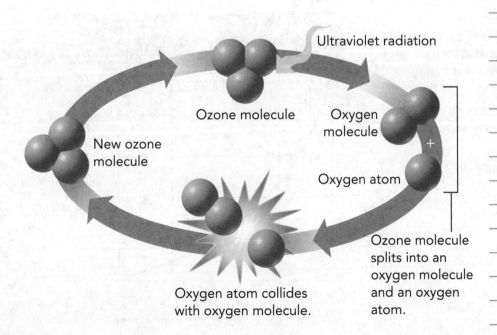

Ultraviolet radiation

Ozone molecule

Oxygen molecule

Oxygen atom

+

New ozone molecule

Ozone molecule splits into an oxygen molecule and an oxygen atom.

Oxygen atom collides with oxygen molecule.

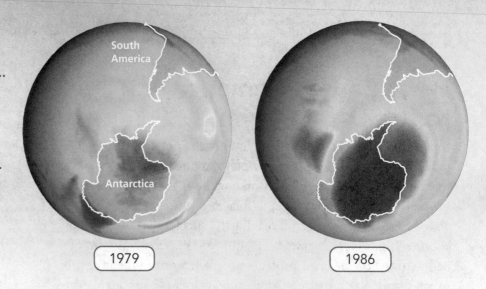

FIGURE 6 ·······················
Ozone Hole
The ozone hole (shown in blue) is over Antarctica. The hole has grown over time, but it varies seasonally and from year to year.

South America

Antarctica

1979

1986

The Ozone Hole In the late 1970s, scientists observed from satellite images that the ozone layer over Antarctica was growing thinner each spring. The amount of ozone in the ozone layer was decreasing. This caused an area of severe ozone depletion, or an ozone hole. In **Figure 6,** you can see the size of the ozone hole in five selected years.

What is to blame for the ozone hole? 🔑 **Scientists determined that the major cause of the ozone hole is a group of gases called CFCs.** CFCs, or **chlorofluorocarbons,** are human-made gases that contain chlorine and fluorine. CFCs had been used in air conditioners, aerosol spray cans, and other household products. CFCs reach high into the atmosphere, and react with ozone molecules. The CFCs block the cycle in which ozone molecules absorb ultraviolet radiation. As a result, more ultraviolet light reaches Earth's surface.

FIGURE 7 ·······················
Ozone and Ultraviolet Radiation
✏️ The amount of ozone in the atmosphere and the amount of UV radiation reaching Earth are linked.

1. **Read Graphs** Label the curve on the graph representing ozone and the curve representing UV radiation.

2. **Summarize** Explain the graph in your own words.

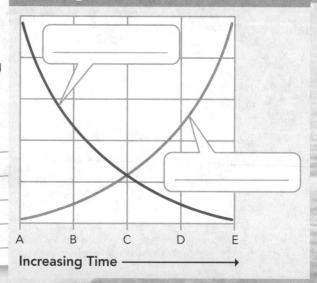

Ozone and UV Radiation Resulting From CFCs

A   B   C   D   E

Increasing Time →

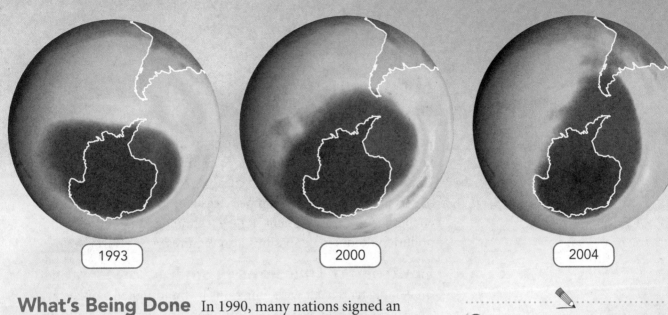

1993   2000   2004

What's Being Done In 1990, many nations signed an agreement to eventually ban the use of ozone-depleting substances, including CFCs. Most uses of CFCs were banned in 2000. Some uses of CFCs are still allowed, but compared to the 1970s, few CFCs now enter the atmosphere. Unfortunately, CFC molecules remain in the atmosphere for a long time. Scientists predict that if the ban on ozone-depleting substances is maintained, the ozone layer will gradually recover.

When scientists discovered that CFCs were harming the atmosphere, they immediately began to search for substitutes. Refrigerators and air conditioners were redesigned to use less-harmful substances. Most spray cans were either replaced by pump sprays or redesigned to use other gases. Researchers developed new ways to make products such as plastic foam without using CFCs. As a result of this research and the development of CFC substitutes, far less CFCs now enter the atmosphere.

Relate Text and Visuals
Based on the photos, describe what happened to the hole in the ozone layer before CFCs were banned. What do you think could happen if the ban is maintained and enforced?

_____
_____
_____
_____
_____
_____

 Do the Quick Lab
Analyzing Ozone.

Assess Your Understanding

2a. Explain How can ozone be both a pollutant and something beneficial to Earth?

_____
_____
_____
_____

b. Solve Problems What can countries do to help the ozone layer recover?

_____
_____
_____
_____

got it? ....

O **I get it!** Now I know the ozone layer was damaged by_____
_____

O **I need extra help with**_____

Go to my science COACH *online for help with this subject.*

How Can Air Pollution Be Reduced?

Air pollution can be reduced if we examine the sources. 🔑 **The key to reducing air pollution is to control emissions.** In the United States, laws such as the Clean Air Act regulate the amount of certain pollutants that can be released into the air. Laws also encourage the development of new technology that reduces air pollution. Reducing emissions also requires your efforts.

Controlling Emissions From Factories At one time, industries dealt with emissions by building tall smokestacks. The stacks released wastes high into the air where they could blow away, but the pollutants still ended up somewhere. Now factories remove pollutants from their emissions with devices known as scrubbers that release water droplets. Pollutants dissolve in the water and fall into a container. The use of scrubbers explains why "smoke" from factories is white—it's not smoke, it's steam.

Controlling Emissions From Vehicles Cars and trucks now contain pollution-control devices. A catalytic converter is a part of the exhaust system that reduces emissions of carbon monoxide, hydrocarbons, and nitrogen oxides. This device causes the gases to react, forming less-harmful carbon dioxide and water. Laws can ensure that people use pollution-control devices. For example, in many states, cars must pass emissions tests to be allowed on the road.

What You Can Do You may not think there is much you can do to reduce air pollution. However, even small changes in your behavior can make a big difference.

You can help reduce air pollution by reducing certain types of energy use. Much air pollution is a result of burning fuels to provide electricity and transportation. Using less energy conserves fuel resources and reduces emissions. Turning off lights, computers, and televisions in empty rooms uses less energy and reduces emissions. When you take public transportation, carpool, walk, or ride a bicycle, there are fewer cars on the road. This means there are less emissions that contribute to air pollution.

FIGURE 8 ·····················
> INTERACTIVE ART

Your Solutions

✎ **Communicate** With a partner, list ways you can reduce air pollution in your everyday life.

_____

_____

_____

_____

_____

_____

_____

Apple Imports

Apples are grown in an orchard in Chile.

Trucks carry apples from the orchard to the airport.

Airplanes carry the apples from Chile to the United States.

More trucks bring the apples from the airport to shipping centers and grocery stores around the country.

FIGURE 9

Where Does an Apple Really Come From?

Many things in our everyday lives, even where food comes from, can contribute to air pollution. ✎ **Analyze Costs and Benefits** Read the comic strip above. Then, fill in the boxes with pros and cons of buying apples that were grown locally instead of those grown in another country.

Pros

Cons

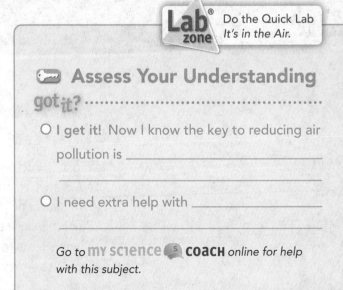

Lab zone
Do the Quick Lab
It's in the Air.

🗝 Assess Your Understanding

got it?

○ **I get it!** Now I know the key to reducing air pollution is _____

_____

○ **I need extra help with** _____

_____

Go to MY SCIENCE ⑤ COACH online for help with this subject.

675

Water Pollution and Solutions

UNLOCK
THE BIG
Q

🔑 **Why Is Fresh Water a Limited Resource?**

🔑 **What Are the Major Sources of Water Pollution?**

🔑 **How Can Water Pollution Be Reduced?**

my planeT DiaRY

DISASTERS

A Flood of Sludge

In December 2008, over 4.5 billion liters of polluted water flooded the area around Kingston, Tennessee. A nearby coal-powered electric plant produced polluted water containing arsenic, lead, and other toxic chemicals. The toxic chemicals and coal ash mixed with water in a holding pond to form a thick sludge. When the dam holding back the pond broke, the water poured into rivers. The sludge water spilled over the land, damaging trees, homes, and other buildings. Local residents feared the flood would be dangerous to their health as well.

Communicate Discuss the question with a group of classmates. Then write your answer below.

Is water pollution a problem in your community? Why or why not?

_____

_____

_____

_____

⊳ **PLANET DIARY** Go to **Planet Diary** to learn more about water pollution and solutions.

Lab® zone Do the Inquiry Warm-Up *How Does the Water Change?*

Why Is Fresh Water a Limited Resource?

Most of Earth's surface is covered by some form of water. Oceans cover nearly three fourths of Earth's surface. Around the poles are vast sheets of ice. From space you cannot even see many parts of Earth because they are hidden behind clouds of tiny water droplets. There seems to be so much water—it's hard to believe that it is a scarce resource in much of the world.

Vocabulary
- groundwater • pesticide • sewage • sediment

Skills
↪ Reading: Outline
△ Inquiry: Design Experiments

How can water be scarce when there is so much of it on Earth's surface? **Water is scarce on Earth because most of it—about 97 percent—is salt water.** Salt water cannot be used for drinking or watering crops. Also, about three quarters of the fresh water on Earth is ice. Most liquid fresh water is **groundwater,** water stored in soil and rock beneath Earth's surface. People use groundwater for drinking, but it is not always found near where people live. Cities in dry areas may draw their drinking water from hundreds of kilometers away.

FIGURE 1 ·····················
Water
Most of Earth's surface is covered with water, but fresh water is still a limited resource.

✎ **Identify** Reread the text. Then, underline the reasons why fresh water is scarce.

Renewing the Supply
Fortunately, Earth's fresh water is renewable. Remember that water continually moves between the atmosphere and Earth's surface in the water cycle. Even though fresh water is renewable, there is not always enough of it in a given place at a given time.

Water Shortages
Water shortages occur when people use water faster than the water cycle can replace it. This is likely to happen during a drought when an area gets less rain. Many places never receive enough rain to meet their needs and use other methods to get water. Desert cities in Saudi Arabia get more than half of their fresh water by removing salt from ocean water, which is very expensive.

Lab zone® Do the Quick Lab
Where's the Water?

🔑 Assess Your Understanding

got it? ···

○ I get it! Now I know that fresh water is limited on Earth because _____

_____

○ I need extra help with _____

Go to **my science** ⑤ **coach** *online for help with this subject.*

What Are the Major Sources of Water Pollution?

Since fresh water is scarce, water pollution can be devastating. Some pollutants, such as iron and copper, make water unpleasant to drink or wash in. Other pollutants, such as mercury or benzene, can cause sickness or even death.

🔑 **Most water pollution is the result of human activities. Wastes produced by agriculture, households, industry, mining, and other human activities can end up in water.** Water pollutants can be point or nonpoint pollution sources, classified by how they enter the water. A pipe gushing wastewater directly into a river or stream is an example of a point source. The pipe is a specific pollution source that can be easily identified. Nonpoint pollution sources include farm, street, and construction site runoff. The exact pollution source is hard to trace and identify.

Agricultural Wastes
Animal wastes, fertilizers, and pesticides are also sources of pollution. **Pesticides** are chemicals that kill crop-destroying organisms. Rain washes animal wastes, fertilizers, and pesticides into ponds, causing algae to grow. The algae block light and deplete the oxygen in the pond.

Household Sewage
The water and human wastes that are washed down sinks, showers, and toilets are called **sewage.** If sewage is not treated to kill disease-causing organisms, the organisms quickly multiply. People can become ill if they drink or swim in water containing these organisms.

FIGURE 2 ·······························

Farm Pollution
This scene may show common things found on a farm, but even common things can lead to water pollution.

✎ **Relate Text and Visuals** Circle the potential sources of water pollution in this scene.

Industry and Mining Wastes
Some plants, mills, factories, and mines produce wastes that can pollute water. Chemicals and metal wastes can harm organisms that live in bodies of water. Animals that drink from polluted bodies of water or eat the organisms that live in the water can also become ill.

Sediments
Water that causes erosion picks up **sediments,** or particles of rock and sand. Sediments can cover up the food sources, nests, and eggs of organisms in bodies of water. Sediments also block sunlight, preventing plants from growing.

Heat
Heat can also have a negative effect on a body of water. Some factories and power plants release water that has been used to cool machinery. This heated water can kill organisms living in the body of water into which it is released. This type of pollution is also known as thermal pollution.

Oil and Gasoline
An oil spill is a very dramatic form of water pollution. It can take many years for an area to recover from an oil spill because the oil floats on water and is difficult to collect. Another water pollution problem is caused by oil and gasoline that leak out of damaged underground storage tanks. The pollution can be carried far away from a leaking tank by groundwater.

↪ **Outline** Look back in the text and fill in the graphic organizer below to outline causes of water pollution.

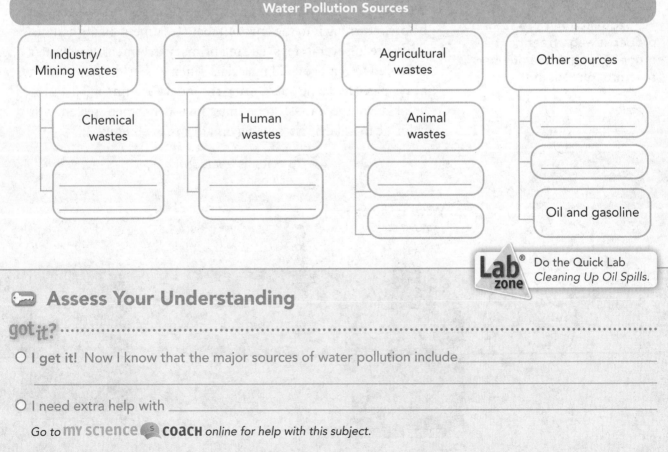

Lab zone® Do the Quick Lab *Cleaning Up Oil Spills.*

🗝 Assess Your Understanding

got it? ....

○ **I get it!** Now I know that the major sources of water pollution include_____

_____

○ **I need extra help with** _____

Go to MY SCIENCE ⑤ COACH online for help with this subject.

How Can Water Pollution Be Reduced?

By working together, governments, industries, and individuals can improve water quality. Federal and state laws in the United States regulate the use of certain substances that can pollute water.

The keys to keeping water clean are effective cleanup of oil and gasoline spills, proper sewage treatment, and reduction of pollutants. There are also some important ways that people can reduce water pollution at home.

Cleaning Up Oil and Gasoline Spills
Nature can handle oil in small amounts. A natural cleaning process slowly takes place after oil spills. Certain bacteria living in the ocean feed on the oil. Of course, oil can cause much damage to an area in the time it takes the bacteria to work, so people often help clean up large spills. The hard work of many scientists and volunteers can minimize environmental damage from large spills.

Gasoline or oil that leaks from an underground tank is hard to clean up. If the pollution has not spread far, the soil around the tank can be removed. But pollution that reaches groundwater may be carried far away. Groundwater can be pumped to the surface, treated, and then returned underground. This can take many years.

Sewage Treatment
Most communities treat wastewater before returning it to the environment. Treatment plants handle the waste in several steps. During primary treatment, wastewater is filtered to remove solid materials. Then it is held in tanks where heavy particles settle out. During secondary treatment, bacteria break down the wastes. Sometimes the water is then treated with chlorine to kill disease-causing organisms. See **Figure 3.**

FIGURE 3 ······························

Wastewater Treatment
There are several steps to proper sewage treatment.

✏️ **Sequence** Put the steps of proper sewage treatment in order by writing the numbers one through four in the circles.

◯ Bacteria break down wastes.

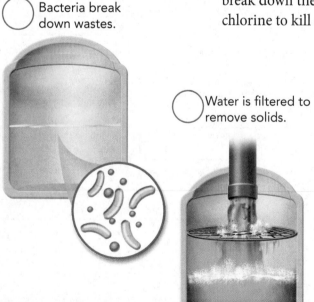

◯ Water is filtered to remove solids.

◯ Water is treated with chlorine.

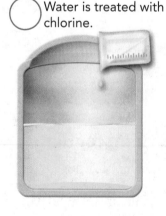

◯ Heavy particles settle in tank.

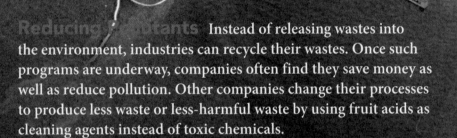

Reducing Pollutants Instead of releasing wastes into the environment, industries can recycle their wastes. Once such programs are underway, companies often find they save money as well as reduce pollution. Other companies change their processes to produce less waste or less-harmful waste by using fruit acids as cleaning agents instead of toxic chemicals.

What You Can Do It is easy to prevent water pollution at home. Some common household water pollutants are paints and paint thinner, motor oil, and garden chemicals. You can avoid causing water pollution by never pouring these chemicals down the drain. Instead, save these materials for your community's next hazardous waste collection day.

apply it!

Bacteria can be used to clean up oil spills. Some companies specialize in creating bacteria for cleaning up oil.

1 Analyze Costs and Benefits Fill in the boxes with some pros and cons of using bacteria to clean oil spills.

Pros	Cons

2 Design Experiments If you were creating bacteria for cleaning oil spills, what characteristics would you want to test the bacteria for? _____
_____

Pollution and Solutions

What can people do to use resources wisely?

FIGURE 4 ···

> REAL-WORLD INQUIRY All living things depend on land, air, and water. Conserving these resources for the future is important. Part of resource conservation is identifying and limiting sources of pollution.

✎ **Interpret Photos** On the photograph, write the letter from the key into the circle that best identifies the source of pollution.

Land
Describe at least one thing your community could do to reduce pollution on land.

_____

_____

_____

_____

_____

_____

_____

_____

Key of Pollution Sources

A. Sediments

B. Municipal solid waste

C. Runoff from development

D. Emissions

E. Oil and gasoline

F. Agricultural wastes

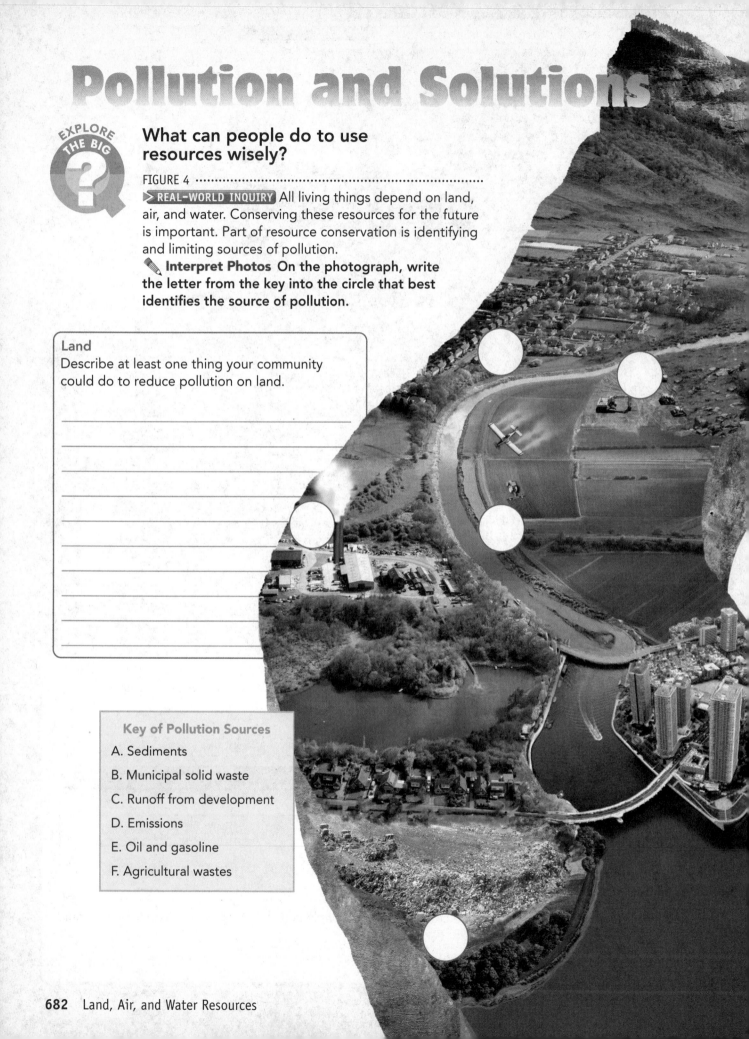

Air
Describe at least one thing your community could do to reduce air pollution.

_____
_____
_____
_____
_____
_____
_____

Water
Describe at least one thing your community could do to reduce water pollution.

_____
_____
_____
_____
_____
_____
_____

Lab® Do the Quick Lab
zone   *Getting Clean.*

🔑 Assess Your Understanding

1a. Define What are sediments?

_____
_____

b. Explain How can bacteria help clean an oil spill in the ocean?

_____
_____
_____

c. ANSWER THE BIG ❓ What can people do to use resources wisely?

_____
_____
_____
_____

d. CHALLENGE Why might a company not want to recycle the waste they produce even if it would reduce water pollution?

_____
_____
_____
_____
_____
_____
_____
_____

got it? ....

○ **I get it!** Now I know that water pollution can be reduced by _____

_____
_____

○ **I need extra help with** _____

_____

Go to MY SCIENCE ⓢ COACH *online for help with this subject.*

17 Study Guide

To use resources wisely, people can reuse or _____ materials and they can properly dispose of hazardous wastes and other _____.

LESSON 1 Introduction to Environmental Issues

🔑 Environmental issues fall into three main categories: resource use, population growth, and pollution.

🔑 To balance opinions, decision makers weigh the costs and benefits of a proposal.

Vocabulary
• natural resource • pollution
• point source • nonpoint source
• environmental science

LESSON 2 Introduction to Natural Resources

🔑 Natural resources include organisms, water, sunlight, minerals, and oil.

🔑 Humans depend on Earth's natural resources for survival and for development.

Vocabulary
• renewable resource • nonrenewable resource
• sustainable use • ecological footprint
• conservation

LESSON 3 Conserving Land and Soil

🔑 Three uses that change the land are agriculture, mining, and development.

🔑 Without soil, most life on land could not exist. Poor soil management results in three problems: erosion, nutrient depletion, and desertification.

Vocabulary
• litter • topsoil • subsoil • bedrock
• erosion • nutrient depletion • fertilizer
• desertification • drought • land reclamation

LESSON 4 Waste Disposal and Recycling

🔑 Solid waste is burned, buried, or recycled.

🔑 Recycling categories include metal, glass, paper, and plastic.

🔑 Hazardous wastes are stored depending on the type and potential danger.

Vocabulary
• municipal solid waste • incineration
• pollutant • leachate • sanitary landfill
• recycling • biodegradeable • hazardous waste

LESSON 5 Air Pollution and Solutions

🔑 A major source of outdoor air pollution is vehicle emissions. Indoor air pollution has a variety of causes.

🔑 The major cause of the ozone hole is CFCs.

🔑 Reducing air pollution requires reducing emissions.

Vocabulary
• emissions • photochemical smog • ozone
• temperature inversion • acid rain
• radon • ozone layer • chlorofluorocarbon

LESSON 6 Water Pollution and Solutions

🔑 Earth's water is about 97 percent salt water.

🔑 Most water pollution is caused by human activities.

🔑 The keys to keeping water clean include cleaning oil spills, proper sewage treatment, and the reduction of pollutants.

Vocabulary
• groundwater • pesticide • sewage • sediment

684 Land, Air, and Water Resources

Review and Assessment

LESSON 1 Introduction to Environmental Issues

1. Coal and sunlight are examples of

   a. environmental sciences.

   b. pollution.

   c. natural resources.

   d. extinction.

2. _____ can take many forms, including chemical wastes, noise, heat, and light.

3. Relate Cause and Effect Fill in the blank circles with the other main categories of environmental issues. How are they related?

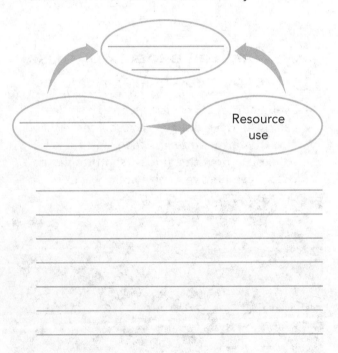

Resource use

_____

_____

_____

_____

_____

_____

4. **Write About It** Suppose your town is considering building a new coal-burning power plant. The benefits of the new facility include providing power and jobs for the town's growing population. What are some of the costs of this project? What do you think your town should do?

LESSON 2 Introduction to Natural Resources

5. Which of the following actions can increase an individual's ecological footprint?

   a. riding a bicycle more often

   b. reducing the use of plastic bags

   c. reusing materials before disposal

   d. turning on the air conditioner

6. Like oil, metals are an example of

_____

7. Apply Concepts When is water a renewable resource? When is it nonrenewable?

_____

_____

_____

_____

LESSON 3 Conserving Land and Soil

8. What is an agricultural use of land?

   a. growing crops on land

   b. collecting water from land

   c. building structures on land

   d. removing minerals from land

9. Plant roots absorb nutrients and water from the layer of soil called _____.

10. Relate Cause and Effect What type of land use can result in nutrient depletion? Explain.

_____

_____

_____

_____

685

LESSON 4 Waste Disposal and Recycling

11. What is one benefit of recycling?

   a. It increases the volume of solid waste.

   b. If it is recycled, a material won't biodegrade.

   c. It conserves resources and energy.

   d. It uses more raw materials that need to be mined.

12. A _____ is a waste that can be harmful to human health or the environment.

13. 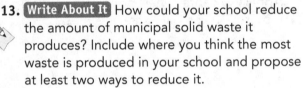 **Write About It** How could your school reduce the amount of municipal solid waste it produces? Include where you think the most waste is produced in your school and propose at least two ways to reduce it.

LESSON 5 Air Pollution and Solutions

14. Which of the following describes a pollutant that has been released into the air?

   a. sewage   **b.** leachate

   c. sediment   **d.** emissions

15. The _____ in the upper atmosphere prevents some of the sun's ultraviolet radiation from reaching Earth.

16. Predict Do you think the hole in the ozone layer will increase or decrease in size? Why?

_____

_____

_____

LESSON 6 Water Pollution and Solutions

17. Why is fresh water a limited resource?

   a. because most water on Earth is in lakes

   b. because most water on Earth is in clouds

   c. because most water on Earth is in the ground

   d. because most water on Earth is salt water

18. A _____ is a chemical that kills crop-destroying organisms.

19. Draw Conclusions Rain may wash fertilizers into bodies of water, such as ponds. How might fertilizer affect a pond?

_____

_____

APPLY THE BIG ? What can people do to use resources wisely?

20. Every individual, including young people, can make decisions to use resources wisely. **Use the terms *reduce*, *reuse*, and *recycle* to explain how the students in the picture below can help minimize solid waste.**

_____

_____

_____

_____

Standardized Test Prep

Multiple Choice

Circle the letter of the best answer.

1. According to the circle graph, what is the most common method of waste disposal in the United States?

Methods of Waste Disposal in the U.S.

33%

54%

13%

Landfills
Recycling
Incineration

A composting   B recycling
C incineration   D landfills

2. In which layer of soil would you expect to find rock fragments, nutrients, and decaying plant and animal matter?

A litter   B topsoil
C subsoil   D bedrock

3. What types of materials could be broken down in a compost pile?

A all recyclable materials
B biodegradable materials
C all materials that can be incinerated
D glass, metal, and other raw materials

4. How can sediments negatively affect an aquatic ecosystem?

A by blocking sunlight
B by causing algae to grow
C by causing plants to grow
D by changing the water temperature

5. What are the main sources of ocean pollution?

A upwellings
B natural causes
C human activities
D waves of sunlight reacting with water

Constructed Response

Use the diagram below and your knowledge of science to help you answer Question 6. Write your answer on a separate sheet of paper.

6. Compare and contrast the role of ozone in each of the images shown above.

Please Don't Pass the Plastic!

An ecosystem includes all the plants, animals, and nonliving resources in a given area. The organisms interact with each other and with all the nonliving components of their ecosystem. The flow of nutrients and energy through food chains and food webs is part of how the organisms and nonliving materials interact. But when did plastic—a nonliving, chemical-based, human-made material—enter the food chain?

Only since the 1940s have plastics become part of our everyday life. Today, large numbers of plastic bags, bottles, caps, and other trash end up in streams, rivers, ponds, landfills, and the ocean. Researchers exploring the remotest areas of Antarctica and the deepest sea trenches have found plastic litter and fragments!

Scientists have identified over 180 species that ingest plastic debris. Birds, fish, crustaceans, turtles, mollusks, plankton, and marine mammals are most susceptible to ingesting different-sized pieces of plastic, from large to microscopic. Many more species are at risk of absorbing harmful chemicals that have leached from plastics. Plastic debris may remain undigested inside an animal—filling the stomach or blocking digestive passages, and contributing to illness or even starvation. Organisms may also be choked or injured by getting tangled in plastic bags or strapping.

Model It Research how waste plastics spread and build up in different ecosystems and in the food chain. Make models of two ecosystems in different locations, comparing and contrasting the organisms in each model that plastic waste may affect. Suggest ways that humans can keep plastics out of the world's environments.

The Big Uncool

When you have a fever, it may last a day or two. But when Earth's atmosphere has a rising temperature, what can be done to reverse it? If the average global atmospheric temperature rises even a few degrees, it could cause major disruptions in climate patterns around the world. This could have devastating effects on the environment and on society.

Greenhouse gases enter the atmosphere both naturally and from human activities. But since the Industrial Revolution, industrial growth—driven by demand from increasing population and development—has caused more and more greenhouse gases, especially CO_2, to enter the atmosphere.

Where does all the CO_2 come from? There are many sources, but the largest has been the burning of fossil fuels—coal, oil, and natural gas. The possibility of major climate changes highlights the importance of developing other fuel sources to power our vehicles, homes, farms, and industries.

Debate It Does driving or riding in an electric vehicle help reduce carbon dioxide and other greenhouse gases in the atmosphere? Vehicles that burn nonrenewable fossil fuels are the second largest contributor of CO_2 to the atmosphere. But up to 70 percent of the electricity in the U.S. is also produced by the burning of fossil fuels. Research more about this question and participate in a class debate about whether switching to electric vehicles can help reduce CO_2 emissions.

CO_2 Emissions From Fossil Fuel Combustion

- Electricity Generation 42%
- Transportation 33%
- Industry 17%
- Homes 5%
- Commercial Buildings 2%
- Other 1%

APPENDIX A

Star Charts

Use these star charts to locate bright stars and major constellations in the night sky at different times of year. Choose the appropriate star chart for the current season.

Autumn Sky This chart works best at the following dates and times: September 1 at 10:00 P.M., October 1 at 8:00 P.M., or November 1 at 6:00 P.M. Look for the constellations Ursa Minor (the Little Dipper) and Cassiopeia in the northern sky, and for the star Deneb, which is nearly overhead in autumn.

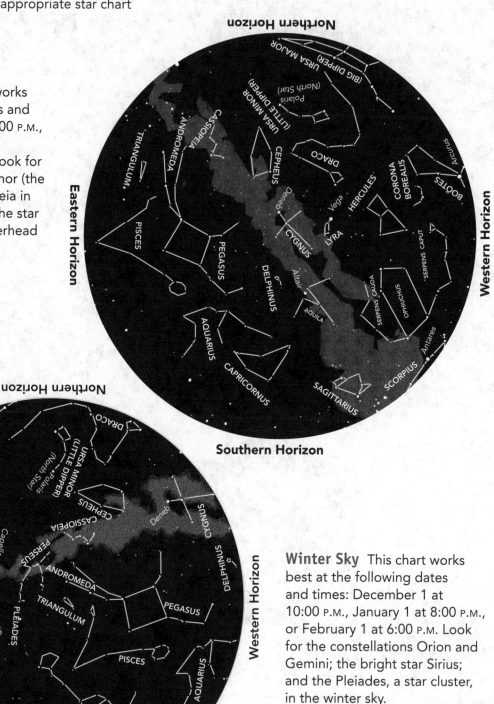

Winter Sky This chart works best at the following dates and times: December 1 at 10:00 P.M., January 1 at 8:00 P.M., or February 1 at 6:00 P.M. Look for the constellations Orion and Gemini; the bright star Sirius; and the Pleiades, a star cluster, in the winter sky.

How to Use the Star Charts

Using a flashlight and a compass, hold the appropriate chart and turn it so that the direction you are facing is at the bottom of the chart. These star charts work best at 34° north latitude, but can be used at other central latitudes.

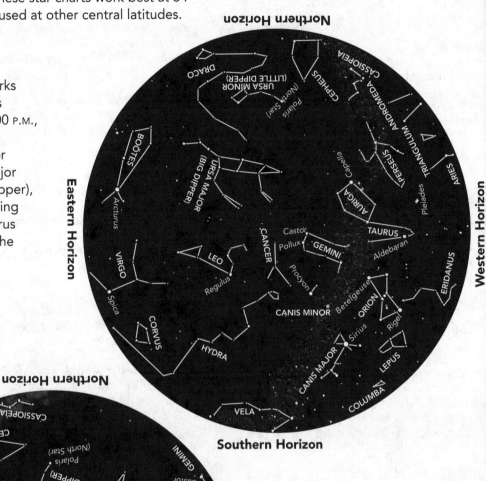

Spring Sky This chart works best at the following dates and times: March 1 at 10:00 P.M., March 15 at 9:00 P.M., or April 1 at 8:00 P.M. Look for the constellations Ursa Major (which contains the Big Dipper), Boötes, and Leo in the spring sky. The bright stars Arcturus and Spica can be seen in the east.

Summer Sky This chart works best at the following dates and times: May 15 at 11:00 P.M., June 1 at 10:00 P.M., or June 15 at 9:00 P.M. Look for the bright star Arcturus in the constellation Boötes overhead in early summer. Toward the east, look for the bright stars Vega, Altair, and Deneb, which form a triangle.

691

GLOSSARY

A

abrasion The grinding away of rock by other rock particles carried in water, ice, or wind. (183)
abrasión Tipo de desgaste de la roca por otras partículas de roca transportadas por el agua, el viento o el hielo.

absolute age The age of a rock given as the number of years since the rock formed. (253)
edad absoluta Edad de una roca basada en el número de años de su formación.

absolute brightness The brightness a star would have if it were at a standard distance from Earth. (611)
magnitud absoluta Brillo que tendría una estrella si estuviera a una distancia estándar de la Tierra.

abyssal plain A smooth, nearly flat region of the deep ocean floor. (351)
llanura abisal Región llana, casi plana, de la cuenca oceánica profunda.

acid rain Rain or another form of precipitation that is more acidic than normal, caused by the release of molecules of sulfur dioxide and nitrogen oxide into the air. (669)
lluvia ácida Lluvia u otra forma de precipitación que es más ácida de lo normal, debido a la contaminación del aire con moléculas de dióxido de azufre y óxido de nitrógeno.

aerosols Solid particles or liquid droplets in the atmosphere. (491)
aerosoles Partículas sólidas o gotas de líquido en la atmósfera.

air mass A huge body of air that has similar temperature, humidity, and air pressure at any given height. (435)
masa de aire Gran cuerpo de aire que tiene temperatura, humedad y presión similares en todos sus puntos.

air pressure The pressure caused by the weight of a column of air pushing down on an area. (381)
presión de aire Presión causada por el peso de una columna de aire en un área.

alluvial fan A wide, sloping deposit of sediment formed where a stream leaves a mountain range. (218)
abanico aluvial Depósito de sedimento ancho e inclinado que se forma donde un arroyo sale de una cordillera.

altitude Elevation above sea level. (384)
altitud Elevación sobre el nivel del mar.

amphibian A vertebrate whose body temperature is determined by the temperature of its environment, and that lives its early life in water and its adult life on land. (273)
anfibio Animal vertebrado cuya temperatura corporal depende de la temperatura de su entorno, y que vive la primera etapa de su vida en el agua y su vida adulta en la tierra.

anemometer An instrument used to measure wind speed. (404)
anemómetro Instrumento que se usa para medir la velocidad del viento.

aneroid barometer An instrument that measures changes in air pressure without using a liquid. (383)
barómetro aneroide Instrumento que mide los cambios en la presión del aire sin usar líquidos.

anticyclone A high-pressure center of dry air. (440)
anticiclón Centro de aire seco de alta presión.

apparent brightness The brightness of a star as seen from Earth. (611)
magnitud aparente Brillo de una estrella vista desde la Tierra.

aquifer An underground layer of rock or sediment that holds water. (343)
acuífero Capa subterránea de roca o sedimento que retiene agua.

artesian well A well in which water rises because of pressure within the aquifer. (345)
pozo artesiano Pozo por el que el agua se eleva debido a la presión dentro del acuífero.

asteroid One of the rocky objects revolving around the sun that are too small and numerous to be considered planets. (586)
asteroide Uno de los cuerpos rocosos que se mueven alrededor del Sol y que son demasiado pequeños y numerosos como para ser considerados planetas.

asteroid belt The region of the solar system between the orbits of Mars and Jupiter, where many asteroids are found. (583)
cinturón de asteroides Región del sistema solar entre las órbitas de Marte y Júpiter, donde se encuentran muchos asteroides.

asthenosphere The soft layer of the mantle on which the lithosphere floats. (14)
astenósfera Capa suave del manto en la que flota la litósfera.

astronomical unit A unit of distance equal to the average distance between Earth and the sun, about 150 million kilometers. (555)
unidad astronómica Unidad de medida equivalente a la distancia media entre la Tierra y el Sol, aproximadamente 150 millones de kilómetros.

atmosphere The relatively thin layer of gases that form Earth's outermost layer. (376)
atmósfera Capa de gases relativamente delgada que forma la capa exterior de la Tierra.

axis An imaginary line that passes through a planet's center and its north and south poles, about which the planet rotates. (515)
eje Línea imaginaria alrededor de la cual gira un planeta, y que atraviesa su centro y sus dos polos, norte y sur.

B

barometer An instrument used to measure changes in air pressure. (382)
barómetro Instrumento que se usa para medir cambios de la presión del aire.

basalt A dark, dense, igneous rock with a fine texture, found in oceanic crust. (13, 63)
basalto Roca ígnea, oscura y densa, de textura lisa, que se encuentra en la corteza oceánica.

batholith A mass of rock formed when a large body of magma cools inside the crust. (169)
batolito Masa de roca formada cuando una gran masa de magma se enfría dentro de la corteza terrestre.

beach Wave-washed sediment along a coast. (230)
playa Sedimento depositado por las olas a lo largo de una costa.

bedrock Rock that makes up Earth's crust; also the solid rock layer beneath the soil. (189, 654)
lecho rocoso Roca que compone la corteza terrestre; también, la capa sólida de roca debajo del suelo.

big bang The initial explosion that resulted in the formation and expansion of the universe. (626)
Big bang Explosión inicial que resultó en la formación y expansión del universo.

binary star A star system with two stars. (621)
estrella binaria Sistema estelar de dos estrellas.

biodegradable Capable of being broken down by bacteria and other decomposers. (662)
biodegradable Sustancia que las bacterias y otros descomponedores pueden descomponer.

biomass fuel Fuel made from living things. (304)
combustible de biomasa Combustible creado a partir de seres vivos.

biosphere The parts of Earth that contain living organisms. (7)

biósfera Partes de la Tierra que contienen organismos vivos.

black hole An object whose gravity is so strong that nothing, not even light, can escape. (619)
agujero negro Cuerpo cuya gravedad es tan fuerte que nada, ni siquiera la luz, puede escapar.

C

caldera The large hole at the top of a volcano formed when the roof of a volcano's magma chamber collapses. (165)
caldera Gran agujero en la parte superior de un volcán que se forma cuando la tapa de la cámara magmática de un volcán se desploma.

calendar A system of organizing time that defines the beginning, length, and divisions of a year. (516)
calendario Sistema de organización del tiempo que define el principio, la duración y las divisiones de un año.

carbon film A type of fossil consisting of an extremely thin coating of carbon on rock. (248)
película de carbono Tipo de fósil que consiste en una capa de carbono extremadamente fina que recubre la roca.

cast A fossil that is a solid copy of an organism's shape, formed when minerals seep into a mold. (248)
vaciado Fósil que es una copia sólida de la forma de un organismo y que se forma cuando los minerales se filtran y crean un molde.

cementation The process by which dissolved minerals crystallize and glue particles of sediment together into one mass. (71)
cementación Proceso mediante el cual minerales disueltos se cristalizan y forman una masa de partículas de sedimento.

chemical rock Sedimentary rock that forms when minerals crystallize from a solution. (74)
roca química Roca sedimentaria que se forma cuando los minerales de una solución se cristalizan.

chemical weathering The process that breaks down rock through chemical changes. (182)
desgaste químico Proceso que erosiona la roca mediante cambios químicos.

chlorofluorocarbons Human-made gases containing chlorine and fluorine (also called CFCs) that are the main cause of ozone depletion. (672)
clorofluorocarbonos Gases generados por el hombre, que contienen cloro y flúor (también llamados CFC) y que son la causa principal del deterioro de la capa de ozono.

GLOSSARY

chromosphere The middle layer of the sun's atmosphere. (562)
cromósfera Capa central de la atmósfera solar.

cinder cone A steep, cone-shaped hill or small mountain made of volcanic ash, cinders, and bombs piled up around a volcano's opening. (166)
cono de escoria Colina o pequeña montaña escarpada en forma de cono que se forma cuando ceniza volcánica, escoria y bombas se acumulan alrededor del cráter de un volcán.

cirrus Wispy, feathery clouds made of ice crystals that form at high levels. (426)
cirros Nubes que parecen plumas o pinceladas y que están formadas por cristales de hielo que se crean a grandes alturas.

clastic rock Sedimentary rock that forms when rock fragments are squeezed together under high pressure. (72)
roca clástica Roca sedimentaria que se forma cuando fragmentos de roca se unen bajo gran presión.

cleavage A mineral's ability to split easily along flat surfaces. (57)
exfoliación Facilidad con la que un mineral se divide en capas planas.

climate The average annual conditions of temperature, precipitation, winds, and clouds in an area. (362, 469)
clima Condiciones promedio anuales de temperatura, precipitación, viento y nubosidad de un área.

coma The fuzzy outer layer of a comet. (585)
coma Capa exterior y difusa de un cometa.

comet A loose collection of ice and dust that orbits the sun, typically in a long, narrow orbit. (268, 509, 585)
cometa Cuerpo poco denso de hielo y polvo que orbita alrededor del Sol. Generalmente su órbita es larga y estrecha.

compaction The process by which sediments are pressed together under their own weight. (71)
compactación Proceso mediante el cual los sedimentos se unen por la presión de su propio peso.

composite volcano A tall, cone-shaped mountain in which layers of lava alternate with layers of ash and other volcanic materials. (166)
volcán compuesto Montaña alta en forma de cono en la que las capas de lava se alternan con capas de ceniza y otros materiales volcánicos.

compression 1. Stress that squeezes rock until it folds or breaks. (121) 2. The part of a longitudinal wave where the particles of the medium are close together.

compresión 1. Fuerza que oprime una roca hasta que se pliega o se rompe. 2. Parte de una onda longitudinal en la que las partículas del medio están más cerca.

condensation The change in state from a gas to a liquid. (420)
condensación Cambio del estado gaseoso al estado líquido.

conduction 1. The transfer of thermal energy from one particle of matter to another. (19, 400) 2. A method of charging an object by allowing electrons to flow from one object to another object through direct contact.
conducción 1. Transferencia de energía térmica de una partícula de materia a otra. 2. Método de transferencia de electricidad que consiste en permitir que los electrones fluyan por contacto directo de un cuerpo a otro.

conservation The practice of using less of a resource so that it can last longer. (651)
conservación Práctica que consiste en reducir el uso de un recurso para prolongar su duración.

conservation plowing Soil conservation method in which weeds and dead stalks from the previous year's crop are plowed into the ground. (197)
arado de conservación Método de conservación de la tierra en el que las plantas y los tallos muertos de la cosecha del año anterior se dejan en la tierra al ararla.

constellation A pattern or grouping of stars that people imagine to represent a figure or object. (510)
constelación Patrón de estrellas que se dice se asemeja a una figura u objeto.

constructive force Any natural process that builds up Earth's surface. (8)
fuerza constructiva Proceso natural que incrementa la superficie de la Tierra.

continental (air mass) A dry air mass that forms over land. (435)
masa de aire continental Masa de aire seco que se forma sobre la Tierra.

continental climate The climate of the centers of continents, with cold winters and warm or hot summers. (472)
clima continental Clima del centro de los continentes, con inviernos fríos y veranos templados o calurosos.

continental drift The hypothesis that the continents slowly move across Earth's surface. (95)
deriva continental Hipótesis que sostiene que los continentes se desplazan lentamente sobre la superficie de la Tierra.

continental glacier A glacier that covers much of a continent or large island. (223)
glaciar continental Glaciar que cubre gran parte de un continente o una isla grande.

continental shelf A gently sloping, shallow area of the ocean floor that extends outward from the edge of a continent. (350)
plataforma continental Área poco profunda con pendiente suave en la cuenca oceánica que se extiende desde los márgenes de un continente.

continental slope A steep incline of the ocean floor leading down from the edge of the continental shelf. (350)
talud continental Región de la cuenca oceánica con pendiente empinada que baja del borde de la plataforma continental.

contour interval The difference in elevation from one contour line to the next. (37)
intervalo entre curvas de nivel Diferencia de elevación de una curva de nivel a la próxima.

contour line A line on a topographic map that connects points of equal elevation. (37)
curva de nivel Línea de un mapa topográfico que conecta puntos con la misma elevación.

contour plowing Plowing fields along the curves of a slope to prevent soil loss. (197)
arado en contorno Arar los campos siguiendo las curvas de una pendiente para evitar la pérdida del suelo.

control rod A cadmium rod used in a nuclear reactor to absorb neutrons from fission reactions. (308)
varilla de control Varilla de cadmio que se usa en un reactor nuclear para absorber los neutrones emitidos por reacciones de fisión.

convection The transfer of thermal energy by the movement of a fluid. (19, 400)
convección Transferencia de energía térmica por el movimiento de un líquido.

convection current The movement of a fluid, caused by differences in temperature, that transfers heat from one part of the fluid to another. (20, 401)
corriente de convección Movimiento de un líquido ocasionado por diferencias de temperatura y que transfiere calor de un área del líquido a otra.

convection zone The outermost layer of the sun's interior. (561)
zona de convección Capa más superficial del interior del Sol.

convergent boundary A plate boundary where two plates move toward each other. (105)

borde convergente Borde de una placa donde dos placas se deslizan una hacia la otra.

convex lens A lens that is thicker in the center than at the edges. (600)
lente convexa Lente que es más gruesa en el centro que en los extremos.

core The central region of the sun, where nuclear fusion takes place. (561)
núcleo Región central del Sol, donde ocurre la fusión nuclear.

Coriolis effect The effect of Earth's rotation on the direction of winds and currents. (361, 407)
efecto Coriolis Efecto de la rotación de la Tierra sobre la dirección de los vientos y las corrientes.

corona The outer layer of the sun's atmosphere. (563)
corona Capa externa de la atmósfera solar.

cosmic background radiation The electromagnetic radiation left over from the big bang. (627)
radiación cósmica de fondo Radiación electromagnética que quedó del Big bang.

crater 1. A large round pit caused by the impact of a meteoroid. 2. A bowl-shaped area that forms around a volcano's central opening. (157, 537)
cráter 1. Gran hoyo redondo que se forma por el impacto de un meteorito. 2. Área en forma de tazón que se forma en la abertura central de un volcán.

crop rotation The planting of different crops in a field each year to maintain the soil's fertility. (197)
rotación de las cosechas Cultivo anual de cosechas diferentes en un campo para mantener la fertilidad del suelo.

crust The layer of rock that forms Earth's outer surface. (13)
corteza terrestre Capa de rocas que forma la superficie externa de la Tierra.

crystal A solid in which the atoms are arranged in a pattern that repeats again and again. (51)
cristal Cuerpo sólido en el que los átomos siguen un patrón que se repite una y otra vez.

crystallization The process by which atoms are arranged to form a material with a crystal structure. (58)
cristalización Proceso mediante el cual los átomos se distribuyen y forman materiales con estructura de cristal.

cumulus Fluffy, white clouds, usually with flat bottoms, that look like rounded piles of cotton. (426)
cúmulos Nubes blancas, normalmente con la parte inferior plana, que parecen grandes masas de algodón esponjosas y redondas.

GLOSSARY

current A large stream of moving water that flows through the oceans. (361)
  corriente Gran volumen de agua que fluye por los océanos.

cyclone A swirling center of low air pressure. (440)
  ciclón Centro de un remolino de aire de baja presión.

D
---

dark energy A mysterious force that appears to be causing the expansion of the universe to accelerate. (628)
  energía negra Misteriosa fuerza que parece acelerar la expansión del universo.

dark matter Matter that does not give off electromagnetic radiation but is quite abundant in the universe. (628)
  materia negra Materia que es muy abundante en el universo y no despide radiación electromagnética.

decomposer An organism that gets energy by breaking down biotic wastes and dead organisms, and returns raw materials to the soil and water. (192)
  descomponedor Organismo que obtiene energía al descomponer desechos bióticos y organismos muertos, y que devuelve materia prima al suelo y al agua.

deep-ocean trench A deep valley along the ocean floor beneath which oceanic crust slowly sinks toward the mantle. (102)
  fosa oceánica profunda Valle profundo a lo largo del suelo oceánico debajo del cual la corteza oceánica se hunde lentamente hacia el manto.

deflation The process by which wind removes surface materials. (233)
  deflación Proceso por el cual el viento se lleva materiales de la superficie.

degree A unit used to measure distances around a circle. One degree equals 1/360 of a full circle. (32)
  grado Unidad usada para medir distancias alrededor de un círculo. Un grado es igual a 1/360 de un círculo completo.

delta A landform made of sediment that is deposited where a river flows into an ocean or lake. (218)
  delta Accidente geográfico formado por sedimento que se deposita en la desembocadura de un río a un océano o lago.

density The measurement of how much mass of a substance is contained in a given volume. (20, 381)
  densidad Medida de la masa de una sustancia que tiene un volumen dado.

deposition Process in which sediment is laid down in new locations. (71, 209)
  sedimentación Proceso por el cual los sedimentos se asientan en nuevos sitios.

desert A dry region that on average receives less than 25 centimeters of precipitation per year. (481)
  desierto Región seca en la que se registra un promedio menor de 25 centímetros de precipitación anual.

desertification The advance of desert-like conditions into areas that previously were fertile; caused by overfarming, overgrazing, drought, and climate change. (656)
  desertificación Paso de condiciones desérticas a áreas que eran fértiles; resulta de la agricultura descontrolada, el uso exagerado de los pastos, las sequías y los cambios climáticos.

destructive force Any natural process that tears down or wears away Earth's surface. (9)
  fuerza constructiva Proceso natural que destruye o desgasta la superficie de la Tierra.

dew point The temperature at which condensation begins. (425)
  punto de rocío Temperatura a la que comienza la condensación.

dike A slab of volcanic rock formed when magma forces itself across rock layers. (168)
  dique discordante Placa de roca volcánica formada cuando el magma se abre paso a través de las capas de roca.

divergent boundary A plate boundary where two plates move away from each other. (105)
  borde divergente Borde de una placa donde dos placas se separan.

divide A ridge of land that separates one watershed from another. (335)
  divisoria Elevación de terreno que separa una cuenca hidrográfica de otra.

dormant Not currently active but able to become active in the future (as with a volcano). (162)
  inactivo Que no está activo en la actualidad pero puede ser activo en el futuro (como un volcán).

drought A long period of low precipitation. (433, 656)
  sequía Período prolongado de baja precipitación.

dwarf planet An object that orbits the sun and is spherical, but has not cleared the area of its orbit. (556)
  planeta enano Un cuerpo esférico que orbita alrededor del Sol, pero que no ha despejado las proximidades de su órbita.

E

earthquake The shaking that results from the movement of rock beneath Earth's surface. (129)
terremoto Temblor que resulta del movimiento de la roca debajo de la superficie de la Tierra.

eclipse The partial or total blocking of one object in space by another. (529)
eclipse Bloqueo parcial o total de un cuerpo en el espacio por otro.

eclipsing binary A binary star system in which one star periodically blocks the light from the other. (621)
eclipse binario Sistema estelar binario en el que una estrella bloquea periódicamente la luz de la otra.

ecological footprint The amount of land and water that individuals use to meet their resource needs and to absorb the wastes that they produce. (650)
espacio ecológico Cantidad de tierra y agua que los individuos usan para cubrir sus necesidades y absorber sus desechos.

efficiency The percentage of input work that is converted to output work. (313)
eficacia Porcentaje de trabajo aportado que se convierte en trabajo producido.

El Niño An abnormal climate event that occurs every two to seven years in the Pacific Ocean, causing changes in winds, currents, and weather patterns for one to two years. (363)
El Niño Suceso climático anormal que se presenta cada dos a siete años en el océano Pacífico y que causa cambios de vientos, corrientes y patrones meteorológicos que duran uno o dos años.

electromagnetic radiation The energy transferred through space by electromagnetic waves. (598)
radiación electromagnética Energía transferida a través del espacio por ondas electromagnéticas.

electromagnetic wave 1. A wave made up of a combination of a changing electric field and a changing magnetic field. 2. A wave that can transfer electric and magnetic energy through the vacuum of space. (392)
onda electromagnética 1. Onda formada por la combinación de un campo eléctrico cambiante y un campo magnético cambiante. 2. Onda que puede transportar energía eléctrica y magnética a través del vacío del espacio.

elevation Height above sea level. (22)
elevación Altura sobre el nivel del mar.

ellipse An oval shape, which may be elongated or nearly circular; the shape of the planets' orbits. (553)

elipse Forma ovalada que puede ser alargada o casi circular; la forma de la órbita de los planetas.

elliptical galaxy A galaxy shaped like a round or flattened ball, generally containing only old stars. (624)
galaxia elíptica Galaxia de forma redonda o semejante a una pelota desinflada, que generalmente sólo contiene estrellas viejas.

emissions Pollutants that are released into the air. (667)
gases contaminantes Contaminantes liberados al aire.

energy The ability to do work or cause change. (5)
energía Capacidad para realizar un trabajo o producir cambios.

energy conservation The practice of reducing energy use. (315)
conservación de energía Práctica de reducción del uso de energía.

environmental science The study of the natural processes that occur in the environment and how humans can affect them. (644)
ciencias del medio ambiente Estudio de los procesos naturales que ocurren en el medio ambiente y de cómo los seres humanos pueden afectarlos.

epicenter The point on Earth's surface directly above an earthquake's focus. (130)
epicentro Punto de la superficie de la Tierra directamente sobre el foco de un terremoto.

equator An imaginary line that circles Earth halfway between the North and South poles. (33)
ecuador Línea imaginaria que rodea la Tierra por el centro, equidistante de los Polos Norte y Sur.

equinox Either of the two days of the year on which neither hemisphere is tilted toward or away from the sun. (520)
equinoccio Cualquiera de los de dos días del año en el que ningún hemisferio se retrae o inclina hacia el Sol.

era One of the three long units of geologic time between the Precambrian and the present. (265)
era Cada una de las tres unidades largas del tiempo geológico entre el Precámbrico y el presente.

erosion The process by which water, ice, wind, or gravity moves weathered particles of rock and soil. (71, 181, 208, 655)
erosión Proceso por el cual el agua, el hielo, el viento o la gravedad desplazan partículas desgastadas de roca y suelo.

GLOSSARY

eutrophication The buildup over time of nutrients in freshwater lakes and ponds that leads to an increase in the growth of algae. (338)
eutroficación Acumulación gradual de nutrientes en lagos y estanques de agua dulce que produce un aumento en el crecimiento de algas.

evacuate Moving away temporarily from an area about to be affected by severe weather. (450)
evacuar Desalojar temporalmente un área que será afectada por mal tiempo.

evaporation The process by which molecules at the surface of a liquid absorb enough energy to change to a gas. (330, 420)
evaporación Proceso mediante el cual las moléculas en la superficie de un líquido absorben suficiente energía para pasar al estado gaseoso.

evolution Change over time; the process by which modern organisms have descended from ancient organisms. (251)
evolución Cambios a través del tiempo; proceso por el cual los organismos modernos se originaron a partir de organismos antiguos.

exosphere The outer layer of the thermosphere. (391)
exósfera Capa externa de la termósfera.

extinct 1. Term used to refer to a group of related organisms that has died out and has no living members. (251) **2.** Term used to describe a volcano that is no longer active and unlikely to erupt again. (162)
extinto 1. Término que se refiere a un grupo de organismos que ha muerto y del cual no queda ningún miembro vivo. **2.** Término que describe un volcán que ya no es activo y es poco probable que vuelva a hacer erupción.

extrusion An igneous rock layer formed when lava flows onto Earth's surface and hardens. (254)
extrusión Capa de roca ígnea formada cuando la lava fluye hacia la superficie de la Tierra y se endurece.

extrusive rock Igneous rock that forms from lava on Earth's surface. (67)
roca extrusiva Roca ígnea que se forma de la lava en la superficie de la Tierra.

F

fault A break in Earth's crust along which rocks move. (107, 254)
falla Fisura en la corteza terrestre a lo largo de la cual se desplazan las rocas.

fertility A measure of how well soil supports plant growth. (190)
fertilidad Medida de cuán apropiado es un suelo para estimular el crecimiento de las plantas.

fertilizer A substance that provides nutrients to help crops grow better. (655)
fertilizante Sustancia que proporciona nutrientes para ayudar a que crezcan mejor los cultivos.

flood An overflowing of water in a normally dry area. (432)
inundación Ocupación de agua en un área que habitualmente permanece seca.

flood plain The flat, wide area of land along a river. (216)
llanura de aluvión Área de tierra extensa y plana a lo largo de un río.

focus The point beneath Earth's surface where rock first breaks under stress and causes an earthquake. (130)
foco Punto debajo de la superficie de la Tierra en el que la roca empieza a romperse debido a una gran fuerza y causa un terremoto.

foliated Term used to describe metamorphic rocks that have grains arranged in parallel layers or bands. (78)
foliación Término que describe las rocas metamórficas con granos dispuestos en capas paralelas o bandas.

force A push or pull exerted on an object. (522)
fuerza Empuje o atracción que se ejerce sobre un cuerpo.

fossil The preserved remains or traces of an organism that lived in the past. (96, 247)
fósil Restos o vestigios conservados de un organismo que vivió en el pasado.

fossil fuel Coal, oil, or natural gas that forms over millions of years from the remains of ancient organisms; burned to release energy. (293, 494)
combustible fósil Carbón, petróleo o gas natural que se forma a lo largo de millones de años a partir de los restos de organismos antiguos; se queman para liberar energía.

fracture 1. The way a mineral looks when it breaks apart in an irregular way. (57) **2.** A break in a bone.
fractura 1. Apariencia de un mineral cuando se rompe de manera irregular. **2.** Fisura de un hueso.

frequency The number of complete waves that pass a given point in a certain amount of time. (354)
frecuencia Número de ondas completas que pasan por un punto dado en cierto tiempo.

front The boundary where unlike air masses meet but do not mix. (437)
frente Límite donde se encuentran, pero no se mezclan, masas de aire diferentes.

frost wedging Process that splits rock when water seeps into cracks, then freezes and expands. (183)
acuñado rocoso Proceso que separa las rocas cuando el agua se filtra entre grietas y luego se congela y expande.

fuel rod A uranium rod that undergoes fission in a nuclear reactor. (308)
varilla de combustible Varilla de uranio que se somete a la fisión en un reactor nuclear.

fuel A substance that provides energy as the result of a chemical change. (293)
combustible Sustancia que libera energía como resultado de un cambio químico.

G
---

galaxy A huge group of single stars, star systems, star clusters, dust, and gas bound together by gravity. (624)
galaxia Enorme grupo de estrellas individuales, sistemas estelares, cúmulos de estrellas, polvo y gases unidos por la gravedad.

gas giant The name often given to the outer planets: Jupiter, Saturn, Uranus, and Neptune. (574)
gigantes gaseosos Nombre que normalmente se da a los cuatro planetas exteriores: Júpiter, Saturno, Urano y Neptuno.

gasohol A mixture of gasoline and alcohol. (304)
gasohol Mezcla de gasolina y alcohol.

geocentric Term describing a model of the universe in which Earth is at the center of the revolving planets and stars. (551)
geocéntrico Término que describe un modelo del universo en el cual la Tierra se encuentra al centro de los planetas y estrellas que circulan a su alrededor.

geode A hollow rock inside which mineral crystals have grown. (58)
geoda Roca hueca dentro de la que se forman cristales minerales.

geologic time scale A record of the geologic events and life forms in Earth's history. (263)
escala de tiempo geológico Registro de los sucesos geológicos y de las formas de vida en la historia de la Tierra.

geosphere The densest parts of Earth that include the crust, mantle, and core. (6)
geósfera Partes más densas de la Tierra que incluye la corteza, el manto y el núcleo.

geothermal energy The intense heat energy that comes from Earth's interior. (305)
energía geotérmica Energía intensa que proviene del interior de la Tierra.

glacier Any large mass of ice that moves slowly over land. (223)
glaciar Cualquier masa grande de hielo que se desplaza lentamente sobre la tierra.

global warming A gradual increase in the average temperature of the atmosphere, thought to be caused by an increase in greenhouse gases from human activities. (494)
calentamiento global Aumento gradual de la temperatura promedio de la atmósfera cuya causa se piensa que es el aumento de emisiones de gases de efecto invernadero ocasionados por actividades humanas.

global winds Winds that blow steadily from specific directions over long distances. (406)
vientos globales Vientos que soplan constantemente desde direcciones específicas por largas distancias.

globe A sphere that represents Earth's entire surface. (29)
globo terráqueo Esfera que representa toda la superficie de la Tierra.

globular cluster A large, round, densely-packed grouping of older stars. (622)
cúmulo globular Conjunto grande y redondo de estrellas viejas densamente agrupadas.

grains The particles of minerals or other rocks that give a rock its texture. (64)
granos Partículas de minerales o de otras rocas que le dan textura a una roca.

granite A usually light-colored igneous rock that is found in continental crust. (13, 63)
granito Roca generalmente de color claro que se encuentra en la corteza continental.

gravity The attractive force between objects; the force that moves objects downhill. (210, 523)
gravedad Fuerza que atrae a los cuerpos entre sí; fuerza que mueve un cuerpo cuesta abajo.

greenhouse effect The trapping of heat near a planet's surface by certain gases in the planet's atmosphere. (397, 570)
efecto invernadero Retención de calor cerca de la superficie de un planeta debido a la presencia de ciertos gases en la atmósfera.

greenhouse gases Gases in the atmosphere that trap energy. (493)
gases de efecto invernadero Gases presentes en la atmósfera que atrapan la energía.

GLOSSARY

groin A wall made of rocks or concrete that is built outward from a beach to reduce erosion. (359)
escollera Pared de piedra o concreto que se construye perpendicularmente a una playa para reducir la erosión.

groundwater Water that fills the cracks and spaces in underground soil and rock layers. (220, 329, 677)
aguas freáticas Agua que llena las grietas y huecos de las capas subterráneas de tierra y roca.

gully A large channel in soil that carries runoff after a rainstorm. (214)
barranco Canal grande en el suelo formado por corrientes de agua durante una tormenta de lluvia.

H

habitat An environment that provides the things a specific organism needs to live, grow, and reproduce. (237)
hábitat Medio que provee lo que un organismo específico necesita para vivir, crecer y reproducirse.

half-life The time it takes for half of the atoms of a radioactive element to decay. (259)
vida media Tiempo que toma descomponer la mitad de los átomos de un elemento radiactivo.

hazardous waste A material that can be harmful if it is not properly disposed of. (664)
desecho peligroso Material que puede ser dañino si no se elimina adecuadamente.

headland A part of the shore that sticks out into the ocean. (229)
promontorio Parte de la costa que se interna en el mar.

heat The transfer of thermal energy from a warmer object to a cooler object. (400)
calor Transferencia de energía térmica de un cuerpo más cálido a uno menos cálido.

heliocentric Term describing a model of the solar system in which Earth and the other planets revolve around the sun. (552)
heliocéntrico Término que describe un modelo del universo en el cual la Tierra y los otros planetas giran alrededor del Sol.

hemisphere One half of the sphere that makes up Earth's surface. (33)
hemisferio Mitad de la esfera que forma la superficie de la Tierra.

hot spot An area where magma from deep within the mantle melts through the crust above it. (155)

punto caliente Área en la que el magma de las profundidades del manto atraviesa la corteza.

Hubble's law The observation that the farther away a galaxy is, the faster it is moving away. (627)
ley de Hubble Observación que enuncia que mientras más lejos se encuentre una galaxia, se aleja con mayor rapidez.

humid subtropical A wet and warm climate found on the edges of the tropics. (482)
subtropical húmedo Clima húmedo y templado que se encuentra en los límites de los trópicos.

humidity The amount of water vapor in a given volume of air. (422)
humedad Cantidad de vapor de agua en cierto volumen de aire.

humus Dark-colored organic material in soil. (189)
humus Material orgánico de color oscuro del suelo.

hurricane A tropical storm that has winds of about 119 kilometers per hour or higher. (446)
huracán Tormenta tropical que tiene vientos de cerca.

hydrocarbon An organic compound that contains only carbon and hydrogen atoms. (293)
hidrocarburo Compuesto orgánico que contiene átomos de carbón e hidrógeno solamente.

hydroelectric power Electricity produced by the kinetic energy of water moving over a waterfall or dam. (303)
energía hidroeléctrica Electricidad producida a partir de la energía cinética del agua que baja por una catarata o presa.

hydrosphere The portion of Earth that consists of water in any of its forms, including oceans, glaciers, rivers, lakes, groundwater and water vapor. (6)
hidrósfera Parte de la Tierra formada por agua en cualquiera de sus formas, ya sea océanos, glaciares, ríos, lagos, agua subterránea y vapor de agua.

I

ice age Time in Earth's history during which glaciers covered large parts of the surface. (223, 490)
glaciación Períodos de la historia de la Tierra en los que los glaciares cubrían grandes partes de la superficie.

igneous rock A type of rock that forms from the cooling of molten rock at or below the surface. (65)
roca ígnea Tipo de roca que se forma cuando se enfrían las rocas fundidas en la superficie o debajo de la superficie.

impermeable A characteristic of materials, such as clay and granite, through which water does not easily pass. (341)
impermeable Característica de los materiales, como la arcilla y el granito, que no dejan pasar fácilmente el agua.

incineration The burning of solid waste. (65)
incineración Quema de desechos sólidos.

index contour On a topographic map, a heavier contour line that is labeled with elevation of that contour line. (37)
curva de nivel índice En un mapa topográfico, curva de nivel más gruesa que lleva rotulada la elevación de esa curva de nivel.

index fossil Fossils of widely distributed organisms that lived during a geologically short period. (255)
fósil guía Fósiles de organismos altamente dispersos que vivieron durante un período geológico corto.

inertia The tendency of an object to resist a change in motion. (524)
inercia Tendencia de un cuerpo de resistirse a cambios de movimiento.

infrared radiation Electromagnetic waves with wavelengths that are longer than visible light but shorter than microwaves. (393)
radiación infrarroja Ondas electromagnéticas con longitudes de onda más largas que la luz visible, pero más cortas que las microondas.

inner core A dense sphere of solid iron and nickel at the center of Earth. (15)
núcleo interno Esfera densa de hierro y níquel que se encuentra en el centro de la Tierra.

inorganic Not formed from living things or the remains of living things. (51)
inorgánico Que no está formado por seres vivos o por los restos de seres vivos.

insulation Material that traps air to help block heat transfer between the air inside and outside of a building. (313)
aislante Material que atrapa el aire para ayudar a bloquear el paso del calor del aire adentro y afuera de un edificio.

intrusion An igneous rock layer formed when magma hardens beneath Earth's surface. (254)
intrusión Capa de roca ígnea formada cuando el magma se endurece bajo la superficie de la Tierra.

intrusive rock Igneous rock that forms when magma hardens beneath Earth's surface. (67)
roca intrusiva (o plutónica) Roca ígnea que se forma cuando el magma se endurece bajo la superficie de la Tierra.

invertebrate An animal without a backbone. (272)
invertebrado Animal sin columna vertebral.

ionosphere The lower part of the thermosphere. (391)
ionósfera Parte inferior de la termósfera.

irregular galaxy A galaxy that does not have a regular shape. (624)
galaxia irregular Galaxia que no tiene una forma regular.

island arc A string of volcanoes that form as the result of subduction of one oceanic plate beneath a second oceanic plate. (154)
arco de islas Cadena de volcanes formados como resultado de la subducción de una placa oceánica debajo de una segunda placa oceánica.

isobar A line on a weather map that joins places that have the same air pressure. (455)
isobara Línea en un mapa del tiempo que une lugares que tienen la misma presión de aire.

isotherm A line on a weather map that joins places that have the same temperature. (455)
isoterma Línea en un mapa del tiempo que une lugares que tienen la misma temperatura.

J

jet streams Bands of high-speed winds about 10 kilometers above Earth's surface. (437)
corrientes de viento en chorro Bandas de vientos de alta velocidad a unos 10 kilómetros sobre la superficie de la Tierra.

K

karst topography A region in which a layer of limestone close to the surface creates deep valleys, caverns, and sinkholes. (221)
topografía kárstica Región en la que una capa de piedra caliza cerca de la superficie crea valles hundidos, grutas y pozos.

kettle A small depression that forms when a chunk of ice is left in glacial till. (226)
cazuela Pequeña depresión formada cuando un trozo de hielo se asienta en arcilla glaciárica.

key A list of the symbols used on a map and their meanings. (30)
clave Lista de los símbolos de un mapa y sus significados.

GLOSSARY

Kuiper belt A region where many small objects orbit the sun and that stretches from beyond the orbit of Neptune to about 100 times Earth's distance from the sun. (583)
cinturón de Kuiper Región en la cual muchos cuerpos pequeños giran alrededor del Sol y que se extiende desde más allá de la órbita de Neptuno hasta aproximadamente cien veces la distancia entre la Tierra y el Sol.

L

La Niña A climate event in the eastern Pacific Ocean in which surface waters are colder than normal. (363)
La Niña Fenómeno climático que ocurre en la parte este del océano Pacífico, en el cual las aguas superficiales están más frías que lo normal.

land breeze The flow of air from land to a body of water. (405)
brisa terrestre Flujo de aire desde la tierra a una masa de agua.

land reclamation The process of restoring land to a more natural, productive state. (657)
recuperación de la tierra Proceso que consiste en restaurar la tierra y llevarla a un estado productivo más natural.

landform region A large area of land where the topography is made up mainly of one type of landform. (26)
región con accidentes geográficos Terreno amplio donde la tipografía está compuesta, principalmente, por un tipo de accidente geográfico.

landform A feature of topography formed by the processes that shape Earth's surface. (23)
accidente geográfico Característica de la topografía creada por los procesos de formación de la superficie de la Tierra.

latitude The distance in degrees north or south of the equator. (34, 408)
latitud Distancia en grados al norte o al sur del ecuador.

lava Liquid magma that reaches the surface. (152)
lava Magma líquida que sale a la superficie.

lava flow The area covered by lava as it pours out of a volcano's vent. (157)
colada de lava Área cubierta de lava a medida que ésta sale por la chimenea del volcán.

law of superposition The geologic principle that states that in horizontal layers of sedimentary rock, each layer is older than the layer above it and younger than the layer below it. (253)

ley de la superposición Principio geológico que enuncia que, en las capas horizontales de las rocas sedimentarias, cada capa es más vieja que la capa superior y más joven que la capa inferior.

law of universal gravitation The scientific law that states that every object in the universe attracts every other object. (523)
ley de gravitación universal Ley científica que establece que todos los cuerpos del universo se atraen entre sí.

leachate Polluted liquid produced by water passing through and dissolving chemicals from buried wastes in a landfill. (660)
lixiviado Líquido contaminado producido por el agua que pasa por y disuelve químicos provenientes de desechos bajo la tierra y en rellenos sanitarios.

leeward The side of a mountain range that faces away from the oncoming wind. (474)
sotavento Lado de una cadena montañosa que está resguardado del viento.

lightning A sudden spark, or energy discharge, caused when electrical charges jump between parts of a cloud, between nearby clouds, or between a cloud and the ground. (445)
rayo Chispa repentina o descarga de energía causada por cargas eléctricas que saltan entre partes de una nube, entre nubes cercanas o entre una nube y la tierra.

light-year The distance that light travels in one year, about 9.5 million million kilometers. (606)
año luz Distancia que viaja la luz en un año; aproximadamente 9.5 millones de millones de kilómetros.

lithosphere A rigid layer made up of the uppermost part of the mantle and the crust. (14)
litósfera Capa rígida constituida por la parte superior del manto y la corteza.

litter The very top layer of fertile soil made of dead leaves and grass. (654)
mantillo Capa superior del suelo fértil, que está formada por hojas y pasto muertos.

loam Rich, fertile soil that is made up of about equal parts of clay, sand, and silt. (190)
marga Suelo rico y fértil formado por partes casi iguales de arcilla, arena y limo.

local winds Winds that blow over short distances. (405)
vientos locales Vientos que soplan en distancias cortas.

loess A wind-formed deposit made of fine particles of clay and silt. (234)
 loes Depósito de partículas finas de arcilla y limo arrastradas por el viento.

longitude The distance in degrees east or west of the prime meridian. (35)
 longitud Distancia en grados al este o al oeste del meridiano cero.

longshore drift The movement of water and sediment down a beach caused by waves coming in to shore at an angle. (230, 358)
 deriva litoral Movimiento de agua y sedimentos paralelo a una playa debido a la llegada de olas inclinadas respecto a la costa.

lunar eclipse The blocking of sunlight to the moon that occurs when Earth is directly between the sun and the moon. (530)
 eclipse lunar Bloqueo de la luz solar que ilumina la Luna que ocurre cuando la Tierra se interpone entre el Sol y la Luna.

luster The way a mineral reflects light from its surface. (53)
 lustre Manera en la que un mineral refleja la luz en su superficie.

M

magma The molten mixture of rock-forming substances, gases, and water from the mantle. (152)
 magma Mezcla fundida de las sustancias que forman las rocas, gases y agua, proveniente del manto.

magma chamber The pocket beneath a volcano where magma collects. (157)
 cámara magmática Bolsa debajo de un volcán en la que está acumulado el magma.

magnitude The measurement of an earthquake's strength based on seismic waves and movement along faults. (132)
 magnitud Medida de la fuerza de un sismo basada en las ondas sísmicas y en el movimiento que ocurre a lo largo de las fallas.

main sequence A diagonal area on an Hertzsprung-Russell diagram that includes more than 90 percent of all stars. (613)
 secuencia principal Área diagonal en un diagrama de Hertzsprung-Russell que incluye más del 90 por ciento de todas las estrellas.

mammal A vertebrate whose body temperature is regulated by its internal heat, and that has skin covered with hair or fur and glands that produce milk to feed its young. (275)
 mamífero Vertebrado cuya temperatura corporal es regulada por su calor interno, cuya piel está cubierta de pelo o pelaje y que tiene glándulas que producen leche para alimentar a sus crías.

mantle The layer of hot, solid material between Earth's crust and core. (14)
 manto Capa de material caliente y sólido entre la corteza terrestre y el núcleo.

map A flat model of all or part of Earth's surface as seen from above. (29)
 mapa Modelo plano de toda la superficie de la Tierra o parte de ella tal y como se ve desde arriba.

map projection A framework of lines that helps to transfer points on Earth's surface onto a flat map. (29)
 proyección de mapa Esquema de líneas que facilita la transferencia de puntos de la superficie terrestre a un mapa plano.

maria Dark, flat areas on the moon's surface formed from huge ancient lava flows. (537)
 maria Áreas oscuras y llanas de la superficie lunar formadas por enormes flujos de lava antiguos.

marine climate The climate of some coastal regions, with relatively warm winters and cool summers. (472)
 clima marino Clima de algunas regiones costeras, con inviernos relativamente templados y veranos fríos.

maritime (air mass) A humid air mass that forms over oceans. (435)
 masa de aire marítima Masa de aire húmedo que se forma sobre los océanos.

mass A measure of how much matter is in an object. (523)
 masa Medida de cuánta materia hay en un cuerpo.

mass extinction When many types of living things become extinct at the same time. (274)
 extinción en masa Situación que ocurre cuando muchos tipos de seres vivos se extinguen al mismo tiempo.

mass movement Any one of several processes by which gravity moves sediment downhill. (210)
 movimiento en masa Cualquiera de los procesos por los cuales la gravedad desplaza sedimentos cuesta abajo.

meander A looplike bend in the course of a river. (217)
 meandro Curva muy pronunciada en el curso de un río.

GLOSSARY

mechanical weathering The type of weathering in which rock is physically broken into smaller pieces. (182)
desgaste mecánico Tipo de desgaste en el cual una roca se rompe físicamente en trozos más pequeños.

mercury barometer An instrument that measures changes in air pressure, consisting of a glass tube partially filled with mercury, with its open end resting in a dish of mercury. (382)
barómetro de mercurio Instrumento que mide los cambios de presión del aire; es un tubo de vidrio parcialmente lleno de mercurio con su extremo abierto posado sobre un recipiente con mercurio.

mesosphere The layer of Earth's atmosphere immediately above the stratosphere. (390)
mesósfera Capa de la atmósfera de la Tierra inmediatamente sobre la estratósfera.

metamorphic rock A type of rock that forms from an existing rock that is changed by heat, pressure, or chemical reactions. (65)
roca metamórfica Tipo de roca que se forma cuando una roca cambia por el calor, la presión o por reacciones químicas.

meteor A streak of light in the sky produced by the burning of a meteoroid in Earth's atmosphere. (509, 587)
meteoro Rayo de luz en el cielo producido por el incendio de un meteoroide en la atmósfera terrestre.

meteorite A meteoroid that passes through the atmosphere and hits Earth's surface. (587)
meteorito Meteoroide que pasa por la atmósfera y toca la superficie terrestre.

meteoroid A chunk of rock or dust in space, generally smaller than an asteroid. (537, 587)
meteoroide Un trozo de roca o polvo, generalmente más pequeño que un asteroide, que existe en el espacio.

meteorologists Scientists who study the causes of weather and try to predict it. (453)
meteorólogos Científicos que estudian las causas del tiempo e intentan predecirlo.

mid-ocean ridge An undersea mountain chain where new ocean floor is produced; a divergent plate boundary under the ocean. (98, 351)
cordillera oceánica central Cadena montañosa submarina donde se produce el nuevo suelo oceánico; borde de placa divergente bajo el océano.

mineral 1. A naturally occurring solid that can form by inorganic processes and that has a crystal structure and a definite chemical composition. (50) **2.** A nutrient that is needed by the body in small amounts and is not made by living things.

mineral 1. Sólido natural que puede formarse por procesos inorgánicos, con estructura cristalina y composición química específica. **2.** Nutriente inorgánico que el cuerpo necesita en pequeñas cantidades y que no es producido por los seres vivos.

Modified Mercalli scale A scale that rates the amount of shaking from an earthquake. (132)
escala modificada de Mercalli Escala que evalúa la intensidad del temblor de un terremoto.

Mohs hardness scale A scale ranking ten minerals from softest to hardest; used in testing the hardness of minerals. (54)
escala de dureza de Mohs Escala en la que se clasifican diez minerales del más blando al más duro; se usa para probar la dureza de los minerales.

mold A type of fossil that is a hollow area in sediment in the shape of an organism or part of an organism. (248)
molde Tipo de fósil que consiste en una depresión del sedimento que tiene la forma de un organismo o de parte de un organismo.

moment magnitude scale A scale that rates earthquakes by estimating the total energy released by an earthquake. (133)
escala de magnitud de momento Escala con la que se miden los sismos estimando la cantidad total de energía liberada por un terremoto.

monsoon Sea or land breeze over a large region that changes direction with the seasons. (475)
monzón Vientos marinos o terrestres que soplan en una región extensa y cambian de dirección según las estaciones.

moraine A ridge formed by the till deposited at the edge of a glacier. (226)
morrena Montículo formado por arcilla glacial depositada en el borde de un glaciar.

mountain range A group of mountains that are closely related in shape, structure, area, and age. (25)
cordillera Grupo de montañas que están estrechamente relacionadas en forma, estructura y edad.

mountain A landform with high elevation and high relief. (25)
montaña Accidente geográfico con una elevación alta y un relieve alto.

municipal solid waste Waste produced in homes, businesses, schools and in a community. (659)
desechos sólidos urbanos Desechos generados en los hogares, los negocios, las escuelas y las comunidades.

N

natural resource Anything naturally occuring in the environment that humans use. (195, 642)
recurso natural Cualquier elemento natural en el medio ambiente que el ser humano usa.

neap tide The tide with the least difference between consecutive low and high tides. (534)
marea muerta Marea con la mínima diferencia entre las mareas altas y bajas consecutivas.

nebula A large cloud of gas and dust in space. (615)
nebulosa Gran nube de gas y polvo en el espacio.

neutron star The small, dense remains of a high-mass star after a supernova. (618)
estrella de neutrones Restos pequeños y densos de una estrella de gran masa tras ocurrir una supernova.

Newton's first law of motion The scientific law that states that an object at rest will stay at rest and an object in motion will stay in motion with a constant speed and direction unless acted on by a force. (524)
Primera ley de movimiento de Newton Ley científica que establece que un cuerpo en reposo se mantendrá en reposo y un cuerpo en movimiento se mantendrá en movimiento con una velocidad y dirección constantes a menos que se ejerza una fuerza sobre él.

nonpoint source A widely spread source of pollution that is difficult to link to a specific point of origin. (643)
fuente dispersa Fuente muy extendida de contaminación que es difícil vincular a un punto de origen específico.

nonrenewable resource A natural resource that is not replaced in a useful time frame. (648)
recurso no renovable Recurso natural que no se restaura, en un período relativamente corto, una vez se utiliza.

normal fault A type of fault where the hanging wall slides downward; caused by tension in the crust. (122)
falla normal Tipo de falla en la cual el labio elevado o subyacente se desliza hacia abajo como resultado de la tensión de la corteza.

nuclear fission The splitting of an atom's nucleus into two smaller nuclei and neutrons, releasing a large quantity of energy. (308)
fisión nuclear Separación del núcleo de un átomo en núcleos y neutrones más pequeños, en la cual se libera una gran cantidad de energía.

nuclear fusion The process in which two atomic nuclei combine to form a larger nucleus, forming a heavier element and releasing huge amounts of energy; the process by which energy is produced in stars. (561)
fusión nuclear Unión de dos núcleos atómicos que produce un elemento con una mayor masa atómica y que libera una gran cantidad de energía; el proceso mediante el cual las estrellas producen energía.

nucleus 1. In cells, a large oval organelle that contains the cell's genetic material in the form of DNA and controls many of the cell's activities. (585) **2.** The central core of an atom which contains protons and neutrons. 3. The solid core of a comet.
núcleo 1. En las células, orgánulo grande y ovalado que contiene el material genético de la célula en forma de ADN y que controla muchas de las funciones celulares. **2.** Parte central del átomo que contiene los protones y los neutrones. 3. Centro sólido de un cometa.

nutrient depletion The situation that arises when more soil nutrients are used than the decomposers can supply. (655)
agotamiento de nutrientes Situación que se produce cuando se usan más nutrientes del suelo de lo que los descomponedores pueden proporcionar.

O

observatory A building that contains one or more telescopes. (602)
observatorio Edificio que contiene uno o más telescopios.

occluded Cut off, as in a front where a warm air mass is caught between two cooler air masses. (439)
ocluido Aislado o cerrado, como un frente donde una masa de aire cálido queda atrapada entre dos masas de aire más frío.

Oort cloud A spherical region of comets that surrounds the solar system. (583)
nube de Oort Región esférica de cometas que rodea al sistema solar.

open cluster A star cluster that has a loose, disorganized appearance and contains no more than a few thousand stars. (622)
cúmulo abierto Cúmulo de estrellas que tiene una apariencia no compacta y desorganizada, y que no contiene más de unas pocos miles de estrellas.

optical telescope A telescope that uses lenses or mirrors to collect and focus visible light. (600)
telescopio óptico Telescopio que usa lentes o espejos para captar y enfocar la luz visible.

orbit The path of an object as it revolves around another object in space. (516)
órbita Trayectoria de un cuerpo a medida que gira alrededor de otro en el espacio.

GLOSSARY

organic rock Sedimentary rock that forms from remains of organisms deposited in thick layers. (73)
roca orgánica Roca sedimentaria que se forma cuando los restos de organismos se depositan en capas gruesas.

outer core A layer of molten iron and nickel that surrounds the inner core of Earth. (15)
núcleo externo Capa de hierro y níquel fundidos que rodea el núcleo interno de la Tierra.

oxbow lake A meander cut off from a river. (217)
lago de recodo Meandro que ha quedado aislado de un río.

oxidation A chemical change in which a substance combines with oxygen, as when iron oxidizes, forming rust. (185)
oxidación Cambio químico en el cual una sustancia se combina con el oxígeno, como cuando el hierro se oxida, y produce herrumbre.

ozone A form of oxygen that has three oxygen atoms in each molecule instead of the usual two; toxic to organisms where it forms near Earth's surface. (668)
ozono Forma de oxígeno que tiene tres átomos de oxígeno en cada molécula, en vez de dos; donde se forma en la superficie terrestre, es tóxico para los organismos.

ozone layer The layer of the upper atmosphere that contains a higher concentration of ozone than the rest of the atmosphere. (671)
capa de ozono Capa superior de la atmósfera que contiene una concentración mayor de ozono que el resto de la atmósfera.

P

P wave A type of seismic wave that compresses and expands the ground. (131)
onda P Tipo de onda sísmica que comprime y expande el suelo.

paleontologist A scientist who studies fossils to learn about organisms that lived long ago. (250)
paleontólogo Científico que estudia fósiles para aprender acerca de los organismos que vivieron hace mucho tiempo.

Pangaea The name of the single landmass that began to break apart 200 million years ago and gave rise to today's continents. (95)
Pangea Nombre de la masa de tierra única que empezó a dividirse hace 200 millones de años y que le dio origen a los continentes actuales.

parallax The apparent change in position of an object when seen from different places. (604)
paralaje Cambio aparente en la posición de un cuerpo cuando es visto desde distintos lugares.

penumbra The part of a shadow surrounding the darkest part. (529)
penumbra Parte de la sombra que rodea su parte más oscura.

period 1. A horizontal row of elements in the periodic table. 2. One of the units of geologic time into which geologists divide eras. (265)
período 1. Fila horizontal de los elementos de la tabla periódica. 2. Una de las unidades del tiempo geológico en las que los geólogos dividen las eras.

permafrost Permanently frozen soil found in the tundra biome climate region. (484)
permagélido Suelo que está permanentemente congelado y que se encuentra en el bioma climático de la tundra.

permeable Characteristic of a material that contains connected air spaces, or pores, that water can seep through easily. (186, 341)
permeable Característica de un material que contiene diminutos espacios de aire, o poros, conectados por donde se puede filtrar el agua.

pesticide A chemical that kills insects and other crop-destroying organisms. (678)
pesticida Químico usado para matar insectos y otros organismos que destruyen los cultivos.

petrified fossil A fossil in which minerals replace all or part of an organism. (248)
fósil petrificado Fósil en el cual los minerales reemplazan todo el organismo o parte de él.

petrochemical A compound made from oil. (297)
petroquímico Compuesto que se obtiene del petróleo.

petroleum Liquid fossil fuel; oil. (296)
petróleo Combustible fósil líquido.

pH scale A range of values used to indicate how acidic or basic a substance is; expresses the concentration of hydrogen ions in a solution. (190)
escala pH Rango de valores que se usa para indicar cuán ácida o básica es una sustancia; expresa la concentración de iones hidrógeno de una solución.

phase One of the different apparent shapes of the moon as seen from Earth. (526)
fase Una de las distintas formas aparentes de la Luna vistas desde la Tierra.

photochemical smog A brownish thick haze that is a mixture of ozone and other chemicals formed when pollutants react with sunlight. (668)
neblina tóxica fotoquímica Nubosidad gruesa de color marrón, resultado de la mezcla del ozono y otras sustancias químicas que se forman cuando los contaminantes reaccionan a la luz del sol.

photosphere The inner layer of the sun's atmosphere that gives off its visible light; the sun's surface. (562)
fotósfera Capa más interna de la atmósfera solar que provoca la luz que vemos; superficie del Sol.

pipe A long tube through which magma moves from the magma chamber to Earth's surface. (157)
chimenea Largo tubo por el que el magma sube desde la cámara magmática hasta la superficie de la Tierra.

plain A landform made up of flat or gently rolling land with low relief. (24)
llanura Accidente geográfico que consiste en un terreno plano o ligeramente ondulado con un relieve bajo.

planet An object that orbits a star, is large enough to have become rounded by its own gravity, and has cleared the area of its orbit. (509, 556)
planeta Cuerpo que orbita alrededor de una estrella, que tiene suficiente masa como para permitir que su propia gravedad le dé una forma casi redonda, y que además ha despejado las proximidades de su órbita.

planetesimal One of the small asteroid-like bodies that formed the building blocks of the planets. (558)
planetesimal Uno de los cuerpos pequeños parecidos a asteroides que dieron origen a los planetas.

plate A section of the lithosphere that slowly moves over the asthenosphere, carrying pieces of continental and oceanic crust. (104)
placa Sección de la litósfera que se desplaza lentamente sobre la astenósfera y que se lleva consigo trozos de la corteza continental y de la oceánica.

plate tectonics The theory that pieces of Earth's lithosphere are in constant motion, driven by convection currents in the mantle. (105)
tectónica de placas Teoría según la cual las partes de la litósfera de la Tierra están en continuo movimiento, impulsadas por las corrientes de convección del manto.

plateau A large landform that has high elevation and a more or less level surface. (25, 127)
meseta Accidente geográfico que tiene una elevación alta y cuya superficie está más o menos nivelada.

plucking The process by which a glacier picks up rocks as it flows over the land. (225)
extracción Proceso por el cual un glaciar arranca las rocas al fluir sobre la tierra.

point source A specific source of pollution that can be identified. (643)
fuente localizada Fuente específica de contaminación que puede identificarse.

polar (air mass) A cold air mass that forms north of 50¡ north latitude or south of 50¡ south latitude and has high air pressure. (435)
masa de aire polar Masa de aire frío que se forma al norte de los 50¡ de latitud norte o al sur de los 50¡ de latitud sur y que tiene presión alta.

polar zones The areas near both poles from about 66.5° to 90° north and 66.5° to 90° south latitudes. (470)
zona polar Áreas cercanas a los polos desde unos 66.5° a 90° de latitud norte y 66.5° a 90° de latitud sur.

pollutant A substance that causes pollution. (660)
contaminante Sustancia que provoca contaminación.

pollution Contamination of Earth's land, water, or air. (643)
polución Contaminación del suelo, el agua o el aire de la Tierra.

precipitation Any form of water that falls from clouds and reaches Earth's surface as rain, snow, sleet, or hail. (331, 429)
precipitación Cualquier forma del agua que cae de las nubes y llega a la superficie de la tierra como lluvia, nieve, aguanieve o granizo.

pressure The force pushing on a surface divided by the area of that surface. (12)
presión 1. Fuerza que actúa contra una superficie, dividida entre el área de esa superficie. 2. Fuerza que actúa sobre las rocas y que cambia su forma o volumen.

prime meridian The line that makes a half circle from the North Pole to the South Pole and that passes through Greenwich, England. (33)
meridiano cero Línea que forma un medio círculo desde Polo Norte al Polo Sur y que pasa por Greenwich, Inglaterra.

prominence A huge, reddish loop of gas that protrudes from the sun's surface, linking parts of sunspot regions. (564)
prominencia Enorme burbuja de gas rojiza que sobresale de la superfice solar, y conecta partes de las manchas solares.

GLOSSARY

protostar A contracting cloud of gas and dust with enough mass to form a star. (615)
protoestrella Nube de gas y polvo que se contrae, con suficiente masa como para formar una estrella.

psychrometer An instrument used to measure relative humidity. (422)
psicrómetro Instrumento que se usa para medir la humedad relativa.

pulsar A rapidly spinning neutron star that produces radio waves. (618)
pulsar Estrella de neutrones que gira rápidamente y produce ondas de radio.

pyroclastic flow The flow of ash, cinders, bombs, and gases down the side of a volcano during an explosive eruption. (161)
flujo piroclástico Flujo de ceniza, escoria, bombas y gases que corre por las laderas de un volcán durante una erupción explosiva.

Q

quasar An enormously bright, distant galaxy with a giant black hole at its center. (624)
quásar Galaxia extraordinariamente luminosa y distante con un agujero negro gigante en el centro.

R

radiation The transfer of energy by electromagnetic waves. (393)
radiación Transferencia de energía por medio de ondas magnéticas.

radiation zone A region of very tightly packed gas in the sun's interior where energy is transferred mainly in the form of electromagnetic radiation. (561)
zona radiactiva Región al interior del Sol de gases densamente acumulados y donde se transmite energía principalmente en la forma de radiación electromagnética.

radio telescope A device used to detect radio waves from objects in space. (602)
radiotelescopio Aparato usado para detectar ondas de radio de los cuerpos en el espacio.

radioactive decay The process in which the nuclei of radioactive elements break down, releasing fast-moving particles and energy. (259)
desintegración radiactiva Proceso de descomposición del núcleo de un elemento radiactivo que libera partículas de movimiento y energía.

radon A colorless, odorless, radioactive gas. (670)
radón Gas radioactivo que no tiene color ni olor.

rain forest A forest that receives at least 2 meters of rain per year, mostly occurring in the tropical wet climate zone. (480)
selva tropical Bosque donde caen al menos 2 metros de lluvia al año, principalmente en la zona climática tropical húmeda.

rain gauge An instrument used to measure precipitation. (429)
pluviómetro Instrumento que se usa para medir la precipitación.

reactor vessel The part of a nuclear reactor in which nuclear fission occurs. (308)
cuba de reactor Parte de un reactor nuclear donde ocurre la fisión.

recycling The process of reclaiming and reusing raw materials. (661)
reciclaje Proceso de recuperar y volver a usar materias primas.

reference point A place or object used for comparison to determine if an object is in motion. (5)
punto de referencia Lugar u objeto usado como medio de comparación para determinar si un objeto está en movimiento.

refinery A factory in which crude oil is heated and separated into fuels and other products. (297)
refinería Planta en la que el petróleo crudo se calienta y fracciona en combustibles y otros productos.

reflecting telescope A telescope that uses a curved mirror to collect and focus light. (600)
telescopio de reflexión Telescopio que usa un espejo curvado para captar y enfocar la luz.

refracting telescope A telescope that uses convex lenses to gather and focus light. (600)
telescopio de refracción Telescopio que usa lentes convexas para captar y enfocar la luz.

relative age The age of a rock compared to the ages of other rocks. (252)
edad relativa Edad de una roca comparada con la edad de otras rocas.

relative humidity The percentage of water vapor in the air compared to the maximum amount of water vapor that air can contain at a particular temperature. (422)
humedad relativa Porcentaje de vapor de agua del aire comparado con la cantidad máxima de vapor de agua que puede contener el aire a una temperatura particular.

relief The difference in elevation between the highest and lowest parts of an area. (23)
relieve Diferencia de elevación entre las partes más altas y más bajas de un área.

renewable resource A resource that is either always available or is naturally replaced in a relatively short time. (647)
recurso renovable Recurso que está siempre disponible o que es restituido de manera natural en un período relativamente corto.

reptile A vertebrate whose temperature is determined by the temperature of its environment, that has lungs and scaly skin, and that lays eggs on land. (273)
reptil Vertebrado cuya temperatura corporal es determinada por la temperatura de su medio ambiente, que tiene pulmones y piel escamosa y que pone huevos en la tierra.

reservoir A lake that stores water for human use. (337)
embalse Lago que almacena agua para el uso humano.

reverse fault A type of fault where the hanging wall slides upward; caused by compression in the crust. (123)
falla inversa Tipo de falla en la cual el labio superior se desliza hacia arriba como resultado de compresión de la corteza.

revolution The movement of an object around another object. (516)
revolución Movimiento de un cuerpo alrededor de otro.

Richter scale A scale that rates an earthquake's magnitude based on the size of its seismic waves. (132)
escala de Richter Escala con la que se mide la magnitud de un terremoto según el tamaño de sus ondas sísmicas.

rift valley A deep valley that forms where two plates move apart. (107)
valle de fisura Valle profundo que se forma cuando dos placas se separan.

rill A tiny groove in soil made by flowing water. (214)
arroyo Pequeño surco en el suelo causado por el paso del agua.

Ring of Fire A major belt of volcanoes that rims the Pacific Ocean. (153)
Cinturón de Fuego Gran cadena de volcanes que rodea el océano Pacífico.

ring A thin disk of small ice and rock particles surrounding a planet. (575)
anillo Disco fino de pequeñas partículas de hielo y roca que rodea un planeta.

rip current A strong, narrow current that flows briefly from the shore back toward the ocean through a narrow opening. (358)
corriente de resaca Corriente fuerte que fluye por un canal estrecho desde la costa hacia el mar abierto.

rock cycle A series of processes on the surface and inside Earth that slowly changes rocks from one kind to another. (80)
ciclo de la roca Serie de procesos en la superficie y dentro de la Tierra por medio de los cuales un tipo de roca se convierte lentamente en otro tipo.

rock-forming mineral Any of the common minerals that make up most of the rocks of Earth's crust. (63)
minerales formadores de rocas Uno de los minerales comunes de los que están compuestas la mayoría de las rocas de la corteza de la Tierra.

rotation The spinning motion of a planet on its axis. (515)
rotación Movimiento giratorio de un planeta sobre su eje.

runoff Water that flows over the ground surface rather than soaking into the ground. (213)
escurrimiento Agua que fluye sobre la superficie en lugar de ser absorbida por el suelo.

S

S wave A type of seismic wave in which the shaking is perpendicular to the direction of the wave. (131)
onda S Tipo de onda sísmica que hace que el suelo se mueva en una dirección perpendicular a la onda.

salinity The total amount of dissolved salts in a water sample. (347)
salinidad Cantidad total de sales disueltas en una muestra de agua.

sand dune A deposit of wind-blown sand. (234)
duna de arena Depósito de arena arrastrada por el viento.

sanitary landfill A landfill that holds nonhazardous waste such as municipal solid waste, construction debris, and some agricultural and industrial wastes. (660)
relleno sanitario Vertedero que contiene desechos que no son peligrosos, como desechos sólidos municipales, de construcción y algunos tipos de desechos industriales y resultantes de la agricultura.

GLOSSARY

satellite **1.** An object that orbits a planet. **2.** Any object that orbits around another object in space. (509)
satélite **1.** Cuerpo que orbita alrededor de un planeta. **2.** Cualquier cuerpo que orbita alrededor de otro cuerpo en el espacio.

saturated zone The area of permeable rock or soil in which the cracks and pores are totally filled with water. (342)
zona saturada Área de roca o suelo permeable cuyas grietas y poros están totalmente llenos de agua.

savanna A grassland located close to the equator that may include shrubs and small trees and receives as much as 120 centimeters of rain per year. (480)
sabana Pradera que puede tener arbustos y árboles pequeños, ubicada cerca del ecuador y donde pueden caer hasta 120 centímetros de lluvia al año.

scale Used to relate distance on a map or globe to distance on Earth's surface. (30)
escala Se usa para relacionar la distancia de un mapa o globo terráqueo con la distancia de la superficie de la Tierra.

scattering Reflection of light in all directions. (395)
dispersión Reflexión de la luz en todas las direcciones.

scientific notation A mathematical method of writing numbers using powers of ten. (606)
notación científica Método matemático de escritura de números que usa la potencia de diez.

sea breeze The flow of cooler air from over an ocean or lake toward land. (405)
brisa marina Flujo de aire frío procedente de un océano o lago hacia la costa.

sea-floor spreading The process by which molten material adds new oceanic crust to the ocean floor. (100)
despliegue del suelo oceánico Proceso mediante el cual la materia fundida añade nueva corteza oceánica al suelo oceánico.

seamount A steep-sided volcanic mountain rising from the deep-ocean floor. (350)
montaña marina Montaña muy inclinada de origen volcánico cuya base es el fondo del mar.

sediment Small, solid pieces of material that come from rocks or the remains of organisms; earth materials deposited by erosion. (70, 209, 679)
sedimento Trozos pequeños y sólidos de materiales que provienen de las rocas o de los restos de organismos; materiales terrestres depositados por la erosión.

sedimentary rock A type of rock that forms when particles from other rocks or the remains of plants and animals are pressed and cemented together. (65)
roca sedimentaria Tipo de roca que se forma a partir de la compactación y unión de partículas de otras rocas o restos de plantas y animales.

seismic wave Vibrations that travel through Earth carrying the energy released during an earthquake. (11)
ondas sísmicas Vibraciones que se desplazan por la Tierra, y que llevan la energía liberada durante un terremoto.

seismogram The record of an earthquake's seismic waves produced by a seismograph. (138)
sismograma Registro producido por un sismógrafo de las ondas sísmicas de un terremoto.

seismograph A device that records ground movements caused by seismic waves as they move through Earth. (132)
sismógrafo Aparato con el que se registran los movimientos del suelo ocasionados por las ondas sísmicas a medida que éstas se desplazan por la Tierra.

sewage The water and human wastes that are washed down sinks, toilets, and showers. (678)
aguas residuales Agua y desechos humanos que son desechados por lavamanos, servicios sanitarios y duchas.

shearing Stress that pushes masses of rock in opposite directions, in a sideways movement. (121)
cizallamiento Fuerza que presiona masas de roca en sentidos opuestos, de lado a lado.

shield volcano A wide, gently sloping mountain made of layers of lava and formed by quiet eruptions. (167)
volcán en escudo Montaña ancha de pendientes suaves, compuesta por capas de lava y formada durante erupciones que no son violentas.

silica A material found in magma that is formed from the elements oxygen and silicon; it is the primary substance of Earth's crust and mantle. (158)
sílice Material presente en el magma, compuesto por los elementos oxígeno y silicio; es el componente más común de la corteza y el manto de la Tierra.

sill A slab of volcanic rock formed when magma squeezes between layers of rock. (168)
dique concordante Placa de roca volcánica formada cuando el magma a través de capas de roca.

soil The loose, weathered material on Earth's surface in which plants can grow. (189)
suelo Material suelto y desgastado de la superficie terrestre donde crecen las plantas.

soil conservation The management of soil to limit its destruction. (197)
conservación del suelo Cuidado del suelo para limitar su destrucción.

soil horizon A layer of soil that differs in color and texture from the layers above or below it. (191)
horizonte de suelo Capa de suelo de color y textura diferentes a las capas que tiene encima o abajo.

solar eclipse The blocking of sunlight to Earth that occurs when the moon is directly between the sun and Earth. (529)
eclipse solar Bloqueo de la luz solar que ilumina la Tierra que ocurre cuando la Luna se interpone entre el Sol y la Tierra.

solar energy Energy from the sun. (301)
energía solar Energía del Sol.

solar flare An eruption of gas from the sun's surface that occurs when the loops in sunspot regions suddenly connect. (564)
destello solar Erupción de los gases de la superficie solar que ocurre cuando las burbujas de las manchas solares se conectan repentinamente.

solar system The system consisting of the sun and the planets and other objects that revolve around it. (555)
sistema solar Sistema formado por el Sol, los planetas y otros cuerpos que giran alrededor de él.

solar wind A stream of electrically charged particles that emanate from the sun's corona. (563)
viento solar Flujo de partículas cargadas que emanan de la corona del Sol.

solstice Either of the two days of the year on which the sun reaches its greatest distance north or south of the equator. (520)
solsticio Uno de los dos días del año en el que el Sol alcanza la mayor distancia al norte o al sur del ecuador.

solution A mixture containing a solvent and at least one solute that has the same properties throughout; a mixture in which one substance is dissolved in another. (59)
solución Mezcla que contiene un solvente y al menos un soluto, y que tiene las mismas propiedades en toda la solución; mezcla en la que una sustancia se disuelve en otra.

sonar A system that uses reflected sound waves to locate and determine the distance to objects under water. (350)
sónar Sistema que usa ondas sonoras reflejadas para detectar y localizar objetos bajo agua.

spectrograph An instrument that separates light into colors and makes an image of the resulting spectrum. (610)
espectrógrafo Instrumento que separa la luz en colores y crea una imagen del espectro resultante.

spectrum The range of wavelengths of electromagnetic waves. (599)
espectro Gama de las longitudes de ondas electromagnéticas.

spiral galaxy A galaxy with a bulge in the middle and arms that spiral outward in a pinwheel pattern. (624)
galaxia espiral Galaxia con una protuberancia en el centro y brazos que giran en espiral hacia el exterior, como un remolino.

spit A beach formed by longshore drift that projects like a finger out into the water. (231)
banco de arena Playa formada por la deriva litoral, que se proyecta como un dedo dentro del agua.

spring tide The tide with the greatest difference between consecutive low and high tides. (534)
marea viva Marea con la mayor diferencia entre las mareas altas y bajas consecutivas.

stalactite An icicle-like structure that hangs from the ceiling of a cavern. (220)
estalactita Estructura en forma de carámbano que cuelga del techo de una caverna.

stalagmite A columnlike form that grows upward from the floor of a cavern. (220)
estalagmita Estructura en forma de columna que crece hacia arriba desde el suelo de una caverna.

star A ball of hot gas, primarily hydrogen and helium, that undergoes nuclear fusion. (509)
estrella Bola de gases calientes, principalmente hidrógeno y helio, en cuyo interior se produce una fusión nuclear.

steppe A prairie or grassland found in semiarid regions. (481)
estepa Pradera o pastizal que se encuentra en las regiones semiáridas.

storm A violent disturbance in the atmosphere. (443)
tormenta Alteración violenta en la atmósfera.

storm surge A "dome" of water that sweeps across the coast where a hurricane lands. (447)
marejadas "Cúpula" de agua que se desplaza a lo largo de la costa donde aterriza un huracán.

stratosphere The second-lowest layer of Earth's atmosphere. (389)
estratósfera Segunda capa de la atmósfera de la Tierra.

GLOSSARY

stratus Clouds that form in flat layers and often cover much of the sky. (427)
estratos Nubes que aparecen como capas planas y que a menudo cubren gran parte del cielo.

streak The color of a mineral's powder. (53)
raya Color del polvo de un mineral.

stream A channel through which water is continually flowing downhill. (214)
riachuelo Canal por el cual el agua fluye continuamente cuesta abajo.

stress **1.** A force that acts on rock to change its shape or volume. (120) **2.** The reaction of a person's body to potentially threatening, challenging, or disturbing events.
presión **1.** Fuerza que actúa sobre las rocas y que cambia su forma o volumen. **2. estrés** Reacción del cuerpo de un individuo a sucesos como posibles amenazas, desafíos o trastornos.

strike-slip fault A type of fault in which rocks on either side move past each other sideways with little up or down motion. (123)
falla transcurrente Tipo de falla en la cual las rocas a ambos lados se deslizan horizontalmente en sentidos opuestos, con poco desplazamiento hacia arriba o abajo.

subarctic A climate zone that lies north of the humid continental climates. (483)
subártico Zona climática situada al norte de las regiones de clima continental húmedo.

subduction The process by which oceanic crust sinks beneath a deep-ocean trench and back into the mantle at a convergent plate boundary. (102)
subducción Proceso mediante el cual la corteza oceánica se hunde debajo de una fosa oceánica profunda y vuelve al manto por el borde de una placa convergente.

subsoil The layer of soil below topsoil that has less plant and animal matter than topsoil and contains mostly clay and other minerals. (191, 654)
subsuelo Capa de suelo debajo del suelo superior que tiene menos materia de plantas y animales que el suelo superior, y que principalmente contiene arcilla y otros minerales.

sunspot A dark area of gas on the sun's surface that is cooler than surrounding gases. (491, 564)
mancha solar Área gaseosa oscura de la superficie solar, que es más fría que los gases que la rodean.

supernova The brilliant explosion of a dying supergiant star. (617)
supernova Explosión brillante de una estrella supergigante en extinción.

surface wave A type of seismic wave that forms when P waves and S waves reach Earth's surface. (131)
onda superficial Tipo de onda sísmica que se forma cuando las ondas P y las ondas S llegan a la superficie de la Tierra.

sustainable use The use of a resource in ways that maintain the resource at a certain quality for a certain period of time. (650)
uso sostenible Uso de un recurso que permite que ese recurso mantenga cierta calidad por un período de tiempo determinado.

symbol On a map, a picture used by mapmakers to stand for features on Earth's surface. (30)
símbolo En un mapa, imagen que usan los cartógrafos para representar los diferentes aspectos de la superficie de la Tierra.

system **1.** A group of parts that work together as a whole. **2.** A group of related parts that work together to perform a function or produce a result. (4)
sistema **1.** Partes de un grupo que trabajan en conjunto. **2.** Grupo de partes relacionadas que trabajan conjuntamente para realizar una función o producir un resultado.

T

telescope An optical instrument that forms enlarged images of distant objects. (600)
telescopio Instrumento óptico que provee ampliaciones de los cuerpos lejanos.

temperate zones The areas between the tropical and the polar zones. (470)
área templada Áreas ubicadas entre las zonas tropical y polar.

temperature inversion A condition in which a layer of warm air traps polluted air close to Earth's surface. (668)
inversión térmica Condición en la que una capa de aire caliente atrapa aire contaminado cerca de la superficie de la Tierra.

temperature How hot or cold something is; a measure of the average energy of motion of the particles of a substance. (398)
temperatura Cuán caliente o frío es algo; medida de la energía de movimiento promedio de las partículas de una sustancia.

tension Stress that stretches rock so that it becomes thinner in the middle. (121)
tensión Fuerza que estira una roca, de modo que es más delgada en el centro.

terrestrial planets The name often given to the four inner planets: Mercury, Venus, Earth, and Mars. (567)
planetas telúricos Nombre dado normalmente a los cuatro planetas interiores: Mercurio, Venus, Tierra y Marte.

texture The look and feel of a rock's surface, determined by the size, shape, and pattern of a rock's grains. (64)
textura Apariencia y sensación producida por la superficie de una roca, determinadas por el tamaño, la forma y el patrón de los granos de la roca.

thermal energy The total kinetic and potential energy of all the particles of an object. (399)
energía térmica Energía cinética y potencial total de las partículas de un cuerpo.

thermometer An instrument used to measure temperature. (399)
termómetro Instrumento que se usa para medir la temperatura.

thermosphere The outermost layer of Earth's atmosphere. (391)
termósfera Capa exterior de la atmósfera de la Tierra.

thunderstorm A small storm often accompanied by heavy precipitation and frequent thunder and lightning. (444)
tronada Pequeña tormenta acompañada de fuertes precipitaciones y frecuentes rayos y truenos.

tide The periodic rise and fall of the level of water in the ocean. (533)
marea La subida y bajada periódica del nivel de agua del océano.

till The sediments deposited directly by a glacier. (226)
arcilla glacial Sedimentos depositados directamente por un glaciar.

topographic map A map that shows the surface features of an area. (37)
mapa topográfico Mapa que muestra los accidentes geográficos de la superficie terrestre de un área.

topography The shape of the land determined by elevation, relief, and landforms. (22)
topografía Forma del terreno determinada por la elevación, el relieve y los accidentes geográficos.

topsoil The crumbly, topmost layer of soil made up of clay and other minerals and humus (nutrients and decaying plant and animal matter). (191, 654)
suelo superior Capa superior desmenuzable del suelo formada por arcilla, otros minerales y humus (nutrientes y materia orgánica de origen vegetal y animal).

tornado A rapidly whirling, funnel-shaped cloud that reaches down to touch Earth's surface. (448)
tornado Nube con forma de embudo que gira rápidamente y que desciende hasta tocar la superficie terrestre.

trace fossil A type of fossil that provides evidence of the activities of ancient organisms. (249)
vestigios fósiles Tipo de fósil que presenta evidencia de las actividades de los organismos antiguos.

transform boundary A plate boundary where two plates move past each other in opposite directions. (105)
borde de transformación Borde de una placa donde dos placas se deslizan, en sentidos opuestos, y se pasan la una a la otra.

transpiration The process by which water is lost through a plant's leaves. (330)
transpiración Proceso por el cual las hojas de una planta pierden agua.

trench A deep, steep-sided canyon in the ocean floor. (350)
fosa Cañón profundo, de lados empinados, en el suelo oceánico.

tributary A stream or river that flows into a larger river. (214, 333)
afluente Río o arroyo que desemboca en un río más grande.

tropical (air mass) A warm air mass that forms in the tropics and has low air pressure. (435)
masa de aire tropical Masa de aire templado que se forma en los trópicos y cuya presión atmosférica es baja.

tropical zone The area near the equator between about 23.5° north latitude and 23.5° south latitude. (470)
zona tropical Área cercana al ecuador entre aproximadamente los 23.5° de latitud norte y los 23.5° de latitud sur.

troposphere The lowest layer of Earth's atmosphere. (388)
troposfera Capa más inferior de la atmósfera de la Tierra.

tsunami A giant wave usually caused by an earthquake beneath the ocean floor. (357)
tsunami Ola gigantesca, generalmente provocada por un sismo que ocurrió debajo de la cuenca oceánica.

tundra An extremely cold, dry biome climate region characterized by short, cool summers and bitterly cold winters. (484)
tundra Bioma de la región climática extremadamente fría y seca, que se caracteriza por veranos cortos y frescos e inviernos sumamente fríos.

GLOSSARY

U

ultraviolet radiation Electromagnetic waves with wavelengths that are shorter than visible light but longer than X-rays. (393)
radiación ultravioleta Ondas electromagnéticas con longitudes de onda más cortas que la luz visible, pero más largas que los rayos X.

umbra The darkest part of a shadow. (529)
umbra La parte más oscura de una sombra.

unconformity A gap in the geologic record that shows where rock layers have been lost due to erosion. (256)
discordancia Interrupción en el récord geológico que muestra dónde las capas rocosas se han perdido a causa de la erosión.

uniformitarianism The geologic principle that the same geologic processes that operate today operated in the past to change Earth's surface. (180)
uniformitarianismo Principio geológico que enuncia que los mismos procesos geológicos que cambian la superficie de la Tierra en la actualidad ocurrieron en el pasado.

universe All of space and everything in it. (606)
universo Todo el espacio y todo lo que hay en él.

unsaturated zone The layer of rocks and soil above the water table in which the pores contain air as well as water. (342)
zona insaturada Capa de rocas y suelo encima del nivel freático en la que los poros contienen aire además de agua.

V

valley glacier A long, narrow glacier that forms when snow and ice build up in a mountain valley. (224)
glaciar de valle Glaciar largo y estrecho que se forma por la acumulación de hielo y nieve en el valle de una montaña.

vein 1. A narrow deposit of a mineral that is sharply different from the surrounding rock. **2.** A blood vessel that carries blood back to the heart. (59)
vena 1. Placa delgada de un mineral que es marcadamente distinto a la roca que lo rodea. **2.** Vaso sanguíneo que transporta la sangre al corazón.

velocity Speed in a given direction. (12)
velocidad Rapidez en una dirección dada.

vent The opening through which molten rock and gas leave a volcano. (157)

chimenea Abertura a través de la que la roca derretida y los gases salen de un volcán.

vertebrate An animal with a backbone. (272)
vertebrado Animal con columna vertebral.

visible light Electromagnetic radiation that can be seen with the unaided eye. (598)
luz visible Radiación electromagnética que se puede ver a simple vista.

volcanic neck A deposit of hardened magma in a volcano's pipe. (168)
cuello volcánico Depósito de magma solidificado en la chimenea de un volcán.

volcano A weak spot in the crust where magma has come to the surface. (152)
volcán Punto débil en la corteza por donde el magma escapa hacia la superficie.

W

water cycle The continual movement of water among Earth's atmosphere, oceans, and land surface through evaporation, condensation, and precipitation. (330, 420)
ciclo del agua Circulación continua del agua por la atmósfera, los océanos y la superficie de la Tierra mediante la evaporación, la condensación y la precipitación.

water table The top of the saturated zone, or depth to the groundwater under Earth's surface. (342)
nivel freático Límite superior de la zona saturada, es decir de la profundidad de las aguas freáticas del subsuelo.

water vapor Water in the form of a gas. (378)
vapor de agua Agua en forma de gas.

watershed The land area that supplies water to a river system. (334)
cuenca hidrográfica Área de terreno que suministra agua a un sistema fluvial.

wave 1. A disturbance that transfers energy from place to place. **2.** The movement of energy through a body of water. (353)
onda 1. Perturbación que transfiere energía de un lugar a otro. **2.** Movimiento de energía por un fluido.

wave height The vertical distance from the crest of a wave to the trough. (354)
altura de una ola Distancia vertical desde la cresta de una ola hasta el valle.

wavelength The distance between two corresponding parts of a wave, such as the distance between two crests. (354, 599)
longitud de onda Distancia entre dos partes correspondientes de una onda, por ejemplo la distancia entre dos crestas.

weather The condition of Earth's atmosphere at a particular time and place. (376)
tiempo meteorológico Condición de la atmósfera terrestre en un momento y lugar determinado.

weathering The chemical and physical processes that break down rock and other substances. (71, 181)
desgaste Procesos químicos y físicos que erosionan la roca y descomponen otras sustancias.

weight A measure of the force of gravity acting on an object. (523)
peso Medida de la fuerza de gravedad que actúa sobre un objeto.

white dwarf The blue-white hot core of a star that is left behind after its outer layers have expanded and drifted out into space. (617)
enana blanca Núcleo caliente y azul blanquecino de una estrella que queda después de que sus capas externas se han expandido y esparcido por el espacio.

wind The horizontal movement of air from an area of high pressure to an area of lower pressure. (403)
viento Movimiento horizontal de aire de un área de alta presión a una de menor presión.

wind-chill factor A measure of cooling combining temperature and wind speed. (404)
factor de enfriamiento por viento Medida del enfriamiento que combina la temperatura y la velocidad del viento.

windward The side of a mountain range that faces the oncoming wind. (474)
barlovento Lado de una cadena montañosa donde pega el viento de frente.

INDEX

Page numbers for key terms are printed in **boldface** type.

INDEX

INDEX

Page numbers for key terms are printed in **boldface** type.

INDEX

Page numbers for key terms are printed in **boldface** type.

INDEX

Page numbers for key terms are printed in **boldface** type.

Prime meridian, **33**, 35
Process Skills. *See* Science Inquiry Skills
Prominences, solar, **564**
Protostar, **615**
Psychrometer, **422**
Ptolemy, 551, 553
Pulsars, **618**
Pumps, 345
Pyroclastic flow, **161**

Q

Quasars, **624**
Quaternary Period, 264, 277, 281
Quiet eruptions, volcanic, 158–159

R

Radiation, **19, 393**
    absorption of, 394–397
    cosmic background, **627**
    electromagnetic, **598**
    and heat transfer, 400–401
Radiation zone, solar, **561**
Radio telescope, **602**
Radioactive dating, 260–261
Radioactive decay, **259**
Radioactive waste, 664
Radon, **670**
Rain. *See* Precipitation
Rain forests, **480**
Rain gauge, **429**
Reactor vessel, **308**
Reading Skills
    graphic organizers, 213, 220, 227, 679
        Venn diagram, 15, 303, 336
    reading/thinking support strategies
        apply concepts, 24, 27, 42, 101, 111, 121, 135, 216, 224, 230, 233, 238, 251, 261, 283, 317, 330, 355, 367, 381–382, 401, 411, 437, 455, 460, 474, 516, 520, 555, 561, 570, 585, 589, 611, 623, 631, 657, 663, 685
        define, 79, 155, 171, 185, 265, 298, 315, 363, 378, 385, 404, 431, 439, 473, 497, 500, 521, 565, 623, 629, 643, 648, 661, 683
        describe, 14, 31, 52–53, 74, 131, 171, 193, 227, 301, 314, 345, 363, 381, 427, 439, 581, 629, 649, 653

explain, 8, 17, 21, 33, 35, 41, 52, 54, 65, 130, 143, 155, 160, 167, 171, 196, 220, 225, 249, 251, 255, 257, 281, 284, 307, 313, 337, 339, 342, 351, 365, 401, 403, 433, 449–450, 457, 480, 499, 513, 517, 531, 541–542, 559, 565, 589, 607, 613, 616–617, 657, 663, 669, 673, 683
identify, 17, 33, 35, 53, 68, 72, 108, 123, 133, 135, 157, 168–169, 193, 199, 213, 223, 225, 229, 231, 249, 261, 269, 281, 293, 309, 331, 335, 354, 383, 393, 396, 400, 404, 409, 441, 449, 473, 475, 479, 484, 500, 517, 525, 619, 654, 670, 677
interpret diagrams, 21, 65, 67, 82, 99, 107–109, 127, 138, 143, 165, 171, 190, 192, 210, 223, 255, 296, 308, 335, 342, 356, 368, 397, 406, 425, 440, 444, 446, 510, 515, 528, 533, 542, 590, 612–613, 628–629, 631, 660
interpret graphs, 13, 15, 134, 144, 158, 299, 328, 343, 347, 389, 477, 494, 525, 672
interpret maps, 29, 34–35, 38, 42, 61, 95, 105–106, 135, 139, 334, 443, 448, 456, 489, 499, 656
interpret photos, 6, 56, 85, 215, 218, 253, 271, 317, 471, 581, 622, 655, 668, 682
interpret tables, 650
list, 9, 27, 56, 143, 163, 191, 213, 221, 231, 257, 274, 329, 351, 378–379, 391, 451, 469, 475, 497, 539, 563, 625, 642, 651
make generalizations, 195, 249, 261, 267, 335, 513, 519, 525, 542, 557, 565, 579, 643
make judgments, 35, 111, 140, 197, 237, 298, 329, 333, 344, 367, 433, 460, 578, 581, 584, 661, 665, 670
mark text, 59–60, 65, 78, 118, 139, 187, 213, 226, 256–257, 261, 273, 301, 309, 312, 327–329, 348, 353, 356, 361, 385, 387, 407, 430, 443, 480, 490, 512, 518, 533, 555, 561, 609, 627, 654–655, 667, 669–670, 677
name, 83, 85, 172, 383, 471, 573, 621, 656, 665, 670

review, 7, 9, 15, 17, 61, 65, 74, 97, 101, 103, 109, 123, 127, 131, 135, 138, 141, 161, 167, 169, 211, 214, 227, 235, 307, 342, 365, 399, 423, 430, 437, 491, 535, 553, 587, 607, 613, 616, 625, 651, 657, 665, 669
solve problems, 75, 238, 283, 315, 318, 345, 451, 539, 568, 644, 663, 673
target reading skills
    ask questions, 7, 97, 190, 234, 395, 493, 524, 600, 602
    compare and contrast, 12, 16, 18, 20, 27, 33, 37, 68, 85, 111–112, 154, 191, 237–238, 248, 294, 303, 317, 337, 341, 354, 362, 368, 378, 394, 411–412, 423, 441, 449, 455, 481, 499–500, 523, 538–539, 541, 563, 570, 580, 587, 589–590, 601, 617, 632, 648, 661
    identify the main idea, 30, 65, 72, 139, 261, 311, 328, 348, 401, 480, 512, 609
    identify supporting evidence, 16, 213, 273, 387, 407, 490, 555, 627
    outline, 160, 446, 576, 679
    relate cause and effect, 9, 20, 68, 78, 85, 103, 106, 125–126, 143, 168, 171, 187, 196, 200, 211, 226, 235, 237–238, 274, 301, 345, 356, 358, 368, 385, 404, 412, 433, 475, 491, 499–500, 521, 533, 535, 541–542, 564–565, 573, 587, 589, 621, 631, 643, 655, 685
    relate text and visuals, 37, 60, 101, 153, 209, 214, 256, 268, 348, 350, 405, 408, 422, 436–437, 441, 470, 529–530, 537, 562, 571, 577, 583, 618, 624, 647, 673, 678
    sequence, 25, 41, 58, 71, 73, 81, 111, 130, 214, 237, 247, 262, 265, 268–269, 274, 284, 317, 331, 338, 397, 411, 421, 474, 485, 515–516, 552, 557–558, 603, 631, 671, 680
    summarize, 13, 16–17, 31, 52, 57, 68, 102, 109, 112, 195, 223, 229, 263, 272, 295, 335, 338, 356, 379, 385, 397, 401, 409, 421, 425, 470, 475, 491, 585, 606, 615–616, 629, 641, 648, 651, 664, 672
vocabulary. *See* Vocabulary Skills
Recycling, 661, 662–663, 681
categories of, 662
See also Waste disposal

INDEX

Page numbers for key terms are printed in **boldface type**.

INDEX

Page numbers for key terms are printed in **boldface type.**

ACKNOWLEDGMENTS

Staff Credits

The people who made up the *Interactive Science* team—representing composition services, core design digital and multimedia production services, digital product development, editorial, editorial services, manufacturing, and production—are listed below:

Jan Van Aarsen, Samah Abadir, Ernie Albanese, Chris Anton, Zareh Artinian, Bridget Binstock, Suzanne Biron, Niki Birbilis, MJ Black, Nancy Bolsover, Stacy Boyd, Jim Brady, Laura Brancky, Katherine Bryant, Michael Burstein, Pradeep Byram, Jessica Chase, Jonathan Cheney, Sitha Chhor, Arthur Ciccone, Allison Cook-Bellistri, Brandon Cole, Karen Corliss, Rebecca Cottingham, AnnMarie Coyne, Bob Craton, Chris Deliee, Paul Delsignore, Michael Di Maria, Diane Dougherty, Nancy Duffner, Kristen Ellis, Kelly Engel, Theresa Eugenio, Amanda Ferguson, Jorgensen Fernandez, Kathryn Fobert, Alicia Franke, Louise Gachet, Julia Gecha, Mark Geyer, Steve Gobbell, Paula Gogan-Porter, Jeffrey Gong, Sandra Graff, Robert M. Graham, Maureen Griffin, Adam Groffman, Lynette Haggard, Christian Henry, Karen Holtzman, Guy Huff, Susan Hutchinson, Sharon Inglis, Marian Jones, Sumy Joy, Chris Kammer, Sheila Kanitsch, Courtenay Kelley, Chris Kennedy, Toby Klang, Alyse Kondrat, Greg Lam, Russ Lappa, Margaret LaRaia, David Leistensnider, Ben Leveillee, Thea Limpus, Charles Luey, Dotti Marshall, Kathy Martin, Robyn Matzke, John McClure, Mary Beth McDaniel, Krista McDonald, Tim McDonald, Rich McMahon, Cara McNally, Bernadette McQuilkin, Melinda Medina, Angelina Mendez, Maria Milczarek, Claudi Mimo, Mike Napieralski, Deborah Nicholls, Dave Nichols, Anthony Nuccio, William Oppenheimer, Jodi O'Rourke, Julie Orr, Ameer Padshah, Lorie Park, Celio Pedrosa, Jonathan Penyack, Linda Zust Reddy, Jennifer Reichlin, Stephen Rider, Charlene Rimsa, Walter Rodriguez, Stephanie Rogers, Marcy Rose, Rashid Ross, Anne Rowsey, Manuel Sanchez, Logan Schmidt, Amanda Seldera, Laurel Smith, Nancy Smith, Ted Smykal, Sandy Schneider, Emily Soltanoff, Cindy Strowman, Dee Sunday, Barry Tomack, Elizabeth Tustian, Patricia Valencia, Ana Sofia Villaveces, Stephanie Wallace, Amanda Watters, Christine Whitney, Brad Wiatr, Heidi Wilson, Heather Wright, James Yagelski, Tim Yetzina, Rachel Youdelman.

Photographs

Every effort has been made to secure permission and provide appropriate credit for photographic material. The publisher deeply regrets any omission and pledges to correct errors called to its attention in subsequent editions.

Unless otherwise acknowledged, all photographs are the property of Pearson Education, Inc.

Photo locators denoted as follows: Top (T), Center (C), Bottom (B), Left (L), Right (R), Background (Bkgd)

Cover
Joel Arem/Photo Researchers, Inc.

Front Matter
vii (TR) Matt Theilen/Getty Images; **xvi** (TR) LOOK Die Bildagentur der Fotografen GmbH/Alamy Images; **xvii** (TR) Eric Nguyen/Photo Researchers, Inc.; **xviii** (TR) Ralph Lee Hopkins/Getty Images; **xix** (TR) Corbis; **xx** (C) Corbis, (TR) ESA/J. Clarke (Boston University)/Z. Levay (STScI)/NASA; **xxii** (TR) UIG via Getty Images; **xxviii** (CL) Arctic-Images/Corbis, (CR) John Cancalosi/Nature Picture Library; **xxix** (TR) Max Rossi/Reuters Media; **xxx** (TR) Image Source/Getty Images; **xxxi** (TL) Jeffrey L. Rotman/Corbis, (TR) NASA; **xxxiv** (B) Whit Richardson/Aurora/Getty Images; (TR) UIG via Getty Images

1 (C) Don Hammond/Design Pics Inc/Alamy; **3** (T) hecke61/Shutterstock, (B) Nature Picture Library; **4** (Bkgrd) Jupiterimages/Thinkstock; **5** (B) hecke61/Shutterstock; **6** (BL) Don Hammond/Design Pics Inc/Alamy, (TL) Kevin Oke/All Canada Photos/Alamy Images, (B) Marvin Dembinsky Photo Associates/Alamy, (CL) InterNetwork Media/Getty Images; **7** (CC) Anna Yu/iStockphoto; **8** (BL) Dietrich Rose/zefa/Corbis, (CR) Philip Dowell/©DK Images; **9** (CR) David Jordan/©Associated Press; **12** (B) Tracy Frankel/Getty Images; **13** (BR) DK Images, (BCR) Harry Taylor/Courtesy of the Royal Museum of Scotland, Edinburgh/©DK Images, (TR) NASA, (CR) Nature Picture Library; **14** (TL) NASA; **15** (TR) NASA; **16** (B) Markus Gann/Shutterstock, (BC) NASA; **17** (TC) Richard Megna/Fundamental Photographs, NYC; **18** (C) Steve Allen Travel Photography/Alamy Images; **19** (CC) Bloomimage/Corbis, (TL) Pancaketom/Dreamstime LLC, (TR) Yuri Arcurs/INSADCO Photography/Alamy; **20** (C) Hall/Corbis, (BR) tbkmedia.de/Alamy Images; **21** (TR) NASA; **22** (TC) Alamy Images, (CL) North Wind Picture Archives/Alamy Images; **24** (BR) Wayne Barrett & Anne MacKay/Getty Images; **25** (CR) Ocean/Corbis, (BC) DLILLC/Corbis; **26** (TL) Angelo Cavalli/Corbis; **27** (TCL) ©Royalty-Free/Corbis, (TR) Egmont Strigl/Imagebroker/Alamy, (CL) Image Source/Getty Images, (BL) Wayne Barrett & Anne MacKay/All Canada Photos/Corbis; **28** (B) Frank Lukasseck/Getty Images; **36** (BL) Kai-Uwe Och/Alamy Images; **37** (B) Corbis, (BR) U.S. Geological Survey; **38** (TR) U.S. Geological Survey; **40** (TR) Don Hammond/Design Pics Inc/Alamy, (BR) Hall/Corbis, (CR) NASA, (T) Tom Bean; **42** (TCR) U.S. Geological Survey; **44** (L) Daniel Sambraus/Photo Researchers, Inc.; **45** (BR) Layne Kennedy/Corbis, (TR) John McConnico/©Associated Press; **46** (B) Matt Theilen/Getty Images; **49** (C) Bill Brooks/Alamy, (T) Javier Trueba/MSF/Photo Researchers, Inc., (B) Sandra vom Stein/iStockphoto; **50** (C) Andrew Romaneschi/iStockphoto; **51** (CR) Arco Images GmbH/Alamy Images, (CC) Rana Royalty Free/Alamy; **52** (CC) ©Harry Taylor/DK Images, (CR) Joel Arem/Photo Researchers, Inc.; **53** (BR) ©Charles D. Winters/Photo Researchers, Inc., (TR, BL, BC) Breck P. Kent Natural History Photography, (TL) Colin Keates/Courtesy of the Natural History Museum, London/DK Images; **54** (BR, BCR, BCL) Colin Keates/Courtesy of the Natural History Museum, London/©DK Images, (BL, BC) DK Images, (TR) Jupiterimages/ PIXLAND/Alamy; **55** (BR) ©DK Images, (BL, BCR, BCL, BC) Colin Keates/Courtesy of the Natural History Museum, London/©DK Images; **56** (TR) Breck P. Kent Natural History Photography, (TL) Florea Marius Catalin/iStockphoto, (BL) Mark A. Schneider/Science Source; **57** (TR) ©Chip Clark/Smithsonian Institution, (TCR) Biophoto Associates/Photo Researchers, Inc., (CC) Colin Keates/Natural History Museum, London/©DK Images; **58** (B) CLM/Shutterstock; **59** (CC) Jane Burton/Bruce Coleman, Inc./Photoshot, (B) Javier Trueba/MSF/Photo Researchers, Inc., (CR) John Cancalosi/Getty Images; **60** (CL) Colin Keates/Courtesy of the Natural History Museum, London/©DK Images, (CR) Gary Ombler/Oxford University Museum of

ACKNOWLEDGMENTS

Natural History/©DK Images; **62** (C) Robert Glusic/Corbis; **63** (CC) Breck P. Kent Natural History Photography, (BL) George Whitely/Photo Researchers, Inc., (C, BCL) Mark A. Schneider/ Photo Researchers, Inc.; **64** (CL) ©DK Images, (BR) Bill Brooks/ Alamy, (TR, TC, CR, CC, C) Breck P. Kent Natural History Photography, (TL) Corbis/Photolibrary Group, Inc.; **66** (TR) Jon Adamson/iStockphoto, (CR) Photo by Jiri Hermann/Courtesy Diavik Diamond Mines Inc./Rio Tinto Diamonds; **67** (BR, BL) Breck P. Kent Natural History Photography, (BCL) Dirk Wiersma/Photo Researchers, Inc.; **68** (TR) Breck P. Kent Natural History Photography; **69** (BL) Keith Levit/Alamy; **72** (CC) ©DK Images, (CR) Breck P. Kent Natural History Photography, (C) Jeffrey A. Scovil, (CL) Joel Arem/Photo Researchers, Inc., (BCL) Lloyd Cluff/Corbis, (BL) Michael P. Gadomski/Photo Researchers, Inc., (BR) Sandra vom Stein/iStockphoto, (BCR) Special Collections Division, University of Washington Libraries; **73** (BCL) Andreas Einsiedel/©DK Images, (BCR) Breck P. Kent Natural History Photography, (BL) Larry Mulvehill/Alamy, (BR) Martin Strmiska/Alamy; **74** (TR) K-PHOTOS/Alamy Images; **75** (B) Daniel Dempster Photography/Alamy Images; **76** (CL) Radius Images/Alamy, (C) Sergey Peterman/Shutterstock; **77** Philip L. Dombrowski; **78** (BL, BCR) Andrew J. Martinez/Photo Researchers, Inc., (BCL) Biophoto Associates/Photo Researchers, Inc., (BR) Jeffrey A. Scovil; **79** (TR) Phooey/iStockphoto; **80** (CR) Adrian Page/ Alamy Images, (C) GlowImages/Alamy; **81** (B) ©Kevin Fleming/ Corbis; **82** (BL) Bern Petit/Breck P. Kent Natural History Photography, (TL) Francois Gohier/Photo Researchers, Inc., (BR) Gregory G. Dimijian, M.D./Science Source, (TR) Simon Fraser/Photo Researchers, Inc.; **84** (BR) ©Kevin Fleming/ Corbis, (CL) Breck P. Kent Natural History Photography; **85** (BC) Don Nichols/iStockphoto; **86** (TR) Andrew J. Martinez/ Photo Researchers, Inc., (TL, TCR) Breck P. Kent Natural History Photography; **88** (T) Loomis Dean/Time Life Pictures/Getty Images; **89** (R) Jane Stockman/©DK Images; **90** (T) Peter Rowlands/PR Productions; **94** (CL) Peter Dennis/©DK Images; **97** (CR) Francois Gohier/Photo Researchers, Inc.; **98** (C) ©The Granger Collection, NY; **99** (TR) moodboard/Corbis; **100** (TCL) OAR/National Undersea Research Program/Photo Researchers, Inc., (BL) Paul Zoeller/©Associated Press, (CL) U.S. Geological Survey; **101** (CR) Sandy Felsenthal/Corbis; **104** (BR) Image Source/Getty Images; **106** (B) Kristy-Anne Glubish/ Design Pics/Corbis; **107** (B) Daniel Sambraus/Photo Researchers, Inc.; **108** (CL) Blaine Harrington III/Corbis; **109** (CL) James Balog/Getty Images; **110** (BR) Daniel Sambraus/ Photo Researchers, Inc.; **114** (B) Emory Kristof/National Geographic Image Collection; **115** (B) Carsten Peter/National Geographic Image Collection, (TL) Radius Images/Alamy; **133** (CL) Corbis; **148** (B) Digital Vision/Photolibrary Group, Inc.; **151** (BL) Justin Bailie/Aurora Photos/Corbis; **152** (C) Carsten Peter/Getty Images; **156** (CR) Colin Keates/Natural History Museum, London/©DK Images, (C) Karl Weatherly/Getty Images; **158** (B) Brad Lewis Photography, (TL) Rainer Albiez/ iStockphoto; **159** (B) Stephen & Donna O'Meara/Getty Images, (CR) Rolf Schulten/imagebroker/Corbis; **160** (BL) Geologic Inquiries Group/U.S. Geological Survey, (CR) Pat and Tom Leeson/Photo Researchers, Inc., (B) Paul Thompson/ PhotoLibrary Group, Inc.; **161** (T) Alberto P. Garcia; **163** (TR) Brad Lewis Photography, (CL) Lyn Topinka/U.S. Geological Survey; **164** (B) Karen Kasmauski/Corbis; **165** (C) Justin Bailie/ Aurora Photos/Corbis; **166** (CR) Jeffzenner/Shutterstock, (BR)

Rob Reichenfeld/©DK Images; **168** (B) Corbis, (BL) Eric Hosking/Photo Researchers, Inc.; **169** (CL) Lee Foster/Alamy; **170** (CR) Stephen & Donna O'Meara/Getty Images, (BR) Lee Foster/Alamy; **174** (B) Bettmann/Corbis, (CL) Ragnar Th Sigurdsson/Arctic Images/Alamy Images; **175** (T) Krafft/ Explorer/Photo Researchers, Inc., (BCR) Tom Van Sant/Corbis; **346** (B) Marevision Marevision/AGE Fotostock/PhotoLibrary Group, Inc., (BL) Mass Communication Specialist Seaman Luciano Marano/U.S. Navy News Photo; **349** (TC) underwaterpics/Fotolia, (TR) Courtesy of Deep Flight Hawkes Ocean Technologies, (CL) Emory Kristof and Alvin Chandler/ National Geographic Image Collection; **351** (CR) U.S. Navy News Photo; **352** (B) Commander Richard Behn/NOAA; **354** (BR) Arnulf Husmo/Getty Images; **355** (R) Felix Möckel/ iStockphoto; **357** (BR) Dita Alangkara/©Associated Press; **359** (BR) Jim Wark, (CL) Karl F Schöfmann/AGE Fotostock, (TL) Steve Dunwell/AGE Fotostock, (T) Sven Zacek/Oxford Scientific/PhotoLibrary Group, Inc.; **360** (CR, C) Dr. W. James Ingraham, Jr/NOAA; **361** (CR, BL) Dr. W. James Ingraham, Jr/ NOAA; **362** (BR) Chris Wattie/Reuters Media, (BC) Eitan Simanor/Robert Harding World Imagery; **363** (TR, TCR) Goddard Space Flight Center Scientific Visualization Studio/ NASA; **365** (TR) PhotoLibrary Group, Inc.; **366** (BR) Ernest A. Janes/Photoshot, (CR) Jim Wark; **372** (B) ©Kevin Fleming/ Corbis; **375** (TL) Bettmann/Corbis, (BCL) David Wall/Alamy Images, (BL) Shutterstock, (TCL) Van Bucher/Photo Researchers, Inc.; **376** (CC) Charles D. Winters/Photo Researchers, Inc.; **377** (B) Bettmann/Corbis; **378** (CC) Digital Vision/Alamy, (TC) Sean Randall/iStockphoto; **379** (C) GSFC Lab for Atmospheres/NASA; **380** (C) Check Six/Getty Images; **383** (TR) Van Bucher/Photo Researchers, Inc.; **386** (B) Melissa McManus/Getty Images; **387** (CR) David Wall/Alamy Images; **390** (TC) LOOK Die Bildagentur der Fotografen GmbH/Alamy Images; **393** (BC) Aqua Image/Alamy Images; **395** (BL) Ermin Gutenberger/iStockphoto, (BCR) Ideeone/iStockphoto, (BR) Jason Major/iStockphoto, (BCL) Mark Yuill/iStockphoto; **398** (C) Helle Bro Clemmensen/iStockphoto; **400** (CL) Mikhail Kokhanchikov/iStockphoto, (B) Xavi Arnau/iStockphoto; **402** (B) Shutterstock; **404** (CL) Geri Lavrov/Alamy/Alamy Images; **405** (CL) Harris Shiffman/Shutterstock; **410** (TL) GSFC Lab for Atmospheres/NASA; **414** (L) NASA; **415** (B) LPI/NASA, (TR) Stefano Bianchetti/Corbis; **416** (B) Eric Nguyen/Photo Researchers, Inc.; **419** (BCL) Gene Rhoden/Still Pictures, (TCL) John Howard/Photo Researchers, Inc.; **421** (C) Jeremy Horner/ Corbis; **424** (C) Gaertner/Alamy; **428** (B) Ng Han Guan/ ©Associated Press; **430** (CR) John Howard/Photo Researchers, Inc., (CC) Liz Leyden/iStockphoto, (TR) Tom King/Alamy Images; **431** (TL) Matthias Hauser/Alamy; **432** (L) Tom Pennington/Fort Worth Star-Telegram; **433** (T) Paul S. Howell/ Getty Images; **434** (B) Digital Vision/Getty Images; **437** (CR) Gene Rhoden/Still Pictures; **442** (B) ©Associated Press; **444** (TL) Peter Menzel/Photo Researchers, Inc.; **445** (R) King Wu/ iStockphoto; **447** (TL, CL) Goddard Space Flight Center Scientific Visualization Studio/NASA, (TR) Joe Raedle/Getty Images; **449** (BL) John Sleezer/Kansas City Star; **450** (BL) Donna McWilliam/©Associated Press; **451** (CL) Chris Mampe/ iStockphoto; **452** (B) Tom Sibley/Corbis; **453** (B) Fitzsimage/ Shutterstock; **454** (CR) David Parker/Photo Researchers, Inc., (CL) NASA/Photo Researchers, Inc., (C) Paul Rapson/Science Photo Library/Photo Researchers, Inc.; **458** (BR) David Parker/ Photo Researchers, Inc.; **462** (T) Brian Cosgrove/©DK Images,

(CL) NASA; **464** (B) Ralph Lee Hopkins/Getty Images; **467** (TL) Corbis, (BL) iStockphoto, (TCL) Photo Researchers, Inc.; **468** (B) Duncan Shaw/Science Photo Library/Photo Researchers, Inc.; **469** (B) Corbis; **471** (TR) Emmanuel Lattes/Alamy Images, (B) Steve Allen/Getty Images; **476** (C) Douglas Peebles Photography/Alamy; **477** (TR) Joseph Sohm-Visions of America/Getty Images; **480** (BL) image100/Corbis; **481** (C) Jennifer Trenchard/iStockphoto; **482** (CL) Dave G. Houser/ Corbis; **483** (T) Kim Karpeles/Alamy Images, (TR) wwoland/ iStockphoto; **484** (TL) Arctic-Images/Corbis, (BL) Content Mine International/Alamy Images; **486** (BR) Petr David Josek/ ©Associated Press, (TR) Rebecca Paul/iStockphoto, (BL) Vienna Report Agency/Corbis; **487** (BL) Atlantide Phototravel/Corbis; **488** (CR) GYRO PHOTOGRAPHY/ amanaimages/Corbis; **491** (CR) Francisco Jose de Goya y Lucientes/Bridgeman Art Library/Getty Images, (TR) Photo Researchers, Inc.; **492** (B) iStockphoto, (TC) Kazberry/ Shutterstock; **496** (CR) Alistair Baker/Getty Images, (C) Long Tran The/iStockphoto; **497** (C) Rudi Sebastian/Getty Images; **498** (B) GYRO PHOTOGRAPHY/amanaimages/Corbis, (TR) Joseph Sohm-Visions of America/Getty Images; **502** (B) Japan Aerospace Exploration Agency, HO/©Associated Press; **503** (CR) Joe Tree/Alamy; **507** (BL) Space Frontiers/Getty, (CR, CL, CC) Photo Researchers, Inc.; **509** (B) Corbis, (TCL, CL) NASA, (CR) T. Rector (University of Alaska Anchorage), Z. Levay and L.Frattare (Space Telescope Science Institute) and National Optical Astronomy Observatory/NASA; **512** (BL) Ted Spiegel/ Corbis; **513** (T) ©Frank Zullo/Photo Researchers, Inc.; **514** (CC) Ellen Rooney/Robert Harding Picture Library Ltd/Alamy Images, (BC) John White Photos/Alamy Images; **517** (CL) Dea/A. Dagli Orti/De Agostini Picture Library/Getty Images, (TC) Werner Forman/UIG/Getty Images, (BCR) SSPL/Getty Images; **521** (TR) Gavin Hellier/PhotoLibrary Group, Inc.; **522** (C) Paul & Lindamarie Ambrose/Getty Images; **526** (TR) Corbis, (C) Jeff Vanuga/Corbis; **528** (L) Eckhard Slawik/Photo Researchers, Inc., (C) John W. Bova/Photo Researchers, Inc./ Photo Researchers, Inc., (R, CR, CL) Photo Researchers, Inc.; **529** (TCR) Space Frontiers/Getty; **530** (T) Fred Espenak/Photo Researchers, Inc.; **532** (BR, BL) Michael P. Gadomski/Science Source; **535** (T) David Chapman/PhotoLibrary Group, Inc.; **536** (B) JPL/USGS/NASA, (BC) Omikron/Photo Researchers, Inc.; **538** (R) Langley Research Center (NASA-LaRC)/NASA, (TR) JPL/USGS/NASA, (B) NASA; **540** (BR) Omikron/Photo Researchers, Inc.; **544** (BL) Andrey Prokhorov/iStockphoto, (CL) Andy Crawford/Dorling Kindersley, Courtesy of the University Museum of Archaeology and Anthropology, Cambridge/©DK Images, (TL) Stephen Strathdee/ iStockphoto; **545** (BL) ©William King/Getty Images, (Bkgrd) NASA; **546** (B) ESA/J. Clarke (Boston University)/Z. Levay (STScI)/NASA; **549** (TL) NASA; **550** (BR, BL) Walter Myers/ ComputerGraphic Vistas/Walter Myers; **552** (BL) Crawford Library/Royal Observatory, Edinburgh/Photo Researchers, Inc., (CR) Detlev van Ravenswaay/Photo Researchers, Inc.; **553** (CR) Pictorial Press Ltd/Alamy Images, (CC) Science Photo Library/Photo Researchers, Inc.; **554** (B) Johns Hopkins University Applied Physics Laboratory/NASA; **556** (BR) Friedrich Saurer/Alamy Images, (C) NASA; **559** (TR) NASA; **560** (B) LOOK Die Bildagentur der Fotografen GmbH/Alamy Images; **562** (BR) SOHO/NASA, (BCR) Space Frontiers/Hulton Archive/Getty Images; **564** (CR) SOHO/ESA/NASA/NASA, (CL) SOHO-EIT Consortium/ESA/NASA; **566** (BC) Bettman/

Corbis, (BCL) Bettmann/Corbis, (BR) Library of Congress, (BL) NASA; **567** (R, CR, CC, C) NASA; **568** (TL, TCL, BR) NASA; **569** (TR) JPL/USGS/NASA, (TL, CL, CC) NASA; **572** (CR) JPL/CalTech/NASA, (B) Mars Exploration Rover Mission/JPL/NASA; **573** (CL) Goddard Space Flight Center Scientific Visualization Studio, and Virginia Butcher (SSAI)/ NASA; **574** (CC) Judy Dole/The Image Bank/Getty Images; **575** (CC) ESA/L. Sromovsky (University of Wisconsin, Madison)/ H. Hammel (Space Science Institute)/K. Rages (SETI)/NASA, (C) JPL/NASA, (CL) JPL/NIX/NASA, (CR) NASA; **576** (BR) JPL/NASA/NASA, (CL) JPL/NIX/NASA, (C) NASA; **577** (R) NASA/NASA; **578** (CR, CL) JPL/NASA, (BL) JPL/ Space Science Institute/NASA/NASA, (TC) JPL/University of Arizona/NASA; **579** (TR) JPL/NASA, (BR) JPL/Space Science Institute/NASA, (TCR) NASA, (BL) Science Source/Photo Researchers, Inc.; **580** (TL) ESA/L. Sromovsky (University of Wisconsin, Madison)/ H. Hammel (Space Science Institute)/K. Rages (SETI)/NASA, (BR) Lawrence Sromovsky, University of Wisconsin-Madison/W. M. Keck Observatory, (TCL) NASA; **581** (CR) L. Sromovsky/P. Fry (University of Wisconsin-Madison)/NASA, (TR, TCR) NASA; **582** (B) Alan Sirulnikoff/ Getty Images; **584** (BR) Detlev van Ravenswaay/Photo Researchers, Inc.; **585** (BR) Jerry Lodriguss/Photo Researchers, Inc.; **586** (L) JPL/Caltech/T. Pyle (SSC)/NASA, (CR) JPL/NASA; **587** (CR) Paolo Koch/Photo Researchers, Inc.; **588** (BR) Jerry Lodriguss/Photo Researchers, Inc., (BL) JPL/NIX/NASA, (C) SOHO-EIT Consortium/ESA/NASA; **592** (B) JPL/Cornell University/NASA; **594** (B) JPL-CalTech/STScI/ Vassar/NASA/Photo Researchers, Inc.; **597** (BCL) Anglo-Australian Observatory, (TL) David Parker/Photo Researchers, Inc., (TCL) NASA, (BL) Shutterstock; **598** (CL) Chip Simons/ Getty Images; **599** (TR, BR) Bjorn Rorslett/Science Photo Library/Photo Researchers, Inc., (BC) Don Farrall/Getty Images; **600** (C) Gerard Lodriguss/Photo Researchers, Inc.; **601** (CR) CXC/Rutgers/J.Warren et al.; Optical: NASA/ STScI/U. Ill/Y.Chu; Radio: ATCA/U. Ill/J.Dickel/NASA, (BR) ESA, HEIC, and The Hubble Heritage Team (STScI/AURA)/ NASA, (BCR) H. Ford (JHU)/G. Illingworth (UCSC/LO)/M. Clampin (STScI)/G. Hartig (STScI)/ACS Science Team/ESA/ NASA, (CC) NASA Hubble Space Telescope Collection/ NASA, (BL) The Hubble Heritage Team (STScI/AURA)/NASA; **602** (B) David Parker/Photo Researchers, Inc., (TCL) Matt York/©Associated Press; **604** (CL) Science Source/Photo Researchers, Inc.; **607** (CL) NASA, (C) SOHO/ESA/NASA; **608** (BL) NASA/CXC/M.Weiss; Spectra: NASA/CXC/SAO/J.Miller, et al./NASA Chandra Space Telescope Collection/NASA; **610** (R) Data Copyrights ESA/ESO/NASA FITS Liberator/NASA Digitized Sky Survey/NASA; **613** (B) Larry Landolfi/Photo Researchers, Inc.; **614** (CR) ESA/CXC/JPL-CalTech/J. Hester and A. Loll (Arizona State Univ.)/R. Gehrz (Univ. Minn.)/STScI/ NASA; **615** (BR) ESA/The Hubble Heritage Team/NASA/ NASA; **617** (T) European Space Agency and Justyn R. Maund (University of Cambridge)/NASA, (CR) NASA; **620** (CL) Kuiper Airborne Observatory/NASA; **622** (CR) JPL/NASA, (BR) Mpia-hd, Birkle, Slawik/Photo Researchers, Inc.; **623** (TL) ESA/C. Carreau/NASA, (CC) Ken Biggs/Photo Researchers, Inc.; **624** (BR) Anglo-Australian Observatory; **625** (CR) David Malin/Anglo-Australian Observatory, (BL) JPL-CalTech/T. Pyle (SSC)/NASA, (CL) Science Source/Photo Researchers, Inc.; **626** (C) Eliot J. Schechter/Getty Images; **627** (BL) NASA; **628** (C) Shutterstock; **634** (L) NASA; **635** (R) Mike

ACKNOWLEDGMENTS

Brinson/ The Image Bank/Getty Images; **636** (Bkgrd) Benedict Luxmoore/Arcaid/Corbis; **639** (BCL)/NASA, (TCL) Getty Images, (TL) Mark Bolton/Garden Picture Library/PhotoLibrary Group, Inc., (TL) Matthew Ward/Peter Griffiths - modelmaker/©DK Images, (BCL) Photodisc/Photolibrary Group, Inc.; **641** (Bkgrd) Frank Krahmer/Masterfile Corporation; **642** (B) Yvon-Lemanour/Photononstop/PhotoLibrary Group, Inc.; **643** (Bkgrd) Steve Schapiro/Corbis; **644** (Bkgrd) Dennis MacDonald/Age Fotostock/PhotoLibrary Group, Inc., (Inset) Mark Bolton/Garden Picture Library/PhotoLibrary Group, Inc.; **646** (CL) AP Photo/©Associated Press, (BC) Derek Dammann/iStockphoto; **648** (TL) Getty Images; **649** (CR) Alfred Cheng Jin/Reuters/Landov LLC, (CL) Liba Taylor/Corbis, (BL) Gary Braasch/Corbis; **652** (Bkgrd) Creatas/SuperStock; **653** (TR) Bethany Dawn/©DK Images, (CR) fotoshoot/Alamy, (BCR) Ron Chapple/Corbis; **654** (Bkgrd) Matthew Ward/Peter Griffiths - modelmaker/©DK Images; **655** (CL) Dana Edmunds/Design Pics/Corbis, (CR) Rest/iStockphoto; **656** (Bkgrd) Robert Harding Picture Library Ltd./Alamy Images; **658** (Bkgrd) Andrew Brookes/Corbis; **660** (CL) Rami Ba/iStockphoto; **661** (TR) Douglas Whyte/Corbis; **662** (BL) Angela Hampton Picture Library/Alamy Images; **663** (CL) Adam Borkowski/iStockphoto, (TR) John Nordell/Christian Science Monitor/Getty Images, (CR) Mark Boulton/Photo Researchers, Inc., (TCL) Martin Williams/Alamy Images, (TL) Michael Nitschke/Imagebroker/Alamy, (TCL) Stan Gilliland/©Associated Press; **664** (TCR, CC, BCR)/©DK Images, (CL) Andy Crawford/©DK Images, (BR) Don Wilkie/iStockphoto, (BCR) Eric Mulherin/iStockphoto, (TCL, BC) Feng Yu/iStockphoto, (CR) Fenykepez/iStockphoto, (BL) gabyjalbert/iStockphoto, (B) James Steidl/iStockphoto, (TC) Paul Wilkinson/©DK Images; **665** (TL) Comstock/Thinkstock; **666** (BR, BL)/San Joaquin Valley Unified Air Pollution Control District; **667** (Bkgrd) Guillermo Arias/©Associated Press; **668** (T) Publiphoto/Photo Researchers, Inc.; **669** (TL) Fletcher & Baylis/Photo Researchers, Inc., (Bkgrd) Will McIntyre/Photo Researchers, Inc.; **672** (Bkgrd) Dorling Kindersley/©DK Images, (TR, TL) Goddard Space Flight Center Scientific Visualization Studio//NASA; **673** (TR, TL, TC) Goddard Space Flight Center Scientific Visualization Studio/NASA; **674** (BL) Charles Orrico/SuperStock; **676** (Bkgrd)/©DK Images, (Bkgrd) Wade Payne/©Associated Press; **681** (Bkgrd) John Gaps III/©Associated Press; **684** (TCR) G. Brad Lewis/©Science Faction; **685** (BCR) XBitter Productions/iStockphoto; **686** (BR) Sonny T. Senser/AGE Fotostock/AGE Fotostock, (TCR) Spencer Grant/PhotoEdit, Inc.; **688** (Bkgrd) ©Narcis Parfenti/Fotolia, (BR) Paulo De Oliveira/PhotoLibrary Group, Inc.; **689** (Bkgrd) ©Ulrich Mueller/Shutterstock

Illustrations
593 Robert (Bob) Kayganich.

this is your book

you can write in it

734

this is your book

you can write in it

736

this is your book

you can write in it

this is your book

you can write in it

740

this is your book

you can write in it

742

this is your book

you can write in it

744

this is your book

you can write in it

746

this is your book

you can write in it